Metric Plywood Panels

Plywood panels come in two standard metric sizes: 1200 millimetres x 2400 millimetres and 1220 millimetres x 2400 millimetres (the equivalent of a 4 foot x 8 foot panel). Other sizes are available on special order. With sheathing and select sheathing grades, metric and imperial thicknesses are generally identical. The metric sanded grades, however, come in a new range of thicknesses.

Metric thicknesses

Sheathing and Select Grades		Sanded Grades	
7.5 mm	(5/16 in.)	6 mm	(4/17 in.)
9.5 mm	(3/8 in.)	8 mm	(5/16 in.)
12.5 mm	(1/2 in.)	11 mm	(7/16 in.)
15.5 mm	(5/8 in.)	14 mm	(9/16 in.)
18.5 mm	(3/4 in.)	17 mm	(2/3 in.)
20.5 mm	(3/5 in.)	19 mm	(3/4 in.)
22.5 mm	(7/8 in.)	21 mm	(13/16 in.)
25.5 mm	(1 in.)	24 mm	(15/16 in.)

Grams, litres, metres

The basic units of the metric system are the *gram* for weight, the *litre* for volume, and the *metre* for length. Other units are related to these units by multiples and divisions of 10. For example, the *kilogram* is 1,000 grams, the *centimetre* is 1/100, or .01, of a metre, and the *millimetre* is 1/1000, or .001 of a metre.

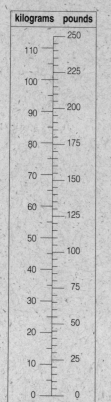

Calculating

Multiply length by width to get the slab area in square metres. Then read across, under whichever of three thicknesses you prefer, to see how many cubic metres of concrete you will need.

Area in square metres (m²) (length x width)	Thickness in millimetres		
	100	130	150
	volume in cubic metres (m³)		
5	0.50	0.65	0.75
10	1.00	1.30	1.50
20	2.00	2.60	3.00
30	3.00	3.90	4.50
40	4.00	5.20	6.00
50	5.00	6.50	7.50

If a greater volume of concrete is required, multiply by the appropriate number. To lay a 100-millimetre-thick patio in an area 6 metres wide and 10 metres long, for example, estimate as follows: 6 metres x 10 metres = 60 metres square = area. Using the chart above, simply double the concrete quantity for a 30-metre-square, 100-millimetre-thick slab (2 x 3 m³ = 6 m³) or add the quantities for 10 m² and 50 m² (1 m³ + 5 m³ = 6 m³).

Fahrenheit and Celsius

The two systems for measuring temperature are Fahrenheit and Celsius (formerly known as Centigrade). To change from degrees Fahrenheit to degrees Celsius, subtract 32, then multiply by 5/9. For example: 68°F – 32 = 36; 36 x 5/9 = 20°C. To convert degrees Celsius to degrees Fahrenheit, multiply the degrees by 9/5, then add 32 to that figure. For example: 20°C x 9/5 = 36; 36 + 32 = 68°F.

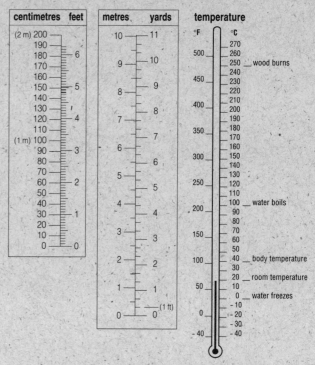

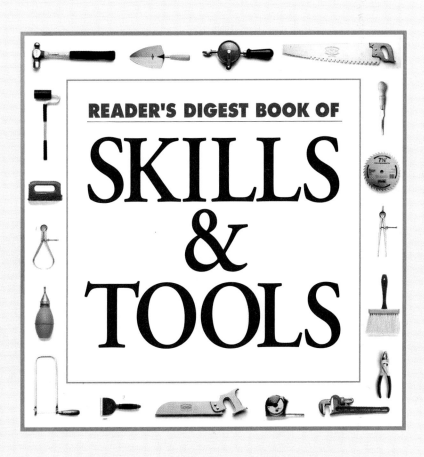

READER'S DIGEST BOOK OF

SKILLS
&
TOOLS

READER'S DIGEST BOOK OF

SKILLS & TOOLS

Reader's Digest

The Reader's Digest Association (Canada) Ltd. Montreal

READER'S DIGEST BOOK OF SKILLS & TOOLS

Staff

Project Editors
Sally French
Robert V. Huber
Alice Philomena Rutherford

Senior Editor
Andrew Byers

Senior Associate Editors
Carolyn Chubet
Fiona Gilsenan
Theresa Lane

Copy Editor
Joseph Marchetti

Research Editor
Wadad Bashour

Art Director
John McGuffie

Designer
Cécile Germain

Senior Art Associates
Marisa Gentile
Morris Karol
Carol Nehring

Art Assistant
Jason Peterson

Coordinator
Susan Wong

Production Manager
Holger Lorenzen

Contributors

Project Art Director
Judy Speicher

Designer
Virginia Wells Blaker

Production Coordinator
Jessica Mitchell

Copy Editor
Katherine G. Ness

Copy Preparation
Enza Micheletti

Editorial Assistants
Elizabeth Eastman
Tracy O'Shea

Indexer
Sydney Wolfe Cohen

Writers
Roy Barnhart
Beverly Bremer
Mark Bremer
Joseph Haviland
Barbara Mayer
Laura Tringali
Joseph Truini
John Warde

Researchers
Beverly Bremer
Mark Bremer
Theo Dominic Corbin
Willard Lubka

Artists
Sylvia Bokor
Mario Ferro
Ray Skibinski
Robert Steimle
Robert Steimle, Jr.

Photographers
Michael Molkenthin (principal)
Richard Felber
Robert Laporta

Consultants

Yvan Aubertin
Daniel Basovitch
Bob Buteyn
Victor DeMasi
Jon Eakes
Phil Englander
Charles N. Farley
Allan E. Fitchett
George Frechter
Eugene Goeb
Lyle Hamre
Wayne Hawk
Walter Kurzmann
Peter Legnos
Jim McCann
Tim McCreight
Charles McRaven
Antonio Maltese
Susan Moore
Americo Napolitano
D. E. Ponzo
Gerald Persico
Lawrence D. Press
Meryl Prichard
Henry H. Printz
Michael Raffio
Michael Sapienza
Seth Stem
Bob Wilcoxson

The acknowledgments and credits that appear on the facing page are hereby made a part of this copyright page.

Printed in the United States of America

Canadian Cataloguing in Publication Data

Main entry under title:

Reader's Digest book of skills & tools.

Includes index.
ISBN 0-88850-210-9

1. Tools. 2. Do-it-yourself work. I. Reader's Digest Association (Canada). II. Title: Book of skills & tools.

TT155.R38 1993   621.9   C93-090322-6

93 94 95 96 97 / 5 4 3 2 1

ACKNOWLEDGMENTS

The editors wish to thank the following organizations and individuals for the assistance they provided:

Aberdeen's Magazine of Masonry Construction
Adjustable Clamp Company
Advanced Technology Inc.
AIN Plastics, Inc.
Allcraft Tool & Supply Company, Inc.
American Clamping Corp.
American Machine & Tool Co., Inc.
American Saw & Mfg. Company
American Tool Companies, Inc.
Ames Lawn and Garden Tools
Andrite, A Division of Wondrastone Co. Inc.
Armstrong World Industries Inc.
Arrow Fastener Company, Inc.
Ball & Ball
Barrasso & Sons, Inc.
Richard J. Bell Company Inc.
S.A. Bendheim Company Inc.
Black & Decker
Boise Cascade Corp.
Robert Bosch Power Tool Corp.
BP Chemicals, Inc.–Filon Products
Brass Accent by Urfic, Inc.
Brick Institute of America
Brico Centre
Bridge City Tool Works, Inc.
C&A Wallcoverings
Canada Mortgage and Housing Corporation
Canadian Centre for Occupational Health and Safety
Canadian General Standards Board
Canadian Paint and Coatings Association
Canadian Portland Cement Association
Canadian Wood Council
Central Hardware & Electric Corp.
Central Supply Inc.
Centre Do-It
Ciment St. Laurent Inc.
Colonial Bronze Co.
Concrete Paver Institute
Congoleum Corp.
Albert Constantine & Son, Inc.

Consumer and Corporate Affairs Canada, Chemical and Biological Hazards Division
Cooper Tools
Delta International Machinery Corp.
Ray Donarski
Tom Doyle
Dremel Power Tools
Eldorado Stone Corporation
Empak Company
Environment Canada, Office of Waste Management
Fibre Glass Evercoat Co. Inc.
Flexi-Wall Systems
Florian Glass
Formica Corporation
Freud, Inc.
Garden State Flooring
Garrett Wade Company
GB Electrical, Inc.
GE Plastics
Glen-Gery Corporation
The Glidden Co.
Goineau-Bousquet
Grinnell Concrete Pavingstones
Grizzly Imports, Inc.
Hafele America Co.
Hager Hinge Co.
Harris-Tarkett, Inc.
Health and Welfare Canada, Health Protection Branch
Hebron Brick Supply Co.
HEWI, Inc.
Hitachi Power Tools U.S.A. Limited
Hi-Way Concrete Products
Hyde Tools
Ilco Unican Corp.
Inter Design Inc.
International Wallcoverings Ltd.
The Irwin Company
Ives: A Harrow Company
Johnson Level and Tool Manufacturing Company, Inc.
Jolie Papier Ltd.
Kentile Floors Inc.
Kentucky Mill Work
Kentucky Wood Floors, Inc.
Keystone Retaining Walls Systems Inc.

Kwikset, A Black & Decker Company
Lasco Panel Products, div. of Tomkins Industries Inc.
Laticrete International
C.R. Laurence Company Inc.
Lazon Paints & Wallcoverings
LBI, Inc.
Lee Valley Tools Ltd.
LePage's Ltd.
McFeely's
Makita U.S.A. Inc.
Mannington Floors
Marion Tool Corp.
Marshalltown Trowel Company
Middletown Plate Glass Co. Inc.
Milwaukee Electric Tool Corp.
Monterey Shelf, Inc.
Benjamin Moore & Co.
Mosaic Supplies
Musolf Distributing Inc.
National Concrete Masonry Association
National Manufacturing Company
National Oak Flooring Manufacturers' Association
National Particleboard Association
National Wood Flooring Association
New Hippodrome Hardware Corp.
NicSand, Inc.
Owens-Corning Fiberglas Corp.
Padco, Inc.
Paxton Hardware
Pfister Industries
Pittsburgh Corning Corporation
Plexi-Craft Quality Products Corp.
Porter-Cable Professional Power Tool Corporation
Potlatch Corporation
Power-Flo Products
PPG Industries
Red Devil, Inc.
Cynthia Rees Ceramic Tile Showroom
Rickel Do-It-Yourself Home Centers

Ridge Tool Company
Rio Grande Albuquerque
Robbins Inc.
Roofing Industry Educational Institute
Roysons Corporation
Ryobi America Corp.
Sandvik Saws and Tools
Schlage Lock Company
Shur-line Inc.
Skil Power Tools
R&G Sloane Manufacturing Co.
Solo Metal Works Ltd.
South Street Ready-Mix Concrete
Standards Council of Canada
Stanley Tools
The L.S. Starrett Company
John Sterling Corp.
Stone Products Corporation
StoneWall™ Landscape Systems, Inc.
Structural Stone Company, Inc.
Tahran Painting & Decorating Center
Target Products Inc.
TECO/Lumberlok
3M Do-It-Yourself Division
Tremco Ltd.
Tremont Nail Company
Triangle Tool Group Inc.
Unicorn Universal Woods Ltd.
Unilock N.Y. Inc.
Vaughan & Bushnell Mfg. Co.
Vermont American Tool Co.
V.T. Industries, Inc.
Wallcoverings Association
Webster and Sons
Wedge Innovations
R.D. Werner Company, Inc.
Wilde Tool Co., Inc.
Willson Safety Products
Ralph Wilson Plastics Co.
Wood Moulding and Millwork Producer's Association
F.W. Wostbrock Hardwood Floor Company, Inc.
Wright Products Corp.

Photo credits

Warning

ABOUT THIS BOOK

The *Reader's Digest Book of Skills & Tools* is tailor-made for you if you enjoy working with tools or if you want to brighten up your home. Whether you're thinking about paving your patio, covering a counter with laminate, painting or papering a wall, or simply having the fun and satisfaction of building something useful and beautiful, this book will fulfill a dual purpose. It will tell you how to do the job and show you what tools and materials you'll need.

The book is divided into eight major sections. The first two, *Tools* and *Hardware,* consist of galleries of color photographs of well over a thousand tools and articles of hardware, with explanations of the use for each item. Included are all the standard hammers and saws, pliers and screwdrivers, and nails and hinges, but there are also specialized and unusual tools, such as a textured paint roller, an around-the-corner bit for drilling curved holes in tight corners, a screw pitch gauge, and a variety of router templates. On any given spread (two facing pages in the opened book) the tools and hardware are photographed at the same focus so that their sizes relative to one another are completely accurate—except that tools enclosed in a ruled box are either much larger or much smaller than the other items on the page.

Each of the six sections that follow is devoted to the skills needed to use these tools and articles of hardware to work with a particular type of material or group of materials. Color photographs show you either the raw materials or the effects that can be created by using them, including woods, metals, moldings, wood finishes, concrete and concrete blocks, stones, pavers, ceramic and vinyl tiles, plastic laminates, fiberglass, glass and glass blocks, paints and wallcoverings, and flooring of every type. Each picture gallery is followed by full step-by-step instructions on working with the materials, giving all the information a beginner needs, and including advanced techniques as well. In the tradition of other Reader's Digest do-it-yourself books, these instructions are brought to life with vivid illustrations—in this case, hundreds of full-color drawings that include all the details you'll need to see.

The *Reader's Digest Book of Skills & Tools* is not a project book that provides blueprints for specific jobs, but it can teach you how to work with a wide variety of tools and materials, giving you the skills and confidence to create your own projects. And when you do, you'll have fun indulging your creative impulses and derive a great deal of satisfaction from the completed work. Although this book is not intended as a manual for large construction jobs (it has no information on electrical work, plumbing, or house framing), the skills it teaches can be put to good use, helping you to save money by doing much of the work in even the largest of projects, leaving only the heavy-duty and highly technical work to the professionals.

Rounding out the book are sections on organizing a safe workshop, working safely with tools, planning a project (including standard measurements for furniture and open spaces in your home), and a buyer's guide to help you find both the common and the unusual items shown in this book. And, in case you do want to tackle a large project, there's also help on selecting and working with a contractor.

—THE EDITORS

CONTENTS

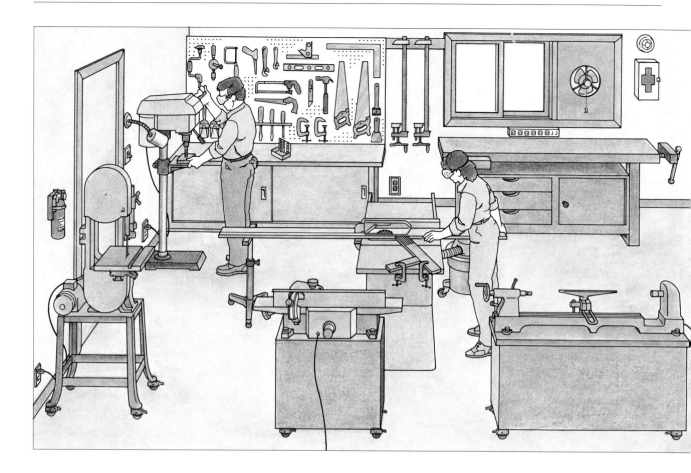

A shop with a sturdy workbench, basic tools, adequate safety equipment, and plenty of well-organized, easily accessible storage space will make it easier and safer for you to complete most jobs. Plan the space with extra room so that you can add tools and accessories as you gain experience and move into more advanced types of work.

Choosing the space. The ideal shop is a closed but well-ventilated room specifically created for that purpose. With such an area, you can lock the door to keep tools and materials from unauthorized use, and save time by letting tools and unfinished projects sit until you are ready to work again.

A workshop should measure at least 8 × 10 feet. Build a new structure or convert an unused utility shed, spare room, or large closet. Garage and basement workshops work well if you add a wall or a large sliding door to sepa-

rate the shop from any cars, water heaters, or laundry facilities. Attic shops are good for small work, but it is difficult to move in large tools and materials and the structure may not be strong enough to support heavy loads. Before moving any heavy equipment into your attic, reinforce the joists.

Electrical work. Once you have selected your space, have a professional electrician put in the proper wiring. Install bright overhead fluorescent fixtures, and use droplights or clamp-on lamps to focus light on your workbench and large power tools. If possible, install an exhaust fan above the workbench area.

Have strategically placed electric outlets for all your power tools, including dedicated circuits and 220-volt outlets for the tools that require them. By installing extra outlets, you can avoid the dangerous practice of laying

cords on the floor or draping them across benches and tools. If you must run a cord across the floor, cover it with a brightly colored wooden bridge to protect the cord and keep it from tripping anyone. Never let a power cord rest on a damp surface. If your shop is damp (or if you work outdoors), see that all the electric circuits have ground-fault circuit interrupters (GFCI's). In case of a fault in the electrical grounding (such as a loose hot wire touching the metal housing of a grounded tool), the GFCI will cut the power off and protect you from shock.

Avoid using extension cords, if at all possible. If using one is unavoidable, be sure that it has a three-prong plug and exceeds the capacity of the tool's cord. To keep the extension and tool cords from unplugging, tie the ends together in a loose knot before plugging them into each other.

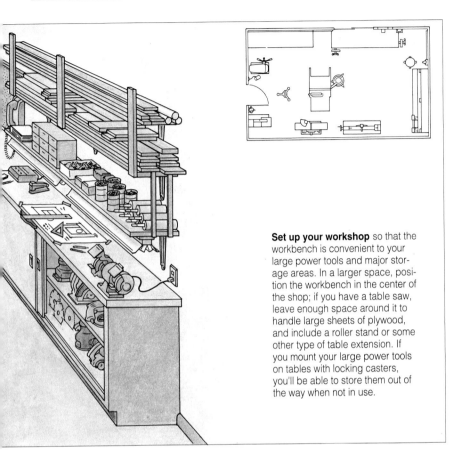

Set up your workshop so that the workbench is convenient to your large power tools and major storage areas. In a larger space, position the workbench in the center of the shop; if you have a table saw, leave enough space around it to handle large sheets of plywood, and include a roller stand or some other type of table extension. If you mount your large power tools on tables with locking casters, you'll be able to store them out of the way when not in use.

For holding workpieces stationary, install a bench vise and hold-downs for the types of jobs you plan to do. If your shop has a concrete floor, place antifatigue mats or carpet scraps in front of your bench and large power tools to help prevent tired legs when standing for long periods and cold feet on chilly fall days.

For support when measuring and cutting long framing materials and sheet materials such as plywood, paneling, and wallboard, you might want to include a good set of sawhorses in your shop. You can also lay a sheet of plywood across sawhorses and instantly create an additional work surface for painting, staining, and finishing work in the shop or on a job site.

Storage. Tools, hardware, and materials should never be left lying about when not in use. A cluttered space is an invitation to fire or accidents.

Store everything in a safe but convenient place. On the wall above or near your bench, install a pegboard panel with hooks for hanging hand tools, arranging them so that the most used are the closest. Be sure to position the hooks in such a way that tools can be removed easily without interfering with one another.

Install metal or wooden shelves for small power tools, use labeled coffee cans or jars for nails and screws, and reserve a long shelf or a dry area on the floor for lumber and other materials. Add cartons for waste materials you want to recycle. More sophisticated storage could include large toolboxes, multiple-unit containers or bins for fasteners and other hardware, lumber racks and bins, and built-in shelves, cupboards, and drawers. Arrange the tools and materials you use most often so that they are the most accessible.

Store flammable and toxic materials (such as paints, thinners, glues, and oils) in a locked fireproof metal cabinet. To protect the environment, check with your local government on how to dispose of these materials properly.

Other safety precautions. Install a fire extinguisher and smoke alarms in the shop. Choose an extinguisher rated A-B-C-D, which is designed to fight wood, oil, gasoline, chemical, and electrical fires. Check periodically that the extinguisher is active and that the batteries in the smoke detectors are good.

Keep a first-aid kit handy and a list of emergency numbers by the telephone. Install childproof switches on your large power tools so that they cannot be inadvertently turned on. You can buy a device that encases and locks the tool's plug or a locking switch that lets you send power to the tool only by turning a key, which you can keep out of the reach of children.

Setting up a workbench. The focus of any shop is the workbench. It must be sturdy and large enough to handle the type of work you plan to do. You can purchase a bench or, better still, build one to fit your space and to suit your particular needs.

You can make a simple workbench for home maintenance and occasional small projects by attaching a set of metal bench legs (sold at home improvement centers) to an expanse of particleboard or plywood. For the serious do-it-yourselfer or craftsman, however, a sturdier bench is called for. Workbenches or kits to make them are available from woodwork suppliers (see pp.348–353). Or you can make one with 2 × 4 lumber, and use multiple thicknesses of plywood and a layer of hardwood for the top to provide a solid surface. Add storage areas underneath the bench by installing shelves, doors, wooden or plastic drawers, and slide-out bins. Workbench plans ranging from simple to elaborate can be found in various books and magazines and at home improvement centers.

Choose tools that suit your budget, space, experience, and the type of work you plan to do. Quality tools are expensive, but you needn't buy a lot of them at first. Start with a few basic hand and power tools, learn to use them, and as you gain experience, add others. Rent tools that you will use only once. For advice on finding the tools you need, see pp.348–353.

Tool maintenance. Take care of your tools to keep them safe and effective. Sharpen, clean, or replace blades, bits, and other cutters before they become damaged or dull. A sharp tool cuts smoothly, accurately, and safely.

Follow the manufacturer's procedures to keep power tools in good working order. Most power tools are permanently lubricated and sealed and require no oiling. On a few tools, however, you may have to oil certain parts, and you may be able to replace worn brushes or power cords or defective switches. Check your owner's manual.

To clean a power tool, unplug it and wipe it with a damp cloth or sponge.

Never submerge the tool in water or clean it with solvents. If a tool's air vents become clogged, remove the debris with compressed air or a vacuum cleaner.

If you have cordless tools, use only the battery and charger that came with the tool. Never charge or store a tool where the temperature is below 40°F (4°C) or above 105°F (40°C). Batteries rely on chemical reactions that slow down in the cold and stop altogether at 32°F (0°C). High temperatures release vapors from the battery and diminish its capacity.

Tool storage. Store cutting tools where their sharp edges won't be damaged, cause injury, or damage other tools. To prevent rust, store tools in a dry place. Spray a rust-inhibiting coating on steel tools or put camphor balls or rust-preventive paper in toolboxes and cabinets. The camphor vapor coats the tools with a rust-preventive film, and the paper gives off a protective vapor or absorbs moisture.

Toolboxes come in a variety of sizes. A small or medium-size box with a

handle and removable tray is used to store small tools and to transport them to a job site. Larger boxes with drawers, trays, and compartments store a variety of tools and hardware. Some have casters for easy mobility in the shop.

When working outside the shop, use a carpenter's pouch, or tool belt, to store and carry basic tools and hardware. A canvas nail apron holds nails, screws, other fasteners, and small tools.

Clothing. Dress appropriately in your workshop and have any helpers do the same. Wear proper footwear, preferably sturdy leather shoes or boots with nonslip soles; sandles and open-toed or canvas shoes are inappropriate. Roll long sleeves up above the elbows, tie long hair back, and never wear dangling jewelry or loose-fitting clothing, especially when operating power tools; they can become entangled in the tool and cause serious injury. Wear gloves to protect your hands when working with rough materials, sharp edges, hot metal, or broken glass and when unloading supplies or cleaning up.

Do not wear gloves when handling most tools. A hand tool may slip from your grasp or twist around and injure you; a power tool's cutter may catch a glove and drag your hand in with it.

Wear kneepads when installing tile, doing masonry work, or working on other projects that require kneeling for long periods. If you don't have kneepads, kneel on a folded blanket or thick newspaper while working.

Eye and ear protection. Wear adequate eye protection whenever you do sawing, grinding, filing, chiseling, or any other work that involves dust, flying chips, or harmful liquids that might splash into your eyes. Safety glasses give general protection, but goggles are more efficient and can be worn over prescription eyeglasses. For full protection, use a face shield.

When using power tools or doing noisy work such as pounding nails, wear hearing protectors or earplugs. They filter out damaging noise but let you hear a person's voice.

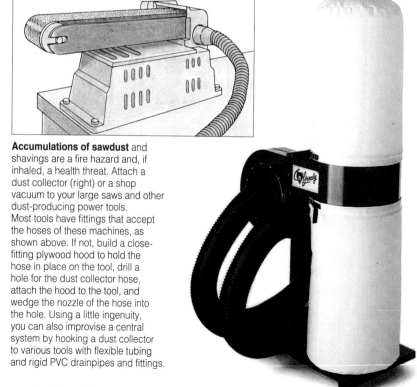

Accumulations of sawdust and shavings are a fire hazard and, if inhaled, a health threat. Attach a dust collector (right) or a shop vacuum to your large saws and other dust-producing power tools. Most tools have fittings that accept the hoses of these machines, as shown above. If not, build a close-fitting plywood hood to hold the hose in place on the tool, drill a hole for the dust collector hose, attach the hood to the tool, and wedge the nozzle of the hose into the hole. Using a little ingenuity, you can also improvise a central system by hooking a dust collector to various tools with flexible tubing and rigid PVC drainpipes and fittings.

Safe work habits. Whether you're working with hand or power tools, think about safety before and with every move you make. Keep your mind on your work, avoid distractions, work at a comfortable pace, and stop before you get tired. Avoid potentially dangerous operations that you don't feel totally comfortable performing. Don't smoke in the shop.

Keep children, visitors, and pets out of your workshop, especially when you are operating power tools. They could cause an accident by distracting you or getting in your way.

Tools are dangerous if used improperly. To ensure safety, always read and follow the owner's manual or instructions that came with the tool. Be careful to use the right tool for the job; never force a tool to work beyond its capacity or your ability. When working with power tools, observe the safety rules listed at right.

Clearing the air. Wood, metal, concrete, and other workshop dust is hazardous when inhaled. Dust created from sanding some woods, including pressure-treated woods, and some stains and finishes can cause harm when it comes in contact with the skin and eyes.

Ventilate your shop by opening windows and doors or by turning on an exhaust fan. Use a dust mask for jobs that generate dust and a respirator for work involving toxic fumes (such as using glues and strippers) or when working with insulation.

The most effective dust masks are "NIOSH-approved" (approved by the National Institute for Occupational Safety and Health in the U.S. In some cases, NIOSH standards are also benchmarks for Canadian safety organizations). Respirators are available with interchangeable color-coded cartridges to filter out toxic dust and the fumes from specific materials, such as paints, lacquers, and adhesives.

Use a dust collector or shop vacuum as often as possible to keep dust and debris from accumulating, and attach one to all the machines you can.

Basic safety equipment includes (moving clockwise): safety goggles, hearing protectors, a dual-cartridge respirator, kneepads, a NIOSH-approved dust mask, and a full face shield.

SAFETY WITH POWER TOOLS

To promote safety when working with power tools, always take the following precautions:
▷ Make sure that the tool you are using is double insulated and properly grounded.
▷ Don't operate a tool if you are tired or under the influence of medication, drugs, or alcohol.
▷ Mentally run through the procedures for using a tool before switching it on.
▷ Never ignore, override, or remove safety devices, such as blade guards, splitters, and antikickback mechanisms on saws.
▷ Don't saw wet wood, and be especially careful when sawing warped or knotty wood.
▷ Check wood for nails, screws, and loose knots before cutting or drilling.
▷ Support large workpieces during operations. When cutting long stock or large plywood panels, get an assistant or use a roller stand to support the stock at the outfeed side of a saw.
▷ Clamp all work securely in place.
▷ Use feather boards, push sticks, or jigs to move stock past a whirling cutter.
▷ Leave no foreign items on the tool's table.
▷ Remove adjusting keys and wrenches from a tool before turning on the power.
▷ Before plugging in a tool, make sure the power switch is off, tighten all of its clamps, knobs, nuts, and levers, and make sure its cutters are securely attached.
▷ Never operate a power tool while standing on a wet surface.

▷ Keep children and pets out of the workshop when operating power tools.
▷ Keep your fingers, hands, and other parts of your body well out of the path of cutters.
▷ Keep power cords away from cutters.
▷ Maintain a firm footing; never reach so far with a portable tool that you become unbalanced. Don't reach over the cutter of any tool.
▷ Stand to one side of a saw in case the blade binds and causes the tool to kick back.
▷ When you finish making a cut, turn off the tool and let the cutters come to a full stop naturally if the machine has no brake; never slow down or stop a cutter with a piece of wood.
▷ Never touch a moving cutter.
▷ If a cutter stalls, switch off the power and unplug the tool before trying to free the cutter.
▷ If you are interrupted while using a power tool, finish the operation you are working on and switch the tool off before responding.
▷ Never clear scraps from a saw table with your fingers; use a long stick.
▷ Turn off and unplug tools when not in use or when making adjustments, performing maintenance, or changing cutters or accessories.
▷ Sharpen or replace any dull or damaged cutters as soon as possible.
▷ Never use the power cord to carry a tool or to pull out its plug.
▷ Don't be overconfident, or you will become careless and have an accident.

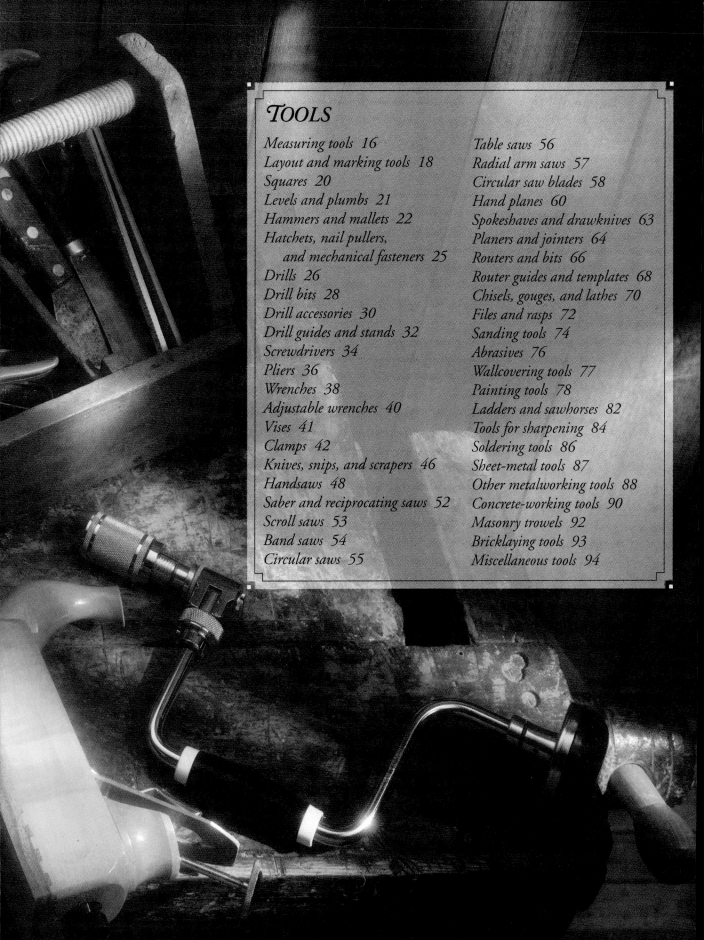

TOOLS

For any job that requires accuracy—from making a simple wooden box to installing a built-in entertainment center—a good set of measuring tools is important for figuring lengths, widths, and angles. Even a small miscalculation can make a difference in the appearance or operation of the finished work; improperly measured pieces will not fit together smoothly when assembled. And if the first step is off, the error can compound itself as you continue, resulting in a significant blunder. A basic assortment of rules, gauges, and calipers is a must for any workshop.

Folding carpenter's rule is useful for measurements where a rigid rule is necessary. Hinged sections fold for easy storage. This model is made of hardwood with a brass sliding extension for inside and depth measurements. It also highlights standard stud spacing. Common lengths for this rule are 6 ft. and 8 ft.

Steel rule has imperial and metric graduations. An accurate straightedge makes the rule suitable for use as a guide for scribing and cutting when straight lines are important. It comes in lengths from 12 to 48 in.

Retractable tape stores a spring-loaded metal rule in a small case. The rule is usually replaceable. A hook on the end of the rule catches on a workpiece, making long measurements a one-person job. Most models feature a metal case with a belt clip and a locking mechanism to prevent retraction. Some retractable tapes have a case that can double as a square (right). Standard lengths are available from 3 to 50 ft.

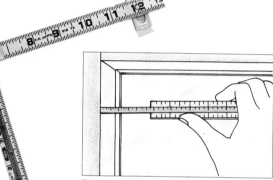

For making inside measurements, slide out brass extension. Add measurements on the rule and on the extension for total distance.

Wrap tape around odd-shaped object; align edges. Start measuring at 2 in.; subtract 2 in. from total.

Micrometer, a high-precision metalworking tool, measures dimensions up to 1 in. in thousandths of an inch. Most indicate outside dimensions, but some show inside dimensions.

Screw pitch gauge offers an easy way to identify the number of threads on a screw, bolt, nut, or in a threaded hole. A series of notched metal blades held in a case correspond to the shape and spacing of the threads. Hold the various blades against the threads until a perfect snug fit is achieved. The number on the blade indicates the correct size.

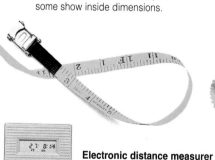

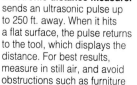

Long tape is made of nonconducting fiberglass (it may stretch a small amount) or a more accurate flexible rust-resistant steel. For one-person measuring, hook the metal loop on the end of the tape over a nail. Retract the tape by using the manual crank. The tape is made up to 300 ft. long for large measuring jobs such as house exteriors, landscaping, and fencing.

Electronic distance measurer sends an ultrasonic pulse up to 250 ft. away. When it hits a flat surface, the pulse returns to the tool, which displays the distance. For best results, measure in still air, and avoid obstructions such as furniture or trees. Look for a model that can also calculate numbers.

Gauge plate comes in different gauge systems to check the thickness of sheet metal or of wire. To use one, push the wire or sheet metal edge into the slots until you find the right size. The number by the slot shows the gauge.

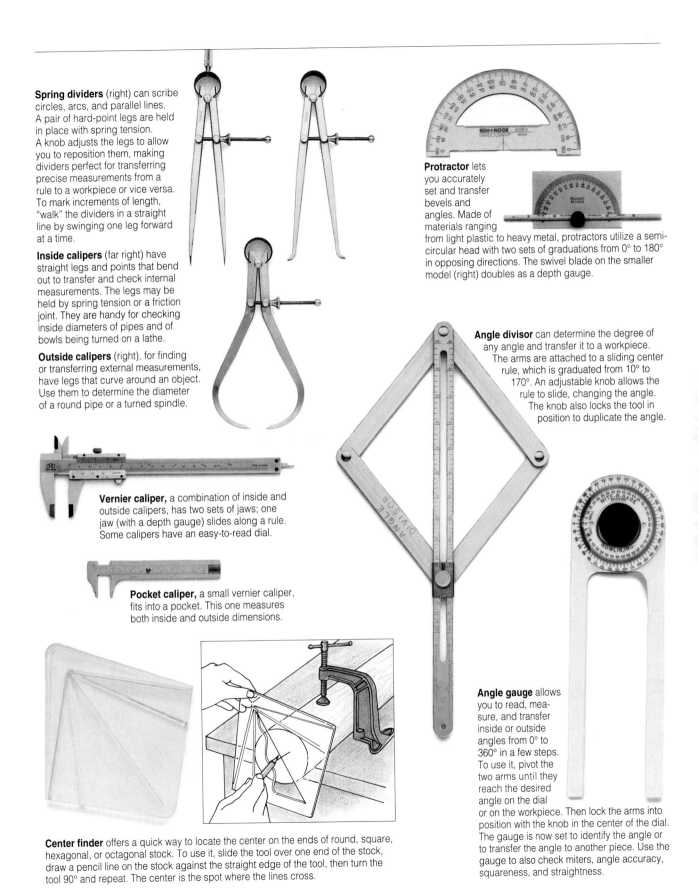

Spring dividers (right) can scribe circles, arcs, and parallel lines. A pair of hard-point legs are held in place with spring tension. A knob adjusts the legs to allow you to reposition them, making dividers perfect for transferring precise measurements from a rule to a workpiece or vice versa. To mark increments of length, "walk" the dividers in a straight line by swinging one leg forward at a time.

Inside calipers (far right) have straight legs and points that bend out to transfer and check internal measurements. The legs may be held by spring tension or a friction joint. They are handy for checking inside diameters of pipes and of bowls being turned on a lathe.

Outside calipers (right), for finding or transferring external measurements, have legs that curve around an object. Use them to determine the diameter of a round pipe or a turned spindle.

Vernier caliper, a combination of inside and outside calipers, has two sets of jaws; one jaw (with a depth gauge) slides along a rule. Some calipers have an easy-to-read dial.

Pocket caliper, a small vernier caliper, fits into a pocket. This one measures both inside and outside dimensions.

Center finder offers a quick way to locate the center on the ends of round, square, hexagonal, or octagonal stock. To use it, slide the tool over one end of the stock, draw a pencil line on the stock against the straight edge of the tool, then turn the tool 90° and repeat. The center is the spot where the lines cross.

Protractor lets you accurately set and transfer bevels and angles. Made of materials ranging from light plastic to heavy metal, protractors utilize a semi-circular head with two sets of graduations from 0° to 180° in opposing directions. The swivel blade on the smaller model (right) doubles as a depth gauge.

Angle divisor can determine the degree of any angle and transfer it to a workpiece. The arms are attached to a sliding center rule, which is graduated from 10° to 170°. An adjustable knob allows the rule to slide, changing the angle. The knob also locks the tool in position to duplicate the angle.

Angle gauge allows you to read, measure, and transfer inside or outside angles from 0° to 360° in a few steps. To use it, pivot the two arms until they reach the desired angle on the dial or on the workpiece. Then lock the arms into position with the knob in the center of the dial. The gauge is now set to identify the angle or to transfer the angle to another piece. Use the gauge to also check miters, angle accuracy, squareness, and straightness.

LAYOUT AND MARKING TOOLS

Many jobs involve laying out angles and curves as well as straight lines. To lay out a design properly, you will need specialized tools and gauges. Protractors and compasses are most commonly used for drawing curves, but other tools are available. A number of combination tools are handy for multiple uses. To transfer points and cutting lines on your work, you will need various scribers, awls, punches, chalk lines, and gauges.

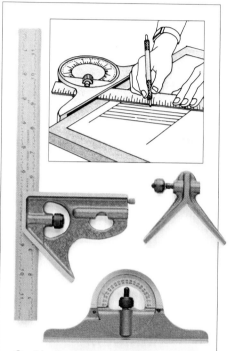

French curves, made of clear acrylic, are used to draw irregular shapes and perspective details. Simply trace along the desired edge to make matching curves in as many locations as you wish.

Compass draws arcs and circles. Insert a pencil into the tool's short leg, set the distance between the two legs to the desired radius, position the metal pivot point at the center of the projected circle, and swing the pencil over the surface.

Sliding T-bevel is an adjustable gauge for setting, testing, and transferring angles. The handle is made of wood or plastic. The metal blade pivots and can be locked at any angle by loosening and tightening the wing nut. Set the angle from an existing one, or set it using a protractor. The end of the blade is angled at 45° for use on mitered corners.

Combination tool consists of a rule, protractor head, squaring head, and center finder. To use protractor, lock it onto rule at correct angle, set flat face of head along edge of work, and scribe line, as shown. To use center finder, lock it onto rule, position its ends on circle, and draw line using rule; reposition and repeat.

Trammel points draw large circles and arcs. Attach them to a yardstick, board, or bar so that the distance between them is equal to the radius of the circle or arc you wish to draw, and use the assembly like a compass.

Another combination tool does the job of seven individual tools: 18-in. rule, square, protractor, bevel, pitch-to-foot indicator, plumb, and level—in fact, a total of four separate levels allow readings from various positions. To use the tool as a square or bevel, mount the steel rule in the revolving turret of the 9-in. stock. The turret shows degrees on one side and pitch on the other.

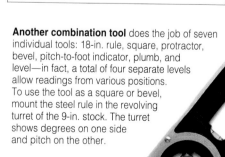

Direct-read compass has a graduated scale for more accuracy in setting. The drawing lead can be replaced with a steel point for scribing metal.

Flexible curve is a bendable vinyl-wrapped bundle of lead strips for forming, transferring, and duplicating unusual shapes. Bend the tool into any shape, hold it in position, and trace the design in as many places as you wish.

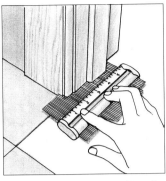

Profile gauge duplicates and transfers an irregular design to a template or piece of stock. The tool is made of a series of movable metal or plastic pins that take on the contour of whatever object they are pressed against.

Punches are steel marking instruments that are used by striking them with a hammer. The center punch (top) and the sharper prick punch (center) have beveled points for starting holes in metal and wood. The pin punch (bottom) has a straight flank and flat tip for knocking out the small pins sometimes used to assemble parts.

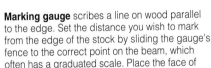

Marking gauge scribes a line on wood parallel to the edge. Set the distance you wish to mark from the edge of the stock by sliding the gauge's fence to the correct point on the beam, which often has a graduated scale. Place the face of the fence against the edge of the wood and draw the pin along the stock. Both a wooden and a metal gauge are shown here. You can set the two slides on the metal gauge for different measurements and use them alternatively.

Mortise gauge scribes double lines on the ends of wood for laying out mortises. Lock the gauge's fence at the exact measurement, hold the face of the fence against the side of the stock, and draw the pin across it.

Metal scriber makes light marks on soft metal. Use it to mark layout and cutting lines or even to write an instruction or direction that will be hidden later.

Awl makes small holes for starting nails, drill bits, and screws, and can be used in place of a pencil for marking very fine layout and cutting lines. The steel shank is sharpened to a point; the tool's handle is plastic or wood. The awl also punches holes in leather or vinyl.

Automatic punch operates on a spring so that you need not hit it with a hammer. Simply grasp the tool in one hand and push down firmly where you want a mark.

Chalk line, a case filled with chalk and 50 to 100 ft. of line on a reel, marks a long straight line between two points. Pull the line from the case, hold it taut, and snap it to leave a chalk mark as a guide. The tool can also be used as a plumb bob.

Pounce wheels make light perforation marks in wood when rolled across its surface. They can be used with carbon paper for drawing dotted lines.

Electronic stud finder locates studs behind wall coverings by measuring changes in the wall's density. Also available are inexpensive magnetic finders that react to the screws or nails that secure wall coverings to the studs. Either type can be thrown off by steel pipes or wires in the wall.

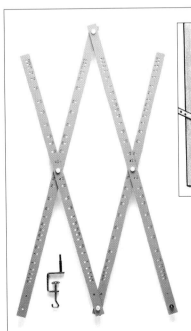

Pantograph copies a design and enlarges it or reduces it in the process. Clamp the tool to a drawing table or flat board, set it up as shown, and adjust it to get the desired scale. Use one hand to trace over the original design with the stylus and the other hand to guide the pencil as it draws the copy.

SQUARES

A type of layout and measuring tool, the square is essential for accurately marking and assembling a project. If it's made in two pieces, the metal or wood handle is called the stock; on a one-piece model, the metal handle is called the tongue. To lay out and mark cuts, place the handle parallel to the object and draw a line against the blade. Models with the blade set at a 90° angle to the handle can also check squareness after cutting and assembling the workpiece. Some models have blades set at different angles.

Adjustable T-square is a heavy-duty layout tool suitable for laying out square and angled lines on large surfaces such as wallboard, plywood, paneling, and other sheet materials. It generally has a 48-in.-long handle; a 22-in.-long pivoting blade locks in position at any angle.

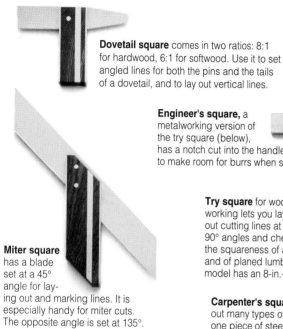

Dovetail square comes in two ratios: 8:1 for hardwood, 6:1 for softwood. Use it to set angled lines for both the pins and the tails of a dovetail, and to lay out vertical lines.

Engineer's square, a metalworking version of the try square (below), has a notch cut into the handle near the blade to make room for burrs when scoring metal.

Try square for woodworking lets you lay out cutting lines at 90° angles and check the squareness of adjoining surfaces and of planed lumber. The most useful model has an 8-in.-long blade.

Miter square has a blade set at a 45° angle for laying out and marking lines. It is especially handy for miter cuts. The opposite angle is set at 135°.

Carpenter's square is practical for laying out many types of projects. It's made from one piece of steel and incremented in inches. Other markings indicate, for example, 30°, 45°, and 60° angles. Sizes go up to a 24-in. blade and a 16-in. tongue.

Framing square, a specialized version of the carpenter's square, has tables and formulas imprinted on it for making quick calculations, including ones for figuring area and volume.

Rafter angle square, like the framing square, is a type of carpenter's square. It's marked with degree gradations for fast laying out, and the square's small size makes it easy to store and transport.

Combination square combines several features of measuring and marking tools. Its blade and sliding adjustable head incorporate a try square, a 45° miter square, and a level in one compact unit.

LEVELS AND PLUMBS

Whether you're hanging a sink, setting a fence post, or putting up a wall, keeping surfaces level and plumb is vital. A spirit level has one or more clear vials filled with a liquid. When you rest the level on a surface, a bubble in the liquid shows that the surface is "true" when it floats in an area marked on the vial. Longer levels are usually more accurate than shorter ones.

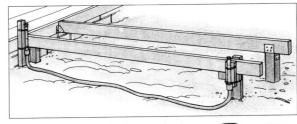

Digital level (right) does everything other levels do but does it electronically. Lights on older models flash red for not level or green for level. Newer models feature a simulated bubble display plus a digital readout of degrees of slope, inches per foot for rise and run of stairs and roofs, and a percentage of slope for drainage problems on decks and masonry.

Torpedo level (below), a shorter 8- to 9-in. version of a carpenter's level, is preferred by plumbers because it can fit into most restricted places. It usually has three bubble vials—which can be read through both top and side windows—to show levelness, plumb, and 45° angle. Some models are grooved on the bottom for resting on pipes and shafts.

Carpenter's level (left, center) comes with a varying number of vials to check horizontal level and vertical plumb. The vials may be adjustable or replaceable. The frames are usually made of aluminum, brass, magnesium, plastic, or wood. Some frames are magnetized to keep hands free for moving the workpiece. Before buying a level, test it on a known level surface. The standard lengths are 24 in. and 48 in. To check the drop of a sloped surface, place a 4-ft. level on the surface; use wood blocks to level the tool. Every inch of wood block equals ¼ in. per ft. of drop.

Mason's level (left), similar to a carpenter's level, includes special features such as heavy-duty bubble vials, a hardwood and brass body, and protective rubber end plates. The frame is longer, up to 72 in., for checking across concrete and brick.

Water level, when attached to a garden hose and filled with water, establishes level heights at a distance that is limited only by the length of the hose. To use it, screw a tube onto each end of the hose; then fill the hose with water. Hold up one tube until the liquid reaches a desired height; the water in the other tube will adjust itself to the same height.

Line level is a handy miniature level with hooks that attach to a taut line stretched between two points. It has a standard vial, and is very useful in masonry, fencing, and landscaping projects.

Angle level uses a dial and needle indicator (like a compass) to determine levelness and various degrees of angle. Some models attach magnetically to a metal straightedge, square, or other metal surface.

Circular level, a 360° disc-shaped level, is also called a bull's-eye level. It's useful for shimming furniture and appliances, and for leveling recreational vehicles and boats. The bubble is centered in a circle when level.

Plumb bob has a weight attached to a line. To establish plumb (a straight vertical line), suspend the line from a height and drop the weight to the ground. Wait for the weight to steady before checking plumb—for example, when aligning wallcoverings or paneling.

HAMMERS AND MALLETS

Most hammers come in a variety of head weights and handle lengths. Choose a quality tool that is precision balanced, fits your hand, matches your strength, and is designed for the work you are doing. A quality hammer will have a forged steel head and a hardwood, fiberglass, graphite, or steel handle. Avoid dangerous cast heads and softwood handles. Faces may be milled (corrugated) to prevent glancing blows and flying nails, but a milled face cannot be used on finished work or it will mar the surface. Most handles are contoured for comfort, and some have slip-resistant grips.

Ball-peen hammer has two faces. One is flat, for striking cold chisels and punches. The other, the *peen*, is rounded, or ball-like, for bending and shaping soft metal. The ball-peen hammer generally has a wood or fiberglass handle from 10 to 16 in. long. Head weights range from 2 to 48 oz. A 20-oz. hammer is good for general use.

Ripping hammer is similar to a curved-claw hammer except that its claw is almost straight. Although not as effective a nail puller as the curved-claw hammer, it is excellent for prying apart or tearing out boards, lath, or sheet materials. The handle is generally 10 to 17 in. long and the head weighs 10 to 22 oz. Heavier ripping hammers are called framing hammers. Some hammers have magnetized heads to hold nails.

Curved-claw hammer, the most familiar of all hammers, can be used for driving common or finishing nails, but not case-hardened cut nails or concrete nails, which can damage it. The head can weigh 10 to 24 oz. and has a sharply angled claw to extract nails. The handle is 10 to 16 in. long.

Soft-faced hammer will not mar surfaces because its 1½- to 32-oz. steel head has replaceable soft and hard plastic faces. The hammer is used for joining, seaming, and assembling or disassembling wood or soft metal projects. Its handle is 8 to 14½ in. long.

Tack hammer, a small lightweight tool, holds and sets tacks, small nails, and brads. It usually has a wooden handle from 10 to 11 in. long. The head, which weighs 5 to 8 oz., has a magnetic face on one end and another striking face or a small claw on the other. The tack hammer is used on cabinetwork, molding, trim, and upholstery.

Bricklayer's hammer usually has a square flat face for setting bricks in mortar and a chisel-shaped face for scoring and cutting bricks and chipping away excess mortar. The head can weigh 10 to 24 oz., and the wood or tubular steel handle is 8 to 14½ in. long.

Cross-peen, or Warrington, hammer has a head with a flat face and a tapered peen. This carefully balanced hammer is a traditional cabinetmaker's tool. You can hold a nail in place with two fingers and start tapping it in with the peen face without smashing your fingers. The head weighs 3½ to 12 oz., and the handle is 10½ to 15 in. long.

Nail set, a punch-shaped tool, countersinks nails in wooden cabinets, furniture, moldings, and trim. Position its point over the head of the nail and strike the top with a hammer. Points range in diameter from $\frac{1}{32}$ to $\frac{5}{32}$ in. to accommodate the various nailhead sizes.

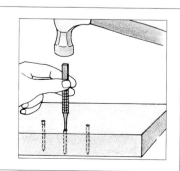

Jeweler's hammer is a lightweight tool that is ideal for working on models, miniatures, and jewelry. Its head is 2½ to 3 in. long, and its handle is 8½ to 10 in. long.

Sledgehammer breaks up concrete or drives heavy spikes, stakes, or chisels into stone, brick, or the ground by the sheer power of the weight of its solid steel head, which ranges from 2 to 20 lb. The wood or fiberglass handle can be as short as 10 in. or as long as 36 in. The heavy long-handled sledges are used primarily for demolition tasks.

Heavy-duty framing hammer, a construction tool for assembling and dismantling framing members, has an even narrower and straighter claw than the standard framing hammer. The hammer has a 17-in.-long hatchet handle, which gives more leverage and is less likely to twist in your hand. The head weighs 23 oz. The model shown here has a milled face.

Carpenter's wooden-head mallet, used mainly for assembling woodworking components and striking chisels, is also good for installing metal parts on equipment without marring them. Its 2½- to 7-in.-long head weighs 6 to 30 oz. and is usually made of beech or lignum vitae.

Carver's mallet drives chisels and other carving tools into wood or stone. Its heavy head (16 to 40 oz.) is made from a single piece of lignum vitae wood that is 4 to 6 in. long. Store the mallet in a plastic bag to keep it from drying out.

Two-faced mallet has a 3½- to 7-in.-long head with a 1⅝-in. round face and a 1⅝- x ¼-in. wedge face. The round face shapes sheet metal into bowls or other concave shapes when hammered inside a wooden form. The wedge face shapes, or *raises*, metal over a solid stake.

Hand-drilling hammer, a broad double-faced construction hammer, is used for striking star drills, hardened nails, punches, and cold and brick chisels. The metal head weighs 2½ to 4 oz., and the handle (generally wood) is 10 in. long.

Rubber mallet is used primarily in assembling components and pounding out dents in metal. The barrel-shaped head is usually made of solid black rubber or nonmarking white rubber, weighing 18 to 32 oz. The handle is generally wood and is 10 to 13 in. long.

Dead-blow hammer head is filled with steel shot and oil that absorb energy when the hammer impacts, eliminating any rebound in demolition and assembly work. The head weighs 8 oz. to 4 lb., and the handle is 10 to 14 in. long.

Rawhide mallet consists of a round head of compressed rawhide, weighing 3 to 30 oz., and an 11- to 12-in.-long wooden handle. It has the same uses as a carpenter's wooden-head mallet.

METALWORKING HAMMERS AND HAMMERING SURFACES

Because so much metalworking involves hammering, a large number of specialized metalworking hammers are available. Before using a hammer to shape metal, be sure that the face is clean and free of pits or scale; the tiniest defect in the hammer head can be imprinted on the work many times over. It is a good idea to keep a piece of crocus cloth or tack cloth handy to wipe off the face of the hammer as you work. Before storing a metalworking hammer for a long period of time, coat the face with petroleum jelly, wax, or oil.

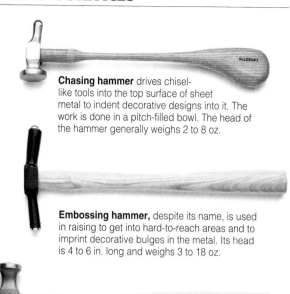

Chasing hammer drives chisel-like tools into the top surface of sheet metal to indent decorative designs into it. The work is done in a pitch-filled bowl. The head of the hammer generally weighs 2 to 8 oz.

Embossing hammer, despite its name, is used in raising to get into hard-to-reach areas and to imprint decorative bulges in the metal. Its head is 4 to 6 in. long and weighs 3 to 18 oz.

Raising hammer shapes deep metal objects, such as bowls or vases, by striking their outer surfaces over solid metal stakes. Standard and extra-narrow heads are available, running from 4 to 6 in. long and generally weighing 8 to 16 oz.

Setting hammer has an angled face for forming and bending sheet metal, and a flat face for flattening seams without marring the surface of the metal. The head is 5 to 6 in. long and weighs 16 to 20 oz.

Planishing hammer flattens and toughens sheet metal as it adds texture to it. The head is 2 to 8 in. long and weighs 2 to 19 oz. Some models have one square and one round face.

Forging hammer is used to shape metal rods or bars. The head is 4 to 6 in. long and weighs 3 to 18 oz. It generally has one slightly domed or flat face and one wedge-shaped face.

Blacksmith's hammer, the traditional tool for shaping heated metal on an anvil, is also used for driving spikes, stakes, rivets, and hardened nails, for striking cold chisels, and for any job that requires a heavy striking face. The head weighs 2 to 4 lb., and one of its faces is flat and the other is wedge-shaped.

Anvil (far right), one of the oldest and most used metal-shaping surfaces, is available in a wide variety of sizes. The familiar shape is flat on top and coned on one end. Metal is also shaped on solid steel stakes, which weigh from 5 to 50 lb. The crossbar of a T-stake may be curved, tapered, or shaped like the horns of a bull. Mushroom stakes and flat circular stakes are also widely used. To hold a stake while hammering against it, slide it into a bolted-down holder, like the one shown, or into a special opening in your workbench or anvil. Rectangular blocks and cone-shaped mandrels are also used as hammering surfaces.

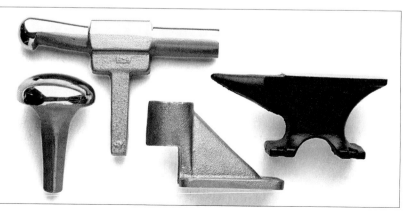

HATCHETS, NAIL PULLERS, AND MECHANICAL FASTENERS

There are a number of other hammerlike tools and driving tools that are related to the hammer. The hatchet, of course, is used for chopping rather than driving or shaping, but many hatchets have a hammer face opposite the cutting face. Other hand and power tools are used for driving brads and staples, and large pry bars and nail pullers do the work that is too difficult for the claws on standard hammers.

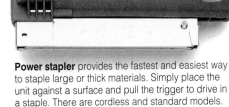

Drywall hatchet, a combination hammer and hatchet, is used to trim, position, and attach wallboard to studs. Use the flat head of the tool to drive and set nails on flat surfaces and close to corners. Use the beveled slot to pull nails, and the sharp hatchet face to make cutouts and score breaks in wallboard. The handle is 12½ to 16 in. long, and the head weighs 12 to 14 oz.

Power stapler provides the fastest and easiest way to staple large or thick materials. Simply place the unit against a surface and pull the trigger to drive in a staple. There are cordless and standard models.

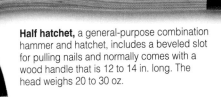

Half hatchet, a general-purpose combination hammer and hatchet, includes a beveled slot for pulling nails and normally comes with a wood handle that is 12 to 14 in. long. The head weighs 20 to 30 oz.

Brad nailer holds small nails in its magnetized spring-loaded barrel while you drive them in by pushing the handle.

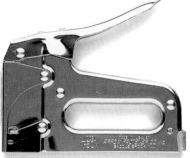

Hand stapler drives staples with a squeeze of the handle. Use it to attach paper-covered insulation, hang plastic sheets, upholster furniture, install screening, or for any major stapling job in your home or workshop.

Power brad nailer drives and countersinks brads 1 to 1¼ in. long with the pull of a trigger—and without marring the surface.

Shingling hatchet is a special tool for installing wooden shingles and shakes. The sharp face cuts the shingles, and a gauge on the side of the face spaces the shingles evenly; move the screw to the desired depth. The handle is 14 in. long; the head weighs 14 oz.

Pry bar utilizes two angled blades. One blade is used as a nail puller, and the other as a prying tool for removing molding and trim and for separating materials that are nailed together. It is 12 to 30 in. long.

Nail puller removes deeply embedded nails, exerting more leverage with its 15-in. length than a claw hammer can. It can be struck with a hand-drilling hammer for even more power. Some models have a cushioned grip.

Hammer tacker drives a staple in one motion. Simply strike the tool against the surface to be stapled. Various sizes of staples can be used in a hammer tacker.

DRILLS

Although a number of hand-powered drilling tools are available, every workshop should have at least one electric drill. Equipped with the right bit or attachment, an electric drill can bore holes in almost any material and do the work of other tools as well. The size of a drill is determined by the largest bit shank its chuck accepts. A drill may run at a single speed, two or three set speeds, or at variable speeds, which you set to suit the job. Generally, the larger the drill the slower it runs but the greater its turning power, or *torque*. Before drilling, make sure the work is firmly supported and clamped down. Make a starter hole with a center punch, awl, or nail to keep the bit from wandering.

Brace works by manually cranking the center handle as you apply pressure toward the bit. The brace is suitable for boring large holes in wood and for driving and removing screws. The bits must have a special end that is designed to fit into the brace's chuck jaw.

Hand drill bores holes in wood, soft metal, and plastics, using twist or countersink bits with ¼-in. shanks. A hand crank turns an interlocking gear to rotate the bit; reverse it to withdraw the bit.

Push drill operates with a repetitive pushing motion that turns a bit and bores a pilot hole up to ¹¹⁄₆₄ in. in diameter. You can use the tool with one hand, leaving the other free to hold the work or guide the tool. The drill accepts *drill points*. In this model, the points are stored in the handle; a knurled knob opens the handle.

Miniature hand drill holds high-speed steel bits as small as #80 (.025 in.). This model has a collet on both ends to accept the bits. A miniature drill is especially handy for working on models, miniatures, and jewelry. You can also use it to make pilot holes for small screws.

Standard electric hand drill comes with ¼-, ⅜-, and ½-in. chucks to hold bits. Select a reversible drill so that you can back out bits or loosen screws, and get one with variable speeds if you want to use it with the various available accessories. Because of its high speed, the ¼-in. model is good for boring small holes, but the ⅜-in. drill (upper left) can handle most household jobs, making it a better choice for the homeowner. The ½-in. drill (left) can bore larger holes, but because it runs at a slower speed, it's unsuitable for sanding and grinding.

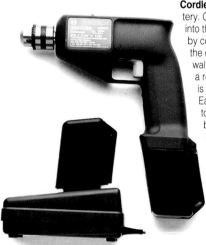

Cordless drill is powered by a battery. One type has a battery built into the drill's handle; recharge it by connecting the transformer to the drill and plugging it into a wall outlet. The other type has a removable battery pack that is recharged in a separate unit. Each pack takes 15 min. to 3 hr. to charge and is designed to be recharged more than 300 times. Buy an extra battery so that you can recharge one while using the other. Never charge (or store) a tool where the temperature is below 40°F (4.5°C) or above 105°F (40.5°C). For longer battery life, turn drill off when it's not in use.

Close-quarters drill has the same capabilities as a standard ⅜-in. electric drill, but its 55°-angled chuck and unique, well-balanced body shape also allow access to hard-to-reach areas. A paddle switch allows you to control speed up to 1,300 rpm. Another switch on the bottom of the drill controls forward and reverse directions.

Drill-screwdriver,
as the name implies,
both drills and drives
screws. Its motor
has greater torque for
driving screws without
burning out; it also pow-
ers the drill through tough
materials quickly. The cordless type,
shown here, is easier to manipulate
and can be used far from an electric
outlet without awkward cords.

Drywall driver is
designed specifically
for driving drywall screws
through wallboard and into
wooden studs. The driver tip
has a depth stop. Set the torque
so that it doesn't overtighten the
screw and tear the material or damage the screwhead. Cordless models
are available.

Hammer drill can bore into concrete and brick.
This tool simultaneously spins a bit and creates a
hammering action, which is rated in bpm (blows per
minute). The variable-speed feature can turn out up to
40,000 bpm. Most models are reversible and can be quickly
switched to a standard rotary-action drill. Some are cordless.
A depth stop and a detachable side handle may be included.

D-handle drill is suitable for driving auger
bits and for other jobs where high torque
is desirable. It comes with a ½-in. chuck and
with single, double, or variable-speed control.
The D-shaped spade handle and side handle provide a secure grip for precise control on large jobs.

Right-angle drill has a right-angled head
for operating in tight spaces where a standard
drill body will not fit. The side handle helps support
the tool. The angled head on this ½-in. model can be
removed to use the drill straight on; some models do
not have this feature. Use high speed for drilling small
holes and low speed for large ones.

Drill press incorporates an electric drill and worktable in one unit. Both freestanding and bench-top
models are available, but either type must be bolted
down. The machine's throat capacity (the distance
between its rear post and the center of the bit) determines the maximum size of the workpiece it can
accept. Secure the work on the machine's table;
lower the bit into the work by pulling down on the
handle. The permanently positioned drill and adjustable worktable make the drill press the most accurate method of drilling square and angled holes.
It's also ideal for sanding and shaping attachments.

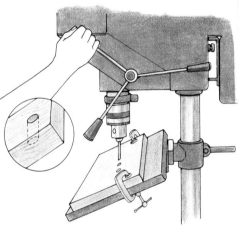

A clamp by the post adjusts the table's height; a
clamp under the table adjusts its angle. Clamp
smaller work and sheet metal to the table; to guide
larger pieces, secure a jig to the table.

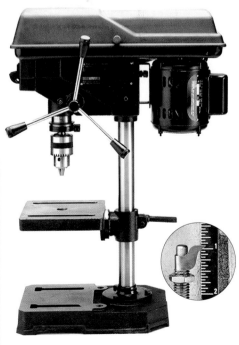

DRILL BITS

In order for them to be versatile—so they can make holes of different sizes and in a variety of materials—drills are designed to accept specialized bits. There are bits for wood, ferrous and nonferrous metals, plastic, wallboard, concrete, masonry, glass, and tile. Some bits make extra-smooth and accurate entrances and exits, which is desirable in fine woodworking; other less expensive bits make accurate holes when used properly, but can create rough exits if too much pressure is applied. Most types of bits are available in a wide range of sizes and quality. For the best results, always use the bit that is recommended for a specific job.

Screw pilot bit comes in several sizes to bore shank and pilot holes for a specific-size wood screw. In the same step you can also create a countersink to recess the screwhead or a counterbore to hide the screwhead. The tapered bit (right) creates a snug fit for wood screws.

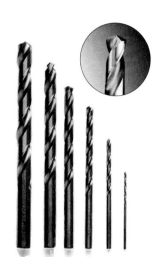

Twist bit made of carbon steel is designed for wood. For metal, use a twist bit made of high-speed steel; lubricate the bit with machine oil when drilling in steel or wrought iron, with kerosene when drilling in aluminum.

Brad-point bit, the best choice for wood, has a center point to position it for the exact, clean holes that are required for fine woodworking applications, especially doweling. Wide flutes eject wood chips to prevent clogging.

Adjustable screw pilot bit has a depth stop or a collar with a setscrew on its side. To set the bit for a flush, countersink, or counterbore hole, release the setscrew to move the depth stop. On the model with a collar, body and thread cutters are also adjustable; before tightening the setscrew, make sure the flat sides of all the cutting elements face the screw. The bits come in various sizes to match the diameters of different screws.

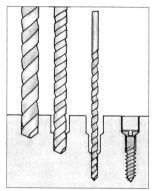

To counterbore a screw without a screw pilot bit, use twist bits slightly narrower than the screw threads and the same width as the head and body. Use a mallet to tap a glued plug into the hole.

Spade bit has a center locating point and two sharp flat cutting edges, which work with a scraping action, to bore holes in wood. Start the drill at a slow speed; as the bit enters the wood, slowly increase the speed. It can leave a rough, splintered exit hole.

Glass/tile bit has carbide tip for boring holes in glass and tile. Drill slowly through pool of turpentine held in by putty dam.

Countersink bit has an angled tip to form a recess for screwheads in wood, plastic, steel, iron,

Masonry bit is designed for drilling holes at speeds below 400 rpm in masonry, concrete, brick, tile, slate, and plaster. The carbide-tipped bit has spiral-shaped flutes to channel dust quickly and efficiently.

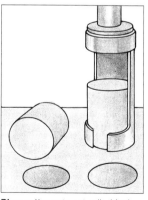

Plug cutter cuts out cylindrical shapes from hardwood to cover screw- and nailheads in counterbored holes. The plug should be a minimum of 1/8 in. deep, a maximum of 1/2 in. deep. Use the bit with a drill press only.

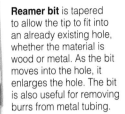

Forstner bit drills shallow hole with a sharp outside rim, leaving smooth-sided holes in wood. It has a small center spur that enables the bit to create a nearly flat-bottomed hole. To form a mortise, cut overlapping holes. Use the bit in a drill press only.

Reamer bit is tapered to allow the tip to fit into an already existing hole, whether the material is wood or metal. As the bit moves into the hole, it enlarges the hole. The bit is also useful for removing burrs from metal tubing.

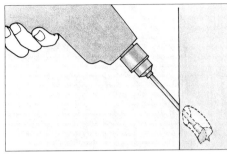

Around-the-corner bit has an angled cutting surface that lets you drill curved holes in tight corners. Gradually feed bit straight into the wood for ½ in. before turning drill to angle the hole. Set the drill at 850 to 1,000 rpm for softwood; for hardwood, set it at 600 to 850 rpm.

Pilot hole and screwdriver bits come as a set to use with electric hand drills and screwdrivers. First make the pilot hole. After the drill comes to a full stop, expose the screwdriver bit by sliding the ring toward the tip of the bit and then pulling off the pilot hole bit.

Self-feeding multispur bit bores holes large enough to run conduit or pipes through wood. To provide a fast feeding action, a replaceable threaded screw point pulls the bit to the work. The bit fits ½-in. drills only and requires extremely high torque.

Drill saw bit bores and cuts holes in both wood and metal. After the tip of the bit drills the hole, the teeth on the side of the bit cut the opening. It can also enlarge already existing holes. For metal, lubricate the tip before drilling.

Auger bit fits into the chuck of a hand brace. The tip of the bit has a point to start holes. The flutes prevent clogging by quickly ejecting wood chips as you drill, an ideal feature for making mortises.

Adjustable bit, or expansion bit, uses adjustable cutters to bore varying diameter holes. It's used to bore holes in wood for installing pipes and wiring, and in areas where a rough cut will suffice. To adjust the cutter, release the setscrew; then use the scale on the cutter to determine the hole size, and secure the setscrew.

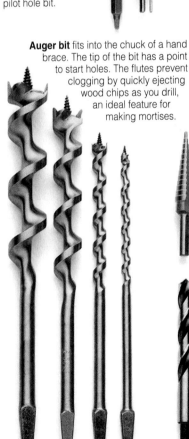

Step bit incorporates up to 13 diameters in one bit. As the bit penetrates the stock, it drills a larger hole, deburring the hole at the same time. Use it in wood, soft metal, and plastic (up to ⅛ in. thickness).

Fly cutter, or circle cutter, is used on a drill press for cutting circles. A shank holds an arm with a cutter; the cutter can be set to different diameters.

Acrylic plastic bit has a tip that can prevent splintering when drilling in plastic. Use scrap plywood or plastic under the work as a backing board. With the work securely clamped to a bench or table, drill slowly with steady pressure. As you near the other side of the work, reduce drill pressure.

Hole saw with tempered hardened-steel teeth cuts large holes in wood, metal, plastic, and wallboard. The saw is mounted on a hole saw arbor (right); the arbor is inserted into a drill. The bit extends slightly beyond the saw teeth to locate the center; then the saw is pushed into the stock.

DRILL ACCESSORIES

Although it isn't necessary to acquire accessories for your drill, they can make the tool more accurate and easier to use, and they can turn the drill into a driver, shaper, sander, grinder, or polisher. Some accessories attach to or hold the drill housing, while others fit into the chuck. If you already have a tool such as a sander or grinder, it's best to use that tool for the appropriate job. But if you don't have the additional tools, these attachments are a suitable substitute.

Chuck key comes with an electric drill to lock bits. Hand-tighten bit in chuck; insert key into holes in chuck and turn clockwise. Always remove key before using drill.

Keyless drill chuck operates without a chuck key by hand-tightening only. You can attach it to a drill that has a standard chuck or purchase one as a replacement part. Some drills are sold with this type of chuck already attached.

Flexible shaft extends the shaft of an electric drill by 36 to 52 in., making the drill more manageable for intricate detail work and for operations in tight places. One end of the shaft fits into the drill chuck; the other end has its own chuck for small drill bits, rotary rasps and files, and sanding and buffing attachments.

Depth stop and drill stop are guides for drilling holes to a specific depth. A steel or plastic drill stop (left) slides onto a bit; a depth stop (right) attaches to the body of an electric hand drill or to a secondary handle and is set to the right position. When either stop contacts the work surface, it stops the penetration of the bit.

Drill gauge, a template for measuring the size of a drill bit, has holes from 1/32 to 1/2 in. Insert a bit into each hole until you find the one that fits best; the correct dimension is marked near the hole.

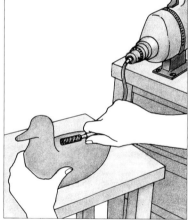

When using a flexible shaft with an electric hand drill, make sure the drill is in a stand secured to a bench. The shaft can also be used with a drill press.

Drill case, available in many styles, organizes bits for quick access. Look for a case that indicates bit size near the bit slot. This model clips onto the drill cord. To remove a bit, rotate the lid until the hole in the lid aligns with the desired bit. Tip the case to slide out the bit.

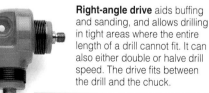

Right-angle drive aids buffing and sanding, and allows drilling in tight areas where the entire length of a drill cannot fit. It can also either double or halve drill speed. The drive fits between the drill and the chuck.

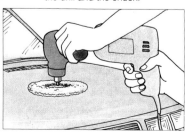

Bit extension adds to the length of a flat or hexagonal bit shaft, allowing you to bore deep holes and to make holes in recessed and hard-to-reach places with a spade or auger-type bit. Insert the bit shank into one end of the extension, and secure it with one or two setscrews. Make sure the bit is seated in a pilot hole before you start drilling. The extension comes in several lengths up to 18 in.

Screwdriver bits let you drive screws with an electric drill; some of these bits have grooved tips to hold screws more securely.

Screwdriver attachment has a clutch mechanism that stops the drill when the screw is driven or pressure is slackened. Fit the attachment to the drill chuck of a variable-speed drill and a screwdriver bit into the attachment.

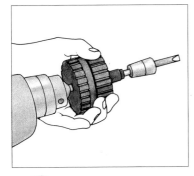

Speed reducer fits on a single-speed electric drill to allow reduced-speed operation for screw and nut driving. Hold the reducer's housing when operating. One collar allows forward rotation of the bit; the other collar reverses the direction of rotation.

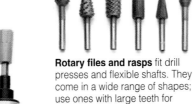

Rotary files and rasps fit drill presses and flexible shafts. They come in a wide range of shapes; use ones with large teeth for wood, with small teeth for metal.

Wire wheel, with wires extending from its perimeter, can rotate at a maximum speed of 3,000 rpm. You can use it on any size electric drill to remove paint, rust, or stains from wood or metal.

Nail spinner attaches to a ¼- or ⅜-in. electric hand drill to start finishing nails. The rotation of the nail prevents the wood from splitting and tearing as it is driven in. The spinner sets the nail almost flush to the surface; use a hammer to finish the job.

Drum sander sands curves and irregular shapes in wood, metal, fiberglass, and plastic. Lock its shank into the chuck of a portable electric drill or a drill press. The drum varies in diameter from ½ to 3¼ in. and in length from ½ to 3 in.

Wire cup brush incorporates wire strands into a circular brush. When mounted in an electric hand drill, it becomes a power scraper for removing paint, rust, or stains from wood or metal. Do not exceed maximum speed of 2,500 rpm.

Flap wheel sander has a number of sandpaper strips attached to a wheel. The spinning strips conform to the flat or contoured surface of the wood, metal, fiberglass, or plastic workpiece for sanding and buffing. It's available in various sandpaper grits.

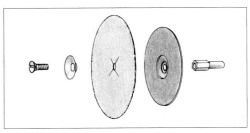

Sandpaper discs convert an electric hand drill to a sander. Some discs are used in combination with a backer pad and wheel arbor. Some systems work with self-adhesive sandpaper or have a Velcro backing. The sandpaper is available with garnet and aluminum oxide, and with coarse through fine grits.

Buffing pad is a soft pad for polishing metals. It is usually made of wool or polyester; most pads are washable and reusable.

Fiber disc sands, grinds, and cuts paint, rust, metal, tile, brick, concrete, and plastic. The disc is made of silicon carbide and attaches to any electric hand drill with a standard backer pad and wheel arbor (right, bottom). Although in some situations it can be used freehand, mounting the drill on a drill stand will allow greater control and safety.

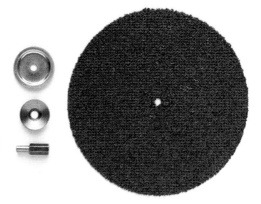

Drilling often requires precision boring that is difficult to achieve when holding an electric hand drill, even with steady hands. A variety of drill stands provide the necessary firm support for drilling holes at any angle. A drill stand also frees both hands to guide the workpiece. With certain drill accessories, such as a rotary rasp attached to a flexible shaft, a stand is essential.

Drill guides ensure accurate hole placement for a variety of drilling applications. The guides on the facing page, except for the spring-action hinge bit and the mortising attachment, can be used either with an electric hand drill or with a drill press.

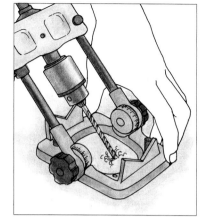

Vertical drill stand is a framework that supports an electric hand drill and turns it into a small bench-top drill press. It has all the basic drill press features: a scaled depth stop, a pull-down handle operation, and a worktable. On some models a mounting bracket swivels the drill to a horizontal position for grinding. On other models the worktable can be tilted to make angled cuts. Before using the stand, bolt it securely to a workbench.

Precision drill stand attaches to the drill in place of the chuck. Its chuck is mounted on a crosspiece that slides up and down two rods, which are attached to a flat base. The rods can be adjusted and locked into place at 5-degree intervals in order to drill holes at various angles. A collar on one rod acts as a depth stop.

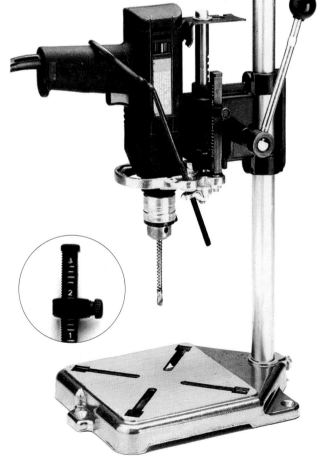

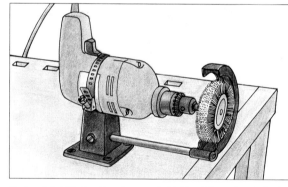

Horizontal drill stand is a base and shield unit that, when bolted to a workbench, holds ¼- and ⅜-in. electric hand drills in a horizontal position. A metal strap holds the drill securely in place on the stand. With various attachments, the drill can then be used for sanding, grinding, wire-brushing, or polishing. The stand also allows the drill to be operated with a flexible shaft (p.30).

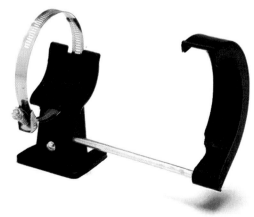

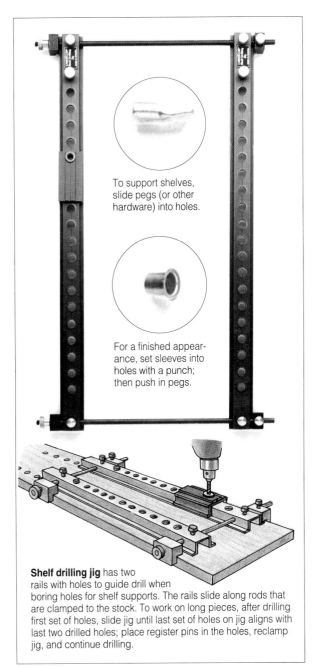

To support shelves, slide pegs (or other hardware) into holes.

For a finished appearance, set sleeves into holes with a punch; then push in pegs.

Shelf drilling jig has two rails with holes to guide drill when boring holes for shelf supports. The rails slide along rods that are clamped to the stock. To work on long pieces, after drilling first set of holes, slide jig until last set of holes on jig aligns with last two drilled holes; place register pins in the holes, reclamp jig, and continue drilling.

Spring-action hinge (Vix) bit has a bit centered in a guide. The bit fits in an electric hand drill chuck and is used for drilling pilot holes for hinge screws. First tape the hinges in position. Then place the bit in a hole in the hinge; the guide centers the bit. Push on the drill to extend the bit from the guide. A setscrew lets you adjust the depth of the pilot hole or replace the high-speed drill bit. The bit can drill into wood, metal, and plastic.

Doweling jig centers any number of holes in ends or edges of wooden workpieces of almost any thickness. The jig clamps to the workpiece; a centered hole guide shows where to bore the hole. The holes accommodate standard-diameter dowels.

Dowel centers align corresponding dowel holes in wood workpieces that are to be joined. Drill holes in one workpiece; push dowel centers into the holes, align with the second workpiece, and push. The points on the dowel centers leave marks to show where to bore holes in the second workpiece.

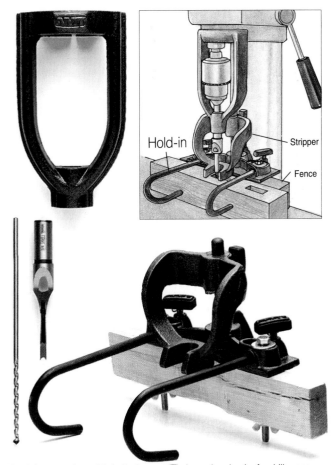

Hold-in — Stripper
Fence

Mortising attachment is bolted on a quill above the chuck of a drill press. A bit removes waste; a chisel shapes the mortise. The attachment includes a fence for guiding the work, and a stripper and hold-ins to support it. When using the attachment, run the drill press at normal speed and work down to final depth in ⅛-in. increments. As the chisel finishes each cut, move workpiece to continue the mortise.

SCREWDRIVERS

Used to insert, remove, loosen, and tighten screws, screwdrivers come in many widths and lengths, with different-shaped shanks, and with a variety of tips. Screws are driven by torque, or turning power, not by downward pressure. The larger the handle diameter, the more torque per turn. Always match the screwdriver tip to the size and type of screw. To drive a screw, hold it and the screwdriver in a straight line. A screwdriver performs under normal use without marring the tip or the screwhead. Never use a screwdriver as a pry bar, punch, or chisel; doing so can damage the tool and the workpiece.

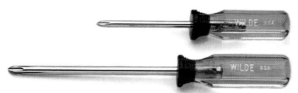

Round-shank screwdriver has a cylindrical *shank,* the steel rod between the tip and handle. The round shape lets you quickly turn the screwdriver by supporting the shank with one hand while rotating the handle with the other.

Stubby screwdriver, designed to be used in restricted areas, has a very short shank. Its large handle permits a firm grip to improve torque.

Square-shank screwdriver is used to drive screws that require a great deal of torque. With an adjustable wrench, grip the square shank and turn the screwdriver; but be careful not to apply too much torque, or the screwhead may be stripped or broken. A rubber sleeve over a plastic fluted handle on some screwdrivers also increases torque by enlarging the grip.

Cabinetmaker's screwdriver has a fat oval handle that is preferred for woodworking; it fits neatly into the palm of the hand. The parallel-sided tip fits into recessed holes to turn slotted flat-head screws without marring the work.

Electrician's screwdriver, designed for working on electrical appliances and equipment, is made with a long shank to reach into deep electrical boxes. It has a plastic tube around the shank to protect the user from electrical shock. Before starting work, unplug appliance or turn off power.

Standard (slotted) screwdriver fits slotted screws. The flared, or winged, tip (left) is best for round- or oval-head screws; parallel-sided tip (see cabinetmaker's) is best for flat-head screws.

Phillips screwdriver, the most common type of cross-head screwdriver, is made to fit snugly into a Phillips-head screw. The cross design of the tip provides a better grip than the straight-tip style.

Torx screwdriver, widely used in automobile repair work, has a star-shaped tip that can be useful for replacing such parts as taillight lenses. Torx screws are found in household appliances as well as in lawn and garden equipment.

Hex-drive screwdriver conforms to screws that can also be operated with hex keys. Suitable for socket-head screws that are recessed, the screwdriver is available in inch and metric sizes.

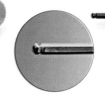

Ball-end hex-drive screwdriver, for socket-head screws, has a round tip that can be angled up to 25° from the surface. This makes it helpful for reaching screws in tight spots. The screwdriver can drive the screw without stripping it.

Pozidriv screwdriver, one of the specialized cross-head screwdrivers (Reed and Prince is another), has a square end instead of a pointed tip. Popular in the automotive industry, it's also used for screws in appliances.

Clutch-drive screwdriver has an hourglass-shaped tip that is especially suitable for applications that require extra holding power, as in cars and appliances. It is also used for security to discourage disassembly by unauthorized persons.

Nutdriver operates in the same way as a screwdriver to turn hexagonal nuts and bolts. It comes with a screwdriver-style handle. Some models come in color-coded or marked sets to make it easy to identify the size.

Robertson screwdriver, usually color-coded according to size, can reach screws that are sunk below the surface in furniture and in mobile homes, recreational vehicles, and boats. The square drive in this screwdriver provides high torque power.

Expansion-tip screwdriver holds a slotted screw as you start to drive it. To use this tool, insert the tip into the screw slot and slide the collar over the split blade, forcing the halves to wedge against each other and to lock into and hold the screw.

Offset screwdriver, handy for driving screws in hard-to-reach spots, is operated with a cranking action. The tips are set at 45° or 90° from the shank; they may be slotted or Phillips or Robertson—or a combination of any two. A ratchet model (far left) lets you drive the screw with a back-and-forth motion without removing the screwdriver.

Cordless power screwdriver, with interchangeable tips, lets you drive a large number of screws without the fatigue of hand-driving. To drive or remove screws, a switch allows you to change the direction of rotation. This model has a locking shaft to permit hand operation as a standard screwdriver for extra torque. To recharge the screwdriver, plug it into a charging unit or place a battery in the unit. Models also come with electrical cords.

Adjustable power screwdriver has a hinge in the middle of its body, which can be snapped into two positions: the conventional straight line of a screwdriver or an angled pistol-grip hold. The torque can also be adjusted on this cordless tool.

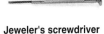

Jeweler's screwdriver is ideal for small screws in items like eyeglasses. To use it, apply pressure to the screwdriver's head with your index fingertip; turn the tools' body with your other fingers.

Magnetic screwdriver accepts interchangeable tips, which come in common types and sizes. A magnetic end holds the tips in place. Some models have a ratchet operation for fast work at high torque, as well as a switch for reversing the direction of the drive. The handle may be hollow to store the tips.

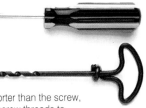

Spiral ratchet screwdriver lets you turn a screw by repeatedly pushing the handle. A ratchet switch changes the direction the shank rotates to allow for both driving and removing screws. The knurled collar just below the switch will lock the shank in the retracted position for use as a conventional screwdriver. In some models the handle provides storage for extra tips.

Screw holder, an attachment that snaps onto most round-shank screwdrivers, allows the placement of screws where fingers cannot reach. To start a screw, slip it between the holder jaws. Before driving the screw in all the way, slide the holder up the shank, out of the way. It's available in several sizes.

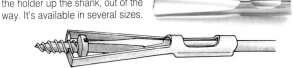

Screw starter (top) and **gimlet** (bottom) are tools for boring pilot holes in wood, thereby making it easier to drive a screw. To use either tool, turn it clockwise. The pilot hole should be narrower and shorter than the screw, leaving enough material for the screw threads to grasp. Gimlets are available in various screw sizes.

Whether they grip a hard-to-hold workpiece or cut wire or other objects, all pliers have the same design: handles on one side of a pivot joint, which allows a scissor-type action, and jaws on the other side. Always use a pair of pliers for the job it was intended to do. The smaller long-nose pliers are delicate; forcing them to do work beyond their capacity can render them useless. Use pliers to turn nuts only in an emergency; pliers can strip the nut, making it difficult to remove with the proper tool. Unless explicitly stated, do not assume that pliers designed for electrical work are insulated, even if the handles have a plastic, rubber, or similar coating.

Slip-joint pliers have both serrated teeth and coarse contoured teeth to grip objects of different shapes. They can be set in two positions to vary the jaw size.

Curved thin-nose slip-joint pliers are made with a specially shaped nose to let you see the work. As with most slip-joint pliers, they have wire cutters in the jaws.

Angle-nose pliers, slip-joint pliers with three adjustable settings, have an offset head for hard-to-reach areas where added leverage is needed.

Groove-joint pliers grip flat, square, round, or hexagonal objects with serrated teeth. The jaws can be set in five positions by slipping the curved ridge into the desired groove.

Straight-jaw locking pliers clamp firmly onto objects. A knob in one handle controls the jaws' width and tension. Close handles to lock the pliers; release a lever to open them.

Large groove-joint pliers, often used for holding pipes, give increased leverage because of long handles. The jaws stay parallel at all settings, giving them a better grip than slip-joint pliers.

Long-nose pliers, or snipe-nose pliers, are used to hold small objects, especially in electrical work. Narrow flat jaws may have serrated teeth. They can fit into confined areas and can grip parts. Some models have a wire cutter.

Needle-nose pliers, a smaller version of long-nose pliers, may have smooth, thin tapered jaws that won't mar or scratch. They are ideal for working with soft metals, especially in jewelry. Some models have serrated teeth, and some have spring-loaded handles.

Curved needle-nose pliers are also ideal for working on jewelry or small electrical items. The bent nose holds the workpiece away from the pliers and in the user's line of vision.

Round-nose pliers, favored by both electricians and jewelers, have smooth, tapered round jaws designed for bending thin wire and sheet metal into different-size loops.

Needle-nose end-cutting pliers work best for cutting thin wire. The cutting area is at the tip of the jaws for cutting items flush or in tight areas.

Diagonal-cutting pliers, also called side-cutting nippers, are designed for cutting wire and thin metal. The cutting area is positioned on the side edge of the jaws to cut precise wire lengths and for cutting flush against a surface or in cramped spaces where larger tools can't fit.

End-cutting pliers, a larger oval-head version of the needle-nose end-cutting pliers, cut heavier wire. Their design keeps knuckles out of the way while cutting the work flush. They also come with angled jaws.

Fence pliers combine several features in one tool to help install wire fencing. The head has wire-cutting slots on each side; the jaws are for pulling and stretching wire mesh; the tool's hammer is suitable for driving staples; and the claw pulls out staples.

Tile nippers chip, shape, and trim irregular contours in ceramic tile up to ½ in. thick. They are ideal for shaping tiles to fit around plumbing fixtures.

Bolt cutters are heavy-duty metal-cutting pliers that chop soft to medium-hard materials such as rods, bolts, and wire. The handles are usually 14 to 24 in. long. The length of the handles along with a well-designed pivot mechanism provides the leverage needed to cut through metals. Use both hands to operate the tool.

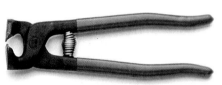

Wire stripper removes insulation from wire. To stop the blades from cutting into the wire, adjust a screw in a handle; it blocks the handles—and the jaws. A band holds the handles closed when not in use.

Wire stripper and cutter removes insulation from a wire and cuts it. To strip a section of wire, place it in a hole, squeeze the handles, and pull off the insulation. To cut the wire, set it between the jaws' sharp flat edges.

Tweezers and tongs

While not technically pliers, these holding tools are necessary for delicate work as well as for protecting hands from heat and chemicals.

Tweezers are used for holding small objects. They are ideal for miniature work and making jewelry, and they can help remove wood or metal splinters. Tweezers come with straight or curved blades and with sharp, rounded, or flat points that are either smooth or serrated.

Automatic wire stripper cuts and strips wire in one squeeze of the handles—unlike other strippers that require you to pull off the insulation after cutting it. This stripper has two sets of jaws: one pair holds the wire; the other pair cuts and pulls off the insulation, exposing enough bare wire for a connection.

Lineman's pliers are a combination of flat-jaw pliers and wire cutters. The outermost portion of the jaws is flat and serrated for a solid grip when pulling and twisting wire. The inner portion of the jaws is a basic cable and wire cutter.

Soldering tweezers are fireproof fine-point tools for holding small pieces of metal during soldering. These cross-locking models can double as clamps. To push the ends apart, apply pressure to the center part of the tool, the point where the arms overlap.

Multipurpose electrician's pliers measure, strip, and cut wire; crimp wire connectors; and cut machine screws. Models vary in functions; buy one that will suit your needs best. As with other wire strippers, the handles do not insulate against electricity.

Copper tongs hold soldered metal while positioning it in a bath of pickling solution for cleaning. Because iron contaminates the solution, iron tongs are not suitable for this job.

WRENCHES

Turning tools that fit around nuts, bolts, or pipe fittings, wrenches provide the needed leverage to loosen and tighten the fasteners. A wrench may be fixed (fit only one size of nut or bolt) or adjustable (expandable to fit different sizes). A fixed wrench comes in English or metric sizes and is used on the exactly corresponding size nut or bolt. No matter how close the size might seem, using a wrench that is "almost right" can damage the hardware. To make hard-to-reach nuts and bolts accessible, one side of the heads on some slender fixed wrenches is open to let the wrench slide in place. Closed box wrenches are stronger, however, and less likely to slip. They come with 8 points to fit square nuts or with 6 or 12 points to fit hex nuts.

Obstruction wrench is a double open-end wrench that has a standard open head on one end of the shaft and a head of the same size on the other end with the opening angled up to 90°. The angled head allows the user to reach fasteners that are otherwise hard to reach.

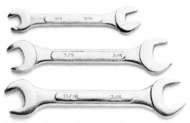

Open-end wrench has a different opening at each end. The openings are close in size, and in some sets, each end will match one on the previous or following size wrench, providing two same-size heads—one to turn the nut, the other to hold the bolt. Extra-thin wrenches are available to fit into tight spots.

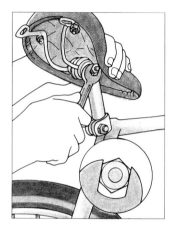

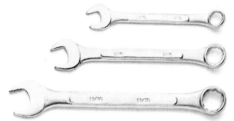

Combination wrench gives you a choice of two different ends of the same size to loosen or tighten a nut or bolt. Use the box end when the job calls for strength and the speedier open end when less torque is needed.

Crow's-foot wrench, an open-end wrench head without a handle, has a square hole that accepts either a socket wrench handle or an extension. Depending on the type of handle you choose, the head can be used parallel to the handle or set at an angle, making it exceptionally useful for tightening or loosening nuts in odd positions.

Torque wrench turns nuts and bolts to an exact tightness. It is ideal for tightening a number of fasteners to the same degree to avoid warping. A scale is attached to the handle of one standard model; the torque (turning force) is indicated by a pointer that remains stationary as the handle bends under stress. All models accept standard square-drive sockets and adapters; measuring devices and the amount of torque vary.

Flare-nut wrench for copper and brass fittings slides over tubing, then down to the fitting. It has a better grip than an open-end wrench.

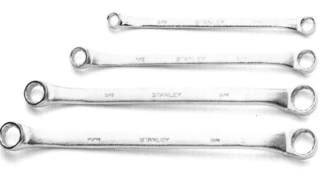

Offset double box-end wrench is designed for hex or square nuts and bolts. Its handle curves away from the work surface, leaving room for gripping. The box ends fit more securely around the fastener than the open-end type. After each turn, lift the wrench and reposition it before continuing.

Combination box wrench, resembling a dog bone, has five different openings on each head. The handle provides little leverage, making it suitable only for light work. Its compact size is ideal for carrying on bicycle trips.

Speed wrench handle uses a cranking motion to remove or install nuts or bolts. Its ⅜- or ½-in. shaft accepts socket heads, adapters, and extensions. The grip remains stationary while the shaft is turned clockwise for tightening fasteners, counterclockwise for loosening.

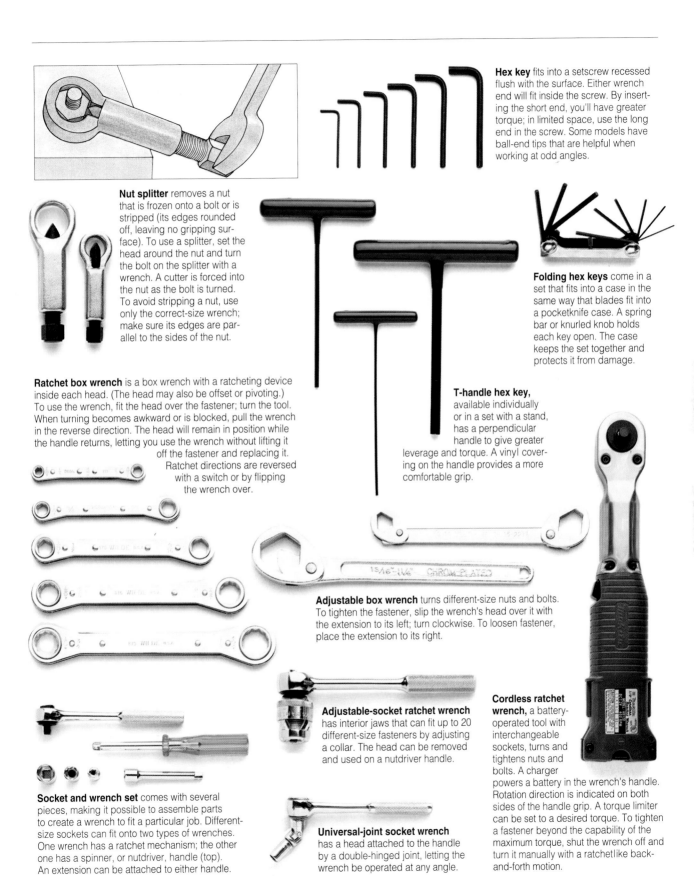

Hex key fits into a setscrew recessed flush with the surface. Either wrench end will fit inside the screw. By inserting the short end, you'll have greater torque; in limited space, use the long end in the screw. Some models have ball-end tips that are helpful when working at odd angles.

Nut splitter removes a nut that is frozen onto a bolt or is stripped (its edges rounded off, leaving no gripping surface). To use a splitter, set the head around the nut and turn the bolt on the splitter with a wrench. A cutter is forced into the nut as the bolt is turned. To avoid stripping a nut, use only the correct-size wrench; make sure its edges are parallel to the sides of the nut.

Folding hex keys come in a set that fits into a case in the same way that blades fit into a pocketknife case. A spring bar or knurled knob holds each key open. The case keeps the set together and protects it from damage.

Ratchet box wrench is a box wrench with a ratcheting device inside each head. (The head may also be offset or pivoting.) To use the wrench, fit the head over the fastener; turn the tool. When turning becomes awkward or is blocked, pull the wrench in the reverse direction. The head will remain in position while the handle returns, letting you use the wrench without lifting it off the fastener and replacing it. Ratchet directions are reversed with a switch or by flipping the wrench over.

T-handle hex key, available individually or in a set with a stand, has a perpendicular handle to give greater leverage and torque. A vinyl covering on the handle provides a more comfortable grip.

Adjustable box wrench turns different-size nuts and bolts. To tighten the fastener, slip the wrench's head over it with the extension to its left; turn clockwise. To loosen fastener, place the extension to its right.

Adjustable-socket ratchet wrench has interior jaws that can fit up to 20 different-size fasteners by adjusting a collar. The head can be removed and used on a nutdriver handle.

Cordless ratchet wrench, a battery-operated tool with interchangeable sockets, turns and tightens nuts and bolts. A charger powers a battery in the wrench's handle. Rotation direction is indicated on both sides of the handle grip. A torque limiter can be set to a desired torque. To tighten a fastener beyond the capability of the maximum torque, shut the wrench off and turn it manually with a ratchetlike back-and-forth motion.

Socket and wrench set comes with several pieces, making it possible to assemble parts to create a wrench to fit a particular job. Different-size sockets can fit onto two types of wrenches. One wrench has a ratchet mechanism; the other one has a spinner, or nutdriver, handle (top). An extension can be attached to either handle.

Universal-joint socket wrench has a head attached to the handle by a double-hinged joint, letting the wrench be operated at any angle.

ADJUSTABLE WRENCHES

Designed to accept pipes, pipe fittings, bolts, and nuts, the adjustable wrench may have two jaws—one fixed, the other movable—or a strap or chain that grips the object to loosen or tighten it. Use one of these wrenches when the right-size fixed wrench is not available or for special tasks such as reaching under a basin. An adjustable wrench usually works best with pressure put on the stationary jaw, not the movable one.

Adjustable wrench, also known as a Crescent wrench, is a versatile smooth-jaw wrench for turning nuts, bolts, small pipe fittings, and chrome-faced pipe fittings. The movable jaw is adjusted with a worm gear, which is accessible on both sides of the head.

Pipe wrench turns threaded pipes. The upper jaw is adjusted by turning the knurled knob. Both jaws have serrated teeth for gripping power. When using the wrench, turn it so that you apply pressure on the movable jaw. That jaw is spring-loaded and slightly angled; it allows you to release the grip and reposition the wrench, without readjusting the jaw, when you remove the pressure.

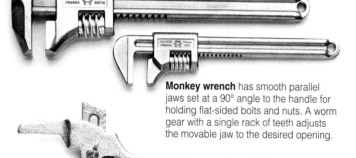

Monkey wrench has smooth parallel jaws set at a 90° angle to the handle for holding flat-sided bolts and nuts. A worm gear with a single rack of teeth adjusts the movable jaw to the desired opening.

Spud wrench loosens and tightens fittings on drain traps, sink strainers, toilet connections, and large odd-shaped nuts. After adjusting the jaws, lock them in place with the wing nut.

Chain-locking clamp and wrench can turn irregularly shaped items and can also clamp objects together up to a 6-in. diameter. Wrap the chain around the object and slide it under the tool's hook. Adjust the thumbscrew to tighten or loosen the chain. Lock the chain in position by squeezing the handles; unlock it by squeezing the lever inside one of the handles.

Chain wrench fits around any large pipe or oddly shaped item. Wrap the chain around the object, secure it on the hook in the handle, and pull the wrench downward (with the hook on top).

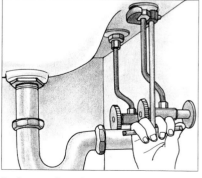

Basin wrench, a plumbing tool for removing and installing sink faucets, has a long handle that reaches up from under a sink to turn nuts on fittings and faucets. The hinged jaw repositions itself after each turn.
Buy one with a reversible jaw.

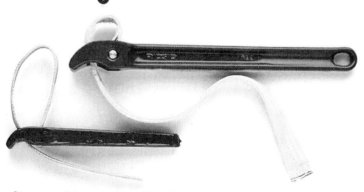

Strap wrench has a canvas webbing that wraps around pipes without marring their finish. Hold the wrench with the claw pointing down; loop the strap around the pipe, then into the opening. Pull the wrench toward the free end of the strap.

VISES

A clamping tool that holds work steady, the vise is attached, permanently or temporarily, to a work surface. Specialized woodworking vises have smooth wood or metal jaws; metalworking vises have serrated teeth on their steel jaws. Be sure to match the vise to the job; improper use can damage the vise or the workpiece. To protect the workpiece, fasten a jaw face between it and the jaws of the vise. For woodworking, use wood or hardboard jaw faces; if the work is metal, bend smooth sheet metal (at least as wide as the jaws) to a right angle over the jaws, or use a fiber liner.

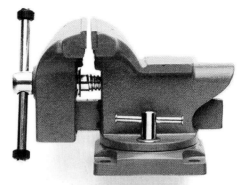

Machinist's vise is permanently bolted to a bench top for metalworking. Many models incorporate a small anvil and have a swivel base that locks in place. Some vises can hold round pipe with round serrated pipe jaws located under the flat jaws.

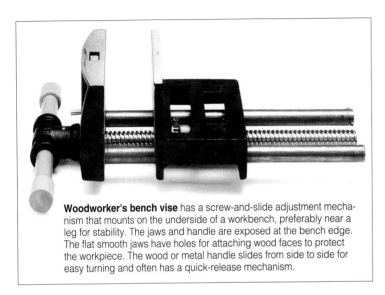

Woodworker's bench vise has a screw-and-slide adjustment mechanism that mounts on the underside of a workbench, preferably near a leg for stability. The jaws and handle are exposed at the bench edge. The flat smooth jaws have holes for attaching wood faces to protect the workpiece. The wood or metal handle slides from side to side for easy turning and often has a quick-release mechanism.

Drill press vise, when bolted on a drill press work-table, holds small and round metal pieces securely for drilling. Some models tilt for drilling angled holes.

Hold-down applies downward pressure on woodwork. It can be mounted on a workbench, along the edge or middle of the top surface or on the bench's side, or on a machine table for a drill press or table saw. The tool usually hooks onto mounting bolts permanently set in the bench. It can be used in unlimited locations by installing additional bolts; simply remove the tool from one bolt and hook it onto another.

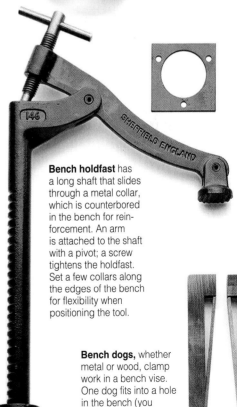

Bench holdfast has a long shaft that slides through a metal collar, which is counterbored in the bench for reinforcement. An arm is attached to the shaft with a pivot; a screw tightens the holdfast. Set a few collars along the edges of the bench for flexibility when positioning the tool.

Clamp-on vise, a small portable machinist's vise that is suitable for light-duty use, attaches to the edge of a workbench with a screw clamp mechanism. The vise can be stored when not in use and set up quickly whenever it's needed.

Bench dogs, whether metal or wood, clamp work in a bench vise. One dog fits into a hole in the bench (you may have to make it); the other dog fits in the movable vise jaw, or it may be part of the vise.

Whenever you need extra hands to hold pieces together temporarily, clamps are the tools of choice. Use them to grip corresponding parts while driving nails or drilling holes for screws, to test-fit pieces before gluing them, or to brace a freshly glued assembly until the glue dries.

Clamps come in many sizes and styles. Some have very specific applications, while others are used in a wide array of situations. Every workshop should have a variety of top-quality clamps; buy them in pairs as you need them. The more clamps you have, the better; according to one rule of thumb, too many clamps are just enough. When using clamps, be sure to apply pressure evenly from two sides to avoid twisting the work.

C-clamp, one of the most common types of clamps, is named for its C-shaped frame. A *shoe* at one end of the screw holds the work against the frame; at the other end is a T-handle. To tighten the screw against the work or change the size of the opening, adjust the screw by turning the T-handle.

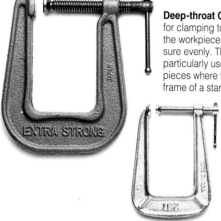

Deep-throat C-clamp is shaped for clamping toward the center of the workpiece, distributing pressure evenly. The deep throat is particularly useful for holding wide pieces where the shallow-throat frame of a standard C-clamp won't fit. As with most clamps, attach a piece of scrap wood to each jaw with double-stick tape to keep the jaws from marring the work.

Square-frame C-clamp is a variation of the standard C-clamp. The square inside perimeter of the frame allows the clamp to fit around the corners of a square workpiece, but it still applies full pressure to the work.

Edge clamp has two or three screws extending from the frame to exert right-angle pressure on the edge or side of a workpiece. A three-way edge clamp (shown) is more versatile for positioning the workpiece. The right-angle, or center, screw can be positioned on or off center on varying thicknesses of workpieces.

Spring clamp operates with hand pressure to open the jaws. Spring pressure forces the jaws closed when the handles are released, allowing the jaws to grip the work. Some models have plastic-coated handles for easier opening and coated tips to protect the workpiece.

Small parallel clamp operates in a similar way to the hand-screw clamp (right), but its jaws are set in a parallel position. It's ideal for working with small or thin pieces without interfering with the workspace.

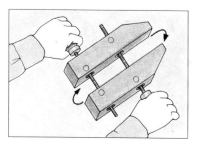

Hand-screw clamp can spread pressure over a broad surface area. Each jaw works independently, allowing them to angle toward or away from each other or to remain parallel. Set the jaws slightly wider than desired by holding the spindles and rotating the clamp. Slip the jaws over the work and tighten the rear spindle.

Fast-action bar clamp consists of a bar with a fixed jaw and a sliding jaw; a spring-locking device secures the sliding jaw in place. Set the workpiece against the fixed jaw and slide the other jaw to the work (with the screw set away from the work). Once the clamp is positioned, tighten the screw to hold the work securely.

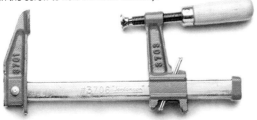

Cam-action clamp has a sliding jaw that adjusts quickly to the size of the work. A handle in the movable jaw is set in a perpendicular position to lock the jaw and work in place. The jaws are padded with cork to prevent damaging the work surface. Its light weight makes this clamp suitable for most delicate work.

Universal clamp holds two pieces of ½- or ¾-in. stock together for gluing. One jaw has a friction grip for holding the stock in place; the other jaw has a screw for increasing the clamp pressure. The clamp is best suited for long work where bar clamps are not practical.

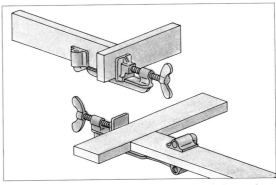

The Universal clamp at top is handy for clamping shelves and drawer supports to the furniture case; the one at bottom is useful for holding butt joints and T-joints.

Pipe clamp comes in a kit to fit on ½- or ¾-in. iron pipe. The length of the clamp is determined by the length of the pipe. A sliding jaw operates with a spring-locking device; a middle jaw is controlled by a screw set in a third, fixed, jaw.

Pipe saddles hold ¾-in. pipes. Mounted on sawhorses and gripping pipe clamps, they support a work surface. On a workbench, they create a clamping station. A thumbscrew retains the pipe.

Scrap wood

Reversible pipe clamp has a sliding jaw that can also be used in the reverse direction, applying pressure away from the clamp instead of between the clamp jaws. As with the standard pipe clamp, set the work against the middle jaw first, with the screw drawn back; set the sliding jaw; then tighten the screw.

Tools 43

MORE CLAMPS

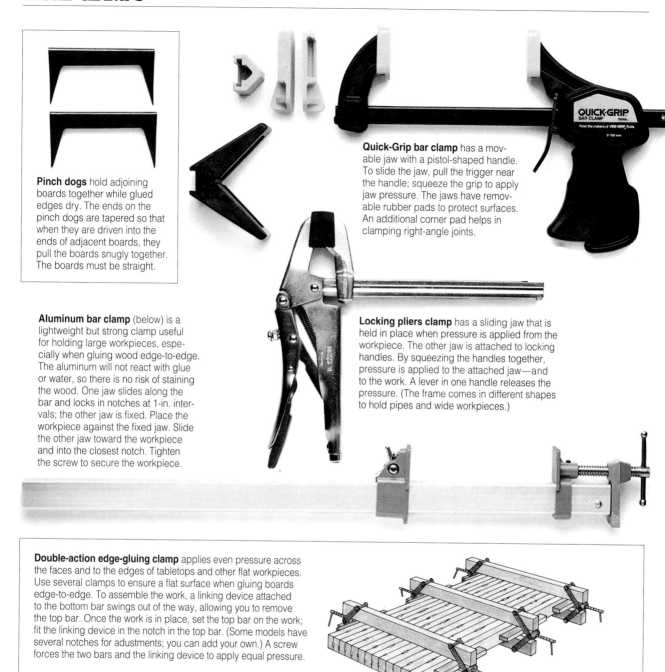

Pinch dogs hold adjoining boards together while glued edges dry. The ends on the pinch dogs are tapered so that when they are driven into the ends of adjacent boards, they pull the boards snugly together. The boards must be straight.

Aluminum bar clamp (below) is a lightweight but strong clamp useful for holding large workpieces, especially when gluing wood edge-to-edge. The aluminum will not react with glue or water, so there is no risk of staining the wood. One jaw slides along the bar and locks in notches at 1-in. intervals; the other jaw is fixed. Place the workpiece against the fixed jaw. Slide the other jaw toward the workpiece and into the closest notch. Tighten the screw to secure the workpiece.

Quick-Grip bar clamp has a movable jaw with a pistol-shaped handle. To slide the jaw, pull the trigger near the handle; squeeze the grip to apply jaw pressure. The jaws have removable rubber pads to protect surfaces. An additional corner pad helps in clamping right-angle joints.

Locking pliers clamp has a sliding jaw that is held in place when pressure is applied from the workpiece. The other jaw is attached to locking handles. By squeezing the handles together, pressure is applied to the attached jaw—and to the work. A lever in one handle releases the pressure. (The frame comes in different shapes to hold pipes and wide workpieces.)

Double-action edge-gluing clamp applies even pressure across the faces and to the edges of tabletops and other flat workpieces. Use several clamps to ensure a flat surface when gluing boards edge-to-edge. To assemble the work, a linking device attached to the bottom bar swings out of the way, allowing you to remove the top bar. Once the work is in place, set the top bar on the work; fit the linking device in the notch in the top bar. (Some models have several notches for adustments; you can add your own.) A screw forces the two bars and the linking device to apply equal pressure.

Band clamp applies even pressure around regular and irregular shapes. Loop the 1-in.-wide nylon band around the workpiece and pull it snug by hand. To apply pressure, tighten the bolt in the clamp head with a wrench or screwdriver. A quick-release device loosens the band. Steel corner pieces allow the band to tighten evenly around the workpiece without catching on sharp corners.

Framing clamp holds all four 90° corners of a frame while glue dries. L-shaped corner blocks have grooves to allow excess glue to escape. To use the clamp, screw the threaded rods into the blocks and adjust them to the frame size; then thread knurled nuts onto the rods near the blocks. Place the clamp around the object; adjust the pressure with the knurled nuts. The clamp fits frames up to 48 in. square, and can also be used for clamping boxes, small shelf units, and other rectangular workpieces.

Web clamp has a 2-in.-wide canvas band that can be set around irregular shapes. Wrap the band around the workpiece; weave the loose band ends into the head, passing the rollers and looping around the cams. Then pull the band snug at both ends; the cams will lock the band in place. To exert pressure against the work, rotate the screw. While the band clamp (above) is suitable for lightweight jobs such as clamping chairs and picture frames, the web clamp is better for heavy-duty applications such as clamping sofa frames.

Miter clamp is designed to hold joints. One type (above) has a removable jaw that rotates, allowing the clamp to be set at different angles; a handle adjusts its placement. By turning a second handle, swivel jaws apply pressure to the work. Another type has screws that press the jaws toward the work.

KNIVES, SNIPS, AND SCRAPERS

Cutting and scraping tools are necessities for everything from opening taped boxes to removing chipped paint from walls. There are two basic types of knives: one has a sharp blade for cutting materials; the other type has a larger, duller blade for applying compounds to walls and ceilings. Scrapers also have sharp blades; they help remove material from a surface. When using a cutting tool, always make sure that the blade is sharp; a dull blade can damage the material it's used on and cause injury to the user.

Utility knife has a variety of blades to cut wood, vinyl, and other materials. A good straight-handle model will have a button that adjusts the length of the blade and retracts the blade into the handle for safety. Replacement blades are often stored in the handle. To expose a stored blade in the offset-handle model, unscrew the cap and pivot the sides.

Snap-blade knife has blades that can be snapped off when dull. The end cap pulls off to allow insertion of the blade cartridge. To snap off a blade, use a slot in the end cap. A locking button adjusts blade position and retracts it into handle.

Razor knife holds a replaceable standard single-edge razor blade. It's ideal for trimming and cutting wallcoverings, paper, and similar materials. The model at left has an attachment to cut overlapping pieces for a perfect butt.

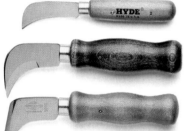

Carpet knife has a blade shape that's best for trimming carpeting in tight areas such as in corners and around doorjambs, vents, and pipes. Use the back edge of the blade to tuck carpet under molding.

Vinyl knife has a blade ideal for scoring hard and soft vinyl and other similar floor coverings.

Flooring knife is also handy for shaping flooring materials, and it can score wallboard. Use the blade edge for scraping.

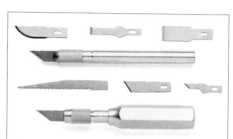

Hobby knife has numerous blades for various tasks, and the handle comes in different sizes. A large handle helps cut hard materials; a small handle is better for precision cuts. Loosen the knurled collar to change blades. Depending on the blade and handle, the knife can cut paper, plastic, wood, cloth, and metal.

Plastic cutter has angled blade edges for scoring acrylic and other brittle materials. Flip the tool over to use it in an offset position.

Shave hook scrapes paint from moldings. Blades may also be teardrop-shaped or triangular to fit different moldings. Some models have interchangeable blades; others come in sets.

Roofing knife, for scoring and cutting asphalt shingles, tar paper, and other roofing materials, can also be used for wallboard and insulation. The model with the straight blade can pry apart asphalt shingles.

Window scraper removes paint from windowpane without damaging the putty. Hold the scraper so that the wheels glide against the window trim; blade scrapes off paint.

Razor-blade scraper uses a single-edge razor blade to scrape paint and stickers off windowpanes. One model (left) has a retractable blade. The blade on the other model (far left) can be locked in several different positions.

Four-edge blade scraper (above) is for quick paint and varnish removal. Use the knob to apply extra pressure. Two blade edges scrape at a time; turn blade over or replace it when dull.

Utility-blade scraper (left) has a guide to help remove paint from window frames and flat surfaces.

Glazier's putty knife combines two functions in one tool. Use the heavy-duty flat chisel blade to remove old putty from a window. Apply and smooth down new putty with the slotted V-blade. To create a bevel edge, hold the tool with the blade at a slight angle.

Tin snips are adequate for cutting lightweight sheet metal. The snips shown here make straight-line cuts or wide curves. Other types have a duckbill head for tight curves or a bullnose head for notching and nibbling heavy stock.

Aviation snips cut sheet metal with less effort than tin snips. A compound lever mechanism provides greater control with less hand pressure. The serrated jaws prevent slippage and withstand heavy use. All aviation snips cut straight lines. Specific heads also cut left curves, right curves, and a combination of all three cuts. The grips are color-coded: yellow for combination cuts, red for left-hand curves, and green for right-hand curves. A latch holds the jaws closed.

Putty knife has a flexible blade to spread and smooth wood putty and filler, glazing or spackling compound, patching plaster, and other similar materials. A knife with a stiff blade scrapes away paint, glue, vinyl and paper wallcoverings, and other materials.

Painter's five-in-one tool has a blade that functions as a paint scraper, putty remover and spreader, gouger, and paint roller cleaner. Use it when making repairs, installing window glass, painting, and hanging wallcoverings.

Hacking knife, for chipping away old putty from a window, has a blade that is thicker on one side for use with a hammer. Hold the slightly angled blade tip with the point against the putty. Drive a hammer against the thicker edge of the blade to remove the putty.

Power nibblers use a replaceable die and punch combination to cut aluminum, stainless steel, and corrugated steel. They are excellent for cutting ductwork, especially in hard-to-reach areas. The nibblers can make straight, right-curve, and left-curve cuts. To make an internal cut, first drill a starter hole.

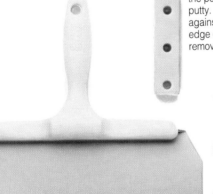

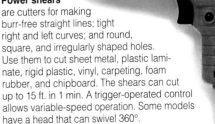

Joint knife, with a large blade for spreading and smoothing wide areas of joint compound over wallboard tape, can also be used to patch wallboard and to smooth wallcoverings.

Right-angle joint knife lets you apply joint compound smoothly to inside corners where walls meet. The handle is offset to allow clearance for fingers.

Power shears are cutters for making burr-free straight lines; tight right and left curves; and round, square, and irregularly shaped holes. Use them to cut sheet metal, plastic laminate, rigid plastic, vinyl, carpeting, foam rubber, and chipboard. The shears can cut up to 15 ft. in 1 min. A trigger-operated control allows variable-speed operation. Some models have a head that can swivel 360°.

Tools 47

HANDSAWS

The best handsaws are made of fine-tempered steel and have well-shaped wooden handles. The main difference among handsaws is the shape, number, and pitch of their teeth, which make them suitable for cutting wood across the grain or with it, along curved lines, or through metal, plastic, or wallboard. To prevent binding, saw teeth are usually set, or angled, away from the blade so that the path, or kerf, it cuts is slightly wider than the blade's thickness. Generally the more points or teeth per inch (tpi) a saw has, the smoother and slower it cuts. (There is always one fewer teeth per inch than points per inch.) Most American and European saws cut on the push stroke.

Wallboard saw, or drywall saw, makes cutouts in plasterboard for electrical outlets or appliances. The average blade is 6 to 9½ in. long with about 10 tpi. The sharp point allows you to make plunge cuts without first drilling a hole to accept the blade.

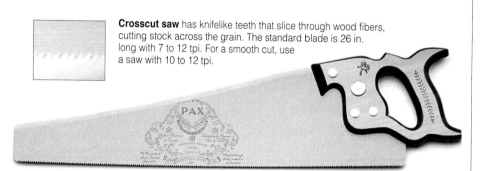

Crosscut saw has knifelike teeth that slice through wood fibers, cutting stock across the grain. The standard blade is 26 in. long with 7 to 12 tpi. For a smooth cut, use a saw with 10 to 12 tpi.

Saw set can be used to bend the teeth of a handsaw to the angle needed to effect the desired cut. Sharpen the saw first. Then turn the wheellike anvil of the saw set to the proper angle, position the jaws of the saw set over a saw tooth, and squeeze the tool's handles together; a plunger will push the saw tooth against the anvil.

Backsaw is a crosscutting saw for making joints, especially miters and tenons. The squared end and stiffened rib along its back keep the blade rigid while cutting. Standard blades are 8 to 14 in. long with 11 to 14 tpi.

Plywood saw has a fine-tooth blade that reduces tearing of the outer plies of a sheet of plywood. An extra set of teeth on the curved upper edge of the blade lets you start a cut on the inside of a panel (away from the edge) without having to drill a starting hole. The standard plywood saw blade is 11 in. long and has 14 tpi.

Ripsaw cuts parallel to wood grain by gouging a groove in the wood with coarse teeth shaped like miniature chisels. The standard blade is 26 in. long and has 4 to 7 tpi. A ripsaw with 5½ tpi gives a smooth, fast cut.

General-purpose saw makes both crosscuts and rip cuts in wood and is ideal if you can have only one saw. Its teeth have three beveled sides, which provide razor-sharp cutting, and deep gullets (spaces between the teeth), which make it easier to clear chips away fast. The blade is 26 in. long with 9 tpi, and cuts fast and smooth.

Japanese saws, unlike Western saws, cut on the pull stroke rather than on the push. The thinner Japanese blades also cut a much finer kerf.

Ryoba saw (left) has two sets of teeth—one set for ripping, the other for crosscutting. Ryoba blades measure 8 to 14 in. in length, with 7 tpi on the rip side and 14 to 20 tpi on the crosscut.

Japanese rip tooth pattern

Japanese crosscut tooth pattern

Dozuki crosscut saw is similar to the Western backsaw. The folding handle protects delicate saw teeth. The standard blade is 9 in. long with 18 tpi.

Veneer saw is a small double-edged tool for cutting thin hardwood veneers. Its narrow curved blade facilitates precision work, and its elevated offset handle makes it possible to cut flush with a surface. The blade is 3 in. long and has 13 tpi.

French flush-cut saw is designed for trimming the ends of dowels, tenons, and other protrusions flush with a surface. Its 6-in. blade is double-edged, with 11 tpi on one side and 20 tpi on the other. To avoid marring the surface adjacent to the cut, the saw teeth have no downward set, but are angled upward slightly to help the blade clear the cut.

Frame saw is used for cutting curved edges. The twisted cord at the top of the frame supplies tension to keep the blade from wobbling during cutting. By rotating the handles, you can turn the blade to cut at any angle. Blades range from 8 to 12 in. long with 8 to 16 tpi.

Folding pocket saw is a handle that accepts saber and reciprocating saw blades that cut wood, metal, plastic, and other materials. It folds to protect the blade's edge and has storage space for extra blades.

Dovetail saw is a small backsaw with a straight handle and fine teeth set to cut a very narrow kerf, making it ideal for fine joints. The blade is 10 in. long with 16 to 20 tpi.

SANDVIK
311

Bow saw is a heavy-duty tool for cutting logs or for coarse sawing of green wood, dry or seasoned wood, or other building materials. The tubular steel frame holds the blade under tension, which can be controlled with the quick-release lever. The replaceable blades are made up of pegged teeth and gullets to allow cutting in both directions.

Tools 49

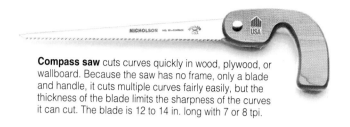

Compass saw cuts curves quickly in wood, plywood, or wallboard. Because the saw has no frame, only a blade and handle, it cuts multiple curves fairly easily, but the thickness of the blade limits the sharpness of the curves it can cut. The blade is 12 to 14 in. long with 7 or 8 tpi.

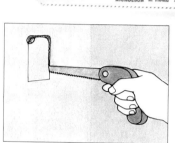

Keyhole saw, a fine-tooth compass saw, cuts light metal as well as wood and wallboard. The average blade is 10 in. long with 9 tpi. To start an inside cut, bore a hole and insert the blade.

Nest of saws consists of a handle and a set of compass or keyhole saw blades of different sizes. Rather than acquiring several saws, you can buy one set of nested saws and change the blade to suit each job. Generally the notch in the base of the blade is pushed into the handle, and a bolt is slid through it and secured with a washer and wing nut.

Slotting saw is a 6-in.-long saw with fine teeth (25 tpi) for cutting very narrow grooves. It is especially handy for creating delicate dovetails and for model work.

Pad saw can cut curves in awkward places, and is more suitable than a compass or keyhole saw for cutting tight curves. The blade of the pad saw is generally 4 to 10 in. long with 8 tpi. It can be inserted into the handle so that it cuts on the pull stroke (like a Japanese saw) for greater control.

Curved pruning saw, a knifelike pruning tool, can be folded up to protect the blade when not in use. The tempered steel blade is 10 in. long, with long slender reverse teeth (5 tpi) set for cutting on the pull stroke.

Pruning saw has a blade of specially hardened and tempered steel for cutting branches. The straight 18-in.-long blade of the saw shown here has two cutting edges. One edge has coarse teeth for sawing green wood more easily. The opposite edge has sharp crosscut teeth (7 tpi) for finish strokes and cutting deadwood.

Plastic pipe handsaw doubles as a special tool for cutting PVC and ABS pipe and a general-purpose saw for cutting plywood, paneling, and wallboard. The blade is 12 in. long with 10 tpi set for cutting on either the push or pull stroke. You can replace the blade by removing the screw in the handle, sliding out the old blade, sliding in the new, and replacing the screw.

Log saw, a heavy-duty tool for crosscutting timber, has an average blade length of 28 in. Longer log saws have two handles, one at each end of the blade, for use by two persons. The forward, or peg, teeth of the blade are designed to make starting easier. The main teeth are filed to cut on both the push and pull strokes. Gaps between the groups of teeth make removal of sawdust easier.

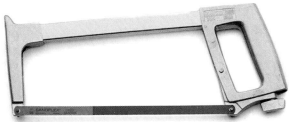

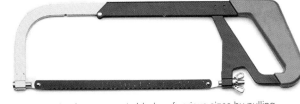

Hacksaw, the traditional handsaw for cutting metal, has extra-hard teeth, a sturdy frame with a pistol-grip handle, and a narrow blade, from 8 to 16 in. long with 14 to 32 tpi. When installing a new blade, apply tension to it by turning the wing nut in the handle. In this model you can store extra blades in the hollow top of the frame.

Adjustable hacksaw accepts blades of various sizes by pulling the front part of the frame out as on a trombone. When using a hacksaw, steady the front of the frame with your free hand.

Coping saw has a steel frame and a narrow, flexible 6-in.-long blade that can be rotated at any angle to cut small curves in wood. The blade, which has 12 to 18 tpi, is pulled taut by turning the handle of the frame. To make an inside cut, drill a starting hole and slip the blade through it before attaching it to the saw frame.

Mini-hacksaw consists only of a handle that holds whole or broken hacksaw blades. Use it to cut metal in awkward places where a full-size saw will not fit. The blade is held steady by a screw on the handle.

Rod saw is a wire with carbide chips permanently affixed. It can be attached to a hacksaw frame for cutting glass, ceramic, plastic, masonry, marble, fiberglass, and metal. Because it can cut in any direction it is ideal for curves and for shaping tiles to fit around door frames or plumbing fixtures.

Fretsaw is a deep-throated coping saw for making cuts farther in from the edge of the stock than a normal coping saw can. Because the blade is extra-fine (up to 32 tpi), it can cut intricate curves. When installing a blade, fasten one end in the frame, press the frame against the edge of a workbench or table to bend the frame in slightly, attach the other end of the blade to the frame, and then release the frame to put tension on the blade and keep it taut.

Miter box holds a backsaw blade in the proper position to make cuts at precise angles. It is often used to cut miters in molding. The simplest miter box is merely a U-shaped wooden structure with a slot through its sides at a 90° angle. The more precise unit shown here comes with its own saw and with clamps to hold work of various sizes and shapes. A dial lets you set the angle of the saw.

Jeweler's saw cuts lightweight sheet metal, such as silver. Its thin, flexible blade is 5 to 6 in. long with up to 80 tpi. Install a new blade as shown at left for a fretsaw.

Flexible pocket saw resembles a burred wire with a handle on each end; it comes in a plastic carrying case. This versatile saw cuts in any direction and can be used on wood, plastic, rubber, bone, and even ice. To use it, loop the blade over the object to be cut, and alternately pull on one handle and then the other, while applying pressure.

In general, a power saw gives a quicker and more precise cut than a handsaw. A saber saw cuts with a blade that moves up and down; a reciprocating saw cuts with an additional front-to-back motion. A variety of blades allow either saw to cut different materials. After making a cut with any type of portable power saw, wait for the blade to stop moving before setting the saw down.

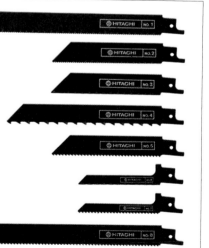

To cut very tight convex or concave curves, first saw straight lines in the waste material, then cut along the curved line. The pieces of waste material will drop off as the blade makes the cut, giving extra clearance for the saw blade to continue.

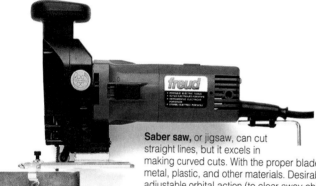

Saber saw, or jigsaw, can cut straight lines, but it excels in making curved cuts. With the proper blade, it can cut wood, metal, plastic, and other materials. Desirable features include adjustable orbital action (to clear away chips and allow faster cutting speed), variable-speed control from 0 to 3,200 strokes per min. (spm) for working on different materials, a baseplate that can be tilted for bevel cuts, and an antichip device.

Scrolling saber saw, a version of the saber saw, has a blade holder that pivots for cutting intricate curves and contours without the operator turning the body of the saw. The saw has an automatic scrolling mode, in which the blade turns in the direction the saw is guided, a manual scrolling setting that lets you control the blade with the top-mounted knob, and settings for normal blade positions.

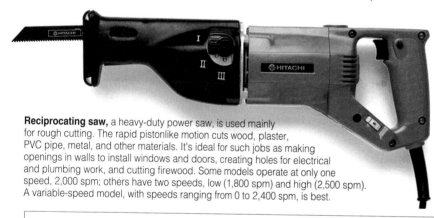

Reciprocating saw, a heavy-duty power saw, is used mainly for rough cutting. The rapid pistonlike motion cuts wood, plaster, PVC pipe, metal, and other materials. It's ideal for such jobs as making openings in walls to install windows and doors, creating holes for electrical and plumbing work, and cutting firewood. Some models operate at only one speed, 2,000 spm; others have two speeds, low (1,800 spm) and high (2,500 spm). A variable-speed model, with speeds ranging from 0 to 2,400 spm, is best.

Saber saw blades are gauged by the number of teeth per inch (tpi). The more tpi, the smoother the cut; blades with fewer tpi make a rougher but quicker cut. The narrower the blade, the tighter the turning radius. Select the blade to fit the job. At top (from left to right) are blades for wood: crosscut, rough-cut, extra-fine, scrolling (also for plastic), and rough-cut for 4 x 4's and logs. At bottom (from left to right) are a flush-cut blade for wood, and medium, fine, and extra-fine blades for cutting metal. Other blades are available for cutting ceramic tile, fiberglass, leather, and plaster.

Reciprocating saw blades range in length from 2½ to 12 in. Some can cut wood as thick as 12 in., others metal up to ¾ in. thick. Use the shortest blade that will do the job. From top to bottom, the first three blades are for cutting steel pipe of different thicknesses and diameters. They are followed by two blades for cutting wood of various thicknesses, a blade for cutting curves in iron, another blade for cutting curves in wood, and a blade for cutting vinyl pipe.

SCROLL SAWS

The tool of choice for making intricate and accurate curved and piercing cuts, the scroll saw is indispensable for creating inlay and marquetry pieces and for making miniatures and fretwork. The saw cuts with a blade suspended between two chucks mounted in arms that move up and down. To reduce teeth marks and blade breakage, look for a saw that holds the blade with a constant-tension arm. Single-speed models are available, but multiple-speed and variable-speed scroll saws are more versatile. Mount the saw on a bench top if it doesn't have its own stand.

Scroll saw blades have ends designed to fit into chucks. Pin-end blades are easier to mount than the smooth ones, but not all saw chucks accept them. All blades can cut very tight curves. Basic blades cut solid wood, plywood, veneer, plastic, and some fibrous materials. Very fine blades cut thin nonferrous metals. A unique spiral-shaped blade allows you to saw in any direction without turning the work.

Sawdust blower keeps workpiece clear of debris, allowing a clear view of the cut. The lock knob holds the drop foot in place. The foot can be raised, but it must rest on the work when the saw is running.

Tension control sets tautness of the blade; turn it to tighten or loosen the blade tension. To convert a smooth-end blade to fit a pin-end chuck, use the blade gauge (right of knob) to attach adapters.

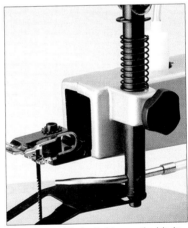

To change a blade, first loosen the blade tension by releasing the tension control. The top end of the blade fits into the upper chuck (top). On some models, you can cut pieces longer than the saw's throat depth by rotating the pin-end blade 90° and feeding the wood away from the throat. (Chuck systems differ.) The bottom end of the blade fits into the lower chuck (right). To reach the lower chuck, remove the table insert (replace it before using saw).

Table adjustment control lets you tilt the saw's table to make bevel cuts up to a 45° angle. Some models can be adjusted up to 45° in the opposite direction.

Ideal for curve cutting and for resawing (making a board thinner), the band saw can also be used to make straight or regular cuts in wood, plastic, and metal. Its blade is looped around a set of wheels; the bottom wheel drives the blade into the work. Before buying a band saw, think about how you'll put it to use. It should have adequate throat capacity (the distance from the blade to the left vertical support); this determines the widest board it can cut. The saw should also have suitable cutting depth (the distance from the worktable to the upper blade guard set at its highest position). Cutting depth in smaller band saws runs up to 4 inches; in larger models, it can be greater than 7½ inches. A variable-speed saw allows better cutting control.

If the blade is too wide to make a curved cut, first cut several passes to remove waste material. If the cut doesn't finish at another edge of the work, turn the saw off at the end of the cut and back the blade out; otherwise, the blade may be pulled off the wheels.

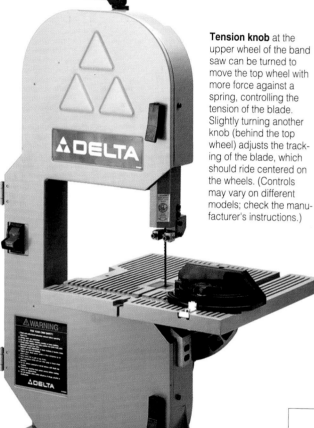

Tension knob at the upper wheel of the band saw can be turned to move the top wheel with more force against a spring, controlling the tension of the blade. Slightly turning another knob (behind the top wheel) adjusts the tracking of the blade, which should ride centered on the wheels. (Controls may vary on different models; check the manufacturer's instructions.)

Upper blade guide and guard move up and down to accommodate work of various thicknesses. The guide should be positioned about ⅛ in. above the work. The upper blade guide and another one under the table help keep the blade aligned.

Table-tilting lock holds the table at various angles up to 45°. A scale below the table shows the angle. When readjusting the table for a 90° cut, use a square to make sure the table is set at 90° to the blade.

Blade is accessed by opening a door or removing a panel on the side of the saw. Blades come in various widths with different numbers of teeth. The more teeth on the blade, the smoother the cut; fewer teeth allow a faster but coarser cut. Generally, use the widest blade possible.

Portable band saw can be used on a workpiece that's too large to fit on a standard band saw's worktable; it's also easier to move to a work site. This saw has a 4-in. cutting depth and variable-speed control. When using it, hold the saw with two hands; clamp the work securely, leaving clearance for the saw. You can buy a stand to hold it, freeing your hands.

CIRCULAR SAWS

The circular saw is used for fast straight cuts in wood or other materials, depending on the blade chosen (pp.58–59). The saw has one of two types of gears: the standard helical gear or the powerful worm-drive gear (not shown); the latter is used mostly in construction. The size of the saw is identified by the diameter of the largest blade it accepts: from 3⅜ to 16¼ inches (7¼ inches is the most common). Select a saw that you can handle comfortably and still accomplish your work; a heavy saw can be fatiguing and hard to control.

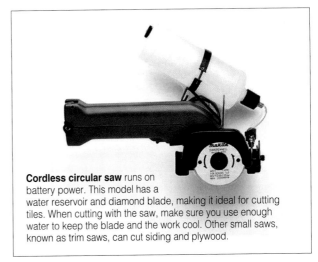

Cordless circular saw runs on battery power. This model has a water reservoir and diamond blade, making it ideal for cutting tiles. When cutting with the saw, make sure you use enough water to keep the blade and the work cool. Other small saws, known as trim saws, can cut siding and plywood.

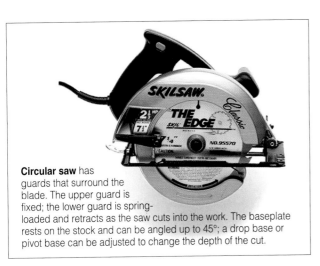

Circular saw has guards that surround the blade. The upper guard is fixed; the lower guard is spring-loaded and retracts as the saw cuts into the work. The baseplate rests on the stock and can be angled up to 45°; a drop base or pivot base can be adjusted to change the depth of the cut.

Miter saw combines a portable miter table and a circular saw to make straight and angled cuts. The saw pivots and locks in position to cut angles from 0° to 45° right and left. Stops are set for common angles. Some models handle stock up to 3⅛ in. thick and 4¾ in. wide; maximum stock width decreases as saw angle increases. Some models can also make compound cuts.

Sliding compound miter saw has a blade assembly that slides along two rods, allowing you to cut wide stock by pulling the assembly toward you. The saw can make miter cuts up to 45°, and it tilts to one side to make compound cuts, also at up to 45° angles. Some models handle stock up to 12 in. wide.

Ideal for making precise straight and angled cuts, the table saw can rip and crosscut long boards and wide panels. A circular blade (pp.58–59) protrudes through a slot in the table; the work is pushed into the blade. (In one model, you can also pull the blade into the work.) The diameter of the largest blade the saw can use establishes its size. The 10-inch table saw is the most common. While a bench-top model (shown) is portable and requires less space, a floor model makes smoother, more accurate cuts.

Blade guard shields the user's hands from the blade and prevents flying chips. The spreader, suspended from the blade guard assembly, keeps the kerf (the cut in the work-piece) open behind the blade. If the kerf is allowed to close, the blade will be pinched by the workpiece, jam, and cause the work to kick back and injure the operator.

Miter gauge can be adjusted to use as a guide for making crosscuts and angled cuts up to 45°. For a long board, support the weight of the work with one hand; while the saw is running, push the miter gauge with the work into the blade with the other hand. For a miter gauge that comes with other table saw models, see band saws, p.54.

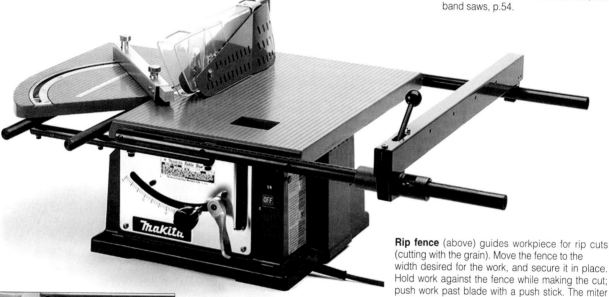

Rip fence (above) guides workpiece for rip cuts (cutting with the grain). Move the fence to the width desired for the work, and secure it in place. Hold work against the fence while making the cut; push work past blade with a push stick. The miter gauge must be removed to make a rip cut.

Depth of cut is adjusted by moving the blade up or down. On this model, you turn a knob to move the blade. (Some table saws use cranks.) You can also tilt the blade to make beveled cuts up to 45°. A scale indi-cates the degree of the angle.

Safety accessories are essential for preventing accidents while you use a table saw. Use the push stick (top) to keep fingers away from the saw blade. The spring-loaded wheel (center) is one of a pair that help hold and guide work on the table and pre-vent kickback. The wheels are attached to a fence—one wheel on each side of the blade. The feather board (bottom) holds the work against the fence while you make rip cuts. (Use two feather boards on a large table saw.)

The blade assembly of a radial arm saw is suspended from an arm and can be rotated, angled, and tilted to make a variety of cuts. The saw excels in making crosscuts—especially in long boards—and you can turn the blade housing and use it horizontally. With the proper attachments (use only those designed for your model), you can turn a radial arm saw into a sander, router, and drill press. The size of the saw is based on the diameter of the largest blade (pp.58–59) it will accept; 10 inches is a versatile size for a home workshop. Before operating the saw, make any adjustments suggested in the manufacturer's manual.

Kerf spreader   Pawl

Saw guard covers blade to prevent injury to user—a safety feature found on all radial arm saws. This guard is made of clear plastic; others are made of steel. Attached to the guard is an antikickback pawl for making rip cuts. If the work starts to move backward, the pawl grips it. A kerf spreader behind the blade keeps the cut open during rip cuts, preventing the blade from jamming in the work.

Worktable can be covered with a protective sheet of ¼-in. hardboard. To cut completely through the work, the blade must penetrate into the worktable surface or the protective sheet. As you need them, cut kerfs (slots) in the table and fence to allow clearance for the blade. The radial arm saw shown is a portable model. It is easy to store and transport to work sites. A heavy-duty floor model, however, will make more accurate cuts.

Arm lock and gauge allow arm to be set in preset stops for making miter cuts up to 22.5° left and 45° right (models vary). The arm can also be locked at other angles between stops.

Yoke controls are used to turn blade assembly to position it for rip sawing. The carriage lock knob secures the carriage in place along the arm, thus setting the width of the cut.

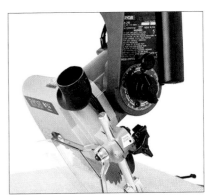

Bevel controls can be adjusted to tilt blade assembly up to 90° in either direction for making a beveled crosscut or rip cut. Adjust arm and bevel controls to make compound cuts.

Having a variety of blades will expand the capabilities of your circular saw, table saw, or radial arm saw. Blades fall into two categories: standard steel, which must be sharpened often, and carbide tipped. The latter stay sharp longer, but they're more brittle and can be damaged if improperly handled. The number of teeth on a blade, the grind of each tooth, and the gullet depth (the space between teeth) determine the smoothness and speed of the cut. Large flat-ground teeth make a fast, rough rip cut; small pointed teeth that alternate left and right cut slowly and smoothly across the grain. To avoid kickback, some blades have a hump behind each tooth. Most blades come in different sizes; match their diameters and arbor holes to your tool.

Rip has large square chisel teeth for making clean cuts parallel to the grain of hardwood and softwood.

Crosscut has small pointed teeth for making smooth cuts perpendicular to the grain in hardwood, softwood, and plywood.

Combination, with alternating large pointed teeth, can make rip cuts, crosscuts, and miter cuts in all wood materials without your having to change blades.

Chisel-tooth combination has large teeth for making fast, rough rip cuts.

Hollow-ground planer provides clearance for cut because blade body is thinner than cutting edge; its combination-ground teeth make smooth crosscuts and miter cuts.

Hollow-ground plywood has alternating fine bevel-ground teeth for splinter-free cuts in plywood and paneling.

Plywood/paneling, with small alternating top-bevel-ground teeth, makes smooth cuts in plywood and paneling.

Nonferrous metal/plastic cutter has alternating top-bevel-ground teeth for cutting brass, aluminum, copper, and plastics. Lubricate with oil or wax before use.

Thin kerf minimizes waste by making fine cuts in woods under ¾ in. thick; it has carbide-tipped teeth. This model, for combination cuts, has vents to prevent overheating.

Combination thin kerf has large carbide-tipped alternating bevel-ground teeth with antikickback humps. Use it for smooth rip cuts and crosscuts in most woods.

Framing thin kerf, with large carbide-tipped square chisel teeth and anti-kickback humps, is for smooth rip cuts in most woods.

Finishing thin kerf has small carbide-tipped alternating bevel-ground teeth with antikickback humps for making fine crosscuts in most woods.

Nail cutter, with large carbide-tipped teeth, can make rough cuts through nails that may be embedded in wood. It's ideal for remodeling and construction work.

Nonferrous metal cutter has carbide-tipped teeth for cutting aluminum, copper, lead, and brass. Lubricate with oil or wax before use.

Nonstick coating is added to hooked carbide-tipped teeth for fine cuts in solid wood, plywood veneers, and plastic.

Dado set includes saw blades and chippers, which are assembled to cut dadoes, rabbets, and grooves in solid wood and plastic laminate. An adjustable dado head comes assembled; it can be reset for various groove widths. Use dado blades on table and radial arm saws only.

Tools 59

A woodworking tool that is basically a blade, or *iron*, in a holder, the plane can trim and smooth wood, bevel and round off wood edges, and straighten irregular edges. Special-purpose planes can cut grooves for joints and shave wood into decorative shapes.

Choose a plane that will accomplish the particular job. Make sure the plane has a readily accessible and easy-to-use depth-adjusting nut or wheel; look for a frog—the underlying plate—that fully supports the iron. For surfacing passes, pick a plane with a grooved sole; to plane edges, select one with a flat sole.

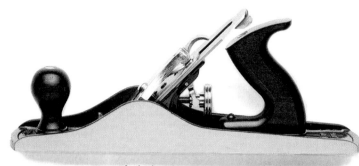

Jack plane has a wide iron and 14- to 15-in.-long body for roughing jobs and wide boards. To use it on freshly cut wood, set the iron cap back 1/16 in.; for final smoothing, move the iron cap until it's 1/32 in. from the cutting edge of the iron. Adjust the iron with the lateral lever and adjusting nut. To remove the iron for sharpening, release the lever cap; remove the lever and iron caps.

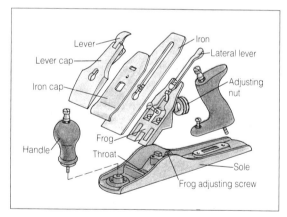

Steel jointer plane is used for edge joining and the initial leveling of wide boards. It has a 22- to 23-in.-long sole to prevent the tool from following bumps and dips. To change the depth of cut, move the iron by adjusting the lateral lever and the adjusting nut.

Lever
Lever cap
Iron cap
Handle
Throat
Iron
Lateral lever
Adjusting nut
Frog
Sole
Frog adjusting screw

Wood jointer plane has a fence to guide the tool for squaring and truing wood edges for tight fits. It's ideal for preparing wood for edge-to-edge gluing. To turn the tool into a smoothing plane, unscrew the fence and remove it.

Smoothing plane finishes a surface after rough planing. Because the small sole is only 7 to 9 in. long, the plane is suitable for working small areas of wood with tricky grain patterns.

Raised panel plane creates a paneled look with an angled sole and iron. It cuts 2-in.-wide strips and comes in right- and left-handed models. A wedge holds the iron in place. To adjust the iron, tap it with a wood or rawhide mallet.

Scrub plane removes large amounts of wood quickly. Its convex-shaped iron is held in place with a wooden wedge. Use short repetitive passes, moving diagonally across the grain. Finish the work with a smoothing plane.

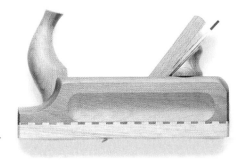

Gent's plane is designed for general finishing work. The handle at the front of the plane is held to give extra pushing power. It's smaller than the standard cabinetmaker's smoothing plane. Although this design makes the plane lighter and less tiring to use, it also makes it unsuitable for heavy-duty work.

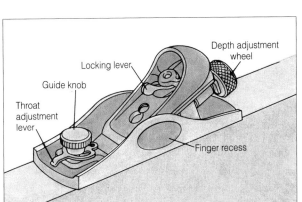

Block plane cuts and trims wood and makes fine finishing cuts. An adjusting wheel under the palm rest controls positioning of the iron. Because of its smaller size, the block plane can be used with one hand.

Low-angle block plane, one of several variations of the block plane, is used for shaping fine trim work and end grain. The blade rests at a 12° angle for finer cuts on cross grains and end grains. The plane is adjustable for making rougher cuts.

Bullnose plane, for fine woodworking, makes stopped rabbets and dadoes. The short nose in front of the iron allows cutting in close quarters.

Palm plane fits into places where a standard-size plane will not fit. It's very useful for intricate detail work. Another model has a raised handle.

Violin plane, for fine detail work, may have a straight iron or come in a set with matching convex- and concave-shaped irons.

Edge plane has an L-shaped body that works like a fence to form true square edges in wood. The blade is skewed for a smooth cut, preventing wood tearout.

Side rabbet plane forms sides of rabbets, dadoes, and other grooves. Two blades allow movement in both directions; a depth gauge adjusts up to ½ in. deep.

Rabbet plane shapes a rabbet in wood. There are two blade positions: center for general use and forward for bullnose applications. Spurs permit work on cross grain. Some models feature an adjustable, detachable fence.

Shoulder plane has sole and body sides at perfect right angles. As the name implies, it trims and squares the shoulders of tenon and rabbet joints.

MORE HAND PLANES

Chamfer plane cuts a 45° bevel, or chamfer, on the corner of a square piece. Adjust the width of the bevel cut with the threaded rods and nuts. Scales at the front and back ensure precise blade adjustment. The V-shaped sole is set at a 90° angle.

Butt mortise plane cuts mortises for hinges, strike plates, deadbolt locks, and similar hardware. It makes accurate square cuts with ease.

Edge finishing plane comes in two versions: one cuts round edges, the other chamfered edges. The front blade makes a rough cut; the rear one finishes it. To set the blades, insert a hex wrench in openings on the side and on top.

Three-in-one plane is a combination rabbet, bullnose, and stop rabbet plane in one tool. The bullnose head (left) makes it easier to control the depth of cut in tight areas. To convert the plane, unscrew one head and attach the other; the screw is located inside the head. To increase the mouth width, add the shims (center).

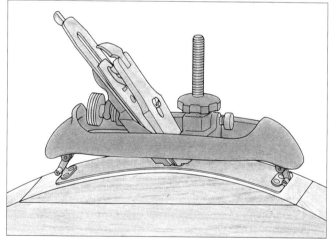

Circular plane, also called a compass plane, has a flexible sole for planing concave and convex surfaces. Place the plane on the work; then, using the adjusting knob to turn the threaded rod, position the sole to fit the contour desired for the work. Once the sole is set, adjust the iron to the correct setting.

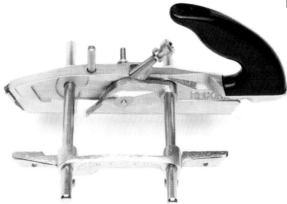

Router plane cuts grooves, dadoes, and other flat-bottomed depressions to a precise depth. It also surfaces the bottom of grooves and dadoes. Some models have an adjustable, detachable guide fence for general or bullnose (close-quarters) work on straight and curved grooves.

Plow combination plane uses an adjustable fence to guide it across the work edge while cutting grooves or rabbets. A conversion kit allows the plane to make bead and tongue cuts. Cutters are available in different widths and styles.

SPOKESHAVES AND DRAWKNIVES

Although all these woodworking tools perform the same basic functions, shaving and shaping wood, each of them is specialized for creating a flat, concave, or convex surface. In general, spoke-shaves are better suited for finishing workpieces, drawknives for roughing out stock. Most of these tools are held with two hands; the worker pushes or pulls the instrument against the work. To create smooth cuts and prevent injury, keep the cutting edges sharp. When using the tools, make sure you follow the grain of the wood.

Adjustable straight spokeshave should have two adjustment nuts to change the blade depth. A third adjustment nut holds a *lever cap,* which applies pressure to the blade. Loosen the nut before adjusting the blade depth. This spokeshave is for flat or convex surfaces. With practice, you need do little sanding after using a spokeshave.

Convex spokeshave (far left) carves a recessed area into a surface. Use it for work that requires hollowing out wood.

Concave spokeshave (left) has a curved blade for shaving rails, posts, and chair legs. The shape it creates fits around the shape carved by the convex spokeshave.

Chamfering spokeshave (far left), guided by two fences, cuts a bevel, or chamfer, on squared work. Thumbscrews adjust the fences.

Combination spokeshave (left) incorporates both a straight and a concave blade. Although this tool performs the same functions as the two individual spokeshaves, its blades are narrower.

Small spokeshave is useful for working in areas where bigger tools won't fit and for creating fine detail. It comes with a flat, round, or spoon-shaped sole. The blade may be flat or convex. To adjust the blade or to remove it for sharpening, remove the screw and washer.

Cabinet scraper holds a blade in a body that resembles a spokeshave. (Some scraper blades are used without a holder.) A thumbscrew is used to adjust the blade. The tool smooths knots and removes dried glue and paper-thin layers of wood.

Inshave, a type of drawknife, has a deeply curved blade for hollowing out wood. It's a practical tool for making recesses in wood but is less controllable than a spokeshave; use it for roughing.

Drawknife removes large or small quantities of wood, depending on how it's pulled by the user. Handles and blades vary. Smaller drawknives are better carving tools; the larger ones have better handle grips for heavy-duty jobs.

Scorp, originally for smoothing inside barrels and buckets, has a circular blade. Use the scorp with one hand to hollow out recesses in wood seats and bowls.

Push knife is a variation of the drawknife. Grasp the handles to push the straight blade through the wood; or with the blade in the reverse position, pull the knife toward you. The blade's tang passes through the handle for added strength—a feature to look for in any type of drawknife.

PLANERS AND JOINTERS

The portable power plane is great for jobs such as shaving down door edges. But if your projects call for perfect-fitting joinery and workpieces, a power jointer and a thickness planer should also be part of your workshop. (Both tools require accurate adjustments to be effective.) With them you can cut boards to less than standard thicknesses, and you can also buy less expensive rough-sawn lumber and smooth its surface yourself. On a jointer, first flatten and straighten a surface, then straighten and square its edges. Finally give the piece an overall equal thickness with the planer. If the work calls for strong joints, it's ready for the biscuit joiner.

Portable power plane is the perfect tool for removing a small amount of stock from a door that no longer swings open because of new carpeting or the wood swelling in humid weather. Balance the door with hand-screw clamps; use scrap wood to create a wider base.

Portable power plane is often used for smoothing and squaring the edges of wood. A set of two rotating blades removes up to ⅛ in. of stock per pass; make a series of passes to remove more wood. Planes are sized according to the width of cut they can make. Maximum cutting width ranges from 3¼ to 6⅝ in., depending on the model. As you plane a workpiece, apply even pressure throughout the pass; at the end of the pass let up slightly on the plane's front end to avoid digging into the work. Besides straightening edges, the plane can also make chamfers and tapers. A fence can be attached to the plane to cut specific angles.

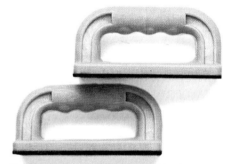

Push blocks are absolutely essential safety tools when working with the jointer. (They can also be used with a table or radial arm saw.) The ones shown have foam pads to grip the work securely, and their handles are angled to keep hands away from the fence.

Jointer flattens, straightens, and squares boards from 4 to 8 in. wide. The machine consists of an infeed table, cutter head, outfeed table, and fence. The height of the infeed table is adjustable to change the depth of cut up to ⅛ in. A guard (open here to show cutter) protects your hands as you feed the work across the cutter; but if the top edge of a board is lower than the fence top, use push blocks. The fence adjusts up to 45° left and right for beveling and chamfering. The tool is available in small bench-top models and larger floor models.

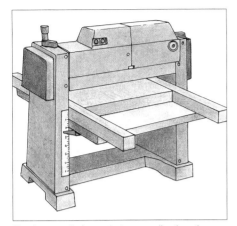

To plane workpieces that are smaller than the manufacturer's recommendations, hot-glue scrap wood to the sides of the work. (Make sure the assembly isn't too wide to fit through the planer.) After passing the work through the planer, tap on the scrap wood to break it off the workpiece.

Biscuit joiner

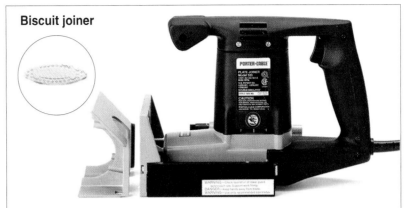

Also called a plate joiner, the biscuit joiner is a unique tool for strengthening butt, miter, and edge joints in wood. A blade cuts corresponding grooves into each of two workpieces; oval-shaped "biscuits" of wood or plastic fit into the grooves and, with a little glue, create a strong joint. (Glue causes the biscuit to expand for a tight fit.) Biscuit joints can be aligned before the glue dries by shifting the pieces laterally. Biscuits are available in several sizes; use the largest one that fits the joint.

Thickness planer sizes stock to a desired thickness after one surface has been straightened or flattened on the jointer. The stock is placed on the table and fed automatically by rollers past rotating blades. It's best to make several passes, removing a small amount of stock each time. The type of wood, its width, and the feed rate determine the amount of stock that can be removed. The slower the feed, the more cuts per inch. The more cuts per inch, the smoother the surface. The thickness planer is available in bench-top models that accept stock from 4 to 12 in. wide and 3/32 to 6 in. thick. Floor models can accept larger stock from 12 to 36 in. wide and 1/8 to 8 in. thick. The planer may operate on single-speed, two-speed, or variable-speed feed rates. Some thickness planers have blades with a cutting edge on both sides. When one side becomes dull, remove any debris and reinstall the blade with the sharp side in the cutting position. Before changing a blade, make sure that you unplug the machine.

An adaptable woodworking tool, the router can be used to make decorative edges or surfaces, top-quality joinery, and freehand or pattern-assisted carvings. It has a ¼-, ⅜-, or ½-inch-diameter collet that accepts matching bit shanks. For light woodworking, a ¼-inch router is adequate, but a larger collet gives greater versatility. The motor sizes range from ½ to 3¼ horsepower. The greater the horsepower, the more work the router can handle. Before buying a router, check that the handles feel comfortable and that the on-off switch is in easy reach.

Router bits can be used singly or several can be used in succession to create different shapes. High-speed steel bits require more frequent sharpening than carbide-tipped bits, which last longer but are more expensive. If the bit has a solid or ball-bearing pilot, it serves as a guide that follows the edge of the work.

Standard router with ⅞ hp and ¼-in. collet has a motor that adjusts up and down. To change the depth of the cut, loosen the knob and reposition the motor in the base. When the motor is on, make sure fingers stay clear of the sharp high-speed bits.

Plunge router, ideal for making interior cuts, is supported with two posts extending up from the base. After setting the depth stop, set the router over the work at the starting point and start the motor; release the plunge locking lever and lower the bit into the work. Some models have variable-speed control.

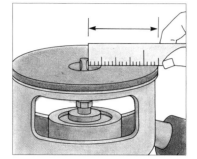

Because bit sizes vary, measure from bit to edge of base before setting a fence or guide. Mark the same distance from the cutting edge.

The router bit spins clockwise and must feed into the work. For cuts on an edge, move the router from left to right; guide it counterclockwise around a continuous piece. For inside cuts, move it clockwise.

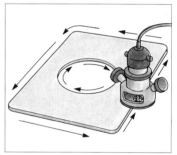

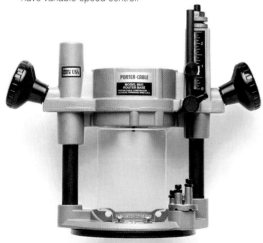

Retrofit plunge base replaces the base on a standard router with a 3½-in.-diameter motor. When attached to the motor, the standard router becomes a plunge router. The plunge base also has a locking lever and a multiposition depth stop.

Laminate trimmer finishes plastic laminate edges on countertops, backsplashes, cabinet doors, and shelves. Attachments include an offset base (top, center) to reach into corners, an adjustable base (top, right) to set trimmer at 0° to 45° angles, and a slitter (bottom, right) to cut laminate sheets.

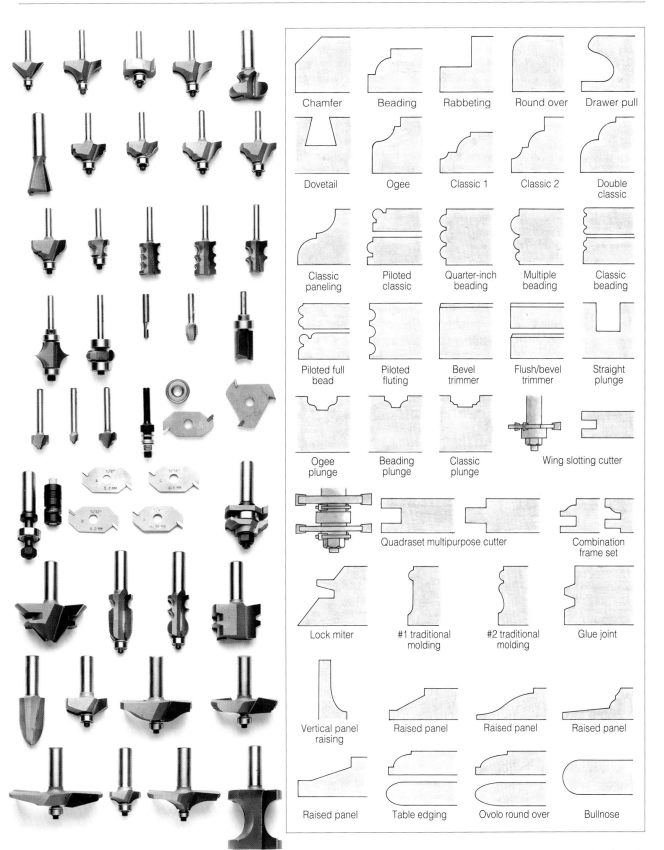

Chamfer

Beading

Rabbeting

Round over

Drawer pull

Dovetail

Ogee

Classic 1

Classic 2

Double classic

Classic paneling

Piloted classic

Quarter-inch beading

Multiple beading

Classic beading

Piloted full bead

Piloted fluting

Bevel trimmer

Flush/bevel trimmer

Straight plunge

Ogee plunge

Beading plunge

Classic plunge

Wing slotting cutter

Quadraset multipurpose cutter

Combination frame set

Lock miter

#1 traditional molding

#2 traditional molding

Glue joint

Vertical panel raising

Raised panel

Raised panel

Raised panel

Raised panel

Table edging

Ovolo round over

Bullnose

ROUTER GUIDES AND TEMPLATES

To make perfect cuts and shapes, a router is often used with a guide or template. Before routing with one of these accessories on the actual workpiece, practice on scrap wood until you feel comfortable with it. Because bits vary in width, when setting up a guide or template, always calculate the distance with the bit in place in the collet (p.66).

Pantograph guides a router to transfer designs from templates to signs, plaques, and other flat surfaces. To use it, attach the router to the pantograph, turn on the router, then trace the design with the stylus; the router will duplicate the design on the workpiece. Some models include letter templates and drawings. You can also make your own templates.

Roller edge guide and guide bushings come in a kit. The roller edge guide, attached to a special baseplate (right), has a bearing that lets you shape decorative profiles when using unpiloted bits. It's also useful for trimming laminate and for edging irregular shapes. Guide bushings (left) and retainer (top) protect precision dovetail, letter, and butt-hinge templates. Never use the roller edge guide and a guide bushing together.

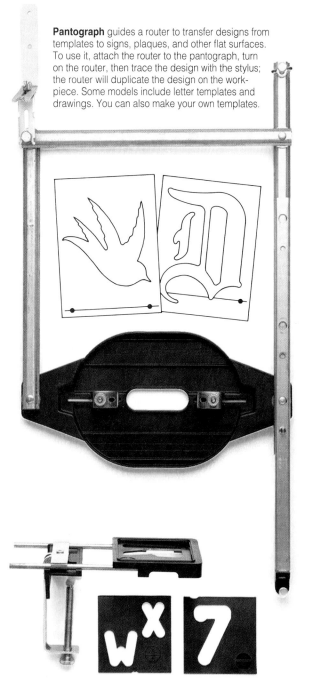

Straight-and-circular guide directs the router for making cuts parallel to the edge of the work. Use it to make straight or circular plunge cuts. The guide has an adjustable fence for straight cuts; an adjustable trammel point holds the guide in place to make circular cuts. Wing nuts are used to make the adjustments. This model also has a micrometer adjustment for accuracy.

Router table transforms a router into a stationary shaper for concise work. Invert the router and mount it underneath the table; make sure the cutter protrudes up through the hole in the center of the table. To rout the work surface or edge, place its good face down on the table and push it into the bit. The table includes a cutter safety guard, a guide fence for edging and slotting, and a miter gauge for angles and crosscuts.

Letter templates are used with a guide bushing and a straight, V-groove, or cove router bit to engrave letters and numbers in wooden signs. A bracket clamps the template and work to a workbench. Letter styles and sizes vary.

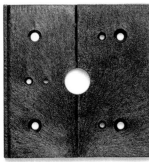

Edge-joining guide is a two-piece subbase that replaces your router's standard subbase. To create a perfect edge joint, make a separate pass against each of the two workpieces, using the enclosed bit.

Mortise-and-tenon jig makes perfect-fitting round mortise-and-tenon joints for constructing furniture and door frames.
The jig can create up to three consecutive mortises and tenons without being moved. The joints can also be angled or mitered. A piloted mortise-and-tenon bit is included.

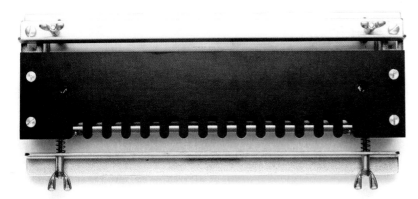

Dovetail template guides router to make strong dovetail joints for fine furniture, cabinet, and drawer construction. It's used in conjunction with a guide bushing and a dovetail router bit. The guide bushing follows the template as the router bit cuts a series of evenly spaced fan-shaped pins and matching recesses simultaneously in the two workpieces. It makes both flush and rabbet dovetails.

Butt-hinge template fits on door edges and jambs to rout mortises for butt hinges from 2½ to 5½ in. wide. It comes in a kit with three templates, letting you make up to three mortises at a time. Adjustable link rails slide into the templates; markings indicate proper placement on 6-ft. 6-in.- to 7-ft.-tall doors. One template has a gauge for the top mortise. Before using a router with the templates, attach a butt-hinge guide to its base.

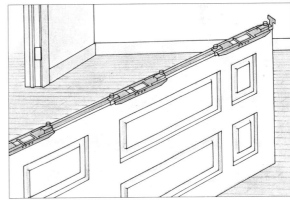

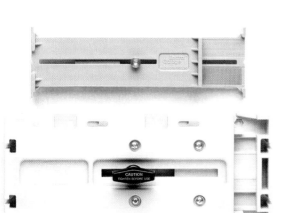

Universal precision positioning jig can become an adjustable fence to make accurate finger and dovetail joints on a router table, and it can act as an adjustable stop for other cuts. The jig (left) can be quickly set at exact stops as small as ¹⁄₃₂ in. apart, up to 8 in. It also operates as a fence on a table saw and has other applications for a radial arm saw and drill press. The multifunction precision gauge (left, top) sets the bit-to-fence alignment and establishes the depth of the cut with the same accuracy as the jig.

CHISELS, GOUGES, AND LATHES

When kept sharp and free of corrosion, a chisel or gouge will last a lifetime. Chisels come in a variety of sizes for working on wood, metal, and stone. They are hand-driven or driven with a mallet. The steel blades may have straight or beveled sides. Straight sides are stronger than beveled, but a beveled blade can reach into tight places. The blade shape may be square, round, or skewed for specific tasks. Gouge blades are curved to make concave or convex cuts. Store chisels and gouges where their blades cannot be damaged by hitting each other or other tools. Never place one where it can be knocked to the floor; the sharp blade can cause a cut.

Butt chisel has a short blade that makes it easier to work with than a standard chisel. It is hand- or lightly mallet-driven. The beveled sides and straight cutting edge make it ideal for undercutting to create dovetail joints.

Mortise chisel has a thick rigid blade, straight cutting edge, and square sides to make mortises and similar joints. The sturdy reinforced handle is struck with a mallet to remove waste.

Skew chisel uses a slicing motion to finish cuts in tight spaces and to trim close to adjacent surfaces. The angled cutting edge (about 60°) gives the chisel its name; the skew on the blade may be right- or left-handed or both. The blade sides are straight for strength. This chisel is only hand-driven.

Framing chisel has beveled sides and a straight cutting edge; it flexes slightly when used in hard-to-reach spaces. You strike the hoop-reinforced handle with a mallet to remove waste when cutting mortises, dovetails, and similar joints.

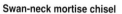

Swan-neck mortise chisel has a blade shaped to clean out grooves and small mortises. Using a chisel slightly smaller than the mortise, set the blade's cutting edge along the mortise's bottom edge. The tool can be used in mortises up to 6 in. deep.

Corner chisel, resembling a punch, is used primarily with a mallet. Another model has a handle for striking and for handwork. The L-shaped cutting edge cleans out square holes and corners with angles of 90° and more; it also trims and fine-tunes mortises.

Dogleg chisel with a straight, right skew, or left skew cutting edge works like a small paring or carving chisel. Uses include fine-tuning joints and adding detail to fine woodwork.

Cold chisel for metalwork is struck with a hammer to cut sheet metal and to chop off rivets, bolts, and nails. You can also use one to reach a plumbing fixture by chipping away ceramic tile.

Paring chisel is ideal for cleaning grooves and slicing away small amounts of stock. The straight cutting edge has beveled sides to access tight spaces. It's made for hand use only; do not strike it with a mallet.

Flooring chisel cuts and lifts flooring materials for removal or repair; it's ideal for tongue-and-groove flooring. The wide blade distributes pressure evenly to prevent damage to adjacent boards.

Crank-neck paring chisel has an offset blade to allow you to hold the tool flat against the work surface, even in the middle of the work, and still have clearance to hold the handle.

Froe splits shingles, clapboards, and other similar materials. First strike the wrought-iron blade (about 15 in. long) into the work; then move the handle in a back-and-forth motion to complete the split.

Blind-nail chisel lifts up a small sliver of wood. After hammering the nail in place, glue the sliver over the nailhead.

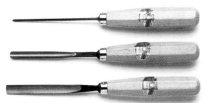

Carving chisel, sold separately or in sets, is used for cutting intricate designs into wood and for sculpting. Some carving chisels are designed to be struck. Their cutting edges include gouge, parting, skew, straight, paring, and V-groove.

Chip-carving knives have blades in a variety of designs for creating low-relief carving and for whittling. Often sold in sets, the knives can be conveniently stored in a canvas pouch.

Miniature carving chisel is for extra-fine detail work. It comes with the same variety of blades as standard carving chisels.

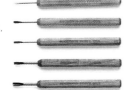

Cabinetmaker's carving chisel has a handle that fits into the palm of your hand.

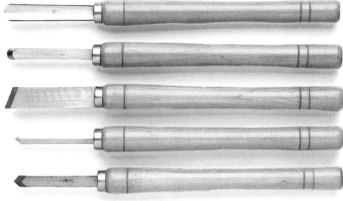

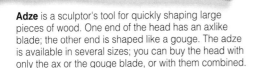

Adze is a sculptor's tool for quickly shaping large pieces of wood. One end of the head has an axlike blade; the other end is shaped like a gouge. The adze is available in several sizes; you can buy the head with only the ax or the gouge blade, or with them combined.

Lathe chisels are used with a lathe to create turned woodwork such as chair legs and rails. A basic set of chisels includes, from top to bottom: gouge for rounding and cutting coves (concave curves); round-nose chisel to form coves and hollows; skew chisel to cut beads (convex curves) and to smooth straight or tapered cylinders; spear-point chisel to cut V-grooves and square shoulders; and parting tool for sizing cuts and to separate the turned work from the waste stock.

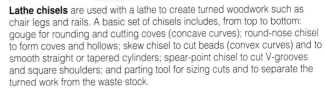

Deep-throat gouge is for bowl work on a lathe. Handled properly, it leaves a smooth finish that needs no sanding.

Finishing scraper is used for inside finishing of work turned on a lathe. It may have a round- or square-shaped blade.

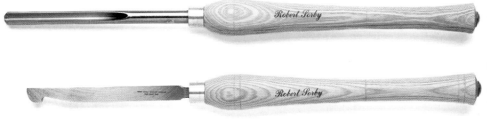

Lathe is ideal for turning wood stock into a cylindrical shape. The headstock holds the wheel; a motor turns the wheel, which turns a spindle. The tailstock also has a spindle; depending on the model, the headstock or tailstock spindle is adjustable. Centers on the spindles grip the work. As the work turns, a chisel held on the tool rest by the user shaves or scrapes it. For bowls and other flat round pieces, attach the work to a faceplate mounted on the headstock spindle; rotate the tool rest 90°.

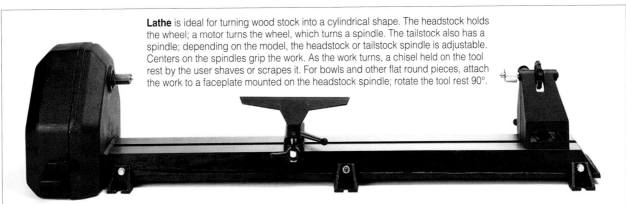

Depending on the individual tool, a file or rasp can sharpen, shape, or smooth while removing metal or wood. Cut, coarseness, length, and shape determine the tool's use. The *cut* refers to the pattern of the teeth. A single-cut file has parallel diagonal rows of ridgelike teeth for smoothing and sharpening metal; a double-cut file has a second set of rows that cross the first for rapid removal of metal stock. The rasp has straight or random rows of individual teeth for fast rough removal of wood or soft metal stock. Single (smooth) cut, second (medium) cut, and bastard (rough) cut indicate the coarseness of a file or rasp, and generally the longer the tool, the coarser its cut. The shape, or profile, of a file or rasp can make it useful for specific jobs.

Flat file (near right), a general-purpose file for fast removal of metal, has a slightly tapered shape and a rectangular profile. It has double-cut faces (above) with a single cut along the edges.

Hand file (near center) is similar to flat file, but it has parallel edges; one edge is *safe*, or uncut, to keep it from marring the work.

Pillar file (far center), a thin file, fits into narrow grooves and slots.

Square file (far right) is shaped to fit into recesses, angles, and square mortises and holes for filing. Like the flat file, it tapers toward the end.

Half-round file (top, far left) has a round and a flat side to file large concave and flat surfaces.

Round file (top, near left) shapes small curves and enlarges and smooths holes. A tapered one is called a rat-tail file.

Triangle file (left) has three sides. Each side is flat and has a single cut.

Saw files sharpen saw blade teeth. From left to right are a chain-saw file, veneer knife file, crosscut file, cant-saw file (for saw blades with teeth angled less than 60°), and taper file (for blades with 60°-angle teeth).

Cabinet file (above) has ridge-like teeth that are staggered in parallel rows. Woodcarvers and cabinetmakers use it for sculpturing.

Wood file (above, right), a half-round file, has teeth that are slightly coarser than those of the cabinet file.

Long-angle lathe file (far left) has a single cut (above) that can leave a smooth finish on lathe metalwork.

Mill file (left, center) is used for lathe metalwork, for fine finishing of metals, for draw-filing, and for sharpening cutters and saw blades.

Auger bit file (near left) is for maintaining the cutting edges on auger drill bits.

Three-square (triangular) file (far left) is tapered and has three flat sides for filing metal at angles under 90°.

Knife file (left, center) is for working on metal pieces with acute angles.

Warding file (left) has a narrow tip to fit into tight areas.

Rifflers—files and rasps used for wood carving and metal crafts—shape and remove stock in irregular and tight spaces. They vary in size and they come in the same shapes, coarsenesses, and cuts as standard files and rasps. Some rifflers have handles, and some are double-ended, with a file at one end and a rasp at the other.

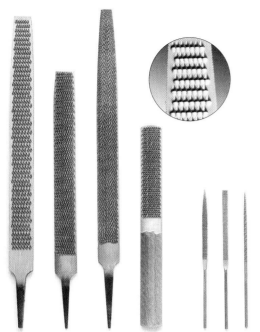

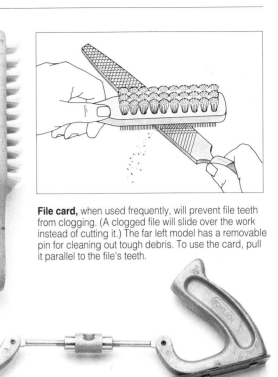

File card, when used frequently, will prevent file teeth from clogging. (A clogged file will slide over the work instead of cutting it.) The far left model has a removable pin for cleaning out tough debris. To use the card, pull it parallel to the file's teeth.

Rasps have individual teeth, instead of ridges, to rough out shapes and remove stock quickly. They work best on wood but can also be used on leather and soft metals. From left to right are a wood rasp with a rectangular profile and coarse teeth, a cabinet rasp with a half-round profile and medium teeth, a patternmaker's cabinet rasp that also has a half-round profile but fine teeth, and a four-in-one rasp, which combines a half-round and a flat profile—each side has a file end and a rasp end. The rat-tail rasp (not shown) has a round profile. Small rasps are ideal for working in restricted spaces.

Flexible file holder provides easy two-handed gripping and filing power. Secure a file in the holder, then adjust the holder to bend outward or inward to suit the stock surface. It can hold files that are from 12 to 14 in. long.

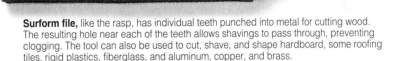

File handle fits on the file's tang, the pointed end of the file, allowing a better hold on the file and protecting the user from the sharp tang. Handles are usually purchased separately from the file. This model has a screw on one end that controls jaws on the other end.

Surform file, like the rasp, has individual teeth punched into metal for cutting wood. The resulting hole near each of the teeth allows shavings to pass through, preventing clogging. The tool can also be used to cut, shave, and shape hardboard, some roofing tiles, rigid plastics, fiberglass, and aluminum, copper, and brass.

Surform plane shapes, planes, and removes stock with a two-handed pushing action. The blades cannot be sharpened but are replaceable; remove the screw usually found beside the handle. Blades come in fine, regular, and medium cuts and in grits from coarse to fine. Use the plane on wood, plywood, chipboard, plaster, vinyl, and linoleum. The regular-cut blade has a feature on one edge for cutting inside corners; the other edge does not cut.

Surform shaving tool works with a pull stroke. Change the depth of cut by adjusting hand pressure. Unlike the other Surforms, the blade simply clips into place.

Surform pocket plane fits comfortably into the palm of your hand. Use it to trim narrow surfaces and to get into tight corners.

Round Surform file is useful for enlarging holes and shaping curved surfaces.

Surform file-plane has a handle that unscrews and moves, allowing the tool to be held and used like a file or a plane.

SANDING TOOLS

Hand and power sanders fitted with abrasive papers can shape workpieces, remove imperfections in wood, and create smooth surfaces prior to finishing. They can also help remove unwanted paint, rust, and finishes from wood, metal, and other surfaces. Hand-sanding is made easier with blocks and pads that hold the abrasive. Power-assisted sanding takes less time but sometimes requires extra skill; you can rent large power sanders, especially floor models. Always wear a dust mask and protective glasses when power-sanding, even if the sander has a dust collection system. Start a power sander before the abrasive touches the work surface; when you finish, wait until the sander stops moving before setting it down. Empty the dust bag often, particularly when changing from a wood to a metal surface; sparks from the metal can ignite wood dust.

Sanding block holds abrasive sheets. It pulls apart to anchor the sheet ends between the two sections.

Flexible block can be adjusted to the contour of the workpiece. To change its shape, pull the two ends of the block apart or push one end under the other.

Stick-It Block is designed to hold self-adhesive abrasive sheets that grip onto a felt backing. Replacing the sheet is as easy as pulling off the old one and sticking on the new one. The block itself has a large handle with a comfortable grip. Use the straight end of the base to sand into tight corners. The rounded end can fit into a concave surface.

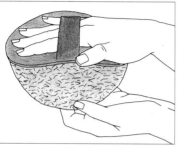

Sanding pad is secured to your hand with a strap, making it convenient for sanding large surfaces. Six-in. abrasive discs are attached to the pad with Velcro. The pad's flexibility allows you to bend it to the work's shape.

Palm orbital sander, for preparing a wood surface before applying a finish, works with an orbital motion. A soft pad (covered with an abrasive sheet) moves in quick, tight circles while the housing remains stationary. The sander's small size allows for one-handed use; hold the base flush to the work. The pad accepts adhesive-backed abrasive sheets; a quarter-sheet square pad for fitting in corners is available. The sander may come with a dust bag.

Pole sander, when attached to an extension pole, is used for reaching ceilings and upper parts of walls. Abrasive sheets are held in place with metal clips.

Random orbital sander, available in single- and variable-speed models, quickly removes stock with coarse abrasive paper; its random action creates a swirl-free finish when using fine abrasive paper.

Finishing sander has a second handle for two-handed operation. It's available in one-, two-, and variable-speed models. Apply light pressure when sanding; excessive pressure can overload the motor. Clamp one-third sheet of an abrasive paper to the pad.

Belt-disc sander, which should be bolted to a workbench, lets you sand, buff, and sharpen narrow pieces of straight, curved, and odd-shaped stock. The belt sander can be raised to fit a job. Attach a buffing belt to polish metals and other materials. The disc sander, with an adjustable worktable, smooths the ends or convex edges of workpieces. Use the miter gauge for precise sanding. Grinding attachments are available.

Portable belt sander uses a continuous-loop abrasive sheet for fast removal of large, flat areas of wood, for trimming off excess wood, and for stripping old paint and finish. Two drumlike rollers control the belt. The back roller is powered by the motor; the front roller is spring-loaded to correct the belt tension. The longer and wider the belt, the heavier and more powerful the tool. Look for a model with a dust collection bag. Before buying a belt sander, hold it to check its feel—is it comfortable? Make sure the sander doesn't twist in your hands when you start it. When using the sander, keep the tool level as you move it across the work.

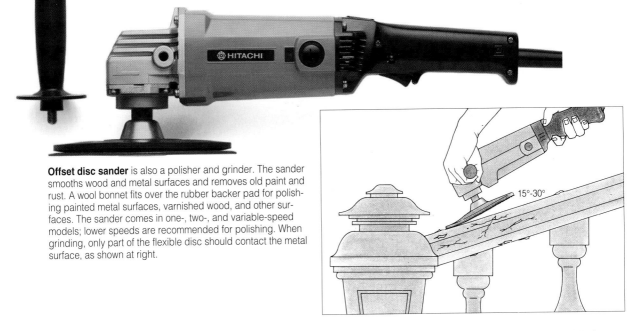

Offset disc sander is also a polisher and grinder. The sander smooths wood and metal surfaces and removes old paint and rust. A wool bonnet fits over the rubber backer pad for polishing painted metal surfaces, varnished wood, and other surfaces. The sander comes in one-, two-, and variable-speed models; lower speeds are recommended for polishing. When grinding, only part of the flexible disc should contact the metal surface, as shown at right.

Tools   75

ABRASIVES

Also known as sandpaper, abrasive paper comes with aluminum oxide, emery, garnet, or silicon carbide particles, or grit, glued to a paper or cloth backing (which is graded by weight). The paper comes in precut sizes or in sheets that can be folded and torn to size; it's graded by numbers that reflect the size of the grit. The higher the number, the finer the grit. Grades include extra-coarse (30–40), coarse (50–60), medium (80–100), fine (120–150), very fine (160–240), extra-fine (280–320), superfine (360–400), and ultrafine (above 400). Other abrasives include metal wools and polishing powders, such as pumice and rottenstone (not shown).

Disc-shaped papers, like other abrasive papers, come in coarse, medium, and fine grits. Use coarse-grit papers for fast stock removal; fine-grit papers are best for sanding finishes on wood, metal, and plastic surfaces.

Precut abrasive papers come in the same grits and coarsenesses as the standard large sheets, but they are cut to fit specific sanders (pp.74–75). Clockwise, the papers fit a sanding block, finishing sander, orbital palm sander with a square pad, portable belt sander, and workbench belt sander. The papers are attached by a form of clamping, an adhesive backing, or with Velcro. Most papers have a closed coat—the paper is completely covered with grains. But to prevent the paper from being clogged with fibers when working on softwoods, choose an open-coat paper with only 70 percent surface coverage.

Abrasive sheets (from top to bottom) are *aluminum oxide paper,* a tough, durable synthetic abrasive for smoothing wood, metal, plastic, and fiberglass, and for removing paint; *emery cloth,* a fine natural abrasive set on cloth, for metalworking; *garnet paper,* with a natural grit that fractures during use to form new cutting edges, for heavy and moderate smoothing on hard- and softwoods, and for preparing wood for sealing and finishing; and *silicon carbide paper,* which uses a synthetic abrasive that cuts fast and smooth, for wet- or dry-sanding between coats of varnish, paint, and other finishes on wood and metal. (Water reduces clogging and extends the life of silicon carbide paper.) The last example is *aluminum oxide* bonded to a pad; it can be rinsed and used a number of times, wet or dry.

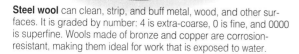

Steel wool can clean, strip, and buff metal, wood, and other surfaces. It is graded by number: 4 is extra-coarse, 0 is fine, and 0000 is superfine. Wools made of bronze and copper are corrosion-resistant, making them ideal for work that is exposed to water.

Drywall sanding screen fits onto a pole sander. Use it for the initial sanding when working with wallboard joint and patching compounds. The open screen allows dust to pass through to prevent clogging.

WALLCOVERING TOOLS

To hang wallcoverings with professional results, you'll find that the tools shown on this page will be helpful. A clean flat surface is necessary to lay the wallcovering down for pasting. If you don't have a large 5- × 3-foot table, make a temporary one by setting plywood on sawhorses (cover it with a plastic sheet, such as a drop cloth); or if you plan to do a substantial amount of wallcovering, buy a pasting table that folds up for storage. For prepasted wallcoverings, you'll need an inexpensive plastic water tray.

Paste brush with 3-in.-long bristles can apply paste and adhesives to wallcoverings that are not prepasted. The brush is 6 in. wide. It's available in wallcovering kits, but you can also purchase the brush separately.

Smoothing brush flattens the wallcovering to create a uniform surface without wrinkles and air pockets. The long-bristle brush works best on paper, cloth, and such delicate coverings as cork, silk, and grass cloth; the gentle bristles won't tear them. The short-bristle model is appropriate for the sturdier vinyl wallcoverings. Both are 12 in. wide.

Seam roller smooths edges of wallcoverings (except embossed). Use rollers with oval barrels for seams, tapered barrels for corners, and flat barrels for door and window frames.

Touching-up kit has a tapered-tip syringe (far left) to repair curled wallcovering corners. To remove an air bubble, slit it with a knife; then inject paste behind the bubble with the needle-tip syringe (left). Smooth down either repair with a seam roller or smoother. Wash area if wallcovering is washable.

Smoother is used on vinyl wallcoverings to produce a uniformly smooth surface and to remove air bubbles. It can also serve as a spreader for spackling compound or as a trim guide. Rounded corners will not mar the work.

Corner trimmer (far left) has an attachment to guide cuts at corners, ceiling lines, and baseboards.

Casing knife (left) trims wallcoverings around outlets, vents, baseboards, and window and door frames.

Wallpaper trimmer (above) comes with a straightedge to remove selvage edges and to cut wallcoverings to size.

Wallcovering shears have sharp blades to cut wallcoverings with great accuracy. The handles are designed to provide a comfortable grip.

Wallpaper scraper is used with a steamer or chemical stripper to peel away old wallpaper. It has a long cushioned handle and a replaceable blade.

Wallpaper steamer speeds up the task of removing old wallpaper. Hold the unit against the wallpaper, letting the steam saturate the paper just enough to soften the paste. Then use a scraper to remove the paper.

PAINTING TOOLS

By taking the time to select the right tools and use the correct techniques, an amateur painter can turn a so-so project into one with outstanding results. Choose the appropriate paint applicators from among the various bristle and foam brushes, rollers, pads, and power sprayers. Each applicator has its own benefits, depending on the type of finish being applied, the size of the area being covered, and the quality and speed of application desired. Special accessories, including tools for preparing the surface and cleaning up afterward, also help to make painting tasks easier and to produce professional-looking results.

Chisel-edge brush has angled bristles for painting clean edges. Hold the brush so that the ends of the bristles apply the paint. With a steady hand, pull the brush with the shorter bristles leading the way.

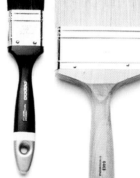

Chinese bristle brush is made with natural animal hairs, which are preferred for applying alkyd paint, varnish, and stain. A good brush will provide long service if treated and cleaned properly.

Wall brush is at least 4 in. wide to cover broad areas. To speed the job, use the widest brush possible without using one wider than the work. This brush, with synthetic polyester bristles (others may be nylon), can apply latex or alkyd paint, varnish, and stain.

Trim brush, available with natural or synthetic bristles for alkyd or latex finishes, comes in several widths up to 2 in. The brush can apply paint to such detail work as baseboards, door and window trim, and moldings. It also "cuts in" paint where rollers cannot reach— such as in corners and where the walls and ceiling meet.

Edger pad has compact fibers to quickly and evenly disperse paint along trim areas. It spreads paint faster than a brush but slower than a roller. One model (right) has guide wheels and a removable pad for cleaning.

Corner pad with two sides angled at 90° is especially designed for painting the inside corners of walls and between walls and ceilings, as well as other right-angle intersections. For other trims, hold the pad with only one side against the work surface.

Wand and sponge applicators can fit into restricted areas. To change angle of handle on wand applicator (left), press the button; move pad to the other side. The sponge applicator (right) uses disposable pads.

Wall pad is 6 to 10 in. wide for large expanses of walls, ceilings, and floors. An extension pole can be fitted into the handle.

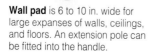

Pad paint tray can be hung over step- or extension ladder rungs. To avoid overloading pad with paint, roll the pad over the revolving wheel in the tray.

Trim rollers have specialized applications. The 3-in.-wide roller (below) comes with its own paint tray for quick touch-up jobs and hard-to-reach areas. Another roller (center) applies paint in corners. The third roller (right) is for narrow surface areas.

Pipe roller has an indented center groove in the cover to conform to the contour of heating pipes. Make sure you apply only heat-resistant paint to the pipe.

Roller and paint tray make it possible to quickly and economically apply paint and other finishes to broad surfaces. The roller uses less paint than a brush, requires less effort to spread a smooth, even coat, and leaves no brush marks. With the paint tray set on a flat surface, pour paint into the deeper well section. Slip a roller cover onto the frame. Place the roller in the well; pull it up to the grooved area, applying slight pressure and rolling it to squeeze out excess paint.

Splatter-shield roller reduces splatters. End caps hold the roller cover in a handle and housing unit. To remove the roller cover, you may have to pry out tight-fitting end caps. The handle can be connected to an extension pole.

Texture roller has a cover made from pieces of leather; only the edges of the leather come in contact with the surface, creating a pattern. The cover fits only on a special-size frame; roller and frame are usually purchased as a unit.

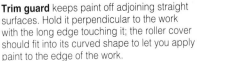

Trim guard keeps paint off adjoining straight surfaces. Hold it perpendicular to the work with the long edge touching it; the roller cover should fit into its curved shape to let you apply paint to the edge of the work.

Roller covers slide onto a frame or the end caps of a splatter-shield roller. If cleaned properly, most roller covers can be used several times. Roller covers come in various naps for use with latex and alkyd paints and for special applications.

Extension pole screws into a threaded roller or pad handle, allowing you to reach ceilings and upper wall areas without using a ladder. It also eliminates bending or kneeling when painting floors and sealing driveways. Extension poles come up to 6 ft. long. Some models telescope to longer lengths.

Self-feeding roller comes with a lid and fill tube that fit on a paint can. Attach the extension pole (assembled with roller cover and splatter shield) to the lid. Pull pole sections apart to siphon paint into handle. Detach pole from lid; push pole section in to send paint to roller.

Electric paint roller employs an electric pump to apply paint, requiring even less effort than using a self-feeding roller. The pump feeds paint directly from the can to the roller through a hose. A push button on the roller handle starts and stops the flow of paint. It's ideal for large projects such as painting several rooms or the exterior of a house.

Pouring spout fits on a standard 1-gal. paint can. It allows you to pour the paint into a tray without spilling or dripping.

Lid opener quickly opens both 1-gal. containers and standard 5-gal. plastic containers of paint, stucco, and similar materials without damaging the lipped lid.

Paint mixer locks into the chuck of almost any standard electric drill. With more consistency and less mess than stirring by hand, the plastic blades easily stir and blend paint, driveway and roofing sealers, and joint compound right in the can.

Paint sprayer applies paint, stain, varnish, and other liquids with a fine mist for fast, even, and run-free covering. It's helpful for hard-to-paint projects such as window shutters and wickerwork.

Stippling brush is pounced over a stencil to leave a decorative pattern on walls, furniture, and other surfaces. Be careful not to overload the bristles with paint.

Varnish brushes have natural bristles for applying varnish, shellac, and other finishes. One brush (right) has bristles with an oval profile to hold varnish and to provide best edge control. The badger-hair brush (far right) can hold more varnish with its "split-end" bristles.

Paint glove, for applying paint to unusually shaped items, is first slipped onto a hand. Dip the glove into paint, then spread the paint over the work.

Paint sponges come in various shapes to apply paints and stains to surfaces. Depending on the sponge, it will leave a smooth or textured pattern.

Striping brush utilizes natural camel bristles that are cut and set in the ferrule to come to a point. Drag the brush through wet stain or glaze to create a wood-grain or marbling effect. The brush can also be used with a steady hand to create delicate line work.

Graining comb creates a pattern in wet stain or paint to simulate wood grain. The comb comes in different sizes; the steel teeth vary in width.

Masking tool dispenses a 7-in.-wide paper strip (or a 21-in.-wide plastic drop cloth) with masking tape along one edge. Use it to protect surfaces that you don't intend to paint.

Rubber grainer has concentric circles imprinted on a rubber base. Experiment with dragging and rolling it in wet stain or glaze to create your own effect.

Brush and roller cover spinner helps with painting cleanup. Soak a brush or roller cover, mounted on spinner, in water or cleaning solvent. Inside a large garbage can, or in an area protected by drop cloths, pump the handle to spin the brush or cover dry. (Also make sure you protect your clothes.)

Three-in-one graining comb has three combs with rubber teeth combined in one tool. This tool is especially suited to round and curved surfaces.

Spiked cleaner helps separate bristles when cleaning a brush. For proper maintenance, always clean out a brush before paint sets.

Wire brush prepares wood, metal, and other surfaces for painting by removing loose paint, rust, corrosion, and other hardened materials. This model has a built-in scraper on the back of the handle.

Heat gun focuses a controlled amount of heat, usually between 250°F (121°C) and 1100°F (593°C), to soften paint so that you can remove it with a scraper. (Do not use on old lead-base paint.) Also use a heat gun to remove glued-down tile and to bend plastic. Start with a low temperature and work your way up.

LADDERS AND SAWHORSES

To reach high places or to create extra surfaces for holding your work, a few ladders and sawhorses—and perhaps a portable work center—are a great help. To prevent accidents, ladders are made to exacting safety standards and are graded by one or more regulating bodies. The rating assigned is called a *load capacity*. The basic load capacities are 200 pounds (light duty), 225 pounds (medium duty), 250 pounds (heavy duty), and 300 pounds (extra-heavy duty).

Caution: Fully open a stepladder and lock its braces before using it. Make sure the ladder is secure and steady. Always face a ladder and hold on when climbing or descending. Never use a broken or damaged ladder. Never work on a ladder outdoors during windy or inclement weather. Keep the ladder far away from electrical or other wires. Never work with two people on a ladder, or underneath someone on a ladder. Climb only as high on a ladder as the manufacturer recommends.

Tripod stepladder, available in heights from 4 to 12 ft., is handy for reaching into high corners where the two back legs of a standard stepladder would push you too far away. The single back leg of a tripod ladder also fits between studs of unfinished walls, allowing you to get as close to the wall as you like. The front legs are braced to balance the ladder.

Stepladder, which comes in heights ranging from 4 to 16 ft., supports itself with a hinged framework and has a foldout shelf for holding paint and tools. The ladder can be made of wood (usually yellow pine), aluminum, or fiberglass. A fiberglass ladder (shown) is lightweight, as is an aluminum one, but it does not conduct electricity as does a metal or a wet wooden ladder.

Sawhorses come ready-made, or you can make your own with 2 x 4's and the bracket kit shown above. Hook-on hardware bins and tool hangers are also available. Use two sawhorses to support a large workpiece, or lay a sheet of plywood across them to make a temporary workbench.

Articulated ladder, or multipurpose ladder, adapts to many needs. Arrange the four self-locking hinged sections to form a straight ladder, a stepladder, a scaffold, or a configuration to fit into such awkward spaces as stairways. Articulated ladders are generally made from high-strength aluminum alloy; they reach lengths of 12½ to 16½ ft. when fully extended.

Portable work center combines a workbench, tool stand, vise, and sawhorse in one compact unit. The wide adjustable jaws clamp workpieces horizontally and vertically. V-grooves in the jaws grip pipe, tubing, and dowels. When fully closed, the jaws form a small workbench that locks at two heights for sawing, gluing, painting, repairing, and similar tasks. The unit folds for convenient storage or for transporting to a job site. A wooden storage shelf can easily be bolted to the brackets in the base.

Extension ladder, primarily for outdoor use, reaches up to 40 ft. high. It consists of two or three single ladders that slide within one another to increase height capacity. Rung latches support the raised sections and lock them into position. Many models have a pulley mechanism that makes it easier to raise the sections. Extension ladders come in wood, aluminum, or fiberglass, all with nonskid feet. Also available are such accessories as paint hooks and stabilizers for straddling windows (below) or for giving support on roofs.

TOOLS FOR SHARPENING

You can sharpen dulled tools on a variety of sharpening stones and grinding wheels and polish metalwork with buffing wheels and a buffing compound. Grinding and buffing wheels are made to fit the chucks of electric drills (for light jobs) or the arbors of a bench grinder (most grinders have two arbors). Before using a wheel, check it by rapping it with a screwdriver handle and listening for a ringing sound. If it makes a buzzing sound, the wheel is chipped or cracked; replace it. Although the grinder has guards, always wear a face shield for necessary extra protection. When turning on the power, stand to one side of the wheel in case it shatters. To prevent overheating, use light pressure and cool the work often in water. Keep your grinding wheels true and even by dressing them with the appropriate tool. After cleaning a stone, store it in a closed box (reapply oil to an oilstone before storing it).

Benchstone made of silicon carbide or aluminum oxide has a coarse grit on one side, medium on the other. Lubricate it with water or oil. If you start with oil, don't switch to water for later uses.

Japanese waterstone sharpens quickly because worn particles on the stone break away, exposing new sharp particles. Before using a medium- or coarse-grit stone, soak it in water for about 6 hr.; soak a fine-grit stone, for only 5 min. Continue to apply water as you work.

Slipstone, with its wedge-shaped profile, has a flat surface for honing straight edges and a round side for irregular shapes; it's ideal for gouge chisels and carving tools. To use the stone, move it against the stationary tool. A storage box comes with the stone.

Arkansas stone, a high-quality natural stone, comes in four grades: Washita, soft, hard, and black hard. Lubricate the stone with oil.

Gouge stone is contoured to fit the round edge of a gouge chisel. Depending on your stone selection, apply water or a light mineral oil to the stone. Rub the stone against the gouge.

Lubricating oil is applied to oilstones to increase grinding speed and to prevent the pores in the stones from clogging. When the the stone becomes sticky, clean off the oil with kerosene or ammonia.

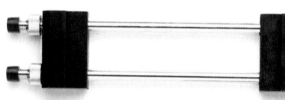

Stone holder keeps stone in place when honing. Grooved rubber soles prevent the holder from skidding. Set the stone in the holder; turn the two knurled wheels to secure it.

Bevel setter and guide sets blades of chisels, planes, and spokeshaves to 25 different angles. Place the guide on the setter with the work edge under the angle block. When it's parallel, secure the work.

Burnisher forms burr, or hooked edge, on scraper. Use round (center) or triangular (bottom) type for general burnishing; only round type with curved scrapers. Dresser (top) is for touch-ups.

Honing guide holds a chisel or plane blade at a set angle for honing. Turn the top knob to hold the blade in place; set the angle of the guide by adjusting the side knob. Wheels let you slide the tool along the stone.

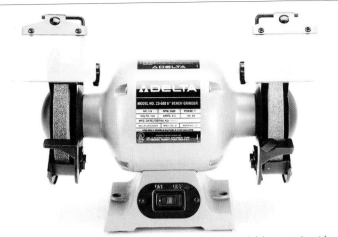

Bench grinder mounts on a workbench or pedestal stand. It has a tool rest for each of the two wheels, spark guards, and protective shields. Grinders come in different sizes; always match a 5-, 6-, 8-, or 10-in. wheel to the correct grinder.

Tapered spindle fits into a bench grinder to hold accessories. The cone-shaped buffer comes in different grades of coarseness and in various shapes. To buff nooks and crannies in metals, use irregularly shaped buffers; to polish rings, use narrow ones.

Buffing compounds, when applied to their own buffing wheels, create final finishes. From top to bottom are emery cake, to remove rust from metals; tripoli, to buff brass, steel, aluminum, and pewter; white rouge, to add luster to chrome, steel, and nickel; and red rouge, to polish silver and other precious metals.

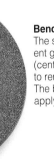

Bench grinder wheels vary in materials. The stone wheel (top) is available in different grits for sharpening. The wire wheel (center) can turn the grinder into a stripper to remove rust and paint from small objects. The buffing wheel (bottom) is suitable for applying a polished finish to metal surfaces.

Strop, a two- or four-sided tool covered with leather and slate, gives the final finishing touch to a honed blade or tool. It's used in conjunction with strop paste. On the four-sided version, three of the sides are covered with different grades of leather.

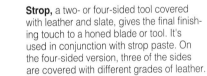

Wheel dressers come in a number of styles to resurface a grinding wheel. The silicon carbide stick (above) cleans and restores a clogged wheel. When the wheel has worn unevenly, hold a hooded star wheel dresser (far left) against it. To true a grinding wheel, use the hardy diamond wheel dresser (left), holding it against the bench grinder's tool rest or a homemade jig.

Drill bit sharpener, powered by a standard electric drill (not a cordless drill), sharpens steel twist bits and masonry bits. Set drill in holder, fitting the spindle of sharpener into its chuck; use collet to hold the bit.

SOLDERING TOOLS

Soldering uses heat to melt a bonding material (solder) and join metal pieces to one another. Soldering irons, guns, and pencils are electric heat-generating tools. Propane or acetylene and butane gas–powered torches produce a flame with significantly more heat. When working with any of these heat-producing tools, be extremely cautious. Keep a fire extinguisher handy, wear eye protection and other protective clothing, avoid explosive atmospheres, and keep the flame away from flammable materials and surfaces.

Soldering gun electrically heats small areas, making it ideal for soldering electronic circuits. The interchangeable tip heats quickly when the trigger is depressed, and cools when it is released.

Electric soldering iron has interchangeable tips that come in a variety of shapes to fit the job. The iron shown is for heavy jobs, such as stained-glass work. Smaller soldering pencils are available for electrical work and light metalworking jobs.

Soft solder comes as solid wire or wire with flux at its center. Use acid-core solder (top, left) to join pieces that can be washed to get rid of the corrosive flux; rosin-core solder (bottom, left) for electronic work; and lead-free solid-core solder (right) for water pipes.

Hard solder flows (melts) at higher temperatures than soft solder. Cut strips, wire, or sheets into tiny chips before using.

Cordless soldering iron holds enough butane gas for up to 4 hr. of work. Ignite it by pushing a button, and use it as a soldering iron or as a hot-air tool. Keep cover on tool when not in use.

Oxygen/fuel torch uses two tanks that combine propane or acetylene gas and oxygen gas or solid oxygen pellets to fuel an extremely hot flame (up to 5000°F / 2760°C) for heavy soldering, cutting metal, brazing, and welding.

Flux is brushed onto metal before soldering to prevent oxidation and help the solder flow. Use a noncorrosive rosin flux for electronic work, a zinc chloride flux for all other soft soldering, and a floride or borax-based flux for hard soldering.

Soldering iron rest can be attached to the edge of the workbench to provide a safe base for the hot iron. Always place the iron on the stand when not using it. Some irons come with small stands of their own.

Torch lighter eliminates dangerous match lighting. Squeezing the trigger causes a spark that ignites the propane or butane gas.

Propane torch uses propane gas that mixes with the surrounding air to produce a hot flame (temperature about 2500°F / 1371°C). Different tips are available for soldering, removing paint from metal (do not use on old lead-base paint), and other jobs requiring localized heat.

Binding wire of black iron can be tied around pieces being soldered to hold them in place. Select 26-gauge wire for general use.

Because of sheet metal's strength, malleability, and versatility, a number of specialized tools are available to cut, bend, shape, join, and stretch it. In addition to the ones illustrated below, you'll need a number of the tools shown on the preceding pages, including a punch or metal scriber and a micrometer to mark and measure the metal; snips, power nibblers, and saws to cut it; drills to make holes in it; various hammers, mallets, stakes, and an anvil to pound and shape it; and a machinist's vise to hold it steady while cutting and bending it.

Hand groover flattens and locks a grooved seam when joining sheets of metal. Choose one to fit the seam, place it over the seam, and tap the tool with a ball-peen hammer or mallet along the entire seam.

Bending brake, or bar folder, bends the edges of sheet metal to form a hem, wire edge, open fold, or angle fold. The sheet is inserted into the tool and a handle provides the leverage needed to easily bend the metal. If you don't have a bending brake, improvise by clamping the sheet metal between two perfectly flat boards at the end of a workbench or table and bending it with a mallet.

Hand seamer bends and flattens sheet-metal edges. Use it to bend sheets into boxes or similar shapes, to fold over sharp edges to form a hem or add rigidity, and to fold over interlocking seams to join multiple sheets.

Hand notcher makes a clean V-shaped cut in sheet metal without slippage. The compound-action handles produce the necessary leverage for fast and easy cutting.

Annealing bowl filled with charcoal chips makes a good surface for annealing metal or holding small pieces while soldering. Filled with pitch, it is used as a bed for chasing or repoussé work.

Hand punch applies more than 2000 lb. of pressure to cut holes in sheet metal, plastic, or leather. The powerful jaws push small metal punches into cylindrical dies, which are interchangeable to create different-size holes.

Chasing and repoussé tools are small blunt punches and chisels that etch decorative designs into metal.

Circle cutter consists of a number of cylindrical pins and a slotted metal base with holes of different sizes. Insert sheet metal into the slot in the base and punch a hole with the pin and a hammer.

Pop riveter fastens metal to metal, plastic to metal, or heavy-gauge fabric to itself or to metal by inserting metal fasteners, called rivets, into predrilled holes.

Sandbag can be used as a malleable backing when pounding dents out of metal. Simply hold the damaged section against the bag and gently pound out the dent with a mallet.

If you work with metal pipes and tubing, you'll need specialized tools for bending, cutting, and joining the sections. If you need to cut threads into any metal rods or plates, you'll also need a set of taps and dies. These tools are made of hardened steel and can cut neatly into any softer metal; they can also be used to restore damaged threads in appliance and automobile parts. Special large-size dies and diestocks are available for threading brass or steel pipes. Finally, if you are working on metal jewelry, you'll find specialized tools to help you do the job; in addition to the ones shown here, you may need smooth-jaw pliers for handling delicate pieces.

Tubing bender provides leverage to bend rigid copper and steel tubing to a maximum of 180°. Push a length of pipe into top of bender to form handle. Insert tubing into curved channel, step on tread, and pull handle until spirit levels in bender indicate the degree of bend you want.

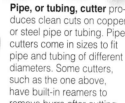

Pipe, or tubing, cutter produces clean cuts on copper or steel pipe or tubing. Pipe cutters come in sizes to fit pipe and tubing of different diameters. Some cutters, such as the one above, have built-in reamers to remove burrs after cutting.

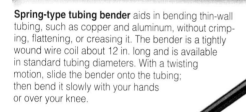

Spring-type tubing bender aids in bending thin-wall tubing, such as copper and aluminum, without crimping, flattening, or creasing it. The bender is a tightly wound wire coil about 12 in. long and is available in standard tubing diameters. With a twisting motion, slide the bender onto the tubing; then bend it slowly with your hands or over your knee.

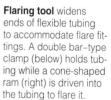

Pipe reamer shaves away rough edges and burrs left inside ends of pipes or tubing after cutting. Turn the reamer as you push it into the pipe. Reamer bits for electric drills are also available.

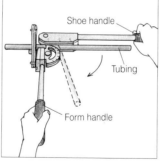

Shoe handle

Tubing

Form handle

Lever bender is operated with two hands to bend tubing. Grasp tool by form handle (or clamp it in a vise) and raise shoe handle. Slide the tubing into the groove of the wheellike bending form, and slowly lower the shoe handle until tubing is bent to desired angle.

Flaring tool widens ends of flexible tubing to accommodate flare fittings. A double bar–type clamp (below) holds tubing while a cone-shaped ram (right) is driven into the tubing to flare it.

Plumber's die and diestock are used to thread brass and steel pipe. Secure the pipe in a vise; fix the die (left) in the diestock (above), and slide it over the pipe. Pressing into the pipe, turn the diestock clockwise until the die begins to cut. Add cutting oil to the end of the pipe, and continue turning the diestock without applying pressure. Add more oil from time to time.

Taps cut or restore internal threads in holes in metal so that threaded fasteners can be used.

Tap wrenches turn the taps in the metal. T-handled wrench (left) gives less leverage than larger model (above).

Diestock is a special wrench for turning die as you thread metal rods or fasteners. This model has an adapter disc that can be inserted to convert the tool to a tap wrench.

Thread-restoring file renews damaged right- or left-handed external threads on any diameter screw, pipe, or rod.

Dies cut external threads on screws, bolts, and rods. Sets including various-size dies and taps, a diestock, and a tap wrench are available. There are also adjustable dies that can be made larger or smaller with the turn of a screw.

Draw plate is clamped in a vise and wire is drawn through the holes with pliers to change its shape or make it narrower. Numbers on the plate show the gauge the wire will be after it is pulled through.

Dapping punch comes in various sizes for use in chasing or repoussé or to shape thin metal on a dapping die (below). Strike the punch with a ball-peen hammer.

Three-in-one tap tree cuts and cleans threads in thin metal or plastic. It is handy for threading electrical boxes. The replaceable taps come in various sizes.

Bolt extractor removes broken screws or bolts. Drill hole in top of fastener and turn extractor at left (above) with wrench. Slide collar over type at center before using wrench. Drill guides at right aid in drilling into hard-to-reach fasteners.

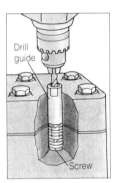

Drill guide

Screw

Extractor

Collar

Dapping die has depressions of various sizes and shapes along its faces for forming silver or other metal for jewelry. Tap the metal into the recess with a dapping punch.

Wire design block lets you shape wire or metal strips into square, rectangular, triangular, or curved shapes. Lay the metal in the appropriate groove and gently hammer it into shape.

Bending jig holds bar metal firmly in place while you hammer it into curves. Secure the jig in a vise, and arrange the pins for the curve you want.

Bracelet bender, an alternative to the mandrel (below), holds a strip of metal in its upturned end as you bend it around the curve of the tool to shape an open-end bracelet.

Bench pin, a wooden brace used in jewelry making, is clamped to the workbench and used as a surface for sawing or filing small metal pieces.

Bracelet mandrel is a form for shaping bracelets. Bend the metal around the mandrel with your hands, and finish by pounding it with a mallet. Turn the bracelet upside down for final pounding.

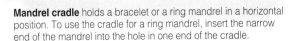

Mandrel cradle holds a bracelet or a ring mandrel in a horizontal position. To use the cradle for a ring mandrel, insert the narrow end of the mandrel into the hole in one end of the cradle.

Ring mandrel works in same way as the bracelet mandrel, but it is graduated to help you shape a ring into the proper size. Turn the ring upside down occasionally to compensate for the mandrel's taper.

CONCRETE-WORKING TOOLS

To work with concrete you'll need a number of general-purpose tools, including measuring and leveling tools, a steel square, a hammer and a saw for building forms, and buckets for measuring cement and adding it to the mix. In addition, you'll need the specialized tools shown below. If you're sinking a pier footing or a post base, you'll need a posthole digger; and if you're mixing your own concrete, a mortar box. Plastic or metal mortar boxes resembling children's sandboxes are available commercially, or you can make one by nailing together a frame of boards and adding a pressure-treated plywood bottom. For larger jobs, rent a rotating-drum mixer or have the mixed concrete delivered.

Screed, or strike-off board, is the first tool used to level freshly poured concrete. When using one, rest its ends on the tops of the forms. Wooden screeds and lightweight aluminum screeds (like the one shown here) are sold in standard lengths, but a long, straight 2 x 4 will also do the job.

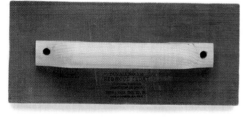

Float smooths concrete after screeding by drawing sand and cement to the surface and pushing aggregate below. Use a magnesium float (top) for air-entrained concrete (concrete with tiny bubbles); otherwise use a wood float (bottom). Floats also come with round edges for curved surfaces.

Edger finishes and rounds the sharp edges of concrete slabs and walkways. The ends of the blade are straight, curved, or a combination of straight and curved for various applications.

Groover cuts grooves in walkways, driveways, and patio floors to control the cracking caused by expansion and contraction.

Square-edged shovel is preferred over a garden spade for concrete work. To eliminate air pockets when filling forms, pull the shovel blade up and down in the concrete; press the concrete against the forms with the back of the shovel.

Mortar hoe is used to mix concrete and mortar, and to spread concrete. The large holes in the blade aerate the mixture for a better consistency.

Posthole digger digs deep, narrow holes without disturbing the surrounding area.

Concrete tamper may be used on flat surfaces. An up-and-down motion, called jitterbugging (see drawing at right), forces wet concrete into position, pushes aggregate below the surface, and removes air pockets. Care must be taken not to overuse the tool. Smaller tampers with solid bottoms are also available.

Darby (below) is similar to a bull float, but it is used with a circular motion on smaller areas. It smooths bumps and ridges left by screeding, fills depressions, and pushes the aggregate below the surface of walkways and small slabs.

Bull float (below) smooths and finishes large areas of wet concrete following screeding and prior to using finishing floats. It has round or square edges and a bracket assembly for attaching a long handle.

Wheelbarrow transports bricks, concrete blocks, and stones to the job site. It can substitute as a portable mortar box, or it can carry building materials, landscaping and gardening supplies, tools, garbage, dirt, and debris. Basic models are metal or plastic and have a hard rubber tire. Sturdier models have a metal tub, an inflatable tire, wooden handles, and heavy-duty rests.

The best trowels have blades cast from a single piece of high-grade steel and handles made of wood, plastic, or leather. Trowels with welded blades are less expensive, but they warp and break easily. When buying a trowel, check the quality of the blade by striking it against a hard object and listening for a ringing sound. A long ring indicates a good blade. Also consider the tool's weight, size, balance, flexibility, and the angle of its handle. After using a trowel, scrape off any mortar with another trowel or a wire brush, and thoroughly rinse and dry the tool. Rub wooden or leather handles with linseed oil.

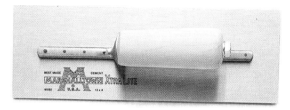

Concrete finishing trowel is used to smooth a surface after the concrete has begun to set. Hold the trowel nearly level and move it in sweeping arcs across the surface. Make two passes for an extra-smooth surface.

Gauging trowel mixes mortar and applies small amounts in confined areas. It is used principally to replace crumbled mortar and to patch concrete. In addition, its rounded nose makes it useful for tucking and pushing insulation into tight areas.

Bucket trowel comes in handy for scooping mortar out of a bucket or mortar box. It is also good for buttering bricks and for small smoothing jobs.

Pool trowel, or round trowel, is a special variation of the concrete finishing trowel. The blade is rounded to prevent it from accidentally digging into the wet concrete, making it ideal for smoothing.

Corner trowels are available for shaping concrete around internal and external corners. The handle is located at the center of the 90° bend in the blade to balance the tool and allow you to apply equal pressure to both sides of the corner.

Step trowel shapes the inside angles on concrete steps. The gentle bend in the blade allows for rounded edges. Trowels for outside angles are also available.

Pointing trowel applies mortar to joints in brick and concrete block work. This smaller version of the brick trowel is also useful for filling small cavities and repairing old crumbling mortar joints.

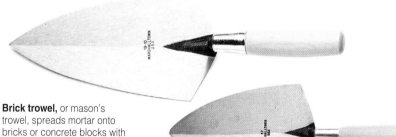

Brick trowel, or mason's trowel, spreads mortar onto bricks or concrete blocks with a technique call *buttering*. The shape of the blade also makes it ideal for smoothing small patches in concrete.

Tile setter is a brick trowel with an extra-wide blade, which holds a greater amount of mortar and smooths easier than the standard brick trowel. It is the best tool for buttering large bricks and blocks.

Margin trowel works mortar into tight spaces and corners where a larger pointed trowel will not fit.

BRICKLAYING TOOLS

When working with bricks, concrete blocks, or even stones, you'll need a number of specialized tools including some of the trowels on the facing page and a number of the hammers, levels, and measuring and squaring tools covered earlier in this section. You'll also need tools for carrying, cutting, aligning, and cleaning the bricks, and tools for working with mortar, as shown on this page. Finally, you'll need a hawk—a flat board with a handle for holding mortar as you work. You can buy a hawk (not shown) or easily make one by cutting a square of plywood and screwing a section of thick dowel or broomstick under its center. You'll also need a plastic or wooden box for mixing mortar.

Tuck pointer is used to pack mortar neatly between bricks or concrete blocks when re-pointing—restoring crumbling mortar in masonry walls.

Skate-wheel jointer rakes out mortar to a depth of ½ in. from a joint. The length of the nail that scrapes out mortar can be adjusted to change the appearance of the joint. After raking, smooth and compress the joint with a narrow jointer.

Jointer shapes mortar in a joint just before it dries, removing excess mortar and adding durability. Standard convex jointer (above, top) leaves a rounded groove. Grapevine jointer (above) leaves a pattern. Sled-runner jointer (left, top) is used for long horizontal joints. V-jointer (left, bottom) leaves a V-shaped groove; it also comes without a handle.

Line blocks are attached to outside corners of walls. A string stretched between two blocks creates a guide for laying each level course of bricks, concrete blocks, or stones. If you can't use line blocks, use metal line pins (not shown here).

Brick tongs make transporting bricks from supply pile to work area easy and fast. The handle quickly adjusts to hold 6 to 10 bricks. There are also tongs (not shown) that pick up a single concrete block.

Brick chisel, or brick set, cuts brick, stone, or concrete block to size and shape when struck with a hammer. Blades range from 3½ in. (bottom) to 5 in.; a 4-in. blade (top) is most common. A wider blade helps you make straighter cuts.

Mason's brush finishes off rough spots in wet joints and cleans brick and concrete block surfaces prior to applying mortar. Joints can be weakened if dust and debris are not removed.

Joint chisel cleans out hardened mortar. Hold chisel in a gloved hand and strike with a hand-drilling hammer. The direction the taper in the blade faces determines if chisel will cut deep or run shallow along joint.

Rub brick is a grooved silicon-carbide stone mounted on a base and handle. Use it to smooth rough areas and to remove form marks from dried concrete.

MISCELLANEOUS TOOLS

Although this section has covered hundreds of tools, there are still many more available for working with specific materials. On this and the facing page you'll find just a few of the additional tools that can make a particular job easier. Whether it's gluing, veneering, tiling, or working with glass or plastic, these tools are worth the money if you'll be putting them to a lot of use. Because some tools are such great timesavers, they can be worth buying even if they are used only once or twice; but you may find it more cost-effective to rent one. Buy tools selectively, only as you need them; with time, you'll find that your workshop will be nicely stocked.

Glue brushes are made with natural hog bristles to spread hot hide glue, white glue, and yellow glue. Long handles make it easier to reach into restricted areas. Unlike brushes that use metal ferrules, the bristles are attached to the handles with glue and string so that rust stains cannot mar the workpiece; this is especially handy when working on fine woodwork. Brushes come in various sizes.

Glass glue pot has a removable brush to apply white or yellow glue to the work. A weight on the handle holds the brush in place and seals the opening in the lid. The handle is spring-loaded; push the brush down to dip bristles into the glue.

Glue roller applies white, yellow, or liquid hide glue quickly and evenly to flat surfaces and edges. Remove the stopper before applying glue. Holding the bottle in your hand, squeeze it as you roll the tool over the work. The harder you squeeze, the more glue will come out of the tool. Wash the roller in hot soapy water after each use. Dried glue can be removed with a dull-bladed tool.

Three-tip glue applicator has exchangeable nozzles for general-purpose, pinpoint, and dowel hole applications. Use the tool to apply white or yellow glue. To prevent glue from drying when not in use, seal bulb opening with plastic film held in place with a rubber band.

Glue injector has a thin nozzle to apply any type of glue in restricted areas without making a mess. The body holds about ½ oz. of glue.

Hot-melt glue gun heats a glue stick that is inserted into an opening at the rear of the gun; by squeezing the trigger, melted glue can be applied to the work. This model is powered by a charger, which also serves as a resting stand. A variety of sticks are available for gluing different materials, including wood, ceramic, and plastic.

Veneer roller applies pressure evenly as it is rolled on veneer that's being glued to a surface. The roller may be as wide as 7 in. Use a narrow roller for joining seams.

Veneer block roller fits into your hand comfortably for applying even pressure to veneer. Hold the tool with the heel of your hand against the flat surface.

Scratch brushes are handy for removing surface dirt or finishing a surface in a restricted area. The bristles are made of stainless steel or brass for metals, nylon or horsehair for gentle abrasiveness, and tampico for holding fluids and polishing.

Toothing blade with serrations is used to scrape a surface before applying glue. The rough surface helps give a stronger bond.

Edge-banding iron uses heat to seal heat-activated veneer strips along plywood edges. As you work, set iron on rest to free your hands. Edge trims come in various wood finishes.

Double-edge trimmer cuts both ends of veneer strips applied to surface edges that are up to 1¼ in. wide. Set tool over work; press its sides together; slide it in direction of arrows.

Miniature rotary tool accepts attachments to carve, grind, polish, sand, cut, and drill wood, metal, glass, and tile. Use it hand-held, or hang it from the hook and attach a flexible shaft. The tool also comes in a cordless model.

Woodburning tool has a 20- to 100- watt element to create designs in wood by darkening the wood color. The tool has interchangeable tips. For greater control over the markings, buy a separate temperature-adjusting rheostat.

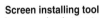

Tile cutter scores and cuts ceramic tile. The long throat accepts tiles up to 12 in. wide. A replaceable wheel under the handle scores the tile as the handle is pulled along a bar. A breaker bar ensures a clean break.

Fiberglass roller has spiral grooves in the roller to work out air bubbles that may form when applying resin to fiberglass cloth. It's available in several sizes, with aluminum or plastic rollers.

Caulking gun holds a tube of caulk or adhesive. To apply the material to the work, squeeze the trigger; the bar will exert pressure on a disc, pushing material out of the tube. Use the spring-loaded clip to release the bar.

Glass cutter wheel scores a line in glass. Separate the glass by holding it on each side of the score with your thumbs and index fingers and bending it until it snaps. The notches can be used to snap thin strips.

Screen installing tool has two wheels to set window screen and spline into a frame. Use wheel with round edge to push the screen into the channel in the frame. The wheel with a concave edge is for pushing the spline into the channel over the screen.

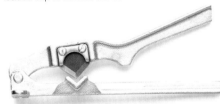

Plastic tube cutter is bolted onto a workbench or other flat surface to cut plastic tubing or rubber hoses. Place the work in the V-shaped rest on the bottom arm of the tool. As the top arm is moved down onto the tubing or hose, the blade cuts the work.

Laminate roller has a smooth rubber roller to apply pressure to sheet laminate while gluing it to the work, thus creating a strong bond.

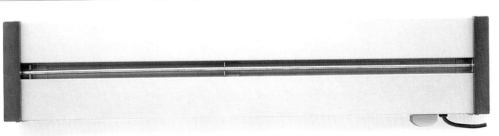

Strip heater is used to heat a sheet of acrylic until it is pliable enough to be formed into any desired shape. It's most often used to make bends or folds in the material. This model can soften acrylic up to 36 in. wide and ⅜ in. thick. Heating time varies from 30 sec. to 4 min. according to the thickness of the material.

HARDWARE

NAILS

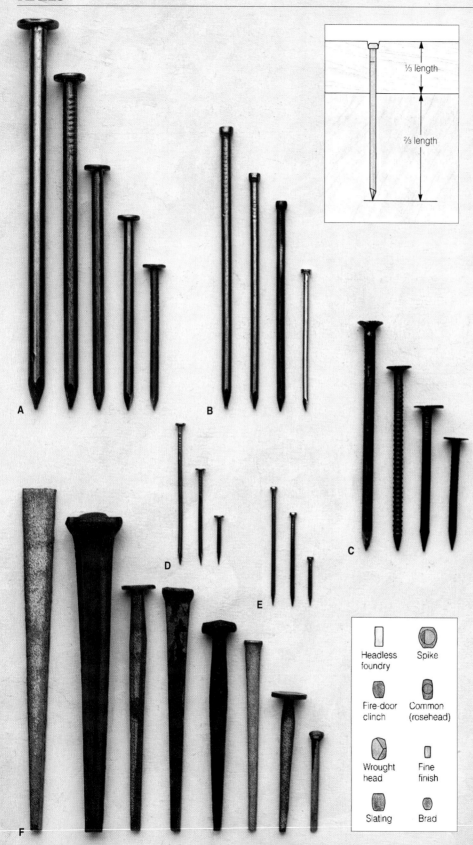

Headless foundry | Spike
Fire-door clinch | Common (rosehead)
Wrought head | Fine finish
Slating | Brad

Fasteners are the most common items of hardware, and the nail, which is used primarily to join items permanently, is the most common fastener. Nails are available in a number of metals, styles, and sizes for driving into a variety of materials.

When nailing a thinner piece of material to a thicker one (left), use nails whose length is 3 times the thickness of the thinner piece. If both pieces are of the same thickness, use two or more nails the length of the combined thicknesses minus ¼ inch.

Common nail (A), a heavy-duty fastener with a flat head that won't pull through the work, is used in carpentry and house framing. It is measured by the penny (p.347), which is abbreviated *d*. The longer the nail, the larger its diameter. The box nail (not shown), a lighter version of the common nail, is used in thin wood to keep it from splitting. It is not found in all areas of the country.

Finishing nail (B) is a thin small-headed nail for cabinetmaking and attaching trim. The nailhead is usually driven below the surface and filled over. The casing nail (not shown) is a heavy finishing nail found in some areas. It has more holding power than the standard finishing nail, and is used for door and window casings or trim.

Drywall nail (C) has a sharp point and broad head for installing wallboard. In ceilings and other areas under pressure, use the ringed type, which has more holding power; or use a nail with an adhesive coating that when driven in, melts from the heat of the friction, cementing the nail in place. The length of a drywall nail is given in inches, its diameter in gauge numbers. The higher the gauge, the thinner the nail.

Wire nail (D), a small version of the common nail, is perfect for light jobs.

Wire brad (E) is a small finishing nail that is used for fine work.

Antique-style nails (F) are available with a variety of different shanks and heads for restoring old furniture and attaching antique hinges. The head styles of the antique nails in the photograph are shown in the drawing at left.

Ring underlay nail (A) has a shank that is ringed with deep, closely spaced grooves. The wood's fiber wedges itself into these grooves, resulting in maximum holding power in soft or medium woods. It's ideal for use in the installation of subflooring, because the increased holding power keeps the subflooring from squeaking or pulling loose.

Roofing nail (B) has a large flat head that keeps it from working through soft roofing materials, such as asphalt shingles. It is generally galvanized to prevent rusting.

Cut flooring nail (C) comes in either steel or iron and is used for installing tongue-and-groove floorboards. Its flat sides and blunt tip minimize splitting of hardwood flooring.

Spiral-fluted flooring nail (D) turns like a screw when driven in, gripping tightly to eliminate squeaking.

Boat nail (E) is a ringed, or annular, fastener made of rust-resistant metal. It is ideal for outdoor use where a strong, rust-free bond is needed.

Escutcheon nail (F) is used for attaching keyhole plates and other backplates, or escutcheons. Sizes range from ⅝ to ¾ in.

Paneling nail (G), a hard, thin nail, often ribbed, is ideal for securing wall paneling to studs. It comes in different colors to match the paneling material.

Molding nail (H), similar to the wire brad, is used to attach molding. Generally the heads of these nails are countersunk and filled.

Double-headed nail (I) is used for putting together temporary structures, such as concrete forms and scaffolding. The second head projects out of the work for easy removal. The double-headed nail comes in bright or galvanized steel. It is sometimes referred to as a duplex nail.

Galvanized nail (J) is coated with zinc to prevent rusting. Use it when exposure to weather is a factor, as on decks.

Masonry nail (K) is made of through-hardened steel that resists bending. The nail is used mostly for nailing furring strips to concrete or masonry walls. The shank may be plain, or it may be fluted to help the nail grip more tightly.

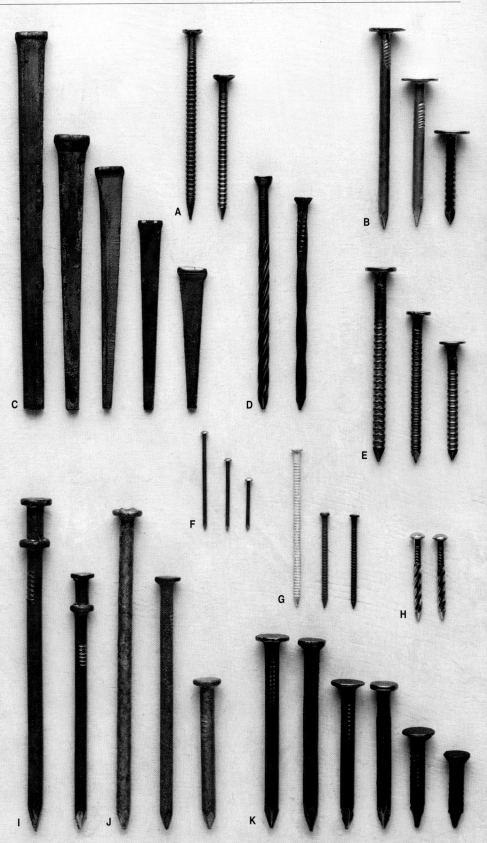

There are five considerations when choosing a screw: the type and thickness of the material to be fastened, the size of the screw, the material it is made of, the shape of its head, and the type of drive. Screws are available for fastening wood, wallboard, masonry, and sheet metal. The diameter of a screw is given by gauge number up to ¼ inch and in fractions of an inch for thicker screws. Lengths range from ¼ to 6 inches, measured from the tip to the part of the head that is flush with the surface when driven in. Screws come in stainless or zinc-plated steel for heavy work; corrosion-resistant brass, stainless steel, aluminum, or bronze; and with decorative finishes. There are various types of heads and drives (see below) and some combination drives, which can be driven by either of two types of driver, such as slotted and Phillips. The one-way screw cannot easily be unscrewed, and so is used for security. Robertson (square) and star-drive screws are found mainly on cars and appliances.

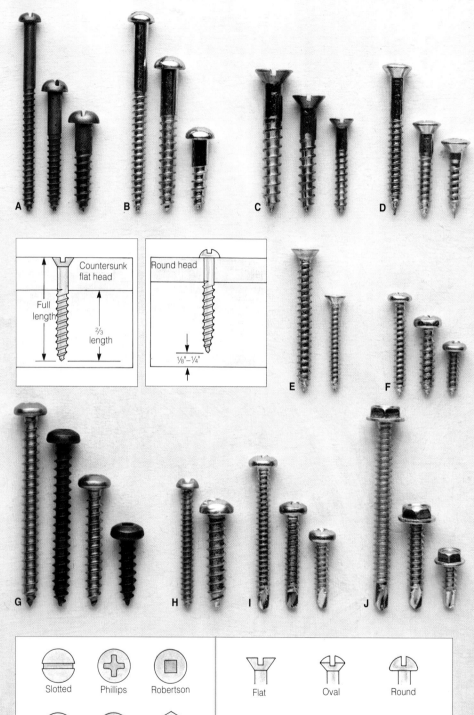

Wood screw holds two pieces of wood together, providing a strong joint that can be dismantled. Shown are brass and zinc-plated round-head screws with slotted drives **(A, B)**, flat-head screws with slotted drives **(C)**, and oval-head screws with Phillips drives **(D)**. When determining screw size, consider the thickness of the woods being fastened. Two-thirds of the screw should enter the second piece; the screw should be ⅛ to ¼ in. shorter than the combined thicknesses of the materials being fastened.

Sheet-metal screw fastens two pieces of metal together. Shown are flat-head **(E)** and pan-head **(F)** screws with Phillips drives, pan-head screws with Robertson **(G)**, and one-way drives **(H)**, and self-drilling screws with Phillips drive pan heads **(I)** and hex washer heads **(J)**. Self-drilling screws have sharp winged tips that cut threaded holes in the metal as they are driven, pulling the second piece in tight.

Screw drives of six major types are used on the various screws. Use a screwdriver with the proper tip to drive them. Use a wrench to drive a hex-drive screw.

Slotted	Phillips	Robertson
Star	One-way	Hex

Screwheads come in various shapes. Flathead is flush with the surface when countersunk; oval head is partly countersunk; the others rest on top. Hex-heads come with or without attached washers.

Flat	Oval	Round
Pan	Hex	Hex washer

Drywall screw (A), a thin, sharp fastener with a bugle-shaped head, cuts through wallboard and anchors itself in wood or metal studs, holding the wallboard tighter than a nail can. Its Phillips or Robertson drive lets you countersink the screw without tearing the wallboard's surface paper.

Lag screw (B), or lag bolt, is a heavy-duty wood screw that comes up to 6 in. long, in diameters of $\frac{3}{16}$, $\frac{1}{4}$, $\frac{5}{16}$, $\frac{3}{8}$, and $\frac{1}{2}$ in. Generally, use a lag screw if you need a screw with lots of holding power. Lag screws are available with hex heads (shown) or square heads. Drive with a wrench or socket.

Concrete screw has sharp widely spaced threads that are driven directly into concrete without an anchor. The screws shown have hex washer heads **(C)** and flat heads **(D).**

Post and screw (E) is used to join case units, such as kitchen cabinets, or to put together frames or assemblies that may later need to be taken apart and reassembled. The screw is driven through the two pieces, and the cap is pushed into a recess in the second piece and screwed on. A light plastic version of this hardware is used on acrylic plastic.

Thumb screw (F) is a machine screw (p.102) with a wide thin head that can be grasped with thumb and forefinger and turned into a threaded plate or bracket. It is used in areas that require frequent adjustment by hand.

Hanger screw (G) is a fastener for installing dropped ceilings with acoustical tiles. Screw the threaded end into a joist, and hook the wire that supports the metal grid of the dropped ceiling into the hole in the unthreaded end.

Hanger bolt (H) has machine-screw threads on one end and regular screw threads on the other. To install one, drill a pilot hole in the wood, and thread two nuts side by side onto the machine-screw end of the hanger bolt, locking them together. Grasp the nuts with a wrench, and drive the screw in.

Dowel screw (I) is used mainly for attaching table legs and other furniture work. Predrill holes, grasp the screw with locking pliers with taped jaws, and screw it into the top of a table leg; then screw the leg into the tabletop.

Finishing washer (J) supplies a hard surface against which to tighten flathead screw without damaging wood.

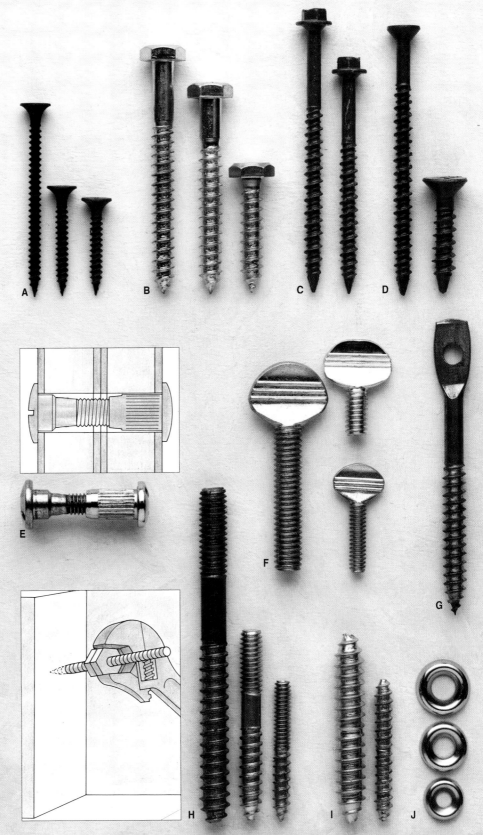

A   B   C   D

E

F

G

H   I   J

NUTS, BOLTS, AND WASHERS

A bolt used with one or two washers and a nut or piece of threaded metal makes the strongest bond and is also easy to take apart without damaging the materials. A bolt should be long enough to protrude through the outside of the nut when assembled, letting at least one of the bolt's threads show. A bolt's size is generally given as the diameter in inches or gauge number, followed by the number of threads per inch, followed by the length of the bolt in inches. For example, a bolt that is marked ¼–20 × 1 is ¼ inch in diameter, has 20 threads per inch, and is 1 inch long. Bolts run from ³⁄₁₆ inch to 6 inches in length. Diameter and thread combinations run from #1–72 to ½–13. The larger the bolt, the fewer threads per inch.

Machine bolt (A) is a strong bolt with a hex or square head.

Stove bolt (B) has a round or flat slotted head that can be countersunk.

Machine screw (C) is similar to the stove bolt, but with the other heads found in screws. It's called a screw because it's often screwed into threaded metal instead of a nut.

Carriage bolt (D) is used in woodworking and sheet-metal work. It has a smooth round head and square shoulders that sink into the wood or fit in a hole, keeping the bolt from turning.

U-bolt (E) holds pipes and other objects snug against a wall or ceiling.

Eye-bolt (F) holds wires, ropes, and other objects in place.

License-plate fastener (G) is a short machine screw with a nut or plastic backplate for attaching license plates.

Turnbuckle (H) has threaded hooks or eyes that move in or out when the sleeve is turned, exerting diagonal pull to keep a gate or screen straight.

Threaded rod (I), or all thread, joins objects over a span of up to 3 ft. It is available with fine or coarse threads.

Flat washer (A) is used under a bolt head or nut to to spread the load and protect the surface. A large flat washer with a small hole is a fender washer. It can cover a hole that is larger than the bolt being used in it, eliminating the need for filling the hole.

Lock washer (B), also known as a split-ring or spring washer, exerts a slight springlike pressure because of its near-spiral shape; this keeps a nut from loosening. When bolting pieces of wood together, it's best to use a flat washer under a lock washer.

Toothed washer (C) has external or internal teeth (or both), which give additional gripping power to a bolt. The washer can also be shaped for use with a flat-head machine screw.

Hex nut (D) screws onto the threaded end of a bolt to tighten the bolt against the pieces being fastened. It may be screwed on over a washer.

Square nut (E) is basically the same as a hex nut, except that it has only four sides instead of six.

Cap nut (F) is a decorative nut that covers the end of the bolt and conceals any exposed threads.

Knurled nut (G) can be turned by hand for fast assembly and disassembly. Its coarse outer design makes it easy to grip between thumb and forefinger. Two styles are shown.

Lock nut (H) has a fiberlike lining next to the threads that prevents the nut from coming loose when subject to vibration or stress.

Push nut (I), or axle nut, is used to cover the end of a rod or to hold a small wheel on an axle. It has no threads, but is simply pushed on. Plastic push nuts with steel spring inserts are also available.

T-nut (J) permits the easy driving of machine screws in wood. Drill a hole and hammer the T-nut into place, with its prongs penetrating the wood.

Wing nut (K) is used to fasten units that will be repeatedly disassembled and reassembled. Always drive a wing nut with your fingers; using pliers may damage the nut.

Threaded insert (L) screws into the wood and becomes a receptacle for a bolt to screw into. It is easier to conceal than a T-nut.

T-nut

Threaded insert

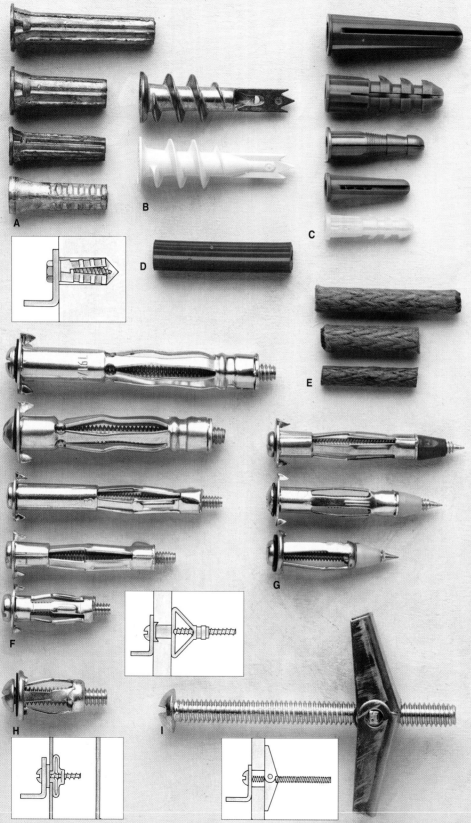

Fasteners tend to pull out of masonry or wallboard, crumbling the material instead of holding fast inside it. Anchors, shields, and toggles are available in various sizes to give a fastener a firm grip. Miscellaneous fasteners are available for other jobs.

Lead anchor (A) is inserted into a hole in plaster or masonry and expands when a screw is driven into it, gripping the edges of the hole and anchoring the screw. To use one, drill a hole just large enough to accept the anchor and push the anchor into it. Drive the screw through the piece being fastened (in drawing, an angle bracket) and into the hole in the anchor.

Wallboard anchor (B) needs no starter hole. Simply push it into the wallboard and drive it in with a screwdriver. Use it for lightweight jobs or for driving many screws into wallboard.

Plastic anchor (C) works like a lead anchor; when a screw is driven into it in the wall, it expands and grips the sides of the starter hole.

Plastic plug (D), a type of plastic anchor, has straight sides and is made of sturdier plastic for heavier jobs.

Fiber plug (E) holds a screw in concrete or masonry. Install it as you would a lead or plastic anchor.

Hollow-wall anchor (F), or Molly bolt, is a machine screw in a sleeve. Push the anchor with the screw into a predrilled hole in a hollow wall. As you drive in the screw, the sleeve will collapse, drawing its shoulders against the inside surface of the wall. Remove screw and use it to mount item.

Hollow-wall drive anchor (G) has a pointed screw in its sleeve. It can be hammered directly into wallboard without drilling a starter hole.

Hollow-door anchor (H), or jacknut, is a small hollow-wall anchor for use on hollow-core doors or similar surfaces.

Toggle bolt (I) is a machine screw with spring-loaded wings. Push the screw, holding the item you are mounting, and the wings through a predrilled hole; then tighten the screw. The wings will fold to pass through the hole, then open against the inner surface of the wall or ceiling. If you remove the screw, the wings will fall off.

Plastic toggle (A) works in the same way as a metal toggle bolt, but it comes with a pointed screw instead of a flat-tipped machine screw and does not require as large an entrance hole. Unlike the metal version, it remains in place if the screw is removed.

Metal drive-in anchor (B) has two pointed legs that stay together as you hammer the anchor into a wall and then spread out against the inside of the wall as you drive in the screw. To remove the anchor, back the screw out three-quarters of the way, then pull it out with pliers. One size anchor fits walls up to ⅜ in. thick. When using in plaster or in thin paneling, predrill a ⅛-in. starter hole.

Machine-screw anchor (C) consists of a hard steel inner core and a lead sleeve. Push the anchor into a starter hole and hammer it in with a special tool; the wedgelike inner core will push against the sleeve, expanding it and holding the anchor in place.

Lag shield (D), or expansion shield, is used for fastening to concrete. It is a lead tube split lengthwise but joined at one end. Install it in a predrilled hole and screw in a lag bolt.

Double-wedge expansion shield (E) is a lag shield with a wedge at each end for greater holding power.

Wood joiner (F) strengthens woodworking joints with eight widely spaced prongs. Drive it straight into the wood.

Corrugated fastener (G) holds lightweight butt and miter joints, such as those on screens and picture frames.

Blind rivet (H) joins sheet metal to sheet metal. It is installed through predrilled holes with a riveting tool.

Cotter pin (I) holds thin rods or shafts. Push it through a hole in the shaft, fold the legs out on the other side of the hole, and wrap them around the shaft.

Tack (J) is used to attach carpet or fabric to wood and for other light jobs.

Upholstery tack (K) comes with a variety of decorative heads to complement the style of the furniture.

Staple (L) comes in various forms for use on fabrics, insulation, or other materials, or for holding wiring flat.

Glazier's point (M) is driven into a window frame to hold in the glass.

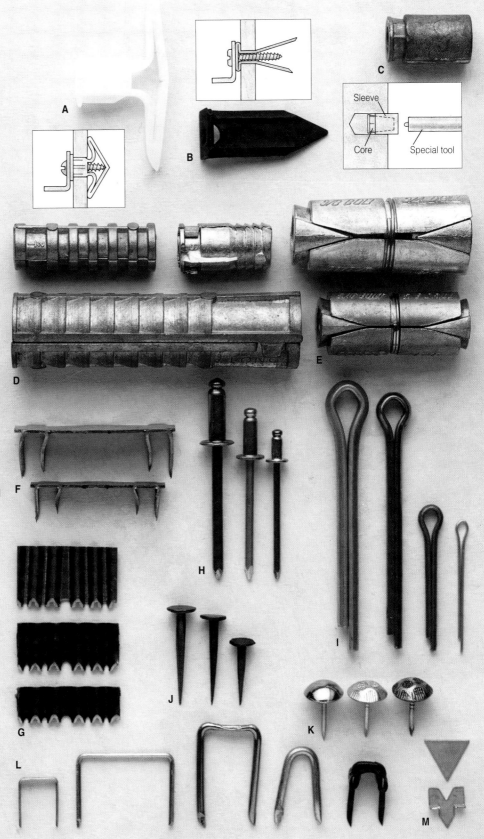

Sleeve

Core

Special tool

HOOKS AND EYES

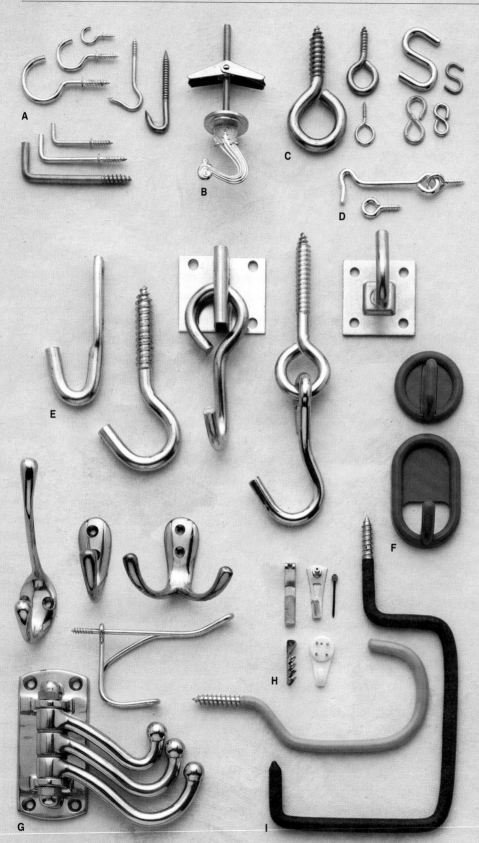

Whether you want to hang a coffee cup or support a clothesline, you'll be able to find a hook of the right shape and size to do the job. Use large hooks for heavy objects; a small hook may pull away from the surface when it's supporting a heavy load. Before installing a hook that screws into place, make a pilot hole with a nail or drill.

Screw hook (A) has a threaded end that screws into wood, walls, or ceilings. The open end supports various items. The rounded-tip hook is for household uses; the pointed-tip hook is for suspended ceilings. The L-shaped hook supports wide objects.

Swag hook (B) combines a hook with a toggle bolt for hanging a swag lamp or a plant from a ceiling.

Screw eye (C) has a ring-shaped end. Use it alone by fitting objects through the ring. Or link an S-hook or 8-hook to it; the linking hook can hold the object.

Hook and eye (D) has a hook attached to a screw eye that screws into a gate or door. The hook fits into another screw eye to keep the gate or door closed; a hook with a clasp (not shown) provides extra security.

Rope hook (E) comes in various designs. From left to right are a general-purpose hook with two holes in the flat stem for screws, a porch-swing hook that is screwed into the porch roof, a hammock hook with a plate to secure it to a flat surface, a hammock hook with a screw eye for a round surface, and a clothesline hook that slips through a plate that is screwed to a flat surface.

Self-adhesive hook (F) made of plastic is for lightweight objects. To install it, wipe the surface clean, remove the lining paper, and press hook in place.

Coat hook (G) may have one, two, or more hooks in various directions for hanging coats and hats. The three-hook model has pivoting hooks.

Picture hook (H) is nailed into a wall. Attach a wire to the back of a picture frame to hang it on the hook.

Heavy-duty hook (I) is for hanging objects in a garage or workshop. For items like bicycles, use them in pairs.

BRACKETS

Sets of two or more brackets are indispensable for supporting a variety of items. Before mounting the brackets, accurately measure and level their placement.

Curtain and shade brackets come in pairs. To install a cafe rod, screw the first brackets shown **(A)** above a window for an outside mount, or attach socket brackets **(B)** to window jambs for an inside mount. Nail roller shade brackets **(C)** inside the jambs (or on other models, outside the jambs or on the wall). A U-shaped curtain rod fits onto outside-mount brackets **(D)**; slip the opening in the rod over the bracket's hook and push the rod into place.

Rail brackets support handrails (screwed into wall studs), footrails, and gallery rails. A flat rail rests on top of a flat rail bracket **(E)**; a round rail slips through a post rail bracket **(F)** or its end fits into a flange bracket **(G)**.

Shelf brackets (H) are attached to a wall to support a horizontal piece (usually ¾-in.-thick softwood or plywood) for storing or displaying items. Screw a bracket into every other stud for a light load or every stud for a heavy load. The almond-color bracket has a decorative cover that slips over the metal support after it's screwed in place.

Spade pins (I) slip into holes drilled in a cabinet's sides, two for each end of a shelf. Make sure that all four holes align horizontally.

Gussetted clips (J) are shown inserted in a side-mounted standard (near right). They support shelves in cabinets or bookcases—use two clips at each end of a shelf. Screw four standards in place (you can recess them); use a level to check plumb. Fit clips into slots at identical height on each standard. Available in various lengths, standards can be cut to size.

Thumbscrew brackets (K) slide into slots in a wall-mounted standard (far right) to support shelves. Screw the standards into studs, using a level to check plumb. When the bracket is in place, turn the thumbscrew to secure it. The hook on the tip of the bracket prevents the shelf from slipping off.

Spring-loaded folding bracket (L) can be raised and locked in placed for an extra work surface. Light pressure on the release lever allows you to fold the surface out of the way.

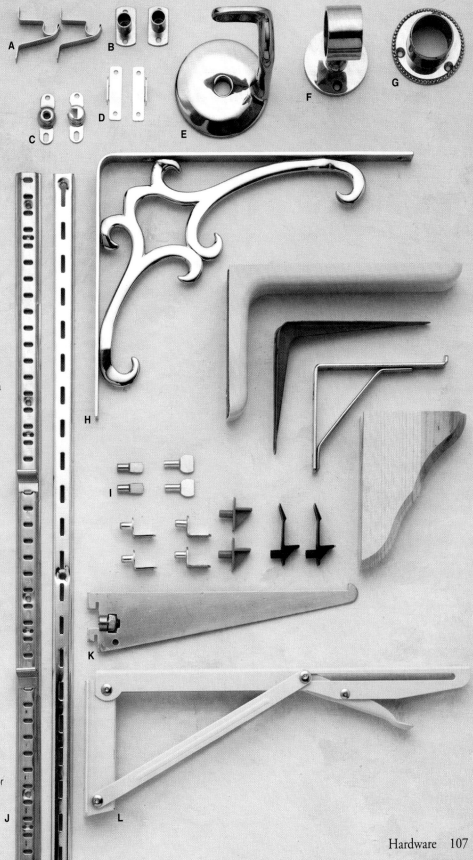

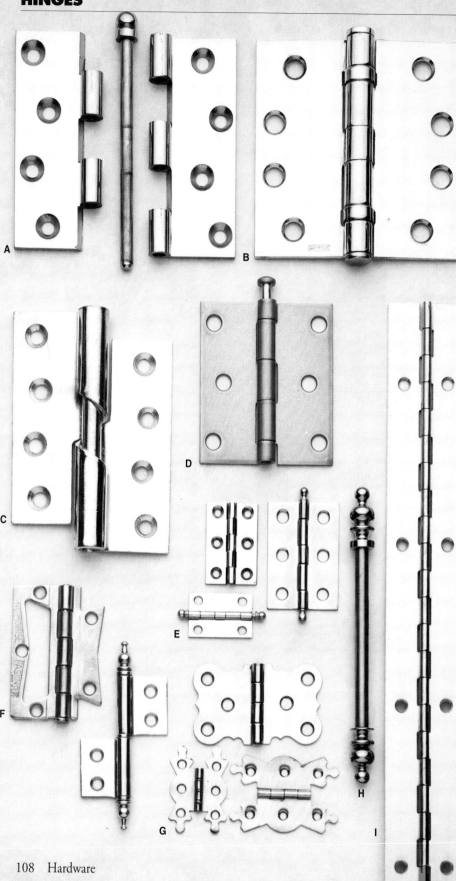

A hinge often has two leaves held together with a pivot pin inside knuckles or a barrel. Most cabinet hinges can be used on either left- or right-handed doors; house door hinges must be correctly "handed." Hinges can be surface-mounted (with the leaves slightly raised), but the leaves create a slight gap between the door and frame when the door is closed. Recessed leaves are mortised flush with the surface.

Loose-pin butt hinge (A) has a detachable pin to allow for door removal without unscrewing the hinge. The head of the hinge pin must always be on top. Some butt hinges have an unremovable "fixed" pin. They are suitable for an exterior door where the barrel is exposed outside; to remove the door, you must unscrew the hinge.

Ball-bearing hinge (B), for heavy doors, has a ball-bearing assembly that's permanently lubricated.

Self-rising hinge (C), for an interior door, has a barrel that is split diagonally. As you open the door, one leaf rides up the other, making the door rise. The door's weight pulls it closed.

Cabinet butt hinge (D) is attached to flush-mounted cabinet doors. It comes with a removable button-top pin.

Small butt hinge (E) may have a fixed or a loose pin. It's often used on small boxes. Attach it with nails or screws.

Flush hinge (F), for a lightweight door, is surface-mounted but doesn't create a gap. To install the type shown at left, screw the small leaf to the door, the large leaf to the frame; when closed, the small leaf fits into the large one. On the other type, the bottom leaf swngs under the top one.

Decorative hinge (G) comes in a variety of ornamental designs for fine wood furniture, cabinets, and boxes.

Decorative-head pin (H) can replace a plain pin in a loose-pin hinge. Pull out the old pin, or tap it out from beneath with a hammer and nail.

Piano hinge (I) is used for table flaps and chest tops where extra strength is important. Made in 2- to 6-ft. lengths, the hinge may be cut to fit. It can be surface-mounted or recessed.

H hinge (A), generally used on furniture, cabinet doors, and small chests, can be mounted vertically or horizontally. The H hinge below is sometimes referred to as a snake hinge.

Lift-off (separable) hinge (B) lets you lift a door off without unscrewing the hinge or removing the pin. It comes in a variety of sizes and styles for cabinet, clock-case, and house doors. You can also use it on dressing-table mirrors or on any hinged object you will want to remove frequently.

Backflap hinge (C) is a fixed-pin butt hinge with wide leaves that provide better support for flaps and lids. It.can be recessed into wood.

Box hinge (D) is small enough to use on delicate jewelry-box lids. The hinge opens only to a 90° angle, preventing the lid from flipping over.

Drop-leaf hinge (E), similar to the backflap hinge, is used on fold-down table flaps made with a rule joint. The hinge's longer leaf should be screwed to the table flap.

Butler's-tray hinge (F) comes with rounded or square corners. It's a small, sturdy hinge for trays and other small tables with leaves that fold up. The hinge surface is flat when open, with no protruding barrel; in the up position, a steel spring holds the leaf at 90°.

Strap hinge (G) is designed for surface mounting. It's available in plain and ornamental styles. Larger sizes are used where strong support is needed—for example, on heavy chest lids, gates, and doors.

Desk hinge (H), a straight strap hinge, is most often found recessed into secretary desks and flaps.

Card-table hinge (I) looks similar to the desk hinge but has a 180° stop, making it suitable for small table flaps that fold out of the way.

Single strap hinge (J) comes in large heavy-duty sizes for doors, gates, boxes, and chests. The steel one shown here is sometimes called a T-hinge. The small decorative hinge is for small boxes.

H-and-L hinge (K) is surface-mounted on a cabinet door. A larger version is available for regular-weight house doors; another variation of the hinge allows you to mortise the jamb leaf.

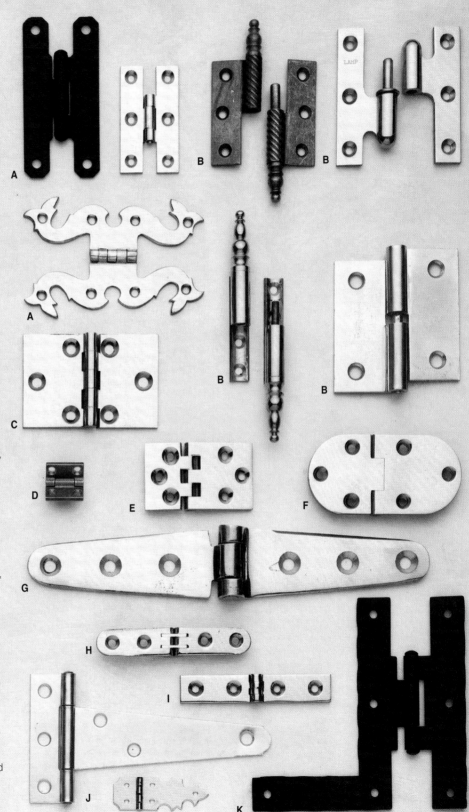

MORE HINGES

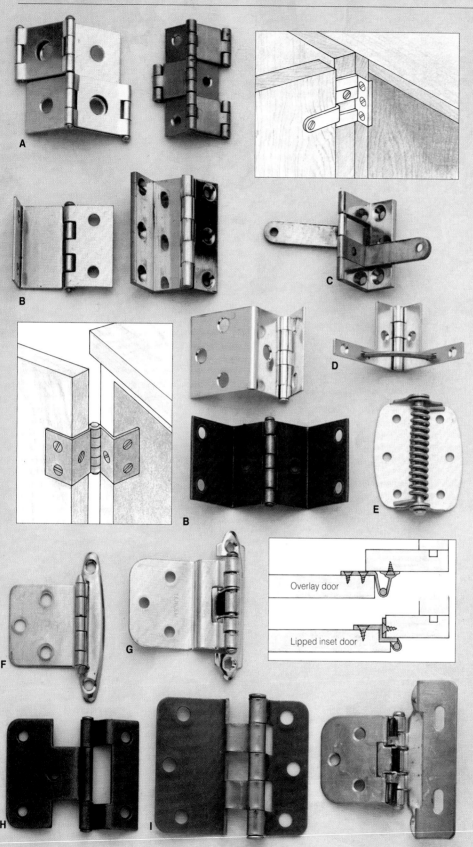

Double-acting hinge (A) is mounted along the side edges of a folding door or screen. The two linked sets of leaves and barrels permit the panels to swing open from both directions. To avoid binding, the leaves of the hinge (less the barrels) must be equal to or less than the thickness of the work.

Wrap-around hinge (B), a version of the fixed-pin butt hinge, is used on flush inset cabinet doors. The size of the hinge must match the door thickness. For extra support, the right-angle leaf attaches to both the edge and the back of the door. Only the barrel shows when the door is closed. The back-to-back wrap-around hinge (bottom) has two right-angle leaves for even greater strength. One leaf is attached to the door, the other leaf to the frame. This hinge is also suitable for a flush inset cabinet door.

Double-flap cranked hinge (C) is mounted on a cabinet's center stile, or partition, to hold two doors. Each door, which overlays half the stile, can be opened independently 180°.

Quadrant hinge (D) is recessed in mortises made in the edges of a small box. It holds the lid open at 100°.

Spring hinge (E) has a coiled spring that returns a door to a closed position. Surface-mount it on a cabinet door and on other places where self-closing doors are desirable.

Overlay hinge (F), for a cabinet door, has a short leaf that is mounted on the exterior surface of the cabinet frame. The long leaf is attached to the back of the door. The hinge allows the door to overlay the frame.

Inset cabinet hinge (G) is similar to the overlay hinge, but the long leaf is offset so that it can be used on a lipped cabinet door. Concealed under a barrel is a spring that, when activated, snaps the door shut.

Semi-concealed overlay hinge (H), for a cabinet door, is almost hidden when the door is closed. A short leaf is offset so that the leaf can be mounted inside the cabinet frame. When the door is closed, only the barrel shows. Use it on overlay doors.

Semi-concealed inset hinge (I), when mounted on a lipped cabinet door, is hidden except for the barrel. The spring-loaded hinge (near left) snaps the door shut when you release it.

Pivot hinge (A) mounts at top and bottom of overlay cabinet door and against cabinet frame. Elongated screw holes permit easy adjustment. When the door is closed, only the pivot pin is visible. Mount the hinge at top as shown; mount both halves of the hinge at bottom horizontally.

Knife hinge (B) comes in a variety of sizes for use on objects as small as a jewelry box or as large as a 200-lb. door. The hinge is recessed into two mortises at the top or bottom of the door, making it almost invisible. With the offset knife hinge (bottom), only the pivot point shows.

Double spring-action hinge (C) is a self-closing hinge that allows the door to swing in both directions. It comes in numerous sizes for a variety of doors. Some types must be mounted to a strip that you hang from the doorjamb.

Glass-door hinge (D), unlike some other hinges for glass cabinet doors, requires no drilling in glass. One leaf is screwed to the cabinet frame. The bottom edge of the glass door slides into the other leaf; secure it in place with a setscrew. A spring-loaded catch in the hinge holds the door closed.

Flush-fitting flap hinge (E) provides a gap-free joint on cabinets and other furniture with down-swinging flaps. For a flush fit, recess the hinge into the bottom edges of the cabinet frame and the flap.

Concealed hinge (F) comes in a variety of styles for small cabinet doors and other lightweight applications. You mount it in a recess made with a drill or router. When the hinge is closed, the leaves lie flat together; the knuckles slide out of sight into gaps in the leaves. Select the hinge size that is close to but less than the thickness of the cabinet stock.

Face-frame hinge (G) has a baseplate that is attached to the front of a cabinet's frame. The cup is recessed into the door. To reposition the door vertically or horizontally, adjust the screws in the baseplate. The hinge can swing open to 105°.

European-style concealed hinge (H), a face-frame hinge that swings open to 176°, is for inset and overlaying cabinet doors. A cup is recessed into the door, and the baseplate is attached to the cabinet side. You can loosen the screws to adjust alignment of the door.

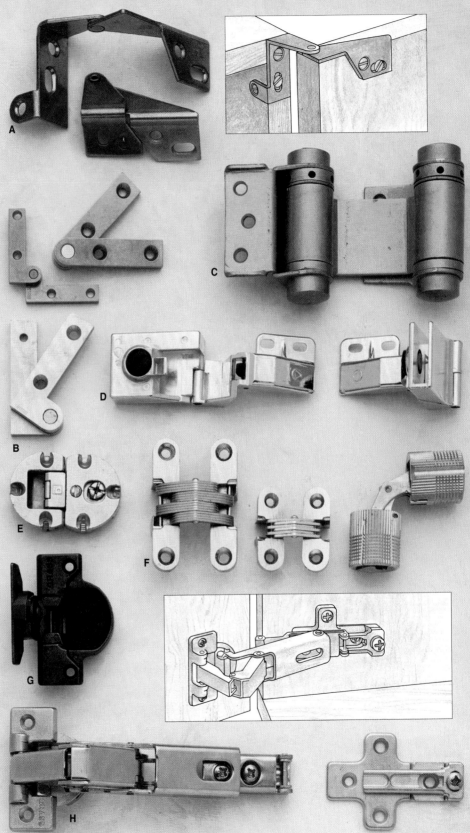

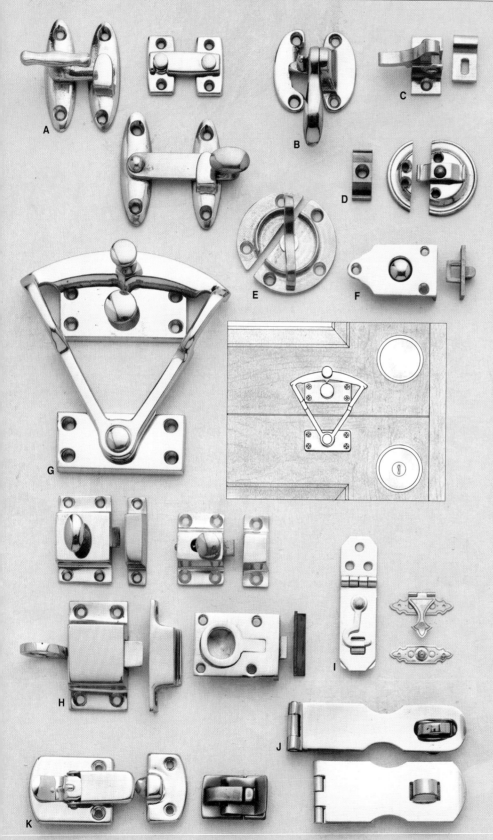

To keep a door or lid closed, latches and catches are mounted on furniture, cabinets, and boxes. They come in a variety of sizes and functions for different needs. Small locks add some degree of privacy, but not security.

Turn catch (A) holds shutters and cupboard, cabinet, and other small doors closed. Space the plates carefully so the arm fits the matching plate. When using the catch on two neighboring doors, secure one door with an interior latch, such as (C), mounted at the top or bottom of the door.

Spring-loaded catch (B) holds small doors closed. To open the door, pull up the catch's handle. A spring pulls the handle down when it is released.

Elbow latch (C) is for small doors. Open it by pushing down the handle—with either your hand or your elbow.

Button catch (D) holds a light-duty door in place with the turn of its catch. Screw it on near the door's edge. It also comes attached to a plate.

Table catch (E) is screwed to the underside of a table that accepts extensions. The catch pulls the sections tightly together and holds them level.

Secretary catch (F) is recessed into the work. The button is attached to a spring clip, which releases the catch.

Dutch door quadrant (G) holds two sections of a Dutch door closed. The plate with the quadrant is screwed to the lower section, the other plate to the top section. For added security, mount a deadbolt to the door's top section.

Cupboard latch (H) has a spring latch that slides into a strike plate. Draw the latch back by turning the knob (top) or pulling out the lever (bottom, left) or the flush ring handle (bottom, right).

Hasp (I) is ideal for holding lids closed on small boxes. The arm is held in place with a snap or hook.

Security hasp (J) has an arm that swings over the screw plate, preventing an intruder from removing screws. A padlock slips onto the keeper.

Box snap (K), for boxes and chests, holds the lid in place with an arm that snaps over the opposite plate.

Bullet catch (A), with a spring-loaded ball in a cylindrical case, fits into the edge of a flush cabinet door. When the door is closed, the ball fits into a recess in the cupboard wall. The strike plate provides a finished look.

Double-ball catch (B) can be used on flush, overlay, and inset cabinet doors. Two balls snap over the strike from the front or side. To adjust the balls' tension, turn the setscrews.

Roller catch (C) operates on the same principle as the double-ball catch. The rollers are spring-loaded.

Spring-pressure catch (D), for a cabinet door, has a roller that fits into the strike's hook. Attach the catch shown at top to the door's bottom edge, the strike to the frame's base. Mount the other catch on the cabinet's vertical frame, the strike on the door. To open the door, push against it.

Magnetic catch (E) holds a cabinet door closed by magnetically pulling in a metal strike plate. Screw the catch to the inside of the cabinet and the strike plate to the inside of the door. Use a pull to open the door.

Magnetic pressure catch (F) combines magnetic and spring-pressure catches. No handles are necessary; simply push the door to open it. Attach a metal strike plate to a wood door.

Glass-door catch (G) works just like the magnetic pressure catch, but the strike plate is designed to slide onto the glass door, eliminating boring through the glass.

Cupboard lock (H) has a bolt that operates left and right. Surface-mount the lock; cut a recess to hold the bolt.

Drawer lock (I) has a double keyhole, letting you set the lock in a vertical or horizontal position. Mount it in a recess in a desk, cabinet, or other furniture.

Mortise lock (J) is ideal for sliding doors, rolltop desks, and other furniture. The model at far right has a spring-loaded dust cover.

Cylinder lock (K) comes in different designs for drawers and cabinet doors. Surface-mount the lock by boring a hole through the surface, or fit it into a mortise. The lower lock at far right is designed to fit glass cabinet doors; to install it, you must bore a hole through the glass.

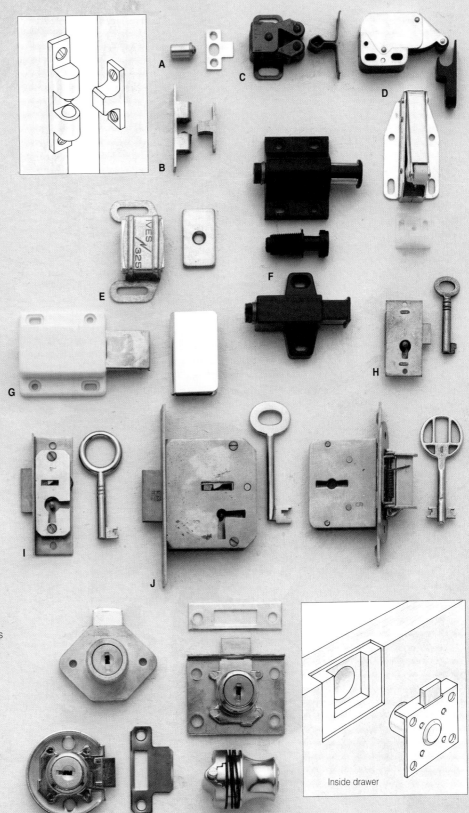

Inside drawer

DOORKNOBS AND LOCKS

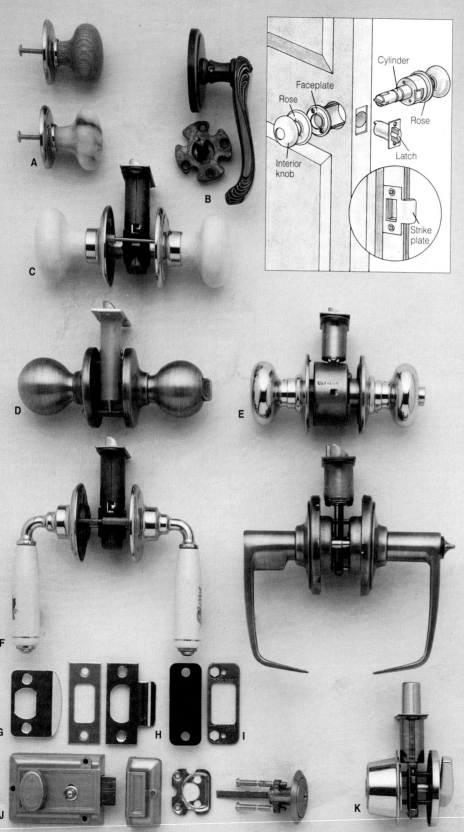

Cylinder

Faceplate

Rose

Rose

Interior knob

Latch

Strike plate

The installation of doorknobs and locks involves boring one or two holes into the door and making a mortise in the door-jamb. Because designs vary, follow the maker's instructions.

Dummy doorknob (A) attaches to a closet door to pull it open. Drill a pilot hole through the door; insert the screw from the closet side of the door; from the other side, slip on the rose and thread the knob onto the screw. To keep the door closed, install a catch.

Dummy lever handle (B) comes with a mounting plate that fits into a 1-in.-diameter hole. For one handle, bore a ¼-in.-deep hole; for two, bore through the door. Slip rose onto plate's stem; slide on handle; tighten setscrew.

Passage lockset (C) has a cylindrical lock with a spring latch to hold the door closed. Use the supplied template to bore a hole through the door face for the spindle and into its edge for the latch. Make a mortise in the doorjamb to accommodate the latch.

Privacy lockset (D) for bedroom and bathroom doors adds a thumb turn or button on the inside knob to lock the door from within. It can be unlocked from outside by pushing a narrow rod or nail into the hole in the outside knob. Install it like passage lockset.

Key-in-knob lockset (E) is a privacy lockset with an outside knob that locks with a key. Installation is the same as the passage lockset. To remove a knob, look for a tab or pin.

Lever lockset (F) is available in passage, privacy, and key-in-lever locksets. The design of the handle allows disabled people, and people with their hands full, to open the door easily.

Strike plate (G) for latches and bolts is installed with 3-in.-long screws into mortise made in doorjamb. Use it alone or, preferably, with a strike box **(H)** and reinforcement plate **(I)**.

Rim lock (J) is mounted at the door's edge 6 in. above the knob for additional security. The bolt slides into the strike plate installed on the jamb.

Deadbolt (K), also for extra security, has a single cylinder that moves only with a key or thumb turn. Install it in a similar fashion as the above locksets.

Exterior lockset (A), used on a front door, comes in a variety of designs. This one has a deadlocking latch; it's similar to a spring latch, but it has a piece projecting in front of the latch that stops it from being pushed back by an intruder. To install, bore holes through the door face and into its edge; make a mortise in the jamb for the latch. From the outside, the latch is drawn back by depressing the thumbpiece or unlocking it with a key; from the inside just turn the knob.

Combination exterior lockset (B) has a spring latch in the lockset but also includes a deadbolt for additional security. The design and finish on the lockset and the deadbolt match. To install the deadbolt (top), you'll have to bore an additional hole through the door face and edge and make a second mortise in the doorjamb, about 6 in. above the lockset mortise.

Interconnected exterior lockset (C) also utilizes a spring latch and deadbolt, but they are joined together by the decorative rose escutcheon. Installation is more difficult because the two sets of holes and mortises must be precisely spaced. A template is supplied to mark out the right locations. As with other locksets, the handles, latch, and bolt can usually be reversed to fit either a right- or a left-hand door.

Interconnected exterior lockset (D), another variety of lockset, uses a deadlocking latch in combination with a deadbolt. In some models, two separate keys operate the lockset. Install it in the same way as other interconnected exterior locksets.

Push-button combination lockset (E) with a deadlocking latch is installed like other locksets that require two holes and a mortise. To unlock the unit, you must push the buttons in a programmed order. The combination can be given out to as many (or as few) people as you wish, and it can also be changed as often as you like. (Make sure you keep the instructions in a secure place.)

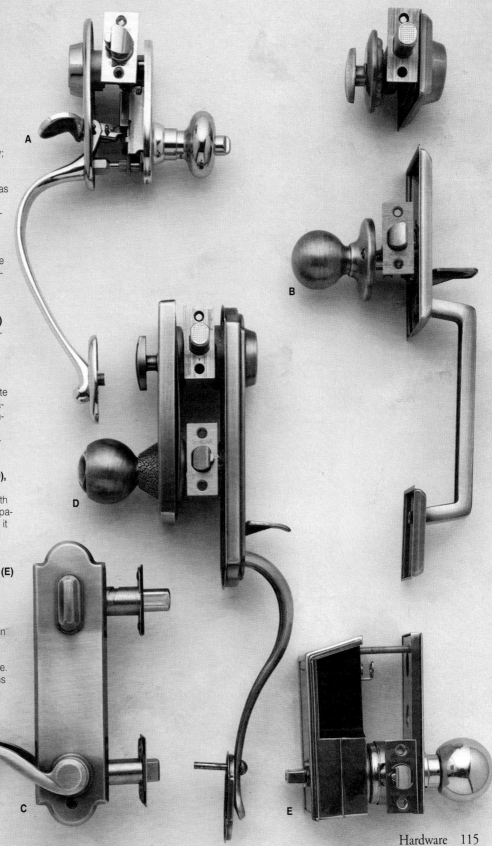

A

B

C

D

E

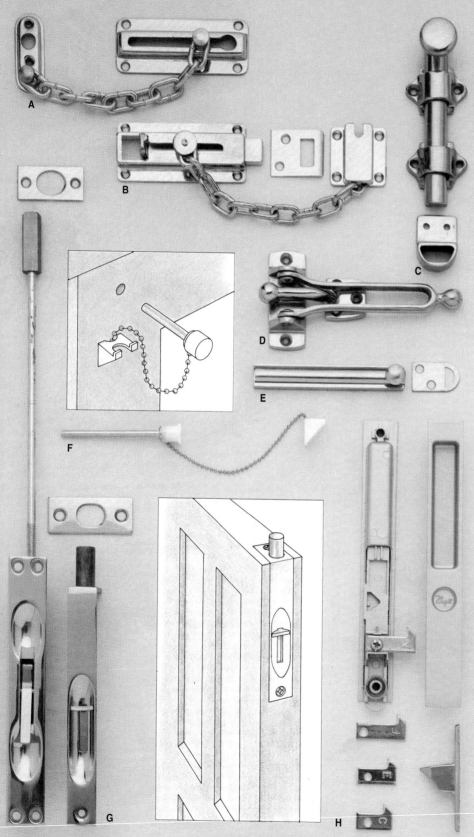

For doors that require minimal security, use the locks on this page. The additional accessories on the facing page add convenience to standard door use.

Door chain guard (A) lets you open a door partway to view visitors or for ventilation. Attach the slide piece to the door; screw the chain piece to the doorjamb or frame. Make sure you use 3-in.-long screws.

Deadbolt and chain guard (B) gives added security with a deadbolt. Attach the long slide plate in a horizontal position on the surface of the door, flush with the edge. Screw the chain plate to the door frame, opposite the slide plate. Position the strike on the doorjamb so the bolt can slide into it; the strike may have to be mortised.

Dutch door bolt (C) is mounted vertically on a Dutch door or conventional door. For a Dutch door, attach the bolt to the top half of the door; secure the strike plate on the surface of the lower half of the door, near the top edge. For a conventional door, attach the bolt at the top of the door; use a flat strike plate (not shown) on the head jamb.

Swing bar guard (D) is stronger than a door chain guard. Attach the long arm piece to the door frame, and the smaller piece to the front surface at the edge of the door, about ¾ in. away from the long arm piece. Both parts should be level, their edges parallel.

Surface bolt (E) can be used in a vertical or horizontal position on doors and cabinets. Position it with the slide bolt on the door and the strike on the jamb, making sure the bolt will easily pass through the strike.

Patio door pin (F) slips through a hole bored through the sliding door and into the stationary door. Secure the plastic pin holder with a screw.

Extension flush bolt (G) holds the inactive door of a pair of doors in place. It's installed in a recess cut into the door's edge. The door must be at least 1⅜ in. thick. The smaller latch (left) is for wood doors; the other one (far left) has a longer bolt for metal doors.

Patio door latch (H) is sold to replace existing latch; select one of the proper length. Place the inside assembly in the door frame; fasten the outside plate to it. Attach the strike plate to the jamb so that the latch engages it.

Baseboard bumper (A) stops an opening door before its handle hits the wall. Allowing clearance for a vacuum cleaner, install the rigid bumper (top) by drilling a pilot hole, then screwing the bumper in place. The flexible bumper (below) bends to make it easier for you to vacuum under it. To install one, screw in its detachable base; push the bumper onto the base.

Floor doorstop (B) screws into the floor to stop a door from opening any farther. Position the stop with the rubber pad flat against the door. (Make sure door handle does not touch wall.)

Hinge-pin bumper (C) fits onto a loose-pin door hinge. To attach one, remove the pin, slip the stop onto the pin, and place it back in the hinge.

Kickdown doorstop (D), attached near the bottom of a door, holds the door open in any position. To use it, kick down the tip so that it rests flat on the floor. When the stop is not in use, the tip should point up.

Wall-mounted bumper (E) stops a doorknob from marring a wall. Screw the bumper onto the wall; make sure it aligns with the knob.

Door knocker (F) comes in a variety of styles. When installing one on an exterior door, center it horizontally 60 in. from the bottom of the door.

Door viewer (G) allows a normal or wide-angle view through a door. Bore a hole through the door; insert the tube and screw it into the threaded ring.

Letter mail slot (H) is installed with a template; using a reciprocating saw, cut a slot in the door. Attach the outside cover plate, then the inside plate.

Pneumatic closer (I) pulls shut a storm or screen door without slamming it. Attach it to the door rail and jamb with brackets and connecting pins.

Door spring (J) comes in several styles. It pulls shut a light door. The top spring slips into hooks fastened to door and jamb; the bottom one is screwed directly to the surface.

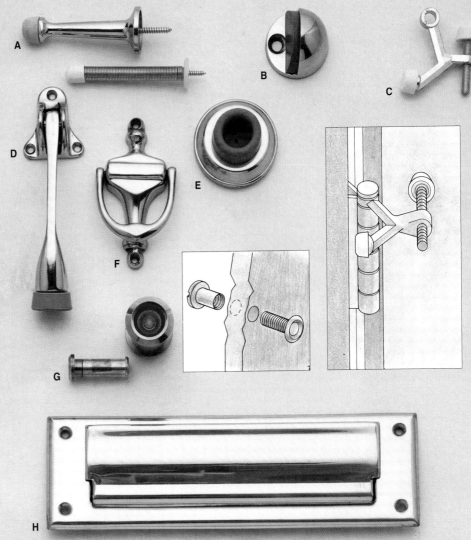

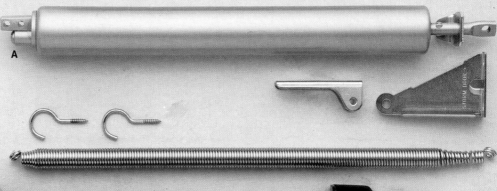

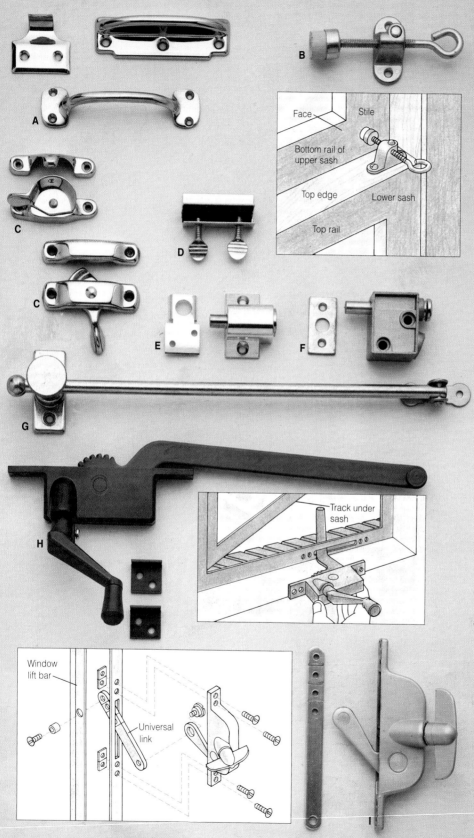

Face · Stile

Bottom rail of
upper sash

Top edge

Lower sash

Top rail

A

B

C

C

D

E

F

G

H

Track under
sash

Window
lift bar

Universal
link

I

Opening, closing, and securing a window is easy when it is fitted with the proper hardware. Some items here are accessories; others are replacement parts.

Sash lift (A) is screwed into the face of the lower sash's bottom rail. Grasp the lift to pull the sash up.

Window bolt (B) holds a double-hung window sash in any desired open position. Screw it to the top edge of the lower sash's top rail; the tip must align with a stile. To hold the sash in place, turn the bolt until the tip presses firmly against the stile. Other bolt styles give extra security by sliding into a hole drilled partway through the stile.

Sash latch (C) draws the two sashes of a double-hung window together to reduce drafts and rattling. The strike plate is attached to the top edge of the upper sash's bottom rail; make sure the plate is centered. Align the other piece; attach it to the top edge of the lower sash's top rail.

Thumbscrew lock (D) keeps a metal double-hung or gliding window from opening beyond a desired point. Slip it onto the track; turn the thumbscrews to tighten the lock in place.

Double-hung sash lock (E) comes with two strike plates to lock the sash closed or slightly open for ventilation. Mount the lock on the lower sash's top edge; attach the plates to the stile on the upper sash. Use a key to open the bolt; to lock it, just push the bolt in.

Gliding window lock (F), also for patio doors, is attached to window's side edge. Drill a hole partway through stationary sash's rail; attach strike plate. To lock window, push in bolt.

Sliding rod (G) operates a casement window. The rod, attached to the rail, slides through a holder installed on the windowsill. Tighten the knurled knob to secure the rod in place.

Casement window operator (H) has an arm that slides along a track on the bottom of the sash. To open or close the window, turn the crank handle to move the arm.

Jalousie operator (I) comes with a universal link to replace most operators. A screw attaches the arm to the link, which is screwed to the window lift bar. Follow maker's directions.

BATHROOM HARDWARE

The easiest way to give your bathroom a face-lift is to replace the existing accessories. Keep in mind that surface-mounted fixtures cannot be installed where recessed ones were removed. Many brass items have a protective finish; to clean, wipe them with a soft dry or damp cloth, then buff with a dry cloth.

Towel bar (A) has a rod that's held in place with two endpieces, or bases, which are secured with toggle bolts or wall anchors. To install it, measure and mark the placement of the bases on the wall. Attach one base; slide the rod into the indentation in its side. Slip the second base over the other end of the rod; secure it to the wall. The porcelain and brass bar has bases that are screwed into the wall. The bases of the white bar slide onto brackets; first screw the brackets into the wall.

Double towel bar (B) has two rods spaced apart, allowing clearance for towels to dry. Brackets hold the bar in place; make sure they are level, correctly spaced, and installed with toggle bolts. Slip the bases onto the brackets; secure them with setscrews on the bottom edge of the bases.

Towel ring (C) needs less space than a towel bar; it's installed with only one bracket. Screw the bracket to the wall; slip the base onto the bracket; tighten the setscrew in the bottom of the base.

Grab bar (D) provides support above bathtub or in shower stall for disabled persons. Screw it to wall vertically into studs or diagonally with toggle bolts.

Toothbrush and cup holder (E) can be screwed in place on the wall above a sink, or it may slide onto a bracket attached to the wall. Secure the glass holder to the bracket with a setscrew; the brass holder has a dome-shaped knob that screws into the bracket.

Soap dish (F) is placed above a sink, using a bracket. The blue porcelain dish is permanently attached with plaster of Paris. Clean the back of the dish and the wall where it will sit; wet both surfaces. Apply the plaster; hold the dish in place until the plaster sets.

Toilet paper holder (G) can be screwed in place, attached like the double towel bar (above), or recessed into a ceramic tile wall as it's installed.

FURNITURE PULLS AND KNOBS

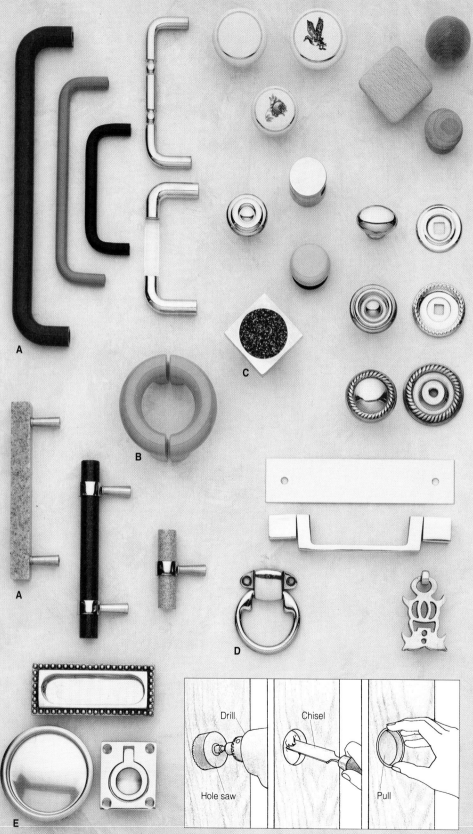

The pulls and knobs needed to open drawers and cabinet doors come in a wide variety of styles, shapes, and materials. Nylon, chrome, marble, plastic, and glass pulls and knobs are ideal for kitchen and bathroom furniture, and they can give other rooms a modern, functional look. Wood, brass, and enamel lend elegance to living room and bedroom furniture, and are available in many modern designs (this page) as well as antique styles (facing page).

Simple pull (A) can be installed vertically on a door or horizontally on a drawer. Position the pull, mark the door or drawer where the ends of the pull touch it, and drill screw holes at these marks. Then hold the pull in position and drive the screws into it from inside the drawer or door.

Semicircular nylon pull (B) can be used singly or paired with a matching pull to make a single circular pull. You can also mount one semicircular pull on each door of a cabinet to form a full circle when the doors are closed.

Furniture knob (C) is installed like a pull but with only one screw. If the knob has a plate, slide it onto the screw between furniture and knob.

Drop pull (D) is only a bit more complicated to install. Drill a screw hole for each post, slide on the backplate, and screw one of the small posts into place with the hole in its surface facing in the direction of the other screw hole. Slide one of the pins in the drop, or *bale*, into the hole in the installed post, slide the other pin into the hole in the second post, and screw the second post to the drawer. If the bale is already attached to the pull, install the pull as you would a standard pull.

Recessed pull (E) is used mainly on sliding doors. To install a recessed pull, chisel out a mortise, or hollow, just large enough to accept the pull. If the pull is circular, use an electric drill with a hole saw to start the mortise, then finish it with a chisel. Sand the edges of the opening smooth, and firmly wedge the pull into place. On some recessed pulls you must glue the pull into place or fasten it with tiny screws, which are supplied.

A

B

C

A

B

D

E

Drill

Hole saw

Chisel

Pull

William and Mary period drop pulls (right) use *snipes* (doubled-over pins) in place of screws. Position the pull and drill a hole for the snipe. Force the bale (drop) over one leg of the snipe and push it down into the bend in the snipe. Then slide the backing plate over the snipe behind the bale, thread the snipe through the hole in the door or drawer, and bend its legs against the furniture, using pliers with the jaws taped to prevent scratching. Gently hammer the ends of the snipe against the inside of the furniture.

Other antique styles (right and below) include Queen Anne, Sheraton, Chippendale, and Hepplewhite. If a pull uses decorative bolts and nuts in place of snipes or screws, countersink the nut on the inside of the drawer or door and saw off the protruding end of the bolt to give a smooth, snag-free surface. If you are replacing a pull and the original bolt holes are up to 1/8 in. too far apart or close together, stretch or push together the arms of the new bale to make it fit. If this doesn't work, install a new pull with a plate that will cover the old holes.

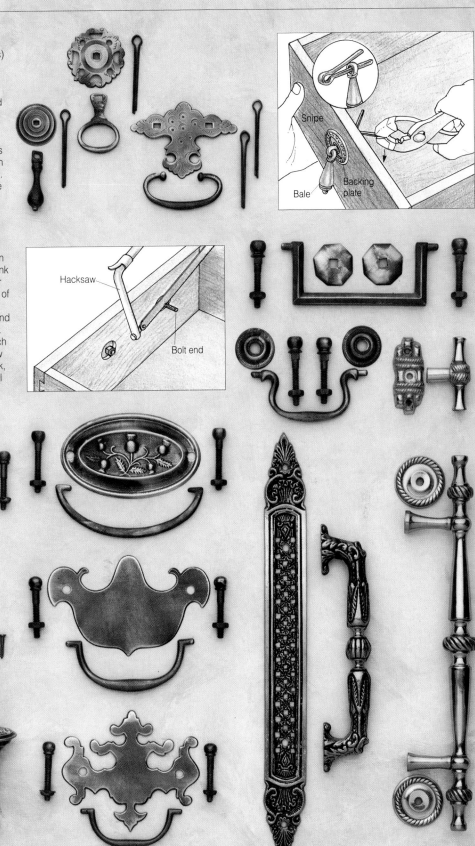

Snipe

Bale

Backing plate

Hacksaw

Bolt end

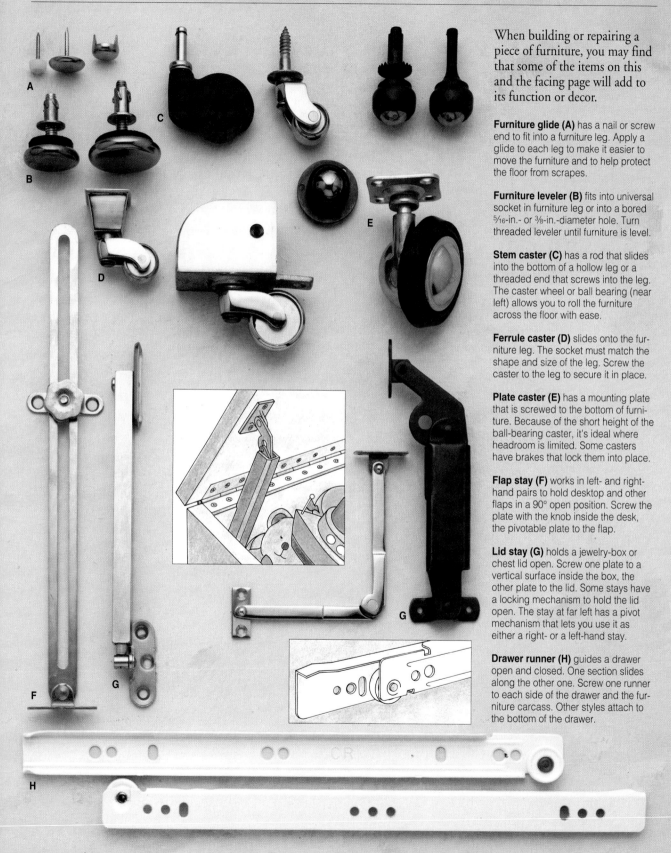

When building or repairing a piece of furniture, you may find that some of the items on this and the facing page will add to its function or decor.

Furniture glide (A) has a nail or screw end to fit into a furniture leg. Apply a glide to each leg to make it easier to move the furniture and to help protect the floor from scrapes.

Furniture leveler (B) fits into universal socket in furniture leg or into a bored 5/16-in.- or 3/8-in.-diameter hole. Turn threaded leveler until furniture is level.

Stem caster (C) has a rod that slides into the bottom of a hollow leg or a threaded end that screws into the leg. The caster wheel or ball bearing (near left) allows you to roll the furniture across the floor with ease.

Ferrule caster (D) slides onto the furniture leg. The socket must match the shape and size of the leg. Screw the caster to the leg to secure it in place.

Plate caster (E) has a mounting plate that is screwed to the bottom of furniture. Because of the short height of the ball-bearing caster, it's ideal where headroom is limited. Some casters have brakes that lock them into place.

Flap stay (F) works in left- and right-hand pairs to hold desktop and other flaps in a 90° open position. Screw the plate with the knob inside the desk, the pivotable plate to the flap.

Lid stay (G) holds a jewelry-box or chest lid open. Screw one plate to a vertical surface inside the box, the other plate to the lid. Some stays have a locking mechanism to hold the lid open. The stay at far left has a pivot mechanism that lets you use it as either a right- or a left-hand stay.

Drawer runner (H) guides a drawer open and closed. One section slides along the other one. Screw one runner to each side of the drawer and the furniture carcass. Other styles attach to the bottom of the drawer.

Decorative plates (A) come in an unlimited number of shapes, sizes, and styles. They can embellish store-bought furniture or pieces that you make yourself. They work especially well on antique reproductions. To install a plate, screw or nail it in place through the small holes in the plate. Some plates have larger holes to accept drawer or door pulls.

Keyhole escutcheon (B), a type of decorative plate, fits over a small keyhole. If you install the lock yourself, place the escutcheon over the hole as the last step. The escutcheon can also serve as a dummy, giving the appearance of a lock where none is installed.

Decorative angle plates (C) are available in a variety of shapes and sizes. Wrap the L-shaped plate and the Y-shaped plate (near right) around a piece where two sides meet; fit the corner plate and the Y-shaped plate (farther right) over corners where three sides meet. Nail the plates in place.

Leg plate (D) firmly holds a chair or table leg in place. Attach the plate to the top of the leg with a bolt; screw the plate to the underside of a chair seat or table surface. Two settings allow you to set the leg straight or angled.

Brace and plate (E) provide extra support on wood joints. Apply them to a piece as it's assembled or when mending a break. The straight plate joins two butt pieces, the T-plate a horizontal and a perpendicular piece. The L-shaped and flat corner braces support right-angle pieces; the three-sided corner brace is for heavy-duty use.

Knockdown fitting (F) joins pieces temporarily, allowing you to take apart and reassemble them when necessary—for instance, to move heavy furniture. They come in many styles.

Shrinkage brace (G) has one plate with a vertical or horizontal slot, allowing wood to move as it shrinks or expands with humidity changes.

Table fork (H), for expandable table, has two plates and a U-shaped fork. Mount one plate under stationary section, the other plate on the leaf; slide the fork into the plates to hold the two sections together. Use two table fork latches for each leaf.

Glass door pull (I) slides over the edge of a glass cabinet door. An inside pad prevents damage to glass.

WOODWORKING

WOODS

A primary building and crafts material, wood offers strength, beauty, or a combination of both. Sizes range from thick beams for houses to paper-thin strips of veneer for furniture.

Of the hundreds of wood species, only a few, mostly native softwoods, are used in the building trade. Wood from trees grown in managed forests is sold in home centers and lumberyards as dimension lumber, boards, and manufactured products such as moldings and doors. The hobbyist or furniture maker uses native woods as well as exotic woods from other countries. Available in forms such as boards and carving blocks, these woods must usually be bought at specialty lumber dealers or through woodworking magazines and catalogs.

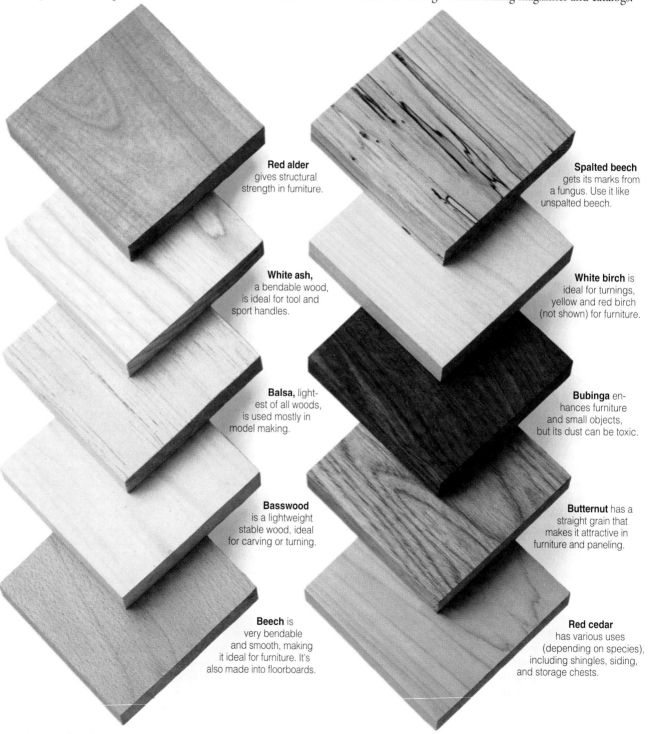

Red alder gives structural strength in furniture.

White ash, a bendable wood, is ideal for tool and sport handles.

Balsa, lightest of all woods, is used mostly in model making.

Basswood is a lightweight stable wood, ideal for carving or turning.

Beech is very bendable and smooth, making it ideal for furniture. It's also made into floorboards.

Spalted beech gets its marks from a fungus. Use it like unspalted beech.

White birch is ideal for turnings, yellow and red birch (not shown) for furniture.

Bubinga enhances furniture and small objects, but its dust can be toxic.

Butternut has a straight grain that makes it attractive in furniture and paneling.

Red cedar has various uses (depending on species), including shingles, siding, and storage chests.

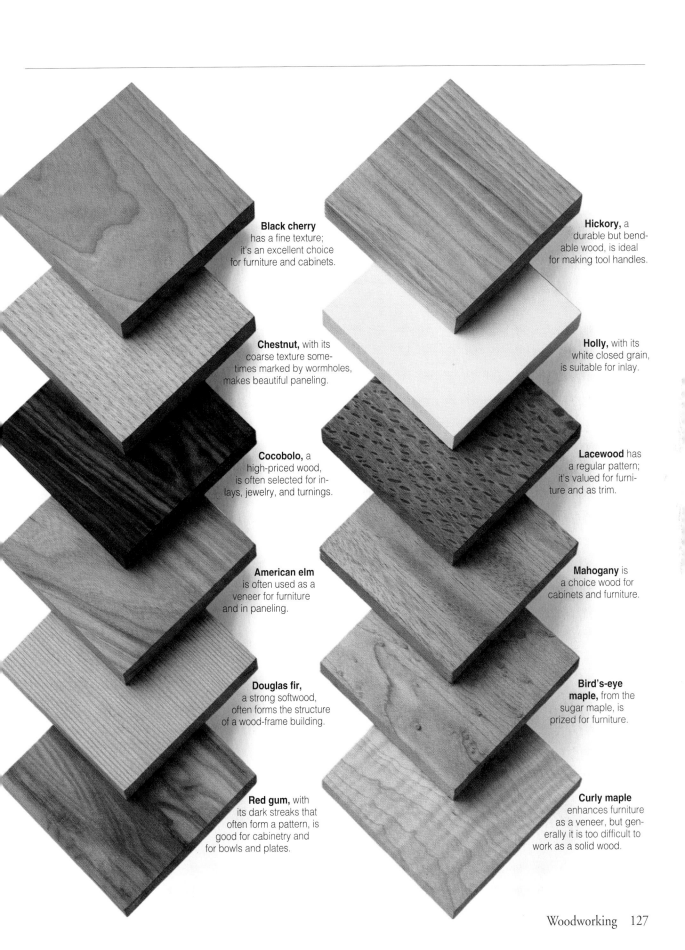

Black cherry
has a fine texture;
it's an excellent choice
for furniture and cabinets.

Hickory, a
durable but bend-
able wood, is ideal
for making tool handles.

Chestnut, with its
coarse texture some-
times marked by wormholes,
makes beautiful paneling.

Holly, with its
white closed grain,
is suitable for inlay.

Cocobolo, a
high-priced wood,
is often selected for in-
lays, jewelry, and turnings.

Lacewood has
a regular pattern;
it's valued for furni-
ture and as trim.

American elm
is often used as a
veneer for furniture
and in paneling.

Mahogany is
a choice wood for
cabinets and furniture.

Douglas fir,
a strong softwood,
often forms the structure
of a wood-frame building.

**Bird's-eye
maple,** from the
sugar maple, is
prized for furniture.

Red gum, with
its dark streaks that
often form a pattern, is
good for cabinetry and
for bowls and plates.

Curly maple
enhances furniture
as a veneer, but gen-
erally it is too difficult to
work as a solid wood.

Red oak is a strong bendable wood, ideal for flooring and sturdy furniture.

Purpleheart, named for its color, is suitable for inlays and trim.

White oak, a bendable wood, is suitable for furniture and furniture veneer.

Redwood weathers well; it's ideal for decks and outdoor furniture.

African padauk has a striped pattern; it's a fine wood for furniture and inlay.

Sycamore is commonly used in furniture and flooring.

Pau amarello's yellow appearance makes it a natural pick for creating decorative inlays.

Teak is excellent for outdoor furniture, boats, and as veneer.

Pine, clear or knotty, is the most common wood for paneling, flooring, and furniture.

Black walnut is frequently used in fine cabinetwork.

Yellow poplar is found in stained and painted furniture, as a veneer on plywood, and in moldings and other trim.

Zebrawood, with its gray, black, and yellow stripes, lends drama to inlays and trim.

MANUFACTURED WOODS

An alternative to solid wood, manufactured wood makes more efficient use of our natural resources by laminating or compressing layers of wood or wood fibers to form panels. Hardwood-veneer plywood panels are sold according to the veneer species, cut (rotary, quarter, rift), and core type (fiberboard, particleboard, or lumber). Softwood plywood, made up of laminated layers of veneers, is graded for interior and exterior use, strength, and the quality of its outer veneers (using one letter for the face and one for the back). The major nonveneer panels are particleboard (compressed wood particles); oriented strand board, or OSB (larger strands); and fiberboard (compressed fine wood fibers, sold mostly in a medium-density grade, or MDF). Particleboard and MDF are bonded with urea formaldehyde; wear a respirator when working with them. If you are sensitive to the gases emitted, avoid these panels. Formaldehyde-free panels are available.

Core thickness varies from ¼ to 1½ in. and thicker. From left to right are a hardwood-veneer panel; two plywood samples (the number of layers are often referred to, for example, as 3-ply or 5-ply); particleboard, which has no layers; and oriented strand board (the long fibers are visibly layered).

Tongue-and-groove panels are suitable as subflooring material. The panels are made from plywood and oriented strand board; the ends have tongues and grooves for tighter installation.

Particleboard (below, top) is sold in several grades: 1-M-1 and 1-M-2 (for veneer substrates), 1-M-1/Underlayment (for under flooring), and 2-M-1 and 2-M-2 (for heat and moisture resistance).

Oriented strand board (below, center) is as strong as plywood but, like all wood panels, may be subject to water damage.

Fiberboard (below, bottom) is stable and machines well. Use it for painted cabinet doors and also as a veneer substrate.

Hardwood-veneer plywood (below, top) is presanded and ready for finishing; the superior-quality outer veneers come in "paint" and "stain" grades. Use the panel where the final look is important. Birch (shown) and oak veneer are the most readily available; others can be ordered.

Softwood plywood made of Douglas fir or Canadian softwood has outer veneers that are graded A, B, and C; they may be knotty (C is the lowest end of the scale). The plywood can be used indoors or outdoors.

All trees belong in one of two broad divisions, *hardwoods* or *softwoods,* depending on whether they are broad-leaved or coniferous. But when it comes to actual characteristics, distinctions between the two types tend to blur. Certain softwoods, like southern yellow pine, are harder than some soft hardwoods, such as basswood. Because hardness and strength go hand in hand, the strongest woods (facing page) are also the most difficult to work and require the sharpest tools. These dense woods are also less forgiving of careless joinery.

All woods have *grain,* a term that describes the direction of longitudinal cells in a board. Relative cell size, which can determine whether a wood needs a filler before finishing, is called *texture.* The attractive patterns of various boards, or *figure,* are caused by deviations from a tree's normal growth.

Freshly sawn lumber has a high moisture content and should be seasoned, or dried, before working. Lumberyards usually sell kiln-dried wood with a moisture content between 6 and 18 percent. Wood that has less than 10 percent moisture content is recommended for furniture-making; the range above 10 percent is suitable for structural uses.

After seasoning, wood continues to shrink during dry spells and swell with humidity. This tendency is critical to the woodworker because it can cause warped boards, loose joints, or swollen-shut drawers. To combat this movement, you can choose a stable type of wood. Buy kiln-dried boards in advance and store them indoors for about a month to acclimate them to the moisture content of your home. After working, apply a sealing finish on all surfaces to retard further moisture exchange.

Wood comes in various grades. In hardwood, *firsts and seconds* (FAS) boards are about 85 percent defect-free; *select* and *#1 common,* about 65 percent. For softwood projects, choose Select Structural for fine finishing, Nos. 1, 2, and 3 for painting. Most hardwood is sold by the *board foot,* a unit 1 foot long, 1 foot wide, and 1 inch thick (144 cubic inches). Softwoods are often sold by the *running* or *linear* foot, which refers to the board's length. Dimensional lumber (2 × 4's, 2 × 6's) is sold in its *nominal size,* the dimension before surfacing or planing, or in its smaller *actual size,* the size after surfacing. Softwood sold in dimensional sizes loses ½ inch in each dimension; hardwood loses about ¼ inch in thickness.

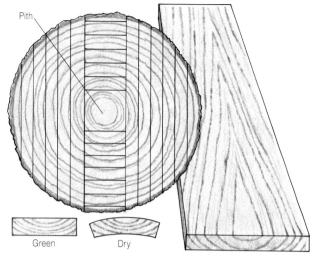

Green   Dry

Plain-sawing, or flat-sawing, yields boards whose growth rings intersect the surface at less than 45°. Boards containing the pith (the soft core at the trunk's center) will cup severely or split, and thus are usually ripped into two narrower boards. Plain-sawn boards warp as they dry.

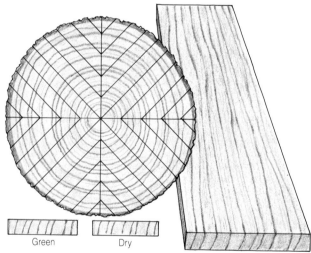

Green   Dry

Quartersawing produces wood with a close, even grain pattern because the growth rings form an angle of 45° to 90° to the board surface. Quartersawing results in more waste than plain-sawing; thus boards milled this way are more expensive. While quartersawn wood may check (facing page), it is less prone to warp.

Types of grain

Straight grain is strong and runs parallel to board edges.

Irregular grain occurs when normal growth pattern is altered by defects in the wood.

Wavy grain, weaker than straight, has attractive figure but is difficult to work.

Spiral grain is a natural growth pattern ascending a trunk. Wood may twist.

Interlocked grain results from successive layers of wood spiraling in opposite directions. These boards, sliced from one block, show how the wood fibers changed course.

Defects in wood

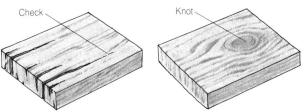

Check   Knot

Wood dries more quickly along the grain than across it. The resulting uneven moisture loss causes cracks, called checks, on board ends. Knots occur when a tree branch dies and the tree trunk grows around it. They can vary from ¼ to 1½ in. in diameter.

Storage: Stacking lumber

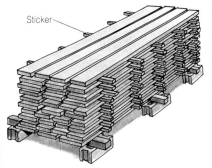

Sticker

To ensure good air circulation and to minimize warp, separate layers of boards with small dry 1- x 1-in. strips of wood, called stickers. Place stickers at each end of the stack and about every 16 in. along the length of the boards.

Types of warp

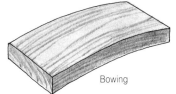
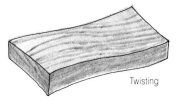

Cupping   Bowing   Twisting

Wood distorts when it shrinks or swells unevenly. The stress thus produced in the fibers causes a deviation from the board's flatness.

Wood types

Wood	Characteristics	Texture	Ease of working	Ease of finishing
Ash	Very strong, very stable	Coarse	Fairly difficult	Sands and stains unevenly
Basswood	Fairly strong, very stable	Fine	Very easy, but dents easily	Easy; usually painted or stained and varnished
Beech	Very strong, stable	Fine	Fairly difficult	Easy to oil or varnish
Birch, yellow	Strong, fairly stable	Medium	Fairly difficult, hard to plane	Easy to oil or varnish, but color may be bland
Bubinga	Very strong, stable	Fine	Difficult	Easy; usually oiled
Butternut	Strong, stable	Medium	Easy, but can dent	Very easy to oil or varnish
Cedar, incense (softwood)	Fairly strong, very stable	Coarse	Difficult because of splits and knots	Fairly difficult because of knots
Cherry, black	Strong, stable	Fine	Easy	Very easy to oil or varnish
Hickory	Very strong, stable	Coarse	Difficult, dulls cutting edges	Easy to oil or varnish
Mahogany	Strong, very stable	Medium	Easy	Easy to varnish; harder to obtain lustrous oil finish; may need filler
Maple, sugar	Very strong, fairly stable	Fine	Fairly difficult	Very easy to oil or varnish
Oak, red	Very strong, stable	Coarse	Easy, but can splinter	Easy to oil or varnish; can be filled
Pine, white (softwood)	Fairly strong, very stable	Medium	Very easy	Very easy to paint or varnish; harder to obtain lustrous oil finish
Poplar	Fairly strong, stable	Fine	Very easy, but dents easily	Easy to paint or varnish; may require many coats of oil for lustrous finish; color may be bland
Redwood (softwood)	Strong, very stable	Coarse	Easy to cut and plane; splits and cracks when nailed	Easy to coat with sealer, but difficult if luster desired
Rosewood	Very strong, very stable	Fine	Difficult, hard to glue	Easy; usually oiled
Teak	Very strong, very stable	Coarse to medium	Easy, but hard to glue	Easy; usually oiled
Walnut	Strong, very stable	Medium	Easy, but can dent	Very easy to oil or varnish

SQUARING, MEASURING, AND MARKING

Squaring: Getting it straight

The first step in any woodworking project is to choose the best board face of each member and make it exactly flat. Additionally, each piece must have one level edge that is squared to the first face. These two surfaces will become the reference for all measuring, marking, and cutting operations on the opposite surface and edge, and at each end.

If you have access to a jointer and a thickness planer, you can buy lumber rough-sawn in nominal dimensions (the least expensive kind) and then mill one face and each edge on the jointer and the other face on the planer. If you have only hand planes, you may want to buy more expensive boards that are surfaced, or dressed, to thickness and width. More expensive yet are those cut to exact length, thickness, and width; even these must be leveled and squared. When planing by hand, use a jack plane, followed by a smoothing plane; then square the edge with a jointer or jack plane (p.134).

Check flatness on best face with straightedge along dotted lines (right). Light will show at low spots. Mark high spots with pencil; plane smooth.

Check for twisting by placing a straight piece of wood at each end of the board and sighting down their top edges. Mark and plane the high spots.

On best edge, check for high spots and squareness of corner, using planed face as reference. Mark spots to be planed both across edge and along it.

Measuring and marking

To reduce the length of rough-sawn lumber to manageable dimensions, mark the boards about 1 inch oversize before cutting. For dressed lumber with accurate reference surfaces, you can cut pieces to their finished lengths. But mark and cut it $\frac{1}{32}$ to $\frac{1}{16}$ inch oversize in width, to allow for smoothing with a jointer plane. Once you've squared the face and edge of a board, mark the reference face with a loop and the reference edge with a V. These marks will help you orient the pieces in the right direction. Then measure and mark the cuts for your project.

A sharp scribing tool is the most accurate for marking, but if you prefer a pencil, choose one with a hard lead, sharpened to a chisel point. Use the same tools for the entire project, and avoid changing marking-gauge settings until you've marked all parts having the same measurements. Locate hole centers with crossed pencil lines; pencil a circle around the cross for clarity. Heavily marked stock can be confusing to interpret, so make pencil notes beside the marks on the waste side of the wood to avoid cutting errors.

Finally, remeasure everything before sawing; finding a mistake after you've made the cut may mean having to start over with a new piece of stock.

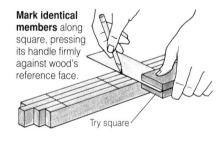
Mark identical members along square, pressing its handle firmly against wood's reference face. Try square

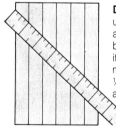
Divide board into uniform widths by angling ruler between board's edges until it gives equal increments. Allow $\frac{1}{16}$ to $\frac{1}{8}$ in. for saw kerfs and planing.

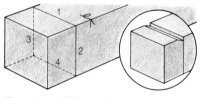
To mark cutoff line, hold try square stock on reference surface; mark lines in sequence. Chisel recess in waste to guide saw.

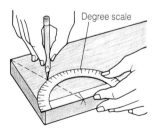
Setting an angle. Align protractor's index line to starting point on board edge; mark. Connect the two points with straightedge.

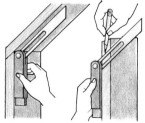
Copying an angle. Adjust the bevel-gauge blade to the angle you want to copy; transfer this angle to new piece.

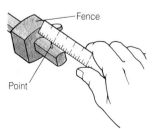
Setting marking gauge. Loosen thumbscrew; push fence away from point with ruler. Tighten screw; check setting.

Drawing a gauged line. Grasp the handle tightly, tilt gauge, and pull toward you (shown here) or push away, trailing pin on line.

Most sawing involves cutting a straight line along the grain (ripping), across the grain (crosscutting), or at an angle to it (miter or bevel cut). Here are the most common woodworking saws: For ripping—ripsaw, bow, table, radial arm, band, circular; for crosscutting—crosscut, bow, table, band, radial arm, circular; for angles—backsaw, coping, circular, table, radial arm, miter, band; for sizing plywood—crosscut, table, circular; for curves—compass, coping, band, saber, jigsaw; for joinery—backsaw, dovetail, bow, table, radial arm.

Wood should not move or vibrate while being cut. When hand-sawing, support the wood on a bench or sawhorses. Hold the saw at about a 60° angle to the wood surface for ripping; at about 45° for crosscutting. Because wood can splinter where the saw teeth exit, place the good side up when cutting with a hand- or table saw, or when crosscutting with a radial arm saw; put the good side down when using a circular saw or when ripping with a radial arm saw. Saw on the waste side of the lines, or the board will be short by the width of the saw kerf (⅛ inch on a table saw).

When you are ripping, the saw may bind (the kerf closes, pinching the blade). A circular saw tends to bind if it twists off a straight line or exposes too much blade. When a circular saw blade binds, the saw will *kick back,* or jump dangerously toward you. To keep hand- and circular saws from binding, drive wedges into the kerf. On a table saw, a splitter is part of the guard or is mounted as an accessory. Boards that are not held securely on a table saw may shoot back at you. To prevent kickback when ripping on a table saw, press the board against the fence with a clamped guide or *feather board.* You can buy one from a supplier or cut kerfs at ¼-inch intervals in an angled board to make "fingers." Another safety tool is the *push stick,* a notched stick that guides narrow pieces.

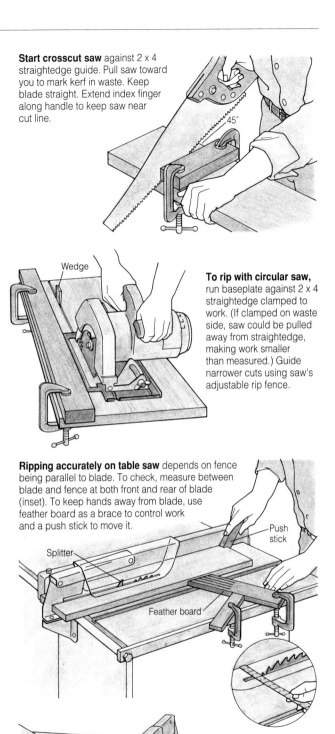

Start crosscut saw against 2 x 4 straightedge guide. Pull saw toward you to mark kerf in waste. Keep blade straight. Extend index finger along handle to keep saw near cut line.

To rip with circular saw, run baseplate against 2 x 4 straightedge clamped to work. (If clamped on waste side, saw could be pulled away from straightedge, making work smaller than measured.) Guide narrower cuts using saw's adjustable rip fence.

Wedge

Ripping accurately on table saw depends on fence being parallel to blade. To check, measure between blade and fence at both front and rear of blade (inset). To keep hands away from blade, use feather board as a brace to control work and a push stick to move it.

Splitter

Push stick

Feather board

Miter cuts on table saw. For safety and accuracy, screw auxiliary fence, made from straight piece of hardwood or plywood, to miter gauge; sand-paper glued to fence will prevent wood from shifting as you slide it into blade.

Auxiliary fence

> ◄ **SAFE PRACTICES** ►

General rules
▷ Let saw reach full speed before cutting; keep work clear of blade until you are ready to cut.
▷ Keep locks and clamps tight. Support work firmly.

Table saw
▷ Make sure guard and splitter, which holds cut stock open after cut, are in place and properly adjusted. Set blade to protrude ⅛ in. above work.
▷ Use a push stick when ripping stock less than 3 in. wide. Clamp a feather board behind saw blade and brace it from the side.
▷ Keep widest part of board between blade and fence. Hold on to work until completely clear of blade. If work is narrow, use a push stick.
▷ Hold stock against fence or miter gauge. Never cut freehand.
▷ To guard against kickback, never stand in area directly behind saw blade and fence.
▷ Make deep cuts in two or more passes; adjust blade each time.

Circular saw
▷ Clamp work firmly so it won't shift. Make sure the blade is sharp and clean.
▷ Never remove or wedge up the retractable blade guard.
▷ Support waste for a long cut.
▷ Stand to one side of the saw, out of the way of kickback.
▷ Stand with weight firmly on both feet; don't reach too far with the saw. Don't let saw drop at end.
▷ Always adjust the blade to the height needed for a particular job. Before adjusting, unplug the saw. (More safety tips, pp.12–13.)

Two types of hand tools shape wood: cutting and scraping. Cutting tools (chisels, drawknives, planes, and spokeshaves) carve the wood, leaving a smooth surface. And because they tear out end grain, they are most efficiently used to work along the grain of straight-grained woods. Scraping tools (files, rasps, and Surform tools) pull the fibers off wood rather than cut them, leaving a fuzzy surface. Use them in any direction, regardless of grain.

Precise planing depends on a keen blade, a flat sole, and correct adjustment. Set the plane throat according to the work: with the opening widest on a jack plane, medium on a jointer plane, and narrow on a smoothing plane. In addition, you may have to file smooth the chip breaker, which keeps the blade from tearing the wood, to make it fit snugly to the plane blade. Move the chip breaker about 1/32 inch away from the blade edge—set it closer for fine work, farther away for rough.

Because taking too thick an initial cut can jam the blade in the wood, adjust the plane for a fine shaving and test the cut; then gradually increase the shaving thickness. For the smoothest surface, finish planing with progres-sively finer cuts. To prevent end grain from chipping, support it by clamping or gluing a piece of scrap wood to the work before you begin planing, or plane end grain from the ends of the wood toward the middle.

Although it's sometimes necessary to work directly across the grain, chisels are best used along the grain, so that the blade doesn't catch or split off hunks of wood. When chiseling a groove, use a chisel that is slightly narrower, or it will chip the groove sides. Control the depth of the cut by working with the chisel's bevel down; raise the handle to go deeper, lower it to cut parallel to the surface. Make a stop cut across the grain to prevent splitting of the grain. For safety, secure the work so it can't move, and always keep your hands behind the cutting edge. Never cut toward yourself.

Drawknives and spokeshaves are useful for curved work. A drawknife resembles a chisel in that it can remove both large and small amounts of wood depending on how you manipulate it. A spokeshave is closer to a plane, with its blade enclosed by a sole. Choose cylindrical handles for an easy grip and ball-shaped handles for carving wood.

Handles level with the blade allow control of heavy cuts, bent handles offer a natural hand position, and dropped handles are good for precise work. When drawknifing, keep both hands on the handles. For safety and accuracy, keep your body balanced as you pull the blade toward you, so you can stop cutting at any moment if the grain splits. Store all cutting tools on a rack—leaving them lying on a work surface is asking for an accident.

Files, rasps, and Surform tools are primarily used to rapidly shape curved work. All cut on the push stroke and leave surfaces that must be smoothed with a plane, cabinet scraper, or sandpaper. For greatest versatility, choose a half-round tool. Work a rasp or file diagonally, with one hand pushing the handle while the heel of the other hand guides the tool toe. A Surform, which is useful for rounding off square corners, is worked the same way, but because it's shaped like a plane, it's easier to hold. The teeth of files and rasps clog; clean them often with a special brush called a *file card*, pulling it in the direction of the file's lines or teeth. To clean a Surform, you must pull the shavings out.

Using a plane

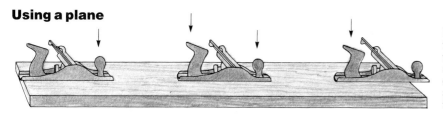

Begin a pass with pressure on the plane's toe, equalize pressure in mid pass, and end with pressure on the heel. Keep the plane sole flat on the wood. Supplement the force of your arms with back and shoulder power, and shift your weight from rear foot to front foot as you finish each stroke.

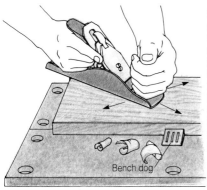

Plane diagonally across wide board with overlapping strokes; this avoids tearing the grain. Stretch your rear index finger along blade edge for extra control. Finish planing along the grain, with blade set to take a fine shaving.

Bench dog

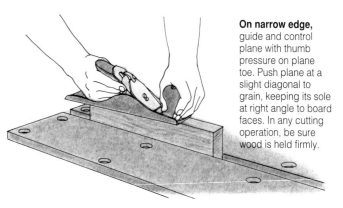

On narrow edge, guide and control plane with thumb pressure on plane toe. Push plane at a slight diagonal to grain, keeping its sole at right angle to board faces. In any cutting operation, be sure wood is held firmly.

Using a chisel

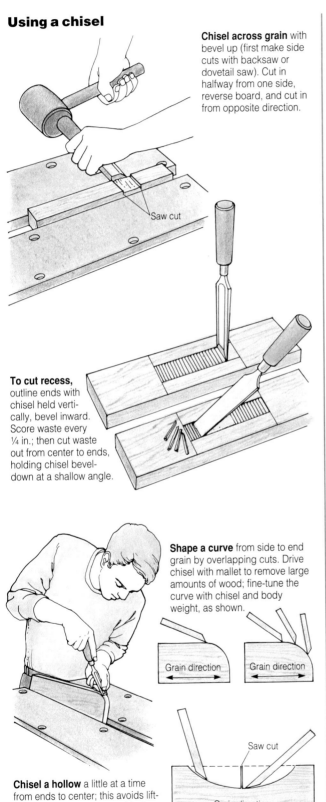

Chisel across grain with bevel up (first make side cuts with backsaw or dovetail saw). Cut in halfway from one side, reverse board, and cut in from opposite direction.

Saw cut

To cut recess, outline ends with chisel held vertically, bevel inward. Score waste every ¼ in.; then cut waste out from center to ends, holding chisel bevel-down at a shallow angle.

Shape a curve from side to end grain by overlapping cuts. Drive chisel with mallet to remove large amounts of wood; fine-tune the curve with chisel and body weight, as shown.

Grain direction

Grain direction

Saw cut

Grain direction

Chisel a hollow a little at a time from ends to center; this avoids lifting the grain. Saw center of hollow to desired depth beforehand.

Using a saber saw

Cut curves in thin stock (under 1 in. thick). Use narrow blades for sharp radii, wider blades for flowing curves. Hold saw with leading edge of baseplate on edge of wood, turn on the motor, and move blade into the work. Keep cutting pressure steady.

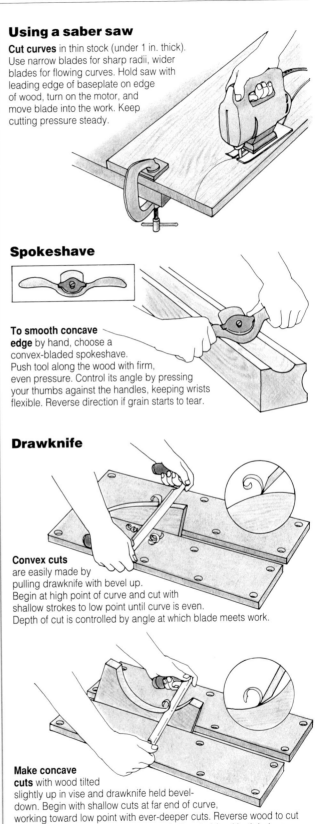

Spokeshave

To smooth concave edge by hand, choose a convex-bladed spokeshave. Push tool along the wood with firm, even pressure. Control its angle by pressing your thumbs against the handles, keeping wrists flexible. Reverse direction if grain starts to tear.

Drawknife

Convex cuts are easily made by pulling drawknife with bevel up. Begin at high point of curve and cut with shallow strokes to low point until curve is even. Depth of cut is controlled by angle at which blade meets work.

Make concave cuts with wood tilted slightly up in vise and drawknife held bevel-down. Begin with shallow cuts at far end of curve, working toward low point with ever-deeper cuts. Reverse wood to cut other half. Take shallow cuts at curve bottom to blend both halves.

SHAPING WOOD ON A LATHE

In spindle turning (center work), the wood, held between the headstock and tailstock of a lathe, is shaped into chair or table legs, stair balusters, and other cylindrical objects. Knot-free straight-grained hardwood with fine to medium texture is easiest to turn; coarse-textured wood may splinter. Softwood is usable, but it's hard to turn crisp details. Wood may be seasoned or wet (green), but green wood may split or shrink unevenly as it dries. Large or very thin pieces take more skill to turn; start with a blank 2 to 3 inches square.

To set up, check that the cup center of the tailstock is tight to the wood, but not so tight that the wood doesn't turn freely. Adjust the tool-rest position so the scraping tool will be at the top edge of the wood's centerline (raise it a bit higher for a cutting tool) and close to the wood (without hitting it). Move the tool rest inward as you reduce the wood's diameter.

Caution: Wear a face shield, and turn off the lathe before you adjust the tool rest or measure your progress.

Scraping tools—round-nose scrapers and diamond-points—are easier for beginners to handle. These tools can carve many shapes, but they leave a rough surface that must be sanded. Experienced turners cut or slice work with cutting tools: gouges, skew chisels, and parting tools. Cutting tools shave the work, leaving a clean finish that needs little or no sanding. All tools must be sharp (pp.198–199).

First, with the lathe running at slow speed, rough out or remove corners of the blank in small sections; as the wood becomes round, increase the speed. Begin the first section 1 inch from one end, and make a series of passes from alternating directions. To avoid splits when starting the next section, move your tool toward the turned section. Rough

Mounting the wood

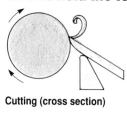

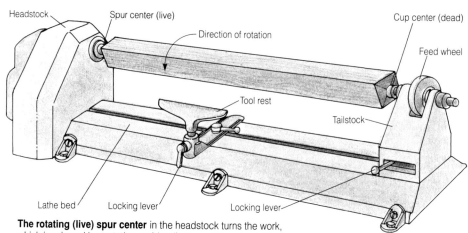

Preparing the blank. Draw two diagonal lines on each end of stock to find exact center. With handsaw on headstock end, score lines; drive spur center into saw cuts. Mark center of X with awl on tailstock end (inset). If stock is more than 2 in. square, plane or saw off each corner so blank is more octagonal.

The rotating (live) spur center in the headstock turns the work, which is gripped by a stationary (dead) cup center in the tailstock. Use lubricant on the wood at the dead cup center end. Begin roughing with the lathe running slowly; smooth rounded work at faster speed; and refine shapes at fastest speed.

How to hold the tool

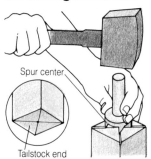

Cutting (cross section)

Cutting (side view)

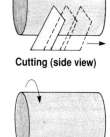

Scraping (cross section)

Scraping (top view)

To cut a shape, rub bevel of skew chisel on wood, then lift handle to angle bottom half of cutting edge into wood; move in direction of work.

To scrape, hold round-nose tool level to floor (or slightly down) and flat on rest, ease edge into work, and scrape lightly along the blank.

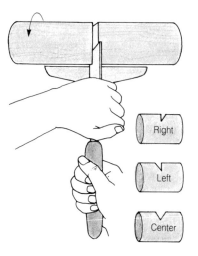

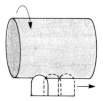

V-cutting. Score centerline of V-cut with point of skew. Then, holding tool 90° to the work, cut V-bottom with heel of skew cutting edge. To make a right or left V-shape (keeping one side of V at 90°), cut right or left side of centerline at 45° or desired angle with bevel edge of skew. For centered V-cut, cut each side to bottom, widening the shape as necessary.

out the end sections with repeated passes moving from the ends toward the middle. To scrape, move a round-nose scraper parallel to the ground along the tool rest. To cut, place the center edge of a square-end gouge against the revolving wood; then roll it slightly in the direction of travel with your lower hand and move it along the rest with your upper hand. To avoid catches, grasp the tool firmly and aim for gentle, steady pressure—never force it into the wood.

To sand your work as it rotates on the lathe, remove the tool rest and press a small pad of sandpaper (backed with a scrap of leather to protect you from heat buildup) against the work, or hold both ends of a sandpaper strip under (not over) it. Start with 180- to 220-grit abrasive on smooth work, 80-grit on rough. Remove work from the lathe with a dovetail saw or parting tool held 90° to the rotating work.

From rough to final shape

Grip gouge overhand to begin rounding. Cup fingers to steady tool; brace handle against body.

Finish truing diameter with round-nose scraper held underhand and parallel to floor.

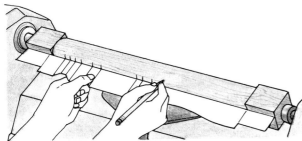

To lay out a design, hold uncut edge of hardboard template against cylinder; mark lines where cuts will be made (shown). Next, hold pencil on rest, its point on marks; hand-rotate wood to sketch lines on cylinder.

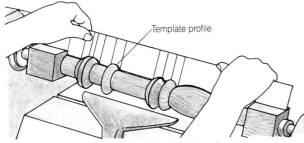

Template profile

Check work against template profile. Stop lathe often to compare your work with a cut profile of your design. For small jobs, measure diameters with outside calipers.

Turned shapes

Spur center

Square shoulder. Score shoulder line with point of skew. With lower half of edge (but not heel), cut away wood leading to shoulder. Then smooth vertical wall of shoulder. Repeat until shoulder cut is correct depth.

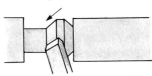

Bead. Make V-cut (facing page) on both sides of bead. Round one side of bead by rolling skew downhill from bead center toward V-cut in one smooth, flowing motion. End with blade edge vertical. Repeat rounding motion on other side.

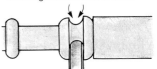

Cove. Start cut with gouge rolled on side. Raise handle to engage wood, and roll tool, rubbing bevel on wood, through cut from a shoulder to cove center. At end of cut, gouge top faces up. Cut in from other shoulder.

Urn shape. Beginning at key wide and narrow diameters, rough out shape with skew to within 1/16 in. of final size. Roll skew from high to low points. Cut small concave shapes with gouge, similar to motion for coves.

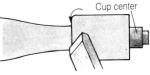

Cup center

Round shoulder. Start cut at highest point of shoulder, engage edge of skew near heel, and roll skew downhill so heel drops into valley. Finish with blade vertical.

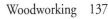

TURNING HOLLOW SHAPES ON A FACEPLATE

In faceplate work, a block of wood, mounted first on a faceplate and then screwed onto the headstock, can be sculpted, as for a bowl. You remove wood across and along its grain. It's best to use finely textured hardwoods because they produce smoother turnings than softwoods and coarse-grained hardwoods, which tear out. Irregular grain patterns show well, but you should avoid wood with knots or splits. If you are just learning, work on blocks that are 6 to 8 inches in diameter and 2 inches thick. Use scraping tools; round-nose and diamond-point scrapers are easier to handle than gouges and chisels and are less likely to mar or catch in the wood.

Before mounting a blank on the lathe, true the base and round off the edges—square corners are dangerous. If a backer is needed, make it from hardwood; softwood and plywood won't hold the screws. Wood up to 12 inches in diameter and 2 inches thick can be mounted to the backer with hot glue from a glue gun. Trace the outline of the backer (to which a faceplate has been screwed) onto the blank; then, working quickly, run a bead of glue around the edge of the backer and inside the matching line on the blank. Hold the pieces together for a minute, then mount the work.

To turn a bowl in one mounting, shape the exterior first. True the outer edge with the lathe running slowly. Then change to medium speed and begin shaping. During the final shaping, switch to higher speed. Keep the tool flat on the rest, and work with a light touch. Before hollowing the interior, measure the stock's thickness and determine the desired bowl depth. (Never cut below ¼ inch thickness.) To sand, remove the tool rest and use 60-, 80-, 120-, and finally 180- or 220-grit paper. To sand large-diameter work, run the lathe at slow speed; for small-diameter work, run it at faster speed. Separate the work and sand the glue off the foot. If desired, shape a base or foot with a chisel.

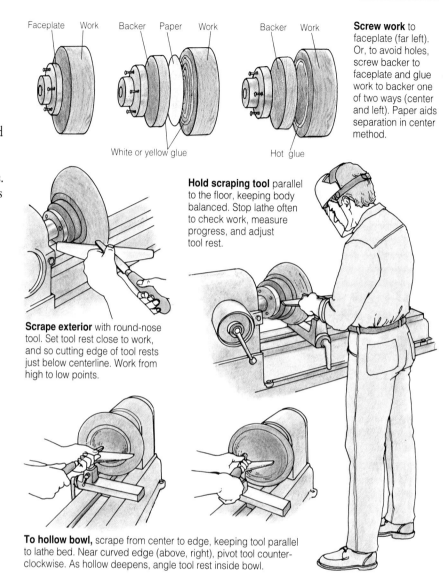

Faceplate   Work   Backer   Paper   Work   Backer   Work

White or yellow glue   Hot glue

Screw work to faceplate (far left). Or, to avoid holes, screw backer to faceplate and glue work to backer one of two ways (center and left). Paper aids separation in center method.

Scrape exterior with round-nose tool. Set tool rest close to work, and so cutting edge of tool rests just below centerline. Work from high to low points.

Hold scraping tool parallel to the floor, keeping body balanced. Stop lathe often to check work, measure progress, and adjust tool rest.

To hollow bowl, scrape from center to edge, keeping tool parallel to lathe bed. Near curved edge (above, right), pivot tool counter-clockwise. As hollow deepens, angle tool rest inside bowl.

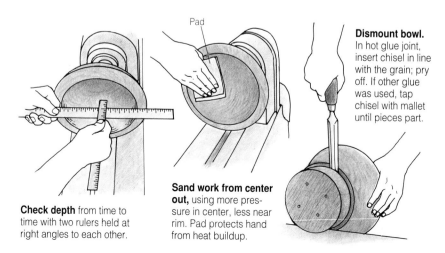

Pad

Check depth from time to time with two rulers held at right angles to each other.

Sand work from center out, using more pressure in center, less near rim. Pad protects hand from heat buildup.

Dismount bowl. In hot glue joint, insert chisel in line with the grain; pry off. If other glue was used, tap chisel with mallet until pieces part.

JOINTS: AN INTRODUCTION

A woodworking project is only as strong as the joints used to build it. Hundreds of joints have been developed, most derived from six groups (see chart). The dovetail, for example, can be made with visible pins and tails (through dovetail) or varied so the pins and tails are half visible (half blind) or fully hidden (blind). Tenons are often mitered when they meet in a mortise, as in a table leg, or are wedged for strength.

How do you pick the best joint for the job? Strength is a major consideration, but appearance, your expertise, and the tools you own are important factors as well. Cutting a joint without the right tools and skills is risky—loose-fitting joints will have a poor glue bond; overtight joints will have to be forced together, which can damage the wood fibers and split one of the pieces of the joint. As a rule, select the least complex joint that will work for the project.

The strength of a joint depends on the amount of gluing surface the joint provides and on whether that surface is long grain (parallel to the wood fibers) or end grain (across the fibers). Long grain holds the glue on the surface for a strong bond; end grain absorbs it, resulting in poor adhesion. The strongest joints interlock, such as dovetail pins and tails, or have maximum long-grain to long-grain gluing surfaces and minimum end-grain surfaces, such as edge joints. Joints that mate end-grain surfaces, such as butt joints, usually are reinforced with nails, screws, splines, or wooden biscuits. These devices can be used to reinforce other joints as well.

Common joints

Type		Tools to use	Uses	Strength	Ease of making
Butt and edge	Butt / Edge	Backsaw or crosscut saw; table, circular, or radial arm saw. Finish edge joints with plane or jointer	Butt: rough carpentry	Butt: weak; reinforce with fasteners	Butt: very easy
			Edge: large surfaces	Edge: strong	Edge: cuts must be accurate, edges straight and smooth
Face and edge miters	Edge miter / Face miter	Miter box, backsaw, and plane; power miter saw; table saw	Frames and moldings	Weak; strengthen with dowels, keys, or splines	Difficult to cut accurately with hand tools; easier with power saw
Lap	Cross lap / End lap	Backsaw and chisel; router; radial arm saw; table saw with dado head	Frames, frame-and-panel doors, and interlocking grid construction	Fairly strong	Easy
Interlocking joints: dovetail, finger	Dovetail	Bow saw or dovetail saw and chisel; router with template; table saw	Drawers, cabinets, and boxes	Extremely strong when cut by hand; strong when cut by machine	Difficult with hand tools; easier with power tools
Grooved joints: rabbet, dado, rabbet-and-dado, tongue-and-groove	Double rabbet / Rabbet / Dado	Backsaw and chisel; router; radial arm saw; table saw with dado head	Drawers, cabinets, boxes, and shelves	Rabbet: fairly strong	Rabbet: fairly easy
				Dado: weak	Dado: easy
				Tongue-and-groove: strong	Tongue-and-groove: fairly easy
Mortise-and-tenon	Through tenon / Through mortise / Bridle or slip joint	Hand drill and chisel; router; drill press; table saw	Frames and legs for tables and chairs, frame-and-panel cabinets	Strong	Fairly difficult with hand tools; easier with power tools

Although wide surfaces in cabinetry are often veneer-covered plywood, some fine table- or desktop projects may call for solid boards joined edge to edge. Because edge joints have plenty of gluing surface and no porous end grain, they may be assembled with glue alone. To help align the boards, you may use dowels, biscuits, or splines. For a precise joint—critical to strength—the mating edges must be smooth, straight, and squared to the faces. Before gluing, dry-clamp the assembly to locate any gaps. Sight along the joints with a lamp shining behind the work; mark high spots (where no light shows through), plane them, and recheck.

When gluing, tighten the clamps enough so that the glue oozes beads, but don't overtighten—this will squeeze out too much glue. To keep excess glue from adhering to the straightedges or reacting with the metal clamps, put a layer of wax paper or plastic wrap wherever they touch.

Butt and miter joints, even when precisely cut, are inherently weak because of the minimal gluing surface and the presence of end grain, which doesn't accept glue well. These joints need reinforcement with mechanical fasteners (nails or screws), dowels, wooden biscuits, keys, or splines, or glue blocks (blocks glued and nailed or screwed to the inside corners of joints). Although visible nails and screws are fine on utility cabinets and shelves, refined work calls for countersunk or counterbored screws and filled nail holes (p.150).

Dowels can be either blind (hidden) or through (ends exposed). A doweling jig aids in drilling perfectly aligned holes to the proper depth, or you can use a homemade guide.

Oval-shaped biscuits are an easy alternative. To install them, you need a machine known as a biscuit, or plate, joiner. Biscuits, made from textured compressed wood, absorb the glue and expand, creating a very strong joint. They come in three sizes—choose the largest that will work with your stock. Biscuits are not recommended for joining warped or bowed plywood panels; instead use dowels or splines.

Caution: Never use a biscuit joiner freehand. Clamp the work, and butt the machine against the work or a stop block. Watch for kickback and keep your fingers away. (For more on miter joints, see pp.133, 149, and 158–159.)

Blind-dowel butt joint

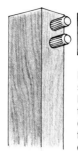

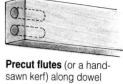

Precut flutes (or a hand-sawn kerf) along dowel length allow excess glue to escape. Drill holes 1/16 in. deeper than dowel to contain excess glue. Chamfer ends for easy driving.

Preassemble frame. Mark dowel positions on faces. Square marks to mating surfaces.

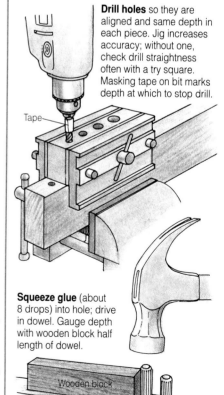

Drill holes so they are aligned and same depth in each piece. Jig increases accuracy; without one, check drill straightness often with a try square. Masking tape on bit marks depth at which to stop drill.

Tape

Squeeze glue (about 8 drops) into hole; drive in dowel. Gauge depth with wooden block half length of dowel.

Wooden block

Making an edge joint

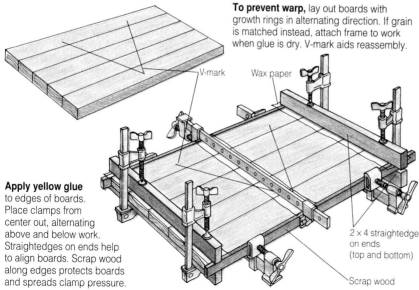

To prevent warp, lay out boards with growth rings in alternating direction. If grain is matched instead, attach frame to work when glue is dry. V-mark aids reassembly.

V-mark

Wax paper

Apply yellow glue to edges of boards. Place clamps from center out, alternating above and below work. Straightedges on ends help to align boards. Scrap wood along edges protects boards and spreads clamp pressure.

2 x 4 straightedge on ends (top and bottom)

Scrap wood

Making biscuit joints

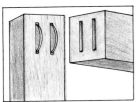
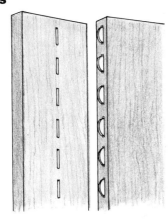

Wood biscuits can substitute for nails, screws, or dowels in butt joints (right). In frame work (above), biscuits can be used instead of mortise-and-tenon joints (though they're not as strong) or splines. Wood must be wider than 1⅞ in., the length of smallest biscuit slot.

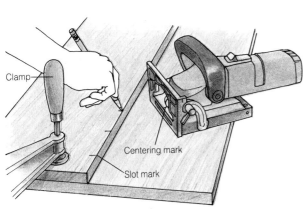

To measure and mark, clamp mating boards together. Mark slots for biscuits in both pieces, using centering mark on biscuit joiner. In butt joints, the closer the slots, the stronger the joint (strengthen frame construction by using two biscuits equally spaced on center).

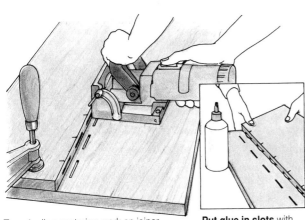

To cut, align centering mark on joiner base with pencil mark, and plunge in the blade; when it springs back, go to next mark. For slots in bottom piece, position joiner vertically with its base against edge of mating board.

Put glue in slots with split-nozzle applicator or thin wood scrap; insert biscuits. Clamp joint until biscuits swell from glue moisture, at least 10 min.

Strengthening miter joints

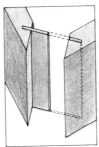

Edge miter joint (p.159) is stronger with spline placed closer to inner corner. Spline is cut from plywood or hardwood scrap.

To cut spline slots, tilt the table saw blade 45°. Hold the work securely against the miter gauge with one hand; press it against rip fence with the other.

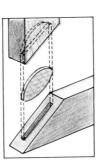

Face miter has biscuit located at 90° angle to miter cut.

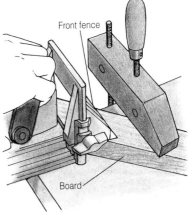

To cut slot in end grain, place biscuit joiner against miter cut on board, and lock front fence into place. Clamp the work securely so that it won't shift.

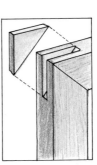

Miter key (triangle of wood) is one-third thickness of joint but may be as thin as ³⁄₃₂ in.

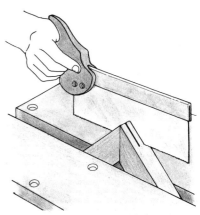

After glued miter joint has dried, cut two parallel slots into corner with dovetail saw. Chisel out waste and test-fit key. Apply glue to key and tap in with hammer. Let dry, saw key flush, and plane smooth.

LAP JOINTS

Easy to cut but somewhat weak, lap joints connect two boards at an angle, usually at 90°. *End lap joints,* at the ends of boards, are made with wide, flat cuts; *cross lap joints,* formed by two notches, join boards at any point between the ends. A third type, called a *middle lap,* has an end lap and an intersecting cross lap and forms a T-shape. Middle laps that have to endure tensile (pulling) stress are best dovetailed.

You can make a lap joint with boards of equal or of unequal thickness. With equally thick boards, cut half their thickness; otherwise, cut no more than half the thickness of the thinner piece. Because the grains of the pieces cross, keep the lap width under 4 inches, or the wood may split when it shrinks and swells as its moisture content changes. Mark the cutting lines on the board edges with a square or

a marking gauge. Mark the shoulders of the dovetail lap with a square; use a marking gauge on the cheek. With a T-bevel, mark the dovetail angle between 8° and 12° (a 1:5 to 1:8 ratio of flare to length).

Although end laps are most easily cut with a table saw equipped with a dado head, you can make repeated cuts with a standard blade. Or use hand tools: after marking the joint on the wood, saw the shoulder (cross-grain cut) with a dovetail saw; then remove the waste by turning the piece on end and sawing along the grain with the same saw. To cut accurate cross laps, first score the shoulder lines on the waste side with a wide chisel held vertically. Then, with the chisel held bevel-up at an angle, remove a sliver on the waste side of the line to form a groove in which to start the saw cut.

End lap joint

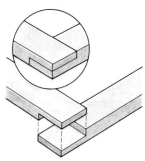

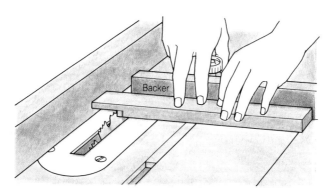

Set height of standard blade using mark on board edge as reference. Screw backer to miter gauge to prevent tearout as blade exits. Fine-tune depth of cut on scrap. Start at end and work toward shoulder, overlapping passes. Pare rough cut with chisel. You can also use a dado head (p.144), or make an initial shoulder cut with a standard blade, then clamp work in tenoning jig (p.147) and remove waste.

Cross lap joint

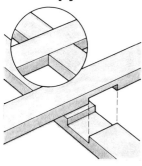

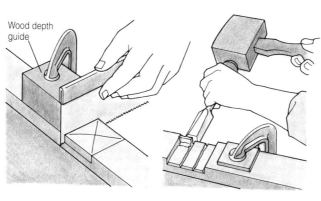

For straight cut when cutting sides of notch, press saw against wood depth guide, which should be just thick enough so that the rib atop the saw hits the guide when cut is right depth. Make a cut at each side, then score the waste at 1-in. intervals with dovetail saw. Remove waste with a mallet and chisel, held bevel-up, and working from edges toward center. Trim corners with chisel held bevel-down.

Dovetail lap joint

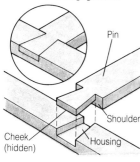

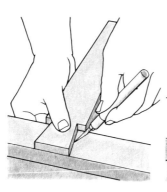

Mark pin's shoulders, cheek, and dovetail angle. Saw dovetail shoulders, cheek, and angle, in that order, with dovetail saw. For an accurate fit, use the finished dovetail as the template to mark the housing on mating piece. Saw and chisel the housing as you did for the cross lap joint.

DOVETAILS WITH A TEMPLATE

These decorative joints are fairly easy to cut with a router and a dovetail fixture. The fixture holds a template and has bar clamps and stop screws to hold both sides of the joint in proper alignment. The router, fitted with a dovetail bit and a guide bushing, follows the template, cutting the tails and the sockets simultaneously. A $\frac{9}{16}$-inch diameter bushing guides a $\frac{1}{2}$-inch bit; a $\frac{5}{16}$-inch bushing, a $\frac{1}{4}$-inch bit.

Make a few test cuts in scrap wood of the same width and thickness as the workpieces. Place each board in the fixture so it butts against its stop screw and is flush with the mating piece (see illustration below). Make the initial shoulder cut in the tail board, guiding the bit along the tips of the template fingers. Advance the router from left to right with slow, steady pressure. Next, guide the bit in and out of the template's fingers, cutting deep into the recesses of the template. Make a second pass from right to left. Test-fit the joint. If the fit is loose, increase the bit's depth of cut. If it's too tight, decrease the depth of cut. If the tails don't fit all the way into the sockets, move the template back slightly. If the tails are too deep in the sockets, slide the template forward.

Once the test joint fits perfectly, you're ready to cut the actual workpieces. If you are making a drawer or box, mark a

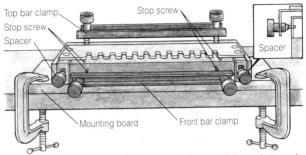

Dovetail fixture. Bar clamps hold two workpieces at right angle to each other. Stop screws establish the proper offset. Spacers hold template; adjust them up and down, forward and back, to correct depth of cut.

letter on the inside surface of all four pieces; mark each bottom edge. Cut the grooves for the bottom panel before routing the dovetails. When clamping the pieces in the fixture, always place the boards with the same edge (either bottom or top) butted against the stop screws, lettered surface facing out. Note that two joints must be cut on the right side of the fixture and two on the left side (see chart). The socket pieces (front part A and back part C) are always clamped to the top of the fixture, the tail pieces (side pieces B and D) to the front.

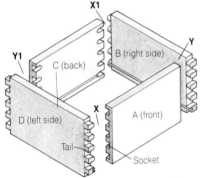

Mark inside surfaces near bottom edge. Cut grooves for bottom piece before routing X- and Y-joints. Front and back pieces have blind dovetail sockets; sides have through tails.

Setting up the workpieces

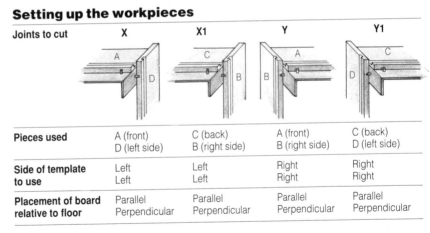

Joints to cut	X	X1	Y	Y1
Pieces used	A (front) D (left side)	C (back) B (right side)	A (front) B (right side)	C (back) D (left side)
Side of template to use	Left Left	Left Left	Right Right	Right Right
Placement of board relative to floor	Parallel Perpendicular	Parallel Perpendicular	Parallel Perpendicular	Parallel Perpendicular

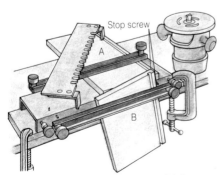

Set up joint Y. Clamp side B as a guide for front piece A. Butt A against side B and top right stop screw. Reposition B flush with top edge of A and bottom right stop screw.

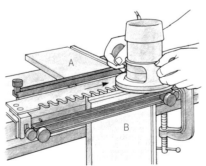

Make the first pass from left to right across tips of template's fingers. This shallow groove helps prevent splintering when the pins and sockets are cut.

Rout tails and sockets, advancing the router from left to right. Keep bushing that guides bit in contact with template at all times. Make another final pass from right to left.

A channel cut across the grain, called a *dado,* and an L-shaped cut along the edge or end of a board, called a *rabbet,* allow you to join wide boards at right angles. The mating piece fits into the dado or rabbet. Rabbeting both pieces, called a *double rabbet,* adds a little more shoulder strength. When combined as a *rabbet-and-dado* joint, the two lock together to resist twisting. The depth of a dado is typically one-third the thickness of the cut board, while a rabbet's depth is between one-half and three-fourths the thickness of the board. When a dado is a corner joint, place the dado as far from the end of the board as possible (see facing page). Assemble all four types with glue and nails or screws. Strengthen the joint, if needed, by fastening a hardwood cleat at each end of the entering board. Glue and screw the cleats to the entering pieces and to the vertical sides or back of the support pieces.

Dadoes can be made by hand with a router plane or with a backsaw and chisel. Or you can use a router with a straight bit or a table saw equipped with a standard blade or a dado head. A dado head consists of two outer blades and four inner cutters, known as *chippers;* it cuts a dado in one pass, whereas a standard blade takes several passes.

To set up a dado head, stack as many chippers as needed between the two blades to obtain the desired width of cut. Replace the saw's narrow throat plate—the slotted plate that frames the blade—with a dado-head throat plate, available from the saw manufacturer, or make one as follows from

Through dado joint

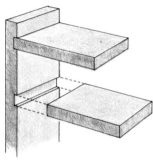

Stopped dado joint

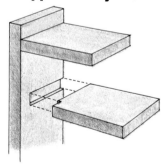

Dovetail dado

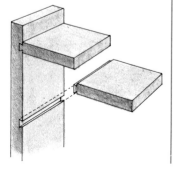

Cutting dadoes on a table saw

Through dado. Mark dado width on work (inset). Add extension to miter gauge. Adjust rip fence so work is desired distance from assembled dado head. Turn on saw; push miter gauge forward.

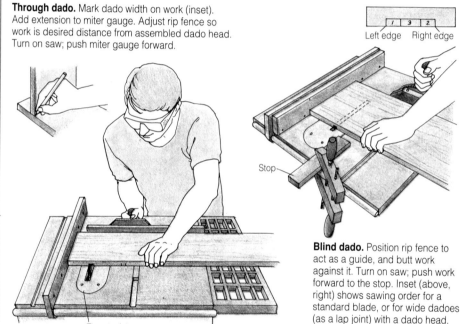

Left edge   Right edge

Stop

Throat plate

Blind dado. Position rip fence to act as a guide, and butt work against it. Turn on saw; push work forward to the stop. Inset (above, right) shows sawing order for a standard blade, or for wide dadoes (as a lap joint) with a dado head.

Dovetail dadoes with a router

Cutting dado. Guide router against T-square. Remove most of waste with straight bit equal in size to narrowest part of correct dovetail bit. Install dovetail bit; finish dado in one pass.

T-square

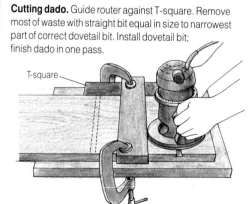

Fence

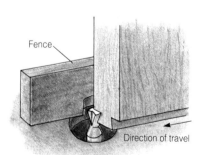

Direction of travel

Mating dovetail. Mount router in table. Make a wood fence with slot for dovetail bit. Clamp fence to router table. Practice on scrap: Start router, push stock against fence, and move it from right to left. Reverse stock and repeat.

½-inch plywood: Remove the standard plate and install the dado head. Cut a plywood blank to match the outline of the standard plate. Hold the plywood blank on the saw table by placing a board over the blank and clamping it to the front and back edges of the table saw. Be sure that the clamped board is positioned on one side of the blank, not where the dado head will come through. Start the motor, and slowly raise the dado head to cut an opening.

Caution: Never use the chippers by themselves without the outer blades.

Test-cut all dadoes in scrap wood. To prevent the saw blade, dado head, or router bit from splintering the workpiece as it exits the cut, back the edge with scrap wood. Cut routed dadoes in two or three passes by increasing the depth of cut with each pass. This reduces vibration and chatter of the router bit and produces a cleaner cut. A blind, or stopped, dado stops short of the board's edge and is hidden from view when assembled. To cut a stopped dado with a router, clamp a stop block to the work and guide the router along the straightedge. If you are using a table saw to cut a stopped dado, guide the work to a stop block that is clamped to the table or to the fence. Square the stopped corners with a chisel. Notch the front corners of the entering piece to fit the stopped end of the dado.

Dovetail, or sliding, dadoes are strong, decorative interlocking joints. This dado, with its angled sides, can be cut with a backsaw or a router fitted with a dovetail bit. When routing a dovetail dado, make the initial cuts with a straight bit. On the last pass, cut the angled shape with a dovetail bit. To rout the mating dovetail ends of the shelves, mount the router in a router table or use a router jig. Practice on scrap wood, test-fit the board, and readjust the bit height or fence.

Rabbet joints can be cut with a router or with a table saw and a dado head. (If you prefer hand tools, use a rabbeting plane or a backsaw and chisel.) Rout rabbets with either a straight bit or a piloted bit. With a straight bit, you must use either an edge guide or a straightedge to control the cut.

Rabbet joints

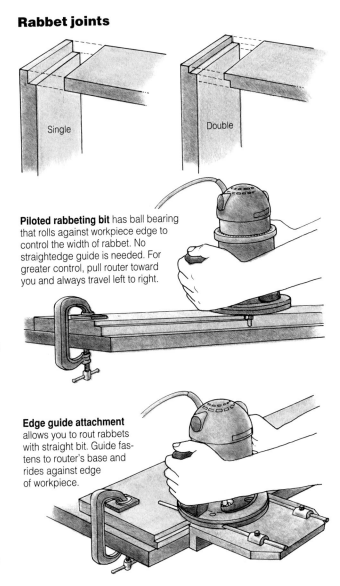

Single

Double

Piloted rabbeting bit has ball bearing that rolls against workpiece edge to control the width of rabbet. No straightedge guide is needed. For greater control, pull router toward you and always travel left to right.

Edge guide attachment allows you to rout rabbets with straight bit. Guide fastens to router's base and rides against edge of workpiece.

Rabbet-and-dado joints

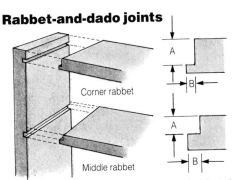

Corner rabbet

Middle rabbet

A

B

A

B

Corner rabbet's depth (A), is ¾ thickness of rabbeted board; width (B) is ¼ thickness of dadoed board. In a middle rabbet, A can equal ½ to ⅔ thickness of the rabbeted board, and B is ⅓ of dadoed board.

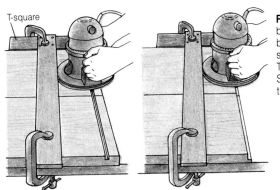

T-square

Rout multiple joints side by side. Clamp squared boards and T-square securely to work surface. Test cut on scrap first. Shoulder plane (below) trims rabbet if fit is too tight.

MORTISE-AND-TENON JOINT

Through mortise-and-tenon

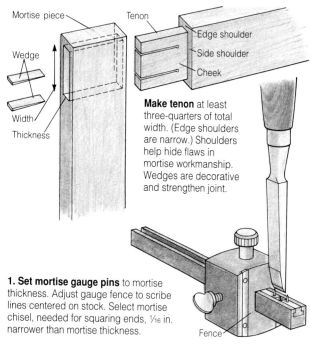

Mortise piece
Tenon
Edge shoulder
Side shoulder
Cheek
Wedge
Width
Thickness

Make tenon at least three-quarters of total width. (Edge shoulders are narrow.) Shoulders help hide flaws in mortise workmanship. Wedges are decorative and strengthen joint.

1. Set mortise gauge pins to mortise thickness. Adjust gauge fence to scribe lines centered on stock. Select mortise chisel, needed for squaring ends, 1/16 in. narrower than mortise thickness.

Fence

In these strong framework joints, the projecting piece, or tenon, should fit snugly into the opening, or mortise. A tight fit allows the large amount of long-grain glue surface on both pieces to adhere well. On wide stock, maximize the long-grain glue surface by spacing multiple mortise-and-tenons evenly across the board (facing page).

Mortise-and-tenon joints may be through or blind (hidden), and each kind can have one to four shoulders. Rounding the tenon profile with a file, a rasp, or a router makes a more decorative but slightly weaker through joint. On wide boards you can make multiple rounded joints by using a jig and a router.

The size of the stock determines the dimensions of the joint. On pieces with like thicknesses, the mortise and each side shoulder of the tenon usually equals one-third the thickness of the stock. A larger mortise piece (as in a table leg) can take a thicker tenon. The edge shoulders of a three- or four-shouldered tenon vary from a fraction of an inch to one-quarter the width of the tenon piece. When marking several mortise-and-tenon joints, always orient the mortise gauge fence against the equivalent stock face. If a piece is to have a tenon on both ends, calculate the distance between the two joints by measuring between the length lines (step 5).

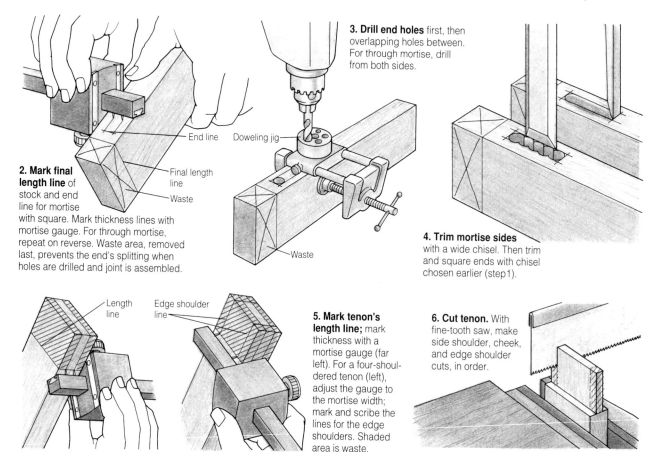

3. Drill end holes first, then overlapping holes between. For through mortise, drill from both sides.

End line
Doweling jig

2. Mark final length line of stock and end line for mortise with square. Mark thickness lines with mortise gauge. For through mortise, repeat on reverse. Waste area, removed last, prevents the end's splitting when holes are drilled and joint is assembled.

Final length line
Waste
Waste

4. Trim mortise sides with a wide chisel. Then trim and square ends with chisel chosen earlier (step1).

Length line
Edge shoulder line

5. Mark tenon's length line; mark thickness with a mortise gauge (far left). For a four-shouldered tenon (left), adjust the gauge to the mortise width; mark and scribe the lines for the edge shoulders. Shaded area is waste.

6. Cut tenon. With fine-tooth saw, make side shoulder, cheek, and edge shoulder cuts, in order.

First, cut the mortise. Set the mortise gauge pins and mark the thickness of the mortise. (Cut a blind mortise ¹⁄₁₆ inch deeper than the tenon length to allow for the glue.) Drill the mortise holes on a drill press, or use a doweling jig and a hand drill fitted with a twist bit (its diameter the same as the mortise thickness). Drill a through mortise from both sides to prevent tearout. Mortises can also be made with a plunge router (see illustration) or with a standard router and jig. For a standard router, clamp the mortise piece and jig to a workbench. Tilt the router; begin cutting slightly short of the end of the mortise; remove ⅛ to ¼ inch of stock on each pass. Cut the tenon to fit with a handsaw or power saw.

Wedges inserted into a through tenon (facing page) strengthen the joint. Before gluing, mark two cuts in the tenon's end, drill a ⅛-inch hole at the base of each cut to prevent splitting, and saw the cuts. Assemble the joint, and tap the wedges into the cuts with a mallet.

The number, width, and thickness of multiple mortise-and-tenons are determined by the size of the tenon piece. To find equal spacing between tenons, as well as the width of the two edge shoulders, measure the width of the tenon piece and decide the number and width of the tenons you want. Add the total tenon width and subtract it from the tenon piece width. Divide the remaining space by the number of tenons plus one. For example: four ¾-inch-wide tenons will be needed on a 5½-inch-wide board. Thus, $4 \times \frac{3}{4}$ inch = 3 inches; 5½ inches – 3 inches = 2½ inches; 2½ inches ÷ 5 = ½ inch between tenons.

Tools that speed the work

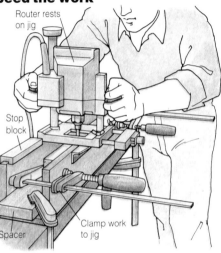

Use plunge router with a straight bit and homemade jig to cut mortise. Jig, a trough made of ¾-in. plywood and glue and screws, supports router base. Front and back stops on one side of jig set mortise width. Spacer blocks bring stock to top of jig. Make repeated passes, removing no more than ⅛ in. of stock per pass. Square rounded ends with a chisel.

Router rests on jig

Stop block

Spacer

Clamp work to jig

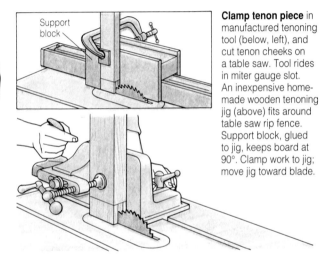

Support block

Clamp tenon piece in manufactured tenoning tool (below, left), and cut tenon cheeks on a table saw. Tool rides in miter gauge slot. An inexpensive homemade wooden tenoning jig (above) fits around table saw rip fence. Support block, glued to jig, keeps board at 90°. Clamp work to jig; move jig toward blade.

Multiple mortise-and-tenons

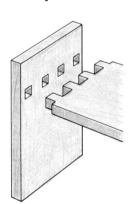

Tenon "fingers" fit into matching mortises in wide stock. Joint may be blind or through.

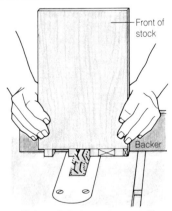

Front of stock

Backer

Cut waste between tenons with a dado head. Support work with backer and miter gauge. Align cuts visually. To prevent tearout, first scribe depth line on back of stock with knife.

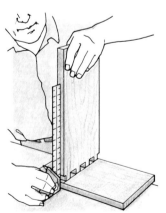

Position and mark mortises using a square and the tenon piece as a template. Scribe and mark waste areas with an X.

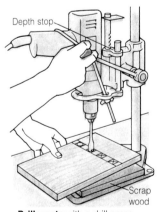

Depth stop

Scrap wood

Drill waste with a drill press and spur bit or brad point bit. Lock depth stop. Clean and square mortises with a chisel slightly narrower than mortise.

GLUING AND CLAMPING

When selecting a glue for a job, ask yourself these questions: What type of materials am I gluing; will the piece be indoors or outdoors; does the glue need to be water-resistant or water-proof; are the joints loose; how much stress will be placed on the glue and the joint? For a repair job, what glue was used before? Use the chart (below) and the container label to help you choose.

Whatever your choice, follow these basic rules: Apply the glue evenly and smoothly on both surfaces. If the end grain of wood is part of the joint, apply two coats; let the first dry before applying the second. Put the project together within the glue's assembly time (how long the glue can be worked and the pieces adjusted). Drying may take longer if a wood's moisture content is above 10 percent or air temperature is below 70°F (21°C). Always allow a way for excess glue to escape (for example, the bottom of a blind mortise is deeper than its tenon).

Caution: When using a toxic glue, follow safety precautions on the label carefully. Work in a well-ventilated area, and avoid getting glue in your eyes or on your skin. Keep glue well away from any open flame. When using epoxy or contact cement, extinguish pilot lights.

Before applying glue, dry-fit (test-assemble) all joints to make sure they fit properly. This allows you to make

Gluing

Apply glue to both pieces. Spread evenly with brush. You can spread white or yellow glue with your fingers.

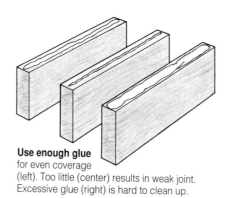

Use enough glue for even coverage (left). Too little (center) results in weak joint. Excessive glue (right) is hard to clean up.

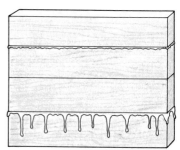

Glue line squeeze-out (top) shows strong joint. No excess (middle) means a weak joint; too much is messy (bottom).

A glossary of glues

Type of adhesive	Assembly time	Clamping time	Uses	Characteristics	Solvent
White glue (PVA, polyvinyl acetate)	7–10 min.	8 hr.	Indoor nonstress wood joints; paper, ceramics	Ready-to-use liquid; nonstaining, odorless, water-soluble; tends to "creep" with age; dries clear	Soap and warm water
Yellow glue (carpenter's, aliphatic resin)	7–10 min.	1 hr.	Indoor furniture and cabinets	Ready-to-use liquid; makes strong joints; spreads and sands easily; water-soluble; dries clear	Warm water
Resorcinol	20 min.	10 hr. at 70°F (21°C), longer if below 70°F (21°C)	Boat repair, outdoor furniture, laminating wood	Liquid mixed with powdered catalyst; waterproof; dries dark red	Cool water before hardening
Epoxy	Follow label instructions	5 min.–12 hr. (depending on type of epoxy)	Dissimilar materials (metal to glass); nonporous materials (china); wood	Liquids mixed in equal parts; water- and oilproof; fills holes; doesn't shrink; sands easily; dries clear or brown; toxic (follow cautions on label)	Acetone (in some nail polish removers)
Urea formaldehyde	20–30 min.	16–20 hr. at 70°F (21°C); 9–13 hr. at 75°F (24°C)	Indoor and outdoor furniture, cabinets, laminating, veneering	Powder mixed with water; water-resistant; fills poorly; dries light brown; won't cure below 70°F (21°C)	Soap and warm water before hardening
Casein glue	5–20 min.	2– 3 hr.	Indoor furniture	Powder mixed with water; good for oily wood (rosewood, teak); fills gaps; stains softwoods	Warm water
Hide glue	1 min. (when cool)	1 hr.	Indoor furniture; antique furniture repairs	Granules soaked in water and heated to 130°F (54°C) in double boiler; water-soluble; fills poorly; incompatible with white or yellow glues	Warm water

adjustments for a better fit, to decide on the number and type of clamps needed, and to establish the assembly sequence—gluing a piece in place too early can cause others to fit badly or not at all. For example, to assemble a bookcase with dadoed sides, place one side with the dadoes facing up. Next insert the shelves in the dadoes, check for fit, and adjust as needed. Then align the dadoes of the other side piece, and readjust if needed. Disassemble, noting the order. In the actual glue-up, follow the same sequence.

When clamping, work on a level surface such as a workbench or, for a large project, the floor. Unless your clamps have covers, their jaws should never touch the work. (Unprotected metal clamps may react with the glue and stain the piece.) Insert plastic wrap or wax paper between the jaws and the work. This prevents the pieces from adhering to the clamp or to the scrap wood used to spread the pressure.

When workpieces are clamped with the right amount of glue, a small bead of glue will be forced from the joint. Immediately wipe off this excess glue with the correct solvent. This is especially critical because wood stains and finishes will not penetrate dried glue. Clamping pressure should never be so tight that it forces out most of the glue (called starving the joint) or deforms the project.

Clamping

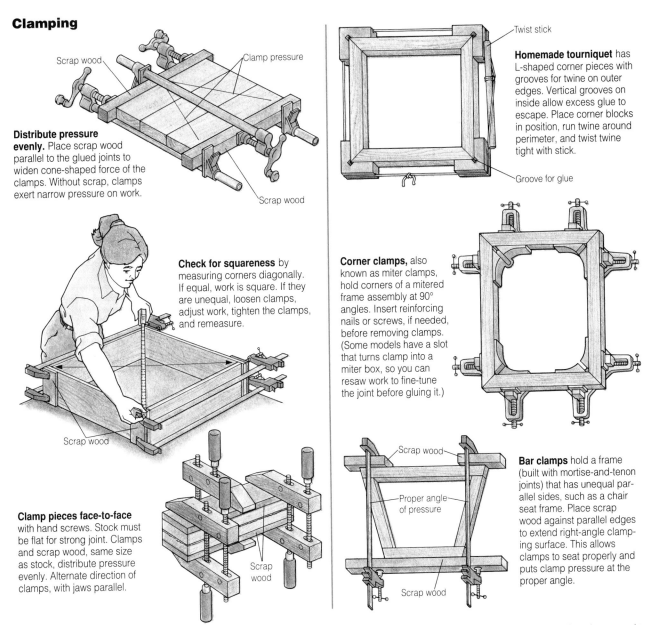

Distribute pressure evenly. Place scrap wood parallel to the glued joints to widen cone-shaped force of the clamps. Without scrap, clamps exert narrow pressure on work.

Scrap wood

Clamp pressure

Scrap wood

Check for squareness by measuring corners diagonally. If equal, work is square. If they are unequal, loosen clamps, adjust work, tighten the clamps, and remeasure.

Scrap wood

Clamp pieces face-to-face with hand screws. Stock must be flat for strong joint. Clamps and scrap wood, same size as stock, distribute pressure evenly. Alternate direction of clamps, with jaws parallel.

Scrap wood

Twist stick

Homemade tourniquet has L-shaped corner pieces with grooves for twine on outer edges. Vertical grooves on inside allow excess glue to escape. Place corner blocks in position, run twine around perimeter, and twist twine tight with stick.

Groove for glue

Corner clamps, also known as miter clamps, hold corners of a mitered frame assembly at 90° angles. Insert reinforcing nails or screws, if needed, before removing clamps. (Some models have a slot that turns clamp into a miter box, so you can resaw work to fine-tune the joint before gluing it.)

Scrap wood

Proper angle of pressure

Scrap wood

Bar clamps hold a frame (built with mortise-and-tenon joints) that has unequal parallel sides, such as a chair seat frame. Place scrap wood against parallel edges to extend right-angle clamping surface. This allows clamps to seat properly and puts clamp pressure at the proper angle.

FASTENING WITH NAILS, SCREWS, AND BOLTS

Holes for screws are usually perpendicular to the stock. A drill press does the job for you, provided its table is level; with a hand or electric drill, use a drill guide or a predrilled hardwood block clamped to the stock to keep the bit straight. When drilling at an angle, mark the starting point with a center punch and start the hole with a smaller bit to keep the final bit from drifting.

Pilot holes, drilled slightly narrower than the diameter of the threads, allow screws and bolts to enter straight and easily. Control the hole depth with a drill stop, a depth gauge, or a piece of tape wrapped around the bit. To prevent tearout on through holes, drill from both sides or drill into a scrap block clamped to the back of the stock.

Screws and bolt heads may be flush with a surface or they may be recessed; if desired, fill the recess with a plug or with wood filler.

Drive a screw with a screwdriver tip the same width as the screw's slot; one too wide gouges the stock, too narrow damages the screwhead. To drive a nail into hardwood, first drill a pilot hole slightly narrower and shorter than the nail. Strike the nail squarely; at the end of the blow, slide the hammer forward or backward to emphasize the level position of the hammer. This lessens the chance of bending the nail.

To remove a bent nail, use a claw hammer or a nail puller. Prevent marring the surface by placing a small piece of scrap wood or metal between the tool and the stock. Grab headless and finishing nails with end-cutting pliers and pull them straight out, wiggling them a little if necessary.

Installing screws and bolts

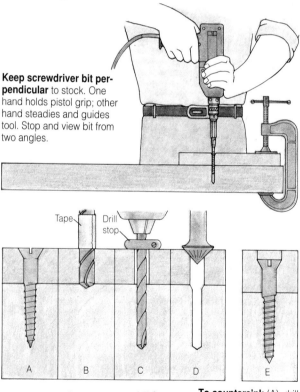

Keep screwdriver bit perpendicular to stock. One hand holds pistol grip; other hand steadies and guides tool. Stop and view bit from two angles.

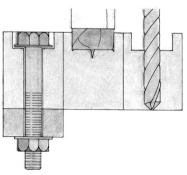

To countersink (A), drill hole size of unthreaded shank (B), then pilot hole the diameter of shank minus threads (C). Finish with countersink bit (D). To drill a counterbored hole (E), first drill recess, then follow countersink steps. To save time, use a combination bit. For bolts (left), first drill recess the diameter of the washer.

Nailing techniques

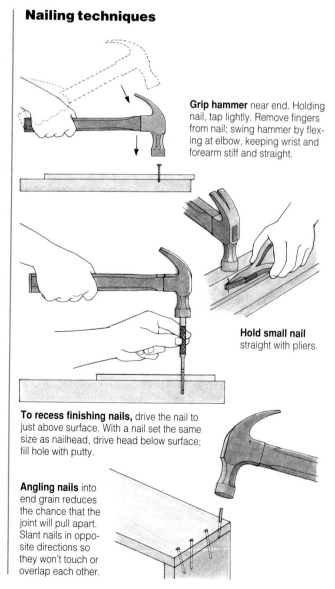

Grip hammer near end. Holding nail, tap lightly. Remove fingers from nail; swing hammer by flexing at elbow, keeping wrist and forearm stiff and straight.

Hold small nail straight with pliers.

To recess finishing nails, drive the nail to just above surface. With a nail set the same size as nailhead, drive head below surface; fill hole with putty.

Angling nails into end grain reduces the chance that the joint will pull apart. Slant nails in opposite directions so they won't touch or overlap each other.

HINGES

The style and placement of the hinge knuckle determines the swing action of a hinge. For a simple hinge with two equal leaves, place the knuckle at the intersection of the two pieces. To mark for a mortise, measure the width of the leaf to the center of the hinge knuckle with a marking gauge. If you are making many mortises of the same size, consider buying or making a jig that you can use with a router.

A drop-leaf table, hinged with one long and one short hinge leaf, has a recess chiseled into the mortise on the tabletop. This recess holds the hinge knuckle. Before mounting a drop-leaf hinge, make a rule joint by routing the mating tabletop and leaf edges with matching cove and rounding-over bits.

On typical house doors, hinges spaced unevenly look even at eye level. Put the lower hinge farther from the bottom of the door than the upper hinge is from the top; place the middle hinge, if any, slightly above the halfway point between the others.

Mortising with a router

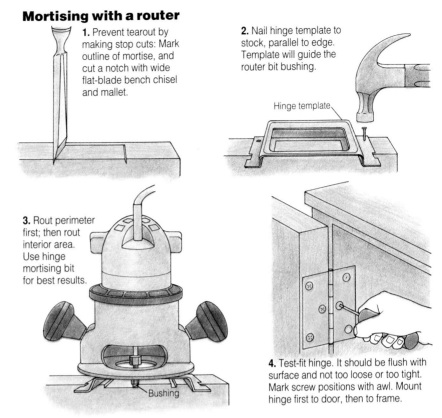

1. Prevent tearout by making stop cuts: Mark outline of mortise, and cut a notch with wide flat-blade bench chisel and mallet.

2. Nail hinge template to stock, parallel to edge. Template will guide the router bit bushing.

Hinge template

3. Rout perimeter first; then rout interior area. Use hinge mortising bit for best results.

Bushing

4. Test-fit hinge. It should be flush with surface and not too loose or too tight. Mark screw positions with awl. Mount hinge first to door, then to frame.

Setting a drop-leaf hinge

1. Center the recess for hinge's knuckle under the routed straight line, or fillet, where the table pieces meet. Mortise on tabletop equals width of short hinge leaf plus the knuckle and part of the long hinge leaf. Long leaf bridges both pieces. Allow 1/32 in. clearance for working pieces to move.

Center knuckle on fillet line
1/32" clearance
Short hinge leaf
Knuckle
Long hinge leaf

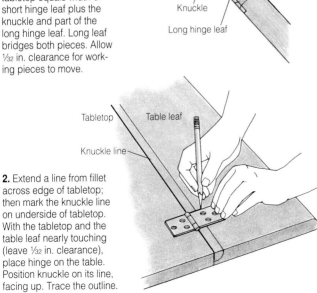

Tabletop
Table leaf
Knuckle line

2. Extend a line from fillet across edge of tabletop; then mark the knuckle line on underside of tabletop. With the tabletop and the table leaf nearly touching (leave 1/32 in. clearance), place hinge on the table. Position knuckle on its line, facing up. Trace the outline.

3. Make stop cuts (step 1 above). Then remove waste with a mallet and chisel, bevel down. Start from center and work with grain toward stop cuts. Check mortise depth periodically.

Tabletop
Table leaf

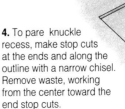

Knuckle line

4. To pare knuckle recess, make stop cuts at the ends and along the outline with a narrow chisel. Remove waste, working from the center toward the end stop cuts.

Layers of real wood, called *plies,* are glued together to make the sheet material known as plywood. Softwood plywood is suitable for construction; hardwood-veneer plywood often substitutes for solid wood in frame-and-panel construction and in furniture. The type of glue that joins the plies determines whether the plywood is for interior or exterior use.

Plywood's large (4- × 8-foot) sheets have advantages over solid wood. The sheets are strong and relatively stable; you can get wide expanses, as for a door or a tabletop, without edge joints. However, its size makes it awkward to transport, handle, and store. Have someone help you with large sheets. When storing, avoid damp areas that will damage plywood fibers and cause warpage.

The secret of plywood's strength and stability lies in the crisscross layering of the plies. The center ply, or *core,* varies

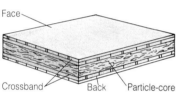

in thickness according to the type of plywood and may be sandwiched between *crossband* layers. The outer plies ($\frac{1}{28}$-inch maximum thickness in hardwood plywood) are the *faces,* or if not of equal quality, the *face* and the *back.* If the outer layers are thin and you must hand-sand them, use very fine grit paper.

When sawed, plywood splinters where the saw exits. To avoid splintering the good face, place it up when cutting with a table saw, down when using a circular saw. With handsaws, use a plywood or tenon saw and work with the good face up.

When joining plywood, choose joints that cover the edge. Tongue-and-groove (facing page), multiple mortise-and-tenon (p.147), router dovetail (p.143), biscuit, and spline joints (pp.140–141) work well. Nails and screws fasten plywood to solid wood or to another piece of plywood. In some cases a combination of nails or screws and glue is necessary. Plywood resists splitting, so nails and screws can be placed close together and close ($\frac{1}{8}$ inch) to the edges of sheets on the face and back. Screws driven into plywood edges will split the layers apart. However, knock-down fittings, such as cross dowels (facing page), create a strong interlocking joint and allow for easy disassembly (and reassembly) of a project. For hinges, choose a wrap-around style that allows screws in the edge and the face of the plywood piece.

Cover exposed plywood edges with molding or with veneer tape that matches the plywood's face. Depending on the type of tape you buy, you will apply it with glue, iron it on, or peel and stick it on. For edges that will get hard use, such as a tabletop, choose solid wood molding.

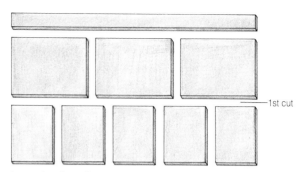

Lay out project pieces on plywood sheet, being careful to avoid odd grain patterns and awkward, unnecessary cuts. Allow for power saw blade kerf (⅛ in.). Make all lengthwise cuts first for easier handling of large sheet. Remeasure after each cut.

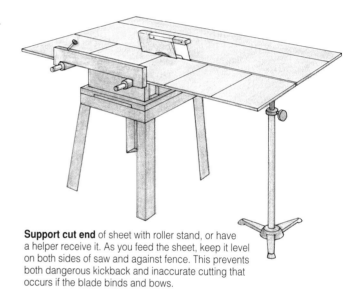

Support cut end of sheet with roller stand, or have a helper receive it. As you feed the sheet, keep it level on both sides of saw and against fence. This prevents both dangerous kickback and inaccurate cutting that occurs if the blade binds and bows.

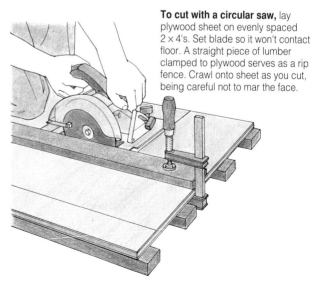

To cut with a circular saw, lay plywood sheet on evenly spaced 2 × 4's. Set blade so it won't contact floor. A straight piece of lumber clamped to plywood serves as a rip fence. Crawl onto sheet as you cut, being careful not to mar the face.

Plywood joints

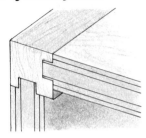

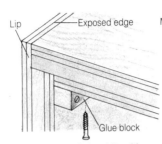

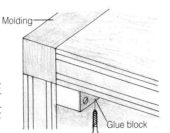

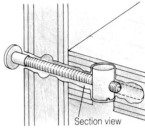

Tongue-and-groove joint is strong. Tongue is one-third stock thickness and should fit snugly into the groove. Corner piece hides plywood ends.

Double rabbet joint. A lip of face veneer and crossband in side piece covers mating piece's edge. Add glue blocks; cover exposed edge with veneer tape.

Hide plywood edges with molding. Align molding and plywood with wood biscuits or splines (pp.140–141), and glue pieces. Glue blocks add more strength.

Cross dowel. Drill bolt's countersink and shank holes, then intersecting dowel hole. Insert dowel; align its opening with screwdriver. Slide bolt into hole through dowel.

Edge treatments

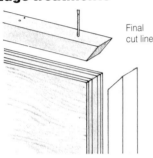

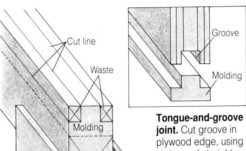

Cover edges with plain or decorative molding. Measure and miter corners carefully. Attach with glue and finishing nails. To prevent hardwood molding from splitting, drill pilot holes for nails.

Tongue-and-groove joint. Cut groove in plywood edge, using router and straight bit or slotting cutter. On table saw use a standard blade or dado head. Next rout, saw, or plane tongue on molding.

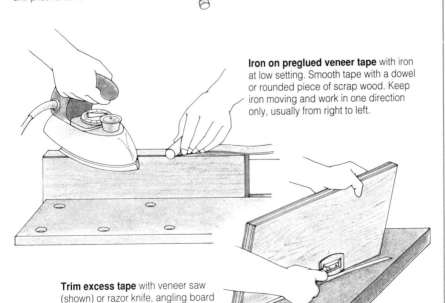

Iron on preglued veneer tape with iron at low setting. Smooth tape with a dowel or rounded piece of scrap wood. Keep iron moving and work in one direction only, usually from right to left.

Trim excess tape with veneer saw (shown) or razor knife, angling board slightly. Lightly sand corners with 120-grit sandpaper.

Frame and panel

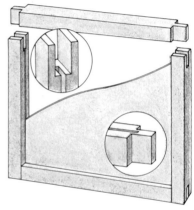

Bridle, or slip, joint is U-shaped mortise and two-shouldered tenon. Cut panel groove in each frame piece first (same thickness as plywood, usually ¼ to ⅜ in.). Extend groove into tenon to accept panel corners. Cut mortise (below); then cut tenon to fit (pp.146–147).

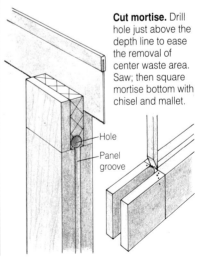

Cut mortise. Drill hole just above the depth line to ease the removal of center waste area. Saw; then square mortise bottom with chisel and mallet.

Plain or fancy, a cabinet is basically a box. Large cabinets often consist of a solid wood frame supporting either manufactured or solid wood panels. Smaller boxes don't require the support of a frame.

The easiest drawer to fit in a cabinet is an overlay drawer, which has a front face that covers part of the cabinet frame. More challenging to build is the flush drawer, which fits within its opening. (Options for cabinet door styles are similar to those for drawers. If the piece has both doors and drawers, make them the same style.)

To make a drawer, rout grooves along the bottom edges of the drawer front and sides to accept a thin plywood or hardboard bottom panel. (The back is narrow and rests on top of the bottom panel; thus it needs no groove.) Cut dadoes for the back in the side pieces, and construct two dovetail, finger, or rabbet-and-dado joints for the front corners. Next assemble the front, sides, and back. Slide the bottom panel into its grooves from the back (this helps square the box), and nail or screw the bottom to the back.

Shelves, if they are adjustable, rest on clips inserted into the holes of a metal track (above, right) or on wood dowels or metal pins inserted into holes drilled in the cabinet sides. Stationary shelves are often dadoed in place.

Doors may be of solid plywood or *frame-and-panel* construction—a solid wood frame around a panel of plywood or solid wood. The frame is joined with mortise-and-tenon, mitered spline, or stile joints (facing page).

Tables, chairs, beds, and the bases of some cabinets use *leg-and-rail* construction, made usually with dowel or mortise-and-tenon joints. If the latter, tenons can be either stub (at least an inch long) or mitered to avoid meeting within the leg. To reinforce leg-and-rail joints, fasten blocks with screws (right).

For more on joints, see pp.139–147; on hinges, p.151; on frames and panels, p.153; on plywood, pp.152–153; on building boxes, pp.143 and 149.

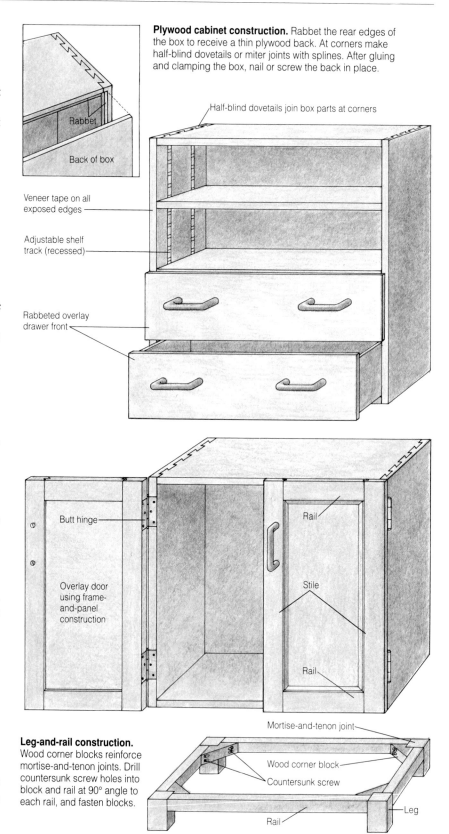

Plywood cabinet construction. Rabbet the rear edges of the box to receive a thin plywood back. At corners make half-blind dovetails or miter joints with splines. After gluing and clamping the box, nail or screw the back in place.

Rabbet

Back of box

Half-blind dovetails join box parts at corners

Veneer tape on all exposed edges

Adjustable shelf track (recessed)

Rabbeted overlay drawer front

Butt hinge

Rail

Overlay door using frame-and-panel construction

Stile

Rail

Leg-and-rail construction. Wood corner blocks reinforce mortise-and-tenon joints. Drill countersunk screw holes into block and rail at 90° angle to each rail, and fasten blocks.

Mortise-and-tenon joint

Wood corner block

Countersunk screw

Leg

Rail

Drawers and supports

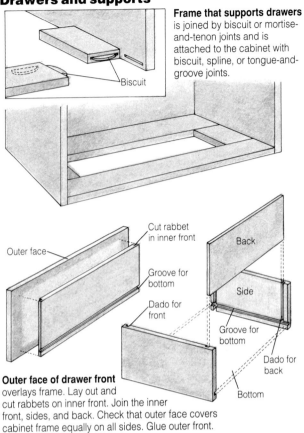

Frame that supports drawers is joined by biscuit or mortise-and-tenon joints and is attached to the cabinet with biscuit, spline, or tongue-and-groove joints.

Biscuit

Cut rabbet in inner front

Outer face

Back

Groove for bottom

Dado for front

Side

Groove for bottom

Dado for back

Bottom

Outer face of drawer front overlays frame. Lay out and cut rabbets on inner front. Join the inner front, sides, and back. Check that outer face covers cabinet frame equally on all sides. Glue outer front.

Side-hung drawers ride on matching wood glides screwed inside the case. Before assembling drawer, rout side grooves. (If grooves end shy of front, they function as a drawer stop.)

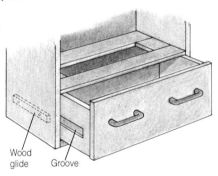

Wood glide

Groove

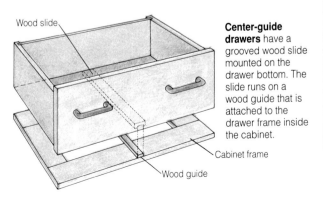

Wood slide

Center-guide drawers have a grooved wood slide mounted on the drawer bottom. The slide runs on a wood guide that is attached to the drawer frame inside the cabinet.

Cabinet frame

Wood guide

Frame-and-panel construction

Rout stile joints with a matched pair of bits called stile and rail cutters. Mount the router upside down in a router table. On the four inner frame edges, cut grooves for the panel with a beading (molding) stile bit (A); change to a beading rail bit; then cut rail ends (B) to fit stile molding.

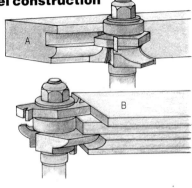

A

B

Rail

Stile

Panel

Rail

Test-fit assembly. Then glue matching rail and stile; spot-glue panel edges and insert into groove. Glue second stile, then second rail. Clamp stile joints.

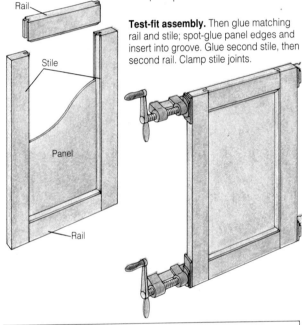

Building a table

Support solid wood top with slotted metal brackets, which let screws move with wood. For maximum length and strength, miter tenon ends (inset); allow $1/16$-in. gap for glue pocket.

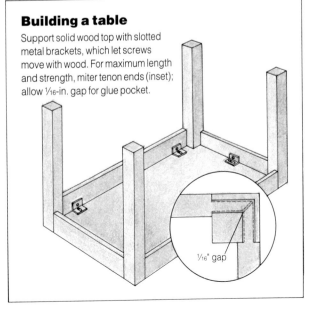

$1/16$" gap

MOLDINGS

Install molding to create an attractive finished look and to hide flawed joints where walls meet floors, ceilings, and door and window frames. Molding also protects vulnerable edges, holds window sashes in place, stops the swing of a door in its frame, and sheds water away from the top of a window.

Carefully select moldings that are to be joined. Each mill makes different profiles, and slight variances occur even in the same profile from the same mill. Make sure that each piece you buy is consistent from end to end and that the pro-

files of all pieces to be used in the same project are matched.

Moldings come in 6- to 16-foot lengths in 2-foot increments. You can buy moldings with "standard" profiles in knot-free grades of white pine and, in some parts of the country, red oak; you can order them in other woods. Prefinished moldings are available in wood to match paneling and in foam, rigid plastic, or veneered wood. Look for them in lumberyards and home centers. Order custom moldings from a mill, or make your own with a router.

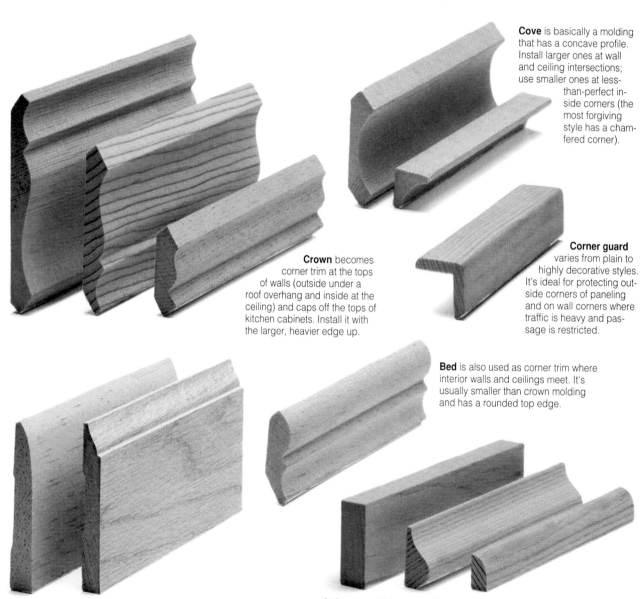

Cove is basically a molding that has a concave profile. Install larger ones at wall and ceiling intersections; use smaller ones at less-than-perfect inside corners (the most forgiving style has a chamfered corner).

Crown becomes corner trim at the tops of walls (outside under a roof overhang and inside at the ceiling) and caps off the tops of kitchen cabinets. Install it with the larger, heavier edge up.

Corner guard varies from plain to highly decorative styles. It's ideal for protecting outside corners of paneling and on wall corners where traffic is heavy and passage is restricted.

Bed is also used as corner trim where interior walls and ceilings meet. It's usually smaller than crown molding and has a rounded top edge.

Base hides joints between walls and floors and protects wall surfaces from damage by vacuums, brooms, furniture, and feet. In general, base molding has an unmolded lower edge, allowing you to add a base shoe. The top is often decorative, making an extra base cap unnecessary.

S4S, or smooth four sides, is a square-edged molding. Use it alone or combine it with other moldings to create a decorative look.

Base cap fits on top of S4S when it's used as base molding; or apply it to paneling as a finishing touch.

Base shoe fits flush against base molding or S4S. It hides edges of carpeting and other flooring.

Quarter round, an easy-to-find molding, fits into corners. You can also combine it with other moldings to build a profile.

Half round is ideal for finishing shelf edges. It also adds a decorative element to furniture and as part of a built-up molding profile such as one that surrounds a fireplace.

Chair rail protects walls against chair backs. It visually lowers wall height and serves as a horizontal dividing line between two surfaces, such as wallcovering and paint.

Picture molding supports paintings and picture frames, which are suspended from it with hooks. The molding should continue around the room's complete circumference, close to the ceiling.

Wainscot cap sits on top of wainscot (wood paneling on the lower portion of a wall). It protects the wood end grains and enhances the overall appearance.

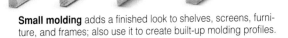

Small molding adds a finished look to shelves, screens, furniture, and frames; also use it to create built-up molding profiles.

Brick molding covers exterior window and door frames. The molding's thickness allows bricks and other types of siding to butt against it.

Casing for windows and doors covers the gaps between the frames (jambs) and the wall. It stiffens the frame and anchors it in the opening. It comes in plain and molded profiles, such as colonial (far left) and clamshell (center), and in several widths. Apron molding (left) can also be applied under windowsills.

Handrail is a thick molding made from sturdy wood to support people as they go up and down stairs. It's often supported by brackets, which must be securely anchored to the studs in the wall.

Casing stop is added to door or window frames to stop the swing of a door or window and to hold a sliding or hung unit in place. It also serves to hide the joint and, to a degree, seals against air infiltration and sound transmission.

Decorative molding finishes the edges of furniture, built-in cabinetry, and rooms. In a room, baseboard molding lies flat against the wall, inside corners joined with coped joints, outside corners with edge miters. Angled ceiling molding, called *crown molding*, is similarly mitered and coped, except that the outside corners are compound mitered —the end of each board has both a face and an edge miter cut (p.141). To saw a compound miter by hand, place the molding in a miter box with the ceiling edge down. On a radial arm saw or a table saw, adjust

the blade and the miter gauge to cut a compound miter.

Before installing molding, locate the studs with a stud finder or by knocking on the wall (listen for a solid sound), and mark their locations. To tightly fit a molding with butt ends, taper each end (cut the face $\frac{1}{16}$ inch long and slightly undercut the back edge); snap the molding into place. To span a long wall, join the pieces with scarf joints (parallel miters). Nail across the joint and into a wall stud. To avoid splits in hardwood molding, predrill all nail holes. Nail molding

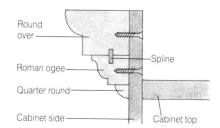

$\frac{1}{2}$ inch from the edges and 1 inch from each end.

With a router and various bits you can create your own moldings. Or use homemade and stock moldings (above) to create more complex profiles.

Crown molding installation

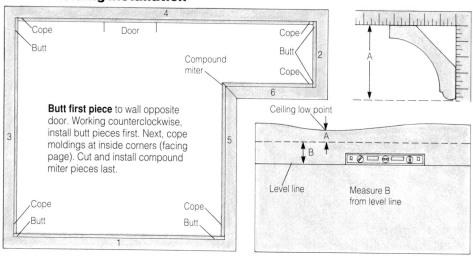

Butt first piece to wall opposite door. Working counterclockwise, install butt pieces first. Next, cope moldings at inside corners (facing page). Cut and install compound miter pieces last.

To find A, the distance from top edge (ceiling) to bottom edge (wall) of a molding, hold it against a square (near left).

Draw a level line around room at a convenient height. Measure up from line at intervals to find ceiling's low point. From this low point, measure down distance A and mark. Then find B by measuring from level line up to A mark. On each wall, transfer same distance (B) from level line for bottom edge of molding.

Install molding with finishing nails anchored in studs and ceiling joists or furring strips (one-third of nail should penetrate framing); recess nails. Fill holes and gaps; sand smooth when dry.

Making a crown compound miter

Exploded view of crown molding shows how it angles away from the corner of a wall. To cut correct angle automatically, place molding in a miter box with the ceiling edge down.

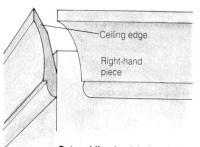

Cut molding for right-hand piece with ceiling edge down and wall edge against fence; waste is to right of saw. For left-hand molding, saw on opposite diagonal, with waste to left of saw.

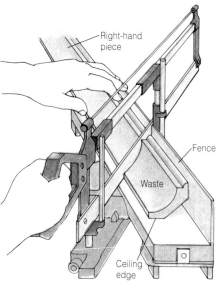

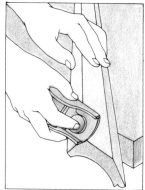

Test fit; if necessary, trim back edge of miter on right-hand piece with block plane. Keep blade away from front molded edge.

Baseboard molding installation

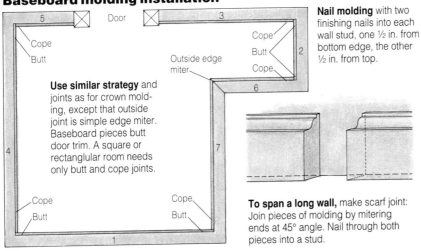

Nail molding with two finishing nails into each wall stud, one ½ in. from bottom edge, the other ½ in. from top.

Use similar strategy and joints as for crown molding, except that outside joint is simple edge miter. Baseboard pieces butt door trim. A square or rectanglular room needs only butt and cope joints.

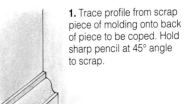

To span a long wall, make scarf joint: Join pieces of molding by mitering ends at 45° angle. Nail through both pieces into a stud.

Coped joints

Cut butt piece and install it to fit tightly between walls. Coped piece is then shaped to fit profile of butt piece.

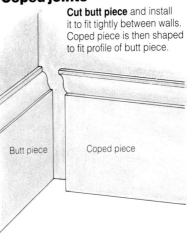

1. Trace profile from scrap piece of molding onto back of piece to be coped. Hold sharp pencil at 45° angle to scrap.

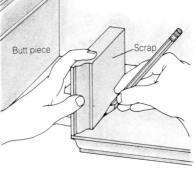

Making an outside edge miter

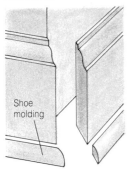

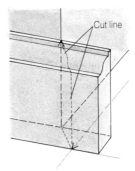

Baseboard edge miters must match exactly for good joint. Shoe molding (quarter round), nailed to baseboard, covers gaps between floor and baseboard.

1. Place uncut baseboards in turn against wall. Draw the lines on the floor where they intersect and V-marks on each piece at wall corner and floor intersection.

2. Draw perpendicular lines from V-marks on front and back of each piece. Connect these lines across top and bottom edges to mark exact cut line (about 45°).

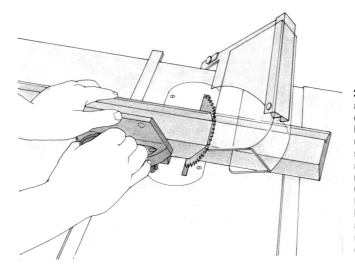

3. On table saw, angle blade for edge miter; place baseboard face up. Test-cut on scrap side of lines about ½ in. from marked miter. Compare cut to lines; adjust the blade. When the angle matches, saw miter cut in one pass.

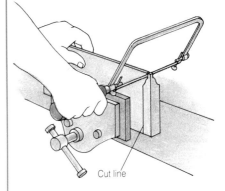

2. With coping saw at 90° to baseboard back and blade angled, saw curved part of profile. Turn piece upside down; cut straight part with dovetail saw or backsaw. Test fit. Use file to adjust profile, then to undercut (bevel) back.

STAINS, FILLERS, AND FINISHES

An array of wood finishing products awaits the amateur, serious hobbiest, and professional. To choose the right one, first determine exactly what you want it to do. Stains, fillers, and finishes can enhance wood's natural grain, cause it to reflect or absorb light, enrich or change its color or texture, or obscure an unsightly surface. Most offer some degree of protection from sunlight, abrasion, water, and chemicals. Some stains and finishes come in a premixed ready-off-the-shelf form. Others must be prepared by mixing powder with solvents; most of these can be altered to create custom products. The skills and tools needed to create and apply, or lay down, a finish vary with the product, surface, and technique.

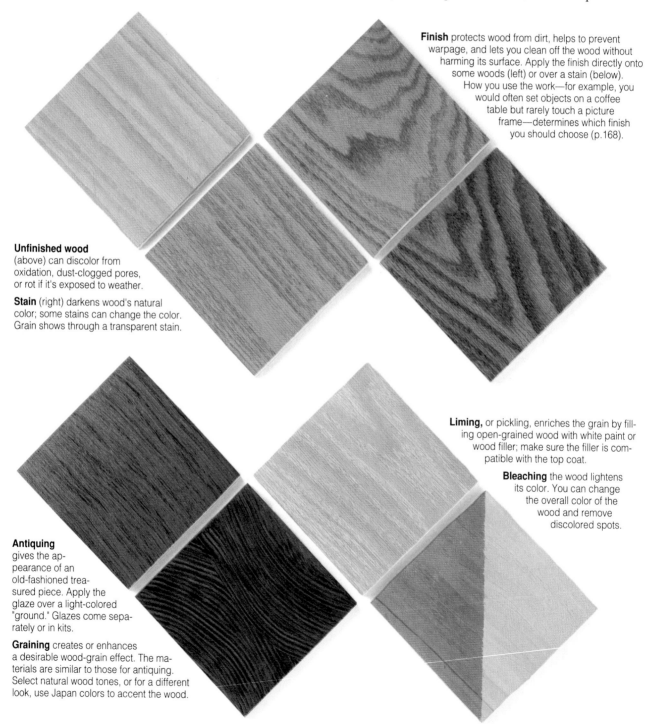

Finish protects wood from dirt, helps to prevent warpage, and lets you clean off the wood without harming its surface. Apply the finish directly onto some woods (left) or over a stain (below). How you use the work—for example, you would often set objects on a coffee table but rarely touch a picture frame—determines which finish you should choose (p.168).

Unfinished wood
(above) can discolor from oxidation, dust-clogged pores, or rot if it's exposed to weather.

Stain (right) darkens wood's natural color; some stains can change the color. Grain shows through a transparent stain.

Antiquing
gives the appearance of an old-fashioned treasured piece. Apply the glaze over a light-colored "ground." Glazes come separately or in kits.

Graining creates or enhances a desirable wood-grain effect. The materials are similar to those for antiquing. Select natural wood tones, or for a different look, use Japan colors to accent the wood.

Liming, or pickling, enriches the grain by filling open-grained wood with white paint or wood filler; make sure the filler is compatible with the top coat.

Bleaching the wood lightens its color. You can change the overall color of the wood and remove discolored spots.

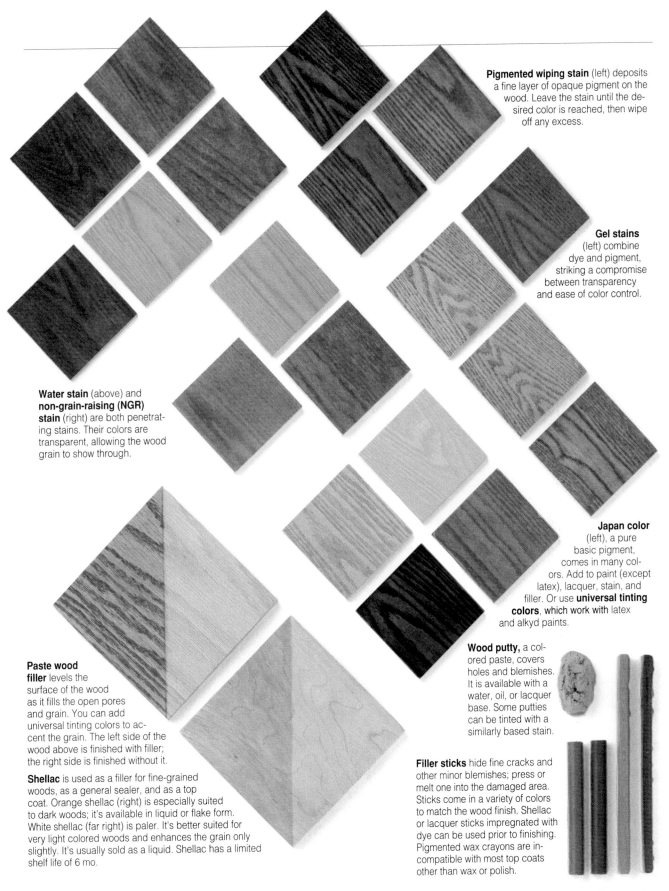

Pigmented wiping stain (left) deposits a fine layer of opaque pigment on the wood. Leave the stain until the desired color is reached, then wipe off any excess.

Gel stains (left) combine dye and pigment, striking a compromise between transparency and ease of color control.

Water stain (above) and **non-grain-raising (NGR) stain** (right) are both penetrating stains. Their colors are transparent, allowing the wood grain to show through.

Japan color (left), a pure basic pigment, comes in many colors. Add to paint (except latex), lacquer, stain, and filler. Or use **universal tinting colors**, which work with latex and alkyd paints.

Paste wood filler levels the surface of the wood as it fills the open pores and grain. You can add universal tinting colors to accent the grain. The left side of the wood above is finished with filler; the right side is finished without it.

Shellac is used as a filler for fine-grained woods, as a general sealer, and as a top coat. Orange shellac (right) is especially suited to dark woods; it's available in liquid or flake form. White shellac (far right) is paler. It's better suited for very light colored woods and enhances the grain only slightly. It's usually sold as a liquid. Shellac has a limited shelf life of 6 mo.

Wood putty, a colored paste, covers holes and blemishes. It is available with a water, oil, or lacquer base. Some putties can be tinted with a similarly based stain.

Filler sticks hide fine cracks and other minor blemishes; press or melt one into the damaged area. Sticks come in a variety of colors to match the wood finish. Shellac or lacquer sticks impregnated with dye can be used prior to finishing. Pigmented wax crayons are incompatible with most top coats other than wax or polish.

VENEERS

Whether you're hiding imperfections in solid wood or covering a manufactured wood, such as particleboard, veneer adds an attractive look to any project. You can apply it to furniture, to an inexpensive door, to shelves, to almost any object where a decorative finish is desired. Veneers offer access to a variety of woods that would otherwise be unavailable because of expense or inappropriateness as a solid wood.

Veneer sheets are stored and sold by suppliers in consecutive order, primarily to facilitate matching procedures (p.170) but also to ensure uniform figure, color, and texture in a finished piece. Veneer is shipped flat or rolled, according to the size of the sheet. Be sure to order on the generous side, allowing about 20 to 30 percent waste for cutting and matching. And handle veneer with great care; it is very fragile.

Veneer sheets (right) are identified according to the wood species, the cutting method used to produce the veneer, the part of the tree from which it was cut (it may have a burl or crotch), and its figure. These variables give an endless selection for your project.

Edge trim (right) comes in strips up to 250 ft. long. It may have an adhesive backing or you may have to apply it with glue. Cover the exposed edges of plywood with it.

Inlay strips (right) create a decorative band around or near the edge of a workpiece. Thin strips of natural wood are preassembled in geometric designs, greatly simplifying the amount of work that goes into a project. They are easily inlaid into shallow grooves that are routed into the workpiece. Order the strips from woodworking catalogs or look for them in specialty shops. They are available in 3-ft. lengths and are ¼ to ¾ in. wide.

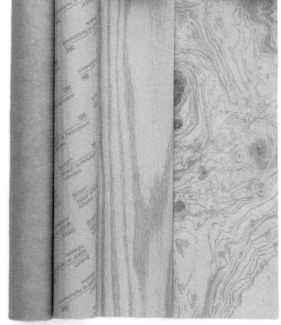

Flexible veneer (above, left) is more pliable than other veneers, making it ideal for curved surfaces. It's available in wide sheets to cover large areas; apply the veneer with contact cement.

Pressure-sensitive veneer (above, right) has a backing that is coated with an adhesive. To apply the veneer, peel off the protective paper, position the veneer, and press it in place.

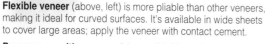

Decorative inlays come in a wide variety of designs. A combination of naturally or artificially colored woods are assembled to create patterns. Recess the veneer into the workpiece, or glue it as an overlay onto the top of the surface.

ORNAMENTAL WOOD TRIM

As the last touch before staining and finishing a surface, create an impressive look by adding one or more ornamental trims. Or add custom-order reproduction trim to replace pieces when restoring an old piece of wood furniture. Most of these trims are available in walnut, oak, cherry, and other hardwoods. They can enhance a cabinet, chest, headboard, bookcase, door, window, staircase, wall, or gazebo.

Ornamental trims are easy to apply, requiring only a little adhesive or a few small brads. And they will accept any type of finish to match the other materials you are working with.

Preshaped pieces come in a variety of configurations and sizes to use on a piece of furniture, such as a chair or baby crib, and for creating architectural details. Some items, such as the galley railing (left), are preassembled.

Decorative carvings have embossed (not carved) patterns in beech, birch, and other hardwoods. They can be found in mail-order catalogs.

Decorative half-round moldings are suitable for cabinetry, picture framing, and trim or borders for walls, ceilings, doors, or windows.

Wood filigree, often seen on antique furniture (especially around glass cabinet doors), comes in a variety of intricate designs. You can apply it to fancy boxes, storage chests, and picture frames. It is available through certain woodworking mail-order catalogs.

PREPARING WOOD SURFACES

The finish you put on a piece will magnify any imperfections in the wood, so prepare all surfaces carefully. (On new construction prepare the pieces before assembly.) Although some hand-sanding is always necessary, the amount can be sharply reduced by using a scraper. Proper scraping leaves lacy shavings. When you create dust instead of shavings, sharpen the blade (pp.198–199).

Power tools speed the sanding process. For rough work use a belt sander, follow with a finishing sander (orbital or oscillating), and end with light hand-sanding. Always work through a sequence of grits. For rough work, use 80 grit. On smooth surfaces, start with 120 grit (fine), then 180 (very fine), and finally 220 or 240. Sand parallel to the grain, or scratches will show. Clean the wood between grits with a tack rag. Make your own rag by dampening a piece of cheesecloth with turpentine, then kneading a little varnish into it. If your finish is water-base, dampen the cloth with water.

Caution: Wear a dust mask. When power-sanding, connect your sander to a dust bag or shop vacuum if possible.

To get a high-shine finish in such open-grain woods as oak or walnut, fill the pores with paste wood filler. This comes in wood tones or neutral; you can tint the latter with universal tinting colors. (See p.167 for special effects.) Filling is unnecessary for a natural look or for wood with small pores, such as pine, maple, and cherry. Follow the maker's suggestions for whether to fill before or after staining.

Before staining, prime wood surfaces and porous end grain with a sealer so they will absorb the stain uniformly (especially important with softwoods). Brush two medium coats on the wood; let each coat dry; then sand the surface with 240-grit paper.

Scraping

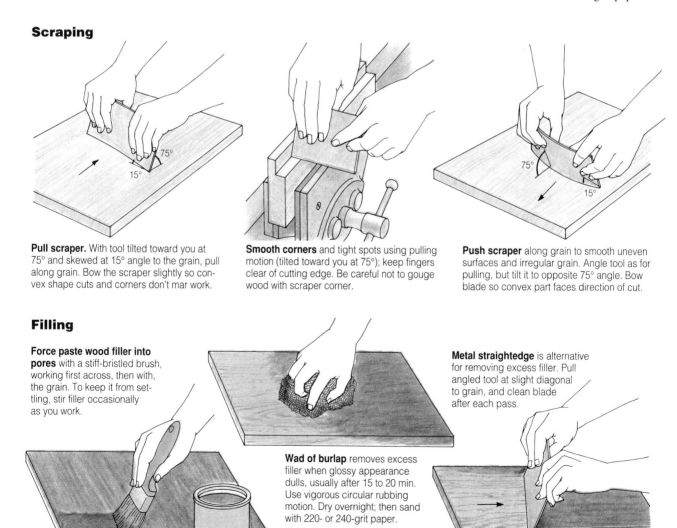

Pull scraper. With tool tilted toward you at 75° and skewed at 15° angle to the grain, pull along grain. Bow the scraper slightly so convex shape cuts and corners don't mar work.

Smooth corners and tight spots using pulling motion (tilted toward you at 75°); keep fingers clear of cutting edge. Be careful not to gouge wood with scraper corner.

Push scraper along grain to smooth uneven surfaces and irregular grain. Angle tool as for pulling, but tilt it to opposite 75° angle. Bow blade so convex part faces direction of cut.

Filling

Force paste wood filler into pores with a stiff-bristled brush, working first across, then with, the grain. To keep it from settling, stir filler occasionally as you work.

Wad of burlap removes excess filler when glossy appearance dulls, usually after 15 to 20 min. Use vigorous circular rubbing motion. Dry overnight; then sand with 220- or 240-grit paper.

Metal straightedge is alternative for removing excess filler. Pull angled tool at slight diagonal to grain, and clean blade after each pass.

Sanding

Move finishing sander with grain in slightly overlapping parallel strokes. Keep a light touch; guide sander without exerting downward pressure.

To sand long turnings (below, left), cup sandpaper (a quarter sheet folded in thirds) over wood and move it up and down. "Shoeshine" short sections (below, right), moving sandpaper strip over area.

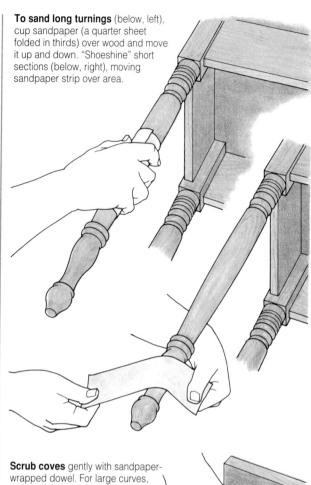

Sand small areas with palm sander, as described above. Start a power sander before it touches the wood surface.

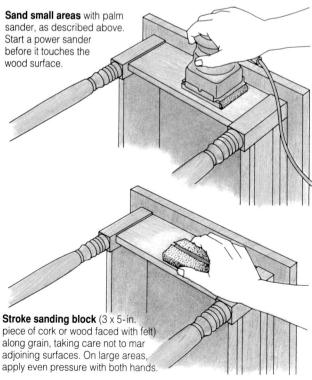

Stroke sanding block (3 x 5-in. piece of cork or wood faced with felt) along grain, taking care not to mar adjoining surfaces. On large areas, apply even pressure with both hands.

Scrub coves gently with sandpaper-wrapped dowel. For large curves, roll dowel from one side to the other.

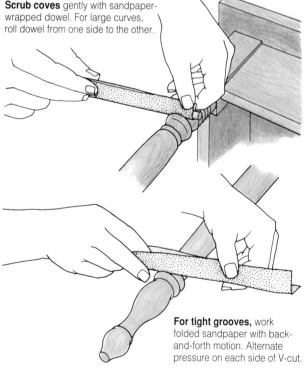

For tight grooves, work folded sandpaper with back-and-forth motion. Alternate pressure on each side of V-cut.

Stains enhance the natural color of wood or dramatically change it, either highlighting or disguising the wood's grain patterns. If you choose a penetrating stain, such as an aniline dye, expect clear, transparent color and emphasized grain, because this type of stain actually soaks into the wood fibers. But because wood absorbs penetrating stain so readily, it can be difficult to avoid streaks and lap marks.

By contrast, pigmented stains, called wiping stains, are easy to apply, but because they leave a thin film of colorant atop the wood, muddy grain often accompanies the rich color. A third category of wood stains, the gels,

combines the advantages of penetrating and pigmented stains. Because they don't splatter or run, they are almost foolproof to apply. Products are also available that combine stain and finish in one step. While these result in a fast finish, it is often inferior to a conventional two-step finish.

When choosing a stain and finish, consider their solvents; the stain and finish must be compatible. (It's always safest to use one manufacturer's products on a project.) Both penetrating and pigmented stains are available in water- and oil-soluble forms. Gel stains and combination products usually have an oil base.

Water-soluble stains are easy to clean up but can be more difficult to apply than oil-soluble ones. Perhaps the biggest disadvantage is that some water-soluble stains can swell the wood fibers, requiring you to raise the grain before staining. Alternatively, a type of water-base stain that doesn't raise the grain, called NGR stain, contains no water. To achieve the best results, NGR stains should be sprayed on.

When selecting a stain, pick a shade slightly lighter than the desired color— it's easier to darken a light stain than vice versa. The color will vary according to the wood, so first test the stain on a hidden area. Apply stain with a lint-free cloth or a synthetic-bristle brush, according to the manufacturer's directions. In small areas use a foam brush.

Some woods, such as pine, fir, birch, and hemlock, do not take stain well. (When properly finished, any wood may be beautiful without staining.) If you stain these woods, seal the wood first (p.164) and choose a water-base or gel type in a color that's a little darker than the natural tone.

You can lighten a wood's overall color by applying a commercial two-step bleach. Follow the label's directions. It is difficult, however, to remove disfiguring stains in wood, unless you know exactly what the stain is. For example, the blue-green to gray-black streaks found on an old mahogany, maple, or oak piece are usually caused by a reaction of iron hardware with the tannin in the wood. Oxalic acid, a liquid commonly sold as a deck brightener, will remove the stain without changing the color of the wood. Apply the acid and allow to dry. Thoroughly wash the dried crystals off the piece.

Caution: Oxalic acid and substances that contain high volatile organic compound (VOC), such as bleaches and alkyd resin- and oil-base stains and finishes, are toxic. (Some products are being reformulated.) Ventilate your work area well, follow the maker's guidelines, and wear rubber gloves and goggles.

Basic techniques

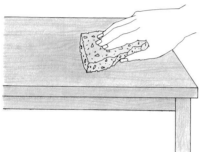

1. Raise wood grain before using water-base stain or if wood still feels rough after final sanding (especially with softwoods). Moisten wood with damp sponge and let dry.

2. Whisk off raised fibers with 180-grit sandpaper (pp.164–165); then vacuum all sanding dust from surface. Don't use a tack rag because it may leave a residue on the wood that will interfere with staining.

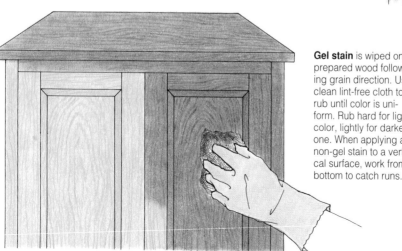

Gel stain is wiped onto prepared wood following grain direction. Use clean lint-free cloth to rub until color is uniform. Rub hard for light color, lightly for darker one. When applying a non-gel stain to a vertical surface, work from bottom to catch runs.

Liming (pickling) and antiquing are two ways to artificially age a furniture piece. Liming involves filling the wood pores with white paint or with paste wood filler before finishing, creating a two-tone effect. Antiquing consists of top-coating enameled or painted wood with a contrasting glaze, then wiping it off to create the illusion of wear. Graining, the art of producing imitation wood grain on bland surfaces, uses the same two-step procedure as antiquing. Because none of these decorative finishes protects wood surfaces (pp.168–169), finish the piece with the surface finish recommended on the label of the products you buy.

Liming

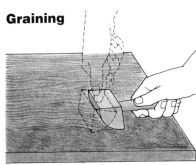

Brush on paste wood filler; then scrub off excess across grain with a wad of burlap, leaving filler in pores. Let dry for 24 hr. before sealing.

Graining

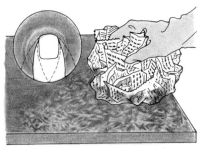

Simulate grain patterns by dragging the coarse side of the graining comb through the glaze with a twisting and rocking motion. Or use a stiff brush or whisk broom.

Create texture by pressing a piece of crumpled newsprint into glaze (experiment on scrap first). To make knots, twist thumb, leaving some "grain" in the knot.

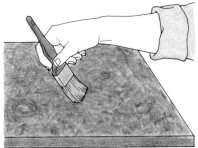

For added realism, brush over completed grain with dry brush. Angle brush as shown, and feather out grain lines with a light stroke.

Unify look of grain by overgraining. Allow first coat of glaze to dry, and then with a pad of coarse cloth, apply a second grain pattern in straight parallel lines.

Antiquing

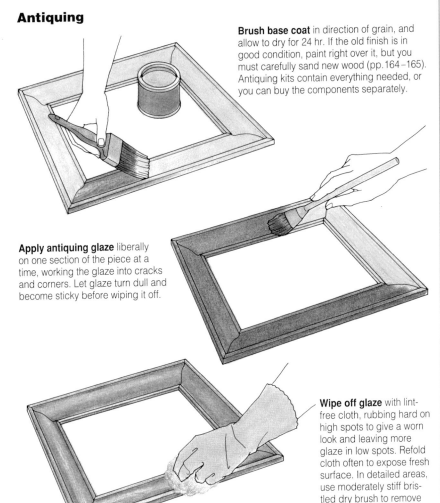

Brush base coat in direction of grain, and allow to dry for 24 hr. If the old finish is in good condition, paint right over it, but you must carefully sand new wood (pp.164–165). Antiquing kits contain everything needed, or you can buy the components separately.

Apply antiquing glaze liberally on one section of the piece at a time, working the glaze into cracks and corners. Let glaze turn dull and become sticky before wiping it off.

Wipe off glaze with lint-free cloth, rubbing hard on high spots to give a worn look and leaving more glaze in low spots. Refold cloth often to expose fresh surface. In detailed areas, use moderately stiff bristled dry brush to remove glaze, wiping brush often on a cloth to clean it.

The type of finish you choose depends on the use the object will receive and the appearance you desire. Surface finishes (varnish, polyurethane, lacquer) build up a protective film on the surface of the wood. Penetrating finishes (oils) sink into the wood, hardening within its fibers.

Surface finishes resist stains and abrasion better than penetrating finishes, but they are more difficult to spot-repair. Surface finishes may look too shiny unless they are hand-rubbed; penetrating finishes produce a soft sheen that emphasizes the wood's color and grain.

Consider, too, the composition of the finishing material. While all penetrating finishes have a solvent base, varnish, lacquer, and polyurethane are also available with a water base. Water-base types are nontoxic and nonflammable, but they can be difficult to apply correctly and may raise the wood grain. In addition, these finishes may not be compatible with oil-base stains and fillers. If there's any doubt about compatibility, contact the manufacturer.

All finishes magnify imperfections in the wood, so you must sand to a very fine grit—at least to 220—before finishing. Treat all parts of the object the same—back, front, underside, and top—so that they will react evenly to moisture changes and won't warp. If working with softwood, seal the wood first (p.164). For best results, the air temperature should be moderate, the humidity low. Consult the label for specific instructions. Allow the finish to dry between coats as recommended on the product label.

Minimize dust while a surface finish is still wet, or unwanted specks could settle in. Air bubbles are another problem: Stir a surface finish slowly, gently, and thoroughly. Never drag the brush against the can rim to remove the excess; instead, tap the brush lightly against the inside edge of the can. Dip a third of the brush into the finish, and flow it on.

For a lustrous sheen, polish a dried surface finish as follows: Apply a liberal amount of rubbing oil to a cloth or felt pad; sprinkle some fine pumice onto the cloth. Rub the oil on the surface, stroking along the wood grain. When the surface is satiny smooth, wipe off the oil with a clean soft cloth, and apply two coats of paste wax. For a glossier look, repeat the process using rottenstone and oil before waxing.

Type	Surface effect	Application	Solvent	Considerations
Alkyd varnish	Durable built-up finish, matte or gloss. Darkens wood slightly	Brush on liquid type; wipe on gel type. Apply 2–3 coats	Mineral spirits or turpentine	General-purpose protection. Spar (marine) varnish good for exterior work. Gel types need more coats to achieve thickness of brushing types
Water-base varnish	Same as above, but may darken wood less	Brush on. Apply 2–3 coats	Water	Environmentally safe. May raise the wood grain. Dries faster than solvent varnishes
Polyurethane	Extremely durable finish, matte or gloss; can look plastic. Darkens wood slightly	Brush on liquid type, wipe on gel type. Apply 2–3 coats	Mineral spirits or turpentine	Extremely durable; good for objects subject to heavy wear
Synthetic-base lacquer	Matte or glossy, accents grain of wood. Darkens wood less than other finishes, but may appear yellow	Brush or spray on; apply at least 3 coats. Brushing types may leave lap marks	Lacquer thinner	More protection than oils but less than varnishes. Highly flammable; apply in explosion-proof spray booth
Water-base lacquer	Same as synthetic-base lacquer, but less tendency to yellow	Brush, spray, or wipe on. Apply 2 coats if brushing or spraying, 3 if wiping	Water	Nonflammable and nontoxic; raises wood grain
Tung oil	Natural-looking matte sheen. Enhances color and grain of wood	Brush or wipe on. Apply 2–3 coats; rub in vigorously	Mineral spirits or turpentine	Suitable for all interior objects, especially carvings. Little protection against abrasion; somewhat resistant to staining
Danish oil	Natural-looking matte finish that enhances wood grain. Clear or colors available; all darken wood	Wipe on. Apply 3 coats, 4 for objects receiving heavy use	Mineral spirits or turpentine	Good for interior objects, but offers less protection than tung oil. Special types available for oily woods
Tung-oil varnish	Durable finish; looks more natural than other varnishes. Darkens wood slightly	Brush or wipe on. Apply 3 coats	Mineral spirits or turpentine	Affords more surface protection than oils but less than other varnishes

Brushing techniques

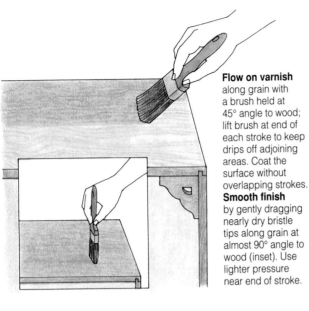

Flow on varnish along grain with a brush held at 45° angle to wood; lift brush at end of each stroke to keep drips off adjoining areas. Coat the surface without overlapping strokes.

Smooth finish by gently dragging nearly dry bristle tips along grain at almost 90° angle to wood (inset). Use lighter pressure near end of stroke.

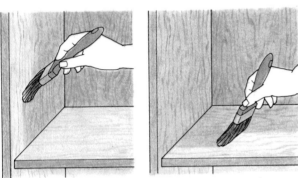

On inside corners, apply varnish first to the vertical surface, from bottom up. Then coat the horizontal surface. Work from the back corner toward front edge, brushing out any drips from the vertical face.

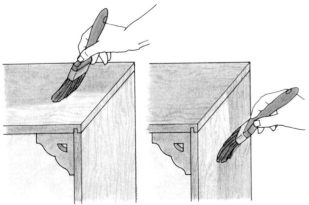

On outside corners, work horizontally, lifting brush at end of each stroke. To keep varnish from sagging, begin vertical stroke from bottom, catching any drips from horizontal face as you work.

Stripping

Paint strippers dissolve the old finish so it can be lifted off the surface. Those containing methylene chloride (a suspected carcinogen) work quickly (usually within 15 minutes) and effectively, but must be used with great caution. Nontoxic water-base strippers work more slowly, and because they may raise the grain, necessitating light sanding after stripping, they may not be the right choice for valuable or veneered pieces. Apply all strippers the same way: Pat on a thick coat with a cheap paintbrush, wait the recommended time, and then scrape off the old finish. Reapply stripper to any stubborn patches.

Caution: Apply methylene chloride stripper outdoors or in an amply ventilated workspace. Wear a respirator fitted with an organic filter that will protect you from harmful vapors (other filters screen out only solid particles). Always wear safety goggles and heavy rubber gloves, not the thin latex type. Protect the floor with newspaper, not plastic dropcloths. Keep fresh water and clean rags nearby, in case the stripper splashes on your skin or in your eyes.

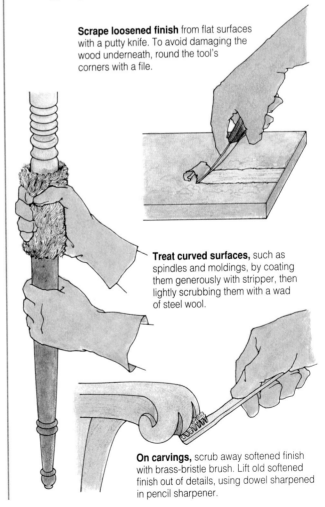

Scrape loosened finish from flat surfaces with a putty knife. To avoid damaging the wood underneath, round the tool's corners with a file.

Treat curved surfaces, such as spindles and moldings, by coating them generously with stripper, then lightly scrubbing them with a wad of steel wool.

On carvings, scrub away softened finish with brass-bristle brush. Lift old softened finish out of details, using dowel sharpened in pencil sharpener.

WORKING WITH VENEER

Veneering is the process of gluing a thin layer of decorative wood over a thicker plain base. Most veneers are between $\frac{1}{40}$ and $\frac{1}{28}$ inch thick for cabinetmaking; thinner, flexible veneers are available for curved surfaces. Veneer is sold by the square foot in pieces of various lengths, in sheets or rolls. Flatten pieces of veneer before use by spraying them lightly with water and then stacking them in a pile; separate the layers with brown paper. Lay a plywood panel atop the stack, and weight it with bricks. When the veneer is flat, let it dry for 5 days in the weighted stack, changing the paper daily.

Veneer is usually either rotary cut or sliced. In rotary cutting, the veneer is peeled off a log held in a giant lathe, much like unwinding a roll of paper towels. The grain of rotary-cut veneer looks stretched out—the growth rings are more widely spaced than in the uncut log. Sliced veneer, which is

Slip matching

Book matching

Diamond pattern

cut across the log, has the lively grain of sawn wood. Veneer is packed in the order it is cut; to keep the slices in sequence, number each one with chalk as you unpack it. The veneers may be arranged different ways. In slip matching, you slip consecutive veneers off the pile, lay them next to each other, and join them edge-to-edge, creating a repetitive pattern. In book matching, you remove sheets from the pile as you

Edge-joining veneer

1. Overlap two veneer sheets by about $\frac{1}{2}$ in.; clamp straightedge along center of overlap. Cut with veneer saw, using multiple light strokes. Remove waste veneer.

2. On good face, tape across joint every 6 in. with veneer tape; then tape along joint. Carefully lift panel to light to check for fit. Light shows through if joint is not tight.

3. Place veneer, tape side down, at edge of work surface; open joint so that one piece hangs down. Apply thin coat of white glue to edges. Close, wipe off excess glue, and cover with wax paper and weights.

Gluing to substrate

Roll or brush yellow glue evenly onto the substrate. Apply veneer to both sides. Protect first veneered side with plain paper. Then weight or clamp as at right.

Veneer

Paper

Veneer

Substrate

Clamp work. Cover caul with plain paper. Place work, paper, and second caul (inset). Clamp center 2 x 4 crosspiece (slightly convex along length), then end 2 x 4 pieces. Check that pressure of all clamps is even.

Paper

Veneer

Caul

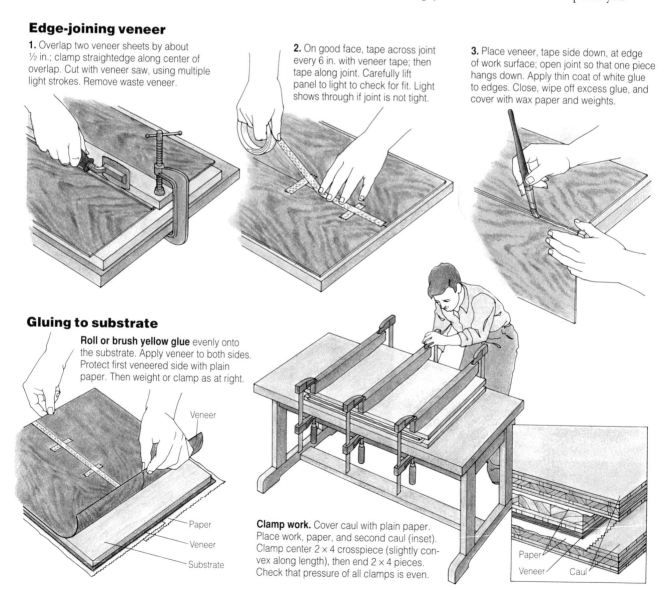

would turn the pages of a book, producing a mirror-image effect. To create a diamond pattern, cut four identical squares or rectangles of veneer so that the grain is diagonal. Then position the squares to form a pattern of either concentric diamonds or radiating lines.

Most materials can be veneered, if they are clean and smooth (bumps telegraph through the veneer). Apply veneer with its grain perpendicular to the grain of manufactured wood. To prevent warping, veneer both sides of each piece.

Cut veneer with a craft knife, single-edge razor blade, or veneer saw held at 90°. Whenever possible, cut with the back face up. Veneer should overhang the surface being covered (the substrate) by about ½ inch on all sides. Trim the waste with a veneer saw after the veneer has been glued but before scraping off the veneer tape. When both sides have been veneered, cut the work to size and cover the edges with veneer edging tape (pp.152–153).

To form a strong glue bond between veneer and its substrate, place even pressure on the work, adding slightly more force on the center. Weight down small areas of veneer with bricks or concrete blocks; if clamping, set one clamp every 9 inches. When using a veneer press, the plywood *cauls* (protective panels) should be larger than the work on all sides and the crosspieces should have convex bottoms. Weight hard-to-clamp areas with a sand-filled plastic bag.

Veneered surfaces break fairly easily, especially on their edges. Before patching, smooth the broken edges of the old veneer and square them with a craft knife so that they are at a right angle to the substrate. Before repairing veneer, make sure that the substrate is smooth and free of old adhesive.

Edge border

Strips of veneer, cut long, frame a center panel of veneer. Hold strips in place with pieces of veneer tape.

Cut mitered corners against straightedge. Work carefully from outer corner in, using many light strokes. Edge-glue strips to the panel (facing page); then glue as a whole to substrate.

Inlaid border

Rout groove from left to right, cutting it slightly shallower than inlay thickness. Square groove ends with chisel. To set guide, measure from router bit's perimeter to base's outer edge; clamp guide that distance from inner edge of inlay groove.

Cut intersecting inlay pieces overlong. Miter and glue as for edge border; press inlay with veneer roller. Sand inlay flush.

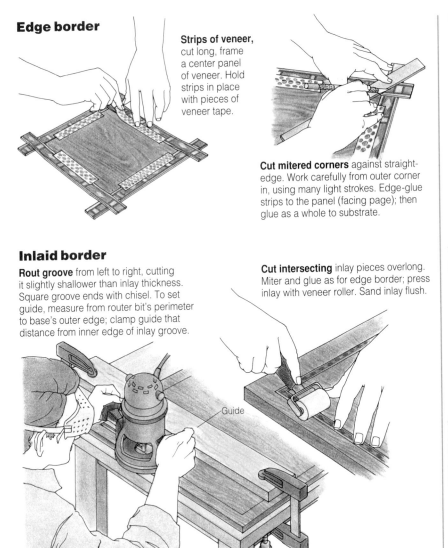

Repairs

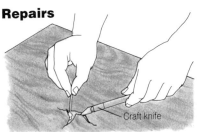

Blister. Slice in line with grain and gently lift veneer. Push in white glue with toothpick or glue injector. Press with flat roller; cover with wax paper and weight with a heavy object.

Raised veneer. Remove dried glue with craft knife or pin. Apply fresh glue with small brush or toothpick, and weight as above.

Hole. With white paper over hole, rub patch pattern with pencil; then rubber-cement drawn template to face side of patch. Cut patch with many light strokes on waste side of cut line. Test-fit patch; trim to fit; then glue and clamp.

Gluing and clamping repairs

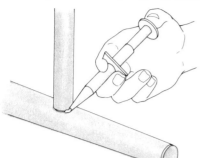

Reglue without disassembly.
Insert glue injector into loose joint; push plunger to force in glue. Small hole may be drilled to accept tip.

Twist stick

Force angled joint together by wrapping rope in figure-8 pattern. Tighten rope with a twist stick.

Try the gentlest approach first when reviving a worn furniture piece. If the finish is sound but lifeless, a thorough cleaning with a mild detergent or a dewaxer may add enough brightness. If not, a finish restorer, which dissolves a thin layer of existing finish and replaces it with a film of fresh finish, may suffice. For alligatored surfaces, try an amalgamator. As the amalgamator dissolves the old finish, blemishes flow together, resulting in a smooth surface when the finish rehardens.

Disguise small scratches with dye-impregnated wood markers, stick shellac, or even crayons. Deeply scratched pieces may require sanding and a complete refinishing.

To remove water rings, dampen a soft cotton cloth (old toweling is fine) with mineral oil, dip the cloth into fine pumice stone or rottenstone, and gently rub the ring until it disappears.

To raise a dent, prick it several times with a pin, cover it with a damp cloth, and press with an iron on the steam setting for a few seconds. Allow the area to dry, and repeat if needed.

Disassemble a piece cautiously when many joints need repair, when a part needs replacing, or when repairing one part will damage another part. Begin by reviewing the overall assembly. Invert tables to see how the apron and top are attached to the legs. Peer inside frame-and-panel cabinets to

locate glue blocks and screws. To aid reassembly, note the order of disassembly and mark mating pieces.

Loose joints can be tapped apart with a rubber mallet, but forcing tight joints can break the pieces. Try softening the glue: Drill or prick several small holes into the joint; then with a glue injector, inject a 1:1 mixture of white vinegar and water; wait 1 to 2 hours and tap the joint apart.

Breaks along the wood grain usually reglue well, but cross-grain breaks do not; strengthen the latter with dowels or splines. Tighten a loose dowel joint by gluing string or a layer of cheesecloth around the dowel to increase its diameter. You can also widen the end of a dowel on a disassembled piece by kerfing the end and inserting a hardwood wedge. Tighten a loose tenon by gluing wood shims to it; then trim them to fit. Build up a loose finger or dovetail joint with veneer pieces. For a good bond, always clean old glue out of all joints before regluing.

Troublesome doors often respond to one of several repairs. Check for high spots by rubbing chalk on the door's edge and then closing the door; plane the spots where the chalk was removed. Plug a stripped screw hole with glue and toothpicks, and redrill. Check hinge mortises. Chisel shallow ones deeper, and shim those that are too deep with pieces of veneer.

Repairing a split

Gently pry apart the pieces of a lengthwise break with a putty knife or an old screwdriver.

Wedge pieces far enough apart to allow insertion of a small glue brush. Coat both surfaces of split with glue. Remove wedge.

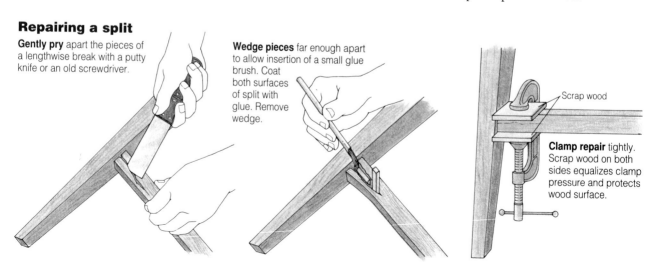

Scrap wood

Clamp repair tightly. Scrap wood on both sides equalizes clamp pressure and protects wood surface.

Fixing a doweled rung

Saw off broken wood on rung. Drill dowel hole. Make hole half the width of rung and ⅛ in. deeper than necessary (for excess glue). (Tape on bit guides depth.) Test-fit new grooved dowel in rung.

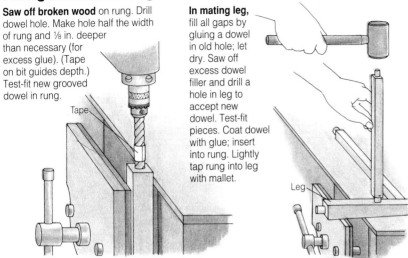

Tape

In mating leg, fill all gaps by gluing a dowel in old hole; let dry. Saw off excess dowel filler and drill a hole in leg to accept new dowel. Test-fit pieces. Coat dowel with glue; insert into rung. Lightly tap rung into leg with mallet.

Leg

Broken mortise-and-tenon

Saw off remains of broken tenon. Within outline of tenon, drill holes for mortise at least 1 in. deep plus ⅛ in. for excess glue. Trim mortise with chisel (p.146). Drill or chisel out remains of tenon in old mortise.

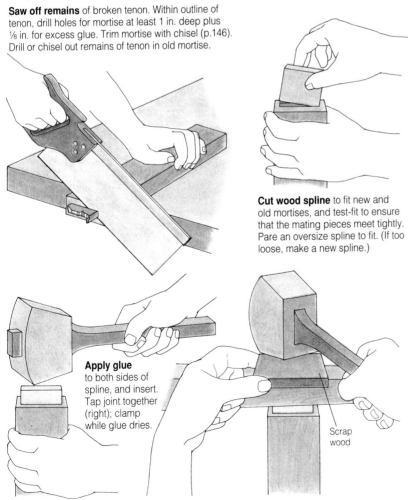

Cut wood spline to fit new and old mortises, and test-fit to ensure that the mating pieces meet tightly. Pare an oversize spline to fit. (If too loose, make a new spline.)

Apply glue to both sides of spline, and insert. Tap joint together (right); clamp while glue dries.

Scrap wood

Drawer repairs

Remove bottom. Pull nails with nippers and slide out panel. Replace, if needed, with ⅛- to ¼-in.-thick hardboard or plywood (⅜-in. for large drawers).

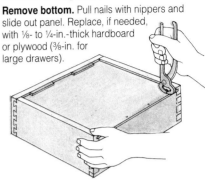

Replace piece. First, knock apart corner joints. Analyze joints to determine direction of mallet blows. Soften glue (facing page). Wood block protects wood during blows. Insert new part, glue, and clamp.

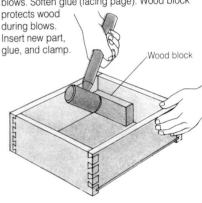

Wood block

Replace uneven or worn runners. Plane down high spots. Shave front corner area with chisel. Cut hardwood strips (maple or birch is best) to fit.

Runner

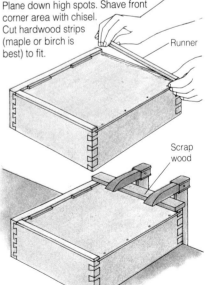

Scrap wood

Glue and align hardwood strips along drawer edges. Place clamps every 6 in.; protect wood with scrap. When dry, test-fit drawer; plane or sand high spots on new strips.

METALWORKING

Although replaced to a degree by plastics, metals are still put to a wide variety of uses around the home, as in flashing, siding, window frames, cabinets, pipes, and ducts. Metals can be soft or hard, beautiful or nondescript, malleable or rigid, thick or paper-thin. They are divided into two broad categories: ferrous (containing iron) and nonferrous, which includes all the other base metals (such as copper, aluminum, nickel, and zinc) and the precious metals (gold, silver, and platinum). Often two or more elemental metals are combined (alloyed)

to alter their visual properties or working and performance characteristics, such as hardness, strength, corrosion resistance, and melting points. The metals you are most likely to work with are sterling silver, copper, brass, steel, and aluminum alloys. Metals are sold in sheets (less than 3/16 inch thick), in plates (1/4 inch thick or more), and in bars, which include strips and flats (narrow sheets and plates), round, square, and hexagonal rods and tubing, angles and channels, and various other shapes.

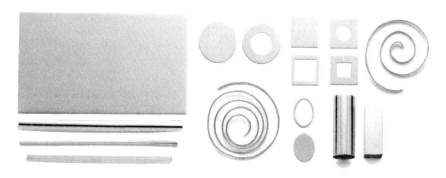

Silver and the other precious metals (gold and platinum) are highly stable chemically and resist oxidation and corrosion from acids. Silver and gold are also plastic and easy to work. They are available in standard or preformed sheets, plates, standard wire, flat bezel wire, tubing, and rods. Also available are foil, leaf, shot (granules) for casting and alloying, and prefabricated chains, clasps, earring posts, and jump rings, called findings, that simplify jewelry making.

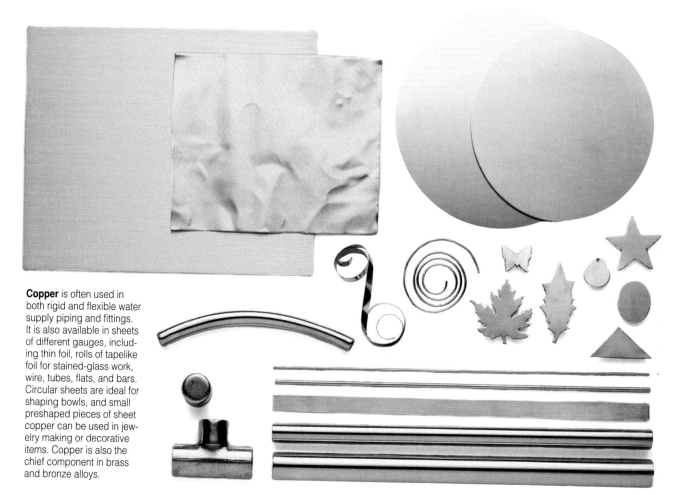

Copper is often used in both rigid and flexible water supply piping and fittings. It is also available in sheets of different gauges, including thin foil, rolls of tapelike foil for stained-glass work, wire, tubes, flats, and bars. Circular sheets are ideal for shaping bowls, and small preshaped pieces of sheet copper can be used in jewelry making or decorative items. Copper is also the chief component in brass and bronze alloys.

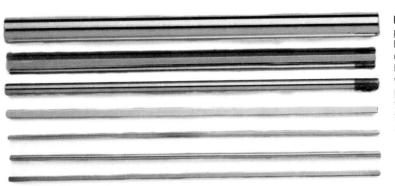

Brass, an alloy of copper and zinc, is sold in sheets, plates, tubes, rods, angles, and wire. It's stronger and harder than copper and resists corrosion, although decorative items are usually coated to prevent tarnish. Thin brass-plated steel pipe is also available. Solid brass is widely used for plumbing pipe and fittings, including nipples and unions and flare, compression, and threaded fittings (below). Banding (bottom) is used for decorating furniture, boxes, lamps, and bowls. Bronze, a copper-tin alloy, has properties and uses similar to those of brass.

Plain carbon steels, alloys of iron and carbon only, are the steels used in home workshops. They come in three varieties: low-, medium-, and high-carbon. The most widely used is low-carbon, or mild, steel, which is easily drilled, cut, and bent. It is available in a vast array of shapes including rods, tubing, angles, and flats, as shown at right, and is ideally suited for threaded heating and gas pipes and fittings (below). Medium-carbon steel, a harder alloy, is found in castings and in many shop tools. High-carbon steel is extremely hard, making it ideal for cutting tools.

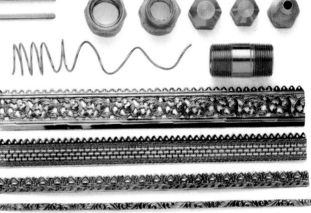

Aluminum, too soft to use alone, is always contained in an alloy. It is lightweight and easily drilled and cut, but it cannot be soldered and is difficult to weld. Although aluminum resists atmospheric corrosion, *anodizing,* an electrochemical coating process, dramatically improves its performance. It comes in sheets, preshaped flashing, and rods, as well as in many other forms, including angles, preformed thresholds, TV antennae, and framework for windows, screens, and greenhouses.

Metalworking 177

Working with metal, whether forming original work or making repairs, requires careful preparation and good materials. Sources for metal and supplies are diverse. For nonferrous metals (copper, brass, or aluminum) try hardware, building, or plumbing supply stores. For ferrous metals (iron or steel) visit a sheet-metal or welding shop, or a scrapyard. Craft shops and jewelry suppliers carry metals, other materials, and special tools for jewelry making.

Metal thickness is usually expressed in gauge numbers; the lower the gauge number, the thicker the metal. The commonest systems (in thousandths of an inch) are Brown & Sharpe (B & S)

or American Wire Gauge (AWG) for nonferrous metals, and U. S. Standard for ferrous metals. When following patterns and ordering stock, use the chart at right to compare systems.

A gauge plate can roughly measure metal thickness, but a micrometer or a vernier caliper is more precise, measuring any piece to thousandths of an inch. Mark the measurement on any leftover metal for future use.

Check angles or find center points with a combination tool. Mark straight lines on sheet metal with an indelible pen or a scriber and a steel rule, curves and circles with dividers, and points with a center punch.

Gauge no.	B & S/ AWG	U.S. Standard	Metric (mm)	Copper sheet
0	.325	.312	8.25	–
2	.258	.266	6.54	–
4	.204	.234	5.19	–
6	.162	.203	4.11	–
8	.129	.171	3.26	–
10	.102	.140	2.59	–
12	.080	.109	2.05	–
14	.064	.078	1.63	–
16	.050	.062	1.29	–
18	.040	.050	1.02	32 oz.
20	.032	.037	.813	24 oz.
22	.025	.031	.643	20 oz.
24	.020	.025	.511	16 oz.
26	.016	.018	.404	12 oz.
28	.013	.015	.330	10 oz.
30	.010	.012	.254	8 oz.

Measuring metal thickness

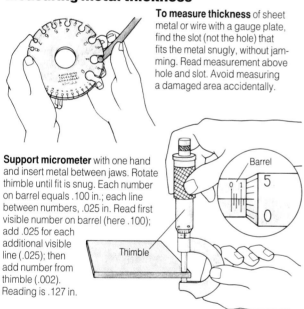

To measure thickness of sheet metal or wire with a gauge plate, find the slot (not the hole) that fits the metal snugly, without jamming. Read measurement above hole and slot. Avoid measuring a damaged area accidentally.

Support micrometer with one hand and insert metal between jaws. Rotate thimble until fit is snug. Each number on barrel equals .100 in.; each line between numbers, .025 in. Read first visible number on barrel (here .100); add .025 for each additional visible line (.025); then add number from thimble (.002). Reading is .127 in.

Barrel · Thimble

Vernier caliper has center scale marked on top in sixteenths of an inch (millimeters on bottom). Above inch scale, each division on sliding vernier scale represents $\frac{1}{128}$ in. Fit metal in jaws; tighten setscrew. Read below "0" (here $\frac{2}{16}$ in.); if a line meets exactly, that's the measurement. If not, look right for first vernier line that meets with a line on the center scale (here at $\frac{4}{128}$ in.). Add $\frac{2}{16}$ in. + $\frac{4}{128}$ in.= $\frac{20}{128}$, or $\frac{5}{32}$ in. (in decimal conversion, .15625 in.)

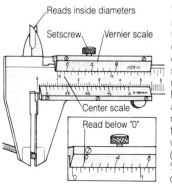

Reads inside diameters · Setscrew · Vernier scale · Center scale · Read below "0"

Marking metal

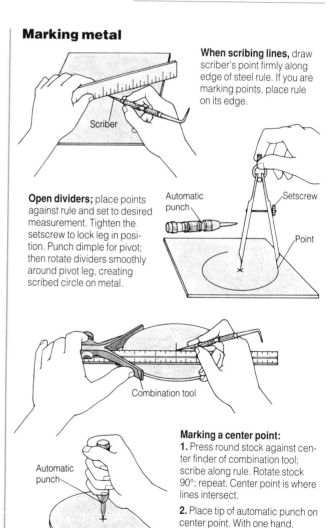

When scribing lines, draw scriber's point firmly along edge of steel rule. If you are marking points, place rule on its edge.

Scriber

Open dividers; place points against rule and set to desired measurement. Tighten the setscrew to lock leg in position. Punch dimple for pivot; then rotate dividers smoothly around pivot leg, creating scribed circle on metal.

Automatic punch · Setscrew · Point

Combination tool

Automatic punch

Marking a center point:
1. Press round stock against center finder of combination tool; scribe along rule. Rotate stock 90°; repeat. Center point is where lines intersect.

2. Place tip of automatic punch on center point. With one hand, press down on sleeve until punch recoils, forming a slight dimple.

Making a pattern

When creating any metal object, start by making a full-size pattern, or template, on heavyweight paper or thin cardboard. Original designs for two-dimensional items, such as plaques or pieces of jewelry, can be drawn on graph paper first, then transferred to pattern paper by tracing over carbon paper. Cut out the pattern and fasten it to the metal with rubber cement. Then cut the metal directly around the pattern. For larger objects—or for such three-dimensional objects as ducts, decorative pieces, or the box shown on this page—make a pattern called a stretch-out, which shows all parts of the object unfolded and flattened.

Draw a stretch-out with a sharp pencil and an accurate straightedge. Check all measurements twice, using one line as a baseline from which to measure; this avoids compounding any errors. Distinguish cut lines from fold lines, and calculate allowances for seams and edges. When you are finished, cut along the cut lines with scissors or a utility knife (use a steel rule to guide the blade); then assemble the pattern to test the design and to establish a logical sequence of work steps to follow when creating the actual object. (For folds, refer to the work sequence on page 182.) For a complicated project, make a written list of these steps so you can refer to them.

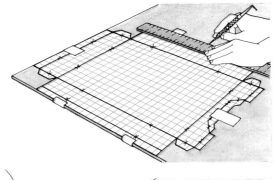
Angle tabs at 30°

Making a stretch-out: 1. For a three-dimensional object, begin by drawing the bottom or base. Extend all dimensions to form the sides, adding the appropriate amounts for seam and edge tabs. Angle the ends of the tabs toward each other at about 30° to make them easier to fold. Mark lines indicating folds with X's. Cut out the pattern and test it by folding it to its final shape, holding the seams temporarily closed with masking tape.

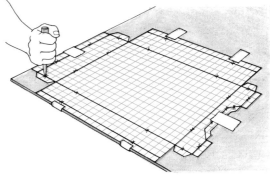

2. To scribe the pattern onto sheet metal, fasten it securely to the metal with masking tape. Using a steel rule as a straight-edge, lightly trace the pattern's outline onto the metal with a scriber. Align rule carefully with the pattern's edges, and always keep scriber's point against the rule's bottom edge.

3. With a scratch awl or a punch, mark fold lines and any internal cut lines by punching gently through the pattern in at least two places along each line. Remove the pattern. Using the scriber and rule, scribe along fold lines lightly to avoid weakening the metal, then scribe over the outline and any other cut lines more firmly, making these lines deeper.

Holding work securely

Accidents happen quickly in metal-working. Avoid them by securing the work with clamps or in a machinist's vise so that it cannot move during an operation. In a home workshop, fasten a machinist's vise at one corner of the workbench, near or over a leg. The vise's fixed jaw should project about half an inch beyond the bench's edge. Read the safety precautions on pages 10–13. In particular, wear eye protection to prevent injury from metal splinters, and heavy gloves and long sleeves to protect against sharp edges.

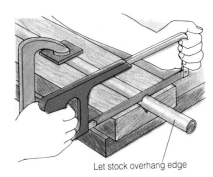
Let stock overhang edge

Swivel lock

For safety and control, tighten swivel and vise jaws firmly. Working close to jaws lessens chattering and movement of metal and reduces strain on vise.

Wooden V-block holds round stock securely for drilling, sawing, or shaping. Clamp stock in single V-block or use two V-blocks in machinist's vise.

There are many ways to cut metal, depending on the type, size, and amount of stock to be cut. Very thin metal, such as aluminum siding, can be cut by scoring with a utility knife several times along the cut line, using a steel rule as a straightedge. Most wire can be cut with side-cutting pliers. For sheet metal thinner than 16 gauge, use snips. Aviation snips, with their compact size and compound leverage, handle well; ordinary tin snips leave a smoother edge. If you have long or multiple cuts to make, choose electric shears or a nibbler. Both make curved and straight cuts quickly, but a nibbler cuts a channel through the metal, leaving a smoother edge. Before cutting with these power tools, lubricate along the cut line with light machine oil.

A circle cutter, available through jewelry suppliers, forms small discs and other shapes (such as half-moons or semicircles) for decorative or jewelry work. For thick metal plate and round stock, cut with a hacksaw or—for soft or thinner metals—an electric saber saw fitted with a metal-cutting blade. A cold chisel struck with a hammer will cut rough openings in metal too thick for snips, and can shear through solid stock such as bolt shafts.

Caution: Read the safety precautions on pages 12–13; in particular, protect your hands and eyes against flying metal chips and sharp edges. Always clamp or grip workpieces securely, and file rough edges smooth immediately after they have been cut.

Cutting techniques

Snips. Grip work with your free hand; slightly angle straight-cutting snips above surface. Work on waste side of cut line; don't close blades completely. Curl waste aside.

Power shears. Let waste overhang work surface. Cut slowly for thick metal or tight cuts, faster for thin sheets or long cuts. Curl waste aside. Wear safety goggles.

For inside curves, first drill or punch a starter hole. Using right- or left-cutting aviation snips, make first cut close to line, then trim remaining metal.

Circle cutter. To make shapes from sheet metal, first remove all pins. Slide metal into groove under hole (for varied shapes, position metal partially under hole). Insert pin in hole; strike with hammer to punch out piece.

Cold chisel. For inside shapes, grip chisel loosely and tilt. Strike chisel with ball-peen hammer, slicing metal with chisel blade.

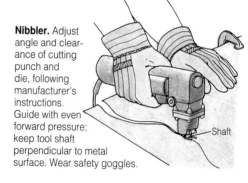

Nibbler. Adjust angle and clearance of cutting punch and die, following manufacturer's instructions. Guide with even forward pressure; keep tool shaft perpendicular to metal surface. Wear safety goggles.

Sawing metal

Hacksaw. Blade should have at least three teeth touching edge of metal for efficient cutting. Hold saw at both ends. Cut on forward stroke; rotate round stock to complete cut.

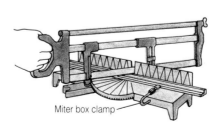

Angled cuts. Cut soft metal to specific angles in a miter box. Clamp or hold metal in box; use metal-cutting blade with miter box saw, or use hacksaw, as at left.

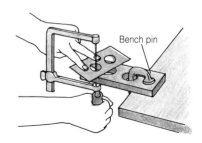

Jeweler's saw. Install blade through drilled hole in metal. Hold work against bench pin with fingers and keep centered in bench pin slot. Keep blade vertical to work; cut on downstroke only.

FILING AND DRILLING

For shaping and smoothing metal edges, mill files are usually the best choice; but for soft metal, particularly aluminum, choose a curved-tooth file with deeply cut teeth. Single-cut files, having a single series of parallel teeth, cut more slowly than double-cut files; the latter have a second row of teeth overlapping the first at an angle. Most files come in three grades—smooth cut, second cut, and bastard (coarsest)—but longer files, regardless of grade, leave a coarser surface than shorter files. Choose a file shape that matches the work, whether round, square, triangular, or flat.

Always put a handle on a file before working; it is safer and gives better leverage. Place the handle on the file's tang, and strike the handle against a hard surface until it is tight.

Hold the file at both ends and push it with long, slow strokes. (Draw-filing, shown on this page, is an exception.) Using your arms and shoulders as well as hands, apply even pressure. Maintain a steady rhythm, but lift the file on the return stroke to avoid dulling its teeth.

Prevent clogged teeth by rubbing chalk over a file before use, and regularly clean files by brushing with a file card.

Cross-file to remove burrs from a cut edge. Lay file diagonally across workpiece edge, square to sides. Push file forward and sideways.

Draw-file to produce smooth, finished edge. Hold file flat against surface, square to work's sides. Pull tool toward you; use fresh teeth for each stroke.

Round file smooths tight curves. Push file forward and sideways along curve (as in cross-filing) while rotating blade.

Drilling holes in metal

Drill holes in metal for fasteners, decoration, or instead of sawing when making large holes. A drill press provides stability, accuracy, and control, but a portable electric drill mounted in a stand can also drill through sheet metal and small stock. Make holes in thinner metal and stationary pieces with a variable-speed portable drill.

Choose sharp high-speed twist bits. Mark the location of the hole by denting the center with a punch (p.178), and back the metal with scrap wood. Apply several drops of light household or motor oil to the bit and the hole as you work. When drilling thick metal or steel, make a well with modeling clay to contain the oil. Drill slowly and exert firm but not undue pressure, slowing the drill speed if the bit squeaks, and pausing if it turns bluish or if smoke appears. Raise the bit frequently to clear waste and to add oil.

Caution: Wear safety goggles to protect your eyes from metal chips, and clamp all workpieces firmly unless they are stationary.

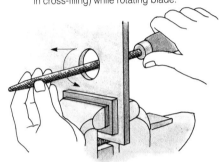

For holes over ⅛ in. wide, back metal with wood. Insert step bit into drill; mark desired diameter on bit with tape. Drive the bit through the metal until bit reaches tape mark and the hole is desired size.

Step bit

To drill holes in tubing, clamp tubing in V-blocks or vise. Insert dowel to reinforce thin walls and to guide bit straight through other side; be sure bit can exit freely.

V-block

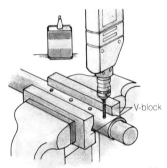

Drill press. For uniformly placed holes, make a two-sided jig. Back metal with wood. Clamp the jig firmly on drill press table; rotate metal for each hole.

Jig

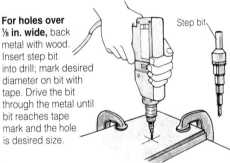

Fly cutter makes large holes in thin-gauge metal. Punch center point for drill bit; clamp work. Insert fly cutter in drill press, center the bit, and lock the cutter blade on the arm. Cut semicircle; turn workpiece over and complete circle.

Fly cutter

FOLDING SHEET METAL

When working with sheet metal, first bend it with gloved hands before moving on to bending and striking tools. Fold gradually by working along the entire fold line in stages, starting in the middle and working toward the ends. A bending brake, available at metalworking suppliers, provides greatest accuracy. A homemade brake can consist of two pieces of hardwood clamped together; align the metal's fold line between them and bend along it.

Complete bends and folds with a flat-faced mallet, and finish edges with a wedge-faced hammer. Never use a damaged wooden, plastic, or rawhide mallet; polish steel hammer faces (p.196) to remove nicks and scratches.

Plan the work sequence beforehand by assembling the stretch-out pattern (p.179). File rough edges smooth and complete any decorative surface work (pp.194–195); then form the edges and seams. Complete the object by making inside folds.

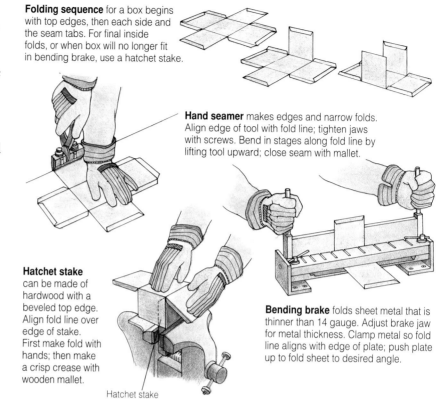

Folding sequence for a box begins with top edges, then each side and the seam tabs. For final inside folds, or when box will no longer fit in bending brake, use a hatchet stake.

Hand seamer makes edges and narrow folds. Align edge of tool with fold line; tighten jaws with screws. Bend in stages along fold line by lifting tool upward; close seam with mallet.

Hatchet stake can be made of hardwood with a beveled top edge. Align fold line over edge of stake. First make fold with hands; then make a crisp crease with wooden mallet.

Hatchet stake

Bending brake folds sheet metal that is thinner than 14 gauge. Adjust brake jaw for metal thickness. Clamp metal so fold line aligns with edge of plate; push plate up to fold sheet to desired angle.

Edges

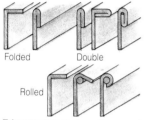

Folded   Double

Rolled

Edge treatment strengthens and smooths edges, and provides neat appearance. Rolled, or wired, edge (right) is strongest.

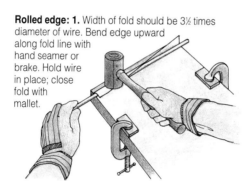

Rolled edge: 1. Width of fold should be 3½ times diameter of wire. Bend edge upward along fold line with hand seamer or brake. Hold wire in place; close fold with mallet.

2. Support seam with block of wood; curl edge around wire with wedge-faced hammer. Snip off excess wire with diagonal-cutting pliers.

Seams

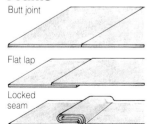

Butt joint

Flat lap

Locked seam

Seams are metal joints that can be soldered or fastened with rivets or screws. Locked seam (right) needs no fasteners or solder.

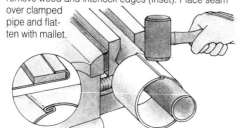

Locked seam: 1. Bend folds of equal width on both edges, one opposite the other. Lay scrap wood inside each fold; hammer down until almost closed; then remove wood and interlock edges (inset). Place seam over clamped pipe and flatten with mallet.

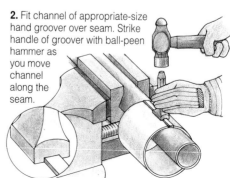

2. Fit channel of appropriate-size hand groover over seam. Strike handle of groover with ball-peen hammer as you move channel along the seam.

SHAPING WITH FORMS

Because metal is ductile—it flows, rather like modeling clay—it can be shaped by striking it against a form with a hammer or a mallet. You can create such objects as vases, bowls, and trays using two basic forming techniques—*raising* and *sinking*.

Deep objects are raised by striking their outer surface against solid forms called *stakes*. Various stakes are available at metalworking suppliers, but you can improvise with pieces of metal or hardwood. Jewelers use tapered stakes called *mandrels* for shaping rings and bracelets (p.193).

When sinking a shallow object, strike its inner surface against a hollow form, such as a sandbag or a mold made by gouging a bowl-shaped depression in the end grain of a hardwood block. Strike the metal squarely with the tool's face, not its edge, and use gentle, even blows. Keep steel hammer faces free of nicks (p.196).

Prolonged beating hardens most metal and it ceases to flow, becoming brittle and likely to crack. *Annealing*, or heating, the metal will restore its malleability. (Do not anneal aluminum, lead, or pewter.) After annealing, remove any oxide residue by cleaning the object in pickle (pp.190–191).

To finish a formed piece, decorate or planish it if desired (pp.194–195), then polish and buff it (p.196).

Annealing. Set piece on firebrick; heat all over with bushy torch flame until metal glows dull red. Allow to cool; then quench in water. Wear gloves and handle metal with tongs.

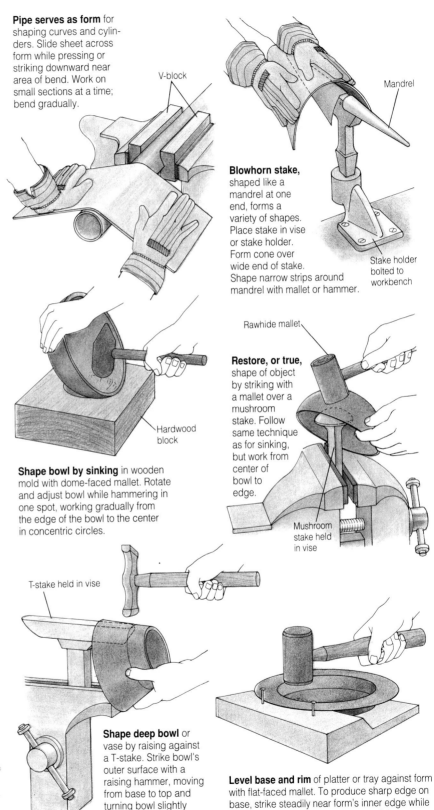

Pipe serves as form for shaping curves and cylinders. Slide sheet across form while pressing or striking downward near area of bend. Work on small sections at a time; bend gradually.

V-block

Mandrel

Blowhorn stake, shaped like a mandrel at one end, forms a variety of shapes. Place stake in vise or stake holder. Form cone over wide end of stake. Shape narrow strips around mandrel with mallet or hammer.

Stake holder bolted to workbench

Shape bowl by sinking in wooden mold with dome-faced mallet. Rotate and adjust bowl while hammering in one spot, working gradually from the edge of the bowl to the center in concentric circles.

Hardwood block

Rawhide mallet

Restore, or true, shape of object by striking with a mallet over a mushroom stake. Follow same technique as for sinking, but work from center of bowl to edge.

Mushroom stake held in vise

T-stake held in vise

Shape deep bowl or vase by raising against a T-stake. Strike bowl's outer surface with a raising hammer, moving from base to top and turning bowl slightly with each blow.

Level base and rim of platter or tray against form with flat-faced mallet. To produce sharp edge on base, strike steadily near form's inner edge while turning metal. Nails establish width of rim.

BENDING BAR METAL AND PIPES

Bar metal is classified as strips and flats as well as shaped rods (pp.176–177). Bending and twisting techniques apply to all varieties of bar metal; in general, ferrous metals are harder to bend than nonferrous. For tubing, use special bending tools.

Most bar metal up to ¼ inch thick and ½ inch wide can be bent cold. However, tight curves can overstretch metal, so make allowances when laying out. A bend of 90° will lengthen the outside of the curve by half the metal's thickness and shorten the inside of the curve by the same amount.

Align the workpiece exactly perpendicular or parallel to the vise jaws, protecting soft metal with V-blocks or scrap wood. Bend gradually and smoothly, by small amounts, checking the angle of the bend several times with a template or T-bevel. Use hand pressure first; then strike the metal with a hammer or mallet. For an exact shape bend around a stationary form, such as a pipe clamped parallel to the vise jaws.

Heating metal makes it easier to bend and increases the amount it will stretch. Heat the area of the bend with a propane torch until you can bend the metal smoothly.

Caution: Remove any nearby flammable objects and direct the torch flame only toward the area of bend. Wear gloves and protective clothing. Do not heat aluminum.

Cold-bending. Mark point of bend on metal strip; clamp metal in vise. Bend by hand for looser curve; for extra leverage, slip a length of pipe over the strip's free end. For tight curve, strike metal just beyond edge of vise.

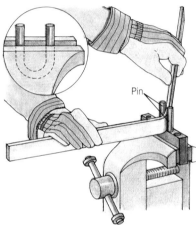

Bending jig makes scrolls and other complex bends. Set distance between pins slightly larger than the metal's thickness; feed metal between pins while bending. Homemade jig (inset) is a U-shaped rod clamped in vise.

Pin

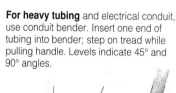

Twisting strips. Clamp one end of strip in vise. Grip other end with adjustable wrench or locking pliers. Twist with steady pressure to produce spiral.

A bending spring shapes copper tubing without kinking. Slide tubing into spring until coils cover area of curve. Bend with thumbs as fulcrum or against knee to desired curve.

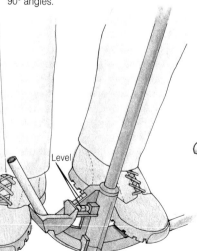

For heavy tubing and electrical conduit, use conduit bender. Insert one end of tubing into bender; step on tread while pulling handle. Levels indicate 45° and 90° angles.

Level

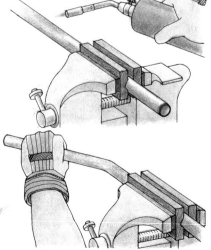

Bend flats, strips, and rods secured in vise by heating area of bend with torch until metal glows red. Extinguish torch; grasp free end of metal with gloved hand and bend sideways.

JOINING PIPE WITH FITTINGS

Rigid bronze and steel pipe are joined with threaded fittings. Flexible copper tubing is joined with compression or flare fittings, and both flexible and rigid copper tubing can be soldered (pp.190–191). Certain fittings require threaded pipe; for these, pipe can be purchased prethreaded or threaded to order at hardware, building, or plumbing suppliers. Special fittings join incompatible materials. When buying fittings, specify the pipe's inside diameter, the material, and whether it forms part of a water supply system or a drainage system.

Make careful calculations before cutting pipe to length—with rigid pipe, adjustments are seldom possible. Calculate both the width of the fitting and the amount it will overlap the pipe. Cut the ends of pipes exactly square, using a tubing cutter or, for bronze or steel pipe, a hacksaw (p.180). To prevent disturbed water flow inside pipes, remove burrs—the rough edges produced by cutting—by reaming the ends.

Tighten and loosen threaded fittings with two pipe wrenches; holding the pipe stationary with one wrench prevents damage to other joints on the line. Hold a pipe wrench so its jaws face the direction in which force is applied.

Caution: Before making modifications to a plumbing system, check with your local building inspector; building and plumbing codes prohibit some repairs and installations unless done by a licensed professional. Shut off the water supply and drain a plumbing pipe before working on it.

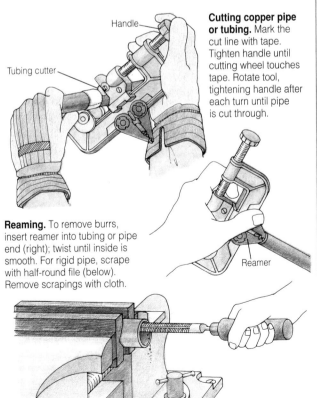

Cutting copper pipe or tubing. Mark the cut line with tape. Tighten handle until cutting wheel touches tape. Rotate tool, tightening handle after each turn until pipe is cut through.

Reaming. To remove burrs, insert reamer into tubing or pipe end (right); twist until inside is smooth. For rigid pipe, scrape with half-round file (below). Remove scrapings with cloth.

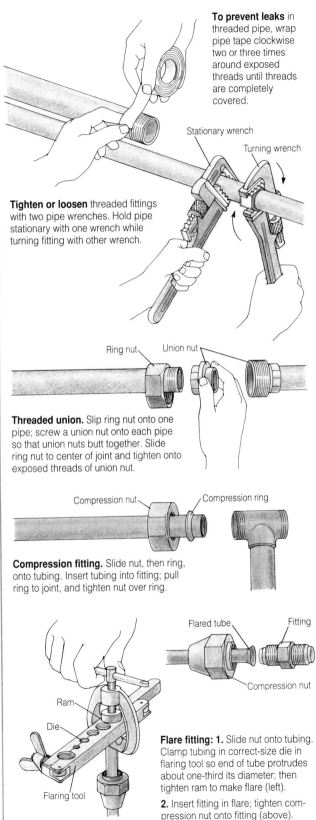

To prevent leaks in threaded pipe, wrap pipe tape clockwise two or three times around exposed threads until threads are completely covered.

Tighten or loosen threaded fittings with two pipe wrenches. Hold pipe stationary with one wrench while turning fitting with other wrench.

Threaded union. Slip ring nut onto one pipe; screw a union nut onto each pipe so that union nuts butt together. Slide ring nut to center of joint and tighten onto exposed threads of union nut.

Compression fitting. Slide nut, then ring, onto tubing. Insert tubing into fitting; pull ring to joint, and tighten nut over ring.

Flare fitting: 1. Slide nut onto tubing. Clamp tubing in correct-size die in flaring tool so end of tube protrudes about one-third its diameter; then tighten ram to make flare (left).

2. Insert fitting in flare; tighten compression nut onto fitting (above).

FASTENING: ADHESIVES, SCREWS, BOLTS, AND RIVETS

Adhesives

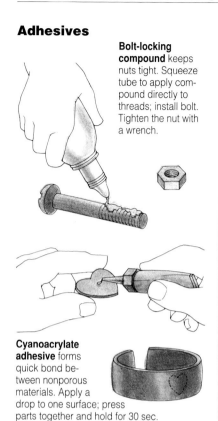

Bolt-locking compound keeps nuts tight. Squeeze tube to apply compound directly to threads; install bolt. Tighten the nut with a wrench.

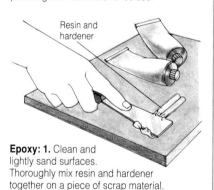

Cyanoacrylate adhesive forms quick bond between nonporous materials. Apply a drop to one surface; press parts together and hold for 30 sec.

Resin and hardener

Epoxy: 1. Clean and lightly sand surfaces. Thoroughly mix resin and hardener together on a piece of scrap material.

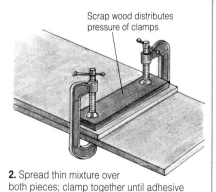

Scrap wood distributes pressure of clamps

2. Spread thin mixture over both pieces; clamp together until adhesive sets. Wipe away excess adhesive immediately.

Adhesives can create a strong bond for metal, but it is important to use the correct high-quality adhesive and to clean the surfaces thoroughly (degrease metal by wiping with denatured alcohol or a commercial degreasing agent). Follow the manufacturer's instructions for application and drying time.

To prevent threaded fasteners from loosening (particularly fasteners installed in engines, appliances, and other vibrating machinery), coat them with bolt-locking compound, available at hardware and automotive stores. Small metal objects that receive little stress, such as costume jewelry and appliance trim, can be bonded with cyanoacrylate adhesive, also known as super glue. Select the right viscosity: liquid cyanoacrylate for tight-fitting flat surfaces; a thicker gel formula for

pieces that fit together more loosely. Use epoxy where moderate stress is likely, when bonding metal to a non-porous material, or where metals are rough-textured and fit loosely. Resin and hardener must be in exactly equal proportions: too much hardener causes a weak joint; too little slows drying.

Caution: Work in a well-ventilated area when using adhesives; don't smoke, eat, or drink. If cyanoacrylate or epoxy adhesive contacts your skin, remove it promptly with acetone (often found in nail polish remover).

Stronger than most adhesives are threaded fasteners and rivets. Fasteners are available in a variety of metals; if possible, match the fastener to the metal being joined. But if the possibility for rust exists, use nonferrous fasteners, such as aluminum or brass.

Screws

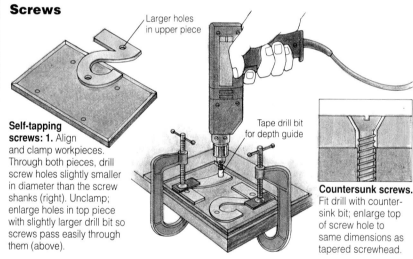

Larger holes in upper piece

Tape drill bit for depth guide

Self-tapping screws: 1. Align and clamp workpieces. Through both pieces, drill screw holes slightly smaller in diameter than the screw shanks (right). Unclamp; enlarge holes in top piece with slightly larger drill bit so screws pass easily through them (above).

Countersunk screws. Fit drill with counter-sink bit; enlarge top of screw hole to same dimensions as tapered screwhead.

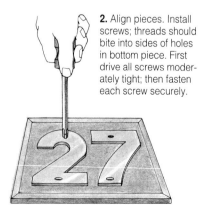

2. Align pieces. Install screws; threads should bite into sides of holes in bottom piece. First drive all screws moderately tight; then fasten each screw securely.

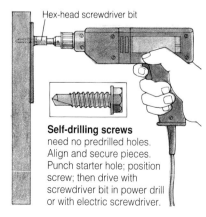

Hex-head screwdriver bit

Self-drilling screws need no predrilled holes. Align and secure pieces. Punch starter hole; position screw; then drive with screwdriver bit in power drill or with electric screwdriver.

Screws for joining sheet metal are usually self-tapping; driven with a screwdriver or a nutdriver, they cut threads inside a predrilled hole. Self-drilling screws create both a pilot hole and the threads inside; check with the manufacturer for the maximum thickness of pieces to be joined. (To remove stuck threaded fasteners, try the methods shown on page 189.)

For thicker pieces accessible from both sides, use bolts. Machine bolts with fine threads have greater holding power than stove bolts. Lag or carriage bolts can be used to attach metal to wood. A tightened bolt should extend beyond the nut by two or three threads. Allow for the additional thickness of washers, which serve to distribute pressure under the bolt head and the nut. A variety of specialized nuts are available; use cap nuts when fastening children's equipment (or wherever safety is a concern) and wing nuts for bolts that will need to be unfastened. If needed, you can thread bolt holes yourself (p.188).

Blind rivets are strong enough only for light sheet metal work like gutters and aluminum siding or for automobile body repairs, but they are easy to install with a blind-rivet tool and are more versatile than tinner's rivets. The work can be accessible from only one side, but there must be room for the rivet to form on the other side.

Bolts

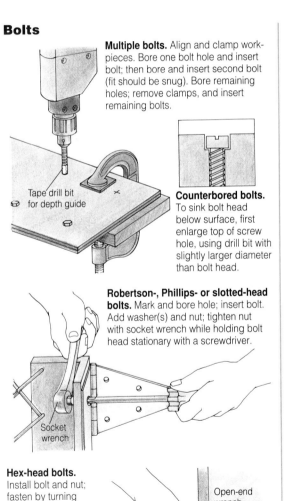

Multiple bolts. Align and clamp workpieces. Bore one bolt hole and insert bolt; then bore and insert second bolt (fit should be snug). Bore remaining holes; remove clamps, and insert remaining bolts.

Tape drill bit for depth guide

Counterbored bolts. To sink bolt head below surface, first enlarge top of screw hole, using drill bit with slightly larger diameter than bolt head.

Robertson-, Phillips- or slotted-head bolts. Mark and bore hole; insert bolt. Add washer(s) and nut; tighten nut with socket wrench while holding bolt head stationary with a screwdriver.

Socket wrench

Hex-head bolts. Install bolt and nut; fasten by turning bolt head and nut in opposite directions with two wrenches, as shown. If access is restricted, hold either the head or the nut stationary with a wrench and tighten other part with a socket wrench.

Open-end wrench

Rivets

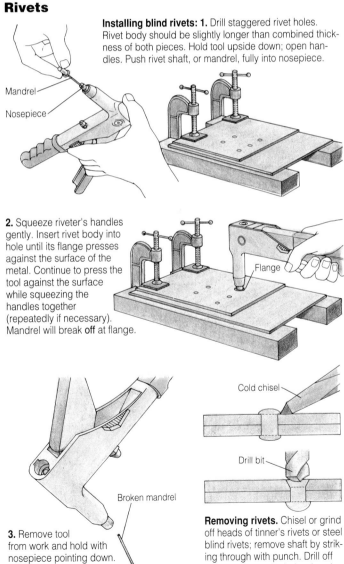

Installing blind rivets: 1. Drill staggered rivet holes. Rivet body should be slightly longer than combined thickness of both pieces. Hold tool upside down; open handles. Push rivet shaft, or mandrel, fully into nosepiece.

Mandrel

Nosepiece

2. Squeeze riveter's handles gently. Insert rivet body into hole until its flange presses against the surface of the metal. Continue to press the tool against the surface while squeezing the handles together (repeatedly if necessary). Mandrel will break **off** at flange.

Flange

Broken mandrel

3. Remove tool from work and hold with nosepiece pointing down. To extract mandrel, fully open handles and either shake riveter or withdraw mandrel with fingers.

Cold chisel

Drill bit

Removing rivets. Chisel or grind off heads of tinner's rivets or steel blind rivets; remove shaft by striking through with punch. Drill off blind or countersunk rivet heads using high-speed electric drill; punch out shaft.

FASTENING: TAPS AND DIES

Taps are used for cutting threads in holes; dies for threading rods. Both tools are often used for renewing damaged threads when repairing automobile parts, small-engine machinery (lawn mowers, garden tractors, chain saws), and household appliances.

Threaded fasteners are commonly designated using the American National Thread System as either National Coarse (NC) or National Fine (NF). General-purpose fasteners usually have the deeper NC threads. This designation is often stamped onto taps and dies, along with their diameter and the number of threads per inch (tpi). Thus a tap that is 5/16-18 NC will cut coarse threads for a 5/16-inch bolt at 18 tpi. (Under 1/4 inch the diameter is given as a number that corre-

Fully tapped hole goes through workpiece.

Blind hole ends inside workpiece.

sponds to a machine-screw size.) Metric taps are similarly designated, but their diameter and number of threads are given in millimeters, and a class number indicates the tap quality (#2 works in most applications).

Drill the hole to be tapped using the drill bit size indicated by a chart (often provided with tap and die sets) or by reading the markings directly on the taps. Complete blind holes with a *bottoming tap*, which cuts threads to the base of the hole.

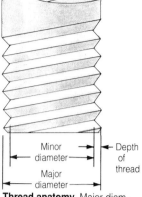

Thread anatomy. Major diameter of threads determines size of tap or die to use for cutting. Drill bit for pilot hole is slightly larger than minor diameter.

Drilling tap holes

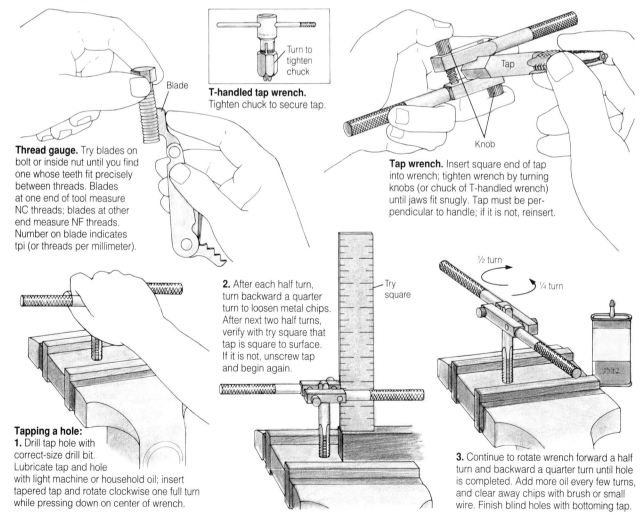

T-handled tap wrench. Tighten chuck to secure tap.

Thread gauge. Try blades on bolt or inside nut until you find one whose teeth fit precisely between threads. Blades at one end of tool measure NC threads; blades at other end measure NF threads. Number on blade indicates tpi (or threads per millimeter).

Tap wrench. Insert square end of tap into wrench; tighten wrench by turning knobs (or chuck of T-handled wrench) until jaws fit snugly. Tap must be perpendicular to handle; if it is not, reinsert.

Tapping a hole:
1. Drill tap hole with correct-size drill bit. Lubricate tap and hole with light machine or household oil; insert tapered tap and rotate clockwise one full turn while pressing down on center of wrench.

2. After each half turn, turn backward a quarter turn to loosen metal chips. After next two half turns, verify with try square that tap is square to surface. If it is not, unscrew tap and begin again.

3. Continue to rotate wrench forward a half turn and backward a quarter turn until hole is completed. Add more oil every few turns, and clear away chips with brush or small wire. Finish blind holes with bottoming tap.

Extracting broken fasteners

A broken or rusted bolt or screw can often be removed by soaking it with penetrating oil for 15 minutes. Then, if the head is accessible, twist out the fastener with locking pliers.

Another method is to strike a prick punch with a ball-peen hammer against one edge of the fastener head, turning the fastener counterclockwise.

For fasteners broken off below the surface, use a screw extractor. Most have left-hand threads; some have straight flutes along the shank. Both are turned counterclockwise with a wrench to extract the broken fastener.

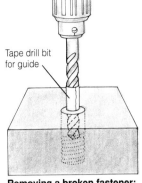

Tape drill bit for guide

Removing a broken fastener:
1. Punch starting point in center of broken fastener. With a drill bit smaller than the fastener, drill at least ⅜ in. into broken shaft.

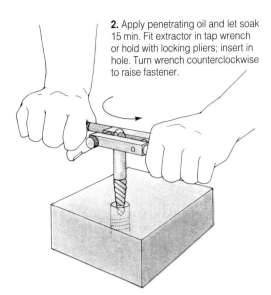

2. Apply penetrating oil and let soak 15 min. Fit extractor in tap wrench or hold with locking pliers; insert in hole. Turn wrench counterclockwise to raise fastener.

Threading rods with dies

Dies are held in a special wrench called a *diestock*. Some diestocks have an adjustable collar called a *diestock guide* that fits snugly around the rod to keep the die perpendicular to the handle.

Most tap and die sets include several dies; choose a die whose diameter corresponds to the size of the rod to be threaded. *Adjustable dies* can be made larger or smaller with a setscrew on one side. To test the fit of an adjustable die, cut the threads first with the die fully open. Screw a nut onto the rod. If the fit is too tight, adjust the die so it is smaller and recut the threads.

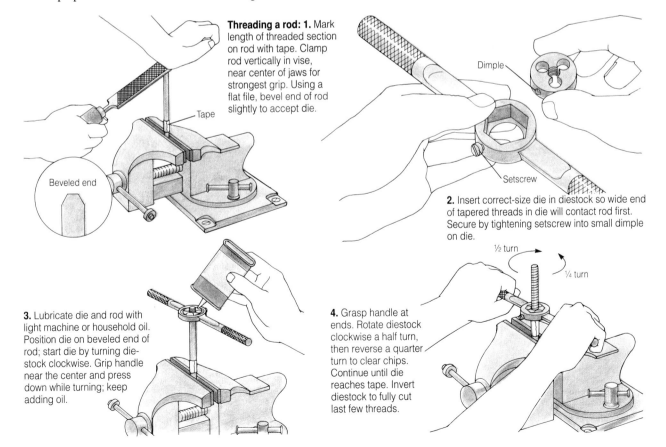

Threading a rod: 1. Mark length of threaded section on rod with tape. Clamp rod vertically in vise, near center of jaws for strongest grip. Using a flat file, bevel end of rod slightly to accept die.

Tape

Beveled end

Dimple

Setscrew

2. Insert correct-size die in diestock so wide end of tapered threads in die will contact rod first. Secure by tightening setscrew into small dimple on die.

3. Lubricate die and rod with light machine or household oil. Position die on beveled end of rod; start die by turning diestock clockwise. Grip handle near the center and press down while turning; keep adding oil.

½ turn

¼ turn

4. Grasp handle at ends. Rotate diestock clockwise a half turn, then reverse a quarter turn to clear chips. Continue until die reaches tape. Invert diestock to fully cut last few threads.

SOLDERING

Soldering joins metals by melting between them an alloy called solder. For *soft-soldering,* used for joining sheet metals and electronic parts, the solder is made chiefly of tin and lead; copper plumbing pipes should be joined with lead-free solder. These solders melt at 700°F (370°C) or under—too low a temperature to affect the metals being joined. *Hard-soldering* creates stronger joints and is needed to join silver or for fine craftsmanship. Hard solder contains precious metals, such as silver, with melting points between 1100°F (593°C) and 1450°F (788°C). Heating a metal to accept hard solder creates microscopic spaces into which the solder can flow; thus hard-soldered joints have more strength than soft-soldered joints and can be filed flush without weakening. *Brazing* is a type of hard-soldering generally used to join steel or dissimilar metals; it requires a brass solder with a melting point between

1800°F (982°C) and 3000°F (1650°C). Brazing requires great skill and the high heat created by an air/fuel torch.

An electric soldering pencil or gun provides sufficient heat for soft-soldering stained-glass joints or small electronic components. To soft-solder metal objects, use an electric soldering iron. A propane torch produces a flame suitable both for soldering copper pipes and for hard-soldering.

Before soldering, cover the surfaces with the appropriate flux to avoid the formation of oxides, a dark scaly film that prevents solder from adhering. For soft-soldering all except electronic items, use a zinc chloride flux, wiping away any excess with a cloth after soldering. Delicate electronic work requires a rosin flux, which is less messy to work with. For hard-soldering use fluxes containing borax or fluoride.

After hard-soldering, remove oxides with *pickle,* a cleaning solution. Pickle can contain sulfuric acid, but non-sulfuric-acid pickles are also available at craft and jewelry suppliers.

Soft-soldering with an iron

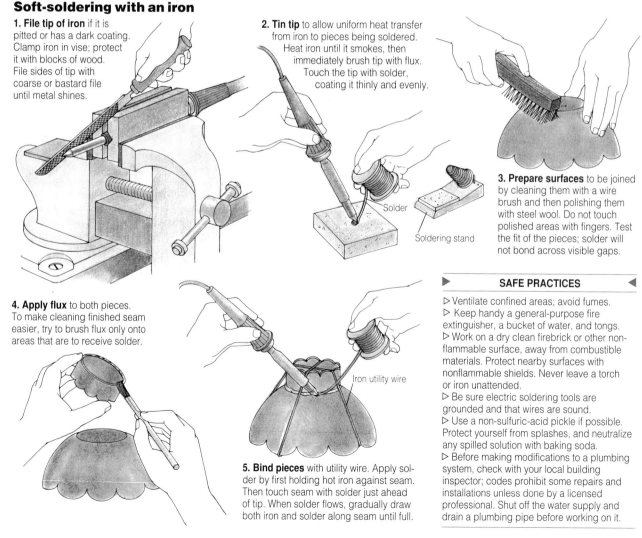

1. File tip of iron if it is pitted or has a dark coating. Clamp iron in vise; protect it with blocks of wood. File sides of tip with coarse or bastard file until metal shines.

2. Tin tip to allow uniform heat transfer from iron to pieces being soldered. Heat iron until it smokes, then immediately brush tip with flux. Touch the tip with solder, coating it thinly and evenly.

Hard solder

Soft solder

Solder

Soldering stand

3. Prepare surfaces to be joined by cleaning them with a wire brush and then polishing them with steel wool. Do not touch polished areas with fingers. Test the fit of the pieces; solder will not bond across visible gaps.

4. Apply flux to both pieces. To make cleaning finished seam easier, try to brush flux only onto areas that are to receive solder.

5. Bind pieces with utility wire. Apply solder by first holding hot iron against seam. Then touch seam with solder just ahead of tip. When solder flows, gradually draw both iron and solder along seam until full.

Iron utility wire

SAFE PRACTICES

▷ Ventilate confined areas; avoid fumes.
▷ Keep handy a general-purpose fire extinguisher, a bucket of water, and tongs.
▷ Work on a dry clean firebrick or other non-flammable surface, away from combustible materials. Protect nearby surfaces with nonflammable shields. Never leave a torch or iron unattended.
▷ Be sure electric soldering tools are grounded and that wires are sound.
▷ Use a non-sulfuric-acid pickle if possible. Protect yourself from splashes, and neutralize any spilled solution with baking soda.
▷ Before making modifications to a plumbing system, check with your local building inspector; codes prohibit some repairs and installations unless done by a licensed professional. Shut off the water supply and drain a plumbing pipe before working on it.

Soldering copper pipes

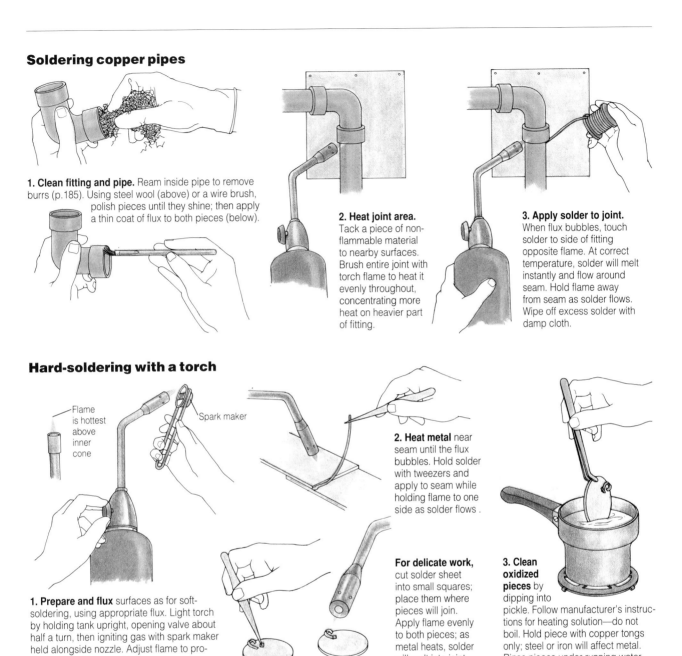

1. Clean fitting and pipe. Ream inside pipe to remove burrs (p.185). Using steel wool (above) or a wire brush, polish pieces until they shine; then apply a thin coat of flux to both pieces (below).

2. Heat joint area. Tack a piece of non-flammable material to nearby surfaces. Brush entire joint with torch flame to heat it evenly throughout, concentrating more heat on heavier part of fitting.

3. Apply solder to joint. When flux bubbles, touch solder to side of fitting opposite flame. At correct temperature, solder will melt instantly and flow around seam. Hold flame away from seam as solder flows. Wipe off excess solder with damp cloth.

Hard-soldering with a torch

Flame is hottest above inner cone

Spark maker

1. Prepare and flux surfaces as for soft-soldering, using appropriate flux. Light torch by holding tank upright, opening valve about half a turn, then igniting gas with spark maker held alongside nozzle. Adjust flame to produce pointed inner cone.

2. Heat metal near seam until the flux bubbles. Hold solder with tweezers and apply to seam while holding flame to one side as solder flows .

For delicate work, cut solder sheet into small squares; place them where pieces will join. Apply flame evenly to both pieces; as metal heats, solder will melt into joint.

3. Clean oxidized pieces by dipping into pickle. Follow manufacturer's instructions for heating solution—do not boil. Hold piece with copper tongs only; steel or iron will affect metal. Rinse pieces under running water.

Welding and blacksmithing

Welding joins metals—usually steel—by melting them so they fuse together. The high heat required can come from a torch that mixes fuel with pure oxygen or from a powerful electric transformer called an *arc welder*. Strong welded joints are required for repairs to machinery, metal furniture, and outdoor equipment, as well as to tools and to metal used for structural purposes. Though fairly simple in theory, welding requires expert instruction and much practice. High schools and vocational schools often offer courses in welding, and rental centers carry welding equipment.

Blacksmithing has seen a revival of interest in recent years. Ample space and equipment is needed, including a forge for heating metal and a selection of hammers and stakes for pounding it into shape. Craft items like fireplace tools, decorative hardware, and cooking utensils are the stock-in-trade of most modern-day smiths. Craft schools and historical organizations may offer courses in blacksmithing. Equipment can be homemade or bought at flea markets and auctions. A smith who shoes horses is a *farrier;* for instruction consult farming, equestrian, or veterinarians' groups.

Wire—round, half-round, square, and rectangular—serves as stock for many jewelry and metalworking projects. Wire can be pulled through a metal drawplate (a process called *drawing*) to change its shape and thickness; it can be decoratively twisted by itself or with other wires; and it can be fashioned into jump rings, then used to form chain or create *findings,* the elements that hold together many jewelry pieces.

Finger rings are made with wire or with strips cut from sheet metal. Use a graduated ring mandrel, which has standard ring sizes marked at intervals along its length, to form new rings or to reshape damaged ones. Calculate the length of metal needed to form a given ring size by using the linear scale provided on some mandrels, or by forming a template from a strip of paper. First wrap the paper around the desired ring size on the mandrel, then add twice the thickness of the metal stock for the template's total length.

The metal found in commercial chain is sometimes filled with solder, which lowers its melting point, making it difficult to repair by soldering. Homemade solid wire jump rings, however, make durable links and chains. Making circular jump rings is shown; you can also create oval and square jump rings by winding the wire around a form with the desired shape.

Buy commercial findings—such as settings for stones, clasps for necklaces and bracelets, and posts for earrings and cufflinks—at crafts or jewelry suppliers, and use them to replace broken findings or to form new pieces. Unless you are experienced, don't try to repair or set valuable stones; it is easy to lose or damage such stones.

Hard-soldering with the technique for delicate work shown on page 191 is the best way to join metal jewelry pieces. For a project with many joints, use solder designated high-, medium-, and lower-temperature in succession to avoid melting completed joints while heating others. Glue together any pieces that can't be heated (p.186).

Working with wire

Drawing wire. File wire tip to 1-in. point; then lubricate it with beeswax or light household oil. Clamp drawplate in vise; insert wire from plate's unnumbered side into smallest possible hole of desired shape. Hold tip; pull wire through hole. Pull through successively smaller holes until wire reaches desired gauge. Anneal frequently (below).

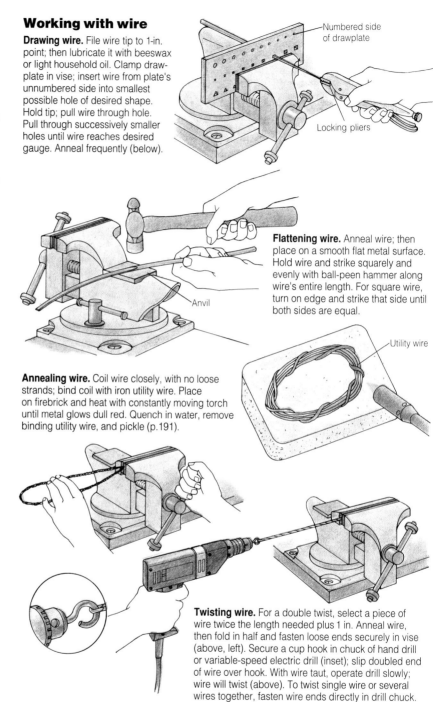

Numbered side of drawplate

Locking pliers

Anvil

Flattening wire. Anneal wire; then place on a smooth flat metal surface. Hold wire and strike squarely and evenly with ball-peen hammer along wire's entire length. For square wire, turn on edge and strike that side until both sides are equal.

Utility wire

Annealing wire. Coil wire closely, with no loose strands; bind coil with iron utility wire. Place on firebrick and heat with constantly moving torch until metal glows dull red. Quench in water, remove binding utility wire, and pickle (p.191).

Twisting wire. For a double twist, select a piece of wire twice the length needed plus 1 in. Anneal wire, then fold in half and fasten loose ends securely in vise (above, left). Secure a cup hook in chuck of hand drill or variable-speed electric drill (inset); slip doubled end of wire over hook. With wire taut, operate drill slowly; wire will twist (above). To twist single wire or several wires together, fasten wire ends directly in drill chuck.

Twisted wire designs

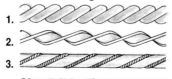

1.
2.
3.
4.

Twisted wire can form rings, patterns on flat brooches, earrings, or bracelets. To make a bracelet, loop wire to desired diameter and solder ends together.
1. Double-twist round wire, then flatten.
2. Twist single strand of flat wire.
3. First twist single square wire, then double-twist round wire and wind together by hand.
4. Twist together several strands of round wire.

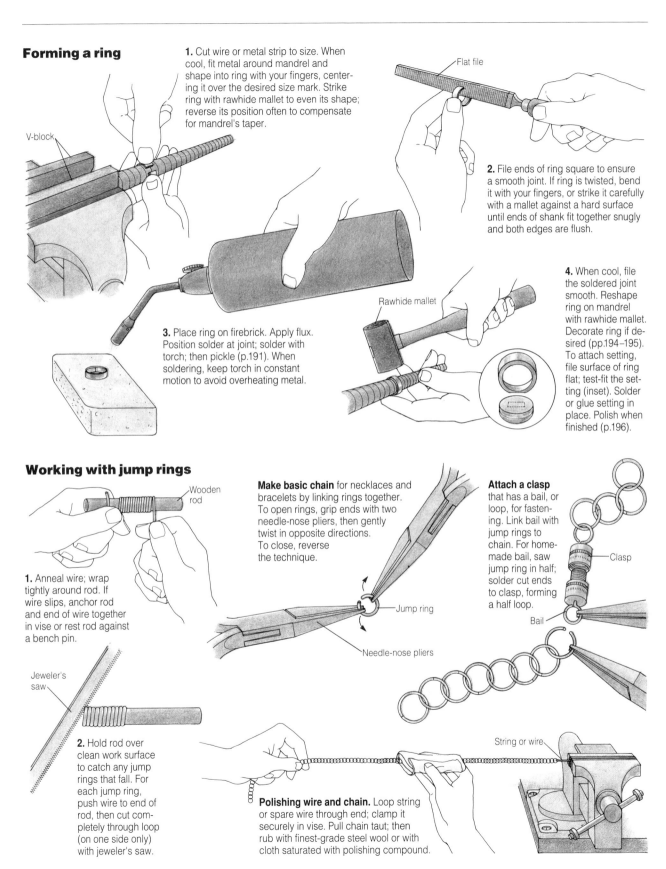

Forming a ring

1. Cut wire or metal strip to size. When cool, fit metal around mandrel and shape into ring with your fingers, centering it over the desired size mark. Strike ring with rawhide mallet to even its shape; reverse its position often to compensate for mandrel's taper.

Flat file

V-block

2. File ends of ring square to ensure a smooth joint. If ring is twisted, bend it with your fingers, or strike it carefully with a mallet against a hard surface until ends of shank fit together snugly and both edges are flush.

4. When cool, file the soldered joint smooth. Reshape ring on mandrel with rawhide mallet. Decorate ring if desired (pp.194–195). To attach setting, file surface of ring flat; test-fit the setting (inset). Solder or glue setting in place. Polish when finished (p.196).

Rawhide mallet

3. Place ring on firebrick. Apply flux. Position solder at joint; solder with torch; then pickle (p.191). When soldering, keep torch in constant motion to avoid overheating metal.

Working with jump rings

Wooden rod

1. Anneal wire; wrap tightly around rod. If wire slips, anchor rod and end of wire together in vise or rest rod against a bench pin.

Jeweler's saw

2. Hold rod over clean work surface to catch any jump rings that fall. For each jump ring, push wire to end of rod, then cut completely through loop (on one side only) with jeweler's saw.

Make basic chain for necklaces and bracelets by linking rings together. To open rings, grip ends with two needle-nose pliers, then gently twist in opposite directions. To close, reverse the technique.

Jump ring

Needle-nose pliers

Attach a clasp that has a bail, or loop, for fastening. Link bail with jump rings to chain. For homemade bail, saw jump ring in half; solder cut ends to clasp, forming a half loop.

Clasp

Bail

String or wire

Polishing wire and chain. Loop string or spare wire through end; clamp it securely in vise. Pull chain taut; then rub with finest-grade steel wool or with cloth saturated with polishing compound.

Metal objects can be decorated by a variety of techniques; among them are hammering, etching, and coloring with chemicals. Decoration must be applied at the appropriate point during construction. For example, items like bowls or vases that are shaped by raising or sinking cannot be decorated until after they are formed. But a box or other item with flat sides can be decorated before it is folded or attached to other pieces. Practice decorative techniques on pieces of scrap metal before attempting them on the actual piece.

Planishing is the technique of hardening and smoothing metal by hammering. A skillfully planished surface has many small indentations that add texture and sparkle to the piece. Polished hammers are reserved for planishing; keep their faces smooth (p.196). A ball-peen hammer can also be used to create patterned surfaces—reflecting the various contours of either the face of the hammer or the surface it strikes. Always wear safety goggles when striking metal with hammers.

Pointed tools and punches are struck with hammers to create intricate designs on metal surfaces. Punching holes to form a pattern in the metal is called *piercing*. In *chasing*, blunt punches are used to create a pattern in shallow relief on the surface. When the pattern is also raised in relief by hammering it from behind, the technique is

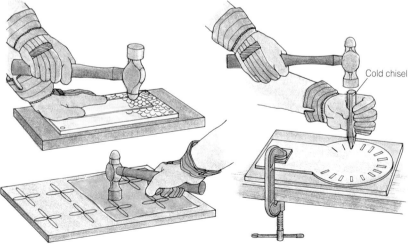

To prevent blemishes, strike concave or flat surface with domed hammer face, convex surface with flat face.

Planishing. Hold piece on stake or against other hard surface. Work with light in front of you. Strike squarely and evenly with planishing hammer, working in a spiral from base to rim, (for a bowl, work from center outward). Deliver blows from wrist; overlap points of impact.

Chasing and repoussé

1. Heat pitch and mount work face-up in pitch bowl so that metal is supported at all points. Trace outline and details with chasing tool by striking tool end lightly with hammer. Hold tools firmly to avoid slips; deliver blows from wrist.

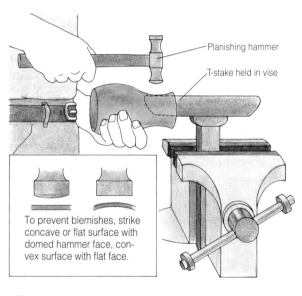

Impact and hammer textures. For dimpled pattern, hold work against a hard surface; strike work with round hammer face (top). To reproduce a surface texture, hold workpiece against surface; strike workpiece all over with flat face until design is imprinted (bottom).

Piercing. Scribe pattern of holes; clamp work on scrap wood. Use nails, a prick punch, or a cold chisel with a sharp edge (shown) to pierce holes in the metal, striking the tool with flat face of a ball-peen hammer. Aim for uniform results over the entire piece.

2. Warm pitch to remove chased work. For repoussé work, anneal (p.183); then mount work face-down in pitch and emboss with repoussé tools, using the same hammer technique as for chasing. Proceed alternately on front and back until design is defined.

called *repoussé*. You strike chasing and repoussé tools with a lightweight chasing hammer, and do both techniques on a surface that yields slightly. Pitch set in a special bowl is ideal (it is available at metalworking suppliers), but softwood or a sandbag can also serve as a work surface. Heat pitch with a torch to soften it before positioning or removing an object, but do not ignite it. To remove excess pitch, soak the metal in lacquer thinner.

In *etching*, a design is created on metal by dissolving part of the surface with a corrosive *mordant*. The mordant for most metals is usually nitric acid; its use is best left to professionals. However, copper and brass can be etched with ferric chloride, a safer, less caustic salt solution available at crafts and electronic suppliers. Elements of the design to be protected from the mordant are coated beforehand with a *resist,* usually a substance called asphaltum.

Exposing metals to certain chemicals creates a thin layer of corrosion that changes their patina, or texture and color. After treatment, polish the metal if desired (pp.196–197), then protect it from further coloration by giving it a coat of lacquer or wax.

Caution: Wear safety goggles and rubber gloves when working with chemicals, and follow any other precautions for handling, storage, and disposal listed by the manufacturer.

Etching

1. Cover areas to be protected from mordant by brushing on asphaltum. Either coat surface and scribe design into asphaltum for etching (above), or cover metal with stencil of design and paint asphaltum over uncovered areas (below), then remove stencil. Let the asphaltum dry.

Metal scriber

Lift piece with cotton string

2. Submerge piece upside down in mordant in glass or plastic container, with patterned face on plastic supports. Stir often with a feather or a string to dislodge bubbles.

3. After 30 min., rinse piece with water and check progress. Repeat every 15 min. until metal has dissolved to desired depth. Remove resist with soft cloth soaked in turpentine.

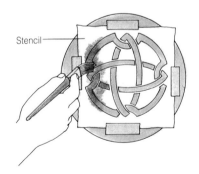

Stencil

Protecting finished surfaces

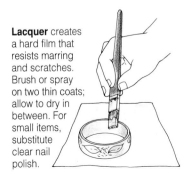

Lacquer creates a hard film that resists marring and scratches. Brush or spray on two thin coats; allow to dry in between. For small items, substitute clear nail polish.

Wax seals out air and moisture where hard finish is not desired. Select a fine-quality furniture wax that contains no silicone. Apply, allow to harden, and then buff with clean soft cloth. Repeat until desired sheen is achieved.

Creating a patina

When treating metal objects to create a surface patina, adjust the recipes below proportionately if greater or smaller amounts are needed for the size of the object. The effect of the treatment will vary depending on the type of metal and the surrounding conditions; try recipes on scrap metal first. Before treatment, wash metal thoroughly in a bucket of water mixed with household detergent and 1 tbsp. of ammonia. (When the metal is clean, water will no longer form beads on the surface.) Dry the metal with a clean soft cloth, and from then on handle it only by the edges. Mix chemicals in a glass or porcelain container and use only distilled water. Check the object frequently to gauge its progress. Follow the manufacturer's instructions for storage and handling of chemicals.

To darken silver or copper, mix 1 tbsp. liver of sulfur (potassium sulfide, available from jewelry and crafts suppliers) in 1 c. warm water. Hold the piece with tongs and dip it into the solution. Rinse under running water.

To darken steel, aluminum, or bronze, apply gun bluing, available at sporting goods stores. Rub the bluing over the metal with fine-grade steel wool until you achieve the desired effect.

To give copper a variegated blue pattern, wet the piece, then sprinkle it with table salt. Place the object beside an open bowl of ammonia, and cover both with a plastic bucket or small plastic tent. Leave until the desired effect is achieved (sometimes several days).

To color copper, brass, or bronze green, mix 1 tbsp. ammonium chloride (sal ammoniac, available from jewelry and crafts suppliers), 1 tbsp. table salt, and 2 tbsp. ammonia in 1 qt. warm water. Pour solution into a plastic spray bottle and spray the piece all over. Allow to dry; repeat until the desired effect is achieved.

To turn copper dark brown, coat your fingers with a thin film of linseed oil, then rub the piece all over, applying just enough oil to cover the surface. Warm the piece evenly with a propane torch just until the oil starts to smoke. Wipe off excess oil with a clean cloth.

The final stages of many metalworking projects are sanding, which smooths the surface, and buffing, which creates luster. (Filing removes rough edges and burrs; see p.181.) Complete polishing consists of rubbing with successively finer grades of abrasive, beginning by hand with abrasive paper (or by using an attachment on a portable ⅜-inch drill), and then buffing with an electric polishing machine, such as a bench grinder.

Start with a medium (100-grit) or very fine (200-grit) abrasive—neoprene is a good choice. When the surface is uniform, switch to an extra-fine (300-grit) abrasive. For a fine polish, work up to at least a 400-grit abrasive, then buff.

Buff on a bench grinder fitted with a cloth disc called a *buffing wheel.* To buff rings and other small objects, fit a *cone buff* over a *tapered spindle,* both of which are available at jewelry and metalworking suppliers. Follow the tool manufacturer's instructions for changing wheels and installing a tapered spindle on the motor shaft—you will first have to remove the side housing panel. It's safe also to remove the eye guard and tool rest from the tool, but wear safety goggles, and allow no one to stand where they might be hit by an item pulled from your grasp by the wheel. Hold large items in your hands; brace smaller or flat items against a board. The wheel should always rotate downward toward you.

Apply buffing compounds directly to the wheel; start with either tripoli or white diamond and proceed to rouge. Install a separate wheel for each compound. After using each, clean the metal by washing it with a mixture of household detergent, water, and a few drops of ammonia. Gloves or rubber finger caps will prevent compounds from soiling your hands.

A portable power drill fitted with a buffing pad attachment and clamped into a horizontal drill stand can substitute for buffing with a bench grinder. Fit a ¼- or ⅜-inch drill into the stand, and run it with the trigger locked. Apply polishing compound and buff as you would with a grinder.

Preliminary polishing. Secure piece; rub metal with abrasive cloth or paper wrapped around stick, file, or dowel. Use two or more grades of abrasive; alternate direction of strokes with each successive grade.

Sanding block

Polishing hammer face. Clamp hammer in vise; polish as described above but with abrasive material wrapped around wood block or secured in sanding block. To buff, coat leather-covered block with white diamond compound; rub hammer face with circular motion.

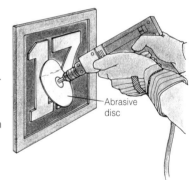

Portable drill speeds polishing. Fit abrasive disc (shown) or buffing pad on a drill arbor according to manufacturer's instructions. If object is not stationary, clamp it securely. Running tool at high speed, move disc across surface at even rate; exert light pressure. Wear goggles and gloves.

Abrasive disc

Buffing with a bench grinder

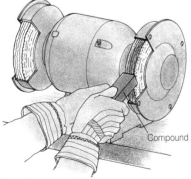

Compound

Preparing wheel. Wear goggles and gloves. Touch end of compound stick to moving wheel below centerline. Coat wheel evenly with compound every 5 min. during use. When surface becomes shiny, hold buff rake (or an old fork) against surface of pad until the cloth is no longer compacted; then reapply compound.

Buffing. Grip work tightly with fingers; hold below wheel's centerline. Turn piece constantly to expose whole surface. Clean work before changing to a wheel that has been coated with another compound.

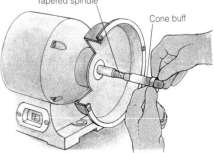

Buffing small items. Install tapered spindle on motor shaft; screw cone buff onto spindle, and coat the buff with compound. Press small items gently and firmly onto spinning buff. Change cones and clean item for new compound. Rubber gloves make handling easier.

Tapered spindle

Cone buff

REPAIRING METAL OBJECTS

Metal objects with minor rust and damage can usually be repaired. But rust destroys metal quickly; prevent it by painting outdoor tools, toys, and other items with rust-resistant paint and storing them in a dry place, and by using galvanized metal for outdoor fasteners, railings, and fencing.

Clean metal with mild detergent and water, and brighten tarnished metal by rubbing it with commercial polish. Careful malleting on a sandbag, stake, or with the aid of a dolly block (a polished steel block available through auto supply stores) flattens dents. Solder small cracks (p.190); or patch cracks and holes with a two-part fiberglass repair kit, available at hardware and auto supply stores. Read the kit manufacturer's instructions before use: these compounds are not suitable for making structural repairs or repairs to containers of liquid or gas.

An alternative to sanding away rust is a *liquid rust converter.* Scrape off any loose rust; then apply the converter. It hardens and seals the remaining rust, creating an irregular but rustproof surface that can be primed and painted.

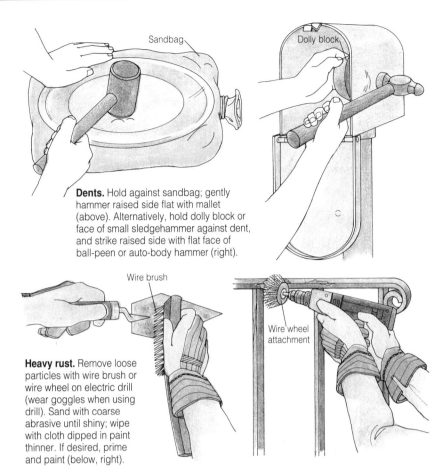

Dents. Hold against sandbag; gently hammer raised side flat with mallet (above). Alternatively, hold dolly block or face of small sledgehammer against dent, and strike raised side with flat face of ball-peen or auto-body hammer (right).

Heavy rust. Remove loose particles with wire brush or wire wheel on electric drill (wear goggles when using drill). Sand with coarse abrasive until shiny; wipe with cloth dipped in paint thinner. If desired, prime and paint (below, right).

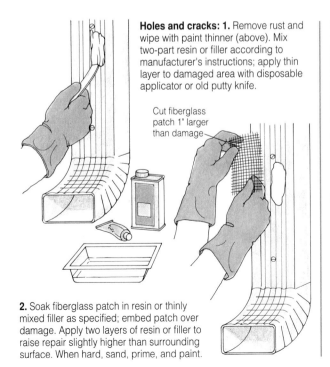

Holes and cracks: 1. Remove rust and wipe with paint thinner (above). Mix two-part resin or filler according to manufacturer's instructions; apply thin layer to damaged area with disposable applicator or old putty knife.

Cut fiberglass patch 1" larger than damage

2. Soak fiberglass patch in resin or thinly mixed filler as specified; embed patch over damage. Apply two layers of resin or filler to raise repair slightly higher than surrounding surface. When hard, sand, prime, and paint.

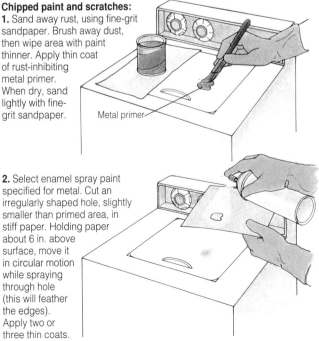

Chipped paint and scratches: 1. Sand away rust, using fine-grit sandpaper. Brush away dust, then wipe area with paint thinner. Apply thin coat of rust-inhibiting metal primer. When dry, sand lightly with fine-grit sandpaper.

Metal primer

2. Select enamel spray paint specified for metal. Cut an irregularly shaped hole, slightly smaller than primed area, in stiff paper. Holding paper about 6 in. above surface, move it in circular motion while spraying through hole (this will feather the edges). Apply two or three thin coats.

Inspect tools before each use; a dull tool is neither efficient nor safe. With practice and good equipment, you can sharpen most straight-edged tools. But saw blades, carbide-tipped tools, and other hardened or contoured edges are best sharpened professionally.

Sharpening causes the sides of a blade to meet at an angle, called a bevel, the steepness of which is crucial to the blade's performance. In general, resharpen a blade to its original bevel. Chisel and plane blades come with bevels ranging from 15° to 30°. You can add a narrow secondary bevel five degrees greater; this speeds honing by reducing the cutting area. *Hollow-grinding* (grinding the primary bevel against the edge of the bench grinder

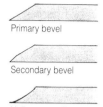

Primary bevel

Secondary bevel

Hollow-ground

wheel until the blade is slightly concave) produces a similar result.

A bench grinder speeds sharpening and is especially helpful for reshaping damaged edges. Buy new grinding wheels as needed; install a medium- and a fine-grit wheel to use as a pair.

When grinding, follow the safety precautions listed below and on pages 12–13. Improper use of a bench grinder not only is extremely dangerous; it can destroy the tool's *temper*—its hardness and resiliency.

Hand-sharpen and hone blades with flat sharpening stones and curved slipstones. A good selection includes a combination 1,000/4,000-grit water-stone, a hard Arkansas oilstone, and a diamond hone. Keep stones well lubricated. For a keen edge, finish up with a leather strop or, better still, with a buffing wheel.

Sharpening with a bench grinder

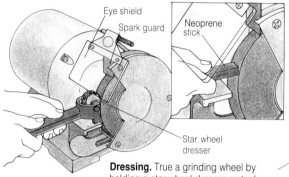

Eye shield

Spark guard

Neoprene stick

Star wheel dresser

Dressing. True a grinding wheel by holding a star wheel dresser on tool rest; while running the grinder, slide dresser lightly from side to side against wheel's edge (above). To restore clogged wheel, use same technique, but with silicon carbide stick (inset).

Hollow grinding. Set tool rest to desired bevel angle. Hold tool with both hands; place on rest and slide from side to side against edge of wheel. Keep forefinger against bottom edge of rest to steady tool.

Tool rest

▶ **SAFE PRACTICES** ◀

▷ Before use, hold a wheel by its center hole and tap it with a hard object. A good wheel will ring; a cracked wheel will make a buzzing sound and must be discarded.
▷ Never grind on the side of a wheel that is not specially designated for this purpose.
▷ Do not remove wheel guards, eye shields, or tool rests. Set tool rest within 1/16 in. of wheel.
▷ Always wear safety goggles or a full face shield.
▷ Don't wear loose clothing or dangling jewelry. Tie back long hair.
▷ Hold tool with bare hands; as you feel the blade getting warm, dip it in a bowl of cool water.

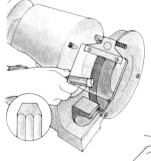

Cold chisel. Grind away mushroomed, or split, head of cold chisel to reduce chances of splintering, which can cause injury. Taper ground end (inset) to reduce chance of future damage.

Drawknife. Before grinding, ensure that blade can move freely across grinder wheel. Bevel blade by sliding it across the wheel, supported on the tool rest. To hone, clamp one handle of tool in vise; start at opposite end and slide sharpening stone along blade's beveled side. To remove burr, reverse tool and repeat on other side.

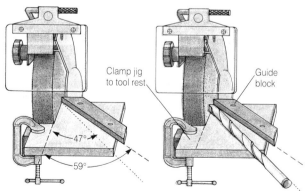

Clamp jig to tool rest

Guide block

47°

59°

Drill bit. Make jig for sharpening twist drill bit against side-grinding wheel. Clamp jig to level tool rest; place on jig against guide block. Press one side of tip against wheel; roll bit clockwise while slowly pivoting it to guideline at 47°. Repeat for other side.

Honing a sharp edge

To prevent uneven wear on stone, move blade in figure-8 pattern. Simpler technique is back-and-forth motion.

Hone primary bevel on chisels, plane irons, and spokeshaves by rubbing blade over medium stone (above, right) until you can feel a burr on blade's flat side. To create secondary bevel, raise blade 5° (inset) and rub over fine stone until burr forms. Remove burr both times (right) by gently rubbing blade's flat side on stone until blade is smooth.

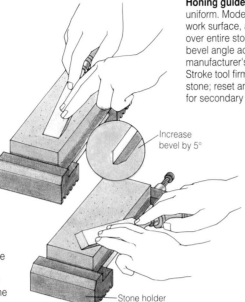

Increase bevel by 5°

Stone holder

Honing guide helps keep angles uniform. Model below rolls along flat work surface, allowing blade to travel over entire stone. Fit tool and set bevel angle according to manufacturer's instructions. Stroke tool firmly along stone; reset angle for secondary bevel.

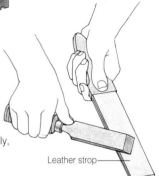

Angle gauge

Roller guide

Strop on leather that has been lightly coated with fine polishing compound. Hold blade against strop; draw back several times on each side of blade. Alternatively, hone on a very fine stone (6,000 grit).

Leather strop

Special techniques

Burnisher

Scraper. Clamp in vise; protect with scrap wood. Make edge perfectly square with file or stone (left). (For beveled cabinet scrapers, file bevel to original angle.) Create burr (hooked edge) by pushing burnisher along edge while pressing down firmly (right). On final strokes, tilt tool downward slightly to make burr curl over.

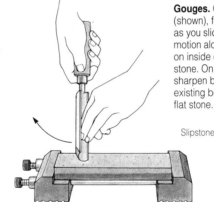

Gouges. On gouge with outside bevel (shown), follow the existing bevel angle as you slide the edge with a rotating motion along a flat stone. Remove burr on inside edge by stroking with a slipstone. On gouge with inside bevel, sharpen by stroking with slipstone at existing bevel angle; remove burr with flat stone.

Slipstone

Knife. With cutting edge leading, draw blade across stone from handle to tip. Maintain bevel angle. Turn blade over and repeat. Use same number of strokes for each side. Strop for razor edge.

Slipstone

Serrated knife. Clamp knife in vise with beveled side of serrations facing you. Sharpen each serration by stroking lightly with curved edge of slipstone held at bevel angle. Remove burrs by rubbing unbeveled side of blade on flat stone.

10°

Scissors. Hold bevel against stone; slide blade forward diagonally along stone, moving from point to pivot. Repeat for other blade. Remove burrs by opening and closing scissors several times.

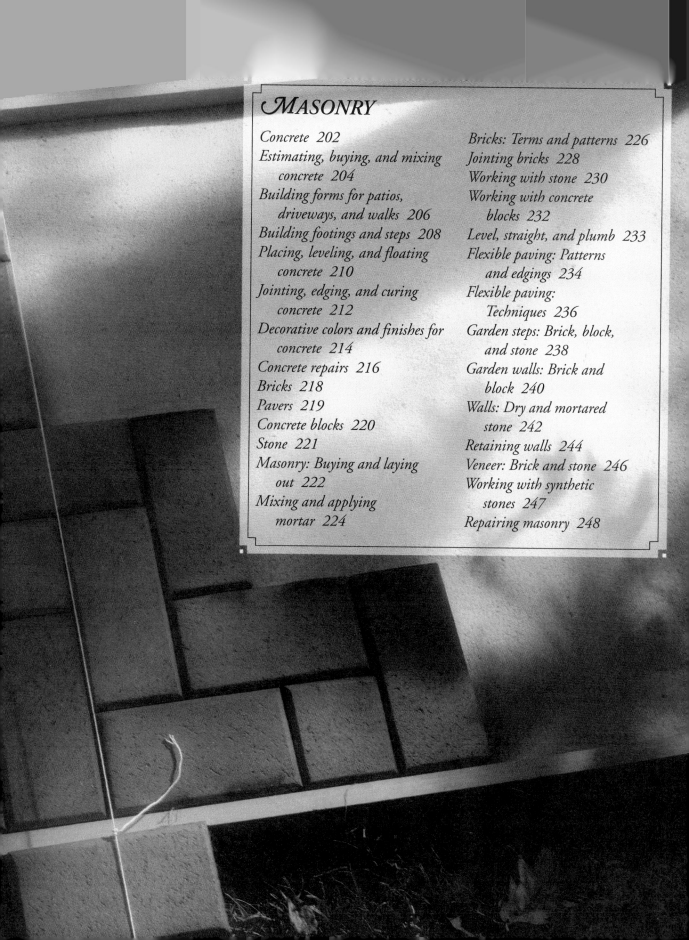

MASONRY

CONCRETE

Concrete is a mixture of sand and coarse aggregates—either gravel or crushed stone—held together by Portland cement. When mixed with water, the cement hardens through a chemical reaction. There are five types of Portland cement manufactured in Canada—10, 20, 30, 40, and 50—but only Type 10 is commonly used. Type 10 is an all-purpose variety that is suitable for most indoor and outdoor projects and that can be blended in such a way that it carries some characteristics of the other types. Type 50, a sulphate-resistant cement, is recommended for certain Prairie areas where soils or groundwaters have a heavy sulphate content. Air-entrained cement must be used where the work will be exposed to

freeze-thaw action or deicing chemicals. In Canada, it is customary to add the air-entrainment mixture during concrete mixing. If you'll be working with 1 cubic yard of concrete or more, you'll probably find it more economical to have ready-mix delivered.

Portland cement is available in gray, white, and sometimes buff. You can create other colors by adding powdered color pigments, combined with color hardeners, to the concrete mix; spray on a sealer after the concrete hardens. You can also liven up a concrete surface before it sets by roughening it, carving designs into it, adding exposed aggregate, or stamping it with a pattern.

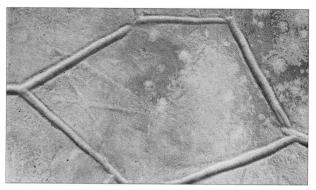

False flagstone effect can easily be hand-tooled into concrete before it sets. If you wish, add a color pigment to the concrete mix. Strike off the poured concrete, smooth it with a float, cut the outlines of flagstones into the surface with a brick jointing tool, and smooth the surface again. Spray on a color sealer when the concrete is hard.

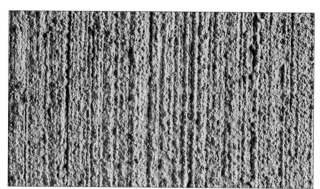

Brooming, achieved by dragging the bristles of a push broom over wet concrete, yields a rough-textured nonslip surface. The "grain" generally runs straight, either along the length of the surface or across it, but there are many decorative variations, including wavy grain, diagonals, and alternating diagonals. Color can be added to the concrete.

Pebbled surface, or exposed aggregate finish, offers a more variable type of rough-textured surface than brooming. Sprinkle decorative aggregate randomly or in a pattern over the surface of poured concrete (colored or not) before it sets. When the concrete is firm, wash and brush the surface to expose the tops of the aggregate.

Decorative aggregates used in textured concrete vary widely in color and shape according to the type of rock; in fact, even pieces of the same type of aggregate may vary. You can use any kind, but rounds and cubes cover best and rough textures bond better than smooth ones; flat stones tend to dislodge.

Basket weave

Herringbone

Square

Hexagon

Charcoal cobblestone

Yellow-ochre cobblestone

Stamping offers a quick method of creating a false finish with a repeated pattern. By pushing a stamping tool into wet concrete (usually colored), you can fashion any number of designs to make a driveway, walk, or patio floor look as though it is paved with bricks, cobblestones, slate, granite, concrete pavers, or tiles.

A few of the patterns available in commercially made stamping tools are shown here. You can use a single pattern for an entire area, or combine two or more to create a more fanciful design or to add a border or separate a section. Seal the stamped concrete after it has hardened.

Compared to hand-laid pavers, stamped concrete does not as readily tilt out of level because of frost heaves, and there are no spaces between units for grass and weeds to grow through. On the other hand, if the surface is damaged, you must replace the entire slab, or at least a large section of it, rather than one or two individual pavers.

Running bond brick

A successful concrete project requires careful planning and preparation. First, determine the composition of your concrete. Choose aggregate that is no larger in diameter than one-third the slab's thickness. Aggregate larger than ¾ inch is hard to spread and compact with hand tools. In addition, select one of several types of cement, the "glue" that holds the coarse aggregate and the sand together (pp.202–203). Also determine how much cement and water you'll need (the thicker the paste, the stronger the concrete), as well as the proportions of sand and aggregate. The recipes below should be checked against your local building code.

As all outdoor projects must withstand freezing and thawing without surface scaling, air-entrained concrete is essential. Tiny air bubbles in the mixture act as shock absorbers, expanding and contracting when the moisture in the cured concrete freezes and thaws.

These bubbles also make this type of concrete easy to work with. To blend the ingredients properly, always mix even small amounts of air-entrained concrete in a power mixer.

To estimate how much concrete you need, use mathematic formulas (p.344) or graph paper (below). Add 5 to 10 percent for contingencies. For strength, walks, patios, and driveways must be 4 inches thick (6 inches for any truck traffic).

Measuring based on weight is more accurate than that based on volume because sand increases in volume when wet. The recipes in the chart below assume wet sand; for damp or overly wet sand, increase or decrease the water. Then make a trial batch and test the consistency (facing page).

For projects requiring 1 cubic yard or more, consider having the concrete professionally mixed and delivered. Call the supplier a week ahead. Specify

the quantity, the strength (generally equal to a load of 4,000 pounds per square inch, or *psi*), the *slump,* a measure of consistency used by professionals (usually 4 inches or less), the air content (5 to 8 percent), and the aggregate size. Have the site prepared and helpers on hand when the truck arrives.

Mix air-entrained concrete or quantities of less than a cubic yard in a rented power mixer. (To make air-entrained concrete, buy air-entraining or Type IA cement.) For small jobs, you can buy premixed concrete with all the dry ingredients correctly proportioned. Just add clean water and blend with a hoe, shovel, or trowel. Or you can buy the dry ingredients in separate bags from building supply stores.

Caution: Contact with wet concrete can cause serious burns. Wear long sleeves, trousers, rubber boots and gloves, and goggles. Wash concrete splashes off your skin with water.

Estimating concrete quantities

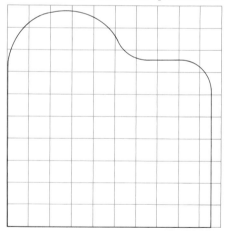

Find volume of irregular shape. Lay out the design on the ground, staking it at its widest points. Measure; then draw the shape to scale on graph paper with one square equaling 1 sq. ft. Count all the filled squares and those that are one-third or more filled. Convert the slab thickness from inches to feet. For example, 4 in.=⅓ ft. Then multiply the area by the thickness to find cubic feet. Divide by 27 to find cubic yards.

Determine moisture content of sand by squeezing. Damp sand won't stick together. Properly wet sand (above) forms ball but leaves no noticeable moisture on palm. Overly wet sand forms ball and leaves palm moist.

To measure by volume, build a bottomless box with inner dimensions of 1 cu. ft. (12 × 12 × 12 in.). Mark sides for partial amounts. Follow one of formulas below. Place box on flat surface. Fill, then lift box away. Transfer measured ingredient to mixing site.

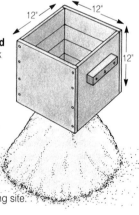

Formulas:	1 cubic foot of concrete (with air)				1 cubic foot of concrete (without air)			
	Maximum aggregate size ⅜"		Maximum aggregate size ¾"		Maximum aggregate size ⅜"		Maximum aggregate size ¾"	
	Pounds	Cubic-foot box	Pounds	Cubic-foot box	Pounds	Cubic-foot box	Pounds	Cubic-foot box
Cement	29	¼	25	¼	29	¼	25	¼
Wet sand	53	½	42	½	59	⅔	47	½
Coarse aggregate*	46	⅔	65	⅔	46	½	65	⅔
Water	1 gal.	1 gal.	1 gal.	1 gal.	1⅕ gal.	1⅕ gal.	1⅕ gal.	1⅕ gal.

*If crushed stone is used, decrease coarse aggregate by 3 lb. and increase sand by 3 lb.

Working with concrete

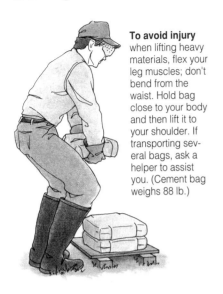

To avoid injury when lifting heavy materials, flex your leg muscles; don't bend from the waist. Hold bag close to your body and then lift it to your shoulder. If transporting several bags, ask a helper to assist you. (Cement bag weighs 88 lb.)

Power mixing

Anchor mixer with sandbags and mix a trial batch. Before starting the mixer, load the coarse aggregate and half the water. Start mixer. Add the sand, cement, and remaining water, in that order. Mix for at least 3 min. or until all ingredients are blended and uniform in color. Shovel a portion onto a flat surface and test the consistency (below).
Caution: To avoid injury, keep your head, hands, and shovel away from the blades when the mixer is on. Don't wear loose clothing that might get caught in outer moving parts.

Mixing concrete by hand: 1. Spread measured amount of sand on mixing surface. Add measured amount of cement; mix until streaks disappear. Add measured amount of aggregate; mix again by turning ingredients at least three times.

2. Mound ingredients and form depression in center. Slowly add two-thirds of the water. Mix by pulling dry ingredients little by little into the center and pushing overwet mixture to the sides. Gradually add remaining water.

3. Test mix for proper proportions by smoothing surface with hoe, then making a row of narrow troughs. Correctly mixed concrete will hold peaks. Aggregate should be barely discernible throughout the mix. If necessary, adjust proportions on paper. If the mixture is lumpy, reduce the aggregate or add more sand, cement, and water. If soupy, reduce the water. Mix a new batch (don't try to adjust a poor one).

BUILDING FORMS FOR PATIOS, DRIVEWAYS, AND WALKS

Site preparation

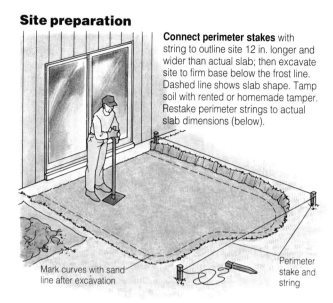

Connect perimeter stakes with string to outline site 12 in. longer and wider than actual slab; then excavate site to firm base below the frost line. Dashed line shows slab shape. Tamp soil with rented or homemade tamper. Restake perimeter strings to actual slab dimensions (below).

Mark curves with sand line after excavation

Perimeter stake and string

Grading the stakes

String guideline

1. Mark high point of slab surface: Drive stakes on both sides 1½ in. outside final slab location (space is allowed for forms to be nailed to stakes). Stretch and level chalked string; then snap it against the house. Drive the tops of stakes level with snapped line. Stretch new perimeter string guidelines to mark placement of graded stakes for the slab.

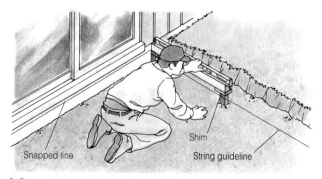

Shim

Snapped line

String guideline

2. Drive stake 3 ft. away from house with inner face of stake resting against string guideline. Nail ¾-in.-thick shim beneath one end of 3-ft.-long straight 2 x 4. Place level and 2 x 4 across stakes, with shim down and away from house; drive stake until 2 x 4 is level. Continue to end; repeat on other side. Nail the forms flush to tops of stakes.

Forms mold and support concrete when it is poured. Because of the extreme pressure wet concrete exerts, forms must be sturdy and well braced, usually with 1 × 2 stakes driven into the ground and nailed to the form. The tops of the forms serve as guides when pouring and as bearing surfaces when smoothing the concrete (pp.210–211).

Most forms are temporary, designed to be removed after the concrete has cured. Double-headed masonry nails aid in disassembly. To make the wooden forms easier to remove, wet them thoroughly, then wipe them with a release agent (available at building supply stores). When constructing forms for a slab to be poured in stages, place and stake temporary partition forms called stopboards. These dividers may have a beveled strip, called a key, nailed to the center of one side, so the concrete sections will be joined (pp.212–213).

Straight forms are made of a Douglas fir plywood designed to be used as forms; regular Douglas fir plywood; or 2 × 4 or wider lumber boards. (A 2 × 4 is actually 3½ inches wide; for a 4-inch slab, fill the gap below the forms with gravel.) Make gradual curves by kerfing 1 × 4's of softwood, sharper curves with plywood or hardboard. Green lumber is easier to bend than kiln-dried lumber, and it draws less moisture from the concrete (which can weaken it) during curing.

Sometimes forms are left in place permanently for decoration, in which case they also serve as control joints, reducing cracking in large slabs (pp.212–213). Select a naturally decay-resistant species, such as cedar or cypress, or use pressure-treated wood. Before use, coat non-pressure-treated lumber with a clear wood sealer. Cover the top edges of all permanent forms with masking tape to prevent staining.

To drain properly, slabs should slope in one direction ¼ inch per foot of length or width. Good drainage makes walks and driveways less slippery when wet and keeps water on an uncovered patio away from the house. (If drainage for a level patio that is separate from the house is not essential, stake the forms 1 inch above grade.) To create a slope, drive stakes to a graded height and fasten forms flush with their tops. To grade from the middle toward both sides of a wider slab, as for a driveway, set the central divider board the required distance higher than the forms along the sides. When screeding the concrete, place the screed across the central form and a side form to grade the slab to the correct pitch.

Prepare the site by excavating below the frost line and deep enough for the slab and a gravel layer, and a foot wider on all sides to provide room for nailing. (Replace the turf when landscaping.) Gravel supports the slab and drains water that collects underneath. Drainage is crucial anywhere the ground freezes, which is virtually everywhere in Canada. In low-lying areas or where the soil is heavy clay, compact a 4-inch-thick layer of ¾-inch gravel beneath a slab. Local building codes regulate concrete construction, so check with the building inspector for your area. You may also have to build a perimeter footing and add reinforcing bars (p.209).

Building a temporary form

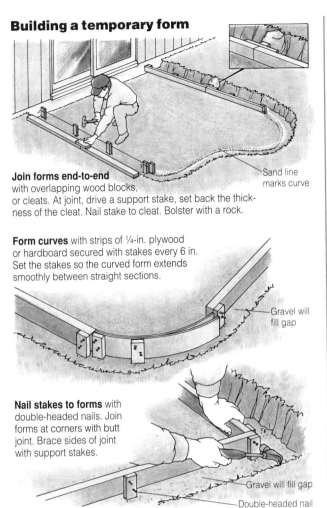

Join forms end-to-end with overlapping wood blocks, or cleats. At joint, drive a support stake, set back the thickness of the cleat. Nail stake to cleat. Bolster with a rock.

Sand line marks curve

Form curves with strips of ¼-in. plywood or hardboard secured with stakes every 6 in. Set the stakes so the curved form extends smoothly between straight sections.

Gravel will fill gap

Nail stakes to forms with double-headed nails. Join forms at corners with butt joint. Brace sides of joint with support stakes.

Gravel will fill gap

Double-headed nail

Making a permanent form

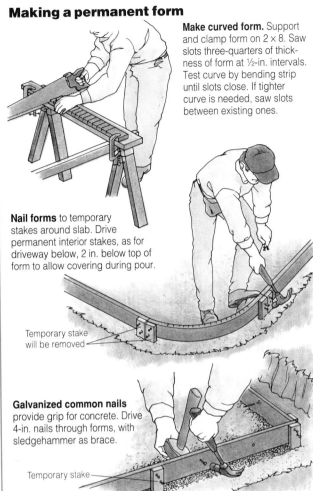

Make curved form. Support and clamp form on 2 × 8. Saw slots three-quarters of thickness of form at ½-in. intervals. Test curve by bending strip until slots close. If tighter curve is needed, saw slots between existing ones.

Nail forms to temporary stakes around slab. Drive permanent interior stakes, as for driveway below, 2 in. below top of form to allow covering during pour.

Temporary stake will be removed

Galvanized common nails provide grip for concrete. Drive 4-in. nails through forms, with sledgehammer as brace.

Temporary stake

Layout for driveway

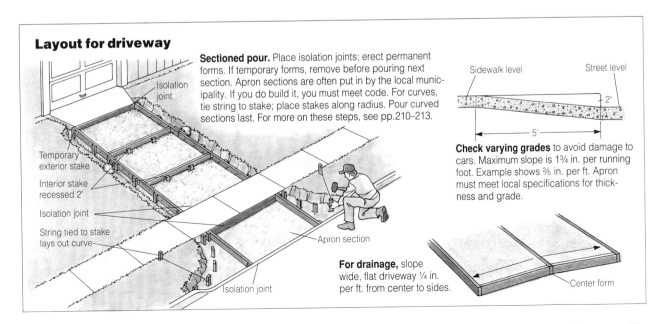

Sectioned pour. Place isolation joints; erect permanent forms. If temporary forms, remove before pouring next section. Apron sections are often put in by the local municipality. If you do build it, you must meet code. For curves, tie string to stake; place stakes along radius. Pour curved sections last. For more on these steps, see pp.210–213.

Isolation joint

Temporary exterior stake

Interior stake recessed 2"

Isolation joint

String tied to stake lays out curve

Apron section

Isolation joint

Sidewalk level   Street level

2"

5'

Check varying grades to avoid damage to cars. Maximum slope is 1¾ in. per running foot. Example shows ⅖ in. per ft. Apron must meet local specifications for thickness and grade.

For drainage, slope wide, flat driveway ¼ in. per ft. from center to sides.

Center form

Masonry   207

BUILDING FOOTINGS AND STEPS

Laying out a footing

1. Place leveled batter boards; lay out the footing corners and outer perimeter with strings (p.233). Dig a trench deep enough for sand and footing, and wide enough for a 1-ft. work area on each side of footing. Place, tamp, and level sand. To mark the outer perimeter, pour contrasting color sand over strings.

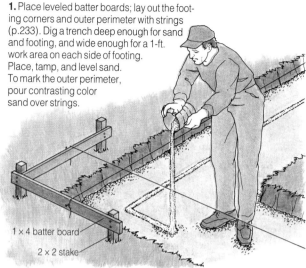

1 × 4 batter board

2 × 2 stake

2. Drive long stakes (equal to footing depth, sand fill, and 4 in. below trench) along outside of sand line. Check with level. Nail forms (pp.206–207). Locate stakes for inner form boards with spacer cut to exact width of footing plus thickness of two form boards.

Reinforcing rod

Spacer

3. Drive inner stakes; nail inner form boards as in step 2. Support stakes with diagonal braces and outer stakes. Nail lubricated spacers 3 to 4 ft. apart across tops of form boards. If code calls for reinforcing rods, prop them on bricks or rock chips so rods will rest in center of footing.

Concrete footings support the weight of vertical structures and hold them in place. In planning a project involving footings, check on the regulations in your local building code. Before excavating, obtain all necessary permits. Follow inspection schedules; for example, some codes require that forms for footings be inspected before the concrete is poured.

A continuous footing, as for a garden wall, has a depth equal to the thickness of the wall above it. The width of the footing is usually twice its depth. It is critical that the footing surface be smooth to ensure a level base and that the sides are straight and plumb (p.233). Pier footings, consisting of concrete columns sunk into the ground, are used as spot supports for fence posts, decks, and storage sheds. For a concrete landing and steps up to 30 inches high (facing page) and pier-and-panel walls (pp.240–241), pier footings should give enough support and require less excavation than a continuous footing. (Steps higher than 30 inches are usually supported by a continuous footing.)

When excavating for footings, dig a trench that is deep enough to hold a layer of tamped coarse sand 4 inches thick. The sand provides a stable support for the footing. The base of the footing should rest below the frost line. Your building inspector will tell you the depth of the frost line in your area and the type of soil you have. In hard, compacted soil, wooden forms may not be needed for continuous footings; a straight-sided trench with a layer of sand in the bottom may do. Pier footings can often be made by pouring concrete into a hole partly filled with gravel; but if the soil is loose or the piers project above ground level, use cardboard tubes called Sonotubes, available at building supply stores.

Concrete steps. When planning, keep safety and ease in mind. The risers and treads must be uniform. Six-inch risers are the easiest to climb; 7 inches is the maximum height. Treads should be deep enough to stand on easily: at least 11 inches, and preferably 12 to 14 inches. To increase the depth of the treads, angle the risers inward 15° from top to bottom. For drainage, concrete treads must slope ¼ inch per foot from back to front. Extend the landing at least 6 inches beyond the door on each side, or as specified by code.

Side forms for steps up to 30 inches high can be made of ¾-inch plywood; riser forms can be plywood or nominal 1-inch-thick lumber. To allow for smoothing the treads prior to removing the forms, bevel the bottom edges of the riser forms. Brace all forms well and lubricate the insides (p.210). To use less concrete, you may fill some space within the forms with compacted gravel; leave at least 4 inches of depth on all sides for the poured concrete.

The grain of the wood forms will show on the concrete. When you remove the forms (from 3 to 7 days after the pour), smooth the step sides by brushing on grout made of 1 part cement to 1½ to 2 parts sand and diluted with enough water to resemble thick paint. Let it dry for 1 to 2 hours; then rub off any excess with dry burlap.

Building steps

Mark perimeter and height of steps with leveled strings stretched between stakes. Excavate down some 6 in. Dig 8-in.-diameter holes 4 to 6 in. below frost line for pier footings at front corners. Compact 4 in. of gravel in holes and fill with concrete. Install isolation joint, then tie steps to house with rebars inserted through isolation joint into foundation wall (p.213).

Layout for landing, treads, and risers. Allow enough area for landing so door can open. To find number of steps, divide height of steps by the riser height. Build riser form with 15° forward tilt, tread with slant of ¼ in. per ft. for drainage.

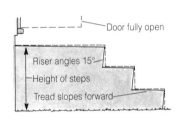

Door fully open

Riser angles 15°

Height of steps

Tread slopes forward

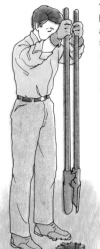

Cut two step profiles, including 6 in. below grade, and riser forms. Stake and brace profiles, then riser forms. Add gravel and compact it. Pour concrete into lowest tread first. Allow it to stiffen about 30 min. (time varies with temperature and stiffness of mixture when placed), so it will resist pressure when successive treads are poured.

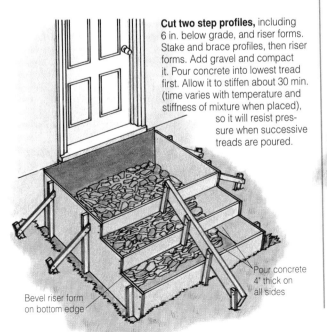

Bevel riser form on bottom edge

Pour concrete 4" thick on all sides

Setting a post

1. Dig posthole. With handles parallel, raise posthole digger and thrust it into ground. Open handles, and rock or rotate tool as you remove it to excavate soil. Repeat until depth is a minimum of half of total post length and at least 4 in. below frost line. For multiple holes or rocky soil, or where the frost line is several feet down, consider hiring a professional with a power auger.

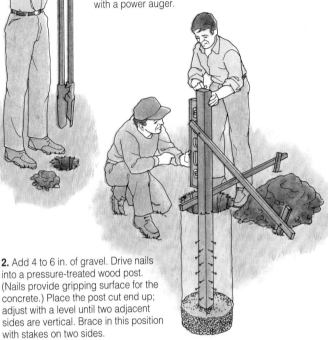

2. Add 4 to 6 in. of gravel. Drive nails into a pressure-treated wood post. (Nails provide gripping surface for the concrete.) Place the post cut end up; adjust with a level until two adjacent sides are vertical. Brace in this position with stakes on two sides.

3. Put second post in its hole; align posts. Hang taut line level between posts; adjust height of second post, if needed, so heights are uniform; adjust second post's vertical position (step 2).

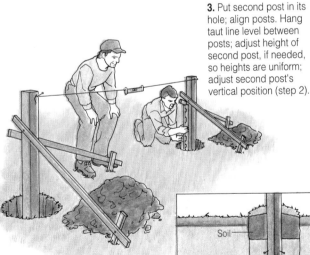

4. Fill postholes with concrete until holes are at least three-quarters full. There should be four times as much concrete as gravel. Fill the remaining space with tamped soil, sloped at the surface to shed water. Remove the braces.

Soil

Concrete

Gravel

PLACING, LEVELING, AND FLOATING CONCRETE

Preparation

1. Prepare forms and gravel bed (pp.206–209). Then wet down all interior surfaces to minimize settling and to keep moisture from being drawn away from the concrete during curing.

2. To prevent concrete from sticking, coat the inside of wet wooden forms with a form-release chemical.

Whether you mix concrete by hand, in a portable mixer, or have ready-mix concrete delivered by truck, you must plan ahead. To prepare for on-site mixing, erect platforms large enough to hold the ingredients and function as the mixing site. Then lay planks for transporting concrete from there to the pouring location via wheelbarrow.

To prepare for delivery of ready-mix, plan a route for the truck. If the truck must travel over unpaved ground or maneuver in tight quarters, ask the company to inspect the site beforehand and help you devise the best route. Normally trucks are equipped with 10-foot chutes for pouring concrete directly into forms. Often producers also have supplementary chutes that can be used. These chutes must be level or inclined downward for the concrete to flow properly. As a last resort, you can haul the concrete from the truck to the site with wheelbarrows on planks.

Several helpers will be needed for distributing and leveling the concrete.

Everyone should wear protective clothing, including goggles, long pants, a long-sleeved shirt, thick work gloves, and knee-high heavy rubber boots, preferably without buckles.

Caution: Concrete is caustic and can cause chemical burns on skin; it will corrode leather, cloth, and other material unless promptly washed off.

Concrete poured in hot weather stiffens rapidly, shortening the time available for finishing. (With ready-mix, you can request that a retarding agent be added.) Surface drying is a problem whenever the humidity is low or the day is windy. Concrete exposed to freeze-thaw cycles must be air-entrained (p.204); do not pour concrete onto frozen ground or into forms containing snow or ice. Regardless of the weather, avoid over-working poured concrete; doing so weakens it. A sheen of water will appear as you level, or strike off, and float the concrete. Delay further smoothing until the sheen has evaporated.

Pouring

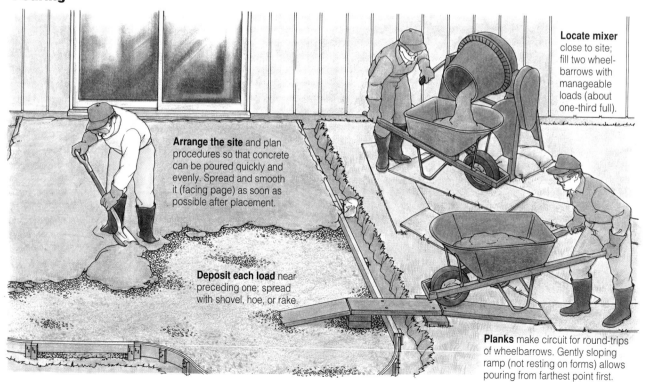

Arrange the site and plan procedures so that concrete can be poured quickly and evenly. Spread and smooth it (facing page) as soon as possible after placement.

Deposit each load near preceding one; spread with shovel, hoe, or rake.

Locate mixer close to site; fill two wheelbarrows with manageable loads (about one-third full).

Planks make circuit for round-trips of wheelbarrows. Gently sloping ramp (not resting on forms) allows pouring from farthest point first.

Spreading

Tamp concrete with a straight 2 × 4 on edge. Start at far end of pour; deliver vertical blows, moving board half its thickness with each blow.

Strike off, or screed, top by sawing back and forth with board used for tamping. Raise the board's leading edge slightly on forward stroke. Excess concrete ahead of board fills hollows.

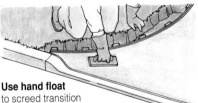

Use hand float to screed transition areas such as apron where driveway meets curb. Tamp, then smooth surface with tool. Fill hollows with spare concrete.

Handling ready-mix

Be ready when truck arrives; otherwise driver may charge overtime after 30 min. Move chute to farthest point of pour. Dampen chute and forms with hose; then signal driver to release concrete. Reposition chute as form fills. If crew lags, direct driver to release concrete more slowly. Signal driver to stop when concrete in chute will complete job.

Plunge spade into the mix to thoroughly fill corners, eliminate voids, and settle the mix.

Tamp to push aggregate below surface; then level by screeding (see left).

Floating

Smooth screeded surface with bull float after surface water has evaporated. Push tool at right angle to screed marks, with front edge slightly raised. Pull tool back with blade flat.

Use darby for smaller areas. Sweep tool in wide arcs, pressing lightly on blade's trailing edge. Work from center to edges. On wide slabs, support yourself on kneeboards.

Move hand float in circles to smooth bull float or darby marks. Lean on second float for support. Keep floating to a minimum. For a skid-resistant surface, finish with broom texture (p.215).

Masonry 211

Isolation and control joints

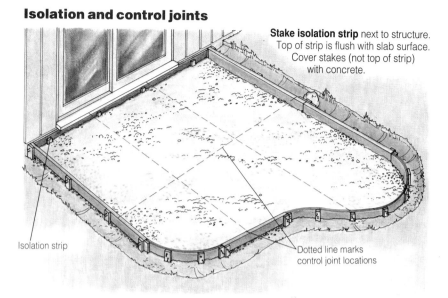

Stake isolation strip next to structure. Top of strip is flush with slab surface. Cover stakes (not top of strip) with concrete.

Isolation strip

Dotted line marks control joint locations

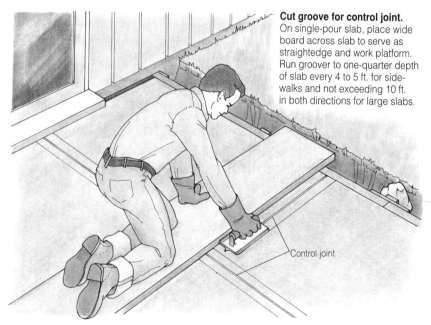

Cut groove for control joint. On single-pour slab, place wide board across slab to serve as straightedge and work platform. Run groover to one-quarter depth of slab every 4 to 5 ft. for sidewalks and not exceeding 10 ft. in both directions for large slabs.

Control joint

Construction joints

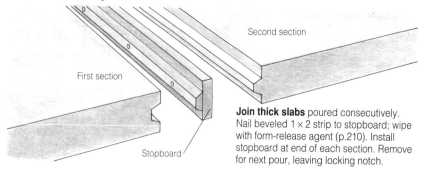

Second section

First section

Join thick slabs poured consecutively. Nail beveled 1 × 2 strip to stopboard; wipe with form-release agent (p.210). Install stopboard at end of each section. Remove for next pour, leaving locking notch.

Stopboard

Concrete shrinks as it dries and hardens. It continues to shrink and expand with seasonal temperature changes. Under these conditions, cracks can develop. Three types of joints—isolation, control, and construction—minimize cracking in different situations.

Isolation joints, or expansion joints, separate new concrete from adjoining building materials or older cured concrete. This allows the new concrete to move at its own rate, unaffected by the different rate of the adjoining material. (If the two were bonded, they would likely crack apart.) Create an isolation joint by placing a ½-inch-thick strip of asphalt-saturated fiber, available from concrete and building suppliers, against an existing material when the new concrete is poured.

Control joints are grooves tooled into fresh concrete or sawn into cured concrete (use a circular saw equipped with a masonry-cutting blade). These grooves create weak areas that induce cracks to occur beneath them, where they are less visible and not harmful.

Use *construction joints* where concrete is poured in sections (with a 30-minute interval or longer). For slabs 4 inches thick, insert a straight-sided temporary form, or *stopboard,* between pours. Join thicker sections with a locking, or *keyed,* joint: fasten a beveled strip to a stopboard that is the same width as the thickness of the slab.

To prevent chipping, round over all edges and joints in fresh concrete with an edger. (In hot weather, cover wet concrete after the initial smoothing. Uncover small areas for finishing, then re-cover them immediately to slow drying.) After jointing and edging, concrete takes time to *cure,* or harden. While it is curing, keep the concrete moist so it will reach its full strength. Concrete with Type 10 Portland cement (pp.202–203) usually cures in 7 days. When pouring in cold weather, keep fresh concrete above 50°F (10°C). Avoid pouring concrete when temperatures are 23°F (−5°C), but if you must do so, add alkaline to the concrete.

Edging and curing

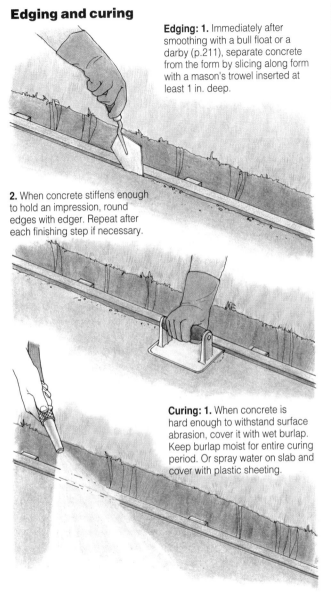

Edging: 1. Immediately after smoothing with a bull float or a darby (p.211), separate concrete from the form by slicing along form with a mason's trowel inserted at least 1 in. deep.

2. When concrete stiffens enough to hold an impression, round edges with edger. Repeat after each finishing step if necessary.

Curing: 1. When concrete is hard enough to withstand surface abrasion, cover it with wet burlap. Keep burlap moist for entire curing period. Or spray water on slab and cover with plastic sheeting.

Curing determines concrete's durability

Concrete must be used (poured or put in place) within three hours of mixing—two hours if the temperature is 77°F (25°C) or more—so mix or order only what you can pour and finish in that time. (Use only air-entrained concrete for retaining walls, and for any work that will be exposed to freeze-thaw cycles or deicing chemicals. Air-entrained concrete must be machine-mixed.)

If possible, pour at temperatures of 70°F (21°C), when there is no wind. Early morning or late afternoon are often the best times. Make sure the concrete remains wet and at a constant temperature for seven days after pouring. If concrete is poured in winter, keep the temperature about 70°F (21°C): curing stops altogether if the temperature is too low.

Cover with continuously wet burlap, curing paper, or plastic sheeting, weighted down to prevent too quick evaporation of water. Concrete that cures too quickly will crack, scale, flake, and lack strength and durability.

In the case of driveways or walkways, avoid heavy use immediately after the seven-day curing period. Prevent this by covering the new concrete with plywood or hard boards for several weeks. Remember, too, that even after the seven-day curing, concrete needs at least 30 days' air-drying time to properly resist deicing chemicals. Better still, avoid deicing chemicals altogether the first winter. Use sand instead.

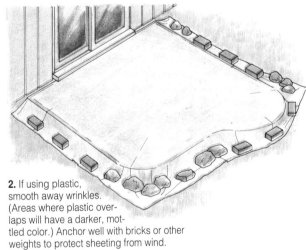

2. If using plastic, smooth away wrinkles. (Areas where plastic overlaps will have a darker, mottled color.) Anchor well with bricks or other weights to protect sheeting from wind.

Anchoring wood posts to concrete

Metal bases embedded in concrete piers (right) or foundation walls secure wooden sills and posts used in house framing. Embed base according to maker's instructions. Bases should be held in position temporarily until concrete has hardened. To position base A, place a wood brace in U of base, and nail. Position Sonotube form in hole; then pour concrete. Place base and brace in wet concrete across top of the form (inset). To position elevated post base B in wet concrete, place it atop 2 × 2 spacer boards. Allow concrete to cure 7 days before attaching the post.

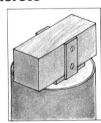

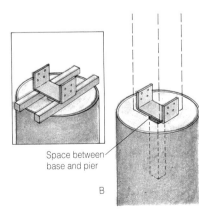

Space between base and pier

A

B

DECORATIVE COLORS AND FINISHES FOR CONCRETE

Coloring the top layer

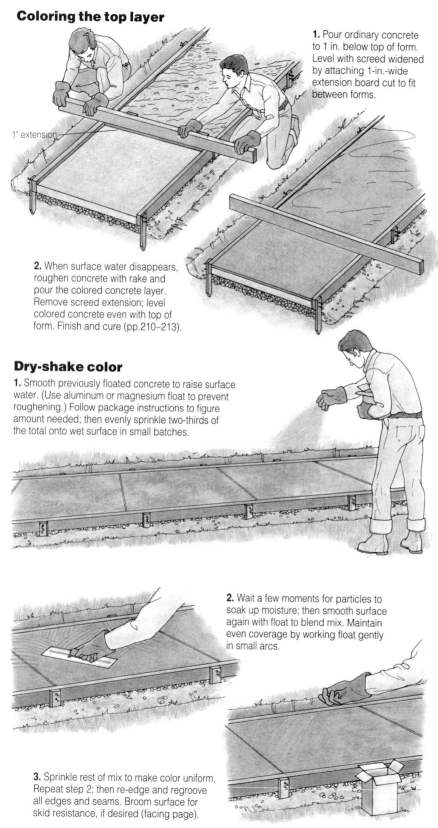

1. Pour ordinary concrete to 1 in. below top of form. Level with screed widened by attaching 1-in.-wide extension board cut to fit between forms.

1" extension

2. When surface water disappears, roughen concrete with rake and pour the colored concrete layer. Remove screed extension; level colored concrete even with top of form. Finish and cure (pp.210–213).

Dry-shake color

1. Smooth previously floated concrete to raise surface water. (Use aluminum or magnesium float to prevent roughening.) Follow package instructions to figure amount needed; then evenly sprinkle two-thirds of the total onto wet surface in small batches.

2. Wait a few moments for particles to soak up moisture; then smooth surface again with float to blend mix. Maintain even coverage by working float gently in small arcs.

3. Sprinkle rest of mix to make color uniform. Repeat step 2; then re-edge and regroove all edges and seams. Broom surface for skid resistance, if desired (facing page).

Concrete surfaces need not be drab; it is fairly easy to add color or texture while finishing concrete. Textured surfaces also make slabs and walks less slippery.

There are two main ways to color concrete: by blending powdered mineral pigment (available from concrete suppliers) with the mix, and by dusting poured concrete with pigment after the concrete has been smoothed with a float (p.211). The latter material, called dry-shake, contains hardeners that increase the surface's resistance to wear. Concrete can also be painted or stained with products made for the purpose; however, the results vary and are not as long-lasting as the other two methods.

Pigments for concrete consist of mineral oxides. Use about 7 pounds of pigment per bag of cement for a strong color; about 1½ pounds per bag usually yields a satisfactory pastel tint. Read the instructions on the container and consult the supplier for specific advice.

For good results with pigment, use white cement instead of the usual gray variety. Using white sand instead of the ordinary tan or beige type, while not necessary, will further improve the color.

To save money on pigment and these premium ingredients, you can use concrete made with standard ingredients (without pigment) for the bulk of the pour. Screed the bottom layer; then immediately mix the concrete for the colored layer, using pigment and the white cement and sand. (Be careful not to add too much water.) Pour, screed, and finish the colored layer.

When finishing the concrete, do not overwork it by smoothing the surface too much. This weakens the slab and can cause powdering. At the curing stage, use damp burlap rather than plastic sheeting. Seal the slab according to the pigment maker's instructions.

To create a textured finish before the surface hardens, roughen it with a broom, embed pebbles in it, carve it with masonry tools, or stamp it with brick design tools (see "Where to Find It," pp.348–353). For complex finishes, pour and finish small sections at a time.

Brooming

Hold push broom at low angle and drag bristles across concrete to produce ridged nonslip surface. Don't let brush strokes overlap or cross each other at angles. Use soft bristles to create fine lines, stiff bristles to make a deeper design.

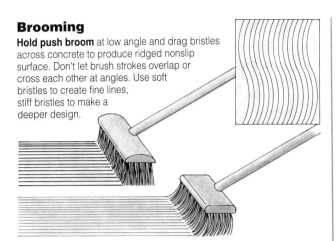

Stamping brick design

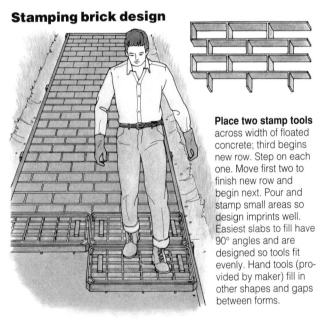

Place two stamp tools across width of floated concrete; third begins new row. Step on each one. Move first two to finish new row and begin next. Pour and stamp small areas so design imprints well. Easiest slabs to fill have 90° angles and are designed so tools fit evenly. Hand tools (provided by maker) fill in other shapes and gaps between forms.

Pebbled texture

1. Wet clean round pebbles or other smooth stones ¾ to 1½ in. in diameter. Pour and screed small section of concrete. Sprinkle pebbles evenly (shown), or create a mosaic pattern on surface.

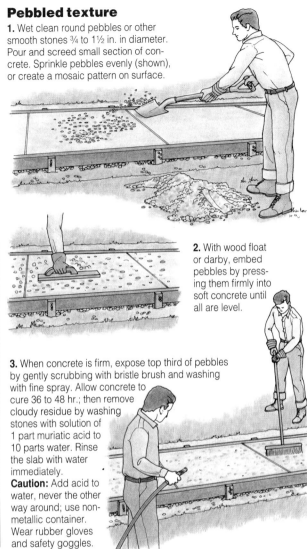

2. With wood float or darby, embed pebbles by pressing them firmly into soft concrete until all are level.

3. When concrete is firm, expose top third of pebbles by gently scrubbing with bristle brush and washing with fine spray. Allow concrete to cure 36 to 48 hr.; then remove cloudy residue by washing stones with solution of 1 part muriatic acid to 10 parts water. Rinse the slab with water immediately.
Caution: Add acid to water, never the other way around; use non-metallic container. Wear rubber gloves and safety goggles.

False flagstone

1. After smoothing concrete with float, carve outlines of flagstone design with a brick jointing tool.

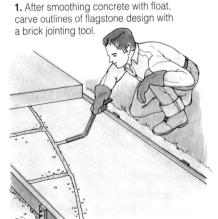

2. Smooth and retool the concrete to finish the flat surfaces and to deepen the outlines.

3. Brush outlines carefully with a dry paintbrush to smooth their edges and remove particles.

Despite its sturdiness, concrete can deteriorate with age and with exposure to severe weather, and it can suffer damage from settling or a heavy blow—being hit by a car, for example. Improper curing and overworking of concrete also weaken a slab. For a successful repair, you must clean the area well and create a good bond between the surface and the patching compound.

You can fill cracks and holes with a homemade compound of 1 part Portland cement, 2½ parts sand, and enough water to make a stiff paste for vertical surfaces, a thin one for horizontal surfaces. However, this mixture doesn't adhere well if applied in a thin layer; the repair surface must be at least 1 inch deep, and the edges must be undercut with a chisel.

An easier method is to buy a patching compound containing latex, epoxy, or other polymers. These don't require the shaping work and they usually bond well, even when filling small cracks and resurfacing scaling surfaces. These products are expensive; an economical strategy for larger holes is to use homemade and commercial products together.

To reduce a dusty or powdery condition, sweep and vacuum the slab, then wash it with soapy water and a wire brush (use strong powdered detergent). Scrub the surface again with more soapy water and a fiber brush; then rinse it with clean water. If the concrete continues to dust, apply a commercial hardener containing magnesium and zinc fluorosilicates or sodium silicate (available from concrete suppliers); follow the maker's directions. The hardener will work best if it is applied before the slab is exposed to weather and use.

To prevent scaling, or flaking, on a new slab that will be subjected to deicer salts, coat the concrete twice before the first winter with a solution of equal parts turpentine and boiled linseed oil or with a commercial penetrating sealer. On an older slab an annual treatment will retard (not halt) scaling.

Caution: Wear safety goggles and long sleeves. Don rubber gloves when applying concrete compounds.

Filling cracks with commercial compound

1. Remove loose or cracked material with small sledgehammer and cold chisel. Hold chisel at slight angle.

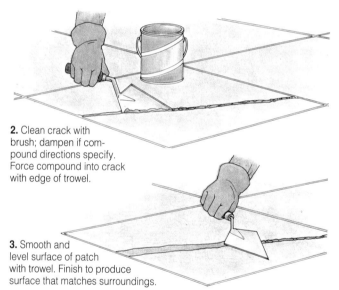

2. Clean crack with brush; dampen if compound directions specify. Force compound into crack with edge of trowel.

3. Smooth and level surface of patch with trowel. Finish to produce surface that matches surroundings.

Patching large holes in layers

1. Chisel sides of hole so they are vertical; prepare hole as for cracks. Brush with grout (mix 1 part cement and 1 part sand; add water to consistency of housepaint).

2. Fill hole to within ¼ in. of surface with homemade compound (see text above). Avoid overwetting mix; this weakens it.

3. Apply finish layer of commercial patching compound, following package directions. Feather edges of patch. Finish to match surrounding concrete.

Rebuilding edges and corners

1. Chisel away loose particles, and brush damaged area thoroughly to remove dust. Mix patching material according to maker's directions. Dampen concrete before applying if directions specify.

Undercut repair area (dotted line) with chisel if using homemade patching mix.

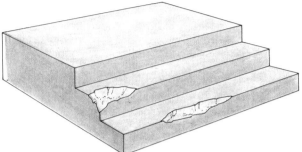

2. Erect, lubricate, and brace form to contain and shape patch. Apply compound. Smooth surface with trowel and edger (pp.206–213).

Replacing a broken slab

Break up damaged slab with sledgehammer. Slab will crack along control joint. Remove broken pieces, and cover with layer of gravel as for new slab (pp.206–207).
Caution: Bend knees as you lift and lower hammer. Straighten knees a little at top of swing. Let the hammer fall of its own weight. Check the hammerhead often for looseness. Wear goggles and heavy work gloves.

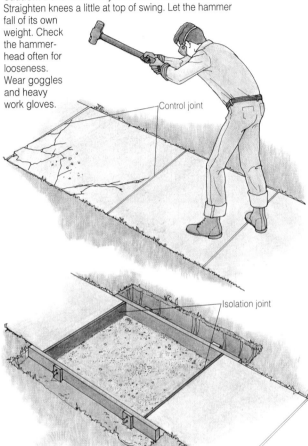

Erect forms level with existing pavement. Install isolation joint material to separate new pour from older concrete. Pour concrete and finish as for new slab. (See pp.206–213.)

Resurfacing

1. Remove damaged surface by chiseling at an angle or by striking with a 3-lb. sledge. Avoid heavy blows that might crack slab. Clean slab thoroughly with wire brush and broom.

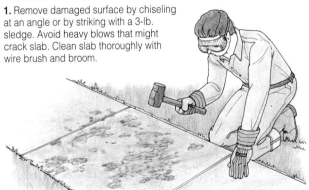

2. Wet slab and allow moisture to soak in if patching compound directions specify. Apply compound; smooth with float. Finish surface with broom to roughen finish, if desired (p.215).

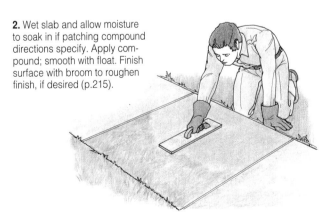

Masonry 217

BRICKS

Brick is a kiln-fired solid masonry unit made with clay or shale. Although some bricks are manufactured essentially the same way they have been for millennia (with soft "mud" in molds), most modern bricks are made by compressing and extruding a stiffer mix through a die to make long bars, which are then wire-cut into shorter units. These "green" bricks are dried, sometimes glazed, and then fired in a kiln to harden them. To a large degree, a brick's color and some of its other properties are determined by the raw materials that make up the mud. However, the final result can be adjusted by adding chemicals or surface coloring to the mud, and by controlling the firing.

Today bricks are available in hundreds of sizes and shapes and in a variety of colors to meet many applications, making brick one of the most versatile of all building materials. Only a few of the available styles are shown below.

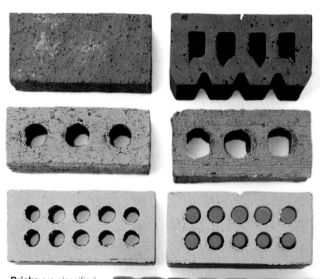

Bricks are classified as *common*, for hidden work, or *face*, for exposed work. They may be solid, cored or have indentations, or frogs, and they may be glazed. Most bricks are modular—they relate in size to each other or to other units, such as concrete blocks, to allow mixing of different units.

Curves and corners may require special bricks. Internal and external radial bricks (top) form sweeping curves. Hinge and octagonal bricks (bottom) offer two different alternatives to simple squared-off corners.

Rounded edges or ends on bricks, originally designed to reduce water penetration, are now used by architects and designers to add dimension to flat walls and to form decorative details. These bricks can also be used to frame doors or windows or to form cornices.

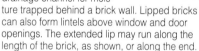

Lipped brick can be placed to form a hidden horizontal expansion joint that accepts flashing or to create a drainage channel for moisture trapped behind a brick wall. Lipped bricks can also form lintels above window and door openings. The extended lip may run along the length of the brick, as shown, or along the end.

Other bricks include copings (above, left) and ogees (above, right), which are designed to cap walls or window or door frames and shed water, preventing undue saturation. Purely decorative bricks, such as the lower two, are available in hundreds of different designs, colors, and shapes; they can be inserted singly or combined to form almost unlimited design details. Furthermore, bricks can be custom-made to fit special designs; but these are expensive, and you may have to submit contractor-approved drawings when ordering them.

PAVERS

Traditionally bricks and flat-cut stones (p.221) have been used as pavers. Bricks are probably the more versatile of the two, as they can be laid in a number of attractive patterns or be set on end at an angle to form a picketlike edging. Equally versatile, however, are pavers that are made of concrete that is pressed in a mold under extreme pressure and compacted with high-frequency vibrators. Both brick and concrete pavers are highly resistant to broad temperature fluctuations and to the corrosive action of winter salts. They also withstand the weight of the heaviest vehicles.

Brick pavers are graded for severe, moderate, or negligible weathering and for heavy, moderate, or foot traffic. Coping pavers with rounded edges (right) are ideal for slight overhangs, as on stairs or pool borders.

Cobblestone concrete paver lets you add a dash of Old World charm to a patio or other outdoor area. These popular pavers are generally available in single units (left), with special edging pieces (far left) to square off the paved area. Double cobblestone pavers (below) are also available. Cobblestones come in a variety of colors, as do the other concrete pavers.

Split-faced paver is made in one piece and then split in half, offering a roughened surface that simulates stone.

Concrete pavers come in shapes and colors to suit just about any purpose. Copy traditional patterns or freely mix shapes, sizes, and colors to create your own design. When developing your own design, work out the pattern on graph paper first.

CONCRETE BLOCKS

Made of Portland cement, graded aggregates, and water, concrete blocks are used around the home primarily in foundation walls, above-grade walls, and retaining walls. In addition to the classic rough gray rectangles, blocks are available in a variety of colors, textures, and shapes for just about any application. Blocks are heavier than bricks, more utilitarian than either bricks or stones, and relatively inexpensive.

Because blocks come in a variety of modular sizes (sizes that fit with one another), structures are easily planned and built without having to cut the building units into smaller sizes, as must be done with stones. Concrete blocks are durable and can be used above grade, and with proper precautions below grade, without harmful penetration of moisture. Hollow-core blocks can be reinforced or filled with insulation.

Stretcher block (right), the basic wall unit, has flanged ends and generally two or three hollow cores (cells) separated by partitions (webs) that taper from top to bottom.

Corner block (far right) has one or both ends flush. This one is called semisolid, with one end of its cells closed for extra bearing or for the tops of walls (closed side up).

Sash block (left) has narrow slots for anchoring a metal sash. This split-faced unit has a rough stonelike appearance.

Half sash (below, left) has traditional texture.

Half sash, half stretcher (below, right) is a fluted split-ribbed unit.

Narrow corner block with both ends flush is one of the vast number of variations on the basic block form. The block shown is a nominal 6 × 8 × 16 in.

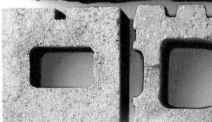

Veneer block adds a false stone surface to a wood-frame house. A single-wythe wall (one block thick) is built outside the wood frame and fastened to the studs with metal ties. The veneer shown is a split-faced concrete block with a rough stone look.

Partition blocks are narrow units designed for partition walls inside a house, garage, or other building. The ground-down surfaces of the blocks shown make them aesthetically pleasing for indoor use. The red block has a single score in its face. The white one is a semi-solid block.

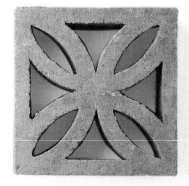

Screen block creates decorative designs in walls and fences. A wall of screen blocks allows for privacy without cutting out all light. Screen blocks are ideal for closing in patios or swimming pools. An almost unlimited number of patterns is available, ranging from simple to intricate and lacy.

STONE

For a combination of strength, diversity, durability, and natural beauty, there is no building material equal to stone. Stone can be roughly shaped, cut to precise dimensions, or used as it is found in nature. Its surface can be rough and irregular, smooth and flat, or polished to a high gloss that is impervious to stain. Because of its versatility, it is used for interior and exterior walls and floors, fireplaces and chimneys, countertops, roofing, walkways and driveways, and countless other landscaping and architectural applications.

Stones for walls or veneer are generally sold by the ton; flagstones, slate, tiles, and other flat units, by the square foot. In rubble masonry, rough uncut stones of various shapes and sizes are fitted together. In ashlar masonry, cut stones with squared-off surfaces are tightly fitted. In either case, the stones may be coursed (layered in rows) or random. Stone walls may be set dry (without mortar) or with or without the mortar showing. Ashlar mortar joints are no more than ½ inch wide; usually they are ⅛ to ¼ inch wide.

River fieldstone (right) is commonly used in mortarless construction. The section of wall shown here is made up entirely of *strips,* as flat stones are called.

Slate (far right) is available in dozens of earthy colors ranging from grays and greens to purples and reds. It is shown here in a section of floor that has been laid in a geometric pattern.

Corinthian granite (right), with its flat surface and irregular shapes, can be laid in a mosaic pattern with ½-in. mortar joints, as demonstrated in the segment of wall shown here.

Salt-and-pepper granite (far right), cut into large squared blocks and strips, is ideal for walls. The section of wall shown here has ½-in. pointed mortar joints.

Gold sandstone (right), a richly colored sandstone, can be arranged in random strips to form a mortarless wall. The variety of sizes keeps spaces between the stones to a minimum.

Rough-textured marble (far right), like all other types of marble, is very difficult to cut; always buy it precut. Pink marble is shown here in a section of an ashlar wall with tight ⅛- to ¼-in. joints.

When planning a masonry project, choose the material that best suits your skill level and the finished look you have in mind.

Bricks and concrete blocks are uniform in size and lend themselves to geometric designs. Although both are available in many sizes, the dimensions of individual units usually are proportionally related. This makes them easy to fit together in patterns, lessens the amount of skill and time required to build with them, and simplifies estimating materials. These projects are relatively easy to design because their dimensions can be based on the size of the individual units. Also, their uniform shape, texture, and color allow you to predict the appearance of a finished project.

Stones that are uniformly shaped, or *dressed,* can be treated like brick or block. Roughly dressed stones (with protrusions cut off, but not squared) and undressed stones vary in size, shape, and surface features. This variety tends to create less structured designs that emphasize texture and color more than precise or repeating geometric patterns.

Working with undressed and roughly dressed stones requires much more creativity, skill, and time than working with bricks, blocks, or dressed stones. Each piece must be chosen or cut to fit with its neighbors like pieces of a jigsaw puzzle. Thus it is necessary to have many stones on hand to choose from. (As a rule, the more irregular the stones, the more stones you will need.) Furthermore, it is difficult to precisely predict the appearance

Grades of undressed stones

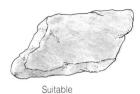 

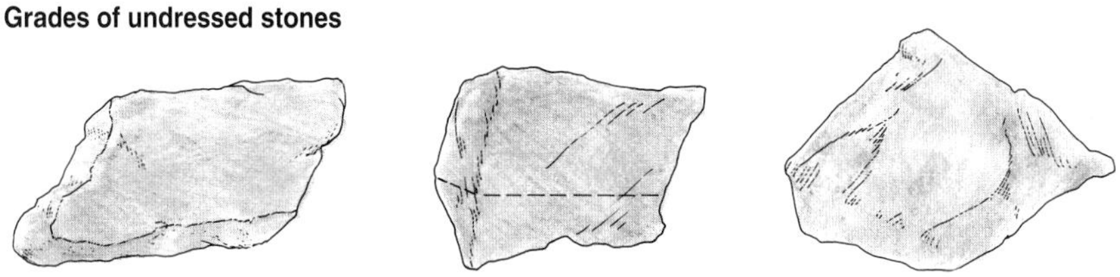

| Suitable | Irregular; needs shaping | Poor (unusable) |

of the finished project. Nevertheless, these types of stones have considerable aesthetic appeal, and the labor associated with this work is well rewarded.

Bricks are rated for their resistance to weathering, specifically the effects of freeze-thaw cycles. (Moisture expands when it freezes, causing them to break.) The most durable brick, SW (severe weathering), is the only kind made here, although weaker MW (medium weathering) bricks are also used in central and northern Canada. NW (no weathering) bricks sometimes seen in U.S. brickyards are seldom seen here. Canada's most frequently used brick size is the *Canadian standard residential (CSR).*

Bricks are customarily sold by their *actual dimensions* although *nominal dimensions,* which include an allowance of either ⅜ or ½ inch for mortar joints, may be used in estimating needed quantities. The actual size of a CSR brick is 3½ × 2³⁄₁₆ × 8⅞ inches, but some slight variations may occur during manufacturing. In the case of other common bricks, actual sizes are: metric modular, 90 × 57 × 190 mm (3½ × 2¼ × 7½ inches); Ontario brick, 4 × 2⅜ × 8⅜ inches; jumbo brick, 3½ × 3½ × 11½ inches; double jumbo, 5½ × 2½ × 11⅝ inches.

To determine the number of bricks needed for a project, calculate the size of the area (p.344) and subtract the areas of openings or unpaved sections. Once you know the size of the area to be bricked, the rule of thumb is that you will need either five CSR or double jumbo bricks, or 8 metric modular bricks, or 7 Ontario bricks, or 4 jumbo bricks per square foot. Add 10 to 25 percent to the total to allow for chippages and breakage.

For large jobs you can use a special slide rule called a brick masonry estimator, available from suppliers. (This estimator will also help you gauge the amount of mortar, and specifically how much sand, cement, and lime, you will need for a given job. See p.224.) For a wall more than one brick thick, multiply the result by the number of bricks making up the structure's thickness. Estimate an extra two bricks per square foot where bricks are to be laid close together without mortar (as in a patio or walk with sand in the joints).

New bricks are usually sold in packaged units of 100, called straps, or in units of 500, called cubes. A cube of standard bricks measures about 4 feet on each side and weighs approximately a ton. When ordering bricks, find out whether delivery will be made to the work site or to the curb. Before delivery, prepare a sturdy wood platform for storing the bricks. For long-term storage, cover them with a plastic tarp.

Blocks are made of concrete and contain a variety of aggregates for different uses. In actual dimensions most blocks are 7⅞ × 7⅞ × 15¾ inches (200 × 200 × 400 mm). If you include ⅜-inch-thick mortar joints in the calculation, the nominal measurement

Estimating bricks

	Actual dimensions	Units per 100 sq.ft.	⅜-in. mortar*
CSR	3½ × 2¹³⁄₁₆ × 8⅞	490	5 cu. ft.
Metric modular	3½ × 2¼ × 7½	720	7 cu. ft.
Ontario	4 × 2¹³⁄₁₆ × 8⅞	600	6 cu. ft.
Jumbo	3½ × 3½ × 11½	300	3 cu. ft.

*Add 25% to 50% more for waste. Amount varies according to size of job and skill of mason.

will be 8¼ × 8¼ × 16⅛ inches. A single course is equal in height to three courses of standard modular bricks laid with mortar. This relationship is useful to keep in mind when laying brick and block together, as for a veneered retaining wall (p.246).

Blocks may have other widths, ranging from 2 to 12 inches. These are usually laid with the width side down. Either way count on about 112 blocks and 6 cubic feet of mortar per 100 square feet. Sometimes, solid blocks may be laid so the width faces out, thus building a dimension other than 8 inches into a project, as for steps with 6-inch risers (p.238).

Depending on the type of aggregate, one 7⅞ × 7⅞ × 15¾-inch block weighs from 22 to 40 pounds. Generally they are sold individually, rather than in packaged units. To avoid having to cut blocks, you can buy half sizes and special shapes for use around door and window frames. If blocks are stored outside, cover with plastic to keep them clean and dry.

Smaller concrete block units, called *pavers* or *paving stones,* are laid without mortar on beds of sand and make durable and decorative paths, patios, steps, and driveways (pp.234–239).

Stones that are dressed, roughly dressed, and undressed can be bought at a stone yard and delivered. Granites are the hardest and often the most expensive; limestones and sandstones range from soft to nearly as hard as some granites; slates are split along their layers to form paving flagstones.

Undressed stone can often be obtained more cheaply from local quarries, construction sites, farms, and streambeds; but hauling stones yourself is heavy, sometimes dangerous, work. (If you do haul your own stones, be careful not to overload your vehicle.) When selecting undressed stones, choose pieces with clearly defined surfaces that will sit level in a wall and will support the stones above with a minimum of shaping or shimming.

Bricks

Place bricks so that successive rows form horizontal increments of 4 or 8 in. Mortar joints of recommended thickness (½ or ⅜ in.) are thus staggered for strength and durability.

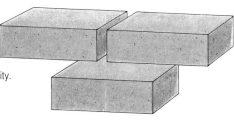

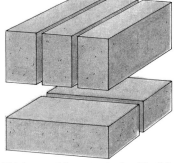

Thickness of three standard residential bricks plus mortar joints equals the length of a similar brick.

Turn a simple corner by alternating position of whole bricks. This offsets the mortar joints at intersecting walls.

Concrete blocks

Webs and face shells taper slightly so blocks can be unmolded at the factory. Others flare, providing a little more mortar surface. Place blocks with thicker side up.

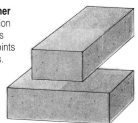

Web

Face shell   Taper

Flare

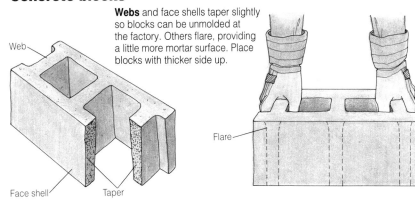

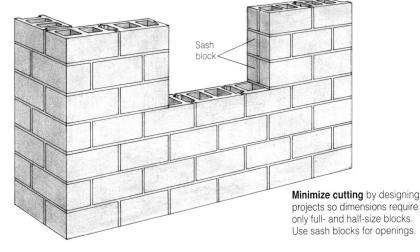

Sash block

Minimize cutting by designing projects so dimensions require only full- and half-size blocks. Use sash blocks for openings.

Mixing mortar

Mix dry ingredients thoroughly; then add water in small amounts. Blend with hoe until mortar is smooth and sides of a test furrow hold their shape without crumbling or sagging.

Mortar is the cement mixture used to bond bricks, concrete blocks, and stones together. Unlike concrete, which weakens if overworked by excessive mixing or smoothing, mortar can be spread and troweled repeatedly until it begins to harden. Masons *throw* mortar beds and *butter* bricks. It is crucial to mix and spread mortar correctly; practice throwing mortar onto a 2 × 4 first.

Select the mortar recipe appropriate to your needs from the chart below. Type M is the one preferred in Ontario and Quebec; type N is the first choice of contractors in Atlantic Canada. Consult an experienced mason about the proper mortar mix for stonework (stones should fit together well and rely on the force of gravity rather than the strength of the mortar) and before restoring brickwork more than 100 years old (mortar that is too strong may cause bricks in such masonry to crack).

There are three ways to mix mortar: from scratch using Portland cement, hydrated lime, and sand; from masonry cement (Portland cement premixed with limestone) and sand; and from bags containing all the ingredients. Buy materials for mortar from a home center or masonry supplier to be sure of getting the right kinds. Sand must always be clean, finely graded, and salt-free. Water should be clean tap water.

Mix mortar in a wheelbarrow or mortar pan in batches of up to 1 cubic foot (about 6¼ gallons). This is about as much as one person can use within 1½ hours, the time it usually takes for hardening to begin. Follow the instructions for mixing concrete by hand (pp.204–205). Add enough water to achieve the right consistency, starting with about 2½ gallons per cubic foot of mix. Mortar that is too wet will run out between the joints; if it is too dry, the bond will be weak. To use a power mixer, add three-fourths of the water, half the sand, and all the masonry cement (or Portland cement and lime) required. Mix briefly, then add the remaining water and sand; mix again for at least 3 minutes.

Caution: Wear waterproof gloves when working with mortar.

Mortar recipes by volume

Type	Use	Strength	Portland cement	Lime	Sand	Masonry cement*	Sand**
M	Load-bearing, freeze-thaw weathering, below grade, stonework, used when Type S is insufficient for the job	Strongest	1	¼	3¾	1	6
S	General use and below grade, internal load-bearing	About 75% of Type M	1	¼ - ½	4½	1	3
N	Basic mortar, non-load-bearing, above-grade work, stonework	About 33% of Type M	1	½ - 1	6	1	3

*Types of masonry cement are M, S, and N, the same as mortar type.
**The volume of sand is always 2¼ to 3 times the volume of the cement mixture used.

Loading the trowel

1. Chop a slice of mortar from the mound on mortar board (2-ft.-square piece of ¾-in. plywood)—enough to cover three or four bricks. When chopping, hold trowel perpendicular to board with thumb extended along top of handle; relax forearm and let blade drop.

2. Without changing grip, use flat surfaces of trowel to shape slice into rounded loaf or wedge, called windrow, whose length equals that of trowel's blade.

3. Rotate wrist to scoop up windrow by sliding trowel underneath it. Forearm and palm of gripping hand should face up. Lift loaded trowel and flick it down and up rapidly to settle mortar firmly on blade.

Throwing a mortar line

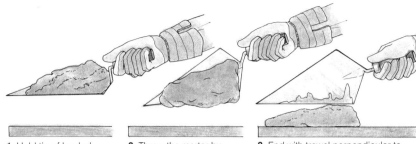

1. Hold tip of loaded trowel at starting point, parallel to ground, with palm of gripping hand facing up.

2. Throw the mortar by rotating your wrist and flicking trowel downward while pulling tool toward you in a straight line.

3. End with trowel perpendicular to surface and mortar along centerline of bricks or practice 2 × 4. If it is not, return mortar to board, remove bricks. Try again using fresh bricks.

4. Draw back of trowel along center of mortar to smooth it into a uniform ½-in.-thick bed that covers entire surface of three or four bricks.

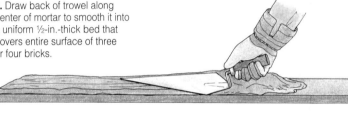

Buttering a brick

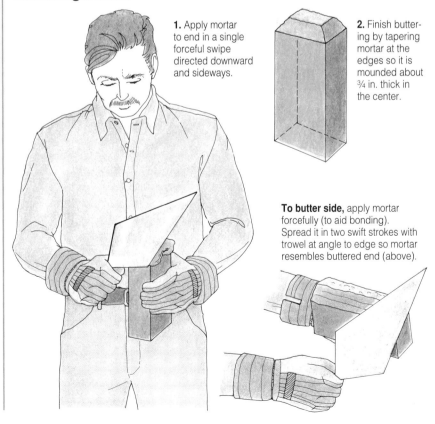

1. Apply mortar to end in a single forceful swipe directed downward and sideways.

2. Finish buttering by tapering mortar at the edges so it is mounded about ¾ in. thick in the center.

To butter side, apply mortar forcefully (to aid bonding). Spread it in two swift strokes with trowel at angle to edge so mortar resembles buttered end (above).

Brick positions

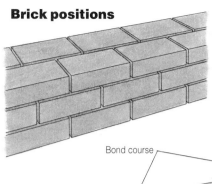

Stretcher is placed horizontally with its long narrow side exposed. This is the most common position for bricks and forms the basis of running, stack, and open bonds.

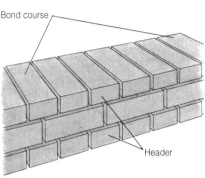

Bond course

Header

Header shows end of brick with wider surface on horizontal. Headers are a common structural bond in double-wythe walls and combine with stretchers to make the decorative feature of many pattern bonds.

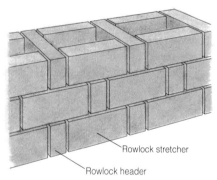

Rowlock stretcher

Rowlock header

Rowlock is laid with long narrow side down. Rowlock stretchers, also called shiners, reveal a brick's long wide surface; rowlock headers reveal ends. The former are used for pattern bonds; the latter for capping walls and windowsills.

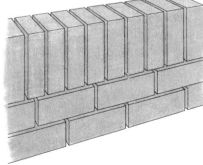

Soldier stands on end with long narrow side exposed. Soldiers are commonly used within pattern bonds to simulate arches over doorways and windows.

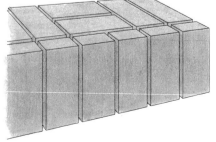

Sailor stands on end with wide side exposed. Narrow support surfaces at top and bottom limit use to nonstructural pattern bonds and edging for paths and patios.

Bricklaying is an intricate skill that has many aspects of an art. Over the centuries, bricklayers have developed colorful yet precise terms to describe every feature of bricks and the ways they are used.

In a wall or other structure, bricks are identified by their position when installed (see left). The exposed surface of an installed brick is called its *face*. The horizontal layer of mortar on which bricks are laid is called a *bed*. A layer of bricks in a structure is called a *course*. A vertical section, or wall, of masonry that is one brick thick is called a *wythe*; a wall two bricks thick is called *double wythe* (facing page). A row of bricks overlapping more than one wythe is called a *bond course*; if the face of a course consists of the ends of bricks, it is called a *header course*.

Any piece that is less than a whole brick is called a *bat*. A *half bat* is a brick split to divide its length in half (the actual dimensions of a Canadian standard residential half bat are $1\frac{3}{4} \times 1\frac{1}{2} \times 4\frac{1}{2}$ inches); a *three-fourths bat* and a *one-fourth bat* are three-quarters and one-quarter of the length, respectively. Short bats that are used at corners to maintain joint spacings are called *closures*.

The term *bond* describes three different ways that bricks are tied together in a structure: A *pattern bond* implies the arrangement of the bricks; a *mortar bond* refers to the adhesion of that material with the masonry units; and a *structural bond* refers to metal ties or anchors used in masonry construction, and to the overlapping of masonry units to stagger and thereby strengthen their vertical joints.

Pattern bonds are named to reflect their appearance; they also may or may not have important structural qualities. Some are suitable only for veneer work (p.246). Before selecting a bond, check with your building department to make sure it is appropriate for your project.

Decorative design

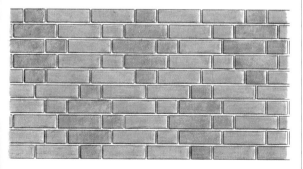

Garden wall pattern places a header after every two stretchers in each course. Use a brick of contrasting color to outline diamond shape. To create a larger diamond pattern, place the header after every three stretchers. Before building, draw your project and its pattern on graph paper.

Forming patterns with stretchers

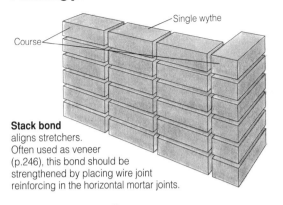

Single wythe

Course

Stack bond
aligns stretchers.
Often used as veneer
(p.246), this bond should be
strengthened by placing wire joint
reinforcing in the horizontal mortar joints.

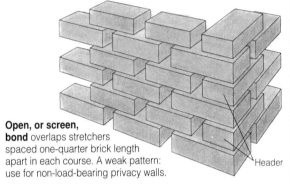

**Open, or screen,
bond** overlaps stretchers
spaced one-quarter brick length
apart in each course. A weak pattern:
use for non-load-bearing privacy walls.

Header

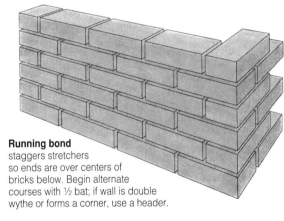

Running bond
staggers stretchers
so ends are over centers of
bricks below. Begin alternate
courses with ½ bat; if wall is double
wythe or forms a corner, use a header.

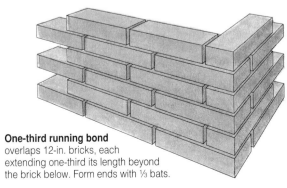

One-third running bond
overlaps 12-in. bricks, each
extending one-third its length beyond
the brick below. Form ends with ⅓ bats.

Combining headers and stretchers

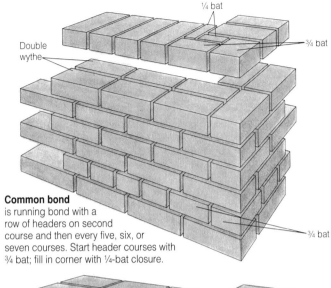

¼ bat

Double
wythe

¾ bat

Common bond
is running bond with a
row of headers on second
course and then every five, six, or
seven courses. Start header courses with
¾ bat; fill in corner with ¼-bat closure.

¾ bat

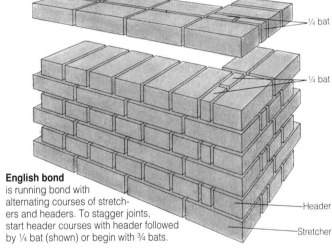

¼ bat

¼ bat

English bond
is running bond with
alternating courses of stretchers and headers. To stagger joints,
start header courses with header followed
by ¼ bat (shown) or begin with ¾ bats.

Header

Stretcher

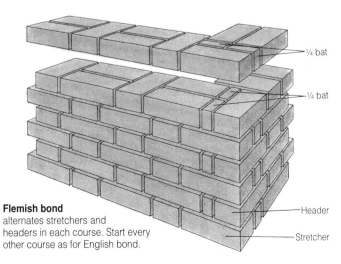

¼ bat

¼ bat

Flemish bond
alternates stretchers and
headers in each course. Start every
other course as for English bond.

Header

Stretcher

JOINTING BRICKS

Joints are the layers of mortar between bricks. They are named for their position in the structure: horizontal joints are called *bed* joints; vertical joints between bricks in a course are *head* joints. If a wall is more than one brick thick, the vertical joint between the wythes is called a *collar* joint.

When laying bricks, apply the mortar forcefully to aid its adhesion (p.225). Then push the bricks into place with one motion; don't move them further except to tap them gently immediately afterward, using the handle of a mason's trowel, to settle and level them. If a brick is too low or is misaligned, remove it together with the mortar in the joint; then clean and replace the brick, using fresh mortar. Check your work often with a level and stretched string (p.233).

The mortar is ready to be finished when it is hard enough to retain a thumbprint without leaving any residue on your thumb. Finishing shapes and compresses the joints, strengthening them and sealing them against moisture. Using a trowel to finish joints is called *striking;* using a special jointing tool is called *tooling.* As a rule, it is best to work from bottom to top.

Some mortar joints are purely decorative and only for indoor use; others are designed to shed water and are best for outdoor work. In housing, weep holes may be created by inserting rope wicks or plastic tubes in the mortar, or by omitting the head joint every now and then along the brick-flashing course at the wall's base, beneath windows, and above windows and doors. After the initial shaping, clean all joints by brushing with a medium-soft bristle brush, burlap cloth, or carpet scrap. After brushing, rework the joints if necessary to sharpen their details and remove any imperfections.

While mortar joints form the main structural bond for masonry, expansion joint material inserted at certain points (facing page) allows the bricks and the mortar to expand and contract with changes in temperature and humidity. These expansion joints are placed every 25 feet in brick walls and at strategic points in rigid (mortared) brick patios and walks. However, you do not need to use expansion joints in a project, vertical or flat, that is less than 20 feet long or in any type of sand-set (flexible) brickwork.

Laying bricks

Stretcher

To place stretcher or header in course, butter one end or side of brick; push brick down and against previous brick to produce uniform head and bed joints. Level by tapping brick with trowel handle.

Header

Closing a course. Butter all surfaces of closure space as well as ends and underside of closure brick. Press brick gently into place from above without disturbing bricks at sides.

Tooling head and bed joints

Trim away tags of excess mortar by slicing upward with edge of trowel. Repeat step after tooling head and bed joints.

Shape head joints first. Press and slide the jointing tool over vertical seams to smooth and compact the mortar before it hardens.

Smooth bed joints next, using the same tool, to create continuous horizontal lines. Avoid gouging joints with tool or knuckles.

Mortar joints and shapes

Weathered. Sheds water well. Form by running trowel tip against underside of upper course while pressing tip inward at 30° angle. Shape of head joints is the vertical equivalent, all slanting in the same direction.

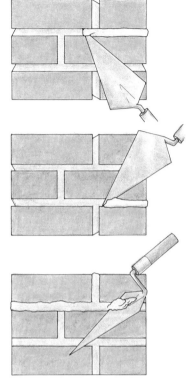

Struck. Opposite of weathered. Sheds water poorly. Work from above to form; recess lower edge of mortar by pressing trowel tip inward against top of lower brick course. Head joints are same as for weathered.

Flush. Moderately water-resistant but not strong because mortar is not compressed. Form by slicing away excess mortar with trowel to leave flat surface. Best for use beneath plaster or stucco.

Concave. Most common joint. Sheds water well. To form, see facing page. You can use pipe, dowel, or back of kitchen spoon instead of convex forming tool. All tools should be ¼ in. wider than joints.

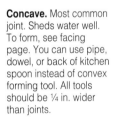

V-. Dramatic appearance. Sheds water well. Form with V-jointing tool or tip of mason's trowel. Practice first to avoid unevenness; centerline of joint must be spaced evenly between brick courses.

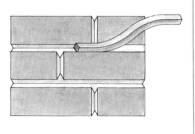

Raked. Not water-resistant; use indoors to create strong shadow lines. Form by removing ¼ to ½ in. of mortar from joints with raking tool. Clean exposed surfaces thoroughly afterward.

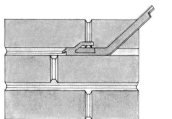

Expansion joints in mortared paving

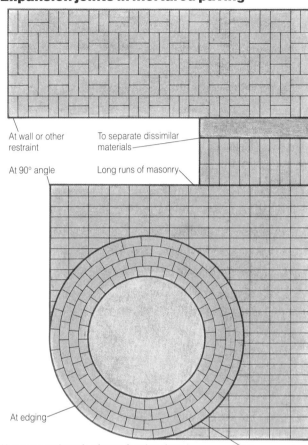

At wall or other restraint

To separate dissimilar materials

At 90° angle

Long runs of masonry

At edging

To separate bond patterns

Neoprene or foam backer rod and sealant expansion joints allow for differing expansion and contraction of bricks and mortar. Pour concrete slab (pp.204–213) prior to laying rigid flatwork.

How to cut a brick

Cut line

Mark cutting line around brick with pencil and straightedge. Place brick on ground or board. Score brick: Place brick set on cutting line, with beveled edge facing waste; then strike tool gently with hammer. To cut brick, place it on edge, insert brick set in scored line, and strike sharply with hammer. Grip brick set around shaft, not blade, to avoid injuring fingers. **Caution:** Wear heavy gloves and goggles.

WORKING WITH STONE

Lifting stones

To lift a stone safely, bring it close to your body. When rising, "hug" the stone, using your thigh muscles to stand. Keep your back straight. Avoid carrying stones more than a few yards; a stone 1 ft. square and 6 in. thick can weigh 75 lb. or more.

Long digging bar levers stone from ground

Pry stone from ground with levers. Start with long steel digging bar; then insert 2 × 4 planks and pry alternately with these until one plank can serve as a ramp on which to slide the stone. Place wood blocks beneath planks to keep them from sinking into sides of hole. Do not reach beneath the stone when rolling it free.

Because stone is heavy and working with it requires physical conditioning, a novice should start a project gradually. Have a medical examination, warm up before working by doing stretching exercises that include touching your toes, and spend no more than 4 to 6 hours daily lifting and moving stones until your muscles are developed. Always wear protective clothing, including heavy leather work gloves, sturdy boots with steel toes, and safety goggles (when cutting).

Rely on mechanical aids to save physical effort and to avoid possible injury. To lift stones, use digging bars, ramps, and hand or power winches. When using a winch, wrap a chain—not the winch cable—around the stone, and attach the winch cable to the chain. A winch cable can break if it is looped around an object and then hooked to itself.

For hauling stones over short distances, get a sturdy wheelbarrow with solid arms and a pneumatic tire. (For maximum maneuverability, load stones so most of the weight is in the rear.) Or place stones on a wooden plank and roll the plank along on logs or pipes. For hauling stones long distances, use a pickup truck with heavy-duty suspension, or a flatbed trailer or a stoneboat attached to a similar powerful vehicle. To avoid losing control, drive cautiously when hauling stones. Inspect the brakes beforehand, and upgrade them if necessary so they are in excellent condition. When hauling flat or thin stones, place them on edge and wedge them to keep them from falling; if laid flat, they can break when bounced.

Dry stone (mortarless) masonry is the best type for novices because it requires fitting stones together and relies on gravity to hold them in place, the key to all stonework. Shaping the stones is an important part of dry stonework; for best results use a 3-pound sledgehammer or a stonemason's hammer and at least two chisels: a broad-bladed *stone chisel* or a *pitching tool* for scoring and for splitting grained stones; and a *point*, tapered on all sides like a sharpened pencil, for focusing blows over small areas. When shaping stones, support them on a firm but resilient surface (p.236). Professional stonemasons use a sturdy homemade wooden table, padded with sawdust or several layers of carpet; the height of such a table should be about 6 inches below the user's waist.

The properties of stone

Type	Physical characteristics	Workability	Durability*	Use
Granite	Hard, dense; coarse-grained or speckled; gray, blue, pinkish	Difficult; hard to cut	Excellent	Walls, foundations, chimneys (not cut to fit)
Limestone	Medium-soft; light to dark gray	Easy; cuts well	Medium to poor	Walls, foundations, chimneys
Sandstone	Soft to medium-hard; brown, gray, reddish	Easy to medium (there are soft and hard sandstones)	Medium	Hard types: walls, foundations, chimneys. Soft types: interior veneer
Slate	Soft; dark gray or black	Medium; splits easily with grain; cut across grain with masonry saw	Medium to poor	Patios, paths, shingles

*Includes resistance to weather

Moving stones

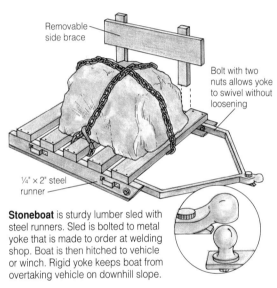

Roll stone onto a plank resting on logs or pipes. Push plank forward, or lever it from behind with a 2 × 4, while removing rollers from rear and setting them in pathway ahead. On soft ground, place boards beneath rollers for support.

Removable side brace

Bolt with two nuts allows yoke to swivel without loosening

¼" × 2" steel runner

Stoneboat is sturdy lumber sled with steel runners. Sled is bolted to metal yoke that is made to order at welding shop. Boat is then hitched to vehicle or winch. Rigid yoke keeps boat from overtaking vehicle on downhill slope.

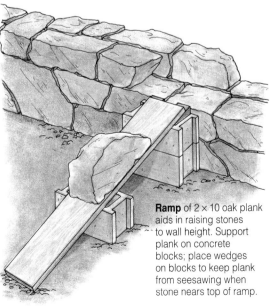

Ramp of 2 × 10 oak plank aids in raising stones to wall height. Support plank on concrete blocks; place wedges on blocks to keep plank from seesawing when stone nears top of ramp.

Splitting stones

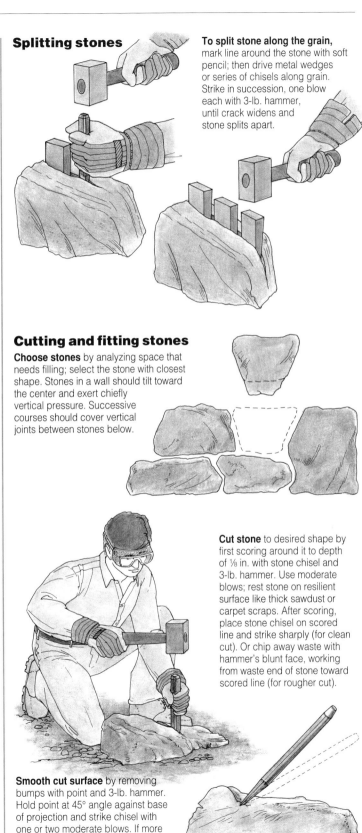

To split stone along the grain, mark line around the stone with soft pencil; then drive metal wedges or series of chisels along grain. Strike in succession, one blow each with 3-lb. hammer, until crack widens and stone splits apart.

Cutting and fitting stones

Choose stones by analyzing space that needs filling; select the stone with closest shape. Stones in a wall should tilt toward the center and exert chiefly vertical pressure. Successive courses should cover vertical joints between stones below.

Cut stone to desired shape by first scoring around it to depth of ⅛ in. with stone chisel and 3-lb. hammer. Use moderate blows; rest stone on resilient surface like thick sawdust or carpet scraps. After scoring, place stone chisel on scored line and strike sharply (for clean cut). Or chip away waste with hammer's blunt face, working from waste end of stone toward scored line (for rougher cut).

Smooth cut surface by removing bumps with point and 3-lb. hammer. Hold point at 45° angle against base of projection and strike chisel with one or two moderate blows. If more blows are needed, lower point to 30°.

WORKING WITH CONCRETE BLOCKS

Laying blocks in courses

1. With blocks on end, trowel mortar onto edges with a downward swipe. Place, using chalk line and level (facing page).

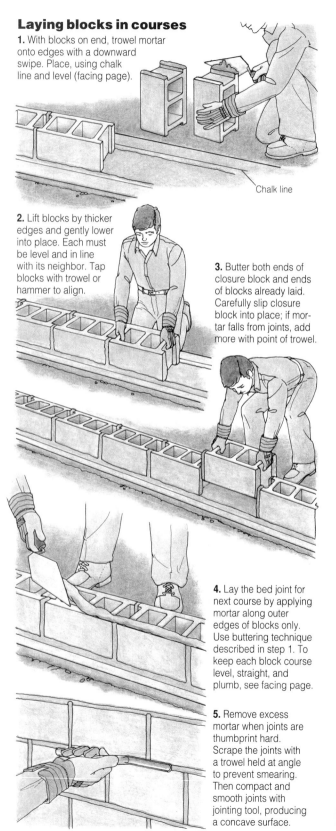

Chalk line

2. Lift blocks by thicker edges and gently lower into place. Each must be level and in line with its neighbor. Tap blocks with trowel or hammer to align.

3. Butter both ends of closure block and ends of blocks already laid. Carefully slip closure block into place; if mortar falls from joints, add more with point of trowel.

4. Lay the bed joint for next course by applying mortar along outer edges of blocks only. Use buttering technique described in step 1. To keep each block course level, straight, and plumb, see facing page.

5. Remove excess mortar when joints are thumbprint hard. Scrape the joints with a trowel held at angle to prevent smearing. Then compact and smooth joints with jointing tool, producing a concave surface.

Many find that laying concrete blocks is faster and easier than laying bricks. You can butter several blocks at one time; in addition, because of their weight, you set the blocks in place without pushing them. Their larger size means that leveling and aligning require less time.

Concrete blocks take the same type of mortar as bricks, and the joints are a standard ⅜ inch. The mortar bed beneath the first concrete block course must cover the entire area; you apply mortar for subsequent block courses only to the blocks' outer edges. Lay blocks with their thicker edges uppermost; the wider surfaces hold more mortar (p.223). Cover stored concrete blocks with a sturdy plastic tarp to keep out moisture and dirt.

In certain walls control joints—deliberately weakened vertical seams—are necessary to reduce cracking by accommodating the movement of the masonry. These walls have large openings, intersect other block walls, are restrained at each end, or have varying heights or thicknesses. In addition, concrete blocks that are joined to other structural materials also require control joints. Locate control joints where the greatest stresses occur and at intervals along the wall's length equal to its height or up to 1¼ times its height. For example, a wall 10 feet high will have control joints every 10 to 12½ feet along its length.

Because control joints act as a focus for cracking and, therefore, occasionally crack themselves, gasket material keeps the wall in alignment as it shifts. You can buy blocks designed to house the various types of gaskets.

Control joints

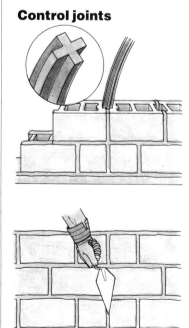

Neoprene gasket strip (inset) maintains alignment of blocks in control joint; it fits channel in specially formed blocks. Install gasket strip in lowest course; build wall using whole and half-size special blocks to make vertical joint within overall bond pattern.

Mortar in control joint acts as backer for caulking compound sealer. Rake out mortar to a depth of ¾ in.; then fill the joint with caulking compound. (First brush primer into the joint if caulking instructions specify.)

LEVEL, STRAIGHT, AND PLUMB

In all types of masonry, aligning the building units accurately is crucial to success. To build straight walls that do not lean or bulge, each brick or concrete block must be checked three ways—lengthwise, across its width, and vertically—as it is set in place, and if necessary, adjusted before proceeding.

To ensure straightness, mark the length of a wall by snapping a chalk line on the footing. So that the chalk line won't be covered with mortar, snap it at a uniform distance—say, 2 inches—from the footing's edge. Each time you lay a brick or block in place, measure between it and the line at both ends to make sure the unit and the line are exactly parallel.

Masons build the ends of a wall first; then they fill in the center of the wall. The built-up ends of walls are called *leads;* if the walls form corners, the ends are called *corner leads.* Stretch a mason's line between the ends as a guide.

A homemade *story pole* allows you to check that your mortar joint is the proper thickness as you build each course. To make a story pole, mark squared lines on a 1 × 2 board at intervals equal to the thickness of your masonry unit plus a mortar joint. Make as many marks as there are courses in the wall. Hold the pole next to the construction to check the mortar joint for each course.

Building a wall lead

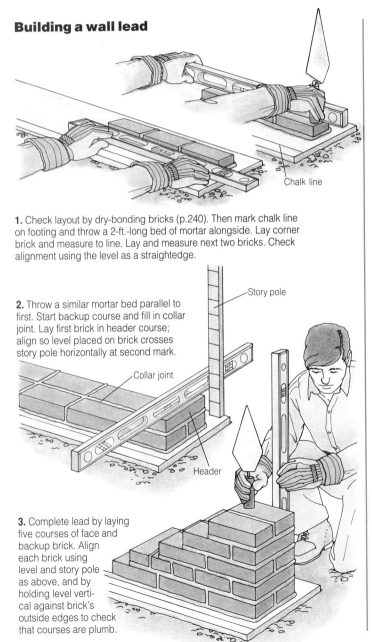

1. Check layout by dry-bonding bricks (p.240). Then mark chalk line on footing and throw a 2-ft.-long bed of mortar alongside. Lay corner brick and measure to line. Lay and measure next two bricks. Check alignment using the level as a straightedge.

2. Throw a similar mortar bed parallel to first. Start backup course and fill in collar joint. Lay first brick in header course; align so level placed on brick crosses story pole horizontally at second mark.

3. Complete lead by laying five courses of face and backup brick. Align each brick using level and story pole as above, and by holding level vertical against brick's outside edges to check that courses are plumb.

Creating a true corner

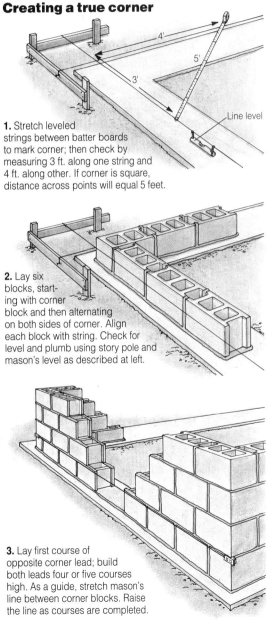

1. Stretch leveled strings between batter boards to mark corner; then check by measuring 3 ft. along one string and 4 ft. along other. If corner is square, distance across points will equal 5 feet.

2. Lay six blocks, starting with corner block and then alternating on both sides of corner. Align each block with string. Check for level and plumb using story pole and mason's level as described at left.

3. Lay first course of opposite corner lead; build both leads four or five courses high. As a guide, stretch mason's line between corner blocks. Raise the line as courses are completed.

FLEXIBLE PAVING: PATTERNS AND EDGINGS

When used in flatwork, bricks and concrete pavers are often laid in sand (without mortar) on a flat, firm base and anchored with an edging. This method, called *flexible paving,* is easy to install and repair.

Brick paving is usually laid in classic patterns: running bond, stack bond, basket weave, and herringbone. Of these, herringbone is the most durable and stable because the bricks interlock at right angles. Concrete pavers are available in many shapes; the more intricate ones come with installation instructions.

Flagstone is also popular for flexible paving. Because no edging is required, it is easier to lay out an area for flagstone than for bricks or concrete pavers. In addition, you can space the sand joints irregularly. But make sure

the flagstones are well supported underneath; otherwise they can break when stepped on. (For more on flagstone paving, see pp.236–237.)

With sandy, well-drained soil in areas where freezing seldom occurs, excavate the site to the depth of the paving plus 2 inches for a bed of tamped sand. (The sand will keep the paving from shifting.) With other soils and in cold climates, excavate 4 inches deeper to add a layer of tamped gravel beneath the sand. The gravel permits drainage and helps prevent masonry from being pushed upward when the ground alternately freezes and thaws.

When laying out a project, base its shape on the dimensions of the paving units in order to minimize cutting. You can cut bricks fairly easily by hand (p.229), but you will need to rent a

splitter to cut pavers. (Pavers that create special patterns usually come with half blocks for filling in outside edges.)

Edging can be anchored with stakes or spikes. Use pressure-treated lumber strips or landscaping ties (or any species that resists decay naturally, such as cypress or cedar). Alternatively, you can anchor strips of polyvinyl chloride (PVC) with $\frac{3}{8} \times 10$-inch metal spikes. Or you can dig a narrow ditch and add a brick edging (facing page). To minimize the effects of frost heave, dig the ditch 2 inches deeper and pour in a layer of gravel before placing the bricks.

To reduce the chance of tripping over wood or PVC edging, place the top surface ¼ inch below the paving; the latter will settle more and the two will eventually be level.

Patterns

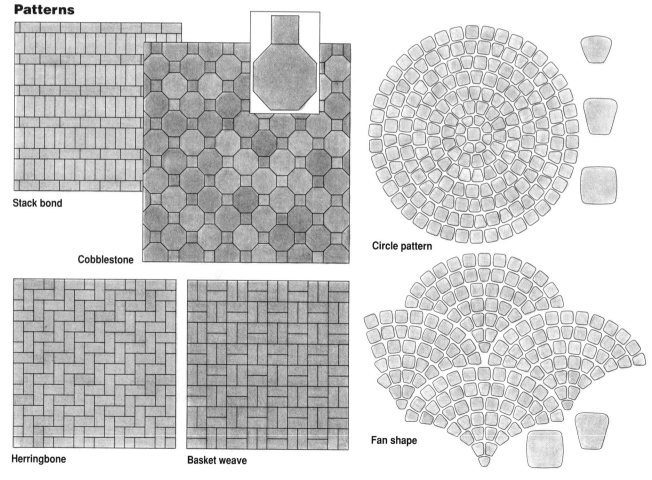

Stack bond

Cobblestone

Circle pattern

Herringbone

Basket weave

Fan shape

Brick edging

Lay out project. Position corner stakes so that connecting strings outline edges of project. Mark edges with a sand line (p.208). Dig a ditch equal to length of bricks (plus 2 in. for gravel, if used). Keep outer sides vertical.

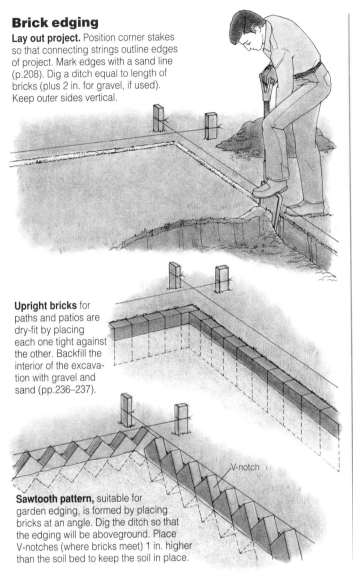

Upright bricks for paths and patios are dry-fit by placing each one tight against the other. Backfill the interior of the excavation with gravel and sand (pp.236–237).

Sawtooth pattern, suitable for garden edging, is formed by placing bricks at an angle. Dig the ditch so that the edging will be aboveground. Place V-notches (where bricks meet) 1 in. higher than the soil bed to keep the soil in place.

V-notch

Wood strip edging

Dig level ditch that is wide enough to allow work area outside perimeter. Place edging. Drive stakes at 3-ft. intervals and where boards join. Recess stakes 1 in. below top of edging. Fasten with nails or screws.

Backfill exterior of ditch to cover stakes; tamp in place.

Two ways to set landscaping ties

Set 6 × 6-in. ties flush with grade. Butt-join them with 10-in. nails driven at an angle and staggered. To hide nails, drive them into sides of ties. Add gravel, sand, and paving. Backfill exterior.

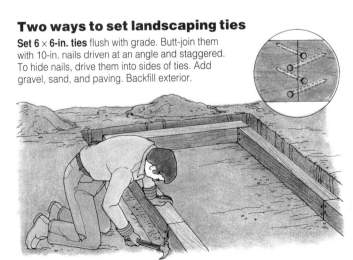

At each end and in center, drill ⅝-in. holes with spade bit. Insert ½ × 18-in. mild-steel rods. With short-handled sledge-hammer, drive rods into holes until flush with edging. Lay paving; backfill exterior.

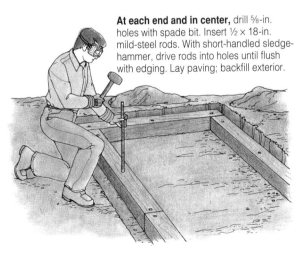

Paving with bricks

1. Spread and tamp gravel over excavated site; then level with a screed and extension (width equal to sand layer plus paver layer). Fill low areas. Add sand; spread with extension equal to paver layer.

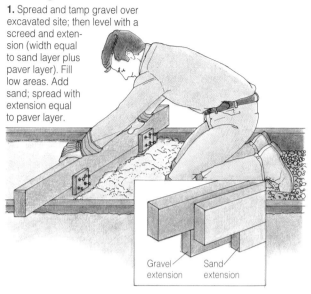

Gravel extension Sand extension

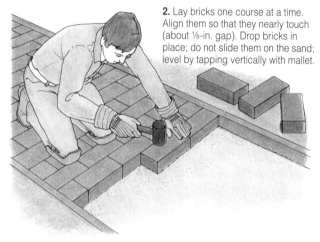

2. Lay bricks one course at a time. Align them so that they nearly touch (about ⅛-in. gap). Drop bricks in place; do not slide them on the sand; level by tapping vertically with mallet.

3. Spread coarse sand over bricks after all are laid; then sweep sand into cracks. Spray site with garden hose to moisten and settle sand. (Do not tamp bricks.) Repeat two or three times, until joints are filled.

To lay out areas for sand-laid paving, tie strings to stakes or batter boards as for poured concrete and mortared masonry projects (pp.206–208, 233). The strings determine the perimeter and establish a height from which to measure downward when excavating the site. To outline curved areas, lay a garden hose or rope on the ground. Drive stakes along the hose or rope outline, and stretch strings between them. (The strings need not follow the exact shape of the curve.)

If the paved surface is to be flat, use a line level to adjust each string. If the surface must slope to promote drainage away from a building, the strings that are stretched in the direction of the slope should slant downward ¼ inch for every foot of their length.

The most crucial step in building with flexible paving is site preparation; a firm and flat site minimizes the settling of the paving. As a rule, it is easier to excavate the entire site to the depth required and then install the edging and paving. If you install anchored wood edging (pp.234–235) before laying the pavers, you can use it as a guide when leveling the sand and gravel beds on which the paving will rest.

To use the edging as a leveling guide, rest the ends of the screed (pp.211, 214) on it and drag the extension over the gravel, then the sand. If the area is wider than the screed, or if you prefer to install the edging last (as you might for vertical or angled brick edging), place temporary strips of wood equal to the height of the edging on the ground before adding the first layer of fill. Use these to support the ends of the screed. After leveling the beds, remove the strips and fill the areas by adding material with a trowel.

Take extra time to make sure that the gravel bed (or the excavation if gravel is not used) is tamped and level. You can tamp small areas with a hand tamper (p.206), but for best results, tamp large areas with a plate vibrator, a motor-powered tool that can be rented.

Caution: Plate vibrators are noisy; wear ear protectors.

Don't tamp a sand bed. Until the paving is laid, protect the bed from rain either by covering the sand with plastic sheeting when you have finished for the day or by spreading the sand in 10-square-foot areas just before installing the paving. Stay off the sand bed by working from outside the perimeter or by kneeling on previously laid sections.

When paving with flagstones, first fit as many uncut stones together as possible to minimize the amount of shaping you have to do. To cut flagstones, support them on sand-covered ground. If you will be cutting a number of stones, raise the work to a more comfortable height and reduce back strain by building a sturdy sand table to rest them on. Make the table surface out of ¾-inch plywood, use 2 × 4's to support the table, and add a rim of 1 × 2's to contain the layer of sand.

Place flagstones with their more level and attractive side up. Avoid using small stones; they tend to sink into the ground or to tip when stepped on.

A patio of concrete pavers

1. Prepare 4-in.-thick gravel base with screed (facing page). To tamp large area, move rented plate vibrator across base several times. Spread and smooth 2 in. of coarse sand; do not tamp.

2. Lay pavers starting at 90° corner. Align edge units precisely; set all pavers in place without disturbing sand. Follow manufacturer's suggested sequence when using irregularly shaped units.

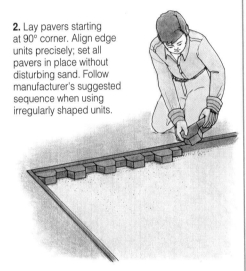

3. Keep pavers aligned by following string stretched parallel with courses. Complete patio; then tamp pavers with plate vibrator. Sweep sand into joints and tamp pavers again with vibrator. Do not wet. Repeat until joints are full.

Shaping flagstones

Place flagstone so edge to be cut overlaps edging or previously laid stone. Determine cut line by eye, and mark both sides with grease pencil.

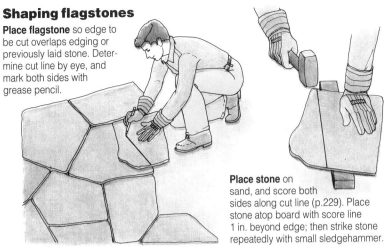

Place stone on sand, and score both sides along cut line (p.229). Place stone atop board with score line 1 in. beyond edge; then strike stone repeatedly with small sledgehammer.

Laying flagstones

1. Lay flagstones about ½ in. apart. Arrange largest stones around perimeter of site to help keep the rest from shifting. Place stone on ground and test fit; then lift stone and regrade area underneath by removing or adding sand to accommodate stone's uneven surface.

2. Tap stones lightly with a mallet to settle them. Lay several stones; then place a mason's level across them in several directions to check that all are the same height and that there are no high edges or irregularities that can cause tripping.

3. Finish project by filling joints with sand and wetting it as for flexible brick walk (facing page). Use scrap wood to tamp sand between stones after each application.

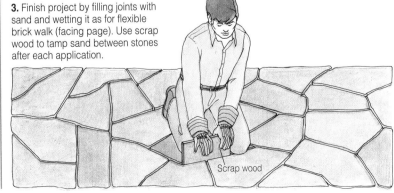

Scrap wood

GARDEN STEPS: BRICK, BLOCK, AND STONE

Aboveground steps generally require a footing to prevent settling and cracking, and often a railing for safety. Steps leading into a building should be wider than the doorway and, if the door opens out, should have a landing that is deeper than the door. Steps that are built into a steep slope may also need retaining walls at the sides (pp.244–245). Before you begin construction, consult your local building inspector to find out what codes apply.

To design aboveground steps so they are easy and safe to climb, apply the 7/11 rule (pp.208–209). Along gently sloping paths, long landings (6 to 8 feet) divided by low risers, or a series of landings interrupted by pairs of identical steps, are often more

comfortable and more appealing than a single compact flight. These designs are safer too, especially if the steps tend to be slippery.

Lay out steps by measuring the slope's *rise,* or height, and its *run,* or horizontal distance. Often the rise is fixed by the physical constraints of the site. For example, the placement of a house entry door and the grade level determine the rise of aboveground steps. When this is the case, the run can usually be adjusted as necessary to fit the steps. With in-ground steps, both rise and run measurements may be more flexible.

To calculate the number of steps, divide the rise (in inches) by a divisor, less than or equal to 7, that goes into

the rise equally. Determine the number of treads by dividing the run measurement by a tread depth (at least 11 and no more than 18 inches) that goes into the run equally. If the rise or the run of the steps happens to divide awkwardly, spread the remainder evenly among the treads or risers, or adjust the overall measurement.

For example, take a 36-inch rise with an 84-inch run. The run divides into seven 12-inch treads, requiring six risers. The rise divides into six risers that are 6 inches high.

You can also design steps by transferring the run and rise measurements to graph paper and sketching uniform riser/tread combinations (to scale) to comfortably and safely fill the space.

Aboveground steps

1. Lay out steps with solid 6-in.-wide blocks (p.223). Pour concrete slab on pier footings (pp.206–209). Slab should be 4 in. wider and 2 in. longer than steps and landing. Dry-bond first course of concrete blocks (pp.240–241) to check their fit. Adjust placement; then lay them with mortar.

Place blocks so 6" width forms safe riser

2. Build sides of steps in modified running bond pattern. (Blocks are the form for poured concrete.) To avoid vertical joints between courses, draw side views of blocks on paper before laying. Form treads by setting each course back from the course below.

¾ block

½ block

Block overlaps 4" to create 12" tread

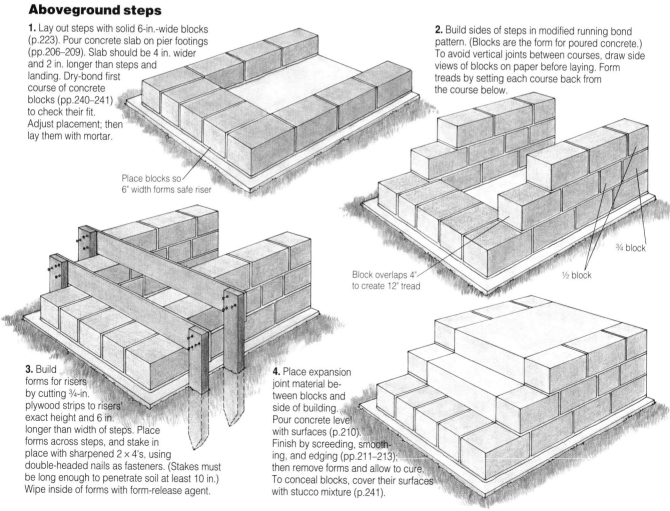

3. Build forms for risers by cutting ¾-in. plywood strips to risers' exact height and 6 in. longer than width of steps. Place forms across steps, and stake in place with sharpened 2 x 4's, using double-headed nails as fasteners. (Stakes must be long enough to penetrate soil at least 10 in.) Wipe inside of forms with form-release agent.

4. Place expansion joint material between blocks and side of building. Pour concrete level with surfaces (p.210). Finish by screeding, smoothing, and edging (pp.211–213); then remove forms and allow to cure. To conceal blocks, cover their surfaces with stucco mixture (p.241).

In-ground steps

1. Drive stakes at top and bottom of slope. Using string and a line level, measure between stakes to find the run. Measure the height of the taller stake from the ground to the string to find the rise. Calculate uniform step dimensions (facing page).

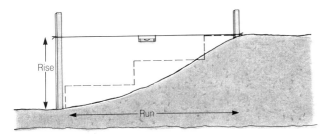

2. Side view of plan for steps shows the placement of (6 × 6-in.) landscaping ties. These ties are 8 ft. long to embed the steps well into the slope. Steel rods anchor each tie to the one below it.

Flagstone steps

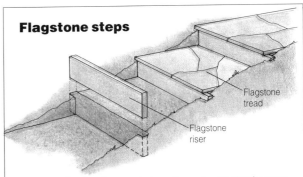

Flagstone tread

Flagstone riser

Lay out as for other in-ground steps. Excavate, allowing for stone tread and 2-in. layer of sand above 4-in. bed of tamped gravel. Then dig narrow, straight trenches for flagstone risers. Install risers; then add fill. Lay flagstone treads so they overlap risers, trimming edges if necessary. Check treads often with a level, and reposition them as needed to ensure flat surfaces (pp.236–237).

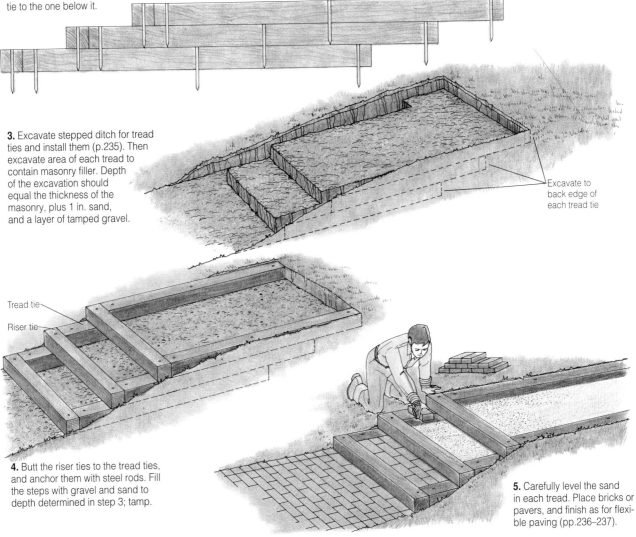

3. Excavate stepped ditch for tread ties and install them (p.235). Then excavate area of each tread to contain masonry filler. Depth of the excavation should equal the thickness of the masonry, plus 1 in. sand, and a layer of tamped gravel.

Excavate to back edge of each tread tie

Tread tie

Riser tie

4. Butt the riser ties to the tread ties, and anchor them with steel rods. Fill the steps with gravel and sand to depth determined in step 3; tamp.

5. Carefully level the sand in each tread. Place bricks or pavers, and finish as for flexible paving (pp.236–237).

GARDEN WALLS: BRICK AND BLOCK

Local building codes govern virtually all types of masonry walls except non-load-bearing walls less than 2 feet high. You should consult your municipality's building inspector before beginning a wall project. You can often obtain sample plans. If you wish to use an original design, you'll need to get it approved.

As a rule, support a wall with a continuous footing that rests below the frost line (pp.208–209). Brick walls higher than 30 inches should be double wythe (pp.226–227), with a ½-inch-thick collar joint between the wythes. To form the collar joint, mortar the rear faces of the stretcher bricks.

An exception to the double-wythe rule is pier-and-panel walls. These are easier to construct than double-wythe masonry and require fewer bricks and

less excavation. The piers rest on footings 18 to 24 inches in diameter and extending below the frost line. (The size of the piers and the panels must be designed to suit the individual site and conditions.) Pier-and-panel walls derive their strength from steel reinforcing rods, called *rebars,* embedded vertically in the piers. Rebars should be spaced properly within grout-filled centers. When placing the first courses, you may need to support the rebars in position with braces staked to the ground on either side of the wall.

Most non-load-bearing walls of concrete block do not require reinforcement. But walls built with screen blocks, a decorative variety used for privacy walls, must be reinforced with pilasters, whose function is similar to

piers. (Like piers, pilasters contain rebars.) In addition, wire joint reinforcing must be embedded horizontally in every other course to compensate for the inherent weakness of the stack bond pattern (pp.226–227) in which screen blocks are usually laid. To keep out moisture and give a finished look, cap all walls. On brick walls, lay a rowlock course or place a course of decorative capping bricks. On concrete block walls, lay a course of solid units or apply a rounded layer of mortar.

Stucco can be applied to masonry for both appearance and protection. A typical formula for stucco is 1 part Portland cement, 1 part masonry cement, and 3¼ to 4 parts very fine sand, mixed with clean water to the consistency of creamy cake frosting.

Double-wythe brick wall

1. Dry-bond first course to test fit. Use finger or wood scrap as spacer to locate the mortar joints. Adjust spaces if necessary to avoid having to cut the bricks. Mark the final brick positions on footing with pencil.

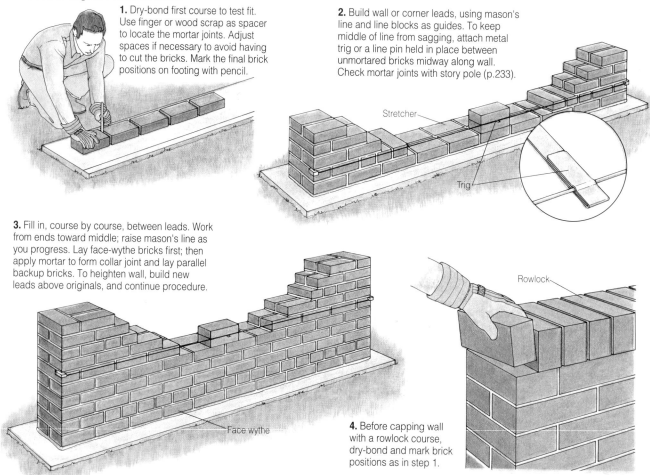

2. Build wall or corner leads, using mason's line and line blocks as guides. To keep middle of line from sagging, attach metal trig or a line pin held in place between unmortared bricks midway along wall. Check mortar joints with story pole (p.233).

Stretcher

Trig

3. Fill in, course by course, between leads. Work from ends toward middle; raise mason's line as you progress. Lay face-wythe bricks first; then apply mortar to form collar joint and lay parallel backup bricks. To heighten wall, build new leads above originals, and continue procedure.

Face wythe

Rowlock

4. Before capping wall with a rowlock course, dry-bond and mark brick positions as in step 1.

Pier-and-panel wall

1. Excavate and pour pier footings. When concrete stiffens, insert rebars cut to wall height; brace bars with spacers and wire ties. Lay each brick course; fill pier cores with grout. Embed wire reinforcing horizontally in every other course as for privacy wall (below).

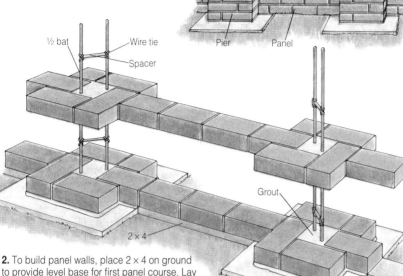

Pier   Panel

½ bat   Wire tie
Spacer
Grout
2 × 4

2. To build panel walls, place 2 × 4 on ground to provide level base for first panel course. Lay first course of bricks (with no mortar bed on 2 × 4). Tie odd and even courses into piers in alternating design. Remove 2 × 4 after wall has cured.

Privacy wall

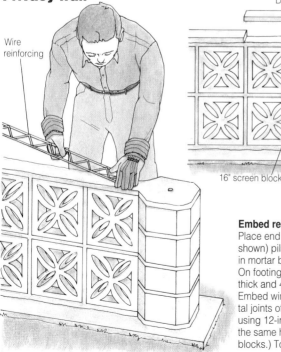

Wire reinforcing

Decorative cap
Rebar

16" screen block   8" pilaster block

Embed rebar in stiff concrete footing. Place end and intermediate (not shown) pilaster blocks around rebar in mortar bed; fill centers with grout. On footing, throw mortar bed ½ in. thick and 4 in. wide; lay screen blocks. Embed wire joint reinforcing in horizontal joints of every second course. (If using 12-in. block, two courses will be the same height as three pilaster blocks.) Top wall with decorative cap.

Stucco wall

1. Stucco is usually applied to rib lathing or copper-alloy steel, but such sheathing is not essential for a low wall. Dampen wall; brush on liquid bonding agent. Apply first coat of stucco ¼ in. thick, spreading it with steel trowel or float.

2. Score first coat with raking tool. Keep surface damp for 48 hr. by spraying or by covering with plastic sheeting. Never apply stucco when temperatures may fall below 50° F (10° C). Second coat should also be at least ¼ in. thick.

3. Apply final coat of stucco ⅛ in. thick with plasterer's trowel. Mix pigment into stucco to add color. To add texture, pattern your strokes.

The courses of a stone wall can be *random,* or irregular, using uncut, roughly dressed, or dressed stones in no particular pattern, or they can be regular, with the stones fitted tightly in level courses.

Walls can be laid with or without mortar. Novices should begin with a *dry stone* wall (one built without mortar) that is a maximum of 3 feet high. Because dry stone walls move with the freeze-thaw cycles, they are more flexible than mortared ones. Dry stone walls need no concrete footing and require an excavation of only about 6 inches.

Gravity is the force that holds well-built walls together and pulls apart poorly laid ones. The following guidelines will help you work effectively with gravity and maximize the friction between the stones: Tilt the stones slightly toward the center of the wall. You can also taper, or *batter,* the faces of a wall a minimum of 1 inch for every 2 feet. (In dry retaining walls you must taper the outer face or slant the inner face, pp.244–245.) Fit each stone so that it contacts the adjacent stones in as many places as possible. Place

Coursed dry stone wall with shaped stones

Random mortared wall with undressed stones

the stones "one over two," staggering vertical joints by laying one stone over the joint between the two below. For stability, make the wall at least two stones thick. (A wall 3 feet high should be about 2 feet thick.) Use a bonding, or *tie,* stone every 10 square feet. These stones, ideally as long as the wall is thick, are laid crossways to hold the stones together.

A mortared, or *wet,* wall can be built with the mortar visible or recessed so that it is hidden from view. Either way, mortar improves the bonding between stones, permitting higher walls and vertical faces. But the same principles for working with gravity apply: Mortar is not as durable as stone, and when it fails, gravity and friction take over.

A mortared wall is relatively inflexible. Instead of moving slightly to adjust to the forces of freezing and thawing or of growing tree roots, a mortared wall cracks. To minimize movement, build a wall on a footing placed just below the frost line. On sloped land install a pipe on the uphill side to drain the water behind the wall (pp.244–245). Never lay more than three courses (or 2 feet of wall height) in a day, so that the mortar can set enough to withstand the weight of the next courses. A standard mortar mixture for stone is 1 part lime, 3 parts Portland cement, and 9 parts sand. Add water slowly until the mixture stands in peaks like whipped cream. Keep the mortar off the stones' faces; the lime will stain the stones.

Caution: Wear waterproof gloves when working with mortar; protect your eyes with goggles.

Keep a just-built wall cool and damp for about a week to extend the curing time and strengthen the mortar. Mist the wall with a hose and cover it with plastic sheeting; if necessary, build a temporary shading device.

Putting gravity to work

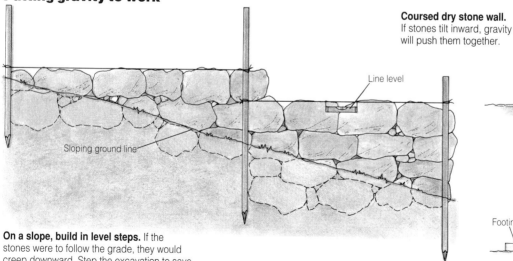

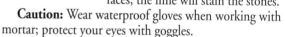

Line level

Sloping ground line

On a slope, build in level steps. If the stones were to follow the grade, they would creep downward. Step the excavation to save unnecessary digging, and step the wall itself to limit its height. Make sure each step is level by running a line level between two stakes. Dig out to accommodate large or irregular stones.

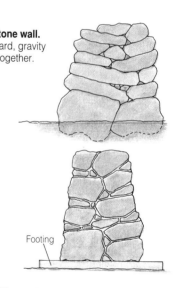

Coursed dry stone wall. If stones tilt inward, gravity will push them together.

Footing

Mortared stone wall. Lay rounded stones so they have maximum contact. Place small wedge-shaped stones to hold the rounded stones in place.

Laying a dry wall

Place the first course on firm, level ground, using stakes and level lines to guide the construction. Place the larger, more irregular stones on the bottom, digging as needed so they slope slightly down toward the center of the wall. Fill the center with smaller stones. As you add courses, stagger the vertical joints.

Turn corners by overlapping long and short stones from each leg in alternating courses. These stones tie the two legs together.

Leg

Tie stone

At wall ends, finish each course smoothly by laying stones that are faced (reasonably smooth and flat).

Building a mortared wall

Lay first course of stones, flat side up and good face out, in a 2-in. mortar bed atop concrete footing (p.208). Small stones fill in center of wall.

Rebar

Fill joints with mortar, leaving no voids that could later trap water. When mortar has dried, fill center with gravel.

Rake out, or strike, about 1 in. of mortar from the joints after it has set (2 to 3 hr.).

Clean the joints with a stiff brush when the mortar is semi-cured, usually the next day.

Cap the wall with large flat stones. Check position with a level. If not level, insert a wedge beneath lower edge. Large stones require fewer joints (where water can enter).

Masonry   243

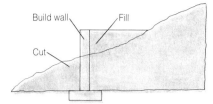

Build wall — Fill

Cut —

On sloping land, retaining walls hold back the soil, preventing erosion and creating a more usable landscape. These walls are commonly made of stone or concrete block—either the standard kind or a variety of interlocking blocks that require no mortar. The design of the wall depends on the building material you choose and such technical factors as the soil type, the wall height, and the site conditions.

A straight vertical wall of concrete block is tied with rebars to a reinforced footing (p.208) that is set deeply into the sloped bank. A stone wall, if laid dry, requires no footing and should slope, or batter, in toward the bank. Whether it is made of stone or concrete block, a gravity wall, which is thick at the bottom and steps up gradually, relies on its mass to hold back the soil.

Soils vary in their ability to absorb or drain water as well as the ways they react when wet or frozen. Generally, soils that drain well and remain stable when wet (such as gravel and sandy gravel) will not put as much pressure on a retaining wall as those that absorb water or lack cohesiveness (such as soft clay and silt). In addition, soils differ in their ability to bear weight—a factor for high walls only. Consult your local building department for advice about local soil conditions. If you learn that the soil conditions are a concern, or if you are unsure, backfill the area behind the retaining wall with gravel rather than the soil found on site.

Site conditions. A rainy climate, a high water table (the level of a site's groundwater), or the presence of a nearby lake, stream, or spring may affect the design of a wall. When soil becomes wet, its load-bearing capacity is reduced, its weight increases, and it tends to move laterally. In cold weather, wet soil freezes and expands, putting tremendous pressure on the wall. To reduce increased soil pressure, install special drainage provisions for all types of retaining walls over 2 feet tall, even dry stone walls. Drainage can be provided by weep holes, gravel backfill, drainage pipe, or a combination of these elements. A dampproofing parge coat prevents water from seeping through the wall itself and prevents the efflorescence water causes (p.248).

Wall height. Retaining walls over 2 or 3 feet high are governed by local building codes and zoning laws. In general, the higher the wall and the steeper the slope of the supported bank, the stronger the wall—and the footing below it—must be. To hold back a steeply sloping bank, a series of low walls (terraced effect) is an attractive and less demanding alternative to a single high wall. Consider having a contractor build walls over 4 feet high, and have an engineer or architect design retaining walls over 8 feet high or those that involve complicating factors—for example, if the wall is below a driveway, it will have to be designed to accommodate truck and car traffic.

Caution: In seismic (earthquake) zones, special designs may be required.

Concrete block retaining walls

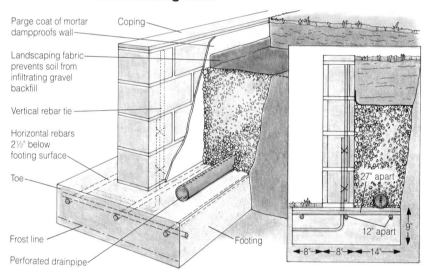

Parge coat of mortar dampproofs wall

Coping

Landscaping fabric prevents soil from infiltrating gravel backfill

Vertical rebar tie

Horizontal rebars 2½" below footing surface

Toe

Frost line

Perforated drainpipe

Footing

27" apart

12" apart

9"

8" — 8" — 14"

Footing for typical 3- to 4-ft.-high retaining wall of 8 × 8 × 16-in. block (above) extends 14 in. into bank. To tie the wall to the footing, vertical #3 rebars run through the block courses every 32 in. and are bent to extend into toe of footing. Horizontal #3 rebars are placed 12 in. apart along the length and 27 in. apart across the width of footing.

Gravity wall (right) has a vertical face and a stepped back profile, with a base equal to at least half the height. This wall depends on its weight and on friction between the wall and the ground for its ability to resist horizontal pressure. Use blocks of 8-in. and 12-in. widths to build stepped wall with staggered mortar joints.

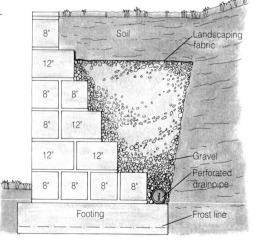

8" — Soil — Landscaping fabric

12"

8" | 8"

8" | 12"

12" | 12" — Gravel

8" | 8" | 8" | 8" — Perforated drainpipe

Footing — Frost line

Dry stone retaining wall

Excavate to firm sub-soil; lay stone courses. Backfill with gravel as you build, extending large stones into the hill. Excess water drains through dry wall joints. For clay soil, add a drainpipe behind wall.

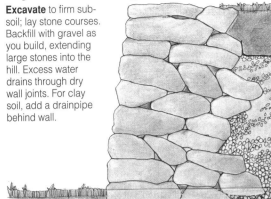

Perforated drainpipe

Vertical-face dry wall

Slant back of wall into slope. Lay narrow base course; backfill with gravel or soil, and pack it with digging bar (p.230). Repeat, laying gradually thicker courses. The top course of a 3-ft. wall should be about 2 ft. thick.

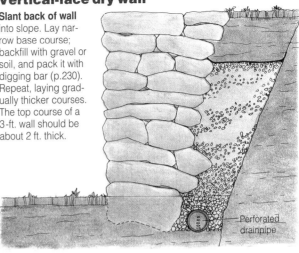

Perforated drainpipe

Check angle with batter board of plywood or nailed boards. Build it as tall as the wall's height, with a base 2 in. long for each foot of height. Add two shims in base to keep it even.

Shim

Mortared retaining wall

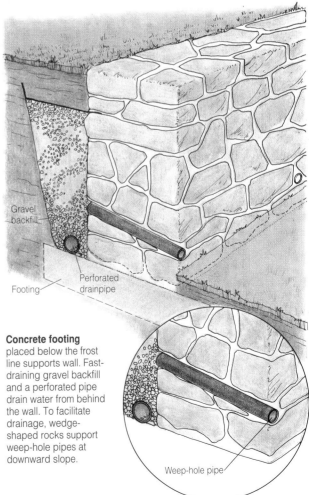

Gravel backfill

Footing

Perforated drainpipe

Weep-hole pipe

Concrete footing placed below the frost line supports wall. Fast-draining gravel backfill and a perforated pipe drain water from behind the wall. To facilitate drainage, wedge-shaped rocks support weep-hole pipes at downward slope.

Place batter board against the wall as you lay each course. For a long wall you can stake several batter boards 3 or 4 ft. apart and add a leveled line.

Masonry   245

VENEER: BRICK AND STONE

Veneer masonry is a decorative sheathing that enhances the face of a structure. It can be made of brick, natural stone, or a synthetic stone that is lighter in weight and easier to install than natural stone. Applying full-size bricks or stones as veneer (bottom of page) requires using traditional masonry techniques. These include building a footing to bear the weight of the

materials (the footing must be below the frost line if the veneer is outdoors) and arranging and mortaring the individual bricks or stones so that those on the bottom support those on top. In addition, metal ties or wire reinforcing is needed to fasten the veneer to the wall or other structure being sheathed.

Veneer bricks, also called *thin bricks,* measure only ½ inch thick and

are lightweight. Individual pieces can be arranged in any pattern. You can also buy them in panels and in kits that contain face and corner units, spacers, mastic, and premixed mortar. To cut thin bricks, use a tile cutter or a circular saw fitted with a masonry blade.

Synthetic veneer masonry. These products come as panels or individual pieces resembling various kinds of bricks or building stones. Many are suited for both outdoor and indoor use; some are designed especially for hearths. Synthetic masonry is easy to install almost anywhere. If it will be visible from the side, install it with corner pieces; these units have a 90° angle that allows the "stones" to turn corners.

When preparing surfaces and installing synthetic veneer, follow the maker's instructions. Set thin bricks in a layer of adhesive, and fill the joints with mortar. For synthetic stones, apply a scratch coat of mortar; then let it dry. (Spread the mortar directly on bare masonry; cover other surfaces with metal lath first.) Next apply mortar to the back of each piece and press them into place; fill the joints with mortar.

Thin bricks for interiors

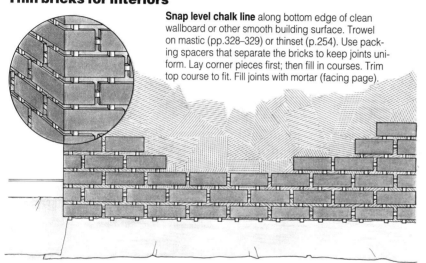

Snap level chalk line along bottom edge of clean wallboard or other smooth building surface. Trowel on mastic (pp.328–329) or thinset (p.254). Use packing spacers that separate the bricks to keep joints uniform. Lay corner pieces first; then fill in courses. Trim top course to fit. Fill joints with mortar (facing page).

Brick-on-block retaining wall

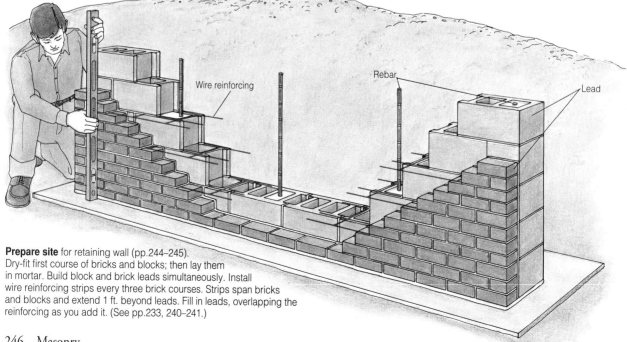

Wire reinforcing

Rebar

Lead

Prepare site for retaining wall (pp.244–245). Dry-fit first course of bricks and blocks; then lay them in mortar. Build block and brick leads simultaneously. Install wire reinforcing strips every three brick courses. Strips span bricks and blocks and extend 1 ft. beyond leads. Fill in leads, overlapping the reinforcing as you add it. (See pp.233, 240–241.)

WORKING WITH SYNTHETIC STONES

Setting the stones

Lay hearth pieces, if any, first (bottom of page); protect them with plastic sheeting. If necessary, staple or nail metal lath to studs in wall at 6-in. intervals. Apply mortar scratch coat. Attach units, working from top down.

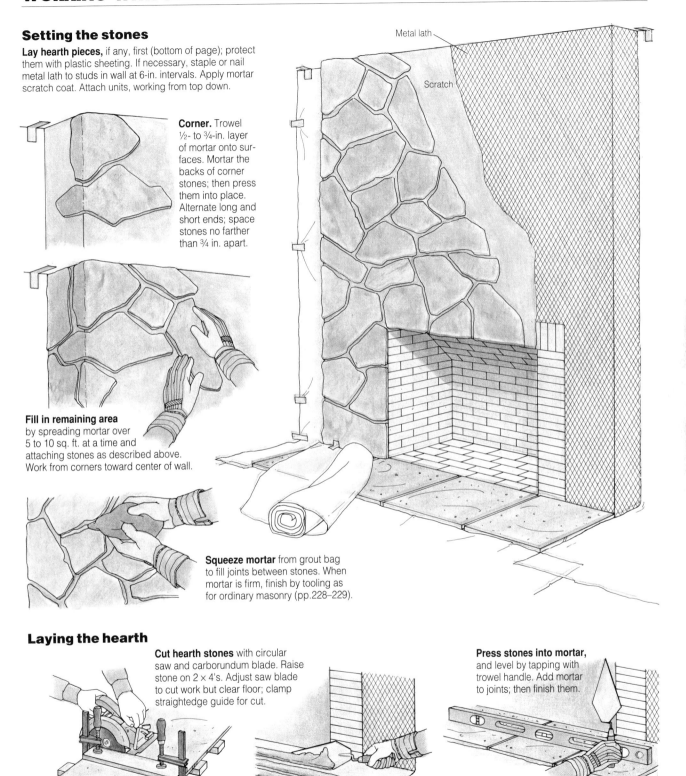

Corner. Trowel ½- to ¾-in. layer of mortar onto surfaces. Mortar the backs of corner stones; then press them into place. Alternate long and short ends; space stones no farther than ¾ in. apart.

Metal lath

Scratch

Fill in remaining area by spreading mortar over 5 to 10 sq. ft. at a time and attaching stones as described above. Work from corners toward center of wall.

Squeeze mortar from grout bag to fill joints between stones. When mortar is firm, finish by tooling as for ordinary masonry (pp.228–229).

Laying the hearth

Cut hearth stones with circular saw and carborundum blade. Raise stone on 2 × 4's. Adjust saw blade to cut work but clear floor; clamp straightedge guide for cut.

Install hearth stones. Throw lines of mortar, each 3 in. wide and ¾ in. thick, on base. Space lines 1 in. apart.

Press stones into mortar, and level by tapping with trowel handle. Add mortar to joints; then finish them.

Masonry should be repaired as soon as the damage is discovered. If neglected, small problems that are relatively easy to fix can become major ones. Most masonry damage is caused by moisture, settling, or impact—in that order.

Efflorescence, a white powder commonly found on new masonry surfaces, is usually caused by moisture introduced during construction. The moisture should dry in a few months, and rain usually washes away the powder.

If efflorescence continues or if it appears on older masonry, look for an entry point for moisture, such as cracks; crumbling mortar; deterioration around windows, doors, and chimneys; and dampness caused by moisture-saturated soil against masonry below ground. Repairing all but the last usually involves replacing damaged

building materials, applying a patch, or caulking. Once you have solved the moisture problem, remove the efflorescence by scrubbing it with a stiff brush and water or a detergent solution.

Before repairing cracks in mortar joints, seal off any entry points of moisture. If cracks redevelop, consult an engineer. For tuck-pointing, use mortar that is 1 part masonry cement, 3 parts sand, and enough water to make the mix the consistency of soft ice cream. Consult a mason before repairing masonry more than 100 years old; special mortar may be required.

Dampness in embedded masonry is more difficult to cure; the soil around the masonry must be drained. If the masonry is a foundation wall, first check that gutters are not clogged and that drainpipes are placed beneath

downspouts to carry runoff away. Sometimes you must regrade the soil so it slopes away from the masonry.

With retaining walls and foundations, drainpipes at the footing level can become blocked. Clear them with a drain auger if you can access their openings (often they empty into a nearby storm sewer). In basements, a high water table causes dampness. Installing a sump pump beneath the floor, and perhaps perimeter drainpipes leading to it, may solve the problem. For severe or persistent moisture problems, consult an engineer. The solution is often to dig along the outside of the wall (or the high side of a retaining wall), install a drainpipe surrounded by a layer of gravel, and place porous drainage fabric against the wall before backfilling (pp.244–245).

Tuck-pointing cracked mortar joints

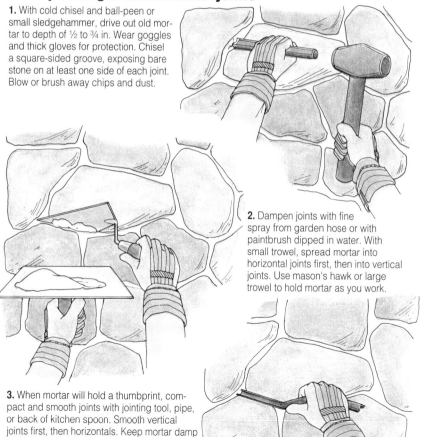

1. With cold chisel and ball-peen or small sledgehammer, drive out old mortar to depth of ½ to ¾ in. Wear goggles and thick gloves for protection. Chisel a square-sided groove, exposing bare stone on at least one side of each joint. Blow or brush away chips and dust.

2. Dampen joints with fine spray from garden hose or with paintbrush dipped in water. With small trowel, spread mortar into horizontal joints first, then into vertical joints. Use mason's hawk or large trowel to hold mortar as you work.

3. When mortar will hold a thumbprint, compact and smooth joints with jointing tool, pipe, or back of kitchen spoon. Smooth vertical joints first, then horizontals. Keep mortar damp for 4 days to complete curing (pp.212–213).

Replacing a broken brick

1. Chisel away damaged brick and surrounding mortar. Clean wall cavity and dampen it; spread mortar on bottom surface.

2. Dampen new brick; mortar top and sides; then slide into place from hawk or trowel. Add extra mortar to joints if necessary.

Filling large cracks

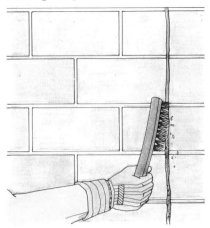

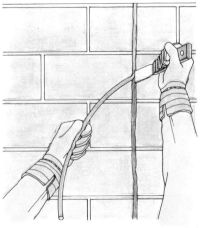

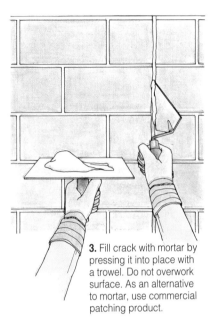

1. Brush or blow out all debris carefully. In concrete block masonry it is better not to chisel out a crack, as you would for concrete. Mortar will adhere to a clean crack in a block, and chiseling may damage the relatively thin face shell of the block.

2. Pack cracks with flexible backer rod (available at building supply stores). Next, dampen the crack and brush all surfaces with a commercial bonding agent or home-made grout (equal parts cement and sand, mixed with water to consistency of thick paint).

3. Fill crack with mortar by pressing it into place with a trowel. Do not overwork surface. As an alternative to mortar, use commercial patching product.

Rebuilding a broken block

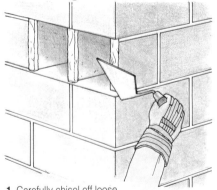

1. Carefully chisel off loose or weak sections of damaged face shell. Dampen area, and apply mortar to webs.

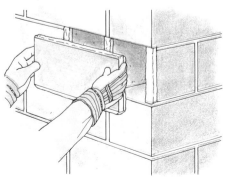

2. Cut face shell from new block. Apply mortar and press block into place. (Mortar fills gaps between cut shell and repair area.) Finish joints as for whole blocks (p.232).

Repairing stucco

1. Correct any structural or moisture problems. Chisel away loose stucco; brush repair clean. Dampen area, then trowel on stucco until it is level with surrounding surface.

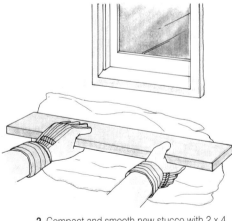

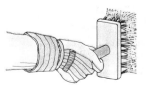

2. Compact and smooth new stucco with 2 x 4 or darby (p.211). Add at least three layers. Disguise repair by feathering stucco beyond borders of patch with trowel. Temperatures should be maintained at 50°F (10°C) during application and the subsequent 48 hours.

3. Keep stucco damp for 5 days until cured. Then mix and apply finish-coat stucco with float or large paintbrush. If desired, add texture by using freehand strokes or by spattering with a brush.

CERAMICS, GLASS, AND PLASTICS

CERAMIC TILES

In addition to being beautiful, ceramic tiles are durable and easy to clean. They come in various colors and may be plain or hand-painted. Grout, the material placed between tiles, comes in colors to match or contrast with the tiles.

When choosing tiles, consider where they will be used; this will determine what the composition should be (p.254). Then think about appearance—large patterns will look out of place in a small room. And remember that although tiling a whole section with hand-painted tiles may be too expensive for most budgets, you can select a few as accent pieces to fit in with more affordable tiles. Because manufacturers make tiles in different thicknesses, whenever you mix tiles be sure that their thicknesses match. When you visit a designer or tile supplier, bring photos, color swatches, and dimensions.

Floor tiles are made to withstand traffic. All of the tiles shown here can be used in heavy-traffic areas with the exception of the small hexagonal tile, which is made for use in light-traffic areas such as bathrooms.

Mosaic tiles are easy to install. They come in mesh- or paper-backed sheets or joined with rubber or plastic; some are also pregrouted. To customize a design, replace individual tiles.

Wall tiles are designed specifically for walls; if you install them on a floor they will most likely crack under the weight of people and furniture; they also scratch easily. You can create your own geometric patterns by selecting plain tiles of different colors and arranging them as you want. Tiles may come designed for complementary arrangements, including tiles with matching patterns (far right, top) or repeating patterns (far right, center). Some manufacturers also make matching border tiles.

Specialty tiles come in a variety of shapes and sizes to create a smooth transition between adjacent surfaces or to give a finished appearance by forming rounded edges or corners. They are usually designed to match standard tiles.

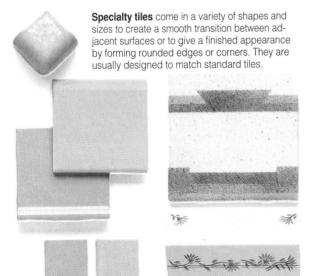

Dual-use tile (above) is suitable for walls and floors. If installed on a floor, make sure dual-use tiles are rated for use in light-traffic areas. These tiles are not suitable for floors exposed to heavy traffic.

Insert tiles (above) accent or border wall tiles. Some are strong enough for floors.

Border tiles come with different patterns and profiles; you can use them in single rows or stack them to create a distinctive look. Use the tiles to accent the tops of tiles that end partway up a wall or to break up a solid block of plain tiles.

Ceramic tile provides a durable, attractive covering for surfaces as diverse as walls, countertops, floors, and hearths. Tiling a surface is not difficult, but careful planning and installation will pay off—careless work can result in cracked, uneven, or loose tiles.

Before choosing a type of tile, consider the degree of water resistance, strength, slipperiness, and stain resistance necessary for the location. Most tiles are classified for use on either walls or floors. Most wall tiles are not strong enough to be set on floors or high-use areas; many floor tiles are too large for countertops and too heavy for walls. Glazed tiles are easier to keep clean; unglazed tiles are less slippery underfoot but are more easily stained. Sealing unglazed tiles with a commercial tile sealant will make them stain-resistant but more slippery; renew the sealer on these tiles annually. Tiles with a textured surface also wear well and are less slippery than regular tiles.

Glazed tiles generally absorb less water than unglazed tiles, but water resistance is gauged by the amount of water the *bisque,* or body, of a tile absorbs. In descending order of absorption, tiles are classified as nonvitreous (readily absorbs water), semivitreous, vitreous, and impervious (absorbs less than .05 percent of its weight). If your dealer doesn't know the classification, ask to see the manufacturer's specifications (usually on the shipping box). Tiles may also be designated as standard grade, second grade, or decorative thin wall tile. Most tile sold is standard grade; second-grade tile may have imperfections in the shape or glaze.

Tiles can be either set on a thick mortar bed (best left to professionals) or laid over a substrate thinly coated with adhesive (known as *thinset installation*). The type of substrate may vary, but it must be clean, flat, and very stable—movement causes tiles to loosen and crack. (If in doubt about the strength of a countertop, add extra cross braces underneath.) An ideal substrate is ½-inch *cement board,* available at tile suppliers and home centers. It can be installed over most flat surfaces, including wallboard and plywood (p.257). A ¼-inch flexible cement board is available for curved surfaces or if a thinner substrate is desired.

The two most common types of adhesive are ready-to-use organic mastic and powdered cement-base adhesive (often called thinset adhesive). Mastics, which are less strong than thinsets, are more easily affected by heat and water. Refer to the chart below when choosing tiles and matching them with the correct substrate and adhesive. Plan the layout, and install the tiles following the steps on pages 256–257. Special techniques for preparing the substrate and installing floor tile are shown on pages 334–336. Mosaic tile sheets, which are commonly set on a mesh backing, are described on page 258. Pregrouted sheets of larger tile are laid out and set in much the same way as individual tiles. However, it's easier to snip or tear individual tiles off the backing sheet before cutting them.

Most tile suppliers will rent or lend tile-cutting equipment. If you have many tiles to cut, a rented wet saw is the best tool. A portable cordless tile saw fitted with a diamond blade can make straight cuts in tile, but make sure the tile is securely held on a stable surface before cutting.

Ceramic tile is extremely hard—use carbide-tipped drill bits and fit power saws with blades specified for cutting ceramic tile. To avoid chipping the glaze, drill and cut through the face of the tile, not the back.

Caution: In addition to following the safety precautions on pages 12–13, inspect all rental tools for sound cutting edges and proper guards before leaving the store. When cutting or drilling tile or mixing powdered adhesive, wear goggles and a dust mask; also wear ear protection when using power tools. When using adhesives, work in a well-ventilated area and extinguish all open flames (including pilot lights). Water keeps bits and blades cool, but never submerge part of the body of a power tool in water.

Choosing tile

Location	Tiles	Substrate	Adhesive
Indoor floors	Glazed floor tiles, pavers (must be sealed), quarry tile, terra-cotta, monocoturra, mosaic	Cement board, concrete slab, plywood	Thinset for dry concrete slab; epoxy thinset for heavy-use areas; thinset with latex additive elsewhere
Outdoor floors	Some glazed floor tiles, mosaic, pavers, quarry tile	Cement board, concrete slab	Thinset with latex additive
Wet walls (such as shower surrounds)	Glazed wall tiles, mosaic	Cement board, moisture-resistant wallboard	Thinset with latex additive
Countertops	Glazed wall tiles (for low-use areas), small glazed floor tiles, mosaic, monocoturra	Cement board, plywood, plastic laminate	Thinset with latex additive, mastic
Indoor walls and backsplashes	Glazed wall tiles, mosaic, small glazed floor tiles	Cement board, wallboard, plaster, plywood	Thinset with latex additive, mastic

Cutting tiles to fit

Tile nippers trim irregular cuts. Nibble away waste from ends to center of cut. To avoid ragged edges, keep jaws parallel to penciled cut line, and place only two-thirds of jaw surface on tile for each bite.

Snap cutter for straight cuts can be rented. Place tile in cutter, and score by drawing marking wheel lightly one time across cut line (inset). To snap tile, set wings on tile close to the rule, then strike handle with heel of your hand. If wings might mar tile, wrap them with masking tape.

Wheel

Wet saw

Wing

Rule

Plate

V-cap

Wood block

Wet, or tub, saw can also be rented to cut many tiles quickly. Fill tray with water and adjust blade as instructed. Hold tile in position; press down and move entire plate forward, feeding tile slowly into blade. To miter corner V-caps for intersecting countertops (above), place tile at correct angle to blade; hold tile steady by placing small wood block underneath (inset).

Water reservoir

Cordless tile saw

Cordless tile saw makes a variety of cuts. Clamp tile securely so cutting line is between two pieces of wood. Fill reservoir with water. Set blade on tile, aligning edge of baseplate with cutting line. Turn on tool and move it slowly along the cutting line.

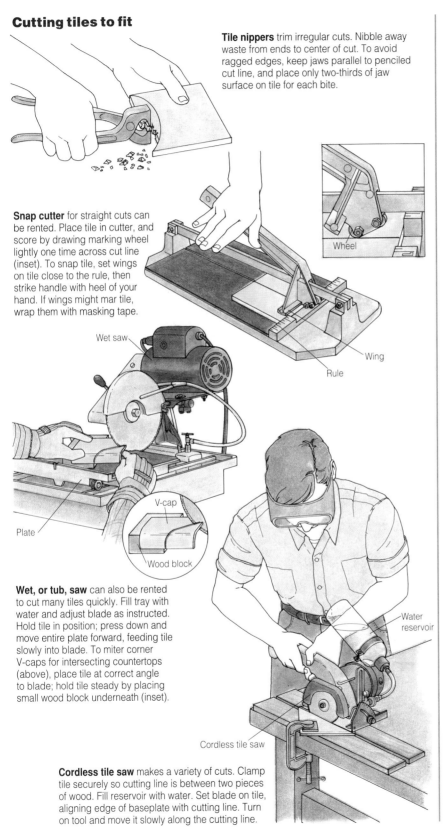

Drilling holes

To cool bit, fill a well of putty with water. Place tile on cardboard. Fit drill with carbide-tipped masonry bit; start drill at low speed, then run at faster speed.

Eyedropper

Water   Putty

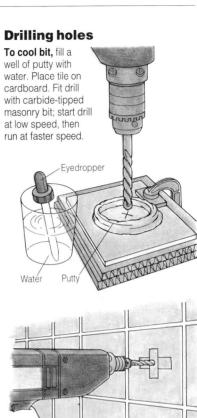

Prevent vertical tile from chipping by drilling through masking tape. Start drill at low speed to prevent bit from slipping; spray bit with water to cool. Insert plastic or lead masonry anchor plug for fastener; tap anchor in gently.

Drill large holes for supply lines and faucets in tile face with hole saw specified for tile. First mark glaze for pilot bit by tapping center punch or drill bit against hole center point. Start at low speed, then run at faster speed.

Hole saw

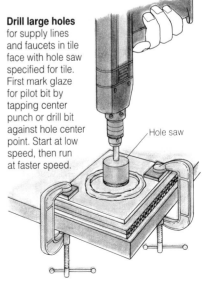

Choose a tile to match the size of your room—large pavers suitable for an expansive entryway would overwhelm a small bathroom. See p.347 to calculate the amount of tile you need; buy 15 percent extra to allow for breakage.

The key to a successful tile job is an accurate layout. The tiles must be equidistant and evenly arranged on the substrate before you set them in adhesive. On a vertical surface, use a layout rod to mark the position of the tiles; for a horizontal surface, you can use the tiles themselves. If it's necessary to cut tiles at the ends of rows, they should be the same size at each end and more than half a tile wide. Working around irregular shapes can be tricky; a round sink, for example, will require curved cuts in all the surrounding tiles.

Grout joints should be ⅛ to ¼ inch wide. Some tiles have built-in lugs to ensure consistent joint size; otherwise, place tile spacers between tiles or use preset sheets of tile (check grout joints between sheets with a straightedge). Spacers are most useful when the tiles are uniform, but for all types, check that the tiles are parallel to the layout lines.

If the surface is not square, you can make corrections in the layout, such as cutting end tiles at a gradual taper. To protect countertop tiles from cracking with any substrate movement, leave a ⅛- to ¼-inch caulk-filled gap between the tiles and the backsplash or wall, or if the tiles continue on the vertical surface, install cove tiles (p.259). Leave a small caulk-filled gap between the substrate and the backsplash, if possible.

Set most tiles with a square-notched trowel—with ⅜-inch notches for tiles with lugs or ribs on the back or with ¼-inch notches for other tiles. Lift a tile from the setting bed to see if its entire back is covered with adhesive; if not, switch to a trowel with larger notches.

Grout can sometimes be colored to match your tile. (Lighter shades are more prone to staining.) A light grout used with dark tiles, and vice versa, can look dramatic but will magnify any mistakes in the installation.

Layout patterns

Jack-on-jack is easier to install than running bond. Turn jack-on-jack 45° for diagonal design.

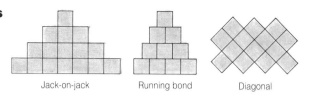

Jack-on-jack   Running bond   Diagonal

Marking the layout

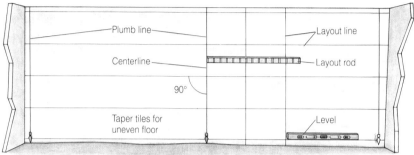

Plumb line — Layout line — Centerline — Layout rod — 90° — Taper tiles for uneven floor — Level

To mark wall layout, first snap a plumb line from ceiling to floor at the wall's centerline or at a focal point (door or window). Then use the layout rod to mark layout lines approximately every 2 ft. in all directions, carefully checking horizontal lines for level. Mark corner plumb lines from the last possible joint on the layout rod; then adjust width of cut tiles on ends as needed. Taper end tiles to accommodate irregularities at wall edges.

To make layout rod, mark tile and joint widths along a 6-ft.-long 1 x 2.

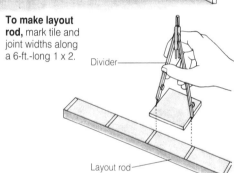

Divider — Layout rod

Straight counter

Centerline

End tile

Trim tile

Mark countertop centerline at counter's center or at a focal point such as the sink above. First determine position of trim or end tiles, then main tiles, avoiding narrow cuts along edges. On an L-shaped counter (above, right), start layout at inside corner and work out in both directions. (Miter trim tiles at corner, if desired.) When layout looks right, snap chalk lines to guide installation in 2-ft. sections. Mark tiles to fit sink and faucet cutouts (right); transfer the cut line to the tile's top for cutting. If possible, install sink and faucet on top of the tile; otherwise, fill space between sink or faucet and tile with caulk.

L-shaped counter

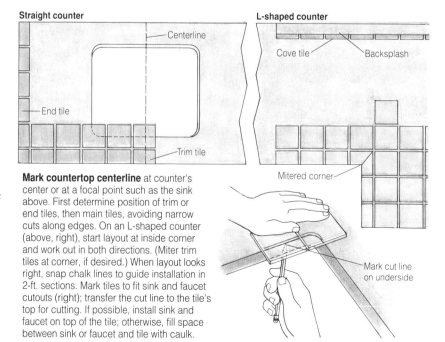

Cove tile — Backsplash — Mitered corner — Mark cut line on underside

Installing cement board

Use cement board for wet areas. Score board with utility knife, then snap along the scored line. Fasten to wall studs or existing surface every 6 in., using galvanized drywall screws. Seams should be ⅛ in. When using thinset adhesive, face textured side of board outward.

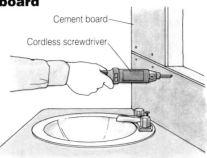

Cement board
Cordless screwdriver

Seal seams between boards with fiberglass tape (to keep out moisture). After taping, use a trowel to apply a coat of thinset adhesive over the tape.

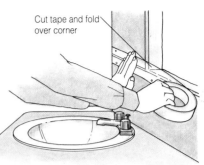

Cut tape and fold over corner

Setting tile

1. Spread adhesive with the trowel's smooth edges; comb with the notched edges to form ridges, keeping the trowel angle consistently at 30° to the surface. Work in 2-ft.-square areas.

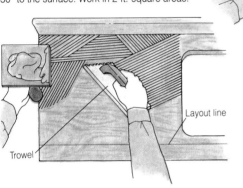

Trowel

Layout line

Spacer

2. Insert spacers, if used, and position tile with firm twisting motion—don't slide. Clean excess adhesive off the face of the tiles and at least halfway into the joints.

3. Seat tiles in adhesive with mallet and wood block. After laying several rows, check that installation is level and square. When finished, remove spacers with utility knife.

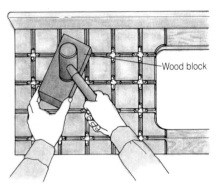

Wood block

Applying grout and caulk

Grout trowel

Pack grout into joints (left) with a grout trowel held consistently at 45° to the tile surface.

Clean off excess grout immediately with damp sponge (right); then remove hazy residue after an hour. When dry, polish with a clean cloth.

Caulk around edges of sink and bathtub with flexible caulk; shape bead with wet finger. Also caulk under rim of sink before installation. To open bathtub seam before caulking, fill tub with water.

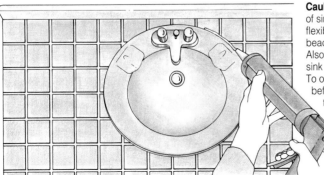

Sealing grout and tiles

Foam sponge applicator

Allow grout to cure for 30 days before sealing grout and tiles with penetrating sealer. (Highly porous tiles, such as terra-cotta, may require specialized sealer.) Brush on several light coats of sealer with foam sponge applicator; wipe sealer off the face of glazed tiles and tiles that will be exposed to food. Keep joints clean with commercial grout cleaner; reseal grout joints once a year.

Ceramics, Glass, and Plastics 257

Trimming edges

Set trim tiles last. For a V-cap, butter the horizontal edge of substrate with adhesive; then butter back of tile's vertical edge (below).

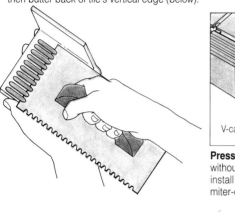

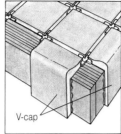

Press tile firmly into place without sliding. At corner, install special trim tile or miter-cut V-caps (p.255).

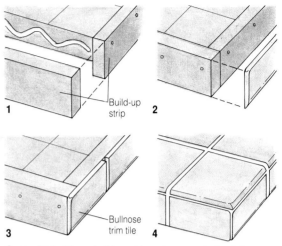

Support trim tile on build-up strips where countertop is too thin. Apply 1 × 2 solid wood or plywood strips to the edges of counter before laying tile. Secure strips with carpenter's glue and nails or screws.

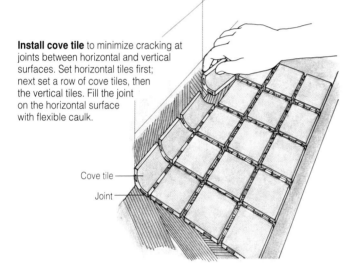

Install cove tile to minimize cracking at joints between horizontal and vertical surfaces. Set horizontal tiles first; next set a row of cove tiles, then the vertical tiles. Fill the joint on the horizontal surface with flexible caulk.

Cove tile

Joint

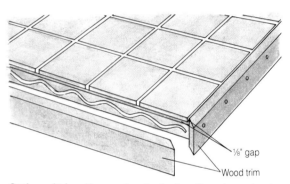

Seal wood trim with several coats of polyurethane to repel moisture. Secure with carpenter's glue and wood screws; countersink screwheads. Allow ⅛-in. gap between wood and tiles, and fill it with flexible caulk.

Installing fixtures

To adhere fixtures directly to wall, set them in latex thinset adhesive or in plaster of paris mixed with acrylic latex grout additive. Coat fixture and wall with adhesive, position fixture, and hold in place overnight with strips of masking tape. Clean off excess adhesive. Do not use fixture for 24 hr.

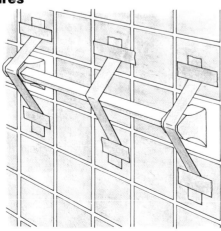

To fit fixtures on existing tile surface, first drill hole for clip-on fixture in center of tile (p.255). Install clip; slide fixture over clip; then caulk narrow joint between fixture and wall.

Fixture

Clip

Installing mosaic tile

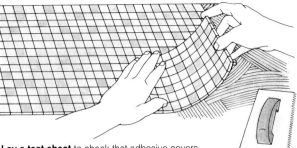

Lay a test sheet to check that adhesive covers entire back of sheet (most mosaics require trowel with triangular ¼-in. notches). To set, loosely roll up sheet, set one edge on layout line, and unfurl in place. Check for square every 24 in.; grout as shown on page 257. Soak off any mounting paper.

Tiling a curved surface

To lay tiles around a gradual curve, first cut tile into lengthwise pieces. Work in 2-ft.-square rows across surface. Align pieces carefully, and fully cover back of tiles with adhesive. (Do not use spacers on curved surface.) For 90° corners, buy corner tiles.

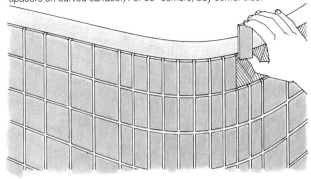

Repairing grout

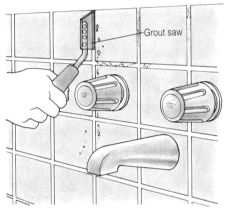

1. Remove damaged or discolored grout with a grout saw or cordless tile saw, working from top of joint (wear goggles with tile saw). Clean away all debris with a damp sponge. If crumbling or cracking of grout is extensive, consult a professional.

2. Dampen joint, and apply new grout with a gloved finger. Make sure to compact grout in joint. For repairs over 1 sq. ft., use a grout float. Seal grout (p.257).

Replacing tile

1. Remove grout around tile as shown at left. Break up tile with chisel and small sledgehammer, or make small plunge cuts with cordless tile saw. Wear gloves and safety goggles.

2. Scrape off old adhesive with a putty knife, without gouging substrate. Clean away all debris; vacuum area around repair thoroughly.

3. Apply new adhesive to substrate and to back of tile. Fit tile in place, twisting it slightly as you position it. Wipe off excess adhesive. Let dry, and regrout.

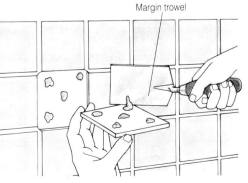

Ceramics, Glass, and Plastics   259

Modern glass has the same humble beginnings as ancient glass—molten silica sand. To create a polished surface, glass is floated on a bath of molten tin. It is then annealed (heated and slowly cooled). When plastic is laminated between two layers of glass, the "sandwich" can be safely used as a car windshield; if it is broken, the pieces remain attached to the plastic. Some glass has wire mesh embedded in it; this glass is ideal where security is an issue, such as in a window next to a front door. Transparent metal coatings on low-emissivity (low-E) glass make it retain heat while admitting light. Subtle texturing makes glass nonreflective for glazing picture frames; dense patterns produce an obscure finish that is ideal for privacy. You can even change a specialty glass from an obscure to a clear finish (and vice versa) simply by flicking a switch.

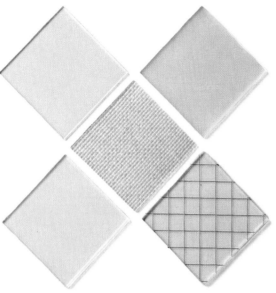

General-purpose glass suits many home uses, including clear glass for windows, light-diffusing ground glass for light fixtures, and patterned glass for bathroom windows. Special glass is laminated with plastic (bottom, left) or has wire set in the glass (bottom, right); this prevents flying shards by holding them in place.

Glass block, the original insulating glass, is available in many textures, sizes, and shapes (including some for curved walls). Use it to make an exterior wall, a translucent room divider, or a floor.

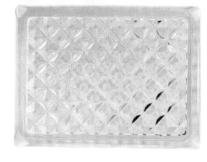

Stained glass is found in the world's most beautiful window murals and lampshades. Specialty houses stock dozens of types of stained glass in a variety of textures and colors, both translucent and opaque. The glass is colored by adding metal alloys such as copper, iron, and cobalt. Antique-style glass is handmade; other glass is machine-made. The names of the glass are as exciting as their appearance: (top to bottom, far left) fracture streamer, ring mottle, stipple; (top to bottom, center) iridized, single glue chip, crackle; (top to bottom, left) hand-blown "antique," opal, and flashed.

WORKING WITH GLASS

Thicknesses and types of glass vary, so ask a retailer which glass is best for your application. Always carry and store glass upright; otherwise it may break under its own weight.

Caution: When you handle glass, protect yourself by wearing goggles and heavy gloves. Dispose of shards in a closed container, or wrap them with several layers of paper; then discard.

Although a supplier will make long cuts, you can make short ones using the techniques shown below and on page 262. First wipe the glass clean with commercial cleaner; then back it with scrap softwood. The cutting—really controlled breaking of the glass—is done in two steps: scoring with a glass cutter, and then breaking the glass along the score (known as *breaking out* the score). Score patterned glass on its smooth side, mirrored glass on its uncoated side. Score curved shapes around a stiff paper template;

slight curves can be broken out in the same way as straight cuts; sharper curves and circles require radial lines.

Lubricate the cutter's wheel with light oil, and grip it comfortably. Score briskly and steadily—a sizzling sound indicates the correct pressure; white flakes mean you've pressed too hard. Never go over an imperfect score; this can damage the cutter. Break out the glass immediately after you have scored it, starting at the score's finished end.

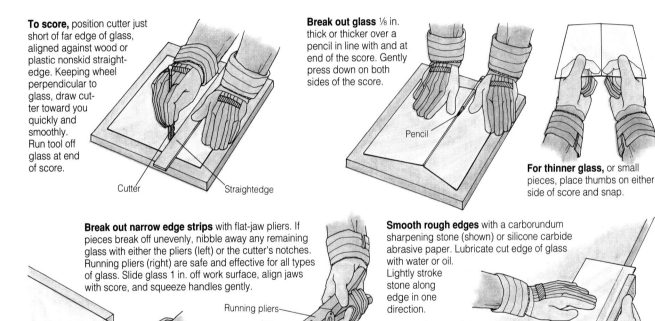

To score, position cutter just short of far edge of glass, aligned against wood or plastic nonskid straight-edge. Keeping wheel perpendicular to glass, draw cutter toward you quickly and smoothly. Run tool off glass at end of score.

Cutter

Straightedge

Break out glass ⅛ in. thick or thicker over a pencil in line with and at end of the score. Gently press down on both sides of the score.

Pencil

For thinner glass, or small pieces, place thumbs on either side of score and snap.

Break out narrow edge strips with flat-jaw pliers. If pieces break off unevenly, nibble away any remaining glass with either the pliers (left) or the cutter's notches. Running pliers (right) are safe and effective for all types of glass. Slide glass 1 in. off work surface, align jaws with score, and squeeze handles gently.

Running pliers

Score

Flat-jaw pliers

Smooth rough edges with a carborundum sharpening stone (shown) or silicone carbide abrasive paper. Lubricate cut edge of glass with water or oil. Lightly stroke stone along edge in one direction.

Sharpening stone

Cutting circles and sharp curves

1. For circles, place glass on corrugated cardboard. Position circle cutter on glass with suction cup in center. Score circle by rotating cutter arm around cup with even pressure. (Score sharp curves against a stiff paper template.) Turn piece over and press down gently along score with thumbs, not quite breaking it out.

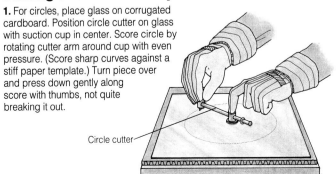

Circle cutter

2. Turn piece back over; remove cardboard; then score freehand radial lines from glass edges to just short of (not touching) the original score. Break out radial lines with running pliers; circle or curved shape will now break out completely.

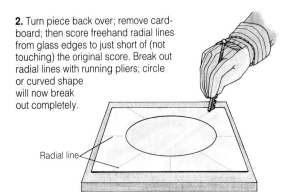

Radial line

Safety glass is available in three types: laminated, wire (security), and tempered. Although tempered glass cannot be cut, both laminated and wire glass can be scored and broken out (p.261), with an additional step of separating the nonglass material. In the case of laminated glass, this material is a sheet of plastic sandwiched between two layers of glass; wire glass has a layer of wire mesh embedded in it. Laminated glass must be scored on both sides; after breaking out each score, sever the plastic sheet as shown below.

Small "bull's-eye" breaks in car windshields can be repaired by using an epoxy solution available as a kit at some auto and glass suppliers. Use it to repair damage up to 1 inch wide on the outside of a windshield.

When removing broken panes of glass, wear heavy gloves and goggles, and work from the top down to prevent injury from falling shards. If the pane does not have broken pieces that make removal easy, tape the glass with masking tape in a crisscross pattern, then break it with a hammer.

Describe the application of the glass to your dealer to help determine the correct type and thickness for its replacement; make a cardboard template for odd shapes, such as diamonds or ovals. To decide whether you need tempered glass at doorways or elsewhere, check local building codes.

Glazing compound, which is used both to bed the glass in the frame and to cover the glazier's points, is available in cans and in cartridges that fit in a caulking gun. You can also bed the glass with a self-adhesive foam strip. Install the foam around the inside of the frame's rabbet, press the glass into place, and insert the points. Then seal the glass with glazing compound, completely covering the points.

Caution: Do not try to replace or repair sealed units or gas-filled high-efficiency windows; they should be worked on only by a professional.

Cutting safety glass

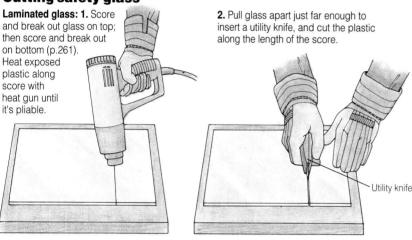

Laminated glass: 1. Score and break out glass on top; then score and break out on bottom (p.261). Heat exposed plastic along score with heat gun until it's pliable.

2. Pull glass apart just far enough to insert a utility knife, and cut the plastic along the length of the score.

Utility knife

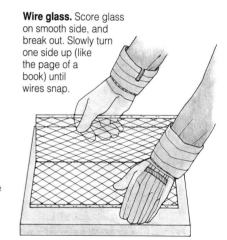

Wire glass. Score glass on smooth side, and break out. Slowly turn one side up (like the page of a book) until wires snap.

Installing fasteners

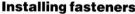

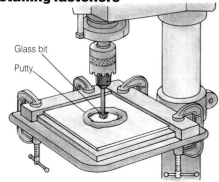

Glass bit

Putty

1. Drill holes up to ½ in. wide in glass with special spade-shaped bit in drill press or hand drill. (Have supplier drill larger holes; or use a circle cutter, p.261.) Drill into a well of putty filled with water. Run bit at low speed, feeding it evenly into glass. Drill no closer than 1 in. to glass edge.

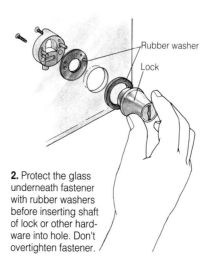

Rubber washer

Lock

2. Protect the glass underneath fastener with rubber washers before inserting shaft of lock or other hardware into hole. Don't overtighten fastener.

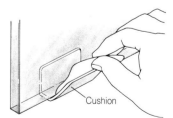

Cushion

Magnetic catch. Install self-adhesive cushion of two-part hardware first; then slide catch into place.

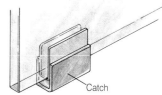

Catch

Replacing glass in a metal frame

Solid frame: 1. With pliers, pry out rubber gasket from frame. If damaged, buy new gasket. Remove any glass, and clean out frame with wire brush. Measure frame from inner edges; cut or order glass 1/16 in. smaller in length and width.

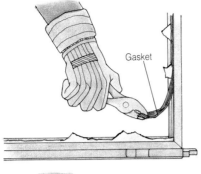

Gasket

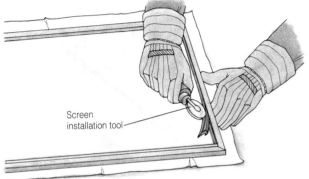

Screen installation tool

2. Coat inside of frame with the adhesive recommended by glass supplier. Position glass in frame. Using screen installation tool or fingers, press gasket under frame lip all around. If gasket is too short, lengthen it by stretching as you insert it.

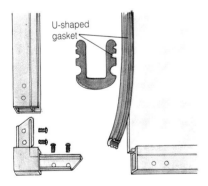

U-shaped gasket

Three-sided frame:
To disassemble frame, unscrew two corners (or remove rivets, p.187), releasing one side. Gently slide out U-shaped gasket and glass. Cut or buy new pane; then fit new gasket around it. Slide glass and gasket into sash, position the side piece, and screw or rivet corners together.

Replacing glass in a wood frame

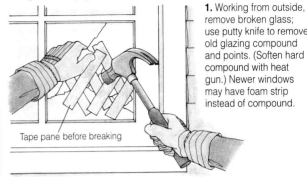

Tape pane before breaking

1. Working from outside, remove broken glass; use putty knife to remove old glazing compound and points. (Soften hard compound with heat gun.) Newer windows may have foam strip instead of compound.

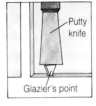

Putty knife

Glazier's point

2. Clean out rabbet with a wire brush; coat with a wood sealer. Measure to inside of rabbet; order or cut glass 1/16 in. smaller in length and width. Lay a thin coat of glazing compound (or foam strip) inside rabbet, then press in glass. Hold pane in place as you press in glazier's points every 4 in.

Glazing compound

3. Cover points and seal glass with glazing compound. Smooth with wet finger or flexible putty knife, forming 45° bevel so that putty is invisible from inside. Paint when compound dries, in several days.

Minor repairs

Fixing a windshield "bull's eye." Align adhesive seal and pedestal over the cleaned damage. Empty the chemicals into injector and shake. Press injector into pedestal; then follow manufacturer's directions to shoot resin into repair. Leave whole assembly in place for 4 hr.; then use a razor blade to scrape away excess resin and free the pedestal.

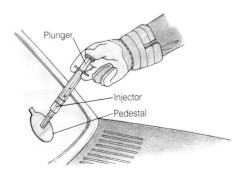

Plunger

Injector

Pedestal

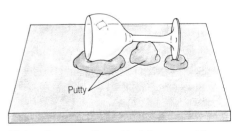

Putty

Gluing glassware. Clean object; then support it with putty (or improvise another way to hold it steady). Glue with epoxy adhesive specified for glass, following safety precautions given with adhesive.

Traditionally pieces of stained glass are arranged in a rigid framework of lead *came* that is soldered only at the joints. Although lead came is suitable for windows and large decorative pieces, it can overpower small or intricate designs. For these, the copper-foil technique shown here is more appropriate. Soldered copper-foil seams look delicate, yet they are strong enough to support sturdy boxes and lamps.

Begin by penciling a full-size drawing, or *cartoon,* on plain paper. Keep your design simple—straight lines are easiest for novices to cut. Then make two copies. Cut one copy into templates for use when cutting the glass; the other copy is a guide onto which you will place the pieces of glass after edging them with foil. Cut the glass and smooth its edges (p.261); then clean it with commercial glass cleaner.

Adhesive-backed copper foil comes in different sizes; for most work, use foil that is ¼ inch wide and .001 inch thick (for the perimeter, you can use slightly wider foil). Wrap outside corners as you would a parcel, folding down one side of the foil, then pressing the second side over the first. To avoid splitting the foil on curved edges, ease it gently around the curve. Immediately after wrapping each piece,

Joining glass with copper foil

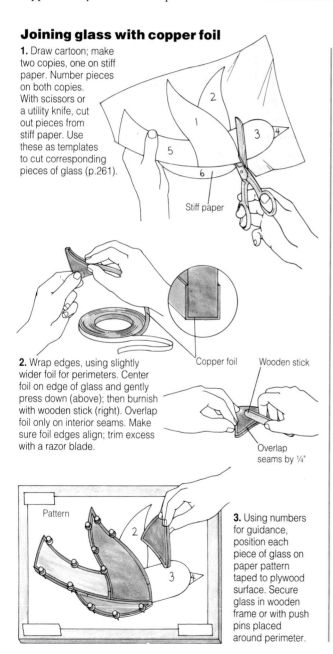

1. Draw cartoon; make two copies, one on stiff paper. Number pieces on both copies. With scissors or a utility knife, cut out pieces from stiff paper. Use these as templates to cut corresponding pieces of glass (p.261).

Stiff paper

Copper foil Wooden stick

2. Wrap edges, using slightly wider foil for perimeters. Center foil on edge of glass and gently press down (above); then burnish with wooden stick (right). Overlap foil only on interior seams. Make sure foil edges align; trim excess with a razor blade.

Overlap seams by ¼"

Pattern

3. Using numbers for guidance, position each piece of glass on paper pattern taped to plywood surface. Secure glass in wooden frame or with push pins placed around perimeter.

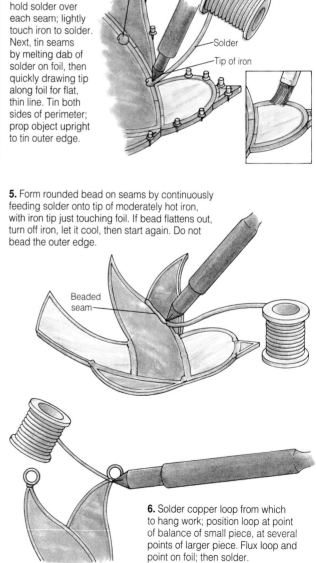

Tacked seam

4. Brush oleic acid flux along seams (inset). To tack, hold solder over each seam; lightly touch iron to solder. Next, tin seams by melting dab of solder on foil, then quickly drawing tip along foil for flat, thin line. Tin both sides of perimeter; prop object upright to tin outer edge.

Solder

Tip of iron

5. Form rounded bead on seams by continuously feeding solder onto tip of moderately hot iron, with iron tip just touching foil. If bead flattens out, turn off iron, let it cool, then start again. Do not bead the outer edge.

Beaded seam

6. Solder copper loop from which to hang work; position loop at point of balance of small piece, at several points of larger piece. Flux loop and point on foil; then solder.

position it on its corresponding number on the paper pattern.

Follow the soldering instructions on page 190. Tin the tip of the soldering iron with the same 60/40 lead/tin solder you'll use for the seams, and flux the seams so the solder adheres. Most copper-foil seams are first *tinned*, which creates a thin flat surface, and then *beaded* for a gently rounded seam; the perimeter need only be tinned.

Manipulating the iron and spool of solder requires practice; if you are having difficulty, switch them to the opposite hands, work more slowly, or change to a more comfortable grip.

Immediately after soldering, dust the work with talc and rub it with a soft cloth. If desired, apply a liquid patina, available at crafts suppliers, to color the seams either copper or black. Wearing rubber gloves, dip a sponge into the patina and wipe it along a seam. Wait a few seconds, and then rub the seam with a dry cloth. To brighten the patina, rub it with brass polish. Prevent dark corrosion from building up on copper foil by rubbing it periodically with fine steel wool.

Caution: Lead is toxic. Ventilate the work area well. Wash hands after handling lead, solder, or patina; dispose of these materials carefully (p.11).

Three-dimensional objects

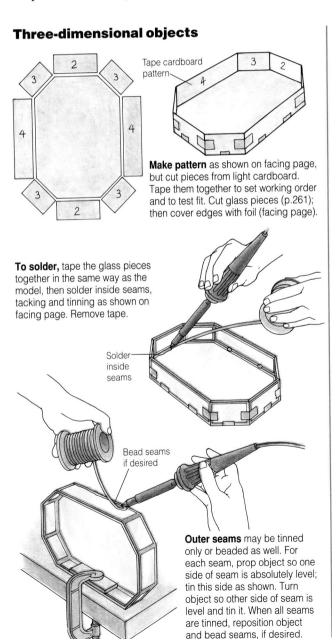

Make pattern as shown on facing page, but cut pieces from light cardboard. Tape them together to set working order and to test fit. Cut glass pieces (p.261); then cover edges with foil (facing page).

Tape cardboard pattern

To solder, tape the glass pieces together in the same way as the model, then solder inside seams, tacking and tinning as shown on facing page. Remove tape.

Solder inside seams

Bead seams if desired

Outer seams may be tinned only or beaded as well. For each seam, prop object so one side of seam is absolutely level; tin this side as shown. Turn object so other side of seam is level and tin it. When all seams are tinned, reposition object and bead seams, if desired.

Repairing lead-came glass

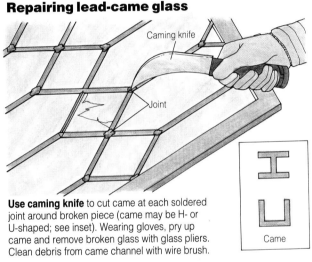

Caming knife

Joint

Came

Use caming knife to cut came at each soldered joint around broken piece (came may be H- or U-shaped; see inset). Wearing gloves, pry up came and remove broken glass with glass pliers. Clean debris from came channel with wire brush.

Trace outline of broken piece on light cardboard. Cut glass to outline, insert glass into came, then lightly push came down on glass. Push glazing putty into opening between glass and came, then fully push came down.

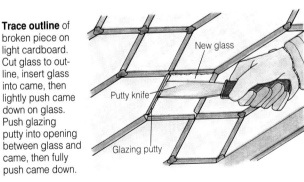

New glass

Putty knife

Glazing putty

To resolder came at joints, first brush on oleic acid flux. Holding solder to seam, touch iron to both came and solder until solder flows; then quickly move iron away. When soldering is done, color seams with patina to match rest of piece.

Glass block makes strong, attractive walls and windows that are easy to maintain and keep clean. The blocks are laid in mortar and require some masonry skills to install, but few special tools are needed. Most supplies, including plastic spacers, expansion strips, reinforcing wire, and panel anchors, can be purchased from your glass block dealer. Before incorporating corner and end blocks in your design, find out if they're offered in the pattern and size you wish to use.

Because glass blocks are non-load-bearing (they cannot support building weight from above), you'll need to frame a block wall with a header (such as a 2×4 or 2×6 secured to the wall studs), a wood or concrete sill, and at least one side jamb—consult the block manufacturer for details on installing block in a particular framework. Show your design to a building inspector or other qualified professional to determine whether extra floor joists and support blocking will be necessary to bear the wall's weight. Panel anchors help secure the wall to its frame, and expansion strips prevent the wall from cracking with any structural movement.

The upper courses of block can squeeze wet mortar out from between the lower courses before it hardens. Avoid this by inserting plastic spacers, which keep the blocks evenly spaced. After the mortar has set, remove the visible part of the spacer, leaving a section between the blocks. Cut the spacers into T- or L-shapes to insert at the edges of each course. Buy at least 50 percent more spacers than blocks.

Use premixed white glass block mortar, or make your own from 1 part white Portland cement, ½ part hydrated lime, and 4 parts clean white sand. (For wet areas, use waterproof cement or a waterproofing additive.) Mix the dry

Preparing the installation

Secure wood sill to jamb. Install header and any other framing for jambs. Brush a coat of asphalt emulsion sealer on concrete or wood sill; let dry for at least 2 hr.

Jamb

Sill

Dry-fit and mark first course of blocks on sill; then mark each course along jamb. Position spacers between blocks, and allow ¼ in. for expansion strips at jamb and header. To fill extra space at header or sill, add a strip of wood.

Spacer

Expansion strip

Staple gun

Loosely fasten expansion strips to jambs and header, using staples or small nails. (Panel anchors will be installed underneath strip as wall rises.)

Laying the first course

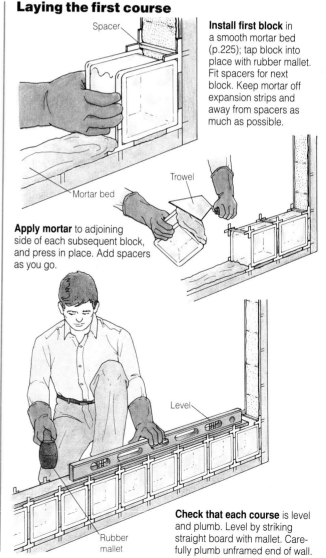

Spacer

Install first block in a smooth mortar bed (p.225); tap block into place with rubber mallet. Fit spacers for next block. Keep mortar off expansion strips and away from spacers as much as possible.

Mortar bed

Trowel

Apply mortar to adjoining side of each subsequent block, and press in place. Add spacers as you go.

Level

Rubber mallet

Check that each course is level and plumb. Level by striking straight board with mallet. Carefully plumb unframed end of wall.

ingredients, then add water—the mortar is thick enough when it no longer slides off a vertical surface (p.224). Mix only what you will use in an hour. Build up a wall in sections of 4 or 5 feet per day, leaving time to strike the joints and ensure that the wall is not out of alignment. As each course rises, check that the wall is level and plumb. If one end of a block wall will be unframed, suspend a plumb bob from the free end of the header and check that the wall is straight.

Glass block can also be purchased preassembled, but you'll need help to position these heavy panels. Panels that are designed to replace windows may come with built-in adjustable louver vents. A mortarless system for installing glass block is also available. You insert thin plastic strips between the blocks and then seal them with silicone caulk; full instructions are provided by the manufacturer of the system.

Building up the wall

Lay mortar bed on course, smoothing with trowel. Fill air gaps in joints (caused by mortar squeezing out of lower joints) by pushing in mortar with damp sponge. Work 4 ft. up wall; let mortar set for 1 hr.

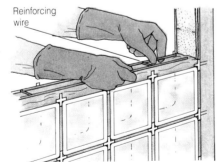

For larger walls (over 25 sq. ft.), embed strip of reinforcing wire in mortar of horizontal joints every third course of 6-in. block, every second course of 8- and 12-in. block.

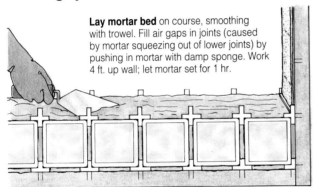

Reinforcing wire

After second course, install panel anchor. Cut 24-in. anchor in half and bend a 4-in. leg. Slit and lift expansion strip; screw leg to jamb. Resecure strip over anchor. Repeat every other course. At second to top course, attach anchors to header in same fashion, running anchors down every other vertical joint.

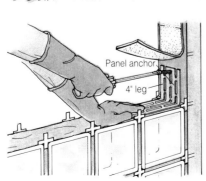

Panel anchor

4" leg

Finishing the wall

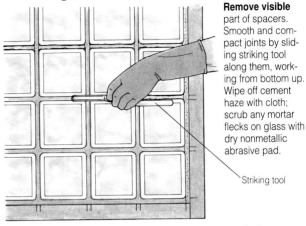

Remove visible part of spacers. Smooth and compact joints by sliding striking tool along them, working from bottom up. Wipe off cement haze with cloth; scrub any mortar flecks on glass with dry nonmetallic abrasive pad.

Striking tool

Caulk

For spaces between expansion strip and blocks at jambs and header, fill with a bead of flexible caulk. (With any structural movement, mortar would crack at these locations.) Smooth caulk with a wet gloved finger.

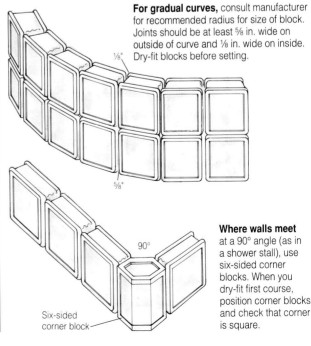

Curves and corners

For gradual curves, consult manufacturer for recommended radius for size of block. Joints should be at least ⅝ in. wide on outside of curve and ⅛ in. wide on inside. Dry-fit blocks before setting.

⅛"

⅝"

90°

Six-sided corner block

Where walls meet at a 90° angle (as in a shower stall), use six-sided corner blocks. When you dry-fit first course, position corner blocks and check that corner is square.

PLASTICS

The variety of plastics on the market makes them among the most versatile of all do-it-yourself materials. For example, chlorinated polyvinyl chloride (CPVC) never corrodes, sweats, or allows scale buildup. As clear as glass, sheet acrylic is easy to shape, resists sunlight, and doesn't break readily. Polycarbonate, a virtually unbreakable but lightweight plastic, is simple to install. Fiberglass patching materials, when layered and saturated with liquid resin, make extremely strong repairs in fiberglass, metal, and wood products. Sheet laminate creates an inexpensive countertop that is easy to maintain. Acrylic and polyester resin solid-surface materials are also ideal for countertops. They cost more than sheet laminate, but they can be custom-edged with your choice of router bit and scratches can be sanded away.

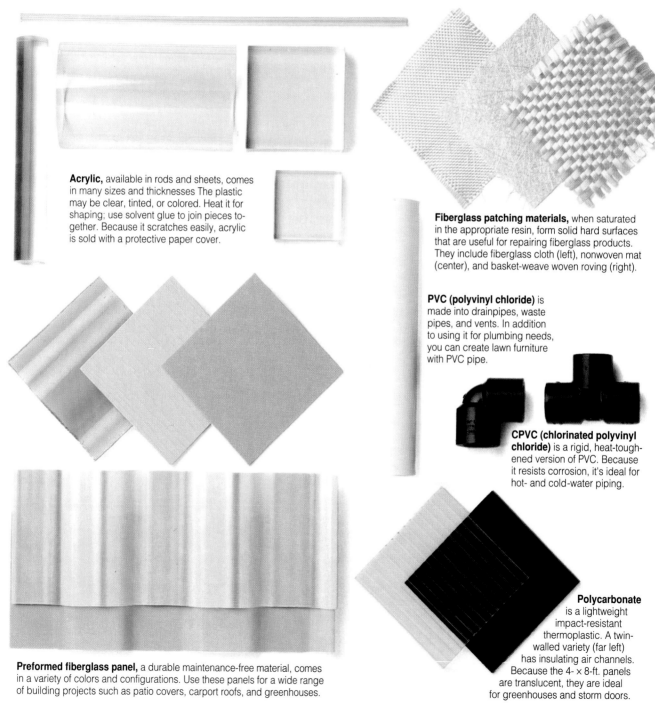

Acrylic, available in rods and sheets, comes in many sizes and thicknesses The plastic may be clear, tinted, or colored. Heat it for shaping; use solvent glue to join pieces together. Because it scratches easily, acrylic is sold with a protective paper cover.

Fiberglass patching materials, when saturated in the appropriate resin, form solid hard surfaces that are useful for repairing fiberglass products. They include fiberglass cloth (left), nonwoven mat (center), and basket-weave woven roving (right).

PVC (polyvinyl chloride) is made into drainpipes, waste pipes, and vents. In addition to using it for plumbing needs, you can create lawn furniture with PVC pipe.

CPVC (chlorinated polyvinyl chloride) is a rigid, heat-toughened version of PVC. Because it resists corrosion, it's ideal for hot- and cold-water piping.

Polycarbonate is a lightweight impact-resistant thermoplastic. A twin-walled variety (far left) has insulating air channels. Because the 4- × 8-ft. panels are translucent, they are ideal for greenhouses and storm doors.

Preformed fiberglass panel, a durable maintenance-free material, comes in a variety of colors and configurations. Use these panels for a wide range of building projects such as patio covers, carport roofs, and greenhouses.

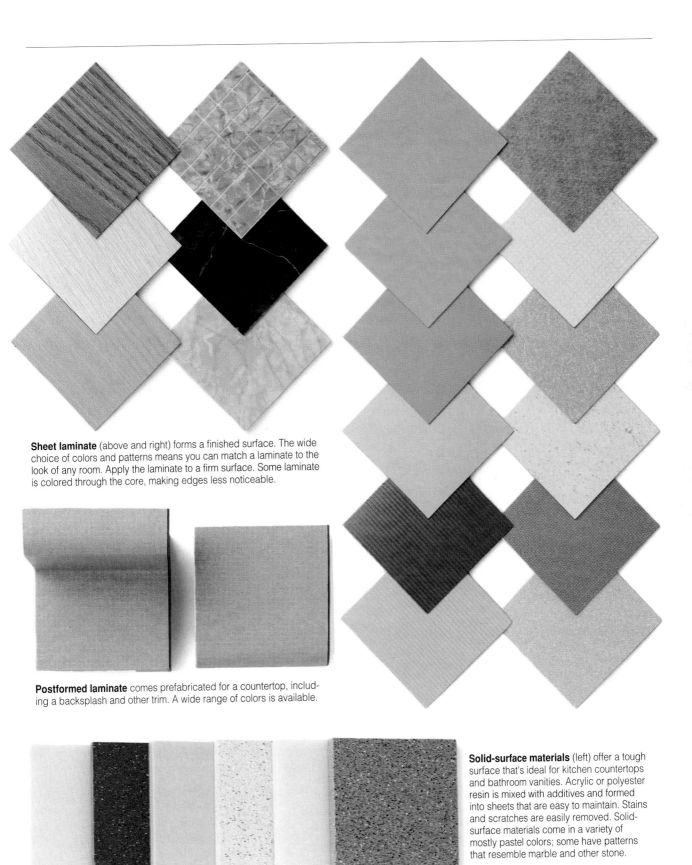

Sheet laminate (above and right) forms a finished surface. The wide choice of colors and patterns means you can match a laminate to the look of any room. Apply the laminate to a firm surface. Some laminate is colored through the core, making edges less noticeable.

Postformed laminate comes prefabricated for a countertop, including a backsplash and other trim. A wide range of colors is available.

Solid-surface materials (left) offer a tough surface that's ideal for kitchen countertops and bathroom vanities. Acrylic or polyester resin is mixed with additives and formed into sheets that are easy to maintain. Stains and scratches are easily removed. Solid-surface materials come in a variety of mostly pastel colors; some have patterns that resemble marble and other stone.

Ceramics, Glass, and Plastics 269

WORKING WITH PLASTIC SHEET AND TUBING

Clear acrylic sheets and other shapes are used in crafts objects, for making furniture, and as a substitute for glass. CPVC (chlorinated polyvinyl chloride) and PVC (polyvinyl chloride) are two types of rigid plastic tubing: CPVC tubing forms hot- and cold-water supply lines; the wider PVC tubing is used for plumbing drainpipes, electrical conduit, and lightweight or outdoor furniture. To work with any of these plastics, you will need a combination of basic woodworking, metalworking, and glazing skills.

Special tools and supplies are available for working with plastics; avoid damaging ordinary tools by following the manufacturer's specific instructions for plastics. For example, when cutting acrylic with a saber saw, running the tool at high speed can melt the plastic behind the blade. The plastic may then fuse together, ruining the cut.

Despite its toughness, acrylic is easily scratched and so comes coated with protective paper. Leave as much of the paper on the plastic as possible until the project is completed. To remove the paper, lift it at one corner and pull it off the sheet. Scratches on plastic are best removed with a commercial scratch remover. To prevent sagging, store acrylic sheets either upright or flat and fully supported.

Acrylic sheets can be joined with threaded fasteners, rivets, or posts and screws, but pieces are usually cemented with a special solvent. The most common technique is cementing along the seams by capillary action (facing page). If solvent spills on an unprotected piece of acrylic, quickly wipe it with a clean soft cloth. CPVC and PVC can also be joined with a solvent cement; use only the cleaner, primer, and cement specifically recommended for joining each plastic.

Most plastics can be bent if they have been heated first, but for CPVC and PVC the temperature must be controlled so precisely that doing it

Cutting and drilling

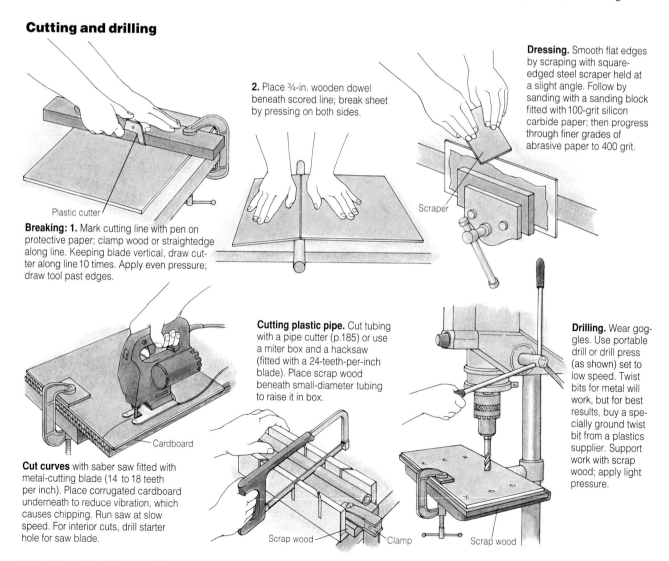

Dressing. Smooth flat edges by scraping with square-edged steel scraper held at a slight angle. Follow by sanding with a sanding block fitted with 100-grit silicon carbide paper; then progress through finer grades of abrasive paper to 400 grit.

2. Place ¾-in. wooden dowel beneath scored line; break sheet by pressing on both sides.

Scraper

Breaking: 1. Mark cutting line with pen on protective paper; clamp wood or straightedge along line. Keeping blade vertical, draw cutter along line 10 times. Apply even pressure; draw tool past edges.

Plastic cutter

Cardboard

Cut curves with saber saw fitted with metal-cutting blade (14 to 18 teeth per inch). Place corrugated cardboard underneath to reduce vibration, which causes chipping. Run saw at slow speed. For interior cuts, drill starter hole for saw blade.

Cutting plastic pipe. Cut tubing with a pipe cutter (p.185) or use a miter box and a hacksaw (fitted with a 24-teeth-per-inch blade). Place scrap wood beneath small-diameter tubing to raise it in box.

Drilling. Wear goggles. Use portable drill or drill press (as shown) set to low speed. Twist bits for metal will work, but for best results, buy a specially ground twist bit from a plastics supplier. Support work with scrap wood; apply light pressure.

Scrap wood

Clamp

Scrap wood

yourself is not recommended. It is easy to bend acrylic using a strip heater, available (often as a kit) from a plastics supplier or hardware store.

Caution: When using power tools to cut, sand, or drill plastic, wear safety goggles and a dust mask. Wear heat-proof gloves while heating and bending plastic. When cementing, follow the precautions listed by the manufacturer; work in a well-ventilated area and do not get solvent on your skin. Before modifying a plumbing system, check with your local building inspector; codes prohibit some repairs and installations. Shut off the water supply and drain a pipe before working on it.

Smoothing edges

Buff edges with ⅜-in. drill fitted with buffing pad; first coat the pad with either tripoli or rouge polishing compound (available at crafts suppliers). Finish with a nonstitched disc of clean muslin or flannel. Do not buff seam edges.

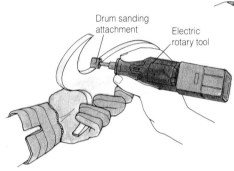

Buffing pad

Drum sanding attachment

Electric rotary tool

Sand and polish curves and tight spots with an electric drill or with a small rotary tool specified for working with acrylic. Sand edges with drum sanding attachment; buff with hard felt and muslin or flannel discs. To avoid overheating plastic, use a light touch and low speed.

Joining plastic tubing

Preparing joints.
With a sharp knife or reamer, remove burrs on cut ends; bevel walls slightly. Smooth ends of fitting and tubing with 120-grit sandpaper. Assemble tubing and fitting to test fit; mark a line across both pieces with a pencil. Detach the pieces and clean them by swabbing with the appropriate cleaning fluid, using the applicator supplied. After cleaner dries, apply primer (to remove gloss); then apply the cement.

Joining. Apply a second coat of cement to tubing, and immediately insert in fitting with marks misaligned by a quarter turn; quickly twist until marks align. Hold together for at least 30 sec.; then wait 24 hr. before applying full pressure. A thin line of cement should be visible entirely around the new joint.

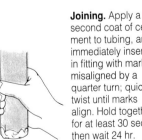

Bending with heat

Heating. Mark area of bend; remove 4-in.-wide strips of paper from both sides of sheet. Center uncovered area just above heating element; turn sheet several times for even heating. Hold for 1 to 5 min., until the plastic softens.

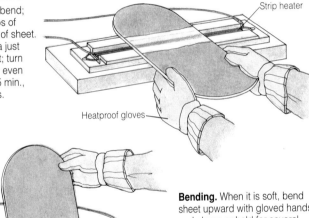

Strip heater

Heatproof gloves

Bending. When it is soft, bend sheet upward with gloved hands, and clamp or hold for several minutes until it cools. To make adjustments, flatten sheet by reheating, then bend again.

Joining acrylic sheets

Remove paper near edges; place pieces to be joined so seams are horizontal. Tape, clamp, or brace pieces together; edges must be even so pieces fit with no gaps. Then carefully draw needle-nose applicator along seam, squeezing gently to dispense solvent evenly. Don't blot excess solvent; allow capillary action to draw it into joint.

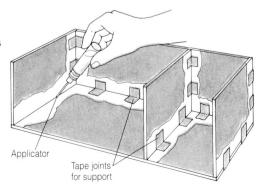

Applicator

Tape joints for support

Fiberglass, a material made from threads or fragments of spun glass, comes in different forms. As a building material, it is molded into hard panels; for shaped objects, it is matted or woven into a fabric, which is then bonded with resin.

Preformed fiberglass panels are easy to work with and can be cut with a saber saw fitted with a fine-tooth blade. For an outdoor project such as a patio roof, heavyweight corrugated or ridged panels are best; for indoor use or where rigidity is not necessary, use lighter flat panels. Supplies for building with the panels, such as sidewall flashing and corrugated closure strips, are also available. To clean the panels, hose them with water; if they discolor, apply a refinisher recommended by the manufacturer. Fiberglass panels will not bear a person's weight; never attempt to walk on them.

Fiberglass laminate is used to make shaped objects such as automobile bodies, boats, swimming pools, and hot tubs. Layers of fabric are bonded together with a liquid resin that cures with the addition of a catalyst, forming a tough, durable shell. Holes up to ½ inch in diameter in fiberglass laminate can simply be filled with putty—a mixture of resin and filler. Larger areas of damage are repaired by patching with layers of fabric and resin. However, if you suspect that the damage may have affected the structural integrity of an object, consult a professional before attempting the repair.

A repair patch (p.274) usually consists of alternating layers of mat and cloth; in large projects, woven roving is sometimes used. A successful repair depends upon choosing the correct fabric and resin; the chart on the facing page will help you determine the best combination for a particular repair.

Polyester resin—used for most laminate repairs—is easier to work with and less expensive than epoxy. There are two types: *Air-dry,* or *tack-free,* contains wax, which floats to the surface of the repair, sealing off the air and allowing the resin to cure with a hard surface. The other type, *air-inhibited,* cures to a tacky surface unless covered with wax paper or polyvinyl alcohol spray (PVA), which can be found at marine supply stores. The PVA is washed off with warm water after the resin cures. Fabric will bond better if you use air-inhibited resin for the inner layers of a repair; if you use air-dry resin for the outer layers, it will harden so that the surface can more easily be sanded.

Epoxy resin cures hard, but slowly. It will bond well with many materials but is more difficult to work with than polyester. If in doubt whether to use epoxy or polyester resin for a repair, contact the manufacturer of the object or try a small test patch on an inconspicuous spot.

The outer finish coat of fiberglass laminate is *gel coat,* a specially formulated polyester resin. Wash the gel coat frequently with detergent and water (or wipe it with a solvent such as acetone), and buff with wax to protect it. Scratches that do not penetrate too far beneath the gel coat can easily be repaired with a mixture of gel coat and filler, often available in a kit at marine supply stores.

Working with fiberglass panels

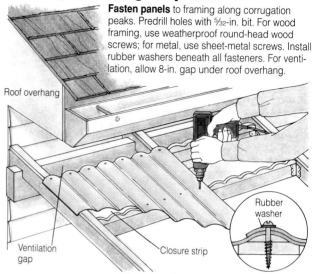

Fasten panels to framing along corrugation peaks. Predrill holes with 5/32-in. bit. For wood framing, use weatherproof round-head wood screws; for metal, use sheet-metal screws. Install rubber washers beneath all fasteners. For ventilation, allow 8-in. gap under roof overhang.

Roof overhang

Rubber washer

Ventilation gap

Closure strip

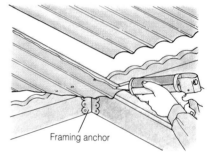

Seal panels by applying permanently flexible (nondrying) mastic or clear silicone caulk to seam area on corrugation's peaks. Also, before installing flashing (below), caulk along length of peaks that will be covered by flashing.

Framing anchor

Shingle

Sidewall flashing

Install flashing where panels meet sidewalls; match aluminum flashing corrugations to those in panels. Slide flashing under siding or shingles. If siding is fastened at lower edge, install flashing over siding with galvanized screws and rubber washers.

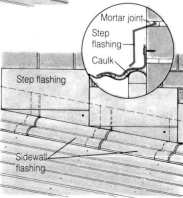

For masonry walls, secure sidewall flashing every 8 in. with masonry anchors. Cover with step flashing: First saw or chisel a small groove in mortar joint. Fold back top edge of flashing, and insert in groove as shown (inset). Fill joint with urethane caulk.

Mortar joint

Step flashing

Caulk

Step flashing

Sidewall flashing

PATCHING FIBERGLASS LAMINATE

Material	Characteristics	Use	Hints
Fiberglass mat	Fairly thick and stiff; easily molded to curves; adds adhesion	Alternated with cloth or roving for general repairs	Use as first and final layers; for thin repairs, use ¾-oz. mat; for thick repairs, use 1½-oz. mat
Fiberglass cloth	Thin and strong; leaves a smooth finish	Alternated with mat for small repairs	Make small cuts in cloth when molding to curved surfaces so fabric lies flat; in general, use 10-oz. cloth
Woven roving	Thick, heavily textured; provides stiffness, strength, and bulk	Alternated with mat for large repairs	Handle carefully as it tends to unravel; do not place directly under gel coat; for large repairs use 18- or 24-oz. roving
Polyester resin	Tough, water-resistant, compatible with many laminated objects; easy to work with	General laminating, especially fiberglass boats; do not use on objects that may contain polystyrene foam	Shelf life may be limited; use within 90 days; use air-inhibited for inner layers of repair, air-dry for outer layer; clean equipment with acetone
Epoxy resin	Creates a stronger bond and is more water-resistant than polyester; can be difficult to work with—cures more slowly than polyester	Bonds fiberglass to dissimilar materials, such as wood, metal, and many household plastics	Requires precise mixing and temperature control; clean equipment with acetone
Gel coat	Hard, glossy, waterproof; can be tinted by mixing with pigment; can be mixed with filler to add bulk	Forms waterproof, protective color coat on finished surface of repair	Air-dry type is best. When mixing, add pigment and test color after adding catalyst; thin with acetone before spraying
Putty	Depending on filler, adds hardness or bulk	Fills flaws that have penetrated beneath gel coat	Use fumed silica filler for small flaws; micro-sphere filler for large areas or where light weight is important; sand after patch dries

Mixing chemicals

Measure ingredients, following manufacturer's instructions carefully. For polyester resins, vary proportions according to temperature: in cool conditions use more catalyst; in warm conditions use less. Do not work in extreme temperatures or direct sunlight. Make several test batches to evaluate curing time and quality of mix. Prepare only as much resin as you can apply in 20 min. (once cured, it cannot be used).

Repairing minor damage

1. Clean damaged area by wiping with acetone. Protect surface around repair with tape. Fit ⅜- or ¼-in. drill or a rotary electric tool with drum sanding attachment; make V-shaped groove along damage.

Drum sanding attachment

2. Sand edges of groove, then blow away dust (do not touch). Mix gel coat with catalyst and filler according to manufacturer's instructions. Pack groove with mixture, building up ⅟₁₆ in. above surface.

Plastic applicator

3. Spray with PVA, or cover with wax paper and push squeegee across surface to force out air. After 2 hr., wash off PVA with warm water or remove paper. Sand and buff area (p.274). (Continued)

PATCHING FIBERGLASS LAMINATE

Preparing the damaged area

Grind damaged area with electric drill fitted with sanding attachment. Use coarse abrasive paper; taper edges back 2 in. from opening (on front and rear if possible). If damage is inaccessible from rear, grind hole to a roughly oval shape. Wipe with acetone.

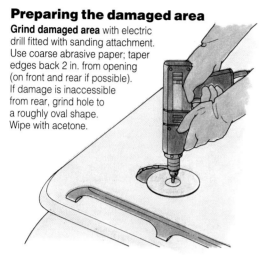

If rear is accessible, tape a piece of cardboard over front of damage. From rear, build up three layers of fabric and resin (p.273), as shown below. Remove cardboard and continue repair from front.

If rear is inaccessible, form backing by covering a piece of cardboard with three layers of fabric and resin (p.273), as shown below. Let cure; remove cardboard; edge backing with bonding mixture of resin and fumed silica. Insert through hole; hold against rear with screw and pliers. Secure with sheet-metal screws; let cure.

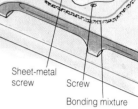

Cardboard

Sheet-metal screw
Screw
Bonding mixture

Building up the patch

Protect area around front of damage with tape. Remove screws. Cut a piece of mat slightly larger than the sanded area; then cut progressively larger pieces of alternating fabric. Saturate first piece of mat with resin, and brush resin around sanded edges. Press piece into place over hole.

Add successive layers of fabric and resin, pressing with laminate roller to remove all air bubbles. Complete repairs more than 1/8 in. thick in two stages, allowing first layers to cure before continuing.

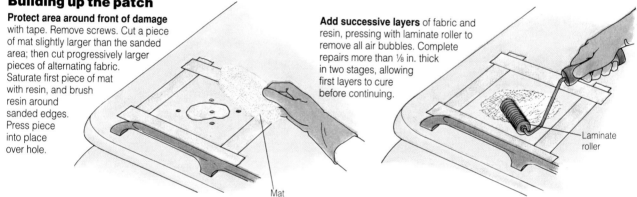

Mat

Laminate roller

Finishing the patch

When patch has cured, sand area with palm sander fitted with medium, then fine, abrasive paper. Wipe area with acetone.

Remove paper, or wash off PVA with warm water. Wet-sand with fine abrasive paper, followed by extra-fine. Remove tape. Coat an electric drill buffing attachment with rubbing compound formulated for fiberglass. Buff the patch (below); then apply auto polish or liquid wax with a soft cloth.

Fill uneven spots with gel coat mixed with filler (p.273). Sand once more; then spray entire area with gel coat mixed with catalyst and thinned with acetone to near-watery consistency. Cover repair with wax paper or spray with PVA. Let cure overnight.

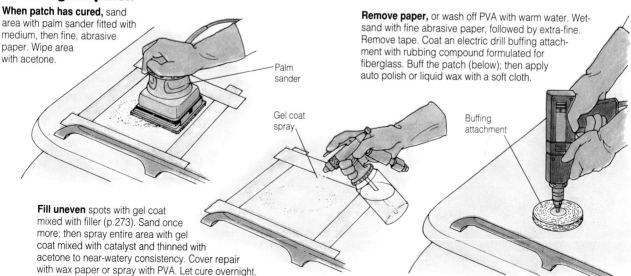

Palm sander

Gel coat spray

Buffing attachment

POSTFORMED LAMINATE

Postformed countertops are made of plastic laminate bonded to a core material (generally plywood or particleboard). The front edge of the countertop is rounded, and often the rear edge also curves up to form a backsplash. They come in standard widths and are cut to length at the building supply center where you purchase the countertop. L-shaped countertops come in two sections with a mitered corner. You join the sections with hardware supplied with the countertop. Also supplied are preglued strips of laminate called *end caps*. Apply these after you have built up the edges as shown on page 276.

Before removing an old countertop, shut off the water, gas, and electricity supply to any fixtures or appliances; then remove the sink and appliances, noting how they are installed so that you can put them back correctly. (Have an electrician disconnect and remove built-in items such as a garbage disposer or a cook top.) Working from inside the base cabinets, remove any fasteners from the countertop; then free it by prying up against it, again from the inside, with a flat pry bar.

Take measurements for a new countertop as shown below; make a detailed sketch of the cabinet layout to take with you when ordering.

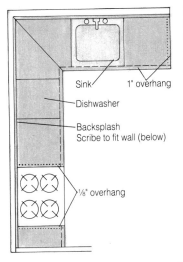

Sink
1" overhang
Dishwasher
Backsplash
Scribe to fit wall (below)
⅛" overhang

Measuring a countertop. For L-shaped top (left), measure along rear of each run of base cabinets, from corner to far end. Also measure from the wall to the front of the cabinets. Add 1 in. where edges overhang cabinets; add ⅛ in. where cabinets abut an appliance or a wall. For a new sink or appliance, measure inside base cabinets.

Leveling. With the countertop removed (right), check if top edges of cabinets and cleats are level. If not, insert shims under or behind cabinets—first loosening the cabinets from the wall if necessary—or tack strips of wood to top edges. If needed, install corner and cross braces to support the new countertop and provide fastening surfaces. Ensure that corners are square; otherwise the countertop will not fit.

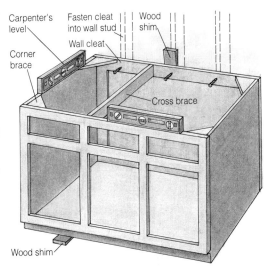

Carpenter's level
Fasten cleat into wall stud
Wood shim
Corner brace
Wall cleat
Cross brace
Wood shim

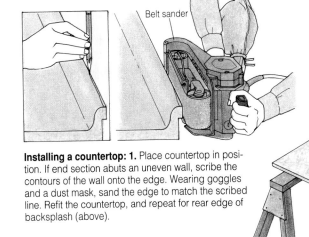

Belt sander

Installing a countertop: 1. Place countertop in position. If end section abuts an uneven wall, scribe the contours of the wall onto the edge. Wearing goggles and a dust mask, sand the edge to match the scribed line. Refit the countertop, and repeat for rear edge of backsplash (above).

Frame

2. To make sink cutout, first mark outline for new sink with the instructions or template provided with the sink. For an existing rimless sink, turn sink upside down and trace rim; draw cutting line ⅜ in. inside traced line. If sink has metal frame, hold frame in position; mark cutting line around the outside of the vertical edge, as shown.

3. To cut sink opening, first drill starter holes in corners of outline, turn piece over, and redraw guidelines. Wearing a dust mask and goggles, remove waste with saber saw fitted with fine-tooth blade. File or sand edges smooth.

Tighten bolt with wrench

4. Spread glue or adhesive caulk along top's mitered edges. Fit sections together so surfaces are flush; secure with fasteners provided (above). Let adhesive dry overnight. Then, with a helper, position top on cabinets. Install wood screws in top's underside through corner braces. Apply clear flexible caulk to any gaps along the backsplash and ends.

SHEET LAMINATE

Sheets of laminated plastic for use on countertops, and on other flat or curved surfaces, are available in hundreds of patterns and colors. Most have a dark core that is visible at the edges, but a variety called color-through laminate has a single color throughout. When choosing laminate, avoid glossy or patterned styles in kitchens—heavy use can dull them. Light-colored laminates show wear less readily and are easier to match. Buy vertical-grade laminate for use on walls and cabinets.

Sheet laminate can be applied over nearly any smooth, level surface. Particleboard is used most often as a substrate for countertops, although plywood (more expensive) is stronger and less likely to absorb moisture, which can cause laminate to lift and buckle. For cabinets, use plywood—it is lighter than particleboard and holds fasteners more securely. Make cutouts for a sink (p.275) or other appliance in the substrate before covering it with laminate. Sand irregularities in the substrate and fill depressions with spackling compound; then wipe clean.

Attach laminate to both sides of the substrate unless (as with a countertop)

Cutting laminate

Scoring and breaking.
Pencil a cutting line on face of laminate. With metal straightedge as a guide, score along line several times with a plastic cutter; then break by lifting edge of sheet. For small strips, clamp straightedge along cutting line, score, and lift sheet.

Plastic cutter

Cutting narrow strips.
For strips 4 in. wide or less, fit laminate trimmer with slitter attachment and solid carbide straight-cutting bit. Clamp laminate to bench; fit piece between slitter's baseplates with guide on edge. Push tool along cutting line.

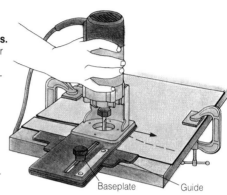

Baseplate   Guide

Laminating a vertical surface

1. Apply contact cement with narrow roller or paintbrush: two thin coats to the substrate, one to the laminate. Allow each coat to dry until adhesive appears hazy and is not sticky.

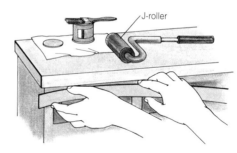

J-roller

2. Carefully align individual strip against edge; press into place, and roll with J-roller or tap with wood block and hammer. (Attach strips to opposite ends of substrate first; trim; then attach any remaining strips.)

Installing preglued laminate.
For bendable strips (and for end caps, p.275), first ensure that surface is clean and dry. Set heat gun to medium; hold several inches from strip. As laminate softens, press strip down.

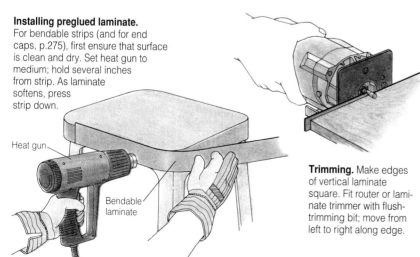

Heat gun

Bendable laminate

Trimming. Make edges of vertical laminate square. Fit router or laminate trimmer with flush-trimming bit; move from left to right along edge.

Edge treatments

Build up an edge
and cover with laminate or preglued end cap. Attach build-up strip of wood with white glue and finishing nails.

Build-up strip

Solid wood edging
is stronger and more durable than laminate. Flanged edging fits groove routed in the substrate panel. Secure with white glue.

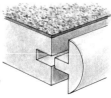

it is securely fastened to a frame; otherwise it will warp. Laminate vertical surfaces before horizontal ones, and fit pieces to the back and sides of an object first, then to the front.

Glue laminate to the substrate with contact cement; other adhesives will work but require extensive clamping. Nonflammable contact cement is safer than the flammable variety.

Laminate can be cut with a laminate trimmer, or with a circular, saber, or table saw fitted with a laminate blade. Keep leftover pieces to use for repairs. Bevel exposed edges with a router or laminate trimmer; then file to prevent chipping, applying pressure on the downward stroke. When trimming with a router or trimmer, use only self-guiding solid carbide bits.

Despite its toughness, sheet laminate is subject to burns, scratches, and stains. Try to remove stubborn stains by dabbing with bleach for 1 minute and then rinsing with water.

Caution: When sanding, cutting, or trimming laminate, wear goggles and a dust mask. If applying contact cement, work in a well-ventilated area and wear a respirator (p.13).

Laminating a horizontal surface

Applying adhesive. Apply contact cement to substrate and laminate. Lay dowels or cardboard strips on substrate (these will not stick) and set laminate on top. Do not let laminate touch substrate until it is in position. Then remove dowels individually, starting at end of surface, as you press laminate into place.

Smoothing. Roll entire surface with J-roller or rolling pin, working from center of panel toward edges. Exert strong pressure to remove all air bubbles.

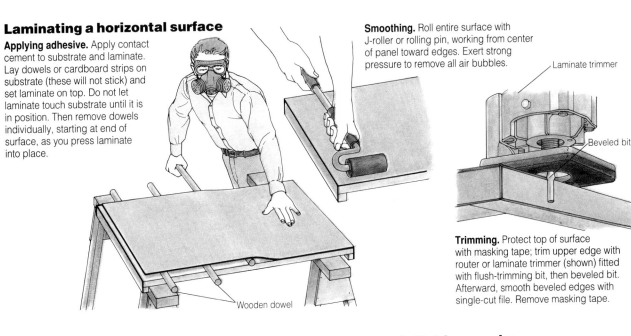

Laminate trimmer

Beveled bit

Wooden dowel

Trimming. Protect top of surface with masking tape; trim upper edge with router or laminate trimmer (shown) fitted with flush-trimming bit, then beveled bit. Afterward, smooth beveled edges with single-cut file. Remove masking tape.

Cutouts and backsplashes

Cutting sink opening.
If there is no sink cutout in substrate, cut opening as shown on page 275. If cutout exists, first apply laminate to substrate, then drill starter hole in laminate. Insert router fitted with flush-trimming bit; guide router to edge of cutout, then clockwise around cutout.

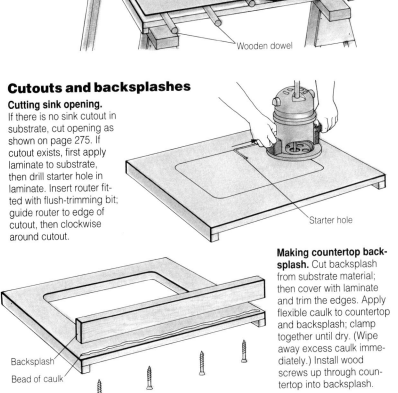

Starter hole

Backsplash

Bead of caulk

Making countertop backsplash. Cut backsplash from substrate material; then cover with laminate and trim the edges. Apply flexible caulk to countertop and backsplash; clamp together until dry. (Wipe away excess caulk immediately.) Install wood screws up through countertop into backsplash.

Making repairs

Mending damaged strip. Trim ragged edge with sharp chisel. Scrape away old adhesive. Cut strip of matching laminate slightly oversize; install with contact cement. When dry, file away excess laminate with single-cut file.

Filling blemishes. Fill minor cracks and depressions with colored laminate seam filler. Use putty knife; sand with 400-grit paper when dry.

SOLID-SURFACE MATERIAL

Solid plastic sheets known as solid-surface material, or solid surfacing, have the best features of marble and alabaster, which they resemble, yet they can be worked with power tools and joined with nearly invisible seams. Usually formed from a blend of acrylic or polyester resin combined with a mined mineral, these synthetics are heavy, durable, and stain-resistant. You must round off all inside and outside corners; custom-profiling (shaping the edges with a router) is optional.

More expensive than many other materials, solid surfacing is available at kitchen and bathroom showrooms. Before selecting a brand, check that its warranty extends to do-it-yourself installation. Study the manufacturer's instructions carefully; if you don't have the basic carpentry skills necessary to work with the material, consult an installer trained by the manufacturer.

Before beginning to work, check that all sheets have the same batch number, and peel off the protective coating. For countertops, measure the

Cutting sheets

Sawing. Support material on 2 × 4's. Rough-cut with circular saw fitted with a carbide-tipped blade; leave ⅛ in. of material for future trimming. Offset seams for U- or L-shaped countertops by 3 in. (see below).

Use 2 × 4 as fence

Sink cutout. To make a template, first calculate the sink outline (p.275). Enlarge outline by the distance between the router bit and the edge of its base; saw a plywood template to this measurement. Clamp template to piece, drill a starter hole, and rout away the cutout, using a ½-in. single-flute straight-cutting carbide bit. Sand edges smooth with 100-grit paper.

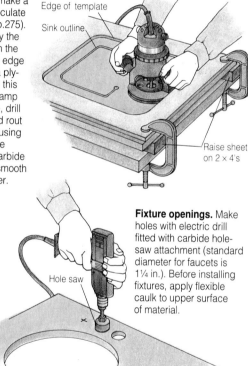
Edge of template
Sink outline
Raise sheet on 2 × 4's

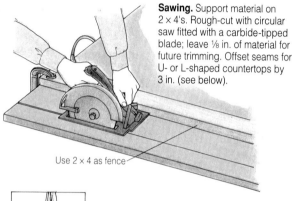
1½"

Outside corners. First make a template to a radius of 1½ in.: Mark a 1½-in. square at the corner of a small piece of plywood. Place a compass on the inside point of the square and scribe an arc across the corner (inset). Cut template along this arc, mark cut line on material, then rough-cut material to cut line with saber saw (left). Clamp template to underside of corner; smooth with router fitted with a self-guiding straight-cutting bit.

Mark cut line using template

Fixture openings. Make holes with electric drill fitted with carbide hole-saw attachment (standard diameter for faucets is 1¼ in.). Before installing fixtures, apply flexible caulk to upper surface of material.

Hole saw

Joining sheets

1. Clamp sheets ¼ in. apart, and rout along edges with double-flute straight-cutting carbide bit. Guide router with straightedges clamped parallel to gap (inset). Clean edges with denatured alcohol, and position sheets ⅛ in. apart. Mix seaming compound and fill seam according to manufacturer's instructions; clamp sheets together until compound hardens.

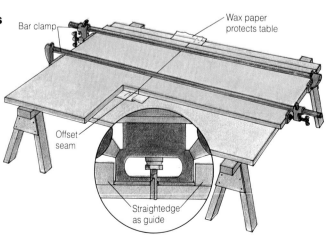
Bar clamp
Wax paper protects table
Offset seam
Straightedge as guide

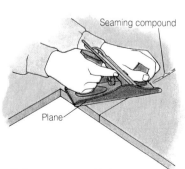
Seaming compound
Plane

2. Remove excess dried compound with sharp plane (to avoid gouging material, round corners of plane iron with file); then sand with 100-grit paper. Finish surface (facing page).

base cabinets as described on page 275. Remove the old countertop, and attach supporting strips (using drywall screws) of 4-inch-wide ¾-inch plywood over the top edges of the cabinets. Add cross braces spaced 24 inches apart if you are using ¾-inch-thick surfacing, or at 18-inch intervals for ½-inch-thick surfacing. Also add cross braces from front to back where sinks and other openings will be located and where countertop seams will lie.

Caution: Wear a dust mask when cutting, routing, and sanding solid surfacing. Seaming compound is very flammable; use it only in a well-ventilated area, and follow all safety precautions listed by the manufacturer.

Adding dropped edges

1. To give the appearance of thicker edges, first turn over piece. Cut 1½-in.-wide strips of surfacing to fit exposed sides. Roughen mating surfaces with 60-grit sandpaper. Test-fit strips; then apply seaming compound to strips. Secure with spring clamps at 4-in. intervals until compound hardens.

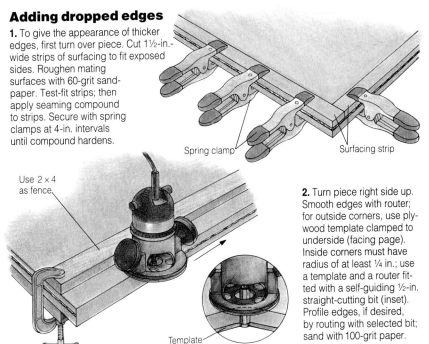

Use 2 × 4 as fence

Spring clamp

Surfacing strip

Template

2. Turn piece right side up. Smooth edges with router; for outside corners, use plywood template clamped to underside (facing page). Inside corners must have radius of at least ¼ in.; use a template and a router fitted with a self-guiding ½-in. straight-cutting bit (inset). Profile edges, if desired, by routing with selected bit; sand with 100-grit paper.

Adding a backsplash

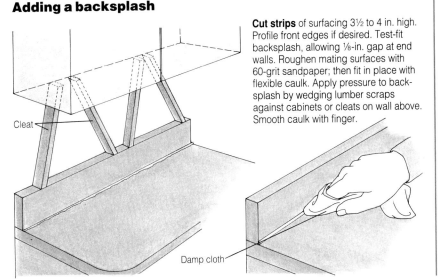

Cleat

Damp cloth

Cut strips of surfacing 3½ to 4 in. high. Profile front edges if desired. Test-fit backsplash, allowing ⅛-in. gap at end walls. Roughen mating surfaces with 60-grit sandpaper; then fit in place with flexible caulk. Apply pressure to backsplash by wedging lumber scraps against cabinets or cleats on wall above. Smooth caulk with finger.

Finishing

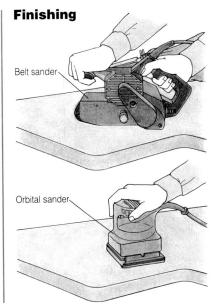

Belt sander

Orbital sander

For matte finish, power- or hand-sand entire surface (top) with 100-grit paper followed by 180 grit; then polish with fine plastic abrasive pad secured to orbital sander (above).

Buffing pad

For glossy finish (for low-use surfaces), sand with 220-, then 320-grit paper. Fit a drill with a buffing pad; polish until glossy with liquid automobile polishing compound.

To remove blemishes, scrub with abrasive cleanser or sand with 100-grit paper. For deep flaws, grind away damage with an electric rotary tool, then fill depression with seaming compound. Finish surface.

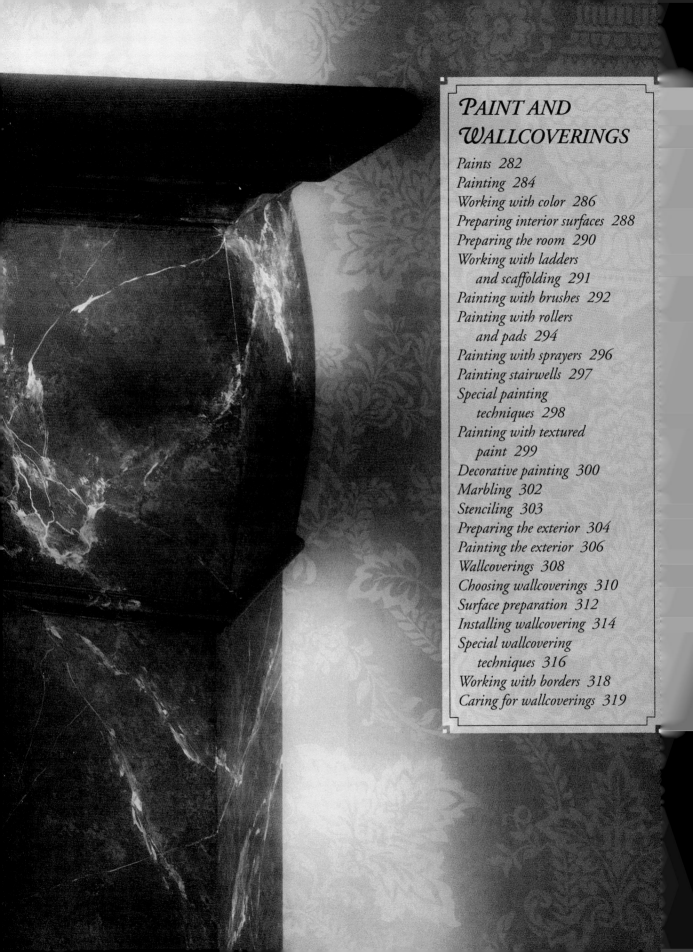

PAINT AND WALLCOVERINGS

PAINTS

Paint is basically pigment, which provides a particular color, and a binder in an oil- or water-base solvent. As the paint dries, the solvent evaporates, leaving an opaque film.

Some oil-base paints have volatile solvents; because their emissions have raised concern about air quality, there may be restrictions on where they can be used. Newer alkyd-oil-base paints leave more brush strokes than their old counterparts, but they also dry faster than the old linseed-oil-base paints.

Most water-base paints have a latex binder, which may be vinyl, rubber, polyvinyl acetate, or acrylic resins. Latex paint offers superior color retention, easy cleanup, and low toxicity, making it the best choice for house paint.

Thick textured paint, with granular additives, hides defects as it adds character to a surface. It comes premixed and as a dry powder. You can create special effects with textured paint (below) or with glaze applied over a paint (facing page).

Textured paints

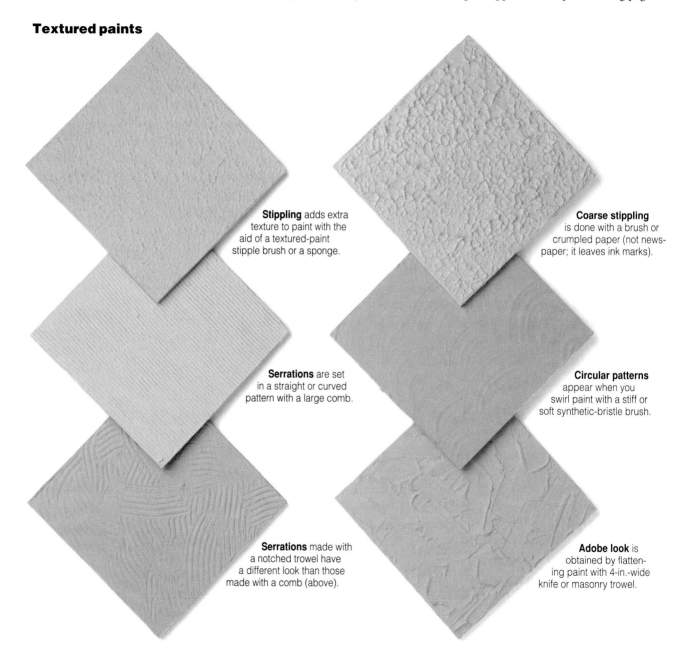

Stippling adds extra texture to paint with the aid of a textured-paint stipple brush or a sponge.

Coarse stippling is done with a brush or crumpled paper (not newspaper; it leaves ink marks).

Serrations are set in a straight or curved pattern with a large comb.

Circular patterns appear when you swirl paint with a stiff or soft synthetic-bristle brush.

Serrations made with a notched trowel have a different look than those made with a comb (above).

Adobe look is obtained by flattening paint with 4-in.-wide knife or masonry trowel.

Glazed paints

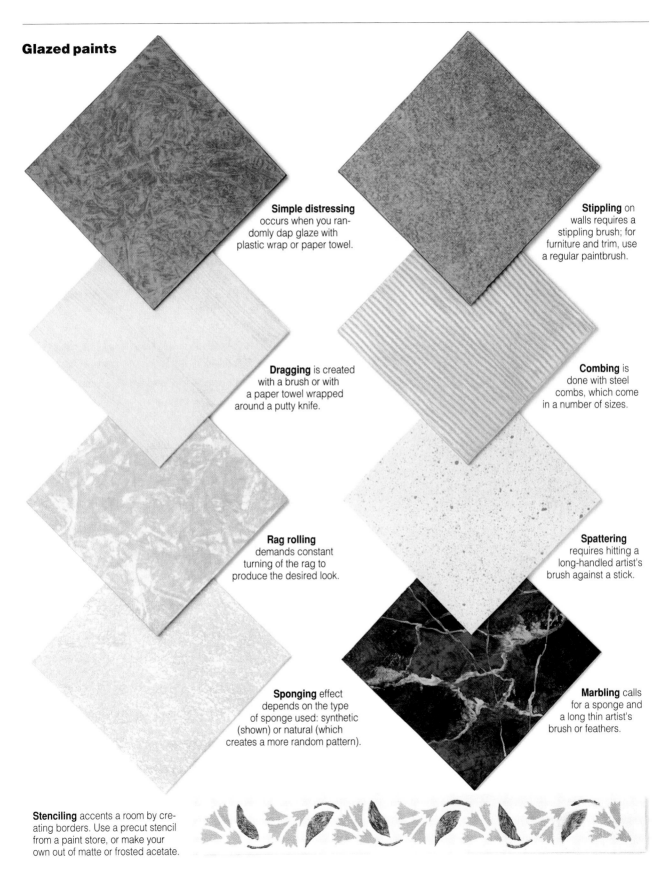

Simple distressing occurs when you randomly dap glaze with plastic wrap or paper towel.

Stippling on walls requires a stippling brush; for furniture and trim, use a regular paintbrush.

Dragging is created with a brush or with a paper towel wrapped around a putty knife.

Combing is done with steel combs, which come in a number of sizes.

Rag rolling demands constant turning of the rag to produce the desired look.

Spattering requires hitting a long-handled artist's brush against a stick.

Sponging effect depends on the type of sponge used: synthetic (shown) or natural (which creates a more random pattern).

Marbling calls for a sponge and a long thin artist's brush or feathers.

Stenciling accents a room by creating borders. Use a precut stencil from a paint store, or make your own out of matte or frosted acetate.

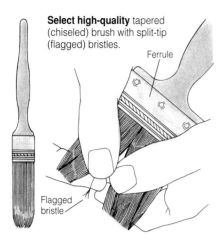

Select high-quality tapered (chiseled) brush with split-tip (flagged) bristles.

Ferrule

Flagged bristle

For an attractive, durable paint job, buy the best-quality tools and materials you can afford. A well-made brush has flagged and chiseled bristles (left) and a sturdy metal ferrule. Because natural bristles absorb water, losing their shape, select synthetic-bristle brushes for latex (water-base) paint. Choose either synthetic- or natural-bristle brushes for alkyd (oil-base) paints. Roller covers (p.294) come in synthetics or lamb's wool. For latex paint, choose a synthetic roller cover; lamb's-wool covers hold and spread

alkyd paints better. Less expensive rollers hold paint poorly and shed lint. Take care of your tools by cleaning them thoroughly after each use and storing them as shown on pages 292 and 294.

Premium paints may seem expensive when compared to their cheaper counterparts, but any saving is usually illusory. Although the less expensive paints may advertise high hiding qualities (the ability to cover the previous color), they generally cover less square footage, may be more difficult to apply

Paint	Location	Characteristics	Comments
Latex (water-base)	Most surfaces, except some metals; many premium brands can be used on aluminum and vinyl siding	Little odor; dries quickly; easy cleanup; withstands sunlight, moisture, mildew, and wood shrinkage or expansion; good color retention; may adhere poorly to problem surfaces; brush marks tend to show	Do not apply over alkyd paint unless it has been sanded and primed; use water as solvent
Alkyd (oil-base)	Most surfaces except aluminum siding; preferred for interior wood trim	Strong odor and fumes; dries slowly; cleanup messier than latex; color may fade; when dry, is easy to wash; brush marks less evident	Do not apply over latex unless it has been sanded and primed; use paint thinner as solvent
Primer	Most surfaces except some metal, such as aluminum; use alkyd for exteriors, wall-coverings, and bare wood; otherwise, use same type as finish coat	Flat; white, unless tinted to match finish coat; rust-inhibiting metal primer is reddish brown	Use appropriate solvent; always check label for information on compatibility of primer with undercoat and finish coat
Masonry paint	Interior and exterior concrete, aggregate, brick, stone, and other masonry	Bonds to concrete and masonry walls; usually flat luster	Specially formulated latex paint
Epoxy	Nonporous surfaces, such as porcelain, plastic, fiberglass, and tile; many bathroom surfaces; concrete floors	Exceptionally durable and moisture-resistant; glossy; color may yellow over time	May be latex or alkyd—use appropriate solvent; may have two parts that require mixing
Heat-resistant paint	Metal objects subject to high temperature, including grills, fireplace screens, radiators, and pipes	Resists heat up to very high temperature; limited luster and color choices available	Specially formulated silicone alkyd paint
Metal paint	Any ferrous metal	Rust- and corrosion-resistant	Specially formulated latex or alkyd paint
Milk paint	Interior surfaces or furniture originally painted with milk paint, or where antique appearance is desired	Flat, grainy, unrefined appearance; available in warm, earthy colors	Specially formulated paint made from milk products and mineral fillers; mixed with water
Porch and floor paint	Interior or exterior wood floors, decks, porches, or steps	Resists wear from foot traffic	Specially formulated alkyd paint
Textured paint	Walls and ceilings where surface pattern is desired	Covers damaged, stained, or uneven surfaces; reduces reflective glare; various patterns can be created (p.299)	Specially formulated latex paint containing texture-producing agents

About gloss

All paints are designated with a certain *glossiness* or *luster.*

Flat, low-gloss, and eggshell lusters are the least shiny and reflective. They are often used on walls and ceilings in living areas and hallways, since they tend not to show surface flaws and brush or roller marks.

Semi-gloss and medium lusters are often used on kitchen and bathroom surfaces, and in rooms where a soft but somewhat shiny look is desired.

High-gloss, enamel, and satin lusters are easiest to wash, and are best for high-wear areas such as kitchen and bathroom surfaces, children's rooms, and woodwork or trim. Higher-gloss alkyds are glossier than similar latex paints, but latex products on the market today, especially acrylic latex, are equally durable and washable, hide defects well, have little odor, and dry quicker than alkyds.

and care for, and don't wear as well as better brands. When applied with a roller, quality paint will go on smoothly, without spattering or forming blemishes. Because the quality of a paint isn't always obvious from the information on the can, follow the advice of a reputable retailer or consult consumer magazines for brand ratings.

Many surfaces can be covered with more than one type of paint. Review the chart at left when choosing paint for a specific location and surface. Because latex paint is easily cleaned up, it is usually preferred for interior walls and ceilings.

Alkyd paint has a stronger odor and requires mineral spirits, turpentine, or another solvent for cleanup. Because alkyd paint is less likely to retain brush marks when dry, it is often used for interior woodwork. However, check your local regulations before using alkyd paint; it poses environmental problems and in some areas its use is restricted.

Both latex and alkyd paints come in all lusters, from flat to high gloss, but latex is never quite as glossy as its alkyd counterpart. If you like the natural look of wood for trim or furniture, consider applying a stain or a clear finish such as varnish (pp.164–167).

An undercoat of primer will help the finish paint coat adhere and keep its color uniform. If you are repainting with the same color and paint type, just spot-prime any stains or patches of spackling compound. But if you are painting fresh wallboard, changing the color of the room, or have done many repairs, prime all surfaces with a primer that you have tinted to match the final coat. If you are unsure whether a previous coat is latex or alkyd, apply primer; latex paint applied over alkyd is likely to peel off in time. When selecting a primer, check the labels to make sure that your primer and finish coat are compatible.

Caution: Follow the preparation and safety recommendations given on page 291. When you are finished, dispose of paint properly (p.307).

Estimating paint quantity

Calculate square footage of walls by adding length of room to width, multiplying by 2, then multiplying result by room's height. Compare square footage with coverage given on paint label; for two coats, double the number of cans.

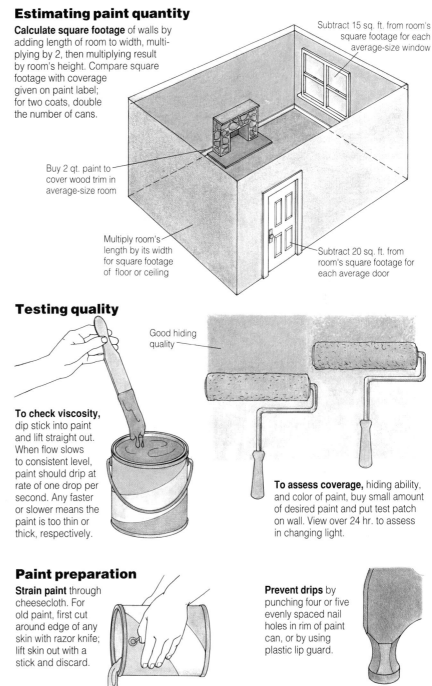

Subtract 15 sq. ft. from room's square footage for each average-size window

Buy 2 qt. paint to cover wood trim in average-size room

Multiply room's length by its width for square footage of floor or ceiling

Subtract 20 sq. ft. from room's square footage for each average door

Testing quality

To check viscosity, dip stick into paint and lift straight out. When flow slows to consistent level, paint should drip at rate of one drop per second. Any faster or slower means the paint is too thin or thick, respectively.

Good hiding quality

To assess coverage, hiding ability, and color of paint, buy small amount of desired paint and put test patch on wall. View over 24 hr. to assess in changing light.

Paint preparation

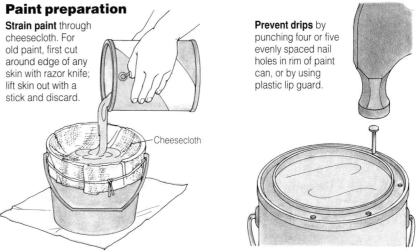

Strain paint through cheesecloth. For old paint, first cut around edge of any skin with razor knife; lift skin out with a stick and discard.

Cheesecloth

Prevent drips by punching four or five evenly spaced nail holes in rim of paint can, or by using plastic lip guard.

When developing a color scheme, work with the color wheel as your basic tool. Combine your own color preferences with the information it provides to achieve the effects you want. Colors opposite one another on the wheel are known as *complementary* colors. They work well together, as do adjacent or related colors (next to each other on the wheel). An accent in a complementary color can enliven a monochromatic scheme (one that has different shades of the same color).

Color influences people's moods; avoid having too little or too much of it in one place. Combine wall colors with the existing elements in the room—artwork, draperies, furniture, and carpeting; exterior colors should be influenced by your home's surroundings. When decorating from scratch, you can begin with the color of one element and then build your scheme around it.

Warm vs. cool. Red and yellow and the combinations made from these primary colors are called warm colors—they energize and heat up a room. In cool climates and in sunny rooms, warm colors create a feeling of coziness. The cool colors are blue, green, and purple. In hot climates, these colors make a room feel cooler.

By adding white, you lighten the shade of a color. Lighter shades can brighten rooms that have little natural light. By adding black, you darken a color's shade. Darker shades create a feeling of intimacy. Light shades appear lighter when placed against a dark background. Against a light background, dark shades seem darker.

Color can help to improve a room's proportions. Lighter shades reflect light, making walls appear to recede and giving the impression of a larger room; darker shades make a room seem smaller and cozier. For a long, narrow room, paint the end walls a darker shade or a warmer color than the side walls; this appears to bring in the end walls and widen the room. To make a room seem larger, paint all the walls and the trim the same color; this will also unify an irregular space. Paint the ceiling a darker shade to

Outer color wheel has 12 colors. Red, yellow, and blue are primaries. Each secondary color (orange, green, and purple) is a combination of two primaries. When you blend colors you change their basic character, creating a wide variety of choices.

Inner color wheel shows how neutrals may be warm (those on right side) or cool (those on left side). Combine neutrals with brighter colors to create satisfying schemes.

visually lower it and a lighter shade to give the effect of height.

Color intensity. An intense color is known as *highly saturated*. Whether it is warm or cool, a saturated color attracts the eye. Use intense colors as accents and for dramatic effect—on a single wall, for instance. In some spaces, such as hallways, an intense color can be chosen as a main color because the room is only for passing through. A high gloss makes any color stand out; the same color in a low gloss is less obtrusive.

To draw attention to a particular wall or to an interesting feature such as a carved molding, introduce a new color or a higher gloss paint. On the other hand, you can minimize an awkward feature, like a misplaced door or a radiator, by painting it the same color as the background and in a less glossy luster.

For variety, introduce new colors in different rooms. But maintain unity by featuring a main color from one room as an accent elsewhere. A multicolored wallcovering, mixing some or all of your colors on some walls (for example, in a hallway), can also unify a color scheme throughout the house.

Choose indoor colors one shade lighter than you think you want. Once they have dried on the wall, they will be darker than they appear on the paint chip. Before making a final decision, try the paint chip test described below, or buy a small can of the desired paint and paint a sample board. Hang the board up for a day, assessing the color as the paint dries and the light changes.

Shades

Adding white or black changes a color's shade, permitting many gradations within a single color. Different colors can also be blended together; brown, for instance, is a mixture of red, yellow, and black.

Paint chips

Use sample paint chips to help you choose shades. Cut the same shade from four chips and tape them together. Compare to furnishings and accessories, and tape to wall to observe in different lighting.

Interior colors

Semigloss coral-red walls make for a stimulating room. Usually red is an accent, but red walls can also wake up a quiet room and lend a cozy, intimate feeling. Try red for dining areas, rooms with northern exposures, and rooms used mainly at night.

Cool colors are serene and relaxing. Here, the soft gray-green of the walls is picked up in accessories such as the throw cushion, picture, and drapery fabric. Use cool colors in hot climates, in rooms that receive morning or afternoon sun, and for modern decor.

Shades of the same color—in this case white—are used to create a simple look that won't go out of style. You can brighten up neutral colors with contrasts (such as the green here). Such a scheme would suit children's rooms, kitchens, and sun porches.

Exterior colors

When choosing paint colors, keep in mind these factors: A small house will seem larger if you paint the entire structure, including trim, the same light color (right). Light colors also make a house appear closer to the street; dark colors make it appear to recede. Any paint with a high gloss will exaggerate surface flaws.

A three-color exterior scheme (below) with neutral or mid-tone walls, darker trim, and a complementary-color door emphasizes architectural features. Change colors only where a surface changes, and harmonize colors with brick or any other features whose color cannot be easily altered. (If you have masonry that needs cleaning, which will alter its color, clean it before selecting colors.)

Sunlight makes any color seem lighter; select a slightly darker shade than the one you actually desire. Strong colors fade more rapidly outdoors than light colors. A house's surroundings change with the seasons; choose colors that will be pleasing year-round.

It is essential that you clean and repair all surfaces before painting. First remove wallcoverings (p.312), draperies, and all hardware except switch plates and outlet covers (remove them only after you have washed the walls). Scrape old paint from screw slots, then back out the screws with a screwdriver. Working up from the bottom, sponge-wash walls and trim with a solution of powdered cleanser (such as phosphate-free trisodium); then rinse. Before washing the ceiling, cover the floor with drop cloths. Observe ladder safety precautions (pp.290–291).

If paint is thickly layered on the trim, remove it with a heat gun, as shown here, or with a chemical stripper. After applying the stripper, let the paint soften, and then scrape and sand as you would when using a heat gun.

Caution: Unless you are absolutely certain the paint does not contain lead (p.307), wear an appropriate respirator (p.13). Dispose of all debris properly.

Patch minor wallboard damage (facing page). For larger holes, saw back to the framing on each side of the damage and screw nailing strips to the framing. Cut a wallboard patch to match the hole, and screw the patch to the strips. Cover the seams with wallboard tape and layers of joint compound. In plaster, large or widening cracks, or cracks radiating from window or door corners, may indicate structural problems; have these professionally evaluated. Also do this wherever you see water damage.

Removing paint

Stripping paint:
1. Soften paint by holding heat gun 3 to 6 in. away. Move it back and forth until paint blisters.
Caution: To avoid scorching wood, keep tool moving. Wear gloves, goggles, and for paint applied before 1980, a respirator.

2. Immediately scrape softened paint from flat surfaces with a narrow putty knife. (Round corners of knife to avoid gouging wood.) Either heat paint or scrape it—doing both at the same time could damage wood.

Shavehook

3. Scrape countoured wood with shave hook or four-edge blade scraper. For intricate carving, use pointed object such as an awl. Do entire surface until bare wood is visible.

4. When most of the paint is gone, let dry; then remove remaining paint with palm sander or sanding block fitted with successively finer grits of abrasive paper.

Repairing wood trim

Scrape away loose paint with a stiff putty knife. Dig away any rotted wood. Brush wood sealer on bare wood and rotted areas.

Patching compound

Fill depressions with latex wood patch; let dry. Smooth and feather edges with coarse, then fine, abrasive paper.

Popped nail

Nail set

Popped nails: 1. For doors, windows, and other trim, reseat nails with nail set. Fill nail holes with compound; fill joints with compound or paintable caulk.

Spray primer

2. Spray wood with a fast-drying primer, or brush on regular primer. Let dry; then sand lightly.

Repairing damaged wallboard

For popped nails, drive new wallboard screw 2 in. below or above nail, then sink nailhead below surface by striking with nail set. Fill any dent (below).

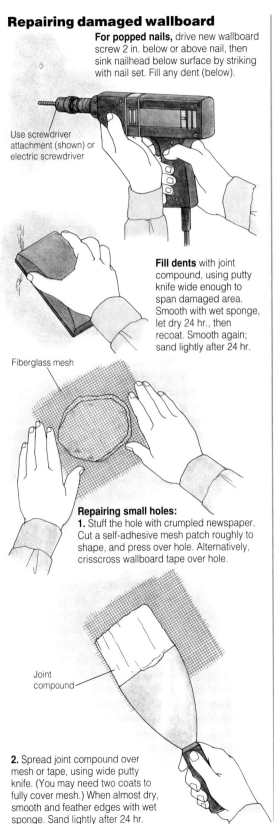

Use screwdriver attachment (shown) or electric screwdriver

Fill dents with joint compound, using putty knife wide enough to span damaged area. Smooth with wet sponge, let dry 24 hr., then recoat. Smooth again; sand lightly after 24 hr.

Fiberglass mesh

Repairing small holes:
1. Stuff the hole with crumpled newspaper. Cut a self-adhesive mesh patch roughly to shape, and press over hole. Alternatively, crisscross wallboard tape over hole.

Joint compound

2. Spread joint compound over mesh or tape, using wide putty knife. (You may need two coats to fully cover mesh.) When almost dry, smooth and feather edges with wet sponge. Sand lightly after 24 hr.

Filling holes in plaster

Scrape away loose paint from area around hole, using large putty knife. (Wear goggles and a dust mask.) Then scrape loose plaster from hole, taking care not to remove sound plaster. Undercut hole's inside edge with utility knife or can opener.

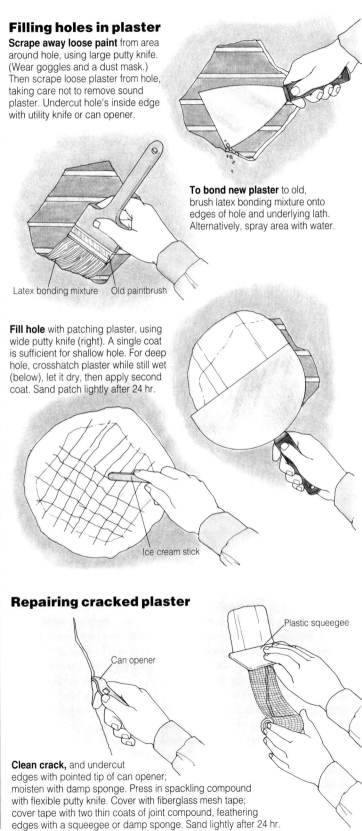

To bond new plaster to old, brush latex bonding mixture onto edges of hole and underlying lath. Alternatively, spray area with water.

Latex bonding mixture   Old paintbrush

Fill hole with patching plaster, using wide putty knife (right). A single coat is sufficient for shallow hole. For deep hole, crosshatch plaster while still wet (below), let it dry, then apply second coat. Sand patch lightly after 24 hr.

Ice cream stick

Repairing cracked plaster

Plastic squeegee

Can opener

Clean crack, and undercut edges with pointed tip of can opener; moisten with damp sponge. Press in spackling compound with flexible putty knife. Cover with fiberglass mesh tape; cover tape with two thin coats of joint compound, feathering edges with a squeegee or damp sponge. Sand lightly after 24 hr.

Reducing clutter and carefully masking your work area will help your project go smoothly and make cleaning up easier. Remove draperies, floor covering, and any light furniture; move the heavier pieces to the center of the room. Wash and repair the walls, ceiling, and trim (pp.288–289). Then vacuum and dust the area thoroughly.

Remove all hardware such as window locks, curtain rods, and picture hooks; tape the fasteners to the hardware so they don't get lost. Use drop cloths or masking material to cover everything that won't be painted. Inexpensive plastic drop cloths are fine for furniture, walls, and cabinets, but

9-ounce canvas cloths are best for floors because they absorb paint splatters. If you do use plastic drop cloths, cover them with newspaper or old sheets to absorb the paint. Cover wood trim with good-quality masking tape or self-adhesive masking paper, available in many widths at paint supply stores. To prevent paint from leaking behind the tape or paper, press its edge down with a flexible putty knife. Remove the masking material when the paint dries; it may damage the trim if left too long.

Before removing the cover plate of a switch or outlet, or wrapping a ceiling or wall fixture in plastic, turn off the electricity to the room. Unscrew

a fixture's cover plate and slide it away from the surface. Don't let a fixture's wires bear its weight; instead, support the fixture with a piece of rope tied through the mounting strap.

Masking window glass can save time, but if you have only one window and a steady hand, it may be easier to scrape dried paint off the glass with a single-edge razor blade. An alternative is to coat the glass with liquid glass coating (a wax-base masking product), but keep it off the frame and muntins.

Caution: Keep children and pets out of the work area. Before leaving for any length of time, clean up or store your paint and materials (p.307).

Preparing to paint

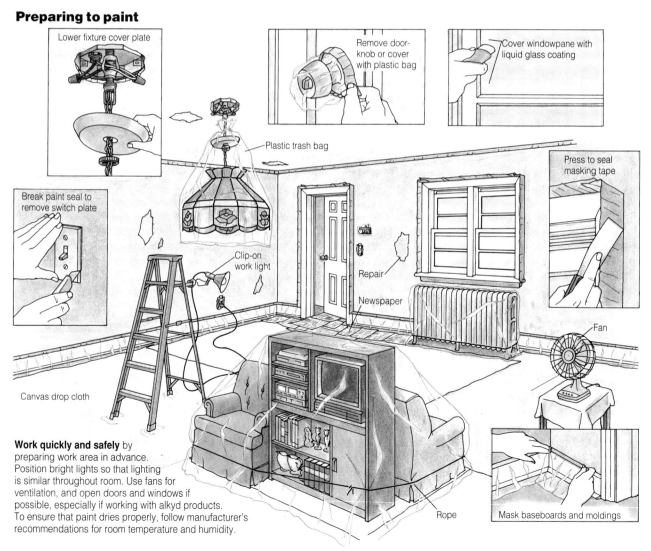

Lower fixture cover plate

Remove door-knob or cover with plastic bag

Cover windowpane with liquid glass coating

Plastic trash bag

Press to seal masking tape

Break paint seal to remove switch plate

Clip-on work light

Repair

Newspaper

Fan

Canvas drop cloth

Work quickly and safely by preparing work area in advance. Position bright lights so that lighting is similar throughout room. Use fans for ventilation, and open doors and windows if possible, especially if working with alkyd products. To ensure that paint dries properly, follow manufacturer's recommendations for room temperature and humidity.

Rope

Mask baseboards and moldings

WORKING WITH LADDERS AND SCAFFOLDING

Usually one ladder is required when painting a room; for exteriors, you will often need at least two ladders. Stairs call for special setups (p.297). Indoors use stepladders; if you need an extension ladder to reach a high ceiling, wrap the tops of its side rails with cloth to protect the wall. Scaffolding can be constructed with ladders and planks; for large setups, you can rent more elaborate scaffolding from a supplier. Keep in mind that you needn't fall far to hurt yourself, so read and follow the basic safety rules given here.

▶ SAFE PRACTICES ◀

▷ Read all instructions that come with the ladder, including load capacity restrictions.
▷ Never use a broken or damaged ladder.
▷ Keep all ladders away from electrical wires, especially outdoors.
▷ Never overlap the two sections of an extension ladder by less than four rungs.
▷ If you set up a ladder or scaffold in front of a door, lock or bar the door.
▷ On a slippery floor, position a nonslip rug under the ladder's feet; on uneven terrain, slide a board under one of the ladder's feet.
▷ Always lock stepladder braces.
▷ Wear shoes with well-defined heels and soles that provide a secure grip.

▷ Never work with two people on a ladder.
▷ Climb a ladder with both hands free; have materials handed to you or haul them up in a pail on a rope.
▷ Climb only as high as the third step from the top; never stand on the braces, extension arms, or paint shelf.
▷ Center your weight between the rails.
▷ Periodically check a stepladder's brace fastenings, and tighten them if loose.
▷ Clean paint and joint compound from the ladder steps after each use.
▷ Store a ladder horizontally in a dry place. If you hang it, support it at three or more points along its length.

Stepladder

Position ladder so feet are level and steady on floor. For balance, lean your body into ladder. When you can no longer comfortably reach work surface, get down and move ladder. Don't overreach, or ladder may topple.

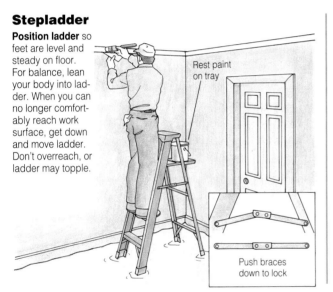

Rest paint on tray

Push braces down to lock

Scaffolding

Construct scaffold from strong, straight 2 x 10 or 2 x 12 plank set between two stepladders. Extend plank at least 1 ft. beyond steps. For spans over 5 ft., double planks for extra strength.

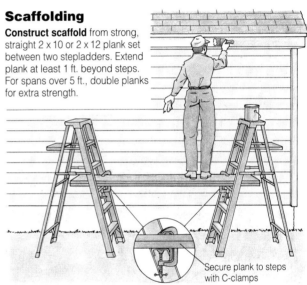

Secure plank to steps with C-clamps

Extension ladder

To raise, set unextended ladder on ground with its feet near foundation, and walk up, hand over hand, against wall. When ladder is in position, extend to desired height and pull base out to correct angle.

Angle ladder so distance between its feet and wall equals one-fourth the ladder's height. Both feet should be an equal distance from the wall, so that ladder does not rock. On a hard or slippery surface, have a helper hold the ladder steady.

¼ ladder's height

Haul up supplies with container on rope, or have someone hand them to you. Hang paint cans and supplies from notched pole that fits through top rung of ladder.

Notched PVC pipe inserted in ladder rung

PAINTING WITH BRUSHES

You can paint the woodwork in a room first, then mask it off (p.290) and paint the ceiling and walls. Or if you are wary of splattering newly painted trim, begin by painting the ceiling and walls, and paint the woodwork last. When painting large surfaces, first use a 2- or 3-inch brush to outline, or "cut in," around windows, doors, and other trim and at the intersections of ceilings and walls where a roller can't reach. Then cover the remaining surface using a wide brush or a roller (pp.294–295). Paint windows and exterior doors early so you can close them at night without the paint sticking.

Start painting in a corner near a window. For an even coat, use the entire tip of the brush to apply the paint. Hold the brush in a comfortable grip, your thumb supporting its underside, but shift your grip now and then to avoid fatigue. When you need to reload the brush with paint, smooth out, or "feather," your strokes by gradually lifting the bristles off the work surface during the stroke. To avoid lap marks, work toward the most recently painted section, slightly overlapping the wet edges. Don't take time off in the middle of an unbroken section; you may end up with color variations.

Using a paintbrush

Load brush, covering one-third of bristle length. To remove excess paint, lift brush straight up and slap it lightly against inside of can. Don't drag brush over rim.

Cut in at ceiling with narrow edge of brush if wall and ceiling colors are different. Keep paint off adjacent surface; remove smudges with a putty knife wrapped in paper towel.

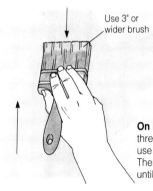

Use 3" or wider brush

On large areas, apply paint with two or three overlapping diagonal brush strokes; use largest brush that is comfortable. Then feather paint with vertical strokes until coverage is smooth.

At corners, around woodwork, and wherever roller won't reach, cut in using width of brush. Work slowly to prevent splatters.

Caring for a paintbrush

Remove excess paint with a brush comb before washing brush. Alternatively, work brush back and forth across newspaper.

Brush comb

Wash latex paint out of brush with warm water, separating bristles with your fingers. For alkyd paint, clean with mineral spirits.

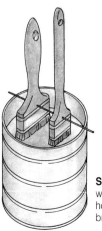

Store brushes overnight in water or paint thinner by drilling hole in handle and suspending brush on piece of stiff wire.

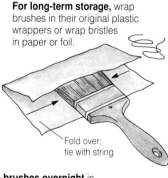

For long-term storage, wrap brushes in their original plastic wrappers or wrap bristles in paper or foil.

Fold over; tie with string

Painting a window

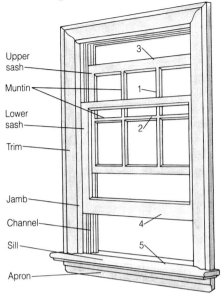

Upper sash
Muntin
Lower sash
Trim
Jamb
Channel
Sill
Apron

Work order: First remove locks and handles. Paint vertical muntins, then horizontal, then the rest of the sash. For double-hung windows, paint as much of upper sash as possible, reverse the sash positions, and paint lower parts of upper sash. Then paint lower sash. Finally, paint jamb, apron, sill, and trim. If you paint sash channels, sand them first. To prevent sashes sticking, move them while paint is still wet.

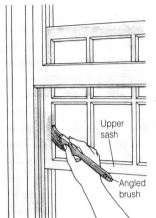

Upper sash

Angled brush

Begin in middle of unpainted area, using 1½-in. sash brush. Brush out in both directions, then stroke toward wet areas. For convenience, put paint in small container.

Lower sash

Check sash corners occasionally for paint buildup and drips—remove by gently dabbing with dry brush. Remove drips at muntin intersections in same way.

Painting a door

Frame
Jamb
Rail
Stile
Wedge

Work order: Before painting, remove or cover doorknob and firmly prop door open with pair of wedges. If door is new, paint bottom edge before hanging, to prevent wood from absorbing moisture and warping. Paint side and top edges of door first. Then paint panel edges. Follow with panel surfaces. Finish with rails, then stiles.

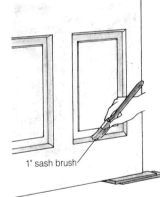

1" sash brush

For panels, paint edge with 1-in. sash brush, working from top to bottom. To prevent drips, dab paint into corners.

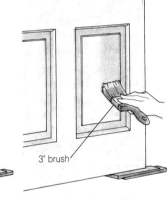

3" brush

Paint panel surfaces with 2- or 3-in. brush, working from center of panel to edge. Feather strokes to smooth paint.

Painting trim

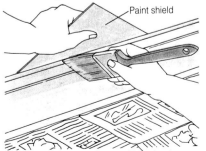

Paint shield

Protect adjacent surfaces with a plastic or metal shield, wiping it frequently with a clean cloth. Paint with the wood grain; use two coats.

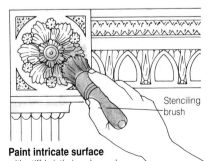

Stenciling brush

Paint intricate surface with stiff-bristle brush, such as a stenciling brush. Force paint into all crevices; remove paint buildups and drips.

Match the thickness of a roller's nap to your job. A ½-inch nap is fine for most flat and semigloss paints on smooth surfaces; for high-gloss paint, choose a ¼-inch nap or a foam roller sleeve. For textured paint (p.299) or concrete, use a ¾-inch nap. Before painting, dampen a roller with water (for latex) or mineral spirits (for alkyd), then blot excess on paper towels.

A power roller requires the same techniques as a manual roller. Even though its speed makes it a tempting investment, the time needed to clean it may cancel out any savings in application time. Painting pads are less messy than rollers, but they can be slower to use. Certain pads are handy for painting over irregular surfaces or over textured paint and for reaching tight spots (p.298); edger pads make it easy to get clean coverage next to trim.

Apply each coat of paint without interruption so that wet paint won't overlap dry. If you must stop, do so at a natural break in the surface, such as a window or door. When painting new wallboard, wait for the first coat of paint to dry, then fill visible seams and repairs before applying the next coat.

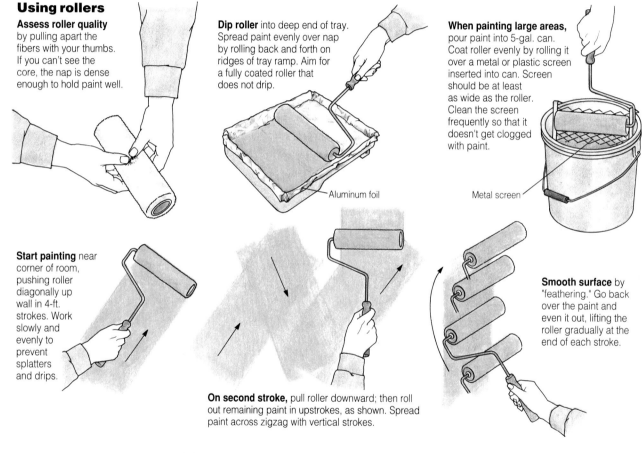

Using rollers

Assess roller quality by pulling apart the fibers with your thumbs. If you can't see the core, the nap is dense enough to hold paint well.

Dip roller into deep end of tray. Spread paint evenly over nap by rolling back and forth on ridges of tray ramp. Aim for a fully coated roller that does not drip.

Aluminum foil

When painting large areas, pour paint into 5-gal. can. Coat roller evenly by rolling it over a metal or plastic screen inserted into can. Screen should be at least as wide as the roller. Clean the screen frequently so that it doesn't get clogged with paint.

Metal screen

Start painting near corner of room, pushing roller diagonally up wall in 4-ft. strokes. Work slowly and evenly to prevent splatters and drips.

Smooth surface by "feathering." Go back over the paint and even it out, lifting the roller gradually at the end of each stroke.

On second stroke, pull roller downward; then roll out remaining paint in upstrokes, as shown. Spread paint across zigzag with vertical strokes.

Cleaning and storing

Remove excess paint with curved side of brush comb. Then wash roller cover with soap and hot running water (for latex paint) or with mineral spirits (for alkyd paint). Wear rubber gloves while rubbing mineral spirits into nap.

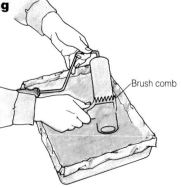

Brush comb

Store cover when dry, wrapped in paper or aluminum foil. If you use plastic, punch a few air holes in it to prevent damage caused by damp or mildew.

Painting ceilings and walls

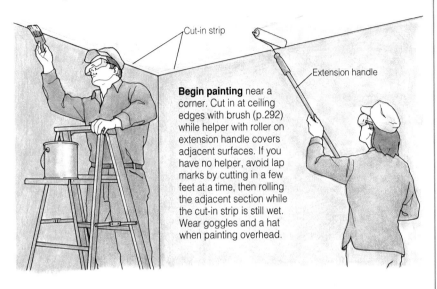

Begin painting near a corner. Cut in at ceiling edges with brush (p.292) while helper with roller on extension handle covers adjacent surfaces. If you have no helper, avoid lap marks by cutting in a few feet at a time, then rolling the adjacent section while the cut-in strip is still wet. Wear goggles and a hat when painting overhead.

Roll on paint in diagonal strokes, as shown on facing page. Cover only a 3-ft. section at a time; then feather the surface to even out coverage. Move from a dry section into a wet one, overlapping edges to prevent streaks. Roll slowly to minimize splattering.

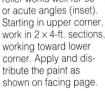

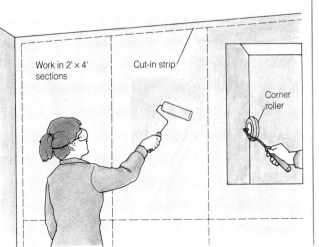

Cut in and paint walls after ceiling. A corner roller works well for 90° or acute angles (inset). Starting in upper corner, work in 2 × 4-ft. sections, working toward lower corner. Apply and distribute the paint as shown on facing page.

Work in 2' × 4' sections

Cut-in strip

Corner roller

Painting with pads

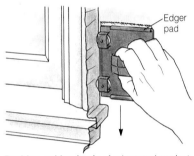

Pad paint tray

Before loading pad, dampen it first (with water for latex paint, mineral spirits for alkyd paint). Then press it into paint until fibers are saturated. Blot off excess on tray's ridges.

Edger pad

Position guide wheels of edger pad against trim, and paint with long, straight strokes. Move pad in one direction only, not with the back-and-forth motion you'd use with a brush.

Clean pad by blotting it on paper to remove paint. Then rinse in water (for latex paint) or mineral spirits (for alkyd paint).

Blot pad on newspaper to remove excess moisture; then air-dry thoroughly. Wrap in paper or aluminum foil for storage.

PAINTING WITH SPRAYERS

Spray-painting saves time, especially when you need to paint irregular surfaces such as fences and furniture, but it takes some practice before you can produce an even, drip-free coating. A typical sprayer requires more paint than a brush or roller for the same surface. And all sprayers require thorough cleaning after use. Before buying or renting a sprayer, balance these factors against the reduced painting time. If you do decide to spray, match the tool to the job. For instance, the 1-quart airless paint sprayer shown here may

not be suitable for painting an exterior (pp.306–307). Although most paints can be sprayed, some sprayers can't spray thick paints. Have the sprayer's operation explained by your dealer or rental agent, and request an instruction manual in case problems arise.

Before filling the sprayer, strain the paint (p.285) to avoid clogging the nozzle; then thin the paint by about 10 percent with water or paint thinner, depending on the type of paint. Select the correct nozzle and clear it of any debris. Because spraying produces a lot

of overspray, mask all surfaces you want to protect. Practice your technique on scrap material. If the paint is thin enough, it will evenly cover the surface in an elliptical pattern.

Caution: A paint sprayer forces paint out at high pressure; you can cause serious injury by actually injecting paint into your flesh. Never point a sprayer at anyone or anything other than the surface you wish to paint. Unplug the sprayer before filling, cleaning, or servicing it. Always wear the appropriate respirator (p.13).

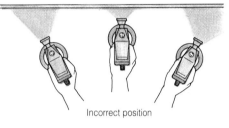

Incorrect position

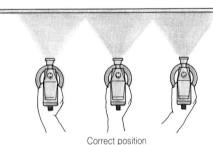

Correct position

Move spray gun parallel to surface, at a distance of about 1 ft. To maintain even coverage, keep sprayer upright and bend your wrist; don't swing sprayer in an arc.

Overlap each pass by about a third of its width (right), stepping from side to side (rather than overreaching) to keep sprayer aimed directly at surface; don't tilt sprayer. If your arm tires, support the sprayer with both hands.

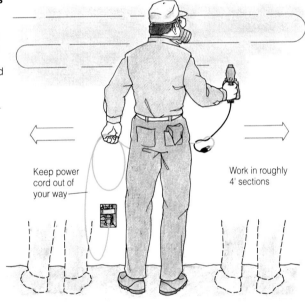

Keep power cord out of your way

Work in roughly 4' sections

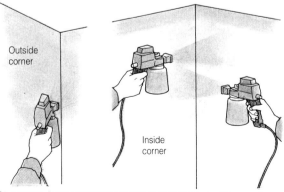

Outside corner

Inside corner

At corners, keep spray gun moving to feather edges of sprayed area. For outside corners, aim directly at intersection of walls; for inside corners, aim at each wall in turn. If ceiling and wall colors differ, cut in at top of wall (p.292).

Extension   Cut in where colors differ

Spray ceiling or floor with a flexible extension. (Paint should be of thinner consistency than for regular spray nozzle.) Support base of sprayer with one hand.

Stick   Provide plenty of masking material

Cover intricate shapes with horizontal strokes. To avoid drips, spray past the edges of object on each pass. For a shutter, hold slats open with a stick.

PAINTING STAIRWELLS

Reaching the ceiling and upper walls of a stairwell usually requires scaffolding. You can rent scaffolding or make your own with 2 × 10 or 2 × 12 planks supported on a combination of sawhorses, extension ladders, and stepladders. Buy the planks at a lumberyard; make sure they're straight and knot-free.

For extra strength on spans longer than 5 feet, double the planks; don't try to span a gap longer than 10 feet without extra support from beneath. When erected, the scaffold planks should be level and should extend beyond the end supports by at least 1 foot. Clamp or nail the planks to their supports. To reduce the risk of falling, position the scaffold no farther than your body's width from the wall and as you work, keep the scaffold free of extra paint, tools, and materials.

Mask and cover the area under and beyond the edge of the work platform. Paint balusters and railings with paint mitts, steps with brushes and small rollers. Cut in around ceilings and walls as you would normally (p.292).

Caution: When working at heights, follow the safety information given on page 291, in particular making sure that your platform is secure. To prevent a ladder from slipping, nail a wooden cleat to the floor to brace its feet (if possible, lift up any carpet to do this). Block access to the stairs, and either leave doors wide open or block them closed to prevent them from being opened into the scaffold.

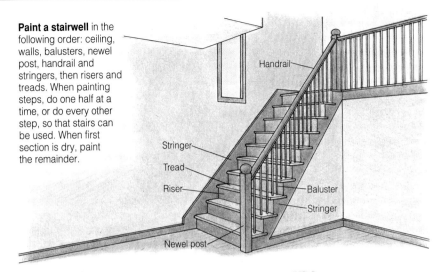

Paint a stairwell in the following order: ceiling, walls, balusters, newel post, handrail and stringers, then risers and treads. When painting steps, do one half at a time, or do every other step, so that stairs can be used. When first section is dry, paint the remainder.

Handrail
Stringer
Tread
Riser
Baluster
Stringer
Newel post

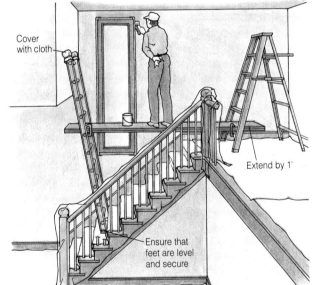

Cover with cloth

Extend by 1'

Ensure that feet are level and secure

Rig a tall scaffold to reach upper wall area by arranging step- and extension ladders as shown. Lodge the extension ladder firmly against a step riser; wrap rails with cloth to protect walls. Run two 2 × 10 or 2 × 12 planks between the ladders, securing them to the rungs with clamps or nails. If space is limited at upper part of stairway, use a stepladder or sawhorse leaned against the upper wall.

Leveling attachment

Some aluminum and fiberglass extension ladders have leveling attachments for positioning the ladder on an uneven surface.

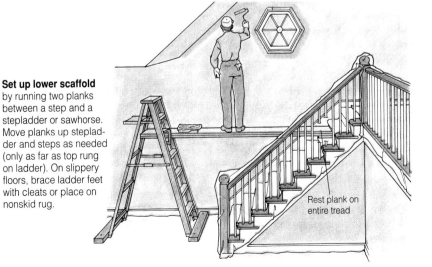

Set up lower scaffold by running two planks between a step and a stepladder or sawhorse. Move planks up stepladder and steps as needed (only as far as top rung on ladder). On slippery floors, brace ladder feet with cleats or place on nonskid rug.

Rest plank on entire tread

Most paint jobs include at least one hard-to-reach area or an irregular surface. While it's possible to paint almost anything with a combination of brushes and rollers, some items require the special techniques or tools shown below.

Reaching all the surfaces of kitchen and bathroom cabinets can be difficult; to maneuver more easily in tight spaces, try a brush with a short handle. Before painting cabinets,

remove the doors, drawers, and hardware, and wash all surfaces. Lightly sand new or previously painted wood. To prevent warpage from uneven moisture absorption, use an equal number of coats of paint on all the cabinet's surfaces.

An airless sprayer (p.296) will quickly paint decorative metalwork and louvered shutters, but you can get similar, if slower, results with a paint mitten or a flexible paint pad.

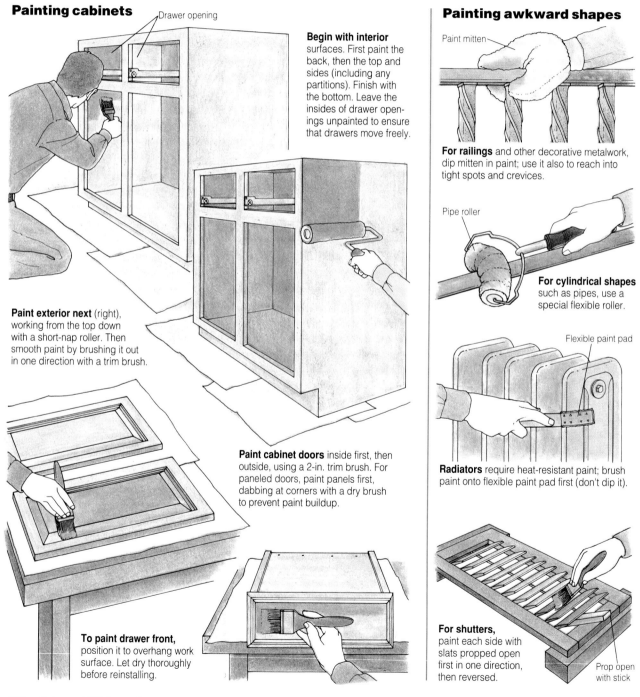

Painting cabinets

Drawer opening

Begin with interior surfaces. First paint the back, then the top and sides (including any partitions). Finish with the bottom. Leave the insides of drawer openings unpainted to ensure that drawers move freely.

Paint exterior next (right), working from the top down with a short-nap roller. Then smooth paint by brushing it out in one direction with a trim brush.

Paint cabinet doors inside first, then outside, using a 2-in. trim brush. For paneled doors, paint panels first, dabbing at corners with a dry brush to prevent paint buildup.

To paint drawer front, position it to overhang work surface. Let dry thoroughly before reinstalling.

Painting awkward shapes

Paint mitten

For railings and other decorative metalwork, dip mitten in paint; use it also to reach into tight spots and crevices.

Pipe roller

For cylindrical shapes such as pipes, use a special flexible roller.

Flexible paint pad

Radiators require heat-resistant paint; brush paint onto flexible paint pad first (don't dip it).

For shutters, paint each side with slats propped open first in one direction, then reversed.

Prop open with stick

PAINTING WITH TEXTURED PAINT

In addition to providing a decorative surface, textured paint hides cracks and other flaws in walls and ceilings. Once applied, it's difficult to remove, but it can be freshened or its color changed with a coat of paint. After you apply the textured paint, pattern it with the simple techniques shown. Premixed latex paints have a thinner texture; powder that you mix with water or latex paint provides a heavier coat.

Before applying the textured paint, practice your pattern on heavy cardboard. Fill any large holes or dents in the surface of the wall (pp.288–289); the paint itself will fill minor flaws. Prime the wall with an appropriate primer, and apply the textured paint. Let it dry for the time specified on the label; then create the final pattern. Before painting textured paint another color, let the finished pattern dry for 24 hours.

Applying textured paint

Mix textured paint to desired consistency. With specified roller, cover 3-ft.square sections until paint is 1/16 in. thick. Create pattern (below); then cover next 3-ft. section.

To color the texture, paint over it with flat latex. First cut in around trim and wall edges with a brush. Dab paint into all crevices, then smooth it out.

For remaining surfaces, use a roller fitted with 3/4-in.-nap roller cover. Roll on latex paint in W or M shape; then fill in spaces. Alternative is to use a paint sprayer (p.296).

A selection of patterns

Circular pattern. Position a slightly damp natural sponge against paint, then rotate.

Ridges. Rake notched trowel across paint in curved or straight motion.

Fine ridges. Comb paint with large-tooth plastic or metal hair comb.

Adobe look. Dab and twist paint slightly with concrete finishing trowel or putty knife.

Swirls. Twist stiff-bristled brush against paint; softer bristles create more subtle look.

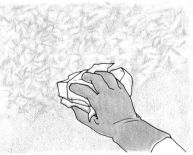

Stipple. Repeatedly place crumpled piece of wax paper or plastic against paint.

With a few improvised tools, glaze that you make yourself, and the techniques shown here, you can decorate surfaces in a variety of ways. More subtle than patterned wallpapers and more elaborate than plain painted surfaces, decorative paint finishes can dramatically alter the appearance of a room. You can treat a whole room or, as is more common, use one effect to accent a single wall, an architectural detail, a piece of furniture, or a craft item.

Glaze is a semitransparent paint that you apply over a base coat. The glaze is *distressed* in such a way that the base coat shows through the glaze unevenly, creating a pattern. The most common technique is to brush or roll the glaze over the base coat, then distress it (facing page), resulting in a smooth, subtle finish. You can also apply the glaze over the base coat with the distressing tool, producing a more clearly defined pattern. Or you can combine these techniques, using several paints or glazes of different colors for a multilayered effect.

Formulas for concocting the glaze abound; a simple, effective recipe that combines alkyd paint, solvent, and glazing liquid is given below. (If you can't find glazing liquid at your paint store, ask them to order it.) Because it's difficult to match consecutive batches exactly, always mix a bit extra. The base coat over which you put the glaze can be either latex or alkyd, but it should have a satin or semi-gloss luster.

Let a new base coat dry for 24 hours before you apply the glaze. Alkyd glazes dry slowly, giving you time to distress the glaze. Latex glazes dry fast, and thus are recommended only for small areas or items.

Once the glaze is dry, you can apply a clear varnish, which provides a protective coating and gives the surface its final sheen. Varnish is almost always used when marbling (p.302), and on furniture or craft objects.

Before choosing a finish, consider the condition of the surface. Combing, stippling, and dragging produce a linear effect that can highlight any imperfections in the surface. Before tackling a project, practice your technique on mat board. Mask and prepare the room as you would for any painting job (p.290). For an entire room, work on one wall, then its opposite, to avoid overlaps in the corners.

Caution: Alkyd-base products are potentially toxic and have strong fumes, so wear a respirator (p.13) and rubber gloves when handling them. Work in a well-ventilated area, keep pets and children away, and dispose of materials properly (p.307).

Making your own glaze

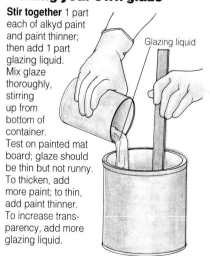

Stir together 1 part each of alkyd paint and paint thinner; then add 1 part glazing liquid. Mix glaze thoroughly, stirring up from bottom of container. Test on painted mat board; glaze should be thin but not runny. To thicken, add more paint; to thin, add paint thinner. To increase transparency, add more glazing liquid.

Glazing liquid

Applying glaze

Glaze

Base coat

On walls, roll glaze over base coat in 2- to 3-ft. vertical strips; then brush it out in one direction, feathering overlaps (p.292) to avoid dark edges. Have helper follow closely behind you, distressing glaze before it dries.

For a linear glazing pattern, such as combing or dragging, smooth glaze over base coat in vertical strokes, then distress.

Foam paint pad

For random distressing techniques, or for marbling (p.302), apply glaze with brush or foam pad, making short angled strokes in all directions.

Ways of distressing glaze

Simple distressing.
Dab firmly at glaze with a paper towel, a clean lint-free cloth, or a piece of lightweight plastic. To keep the pattern random, rotate material in your hand often. Periodically expose clean surface of material or change to a fresh piece.

Sponging. Pat solvent-dampened sea sponge against surface, frequently changing its position in your hand. Hold the sponge delicately, without squeezing it. Man-made sponge gives a more defined, regular look.

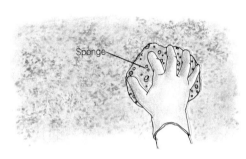

Sponge

Stippling. Firmly press stippling brush (or less expensive stainer's brush) into wet glaze; for crisp pattern, avoid sliding. Frequently wipe glaze off brush with clean cloth. Keep bristles at right angle to surface.

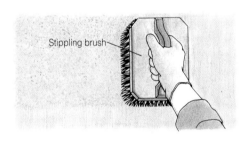

Stippling brush

Rag-rolling. For pattern resembling crushed velvet, shape a clean lint-free cloth about 1 ft. square into a loose sausage shape, and roll it down the surface in vertical strips. Overlap the strips slightly.

Combing. Place steel or rubber comb at 45° angle to surface; drag down to etch pattern into glaze, forming straight, wavy, or zig-zag lines, as you prefer. Don't overlap rows; clean comb at end of each row. Use comb with narrow teeth for tight spots.

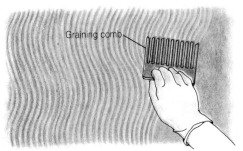

Graining comb

Spattering

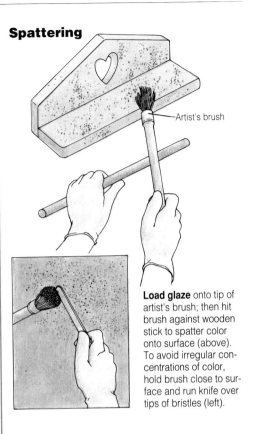

Artist's brush

Load glaze onto tip of artist's brush; then hit brush against wooden stick to spatter color onto surface (above). To avoid irregular concentrations of color, hold brush close to surface and run knife over tips of bristles (left).

Dragging

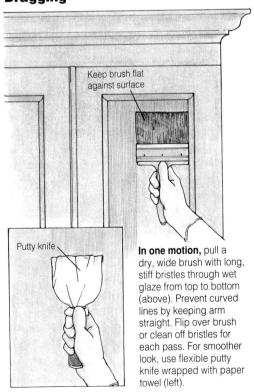

Keep brush flat against surface

Putty knife

In one motion, pull a dry, wide brush with long, stiff bristles through wet glaze from top to bottom (above). Prevent curved lines by keeping arm straight. Flip over brush or clean off bristles for each pass. For smoother look, use flexible putty knife wrapped with paper towel (left).

MARBLING

The easiest way to create the look of marble is to gradually build up a clouded effect over a base coat with one or two colors of glaze, blending them with distressing tools to create a subtle effect. After this clouding has dried, use a feather or an artist's brush to paint on the glaze veins.

Two often-reproduced marbles are *verde* (which is shown here and has a black base with green clouding and gray veins) and *Carrera* (composed of a white base with light gray clouding and medium gray veins).

Before beginning to work, assemble the tools and glazes (pp.300–301) you will need. Then practice your technique (especially the veins) on a sample board. Refer to a real piece of marble or to a photograph for help in making your "marble" realistic.

Good marbling projects for beginners are objects that could actually be made of marble, such as tabletops or fireplace mantels. If you choose to tackle a larger area, such as a wall or a floor, divide it into 1-foot-square sections and work on one at a time. However, for a realistic effect, flow the clouding and veins across the sections.

Just about any paintable surface can be marbled, as long as it is clean and smooth. Remove old paint only if it is thick or flaking. Sand the surface smooth with fine abrasive paper, and then apply the base coat, which can be either latex or alkyd enamel paint (but make sure that it is compatible with the existing surface).

Most marbled projects are finished with several coats of clear oil- or water-base varnish (p.168), to enhance the deception. All varnishes yellow somewhat with age, oil-base ones more than water-base. This can eventually dull a marbling job, so a water-base varnish is preferable. A too glossy finish will highlight any surface irregularities. Ask your paint dealer about the best type of varnish for your marbling project.

Caution: When you are working with alkyd-base glazes, follow the safety measures described on page 300.

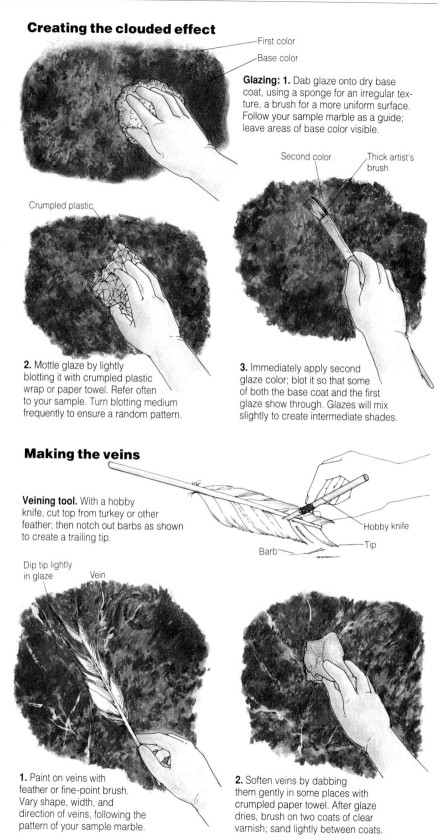

Creating the clouded effect

First color
Base color

Glazing: 1. Dab glaze onto dry base coat, using a sponge for an irregular texture, a brush for a more uniform surface. Follow your sample marble as a guide; leave areas of base color visible.

Crumpled plastic

Second color — Thick artist's brush

2. Mottle glaze by lightly blotting it with crumpled plastic wrap or paper towel. Refer often to your sample. Turn blotting medium frequently to ensure a random pattern.

3. Immediately apply second glaze color; blot it so that some of both the base coat and the first glaze show through. Glazes will mix slightly to create intermediate shades.

Making the veins

Veining tool. With a hobby knife, cut top from turkey or other feather; then notch out barbs as shown to create a trailing tip.

Hobby knife
Tip
Barb

Dip tip lightly in glaze
Vein

1. Paint on veins with feather or fine-point brush. Vary shape, width, and direction of veins, following the pattern of your sample marble.

2. Soften veins by dabbing them gently in some places with crumpled paper towel. After glaze dries, brush on two coats of clear varnish; sand lightly between coats.

STENCILING

Creating the stencil

Draw design on paper, indicating colors of elements. For symmetrical design, fold paper over, draw half the design, and cut. (You can also draw the design directly on acetate with lead or wax pencil.)

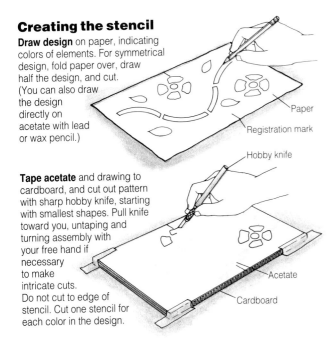

Paper

Registration mark

Hobby knife

Tape acetate and drawing to cardboard, and cut out pattern with sharp hobby knife, starting with smallest shapes. Pull knife toward you, untaping and turning assembly with your free hand if necessary to make intricate cuts. Do not cut to edge of stencil. Cut one stencil for each color in the design.

Acetate

Cardboard

Marking the wall

Mark horizontal guideline for top of stencil. Use a level, and mark very lightly with a sharp, hard lead pencil.

Walls, ceilings, floors, furniture, and decorative objects all can be made brighter or given a more traditional look with the application of a stenciled pattern. This pattern can be a continuous border, a design that completely covers a surface, or simply an accent for a focal point. You can purchase stencils ready-made, copy a design from a pattern book (available at paint and art supply stores), or create your own design. Enlarge or reduce the pattern as necessary (p.338).

Stenciling requires few materials. If you're making your own stencil, you'll need acetate or stencil paper. Acetate is easier to cut, and because it's transparent, it's easier to align with registration marks. Protect the work surface with heavy cardboard, and cut out the stencil with a sharp hobby knife.

When painting, tape stencils to the surface with drafting tape. Paint the stencil with either special stencil paint or artist's acrylics. Thin paint can bleed behind the stencil and smudge, so if necessary, thin the paint just to a creamy consistency with paint thinner (for oil-base paint) or water (for latex paint). Apply the paint with a stippling brush or, for a more mottled look, a sponge. You can stencil on most surfaces, but for best results, stencil over flat latex or alkyd paint.

Follow the steps at left to measure and mark out registration marks along a horizontal wall border, fine-tuning the spacing as necessary to compensate for uneven walls or obstacles. Complete one color at a time, and let the paint dry before positioning the stencil sheet for the second color—wet paint can easily be smudged. If you have a complicated design (even if using only one color), you can also avoid smudging by "leapfrogging" around the room, doing every other stencil repeat. When you have finished, go around the room again to fill in the missing spaces.

Registration mark

Length of stencil

Divide each wall by length of stencil to determine number of pattern repeats. Adjust spaces between repeats to avoid awkward pattern breaks at corners and obstacles. Lightly pencil registration marks along horizontal guideline, working out from center of each wall to both corners.

Painting the stencil

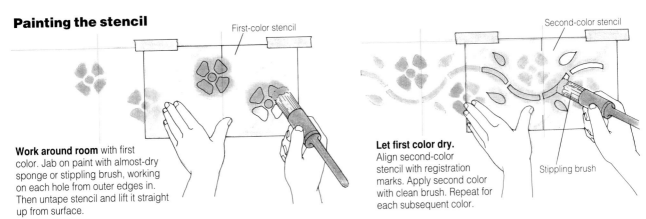

First-color stencil

Second-color stencil

Work around room with first color. Jab on paint with almost-dry sponge or stippling brush, working on each hole from outer edges in. Then untape stencil and lift it straight up from surface.

Let first color dry. Align second-color stencil with registration marks. Apply second color with clean brush. Repeat for each subsequent color.

Stippling brush

If you spend time properly preparing your house for painting, you'll be rewarded with professional-looking, durable results. Start by diagnosing any problems. For example, peeling paint on the wall outside a kitchen can indicate a need for improved ventilation. Mildew may be caused by heavy shade or overgrown shrubbery; trim the trees and shrubs, and choose a paint containing a mildewcide.

With the drawing below as a guide, work your way around the house, making repairs as needed. Then remove hardware (such as a mailbox or lamps), shutters, awnings, and storm windows. Cover the perimeter with canvas or plastic drop cloths (taking care not to damage delicate plants); enclose every-

thing else you don't want painted, such as electric meters, in plastic bags.

All surfaces must be thoroughly cleaned. A rented power washer is fast and also removes most peeling paint. Then prime all bare wood, repairs, and chalking surfaces. (Chalking produces a fine light powder that can stain dark wood or masonry; power-washing will remove it, but you must prime in order to prevent it from recurring.) Select a primer based on the recommendations of your paint manufacturer. An alkyd primer followed by two coats of flat exterior latex is suitable for most siding; a glossier paint is often used for trim. To ensure a strong bond between the paint and the primer, paint the house within two weeks of priming it.

To calculate the number of gallons of paint needed per coat, multiply the house's height by its perimeter, then divide the result by the coverage on the paint can. Buy 1 gallon of trim paint for every 5 gallons of siding paint. Pick a dry, clear day to paint. Start with the siding, then paint the trim and windows. Finish with doors, porches or decks, thresholds, steps, and shutters.

Caution: Wear goggles when sanding and scraping paint; and unless you are certain that the paint does not contain lead (p.307), wear a respirator (p.13). Dispose of all debris properly. When power-washing, wear goggles and protective clothing, and aim only at wood or masonry—the spray can break glass or injure someone.

Preparing to paint

Gutters, downspouts. Clean out debris; repair leaks (p.197); tighten hangers. Remove downspouts to paint them and gain access to corners.

Wood trim. Repair damaged wood. Renail loose pieces. Fill large gaps with caulk (facing page).

Stone, masonry. Replace missing pieces; repair crumbling mortar joints (pp.248–249). Let new mortar cure at least 60 days before painting. Do not paint stone.

Wood siding. Repair and recaulk. Set protruding nailheads and fill holes with putty; seal rusting nails with shellac. Prime any areas of bare wood.

Flashing. Replace missing or damaged pieces; repair holes (p.197); apply caulk or roofing cement around seams.

Fascia boards and soffits. Repair damaged wood; fill gaps with caulk. Clean off any mildew (facing page).

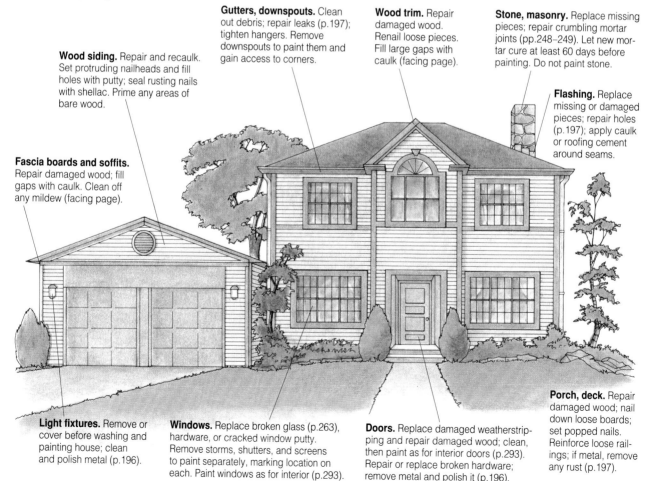

Light fixtures. Remove or cover before washing and painting house; clean and polish metal (p.196).

Windows. Replace broken glass (p.263), hardware, or cracked window putty. Remove storms, shutters, and screens to paint separately, marking location on each. Paint windows as for interior (p.293).

Doors. Replace damaged weatherstripping and repair damaged wood; clean, then paint as for interior doors (p.293). Repair or replace broken hardware; remove metal and polish it (p.196).

Porch, deck. Repair damaged wood; nail down loose boards; set popped nails. Reinforce loose railings; if metal, remove any rust (p.197).

Cleaning exterior surfaces

Car brush attachment

Remove dirt from small areas with garden sprayer; for tougher stains, use car brush attachment. Scrub mildew with solution of 1 qt. bleach, ⅓ c. household detergent (no ammonia), and 3 qt. warm water.

Wand

Wash large areas with rented power washer rated between 1,200 and 2,500 pounds per square inch (for cedar shingles, rent a less powerful washer). For badly soiled siding, add nonphosphate trisodium to water. Hold wand at 45°, if possible, and at least 1 ft. from surface, working up from bottom of house to avoid streaking. Wait 2 days before painting.

Preparing exterior surfaces

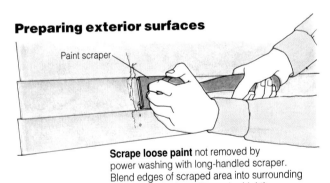

Paint scraper

Scrape loose paint not removed by power washing with long-handled scraper. Blend edges of scraped area into surrounding paint by feathering with sander (right).

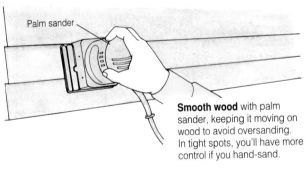

Palm sander

Smooth wood with palm sander, keeping it moving on wood to avoid oversanding. In tight spots, you'll have more control if you hand-sand.

Cut tip at 45° angle

Scrape joints between siding and window or door trim; remove old, crumbling caulk. Refill joints with paintable caulk. Add caulk under windowsills and thresholds.

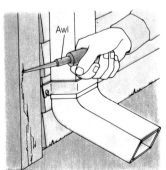

Awl

Probe rotted wood with awl to determine depth of damage. If minor, sand or scrape down to sound wood. Powdered wood and tiny holes indicate insect damage; consult a professional.

Fill deep rot pockets with epoxy wood filler, after mixing according to product instructions. Sand dried filler before painting it.

PAINTING THE EXTERIOR

When all the surfaces of your house are clean and smooth, you are ready to begin priming and then painting. To avoid unattractive lap marks in the finish coat (caused by the edge of a paint stroke drying out before you overlap it with the next stroke), work on the shady side of the house so that the sun won't dry the paint too quickly. Begin at the top of the walls and work down, moving from left to right, and try to work from one natural break to the next, such as from a window to a door. Where there are no natural breaks, paint across the width of the house, coating only as many courses of siding as will allow you to keep blending the paint before it dries.

After completing the walls, tackle the other parts of your house, following the order of work described on page 304. Paint doors and windows the same way as their interior counterparts (p.293). When painting the edges of an exterior door, match the color of the hinge edge to the color of the exterior, the color of the latch edge to the interior trim. When painting steps, porches, or decks, block off their entrance with sawhorses or rope to prevent traffic over wet paint.

Fences and other outdoor structures are probably best painted with a paint sprayer. A portable sprayer (p.296) will cover small areas, but a larger airless or compressor-type sprayer will speed major jobs. Select one with a capacity of at least 5 gallons and a long hose. If you rent the sprayer, ask the rental agent to show you how to use and clean it. Read the information given on page 296 before beginning.

Siding

Begin by coating bottom edge of each course of boards with a brush. Clear up drips immediately with your brush. Do several courses at a time.

Next, paint along length of each course with short strokes of wide brush. Force paint into any cracks. To avoid lap marks, do entire course before starting next one.

Shingles

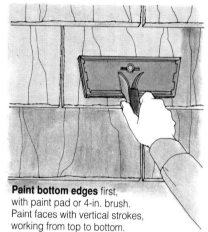

Paint bottom edges first, with paint pad or 4-in. brush. Paint faces with vertical strokes, working from top to bottom.

Exterior trim

Hold trim guard over areas adjacent to trim to protect them from paint. Alternatively, cover these areas with masking material.

Porch or deck

Use soft broom (with synthetic bristles) to force paint into gaps between widely spaced boards.

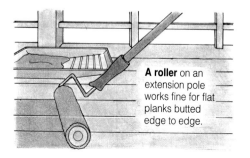

A roller on an extension pole works fine for flat planks butted edge to edge.

Concrete

Apply masonry paint by stroking a 4- to 6-in. coarse-bristle brush first in one direction, then the other. Force paint into angles and surface irregularities. Mask base of railings with tape.

Using a sprayer

Spray siding or shingles in two steps. Paint bottom edges first (inset). To paint the faces, hold spray gun 8 to 10 in. from surface and at right angle to it (p.296). For even application, overlap strokes by about one-third on each pass.

For fences, furniture, and other items that don't have solid surfaces, choose a wind-less day and block overspray with a shield such as a large piece of cardboard braced against a ladder.

Wear goggles and a respirator

Hold gun upright

Cover shrubbery

Paint sprayer

Spray bottom edge of each course with gun held side-ways as shown. Then hold gun upright to finish siding.

Cardboard

Cleanup and disposal

The worst way to dispose of leftover paints and solvents is to pour them down the drain or onto the ground, where they can contaminate the groundwater supply. Ideally, try to have as little leftover material as possible by buying only the amount you'll need (pp.284–285), even if a smaller quantity is more expensive.

If you are saving extra paint for future touch-ups or other projects, pour it into a container matched in size to the amount of liquid (this helps prevent it from drying out). Never re-place the contents of a container with-out giving it a new label. Keep paints and solvents in a locked cabinet out of the reach of children. Linseed oil is highly combustible; store it in a tightly

sealed metal or glass container in a cool, dark area.

Before disposing of leftover latex paint, let the paint in the can dry completely; any cloth or paper covered with paint should also be allowed to dry before you discard it. Some munic-ipalities let you put such materials in your regular garbage; others want them treated as hazardous waste and provide a pick-up service or a drop-off depot. Check with your local authority.

Always keep alkyd paints, solvents, and used tools and materials for your area's hazardous waste pick-up. Never throw tools or cans that contain wet alkyd paint or solvent into the trash, because the liquid could spontaneously combust. To recyle solvents, pour the

used liquid into a container, seal it, and allow the paint particles to settle out. Then pour off the clean solvent for reuse. Add cat litter, sawdust, or sand to the residue, let it dry completely, and dispose of it with your hazardous waste.

Any house built prior to 1980 may contain lead paint, which is extremely toxic if inhaled as dust or vapor or if ingested as chips. Children are especially susceptible to lead poisoning. Unless you are sure the paint on your house is lead-free, consult a contractor who specializes in lead paint removal. Any lead-paint scrapings, dust, or other debris is considered toxic waste; it should be handled and disposed of according to local regulations.

WALLCOVERINGS

Because of the wide variety of patterns and styles available, choosing a wallcovering can be difficult. Before selecting a covering for a particular room, consider its dominant architectural style and its furniture and furnishings; the covering should be compatible with its surroundings.

The covering's color, pattern, texture, and overall design will influence a room's look. "Advancing" warm and dark colors make surfaces appear closer or larger, whereas "receding" cool colors make surfaces seem farther away or smaller.

Vertical stripes or patterns with an upward movement add height. Borders and friezes can be used effectively near ceilings, as chair rails, and as frames around architectural elements to enhance or alter a room's appearance.

Generally, choose patterns in proportion to the room size, and if you're mixing coverings, keep the colors alike but vary the pattern sizes. Don't forget to look at the whole picture, especially if rooms flow into one another. And remember that many coverings have companion fabrics and borders.

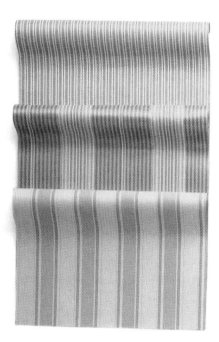

Stripes (left) are easy to match. But if the walls are bumpy or aren't plumb, the straight lines will show up these defects.

Random patterns (right) don't need matching unless one side of the sheet is "shaded" (darker than the other). Wall defects will not be as noticeable as with striped coverings.

Small patterns (below, left) are best used in small areas, such as in a kitchen where cabinets leave little uncovered wall space, but they can also be used in large rooms with matching upholstery. When hanging sheets, some patterns will match straight across; others are drop patterns—the sheets must be staggered to align the patterns.

Large patterns (below, center and right) are best suited to big rooms. Light colors are less likely to overwhelm the room. You may want to use a large pattern on one wall and a smaller related pattern on the other walls.

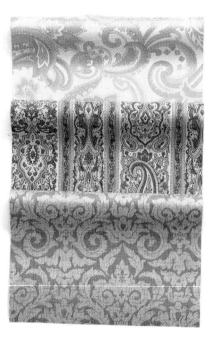

High-relief and expanded vinyls are embossed. High-relief vinyls (top three) have patterns that stand out noticeably; apply paint after hanging the covering. Expanded vinyl (bottom) is raised slightly to add texture.

Natural-look coverings include string, burlap, and grass-cloth materials. Although the textures don't require matching, the color will vary from roll to roll. The individual rolls may also "shade." Before hanging these coverings, arrange the sheets to match the color.

Exotic coverings include, from top to bottom, rice paper backed with paper (unbacked versions have a translucent look); ceramic chips and false stone (their bumpy surfaces make it more difficult to cut clean seams); and cork, which should be hung over a lining.

Lining (right) is necessary under silk, unbacked fabrics, cork, foils, and Mylar. It gives a smooth, uniformly porous surface that has a neutral pH. It may also eliminate shrinkage and absorb excess moisture.

Plaster-saturated coverings are ideal for covering wallboard, concrete block, cracked plaster, and other problem walls.

Borders are made to complement wallcoverings and to be used by themselves as trim on painted walls. They may have, for instance, floral designs or patterns that appeal to young children, or the borders may be embossed to imitate architectural details.

CHOOSING WALLCOVERINGS

Three kinds of patterns

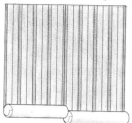

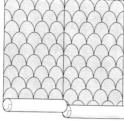

Random match. Easy to hang; design either may not align or may align anywhere.

Straight-across match. Easy to hang; design flows across strips when top edges align.

Drop match. Harder to hang; design runs diagonally; every other strip aligns at ceiling.

Creating illusions with wallcovering

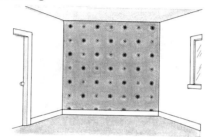

Create a cozy feeling in a high-ceilinged room by adding a wide border at the top and bottom of the walls.

Foreshorten a long, narrow room by covering one short wall; choose a pattern that is in scale with the room proportions.

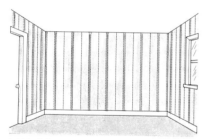

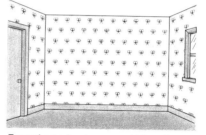

Add height to a room by choosing a vertical pattern, but avoid straight-line designs if walls are badly damaged.

Expand a confined space, or hide wall irregularities, by covering the walls with a medium-size overall pattern.

Estimating quantity

Find square footage of room by multiplying length by width, multiplying the result by 2, and then multiplying that result by the room's height. To determine number of rolls needed, divide square feet of room by that of roll; then add 1 roll. Straight-across patterns with large repeats may require extra rolls.

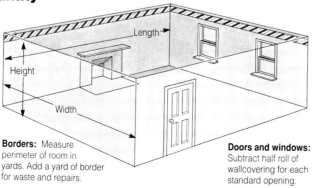

Borders: Measure perimeter of room in yards. Add a yard of border for waste and repairs.

Doors and windows: Subtract half roll of wallcovering for each standard opening.

Wallcoverings are categorized by the base material, or ground, onto which the design is printed—it may be paper, vinyl, or fabric. Often this ground provides the background color for the design. In thicker products, the ground is laminated to a backing, or substrate; in thinner ones the ground and the substrate may be one and the same. Other terms you may come across when shopping for wallcovering refer to ease of care and removal. *Washable* coverings can be sponged off with mild detergent; *scrubbable* ones can withstand more vigorous scrubbing (p.319). Both the ground and the substrate of a *strippable* material can be removed, but the substrate of a *peelable* covering must be removed separately (p.312).

When choosing wallcovering, take along some fabric samples and paint chips from the area you are decorating. If you plan to mix two patterns, remember that the colors must match but the scale needn't; in fact, the greater the difference in scale, the better. Even a flowered border can complement a striped covering if the colors are a good match. Keep durability (see table) and ease of installation in mind. Many coverings come prepasted; you can either cover the back with water or soak the strips in a water tray. Cover the back of unpasted wallcoverings with the appropriate adhesive.

The sample book or the roll's packaging should indicate the amount of wall space a roll will cover. A single standard roll contains about 36 square feet; European wallcoverings come in metric sizes. (To convert square metres into square feet, multiply the square metres by 10.8; multiply square feet by 0.09 to get square metres.) To avoid color variations, make sure all rolls have the same lot number. (To minimize variations between strips on some random-match patterns, install them with alternate strips reversed top to bottom.) Take sample swatches of your choices home and tape them to the wall for 24 hours to judge them under changing lighting conditions.

Sorting out wallcoverings

Type	Description	Typical location	Ease of hanging	Cleaning	Durability	Cost*
Paper	Traditional wallcovering; consists of single layer of patterned or colored paper	Dry medium- to low-wear areas, such as living rooms, bedrooms	Medium (tends to tear easily)	Non-washable	Poor	$
Vinyl-coated paper	A paper substrate with a thin layer of vinyl sprayed on during manufacture. Usually prepasted. Strippable	Any room	Easy	Medium	Medium	$
Fabric-backed vinyl	Fabric substrate covered with solid vinyl ground	Any room	Easy	Easy	Very durable	$$
Solid vinyl	These have a paper or fabric substrate onto which has been laminated a solid vinyl film	High-wear areas such as children's and recreation rooms, or rooms prone to moisture, such as bathrooms, laundry rooms, and kitchens	Medium	Easy	Very durable	$$$
Expanded vinyl	During manufacture the surface of a solid vinyl sheet is "expanded," raising relief patterns for an embossed look. Sometimes called "foamed vinyl"	Medium-wear areas, such as bedrooms, living rooms, dining rooms. Good for uneven surfaces	Easy	Medium	Medium	$$
High-reliefs (Lincrusta, Anaglypta)	Molded wallcoverings with highly defined relief patterns. Some are permanently attached to the surface; others are used for borders	Good for cracked or uneven surfaces	Medium to difficult (requires painting after mounting). Some require professional installation	Medium	Very durable	$$$
Mylar	Metallic-looking wallcoverings with paper or fabric substrate. May have a thin vinyl coating	Smooth surfaces only. Used for decorative effect in hallways, small rooms. Bright sun or lighting creates undesirable reflective glare	Difficult **	Medium	Medium	$$
Hand prints, screen prints	Handmade patterns applied over wall-covering with paper or fabric substrate. Most have thin vinyl coating over pattern. Paint texture creates relief in some; others can be custom-colored	Dry low-wear surfaces	Difficult **	Medium	Least durable	$$$
Naturals	Made of grass cloth, string, or other material over paper substrate	Clean, dry low-wear surfaces	Difficult **	Non-washable	Poor	$$$
Cork	Layers of cork over paper substrate. Available in varying thicknesses and textures	Low-wear surfaces where additional sound insulation is desired.	Difficult **	Medium	Medium	$$$
Fabrics	Wallcoverings made of a textile or fabric, usually with no substrate	Clean, dry low-wear surfaces	Difficult **	Non-washable	Poor	$$$
Rice paper	Translucent type has no substrate; opaque type has paper substrate. Usually has a thin vinyl coating	Low-wear surfaces	Difficult **	Non-washable	Poor	$$$
Ceramic chip, false stone	A layer of tiny rough chips or flakes on a paper substrate	Medium- to low-wear areas, such as living rooms, bedrooms	Difficult	Non-washable	Poor	$$$
Plaster-saturated	Gypsum-saturated material. Can be covered with other wallcovering	Damaged, unsightly surfaces	Difficult	Easy	Very durable	$$
Lining paper	Unpatterned paper or fabric. Often applied under delicate specialty coverings or used to cover damaged surfaces	Damaged or uneven surfaces, or wherever specified for installation under specialty coverings	Easy (pp.312–313)	Not necessary	Very durable	$

*Cost: $—Inexpensive, $$—Medium price range, $$$—More expensive
** Requires professional installation

Although you can apply new wallcovering over old, it's generally better to strip off the old covering and adhesive (and if you are hanging vinyl wallcovering, it's essential). Buy a commercial remover product from your wallcovering supplier or a home center; follow the manufacturer's instructions for mixing it into a solution.

To remove built-up layers of wallcovering, or covering that has been painted over, rent a steamer from your wallcovering supplier or a home center. Learn how to operate the steamer before leaving the store, and check occasionally during use to make sure that the water tank doesn't run dry. Follow all safety instructions included with the tool, and wear goggles and gloves.

Whatever stripping method you choose, protect the room (p.290) before starting. Lay a disposable drop cloth on the floor and tape it to the baseboards; then cover it with newspapers to absorb the solution. When you have finished, gather up the papers in the drop cloth and dispose of them.

If your walls are rough-textured or damaged, disguise the flaws by choosing a high-relief or fabric-backed vinyl covering. Even after repairing holes and dents (pp.288–289), you may need to cover irregular surfaces with

Removing wallcovering

Pull down, not straight out.

For strippable and peelable coverings: Loosen covering at corner and gently peel each strip from wall. For peelable covering, soak remaining substrate and adhesive with wallcovering remover for 10 min., then scrape with wide putty knife.

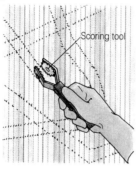

Scoring tool

Stripping with solution: 1. First score covering in crisscross pattern with scoring tool or utility knife so that solution can penetrate to the adhesive layer. Be careful not to damage wallboard or plaster.

2. Roll or sponge solution onto walls (or spray onto surface with a tank-type garden sprayer). Let soak into covering for amount of time specified on remover's label. When paper bubbles up, it's ready to be stripped.

3. Soak tight spots (such as corners or narrow strips beside cabinets) by applying solution with a plastic spray bottle.

Wallcovering scraper

4. Scrape off wallcovering with scraper or wide putty knife. Then saturate adhesive with remover solution and scrape off. Rinse surface with clean hot water; allow it to dry; then apply sealer or size.

Using a steamer

Steamer

1. Fill unit with clean water before plugging it in. Steamer is ready to use when vapor emerges from holes in baseplate.

Baseplate

2. Hold steamer against (but not touching) surface for 15 sec. or until area around plate is moist. Scrape with scraper or wide flexible putty knife with one hand while steaming adjacent area with the other.

Stiff nylon brush

3. After scraping, clean surface by scrubbing with nylon brush and solution of either phosphate-free cleaning products or 1 part bleach to 4 parts water. Allow surface to dry; then apply sealer or size.

lining paper. This improves both the appearance and the adhesion of a wall-covering, and it is essential for certain delicate coverings. Leave a ¹⁄₁₆-inch gap at the edges and seams of lining paper, and plan the wallcovering seams to fall elsewhere than on the paper seams.

Some surfaces should also be prepared with a primer/sealer. A sealed wall is uniform and will prevent moisture and residue from affecting the covering's adhesive. A "universal" acrylic latex primer is easy to clean up and can be tinted to match the background of the wallcovering. Use it in high-moisture areas such as bathrooms and over new wallboard, existing wallcoverings that cannot be removed, and surfaces that have been repaired.

You can also improve the adhesion of a wallcovering by first applying liquid *size* to a prepared wall. In addition, size makes it easier to slide the wallcovering into place. Size is not required if you use a premixed vinyl adhesive.

Wash painted surfaces with detergent or phosphate-free trisodium. (The latter gives "tooth" to glossy surfaces, improving the adhesion of the wallcovering.) Rinse with clean water and let dry. After preparing the surfaces, paint the ceiling and trim to avoid splattering paint on the new wallcovering.

Applying sealer and size

Spread sealer or size evenly over surface with short-nap roller or 6-in. paste brush. Allow to dry for 1 hr. before hanging wallcovering.

After repairing painted walls, cover repairs with sealer, then wash walls.

Hanging lining paper

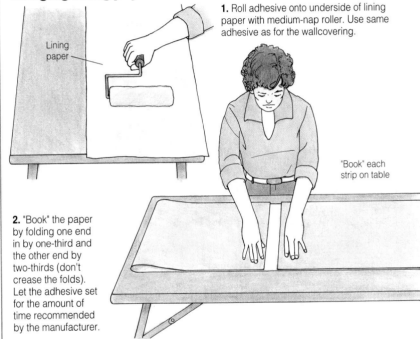

Lining paper

1. Roll adhesive onto underside of lining paper with medium-nap roller. Use same adhesive as for the wallcovering.

"Book" each strip on table

2. "Book" the paper by folding one end in by one-third and the other end by two-thirds (don't crease the folds). Let the adhesive set for the amount of time recommended by the manufacturer.

Begin at plumb line

3. Carry liner to wall and unfurl on wall as you smooth it with a 12-in. smoothing brush. Leave a slight space at wall edges and trim.

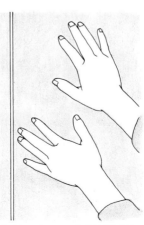

4. Do not butt strips at seams. Let paper dry for 36 hr., or until it does not indent when pressed with a finger.

INSTALLING WALLCOVERING

Planning the layout

Plan a mismatch in an inconspicuous corner. You may start hanging at this point, or use it as an end point, beginning directly across the room and working back toward it, first from one direction, then the other.

If pattern is large or room has strong focal point or wall, center a strip (or seam) at its center. Work out from both sides until you reach the end point.

Mark location of each strip around room with level (mark width of strip on level with tape). Rearrange guidelines as needed to avoid awkward pattern breaks and so that strips at corners will be no less than 3 in. wide.

To guide installation, snap chalked plumb line at starting point for each wall.

Before you begin, establish both where you will start and where you will finish hanging the strips, and decide how you will handle potentially awkward areas such as corners and around windows and doors (pp.316–317). To help prevent errors, pencil in guidelines to indicate the placement of each strip. Because paper and prepasted strippable wallcoverings may expand up to ½ inch when wet, you must determine a strip's true width before marking guidelines. To do so, cut a 2-inch strip from the roll, briefly submerge it in water, and let it expand for 10 minutes; then measure its new width.

Some wallcoverings have arrows printed on the back to indicate which way the pattern should run. Decide how you want to break the pattern at the intersection of the wall and the ceiling; it's usually best not to cut through a design element, particularly if the design is strong. Remember that you'll be adding 2 inches to both the top and the bottom of each strip for trimming at the ceiling and baseboard, so factor this into your measurements. For a drop-match pattern, align the second strip to the first by eye before cutting it (facing page). Cutting a drop-match pattern from alternating rolls reduces waste; with a straight-match pattern you can cut as many strips as possible from each roll.

Check for any flaws in each roll by rerolling it in the opposite direction; this also helps to uncurl and loosen the wallcovering. Plan to cut and paste two strips of covering first—then if there are no problems, continue to cut several strips at a time (most manufacturers will not accept returned rolls from which more than two strips have been cut). Sometimes unpatterned or textured wallcoverings will be overinked, and thus slightly darker, along one edge. To even out the color across the wall, turn every other strip upside down so that similarly shaded edges meet.

To hang unpasted covering, you'll need a good-size work table and a paint roller or paste brush for applying the paste. Choose the type of paste recommended by the wallcovering manufacturer, and follow the directions for mixing it; a kitchen whisk is useful for stirring out lumps.

You can purchase a special water tray in which to wet a prepasted covering. Follow the instructions on the wallcovering about soaking time; oversoaking can cause some of the adhesive to wash away. An alternative to soaking a prepasted covering in a tray is to place the covering on the table and use a damp paint roller to wet the back of the strip thoroughly. Don't add any paste to a prepasted wallcovering; it may be incompatible with the existing adhesive.

After hanging each strip, smooth out any air bubbles with a 12-inch smoothing brush (choose short bristles for vinyl, longer for paper) or a plastic smoother; you'll also need a seam roller to smooth seams and edges. As you finish hanging each strip, sponge off excess adhesive with clean water, then dry the covering with a clean cloth. It's best to keep all surfaces clean while you're working; if you try to remove dried adhesive later, you can damage the covering.

Cutting a drop-match covering

Cut strip from first roll (A) to length plus 2 in. at top and bottom (for trimming), using utility knife and straightedge. Mark top with T. Weight down strip to prevent it slipping off table.

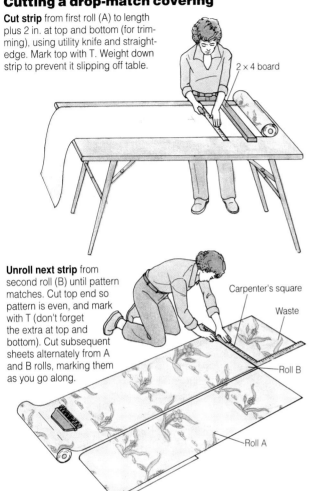

2 × 4 board

Unroll next strip from second roll (B) until pattern matches. Cut top end so pattern is even, and mark with T (don't forget the extra at top and bottom). Cut subsequent sheets alternately from A and B rolls, marking them as you go along.

Carpenter's square

Waste

Roll B

Roll A

Pasting the strips

Reroll prepasted covering from bottom to top (with pattern facing in), and submerge in water tray (right) for about 10 sec. Or unfurl strip on table and wet back with saturated paint roller (see box below).

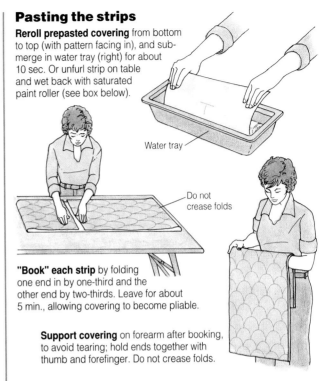

Water tray

Do not crease folds

"Book" each strip by folding one end in by one-third and the other end by two-thirds. Leave for about 5 min., allowing covering to become pliable.

Support covering on forearm after booking, to avoid tearing; hold ends together with thumb and forefinger. Do not crease folds.

"Book" end

For unpasted covering, keep extra adhesive off work surface (where it could damage the covering) by working out from center of strip toward surface edge, repositioning covering as shown. Make sure to paste all edges completely.

Hanging the covering

Plumb line

Align first strip against plumb line, smoothing upper section first and overlapping ceiling by 2 in. (left). Then unbook and position lower section. Work out air bubbles from center to edges with smoothing tool. Trim top and bottom by holding straightedge tool against end and cutting with utility knife (below).

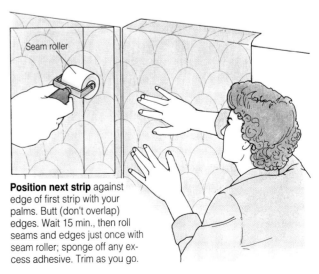

Seam roller

Position next strip against edge of first strip with your palms. Butt (don't overlap) edges. Wait 15 min., then roll seams and edges just once with seam roller; sponge off any excess adhesive. Trim as you go.

SPECIAL WALLCOVERING TECHNIQUES

Fitting around doors and windows

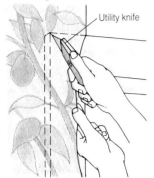

Let strip hang over door or window. Cut to rough shape, leaving 2 in. extra all around for trimming. Then make a diagonal cut from the outer corner of the frame.

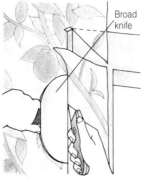

Smooth the covering into place against side of frame; then trim away excess with razor or utility knife, guiding the blade against a tool with a straight edge.

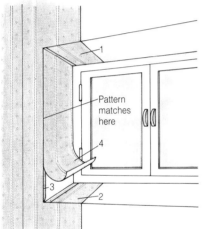

Recessed window. Let strip hang over recess. Cut horizontal line to 1 in. from edge of recess; then cut and paste to upper (1) and lower (2) parts of recess. Trim at edges. Paste 1-in. vertical flap around side edge (3). Cut an additional strip of covering to fit side of recess (4), making sure to match the pattern with strip on wall. Overlap this strip at upper and lower edges.

The walls of most rooms are likely to present some challenges; at the very least, you'll have to fit wallcovering around one door and usually one window. Use the techniques shown here to make clean edges at windows, doors, fireplaces, built-in bookcases, and cabinets. Never try to measure and precut wallcovering around obstacles. It is much easier to fit when it's up, and if you make a mistake, there's usually time to reposition the wallcovering before it dries.

The broad, unobstructed surface of a typical ceiling makes it relatively easy to hang wallcovering there, but because you have to work overhead, the job can be tiring. If possible, enlist the aid of a helper to unfold the wet strips and hand them to you for positioning and smoothing. A sturdy scaffold (p.291) is a necessity for most ceiling work. If you plan to cover both the ceiling and the walls, do the ceiling first; otherwise, you may damage the finished walls.

When you are using a patterned wallcovering on both ceiling and walls, remember that you will probably be able to achieve a perfect match at only one wall/ceiling intersection, so make this match at the most conspicuous place. Mismatches are less obvious in small random patterns.

If you are working on stairwell walls, you may need to stand on a scaffold (p.297). While you are on the scaffold, fitting the covering to the upper part of the wall, have a helper stand on the stairs below to fit and smooth each strip to the lower part of the wall. Be especially careful not to splash water from a wallcovering tray onto a scaffold or ladder, where it could easily cause you to slip.

Covering a room's switchplates to match the walls is a common way to finish off a wallcovering job. If you don't want to cover the plates yourself, you can buy kits at your wallcovering store that allow you to simply insert a piece of the covering behind a clear plate.

Turning a corner

Inside corner: 1. Measure from edge of last strip to corner at top, middle, and bottom; cut the next strip ⅛ in. wider than the widest dimension.

2. Hang cut strip, wrapping ⅛ in. around corner. Measure narrowest part of remainder of cut strip; mark plumb line on new wall this distance from corner.

3. Position remainder of strip with factory (uncut) edge against plumb line. Smooth covering into corner on top of ⅛-in. overlap. Trim at top and bottom.

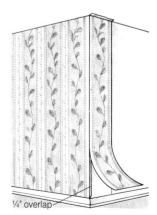

Outside corner. Measure first strip as for inside corner, but add ¼ in. allowance for corner overlap. Plumb second wall and hang strip as for inside corner.

Covering ceilings

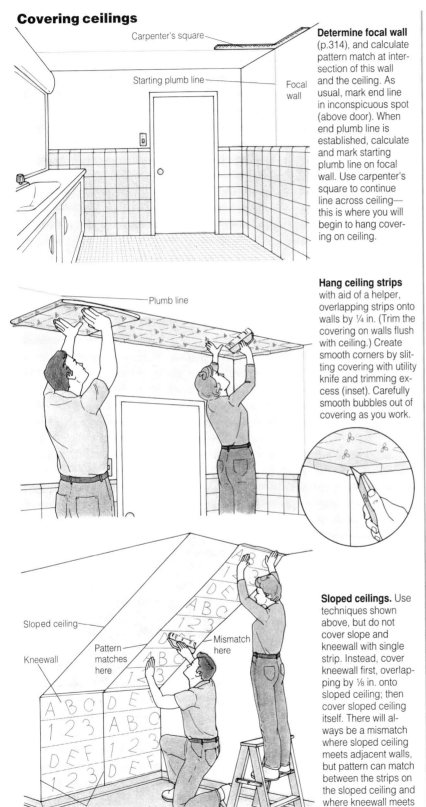

Determine focal wall (p.314), and calculate pattern match at intersection of this wall and the ceiling. As usual, mark end line in inconspicuous spot (above door). When end plumb line is established, calculate and mark starting plumb line on focal wall. Use carpenter's square to continue line across ceiling—this is where you will begin to hang covering on ceiling.

Hang ceiling strips with aid of a helper, overlapping strips onto walls by ¼ in. (Trim the covering on walls flush with ceiling.) Create smooth corners by slitting covering with utility knife and trimming excess (inset). Carefully smooth bubbles out of covering as you work.

Sloped ceilings. Use techniques shown above, but do not cover slope and kneewall with single strip. Instead, cover kneewall first, overlapping by ⅛ in. onto sloped ceiling; then cover sloped ceiling itself. There will always be a mismatch where sloped ceiling meets adjacent walls, but pattern can match between the strips on the sloped ceiling and where kneewall meets adjacent walls.

Covering curved archways

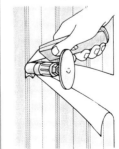

1. Trim covering on both sides of arch, leaving a 1-in. band to wrap into arch.

2. Cut V-notches in band about ½ in. apart, leaving ¼ in. between notch tops and band top. Smooth notched covering around edge with damp sponge.

3. Cover arch with two pieces cut to exact width. Make a matching seam at midpoint.

Working around obstacles

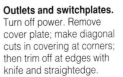

Fixtures. Cut from closest seam to fixture; fold covering back and trim around fixture, using notch-shaped cuts. Press covering down; roll seam.

Outlets and switchplates. Turn off power. Remove cover plate; make diagonal cuts in covering at corners; then trim off at edges with knife and straightedge.

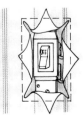

A border near the ceiling can make a room feel cozier; at chair-rail height it makes a room feel loftier. Borders can also add interest to a plain room (particularly a child's room), fill a narrow space between cabinet tops and the ceiling, or frame windows and doors. As with any wallcovering, first take home samples so that you can check them with your decor and lighting.

Prepare painted walls by sanding them with fine sandpaper. Then wash away the dust and apply a coat of wall-covering primer. On covered walls, coat the area that will accept the border with wallcovering primer (with tack). Apply a border over new wall-covering only after the latter has dried for at least 48 hours. However, if you allow for the border while planning the wallcovering layout, you can then cut each wallcovering strip to allow the border to be inset above or within it. This method yields smoother seams, but it also requires more time and skill.

Borders are usually sold in 5-yard rolls. Cut pieces the length of each wall, plus ¼ inch to wrap into the corners. To avoid awkward design placement at corners or obstacles, calculate the border's positioning before you hang it. If the border will frame a window or a door, avoid the problem of having a directional pattern going sideways or upside down by selecting a random pattern. When framing with a border, miter the corner seams, as shown. Use only an adhesive recommended by the border manufacturer.

Hanging a border

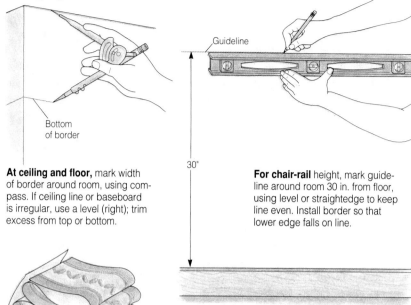

At ceiling and floor, mark width of border around room, using compass. If ceiling line or baseboard is irregular, use a level (right); trim excess from top or bottom.

For chair-rail height, mark guideline around room 30 in. from floor, using level or straightedge to keep line even. Install border so that lower edge falls on line.

Wet or paste border, depending on type (p.315); then fold accordion-style and "book" it for several minutes. Fold loosely; do not crease the folds.

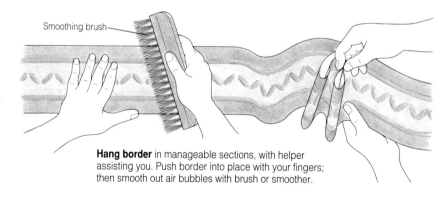

Hang border in manageable sections, with helper assisting you. Push border into place with your fingers; then smooth out air bubbles with brush or smoother.

Making tight seams

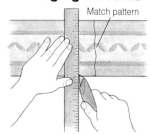

Butting seams: 1. Overlap ends; cut through both layers with a utility knife along a straightedge.

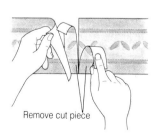

2. Remove cut pieces of both layers. Smooth ends in place with sponge; wait 15 min.; then roll seam smooth.

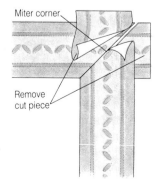

Miter-cut corners by overlapping pieces, then cutting through both layers at 45° angle (left). Remove cut pieces of both layers, and roll seam smooth (below).

CARING FOR WALLCOVERINGS

Clean wallcoverings twice a year, following the manufacturer's directions. Wash scrubbable coverings with a brush and mild detergent; washable coverings can be lightly rubbed with a solution of water and mild detergent applied with a damp cloth or a nearly dry sponge. You can vacuum some cloth and flocked wallcoverings with a brush attachment, but delicate wallcoverings such as silk or burlap (p.311) must be cleaned by a wallcovering professional. Commercial cleaning solutions are also available for various types of wallcovering. Whichever product or technique you choose, first test-clean a small patch in an inconspicuous area to ensure the cleaner won't stain or damage the wallcovering.

Many stains on nonwashable coverings can be removed with either an artist's gum eraser or wallcovering cleaning dough (available at wallcovering stores). Stroke the eraser or dough downward against the wallcovering, overlapping strokes until the stain lifts off. As the material picks up dirt, turn it to expose a fresh surface.

To remove grease or wax, cover the stain with blotting paper or paper towels, and iron over it on low heat for several seconds. Repeat, using clean paper each time, until the spot is gone. If this doesn't work, wipe the stain with cheesecloth dampened with turpentine. If ironing causes the wax from crayons to be absorbed, gently rub off the colored residue with moistened baking soda on a damp cloth.

Stains that can't be removed any other way may be patched (below). Whenever you redecorate, save extra wallcovering for this purpose; but remember that due to aging, a patch is bound to be a slightly different shade than the installed wallcovering. Use ordinary premixed wallpaper paste or seam adhesive for patching.

Loose or torn seams and edges

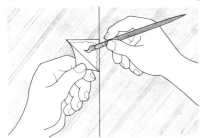

1. Brush adhesive onto wall surface and underside of covering. Press covering into place and hold for several minutes.

2. Smooth flat, and remove excess adhesive with a slightly dampened sponge. Roll seam after 15 min.

Fixing bubbles

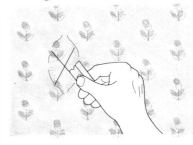

Slit bubble in X-pattern with razor blade, fold back edges, and tweezer or brush out any grit. Insert adhesive as shown at left; smooth with sponge.

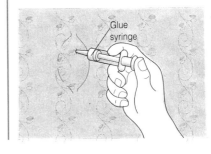

Glue syringe

For glue syringe, (often available in a kit), first make small slit with razor blade. Press out air; inject adhesive. Smooth area with seam roller or sponge.

Patching a hole or stain

Damage

Patch

Cut patch 3 in. larger than damaged area, making sure pattern matches. Tape patch over damage with drafting tape.

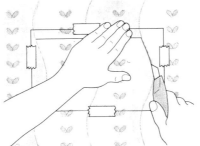

Cut through both layers beyond edge of damaged area. If possible, cut along design elements to disguise cut lines.

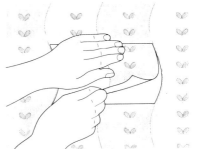

Remove both layers of wallcovering, scraping old covering if necessary (p.312). Paste patch in position; after 15 min., roll edges.

WOOD FLOORING

More resilient than stone or tile, wood flooring has a natural warm appearance that enhances almost any home. It's available in blocks, strips, and planks (either solid or laminated); the flooring is sold unfinished, which requires sanding and finishing, and it's also available prefinished. The final look of the floor will depend on what you choose: the type of floor-ing (planks or blocks), the species and grade of the wood, and the finish. Because some building codes require specific materials, such as hardwood or a urethane finish, speak with a qualified flooring specialist before making your selection. Be sure to describe the intended use of the flooring as well as what you want visually.

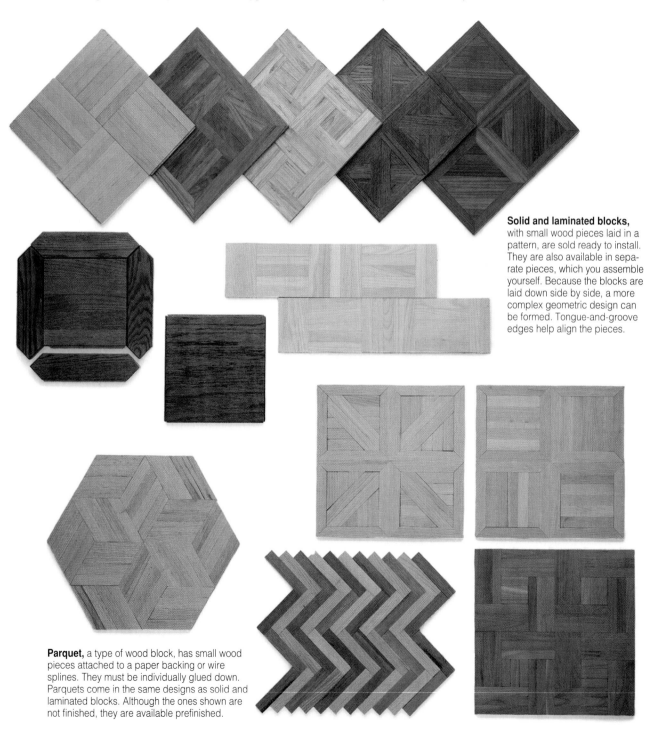

Solid and laminated blocks, with small wood pieces laid in a pattern, are sold ready to install. They are also available in separate pieces, which you assemble yourself. Because the blocks are laid down side by side, a more complex geometric design can be formed. Tongue-and-groove edges help align the pieces.

Parquet, a type of wood block, has small wood pieces attached to a paper backing or wire splines. They must be individually glued down. Parquets come in the same designs as solid and laminated blocks. Although the ones shown are not finished, they are available prefinished.

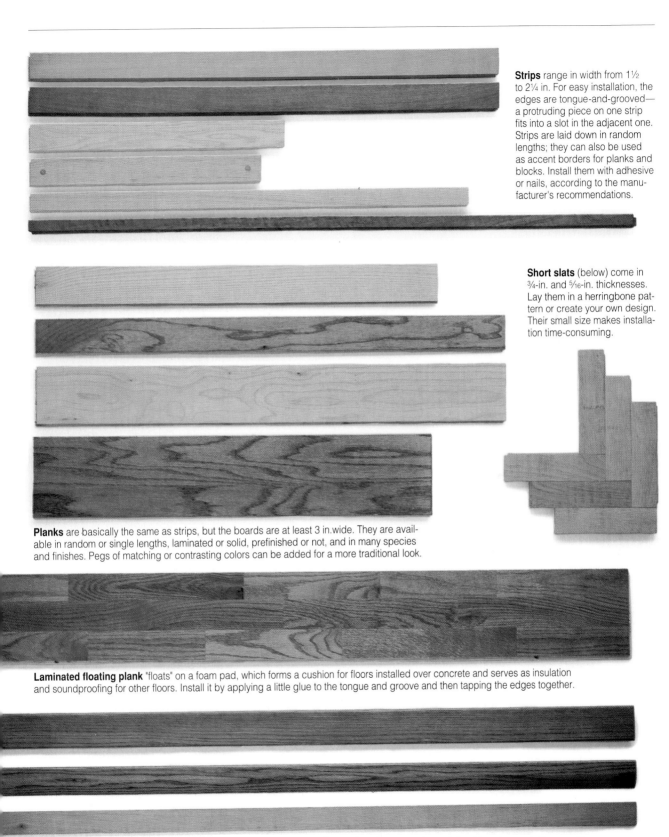

Strips range in width from 1½ to 2¼ in. For easy installation, the edges are tongue-and-grooved—a protruding piece on one strip fits into a slot in the adjacent one. Strips are laid down in random lengths; they can also be used as accent borders for planks and blocks. Install them with adhesive or nails, according to the manufacturer's recommendations.

Short slats (below) come in ¾-in. and 5⁄16-in. thicknesses. Lay them in a herringbone pattern or create your own design. Their small size makes installation time-consuming.

Planks are basically the same as strips, but the boards are at least 3 in.wide. They are available in random or single lengths, laminated or solid, prefinished or not, and in many species and finishes. Pegs of matching or contrasting colors can be added for a more traditional look.

Laminated floating plank "floats" on a foam pad, which forms a cushion for floors installed over concrete and serves as insulation and soundproofing for other floors. Install it by applying a little glue to the tongue and groove and then tapping the edges together.

Reducer strips create a transition between two types of flooring at different elevations: one of wood; the other of ceramic tile, carpeting, vinyl, or another wood. These strips are useful where two rooms, such as a dining room and living room, flow into each other.

Because it is affordable and easy to install and maintain, resilient flooring is a good choice for bathrooms and kitchens. Today's resilient flooring is usually made of vinyl (the actual vinyl content varies from product to product). It's available in 9- and 12-inch square tiles and in 6- and 12-foot-wide rolled sheets. Tiles are either solid vinyl or a vinyl composition; the latter resists stains better. Sheet flooring has a base layer topped with a vinyl resin or, for added scuff resistance, a vinyl resin–urethane or vinyl resin–melamine finish; it may be cushioned with a high-density foam. Designs with texture and color variations are better at concealing seams, scratches, substrate irregularities, and dirt.

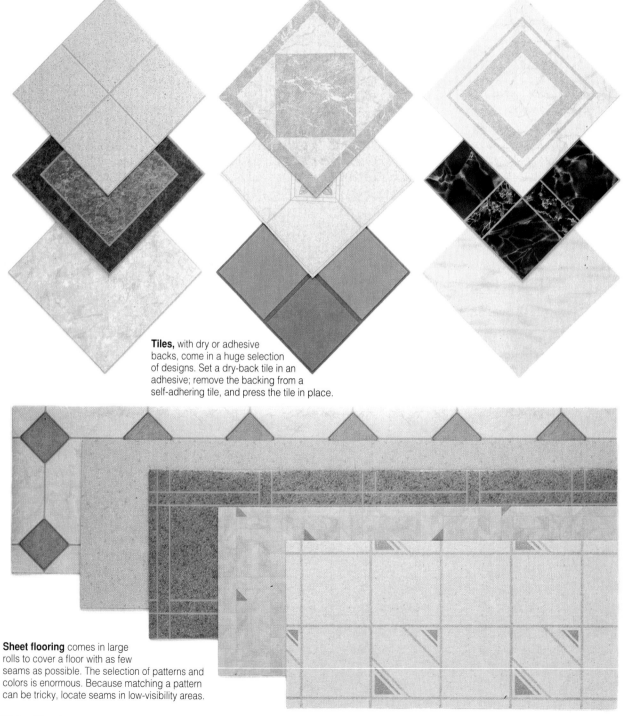

Tiles, with dry or adhesive backs, come in a huge selection of designs. Set a dry-back tile in an adhesive; remove the backing from a self-adhering tile, and press the tile in place.

Sheet flooring comes in large rolls to cover a floor with as few seams as possible. The selection of patterns and colors is enormous. Because matching a pattern can be tricky, locate seams in low-visibility areas.

Before installing wood or resilient flooring or ceramic tile, make sure the surface beneath is flat, smooth, stable, and structurally sound. If it is not, the new flooring may crack or buckle in time.

The existing floor need not be made absolutely horizontal to prepare it for a new covering. Many floors in older houses sag or tilt because of settling, and if the condition is not severe, new flooring usually can be installed over the old with satisfactory results. But be alert to sagging caused by structural damage. Have a professional building inspector or engineer examine subflooring, joists, and other framing that appears to be weak or decayed.

To prepare an existing subfloor or a finished wood floor, vacuum and clean it thoroughly and reseat any protruding fasteners. Then walk over the entire floor, bouncing on it as you go. Squeaks signal loose flooring; springiness indicates weak support underneath.

Also check the floor for bumps and hollows. Uneven wood flooring can be sanded (pp.332–333), but often the best way to obtain a flat, smooth surface is to cover it with liquid floor-leveling compound, a filler available at hardware and flooring supply stores. Choose a compound that is compatible with the subfloor and the new flooring adhesive. Mix the compound according to the manufacturer's instructions, and follow any safety precautions.

Both resilient flooring and ceramic tile can be covered directly with flooring, but apply floor-leveling compound first if the surface is uneven. Before applying compound or any new flooring to a concrete slab, perform a test (right) to check for excess moisture seeping through the concrete.

Caution: Never sand or remove existing resilient flooring unless you are absolutely certain that it does not contain asbestos. (If it does, the dust created would be hazardous.) Before removing even loose resilient flooring, call your local health department for advice on safe handling techniques and any local regulations.

Checking for flatness

Use straightedge board or long level to find bumps and hollows over ⅛ in. high; sand or fill. If possible, level raised flooring by resecuring or removing it.

Stiffening a springy floor

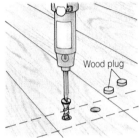

Eliminate squeaks by driving glue-coated shims between joists and flooring (far left). Do not use wedges; they will lift flooring. If repairs cannot be made from underneath, fasten loose flooring to joists with screws from above (left); fill holes with wood plugs.

Close a long gap between flooring and warped joist by attaching 2 × 4 or wider lumber along upper edge of joist (right). Brace springy joists by installing rows of wood or metal cross-bridging strips at 6- to 8-ft. intervals (far right).

Applying floor-leveling compound

Spread leveling compound with trowel or wooden float. For concrete slab, first perform a moisture test (inset): Clean and sand a small area and cover it with multipurpose vinyl adhesive. Tape down a patch of resilient sheet flooring. Remove after 72 hr.; if adhesive is still wet, moisture is seeping through slab.

An underlayment provides a smooth, flat surface for all types of new flooring. It gives extra support for heavy materials such as ceramic tile, provides a good nailing surface for a solid wood floor, and can provide moisture resistance. Choose an underlayment that is appropriate for the type of flooring you wish to install; be sure that it is thick enough to cover any unevenness and imperfections in the subfloor.

Removing molding

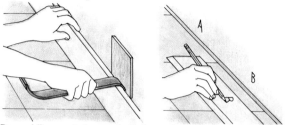

Pry molding gently from wall with flat pry bar or stiff-bladed putty knife (left); work gradually to minimize chipping or splintering. Protect wall with scrap wood. Label pieces and wall areas with matching letters to simplify reinstallation (right). If molding is old and damaged, or if splintering and chipping are unavoidable, consider replacing the molding.

Installing plywood underlayment

Place panels so surface grain is 90° to joists. Stagger end joints. Leave ⅛-in. gap between panels and ½-in. gap between panels and walls. Nail panels through joists (located 16 in. apart on center). Fasten every 6 in. at the joists at panel edges and every 10 in. at inner joists.

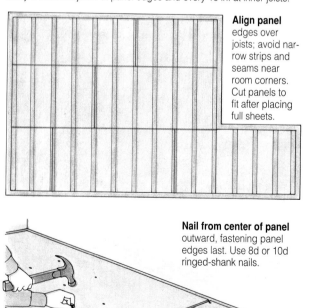

Align panel edges over joists; avoid narrow strips and seams near room corners. Cut panels to fit after placing full sheets.

Nail from center of panel outward, fastening panel edges last. Use 8d or 10d ringed-shank nails.

Before installing new flooring, you can take measures to reduce moisture and increase comfort. For example, if the floor is over an unheated crawl space, lay 6-mil polyethylene film on the dirt to act as a vapor retarder. If the floor is above a living space, add a layer of insulation to muffle sounds.

Existing floors. Some types of flooring can be installed directly over existing flooring; however, you should always remove any carpeting and make sure that the floor is clean, dry, and grease-free. (Consult your flooring dealer or a building professional to determine specific underlayment requirements.) Underlayment panels can be installed over flooring that is dry, flat, and securely attached to the subfloor. Adding an underlayment and the new flooring will raise the floor's height; if the difference is pronounced, install threshold reducer strips and cut doors and frames as necessary (p.329).

Caution: Resilient flooring can create hazardous dust and waste when it is removed. If it contains asbestos, it should be removed by an experienced professional.

To prepare a floor for ceramic tile or wood parquet, use two layers of ½-inch sheathing or select-grade plywood; for other wood flooring and for resilient flooring, use one layer of ¾-inch similar-grade plywood. (Never use fiberboard or

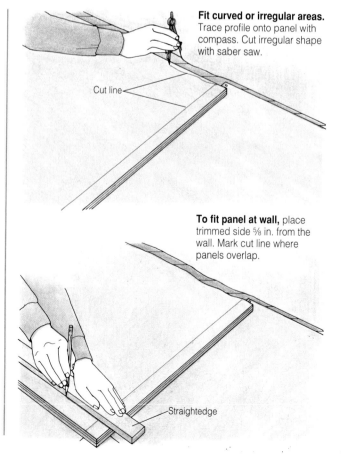

Fit curved or irregular areas. Trace profile onto panel with compass. Cut irregular shape with saber saw.

Cut line

To fit panel at wall, place trimmed side ⅝ in. from the wall. Mark cut line where panels overlap.

Straightedge

particleboard as underlayment.) Lay cement board wherever extra moisture resistance is needed underneath ceramic tile. Whether you install cement board or plywood, always leave a small gap between the panels, and between the walls and the underlayment, to allow the panels to expand or move. Fill the gaps between the cement board and the wall with a flexible caulk; leave the gaps in a plywood underlayment unfilled.

Concrete slab. Parquet, laminated strip and plank flooring, ceramic tile, and all types of resilient flooring can be glued with adhesive or mastic directly to dry, sealed concrete (p.325). (Never glue down planks or strips of solid wood.) If the concrete slab is below ground level, you will need to provide a moisture barrier. For solid wood flooring, embed short lengths of 2 × 4 lumber, called *screeds* or *sleepers,* in mastic as shown at right. Strip or plank flooring up to 4 inches wide can be attached to the screeds; to support wider planks, attach a plywood underlayment. For ceramic tile, spread thinset adhesive and lay in it a moisture barrier of chlorinated polyethylene (CPE) specifically designated for this purpose.

Exterior concrete slab. Ceramic tile can be laid over an exterior concrete slab if it drains well and has been laid with the correct expansion joints (pp.206–207, 212–213).

Installing cement board

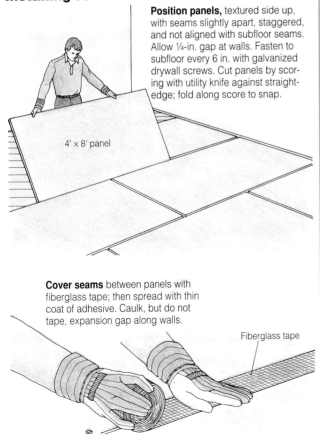

Position panels, textured side up, with seams slightly apart, staggered, and not aligned with subfloor seams. Allow ¼-in. gap at walls. Fasten to subfloor every 6 in. with galvanized drywall screws. Cut panels by scoring with utility knife against straightedge; fold along score to snap.

4' × 8' panel

Cover seams between panels with fiberglass tape; then spread with thin coat of adhesive. Caulk, but do not tape, expansion gap along walls.

Fiberglass tape

Preparing a concrete slab

1. Clean a slab when it is completely dry, and if necessary even it out with leveling compound (p.325). Then spread waterproofing mastic with a notched trowel. Start at far corner and work toward doorway.

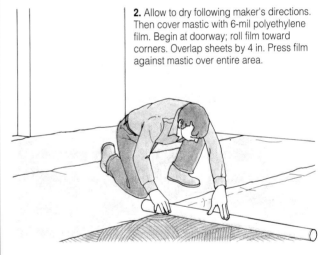

2. Allow to dry following maker's directions. Then cover mastic with 6-mil polyethylene film. Begin at doorway; roll film toward corners. Overlap sheets by 4 in. Press film against mastic over entire area.

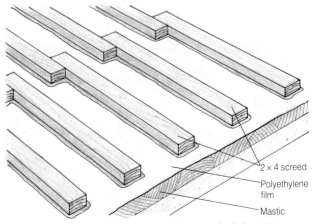

2 × 4 screed

Polyethylene film

Mastic

3. To attach screeds, spread runs of mastic onto polyethylene at 12-in. intervals on center and perpendicular to direction of finish flooring. Embed 2 x 4 lumber strips (screeds) in mastic, overlapping strips by 4 in. (In areas of high humidity, cover screeds with an additional layer of polyethylene.) Add a ¾-in. underlayment for planks wider than 4 in.

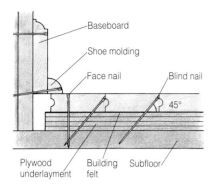

Baseboard

Shoe molding

Face nail

Blind nail

45°

Plywood underlayment

Building felt

Subfloor

Strip and plank boards require a strong support system that will hold the fasteners securely; the flooring can run either perpendicular to or diagonally across the floor joists or screeds. Leave a ¾-inch expansion gap between the flooring and the two walls that run parallel to the flooring (none is needed at the end walls).

First of all, find out how square the room is and how parallel the walls are. (Some variation is likely; cut and taper pieces to fit as described.) To determine how close to square the corners are, measure between the diagonal corners (p.149); to locate unparallel areas, measure between the walls that will be parallel to the flooring strips. Variation between the end walls matters less because you can easily cut the ends to fit.

To accurately align the flooring, string a baseline on the floor parallel to the intended direction of the floorboards. In a small or average-size room, locate the baseline close to the longest or most noticeable wall; in a room over 20 feet wide, locate the baseline near the center so that the flooring can be installed by working outward from it in each direction.

Measure between the baseline and the wall every foot or so. If the wall is bowed or snakes, use a saber saw to shape the first course, or row, of boards. If the room is less than 1 inch out of parallel, taper the last course; if more than 1 inch, divide the variation between the first and last courses. Mark the pieces that need tapering (p.326); then rip the boards to the correct taper. To make the adjustment less obvious, plane the grooved edge and the tongue (or deepen the groove) of pieces in several courses. Install the shaped pieces where least noticeable.

Select the straightest pieces for the first two or three and the final three or four courses. Slightly warped boards can be pried into place; check severely warped boards for straight sections that can be cut off and used.

Face-nail the first course of flooring, its grooved edge toward the wall, with a row of 7d or 8d nails driven vertically 1 inch from the groove; don't nail through the groove. Before finishing, sink the nails with a nail set and fill the holes. Continue fastening the first course by *blind-nailing* it at an angle through the tongued edge and into the bottom of the floorboard and the subfloor (the face and blind nails are staggered); drive these heads flush. Blind nails are hidden when the next board is put in place. Blind-nail all but the final courses. Face-nail the last two courses.

Getting started

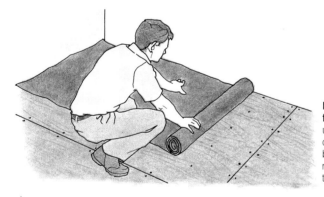

Locate baseline. Near each corner of the wall where you will begin installing boards, measure and mark the width of your flooring plus ¾ in. for expansion joint.

Roll out building felt over plywood underlayment, overlapping pieces by 4 in. Felt minimizes squeaks in the flooring.

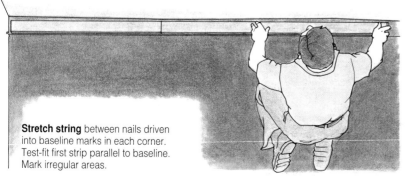

Stretch string between nails driven into baseline marks in each corner. Test-fit first strip parallel to baseline. Mark irregular areas.

Lay out several courses before nailing. Arrange strips so that joints are staggered at least 6 in. apart from course to course. Avoid clustering short boards and creating patterns like "staircases" and H-joints. Strips at ends of courses should be at least 8 in. long.

Fitting pieces

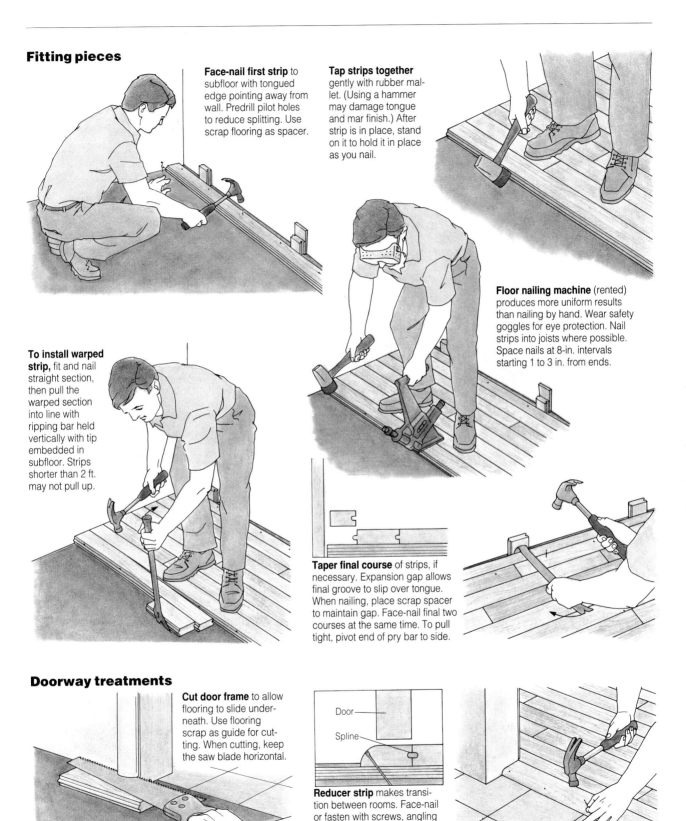

Face-nail first strip to subfloor with tongued edge pointing away from wall. Predrill pilot holes to reduce splitting. Use scrap flooring as spacer.

Tap strips together gently with rubber mallet. (Using a hammer may damage tongue and mar finish.) After strip is in place, stand on it to hold it in place as you nail.

Floor nailing machine (rented) produces more uniform results than nailing by hand. Wear safety goggles for eye protection. Nail strips into joists where possible. Space nails at 8-in. intervals starting 1 to 3 in. from ends.

To install warped strip, fit and nail straight section, then pull the warped section into line with ripping bar held vertically with tip embedded in subfloor. Strips shorter than 2 ft. may not pull up.

Taper final course of strips, if necessary. Expansion gap allows final groove to slip over tongue. When nailing, place scrap spacer to maintain gap. Face-nail final two courses at the same time. To pull tight, pivot end of pry bar to side.

Doorway treatments

Cut door frame to allow flooring to slide underneath. Use flooring scrap as guide for cutting. When cutting, keep the saw blade horizontal.

Door

Spline

Reducer strip makes transition between rooms. Face-nail or fasten with screws, angling them toward new flooring. If no tongue and groove, glue spline into routed grooves.

Laying a floating floor

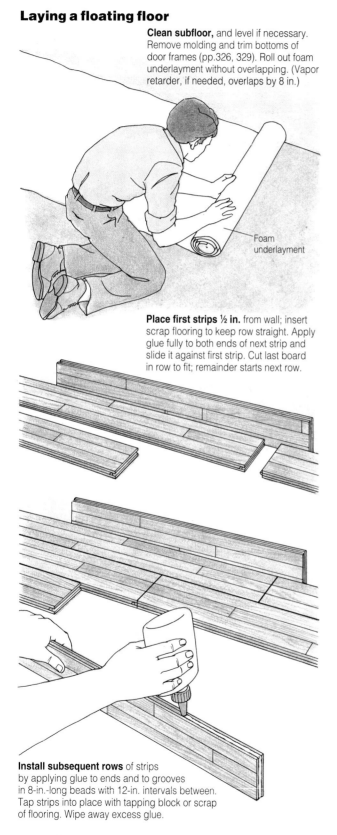

Clean subfloor, and level if necessary. Remove molding and trim bottoms of door frames (pp.326, 329). Roll out foam underlayment without overlapping. (Vapor retarder, if needed, overlaps by 8 in.)

Foam underlayment

Place first strips ½ in. from wall; insert scrap flooring to keep row straight. Apply glue fully to both ends of next strip and slide it against first strip. Cut last board in row to fit; remainder starts next row.

Install subsequent rows of strips by applying glue to ends and to grooves in 8-in.-long beads with 12-in. intervals between. Tap strips into place with tapping block or scrap of flooring. Wipe away excess glue.

The easiest type of flooring to install is laminated strip flooring. It requires no nailing; you either glue the pieces to each other, creating a *floating* floor, or embed them in mastic applied to the subfloor, creating a *glue-down* floor.

To prepare for a floating floor, flatten the subfloor with floor-leveling compound (p.325); then cover it with a layer of foam sheeting supplied by the flooring manufacturer. On a concrete slab, place a layer of 6-mil polyethylene sheeting beneath the foam as a vapor retarder.

A glue-down floor also requires a flat subfloor, and if the floor is belowground, a layer of polyethylene sheeting set in mastic. If the floor is concrete, dry, and aboveground, you can adhere most types of laminated flooring directly to it. But if the slab is at or below grade, first glue down a sheet of polyethylene film and install a subfloor of sleepers and plywood underlayment. Then lay the flooring in mastic on the plywood. (For more on preparation, see pp.325–327.)

Parquet patterns may look best only when running in a certain direction; arrange a dozen or more squares on the floor as a test. Parquet, like ceramic and vinyl tiles, requires two perpendicular baselines that act as guides for the alignment of the tiles. Follow these lines precisely when laying parquet—the tiles are often not exactly square.

For best results, use the special installation tools, materials, and adhesives recommended or supplied by the maker. Tools include tapping blocks and pry bars designed for fitting strips into place without damaging their tongued edges or disturbing the mastic, and a trowel with precisely notched edges for applying the mastic. Cork material (available in strips or 1 × 3 sheets that must be cut to fit) fills an expansion gap that is needed between the flooring and the walls.

Mastics vary in their content, but all require a waiting period after they are applied (the length of time depends on the type). Mastic is ready to accept the tiles when it has become tacky. It stays that way for a specified time; set the tiles during this *open* period. Trowel mastic over only as much area as you can tile in that time.

Caution: The solvents for many mastics are toxic and may be flammable. Follow the maker's safety precautions.

As you work, select squares randomly from several cartons to maximize color uniformity over the entire floor. Before kneeling on just-laid squares, cover them with a plywood sheet. This helps embed the squares and prevents them from sliding apart. Before the mastic hardens, walk on each square or roll the floor with a rented 150-pound roller to make certain the squares adhere completely. Finish the floor except for the perimeter; trowel mastic onto this area only after all the tiles have been cut to fit.

Caution: Trim parquet by hand or with a band or a saber saw; a table saw or a radial arm saw will cause kickback.

Allow new flooring to harden for 24 hours or as long as the maker suggests. Then cover the gaps with molding, and install a reducer strip where different floorings meet (p.329).

Layout for parquet

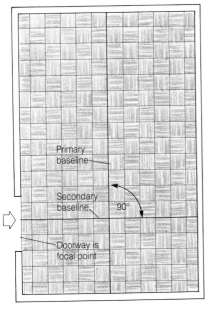

Primary baseline

Secondary baseline 90°

Doorway is focal point

Snap primary baseline parallel to longest wall. Then mark secondary baseline at 90° angle to primary line; they should cross at focal point or room's center. To check corner for squareness: Measure 3 ft. on one line, 4 ft. on other; distance between must be exactly 5 ft.

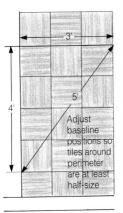

3'

4'

5'

Adjust baseline positions so tiles around perimeter are at least half-size.

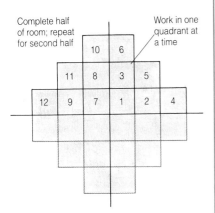

Complete half of room; repeat for second half

Work in one quadrant at a time

		10	6		
	11	8	3	5	
12	9	7	1	2	4

Starting where baselines cross, lay squares in a pyramid pattern, placing squares next to baseline and tile or in a corner formed by two tiles. This technique ensures straight rows.

Installing parquet

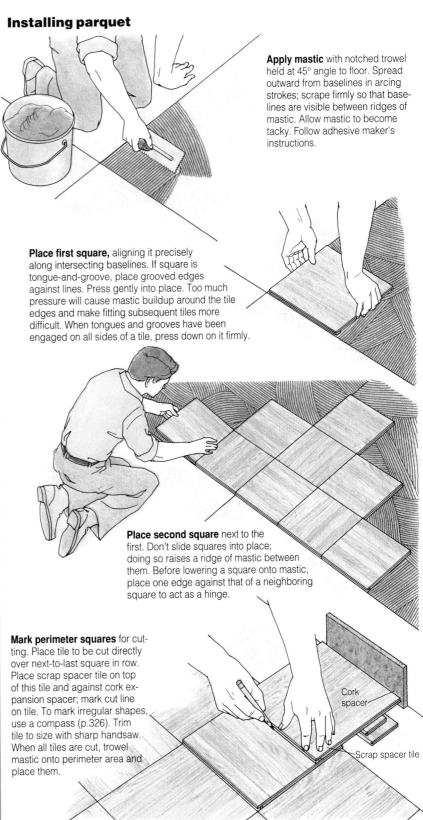

Apply mastic with notched trowel held at 45° angle to floor. Spread outward from baselines in arcing strokes; scrape firmly so that baselines are visible between ridges of mastic. Allow mastic to become tacky. Follow adhesive maker's instructions.

Place first square, aligning it precisely along intersecting baselines. If square is tongue-and-groove, place grooved edges against lines. Press gently into place. Too much pressure will cause mastic buildup around the tile edges and make fitting subsequent tiles more difficult. When tongues and grooves have been engaged on all sides of a tile, press down on it firmly.

Place second square next to the first. Don't slide squares into place; doing so raises a ridge of mastic between them. Before lowering a square onto mastic, place one edge against that of a neighboring square to act as a hinge.

Mark perimeter squares for cutting. Place tile to be cut directly over next-to-last square in row. Place scrap spacer tile on top of this tile and against cork expansion spacer; mark cut line on tile. To mark irregular shapes, use a compass (p.326). Trim tile to size with sharp handsaw. When all tiles are cut, trowel mastic onto perimeter area and place them.

Cork spacer

Scrap spacer tile

FINISHING WOOD FLOORS

Solid wood floors that are at least ¾ inch thick can be restored several times during their life by sanding off the old finish and applying a new one. Thinner floors and some parquet flooring can be restored this way once or twice. Laminated flooring has a thin surface layer, and sanding will likely expose the backing underneath; for this reason, it is usually sold prefinished.

Sanding a floor is a big job that must be done carefully. Rather than using an ordinary belt sander or a disc sander attached to an electric drill, which can easily gouge the wood, rent three large power tools—a drum sander, a special disc sander called an edger, and a buffer. The drum sander does the bulk of the work; the edger sands the perimeter of the room and wherever the drum sander cannot reach; the buffer prepares the sanded floor for each finishing coat. These

machines must be handled carefully to avoid gouging the wood. Have a salesperson show you how to load and operate them. Obtain plenty of sandpaper, steel wool, or screen for each tool; you can return unused portions.

Before you begin sanding, empty the room and seal all interior openings to contain the dust. Then inspect the floor for protruding nails, staples, or tacks. Glue down any large splinters.

Sand the entire floor with coarse (60-grit) aluminum oxide sandpaper. Next, vacuum the floor and sand it again with medium (80-grit) aluminum oxide paper. Vacuum again and sand the floor with fine (120-grit) aluminum oxide or garnet sandpaper. Then fill any cracks and flaws in the floor with filler. When it has dried, sand the floor with the buffer fitted with a 100-grade screen disc or 00-grade steel wool. Using a screen,

called *screening,* gives a smoother surface than the steel wool.

Next apply either a stain or the first coat of finish. When it is dry, screen the surface with the buffer, and then thoroughly vacuum the floor and wipe it with a tack cloth (p.164). Repeat the process until as many coats of finish as necessary have been applied.

Caution: Follow the manufacturer's instructions exactly. Non-water-base products are toxic, and even water-base versions can be harmful. Ventilate the area well and wear safety goggles, a NIOSH-approved respirator, and rubber gloves. Extinguish all pilot lights, stoves, and electric motors to avoid an explosion. To prevent exposure to fumes, inhabitants should stay away from the premises for at least 24 hours after the finish is applied.

For more on sanding, staining, and finishing wood, see pp.164–169.

Sanding direction

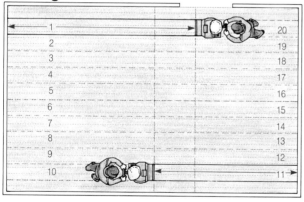

Move parallel to grain of strip and plank floors. Begin near door; cover two-thirds of room by moving sander back and forth. When reversing, retrace your steps without turning machine. On forward cuts, overlap previous pass by 2 to 4 in. When ready to sand final third of floor, switch off machine and turn sander 180°. Overlap the sanded area by 2 ft.

Sand parquet floor with medium-grit paper at a 45° angle, using similar sequence as for strip and plank flooring.

Make second pass with fine grit at 90° angle to first pass. Start at diagonally opposite corner.

Final pass with extra-fine grit should be parallel to room's long walls. Finish sanding with buffer and a screen.

Wood floor finishes

Finish type	Durability	Application	Upkeep and repair
Polyurethanes	Oil-base type is extremely durable; water-base type has fair durability. Both have excellent water resistance	Brush on with lamb's-wool applicator. Oil-base type dries in 12–24 hr., is easier to apply. Water-base type dries in 2–4 hr.; spread carefully to avoid surface bubbles	Damp-mop to keep floor free of grit. Never apply wax or cleaner containing oil. Sand dull floor; recoat with new finish
Varnishes	Moderate durability and water resistance. Avoid spar (marine) varnish, which is too soft for flooring	Spread with brush; usually needs 3 coats. Water-base type dries faster than solvent- or oil-base types but may raise wood grain. Keep room dust-free until dry	Dust often to remove grit. Apply wax to protect against moisture. Most repairs require stripping and refinishing
Penetrating sealers	Fair durability; strengthens and seals wood but does not protect surface	Easiest finish to apply. Spread with lint-free cloth or lamb's-wool applicator; let stand for a time (see directions); then wipe off excess	Dust often to remove grit. Apply wax to protect against moisture. To repair, sand and apply new finish or refurbisher

Sanding and filling

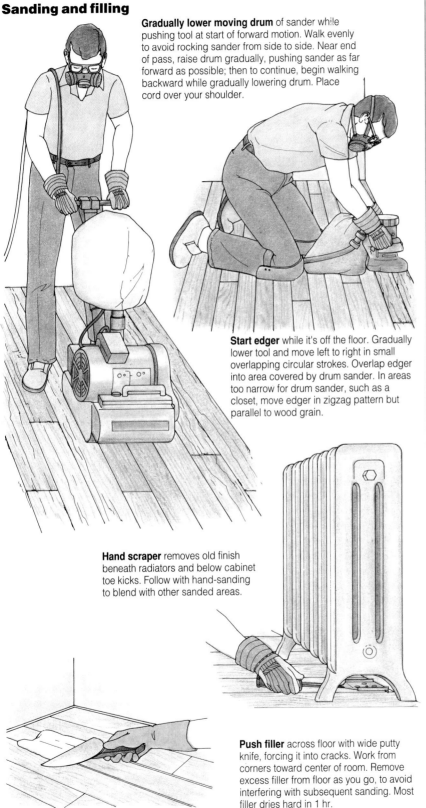

Gradually lower moving drum of sander while pushing tool at start of forward motion. Walk evenly to avoid rocking sander from side to side. Near end of pass, raise drum gradually, pushing sander as far forward as possible; then to continue, begin walking backward while gradually lowering drum. Place cord over your shoulder.

Start edger while it's off the floor. Gradually lower tool and move left to right in small overlapping circular strokes. Overlap edger into area covered by drum sander. In areas too narrow for drum sander, such as a closet, move edger in zigzag pattern but parallel to wood grain.

Hand scraper removes old finish beneath radiators and below cabinet toe kicks. Follow with hand-sanding to blend with other sanded areas.

Push filler across floor with wide putty knife, forcing it into cracks. Work from corners toward center of room. Remove excess filler from floor as you go, to avoid interfering with subsequent sanding. Most filler dries hard in 1 hr.

Finishing

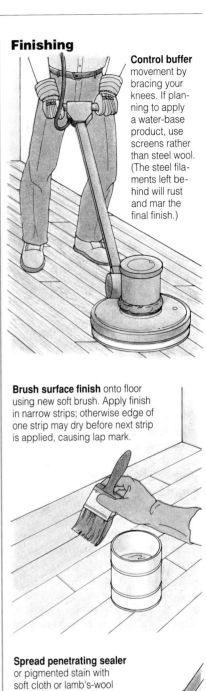

Control buffer movement by bracing your knees. If planning to apply a water-base product, use screens rather than steel wool. (The steel filaments left behind will rust and mar the final finish.)

Brush surface finish onto floor using new soft brush. Apply finish in narrow strips; otherwise edge of one strip may dry before next strip is applied, causing lap mark.

Spread penetrating sealer or pigmented stain with soft cloth or lamb's-wool applicator. Apply generously, parallel to wood grain; then wipe up excess.

Installing resilient and ceramic tile is similar to installing parquet flooring and ceramic tile countertops. The floor must be flat, and an underlayment is needed for support (pp.325–327).

Modern no-wax resilient tiles are usually made of vinyl, come in a wide range of colors and patterns, and are typically 12-inch squares. Accent tiles—larger or smaller or in different shapes—are also available; with these you can create borders or design your own patterns. Newer resilient tiles can usually be removed by heating them with a heat gun. This allows you to change accent tiles to update the floor's appearance, rather than changing the entire floor. However, do not remove existing tiles if there is any chance that they contain asbestos (p.325).

Most resilient tile is fastened by gluing it to the floor with special adhesive. (The tile manufacturer or dealer will specify which kind to use.) Some tiles are self-adhering; their backs are coated with contact cement covered by paper or plastic film; you remove the covering just before installation. Both types of tiles must then be pressed down with a floor roller to secure them completely. You can rent a floor roller; they usually weigh 100 pounds but come disassembled for easier carrying.

Ceramic floor tiles are similar to those used for countertops and walls but are generally larger and stronger. Powdered thinset adhesive is the best choice for do-it-yourself installation; wear a dust mask when mixing it with

Planning a diagonal layout

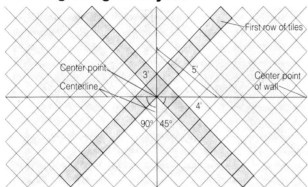

Draw a plan on graph paper, letting each square represent a tile (add grout spaces for ceramic tiles). Find the room's center point by snapping chalk lines between the center points of opposite walls. To verify 90° angle, mark out from center point 3 ft. along one line, 4 ft. along the other. Distance between two marks should be 5 ft. If necessary, adjust by redrawing one centerline without changing center point. Bisect 90° with carpenter's square for 45° angle; verify with combination square.

Border of tiles placed parallel to walls simplifies trimming to compensate for room that is out of square.

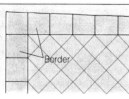

Lay down first row (without adhesive) along 45° line; if necessary, adjust the row without changing its angle so that the end tiles are equal in size and at least half a tile wide. Mark additional guidelines every 2 ft.; mark border with separate color to avoid confusion.

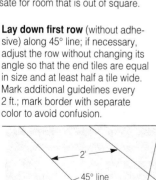

Installing resilient tiles

Remove backing from self-adhering tile, or spread tile adhesive with notched trowel (facing page). Lay tile in place without twisting, using edge of adjoining tile as a "hinge."

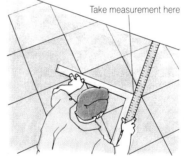

To mark perimeter tiles that are not full-size, run a straightedge ruler from the wall to the corner of the tile in preceding row (ensure that straightedge is at 90° to wall by holding a carpenter's square across centerlines of adjoining tiles). Transfer measurement to new tile; cut tile with utility knife held against straightedge.

To fit tiles around obstacles, make a cardboard template and trace the shape onto the tile. Cut tile along outline.

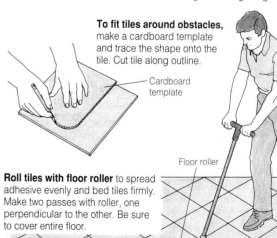

Roll tiles with floor roller to spread adhesive evenly and bed tiles firmly. Make two passes with roller, one perpendicular to the other. Be sure to cover entire floor.

water. For more information on choosing, cutting, and repairing ceramic tiles, see pp. 254–259.

Typically, tiles are laid either parallel to the walls or at a 45° angle to them. When designing a parallel layout, follow the same procedures as for parquet floors (pp.330–331), but allow for the width of grout joints with ceramic tile. Where a room is significantly out of square or has many obstacles, adapt the layout method on pages 328–329. Select one wall as a focal point, mark a baseline two or three tile widths from it, and then proceed with a parallel or diagonal layout.

Tiles can hide a room's defects: vertical lines appear to lengthen a room; a border will make it appear smaller. Hexagonal tiles should be laid with their sides, not their corners, parallel to two opposite walls. For your first tile floor, keep the design simple.

Whatever the layout, work first on graph paper. Estimate the amount of tile you need based on the size of the room and that of your chosen tile (plus any grout joints), adding 10 percent extra for breakage and for future repairs. Test the design first by doing a dry run on the floor, making adjustments as needed to compensate for obstacles and the room's dimensions.

Be careful not to apply adhesive over areas that are too large to cover with tiles before the adhesive hardens. Similarly, never apply more grout than you can easily spread and clean before it begins to set.

Laying ceramic tiles

Work in small sections, beginning in one corner of the room. Spread thinset adhesive over a 2-ft. square area; then lay and level tiles (below). Spread adhesive with smooth side of trowel; then comb with notched side to create ridges.

Notched trowel
Guideline
Spacer

Lay tiles in adhesive, fitting them in place with a slight twist to spread the adhesive; remove excess from joints with knife or grout saw. Place spacers at corners to maintain uniform gap between tiles (inset). Never walk on newly laid tiles.

Level tiles and spread adhesive by hammering against tiles with rubber grout float or by striking 2 × 4 covered with carpet or thick toweling. To raise a tile that is too low, pry it up, apply fresh adhesive to the back, and reset the tile.

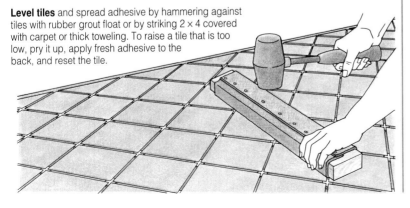

Grouting and cleaning the tiles

Wait 24 hr., then remove spacers before applying grout (left). Scrape away any adhesive that has oozed into joints between tiles; then vacuum joints free of particles.

Spread grout over tiles with rubber grout float held firmly at 30° angle. Wipe away excess immediately by scraping with float held nearly perpendicular to floor.

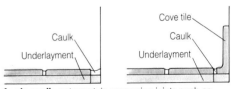

Cove tile
Caulk
Caulk
Underlayment
Underlayment

Apply caulk, not grout, in expansion joints such as joint around perimeter of floor (left) or where cove and floor tile meet (right). Use caulking gun to push flexible waterpoof caulk firmly into joint.

Clean tiles before grout dries. Wipe several times with sponge squeezed nearly dry (rinse sponge often); then remove hazy residue with clean towel.

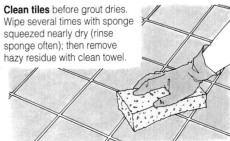

Laying the flooring

1. Ventilate the area well. Unroll flooring starting at longest uninterrupted wall. Allow excess to curl up at edges; adjust sheet so pattern is square to walls.

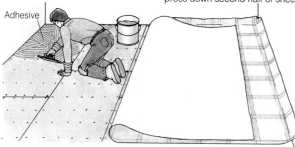

2. Fold back half of sheet, without creasing, to expose underlayment. Apply adhesive to floor with notched trowel; immediately press down sheet. Fold back other half of sheet, cover remainder of floor with adhesive, and press down second half of sheet.

Adhesive

3. Flatten sheet with floor roller or rolling pin to spread adhesive and remove bubbles. Work from center of floor outward.

Floor roller

Usually made of vinyl, resilient sheet flooring comes in many different colors, patterns, and textures. Quality and prices vary; premium grades have a durable top, or wear layer, that disguises underlayment flaws. So-called no-wax types have a wear layer made of thermoplastic or other resins.

Most sheet flooring is available in rolls 6 or 12 feet wide. Whenever possible, select a width that allows you to cover the floor with a single piece. Sheets can be joined, but it is difficult to match patterns and textures at a seam. If a seam can't be avoided, plan so that it will occur in an inconspicuous area.

You can apply sheet flooring over almost any smooth hard surface, even over existing resilient flooring. (To flatten or strengthen the underlayment, see pp.325–327.)

The flooring manufacturer will specify whether the flooring should be laid using the full-adhesion method shown here or whether it should be laid loose. To loose-lay flooring, follow the steps shown here to position and trim it, but leave a ¼-inch gap along the walls and do not apply adhesive. Then secure the edges as directed by the manufacturer.

Resilient flooring can be difficult to manipulate. Avoid bending it sharply as you lay it, or it may crease or rip. Even after it has been rolled, fully adhered flooring usually develops bubbles, caused by gas escaping from the adhesive. If these have not disappeared within a week, prick them with a pin in an inconspicuous spot and then press the flooring flat.

When moving heavy items over resilient flooring, lay down a sheet of thin plywood or heavy cardboard to protect it. Clean flooring often with a slightly damp mop (the flooring is not waterproof). Special cleaners recommended by the flooring manufacturer will preserve or restore a glossy finish.

Trimming

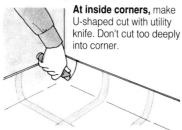

At inside corners, make U-shaped cut with utility knife. Don't cut too deeply into corner.

At outside corners, trim with utility knife, making vertical slits through excess flooring.

Trim excess along walls by pressing flooring close to wall and using straightedge as a guide; leave a ⅛-in. gap between flooring and wall.

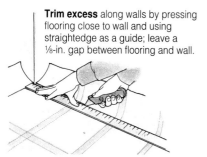

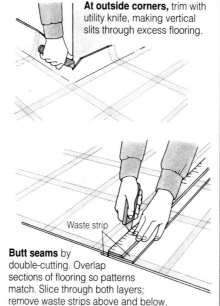

Waste strip

Butt seams by double-cutting. Overlap sections of flooring so patterns match. Slice through both layers; remove waste strips above and below.

Finishing touches

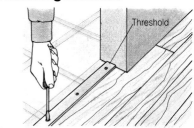

Threshold

Cover flooring at doorways and where flooring meets different material. Cut strips of metal or other threshold material to precise length; fasten with matching fasteners.

Install shoe molding to cover flooring edges along walls. Secure with finishing nails to baseboard or wall, not floor.

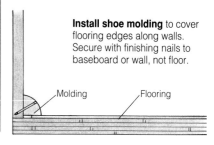

Molding   Flooring

Strip and plank flooring

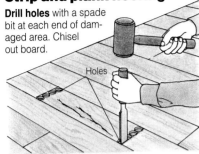

Drill holes with a spade bit at each end of damaged area. Chisel out board.

Holes

Cut to length a new strip of tongue-and-groove flooring; reverse board and remove lower lip of groove with chisel, saw, or plane.

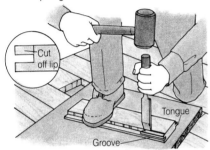

Cut off lip

Tongue

Groove

Fit tongue of new board into groove of adjacent floorboard. Tap into place with mallet and scrap block; fasten with nails. Finish to match floor.

To stretch the time between major refinishings, dust floors frequently to remove grit; wipe up spills promptly to avoid stains. For general cleaning, and to maintain a bright finish, use commercial cleaners recommended by the flooring manufacturer or installer.

On wood floors, avoid water-base products. On floors finished with polyurethane, don't use cleaners containing any kind of oil, grease, or solvent. Synthetic floor finishes—such as Swedish finish and acrylic—resist penetration by most liquids. On the other hand, floors finished with shellac, lacquer, conventional varnish, and wax are easily damaged by almost any liquid that is allowed to remain for more than a few minutes, especially liquids containing solvents like alcohol.

To repair minor scratches in a non-synthetic finish, rub the spot with very fine steel wool (No. 0000) and then apply a dab of paste wax. Extensively damaged or stained finish may have to be stripped and replaced. To repair a synthetic finish and the finish on resilient flooring, use only the products and techniques recommended by the flooring manufacturer.

Stained wood flooring can sometimes be sanded or bleached; if not, or if floorboards are splintered or broken, the damage must be removed and patched, as shown (far left).

Lighten stained ceramic tile grout with special cleaners, available at tile suppliers. For instructions on sealing tiles and grout and repairing damaged ceramic tile, see pages 257 and 259.

In resilient flooring, you can sometimes patch small gouged areas with a paste made of grated flooring material and clear nail polish. (Grate resilient flooring only if you are certain that it does not contain asbestos, p.325). However, you'll usually get better-looking results by patching the area.

Parquet tile

Drill holes from corner to corner to slightly less than the depth of the tile. Chisel away all sections.

Scrape off old adhesive; then apply new layer and fit replacement tile in place.

Resilient tile and sheet flooring

Soften adhesive with a heat gun; scrape off the damaged tile and old adhesive. Apply the new adhesive and fit the new tile in place.

Patch

Patching sheet flooring:
1. Place a patch on top of damage, aligning pattern precisely. Tape in place; then cut through both layers with a utility knife.

2. Remove patch (below) and set it aside. Heat and pry away damaged flooring and adhesive as you would for a damaged tile.

Patch

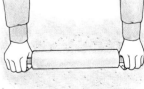

3. Spread new adhesive, using notched trowel. Fit patch into place; then press flat with rolling pin.

PLANNING PROJECTS

You will save time, money, energy, and a lot of frustration if you think a project through and carefully plan each step before beginning. For almost any undertaking, large or small, you will benefit by drawing up your plans on paper. A good set of plans lets you see what tools you'll need and aids in estimating the amount and cost of the materials you'll use. It also helps you see the complexity of the entire job, so that you can determine whether or not you'll need professional help.

Drawing up plans. Begin by making a sketch or diagram of the project. It needn't be elaborate or artistic—simply clear enough to illustrate what you mean to do, showing all the parts and indicating the materials you plan to use. You can make simple outlines of the parts and use heavy dots or X's for the nails, screws, or bolts.

Then, to ensure accurate results, transfer the sketch to graph paper, letting each square on the paper equal 1 foot or some other clear-cut measurement. Or use measuring and layout tools to draw the plans to scale.

To make a full-size pattern from a small picture or drawing, use a pantograph (p.19), or draw a grid of intersecting vertical and horizontal lines over the original drawing and transfer the design onto graph paper square by square. Be thorough and accurate.

When designing furniture and cabinets, consider the average person's comfort and use standard dimensions. Also be sure to leave enough open space around each item (pp.340–343).

For large projects, if you don't want to draw your own plans, you can alter existing ones, purchase ready-drawn plans at home centers, or copy plans from books or magazines. Or you can buy two- or even three-dimensional kits that have scaled pieces of cardboard or plastic representing furniture, cabinets, and other features. These small pieces can easily be moved about inside a grid floor plan to find the best arrangement. Also available is computer software for designing a room or an entire house or for landscaping a garden. Some home centers provide personalized computer planning.

Outlining the steps. Once the plans for a project are drawn up, think the whole job through and make a list of the major steps. Put the steps in order, break them down into substeps, and number the steps and substeps.

When planning a large project, break it down into a series of small, manageable projects (see below). This allows you to make timely purchases, organize your time, and spot any specialized work that goes beyond the level of your skills and requires a professional. Checking through the steps, make a list of all the tools you will want to have on hand. Then examine the steps and the plans to determine the amounts of materials you will need (pp.344–347), including fasteners and other hardware.

Other considerations. For your safety, be sure to line up one or more helpers if the project will involve transporting or working with materials that are heavy or awkward to handle. Also, plan and set up a space, either in your workshop or on site, for working on the project and storing the materials.

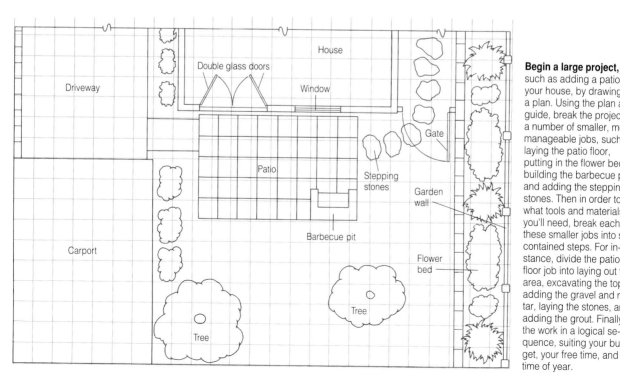

Begin a large project, such as adding a patio to your house, by drawing up a plan. Using the plan as a guide, break the project into a number of smaller, more manageable jobs, such as laying the patio floor, putting in the flower beds, building the barbecue pit, and adding the stepping stones. Then in order to see what tools and materials you'll need, break each of these smaller jobs into self-contained steps. For instance, divide the patio floor job into laying out the area, excavating the topsoil, adding the gravel and mortar, laying the stones, and adding the grout. Finally, do the work in a logical sequence, suiting your budget, your free time, and the time of year.

If a project is going to generate a lot of waste materials, decide in advance how you will recycle or dispose of them. If your municipality will not pick up such materials, rent a dumpster and haul the debris to a landfill.

Remember that materials such as oils, paints, lacquers, and varnishes, as well as thinners, strippers, and other solvents, are flammable or toxic; some are hazardous to the environment. Use them up according to the instructions on the labels, seal the empty containers, wrap any remaining sludge in newspaper and seal it in an airtight plastic bag or container, and bring the packages to a disposal center. Or store the packages in a fireproof metal cabi-net and dispose of them on hazardous-waste collection day, or contact your local government for information on how to dispose of them properly.

Codes and permits. Before finalizing any building or renovation plans, review them with your local building department, making sure that you are familiar with any related codes, restrictions, or requirements. Generally there are separate codes for construction, plumbing, and electrical work, and these codes may cover every aspect of the job, even down to the types of nails you must use. You may also have to have some of the work done by a professional or have it inspected at various stages of completion.

Get a permit if you need one, and schedule any neccesary inspections. Permits are usually required for major renovations, such as turning a garage into a guest room, but they may also be required for small jobs, such as walling in a patio, building a barbecue with a high chimney, breaking through a curb to install a driveway, and many plumbing and electrical jobs.

When working on a project that requires digging or excavating, such as putting in a sidewalk, ask your local utility and cable companies to mark the locations of underground cables or pipelines before you start digging. This will protect you from possible injury, liability, and disruption of services.

Hiring a Contractor

The skills portion of this book shows you what's involved in working with various materials, demonstrating all the basic techniques and some advanced ones. It can also help you assess what's involved in any projects you may plan and determine your role in them.

If, after gathering information and assessing the job's complexity, you decide to undertake a large project that involves work you don't feel comfortable doing, consider hiring a contractor to do part or all of the job. For example, for the patio project shown on the facing page, you might serve as general contractor and do some of the work yourself, but hire a laborer to excavate the soil, an electrician to install the outdoor lighting, and a plumber to put in the garden sprinkling system.

To find a contractor, compile a list of names by talking to your friends and relatives who have had similar work done, looking in the Yellow Pages of your phone book, and calling local building and construction organizations. Contact several of the listed contractors who do the type of work you need, asking for references from customers who have used their services recently for a project similar to yours. Call the references and ask to look at the work.

Narrow your list to contractors with good references. Check with your local Better Business Bureau for complaints against them, and make sure they have the appropriate licenses.

Finally, ask two or three of the contractors to bid on the work, furnishing them with drawings and specific information on the materials you want. (Most contractors provide their own materials because part of their profit is derived from the discount they receive from suppliers.)

When the bids are in, study them carefully and choose the contractor you think is best for the job. But remember, the lowest bid is not always the best. Contractors may cut corners to bring down the price.

For your protection, get everything in writing. The contract should include start-up and completion dates, a detailed account of the work to be done, the types of materials to be used (including the brand names, if important), how and when garbage disposal will be handled, procedures for making changes in the original plans, warranties, and termination conditions.

Be sure to include the full cost of the project and a schedule of payments. Never pay everything up front; it's common to make a down payment of no more than one-third the total cost, several payments as the work progresses, and a final payment when everything is completed and you have approved the work.

Your contract should also include a lien waiver clause, requiring the contractor to show proof that suppliers and subcontractors have been paid so that you cannot be sued for nonpayment of bills. It is also a good idea to have the contractor obtain needed permits and take full responsibility for following the local codes. Demand certificates of damage and liability insurance from all contractors and subcontractors.

Once the work begins, keep close tabs on its progress and quickly bring any problems to the attention of the contractor—not his workers. If you want to make a change in the plans, ask how it will affect the total cost of the project and get it all in writing. Sometimes making a small change necessitates expensive changes elsewhere. For example, to add a lighting fixture an electrician may have to run an extra circuit at great expense, but he might not tell you until he presents the bill at the end.

When the job is finished, examine it carefully before making the final payment. Never pay for work that has not been done.

STANDARD MEASUREMENTS FOR TABLES AND CHAIRS

When designing furniture and arranging it in a room, it's best to adhere to the standard dimensions that architects have established for the average person. A table or desk must be the proper height, for example, to eat or work at comfortably. In addition, allow sufficient space for people to pass easily through a room or to walk or work around the furniture.

DINING TABLE SIZES

	People	Minimum	Average	Ample
Square tables	2	24" × 24"	28" × 28"	30" × 30"
	4	30" × 30"	32" × 32"	36" × 36"
	8	44" × 44"	48" × 48"	52" × 52"
Rectangular tables	2	22" × 28"	24" × 30"	28" × 32"
	4	28" × 44"	32" × 48"	36" × 52"
	6	34" × 50"	36" × 66"	42" × 72"
	8	34" × 72"	36" × 86"	42" × 90"
Round tables	2	22"	24"	28"
	4	32"	36"	42"
	6	42"	50"	54"
	8	56"	62"	72"

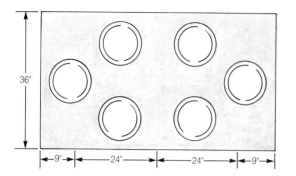

Coffee, or cocktail, table must be within easy reach of someone seated on a sofa or an armchair but far enough away to allow leg room.

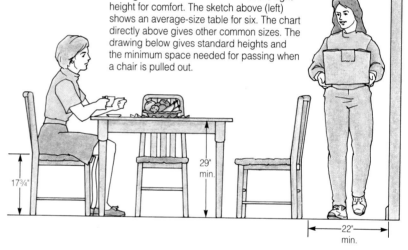

Dining table and chairs must be at the right height for comfort. The sketch above (left) shows an average-size table for six. The chart directly above gives other common sizes. The drawing below gives standard heights and the minimum space needed for passing when a chair is pulled out.

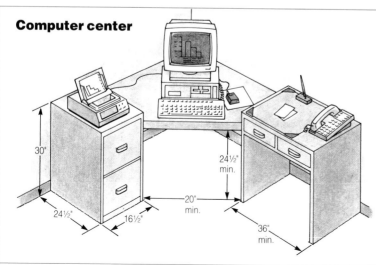

Computer center

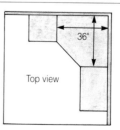

Top view

By building your computer center into a corner, you gain more room for the monitor and keyboard, and provide a partial wraparound workspace that lets you work with a minimum of movement.

Either build or buy the elements for a computer center. In the arrangement shown, the center table, for the keyboard (and monitor), is 5½ in. lower than the rest because that is generally a more comfortable height for typing. The area at right can be reserved for writing, and the printer can be placed at left. Reverse the arrangement for a left-handed worker.

STANDARD MEASUREMENTS FOR STORAGE AREAS AND BEDROOMS

In planning storage space, always take into consideration the size of the people who need access to it. Some standard measurements are given here, but you may have to change them to suit the needs of individuals. For example, you might build low shelves in a child's bedroom but put high ones in another room for storing harmful materials out of the reach of young children. If you add extra-high shelves, use a steady ladder or step stool to reach them. Bookshelves should be shallower than closet shelves, and they should not be more than 36 inches long to sustain the weight of the books without sagging. When furnishing a bedroom, leave enough space for dressing and moving about.

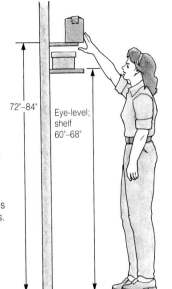

Shelves (right) should be within reach of everyone who uses them without their having to stand on tiptoes. Make high shelves shallower than lower ones.

Closets (left) hold more if packed tightly; buy or build a closet organizer. Install rods for hangers at least 12 in. from wall.

Allow access space in front of cabinet doors or drawers (below).

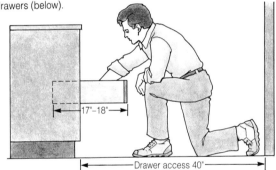

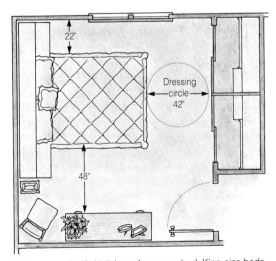

Bedroom wall unit (right) can frame any bed. King-size beds measure 76 × 80 or 84 in.; queen-size, 60 × 80 or 84 in.; double, 54 × 75 in.; and twin, 39 × 75 in. Allow 22 in. between twin beds. A platform bed with drawers gives extra storage space. The amounts of space shown around bed (above) are minimums.

STANDARD KITCHEN AND BATH MEASUREMENTS

Perhaps more than any other parts of your home, the kitchen and bathroom benefit from careful planning. A well-designed kitchen can put everything at your fingertips and dramatically reduce the time you spend preparing food. A carefully laid-out bathroom ensures maximum comfort and avoids cramped spaces that cause you to bang your knee or stub your toe. You might also consider installing a hand-held shower and grab bars at convenient heights for anyone who might be unsteady on their feet. If someone in your household is confined to a wheelchair, you may want to make some of the adjustments shown below and on the facing page.

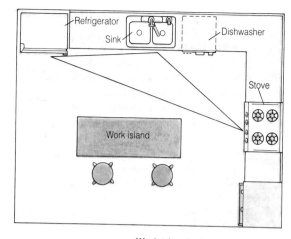

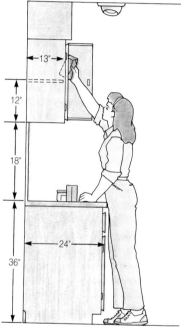

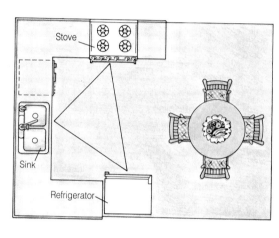

Work triangle that puts the sink, refrigerator, and cooking range at its three corners is the most efficient arrangement for a kitchen. A U-shaped work triangle is shown in the layout at left, and an L-shaped kitchen with a longer, narrower work triangle is shown above. When planning a kitchen, be sure to leave enough counter space between the three points for preparing food, serving, and cleaning up, but make the length of the legs of the triangle short enough to minimize walking. Never place a heat-making appliance, such as the range or dishwasher, next to the refrigerator.

Base cabinets in kitchen are deeper than the wall cabinets, and so the top shelves cannot be as high as shelves with no obstruction below them.

Leave crouching space in front of a low oven (below) or a cabinet with swing-out doors.

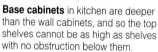

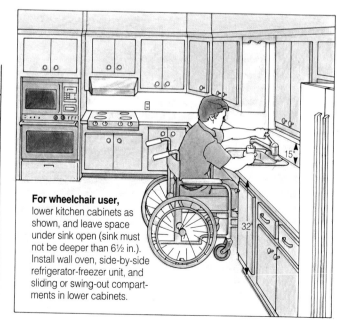

For wheelchair user, lower kitchen cabinets as shown, and leave space under sink open (sink must not be deeper than 6½ in.). Install wall oven, side-by-side refrigerator-freezer unit, and sliding or swing-out compartments in lower cabinets.

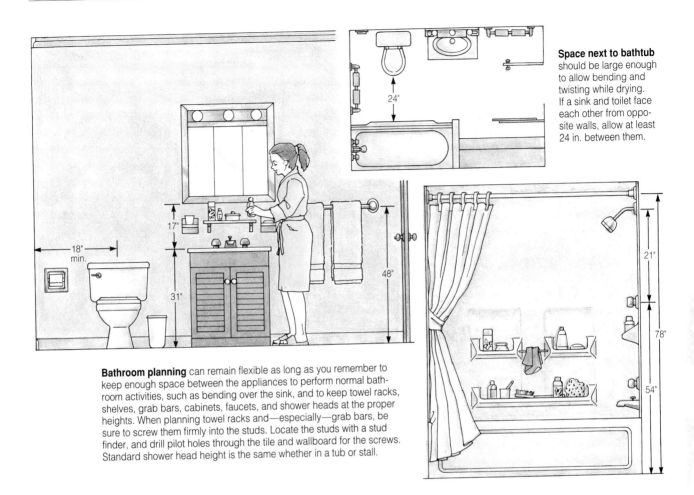

Bathroom planning can remain flexible as long as you remember to keep enough space between the appliances to perform normal bathroom activities, such as bending over the sink, and to keep towel racks, shelves, grab bars, cabinets, faucets, and shower heads at the proper heights. When planning towel racks and—especially—grab bars, be sure to screw them firmly into the studs. Locate the studs with a stud finder, and drill pilot holes through the tile and wallboard for the screws. Standard shower head height is the same whether in a tub or stall.

Bathroom for handicapped needs more grab bars and a hand-held shower. You should also lower the medicine cabinet and position it beside the sink (right). Leave enough space next to the toilet to park a wheelchair, and a circle of space at least 5 ft. across in the center of the room to turn the chair freely (below).

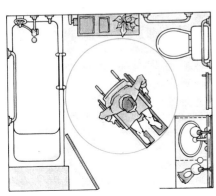

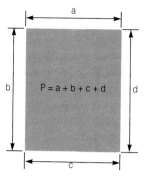

Perimeter of (distance around) a rectangle, triangle, or other straight-sided shape is found by adding the lengths of all its sides.

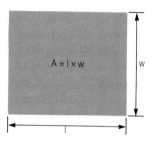

Area of a rectangle is found by multiplying its length by its width.

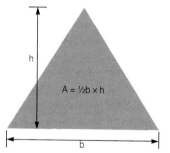

Area of a triangle is determined by multiplying half the length of its base by its height.

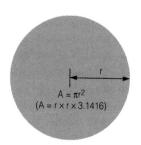

Area of a circle is found by multiplying the square of the circle's radius (half the distance across the circle) by π (3.1416).

Once you have drawn up plans for a project, begin compiling lists of the materials and hardware you will need. First consider the nature of the project: How much will it be used? Is it to be permanent or temporary? Will it be visible or hidden, utilitarian or decorative? Should it match or coordinate with existing materials? Is it going to be indoors or outdoors? Will it be used by children or a handicapped person? Should its cost be keep below a certain dollar amount? With these factors in mind, choose the type and quality of materials you want to use, and, if applicable, pick the finish (paint, stain, or natural) you wish them to have. Don't forget that you may be required to adhere to local building codes in selecting materials and hardware.

After you have decided upon the types of materials, you'll need to figure out the quantities. For materials that are installed in straight lines, such as pipes or wall molding, simply measure

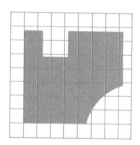

Sketch complex areas on graph paper, letting each square on the paper equal 1 sq. ft. or 1 sq. in. Add up whole squares and those more than one-third filled.

the length needed in feet. For materials that frame or border, measure the perimeter or circumference of the piece or area to be enclosed. For many other materials, you'll need to calculate either the area to be covered or the volume to be filled. Use the formulas illustrated here to make these estimates. Then determine the amounts of materials you'll need based on these calculations. When using any formula, remember to compute like things. For instance, you can't multiply inches by feet; either convert the inches into feet by dividing by 12 or convert the feet into inches by multiplying by 12.

Some materials are sold and estimated in several ways. The most common are given in the pages that follow. If you want to be sure how a material is sold, call and ask the supplier.

The best way to organize an estimate of the materials required for a job is to break the job down into its individual steps (p.338), recording the type and quantity of the materials needed at each step. List every item required for building or installation, including hardware, fasteners, caulk, and abrasives. Also list any tools that you may have to buy or rent.

A rule of thumb when estimating materials is to add 10 percent to allow for miscalculations, errors, damage and waste, and future repairs. Once you have determined the quantities, multiply the amount by the cost per unit to find the total cost of the materials.

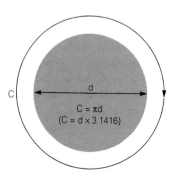

Circumference of (distance around) a full circle is found by multiplying the circle's diameter (the distance across it) by π (3.1416).

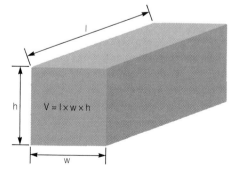

Volume, or cubic dimension, of a square or other rectangular space is determined by multiplying the length by the width by the height.

ESTIMATING LUMBER NEEDS

Conversion table: linear to board feet

Linear feet	5	10	20	30	40	50	100	250	1000
Stock					Board feet				
1 × 2	.83	1.7	3.3	5	6.7	8.3	16.7	42.7	166.7
1 × 3	1.25	2.5	5	7.5	10	12.5	25	62.5	250
1 × 4	1.7	3.3	6.7	10	13.3	16.7	33.3	83.3	333.3
1 × 6	2.5	5	10	15	20	25	50	125	500
1 × 8	3.3	6.7	13.3	20	26.7	33.3	66.7	166.7	666.7
2 × 4	3.3	6.7	13.3	20	26.7	33.3	66.7	166.7	666.7
2 × 6	5	10	20	30	40	50	100	250	1000
2 × 8	6.7	13.3	26.7	40	53.3	66.7	133.3	333.3	1333.3
2 × 10	8.3	16.7	33.3	50	66.7	83.3	166.7	416.7	1666.7
2 × 12	10	20	40	60	80	100	200	500	2000
4 × 4	6.7	13.3	26.7	40	53.3	66.7	133.3	333.3	1333.3

Before estimating the amount of lumber you will need for a project, select the type and grade (pp.130–131), and find out how your supplier sells it. Softwoods are generally sold by the running, or linear, foot—the board's actual length. Most hardwood, however, is sold by the board foot—a unit about 12 inches long, 12 inches wide, and 1 inch thick (144 cubic inches).

Boards and dimensional lumber. Softwood boards (1 × 2's to 1 × 12's) and dimensional lumber (2 × 2's to 4 × 12's) are generally sold in their nominal size, the size the wood was before it was planed at the mill. Actual measurements are ¼ to ¾ inch smaller in thickness and width (see the table at right). Hardwood's nominal sizes are different from those of softwood. The thicknesses are given in quarter-inch increments, ranging from 4/4 (1 inch thick) to 8/4 (2 inches thick). Planed hardwood is about ¼ inch thinner than its nominal size indicates.

To calculate needed amounts of lumber sold in linear feet (including boards, dimensional lumber, dowels, and moldings), simply measure the length needed in feet. In the case of project components, measure each component separately, and add all the measurements together to calculate the total amount of lumber.

To convert linear feet to board feet, use the table above. For sizes that are not included in the table, multiply the nominal size in inches by the total length in feet and divide by 12. For example, to find out the number of board feet in a 12-foot-long 1 × 8 , multiply 1 × 8 × 12 to get 96, and then divide by 12 to get 8 board feet.

Calculating the number of board feet you'll need for a project is a little more complicated and generally results in more waste. Lumber that is sold by the board foot comes in varying lengths, widths, and thicknesses, and so you may have to resaw or plane the boards for components that need to be of uniform width and thickness. You may even have to glue up stock to get the width you need. And finally, you may need extra wood to match the grain direction.

To find the board feet for the components of a project, multiply the thickness by the length by the width (in inches) of each component. Add the resulting figures for all the components, and divide the total by 144 (the number of inches in a board foot).

Sheet materials. Plywood, particleboard, paneling, and other sheet materials come in various thicknesses. The most common sheet size is 4 × 8 feet (1,200 × 2,400 mm). Larger sizes

(both longer and wider) may be available by special order—usually at a premium price—and some suppliers sell cut panels, or cut them to order if you pay for the waste and the cutting.

To calculate the number of panels needed for a large project, such as wall sheathing, simply divide the area (in square feet) of the space to be covered by the area of a single panel (32 square feet for a standard-size panel). Then add a standard waste factor of from 5 to 10 percent, allowing for more waste when dealing with odd angles, curves, or irregular shapes.

If you are working on a small project or one that requires a sheet to be cut into numerous pieces, lay it out on graph paper to determine the best size sheet to buy and to devise a cutting plan that will make the most efficient use of the material, keeping in mind that plywood is stronger along its length. If it matters, show the orientation of the grain; you may need additional material to match grain patterns.

Lumber sizes

Nominal size	Actual size
1 × 2	¾" × 1½"
1 × 3	¾" × 2½
1 × 4	¾" × 3½"
1 × 5	¾" × 4½"
1 × 6	¾" × 5½"
1 × 8	¾" × 7¼"
1 × 10	¾" × 9¼"
1 × 12	¾" × 11¼"
2 × 2	1½" × 1½"
2 × 3	1½" × 2½"
2 × 4	1½" × 3½"
2 × 6	1½" × 5½"
2 × 8	1½" × 7¼"
2 × 10	1½" × 9¼"
2 × 12	1½" × 11¼"
3 × 4	2½" × 3½"
4 × 4	3½" × 3½"
4 × 6	3½" × 5½"
6 × 6	5½" × 5½"
8 × 8	7¼" × 7¼"

ESTIMATING OTHER MATERIALS

In addition to wood, you'll have occasion to estimate the amounts needed of various other building materials and hardware. Some of the most common items are discussed below.

Bricks. To estimate the number of bricks you'll need for a project, calculate the number of square feet to be covered and divide by the number of square feet in the face of the type of brick you are using. Use the nominal dimensions of the brick for a project with mortar; use actual sizes for a mortarless project, such as a patio or walkway. Allow 10 to 25 percent for waste.

Per square foot, you'll need about 5 CSR or double jumbo bricks, or approximately 7 Ontario, 8 metric modular, or 4 jumbo bricks. Because new brick is usually sold in packaged units of 100, called straps, or in units of 500, called cubes, you'll have to adjust your order accordingly. (See p.222.)

Concrete and concrete blocks. Concrete is sold in cubic yards and cubic metres. Calculate the volume required by multiplying the project's length by its width, then multiplying the result by the thickness of the concrete. In estimating cubic yardage, calculate the area in square feet and multiply that number by the thickness of the concrete in feet. Divide the cubic feet by 27, the number of cubic feet in a cubic yard. If you are pouring a 4-inch-thick slab that is 25 feet by 15 feet, for example, multiply 25 by 15 by $\frac{1}{3}$ (4 inches equals $\frac{1}{3}$ foot) and divide by 27; the total is 4.63 cubic yards. Buy or mix 5 cubic yards to be safe.

You can roughly estimate the number of blocks you'll need for a project by dividing the number of square feet the project will cover (less any doors, windows, or other large openings) by the number of square feet in the face of the block. Usually enough corner blocks for most jobs are included with an order of stretchers, but check with your dealer. Specifically order any other specialty blocks, such as sash blocks for windows or solid blocks for the top courses of bearing walls. To be on the safe side, however, have your supplier help you make the estimate based on your plans, which should be drawn to scale or marked with exact dimensions.

Your supplier can also help you estimate the amount of mortar you'll need for a concrete block project. Generally you'll use about 6 cubic feet of mortar for every 100 feet of solid wall, but the type of cement and the proportions of cement, sand, and lime vary with the type of project.

Concrete pavers. Manufactured concrete pavers come in different sizes and shapes; some interlock. Check with the supplier for actual sizes.

To estimate the number of pavers needed for a job, divide the square footage of the space to be covered by the square footage of each paver. For example, the area of a 12 × 6-inch paver is $\frac{1}{2}$ square foot (1 × $\frac{1}{2}$ foot). To estimate the number of pavers for a 10 × 12-foot patio, first multiply 10 by 12, which gives 120, the square footage of the patio; then divide 120 by $\frac{1}{2}$, the square footage of the paver; you'll need 240 pavers.

Flagstones. Flagstone, any flat stone used for a patio or walkway, can have regular or irregular dimensions. Squares and rectangles are available in 6-inch increments up to 24 × 48 inches; rounded stones are available in diameters of 12 to 30 inches. The stones range from $\frac{3}{4}$ inch to more than 3 inches in thickness. Stones are often sold by the ton and may cover from 50 to 60 square feet of ground per ton, but a ton of thin stones covers twice the space a ton of thick stones covers. Some stones, such as regularly shaped bluestone, may be sold by the square foot. Whatever stone you use, it is best to review your plans with your contractor or supplier.

Finishes. Paint, stain, and other finishes come in containers holding from 1 to 40 litres ($\frac{1}{2}$ pint to 5 gallons), depending on the finish and whether or not it is custom-mixed. Labels on the containers indicate what areas the finish should cover.

In general, to calculate the amount of finish you'll need, divide the total area to be covered (in square feet or square metres) by the coverage indicated on the container; then multiply the result by the number of coats you plan to apply. For large areas such as walls, deduct for doorways, windows, and other large openings (p.285).

If you apply too little paint (as most nonprofessionals do), you will either get away with using less paint or will need more paint for an extra coat. The type of applicator you use will also affect the amount of paint you need. Allow 10 to 15 percent waste if you use a paint-feeding tool, such as a power roller or a spray applicator. If the surface to be painted is unusually porous, as is concrete block or new wallboard, allow 25 percent more paint for the first coat (usually a primer). Finally, if you are applying a light color over a dark one, you'll need to apply a heavier coat or add a coat.

Wallcoverings. Wallpaper and other wallcoverings usually come in standard rolls of 36 square feet each. (European coverings contain about 28 square feet per roll.) To estimate the number of rolls you'll need, calculate the square footage of each wall and add all the measurements together; then subtract 20 square feet for each door and window; divide the result by 30, rather than 36, to allow for waste and matching patterns.

To determine the number of rolls for a ceiling, multiply the length by the width in feet and divide by 30. Borders are sold by the foot or yard. Measure the perimeter of the room in feet. To convert to yards, divide by 3.

For wallcoverings that are not pre-pasted, a pound of paste will hang approximately 10 rolls of paper. Liquid sealer or sizing may be needed to prepare certain surfaces before adding the wallcovering. If so, estimate the amount you need as you would paint.

Plastics. Plastic laminate, for countertops and cabinets, is sold by the linear foot in widths of 24, 30, 36, 38,

Approximate number of nails per pound																
Size	2d	3d	4d	5d	6d	7d	8d	9d	10d	12d	16d	20d	30d	40d	50d	60d
Length	1"	1¼"	1½"	1¾"	2"	2¼"	2½"	2¾"	3"	3¼"	3½"	4"	4½"	5"	5½"	6"
Common nails per pound	847	543	294	254	167	150	101	92	66	61	47	30	23	17	14	11
Finishing nails per pound	1,473	880	630	535	288	254	196	178	124	113	93	65	–	–	–	–

and 60 inches and in lengths ranging from 5 to 12 feet. Measure the length and width of the area to be laminated and order a piece that is at least ½ inch wider and of equal length.

Acrylic sheets are commonly ⅛, ¼, or ⅜ inch thick, 8 feet long, and 4 feet wide, but suppliers often sell smaller pieces. Calculate the area to be covered and order accordingly.

Glass. You can buy glass cut to order or buy a large sheet and cut it yourself. If you are buying glass to replace a broken windowpane, measure the cracked pane, if possible, or measure the length and width of the inside of the window frame. For ease of fit, cut or buy a piece of glass ⅛ inch smaller than the maximum opening. For a large, expensive piece of glass or mirror, it's best to have the glass company assume the responsibility of taking the measurements, particularly if it must fit an opening that may not be perfectly square.

Glass blocks are available in standard thicknesses of 3⅛ and 3⅞ inches. The faces come in 6-, 8-, and 12-inch squares or in 4 × 8- or 6 × 8-inch rectangles. The face measurements are nominal, allowing for ¼-inch mortar joints. Glass blocks are also sold in preassembled panels that can be slipped into place.

Preassembled or not, determine the number of courses you'll need by measuring the height of the space to be filled and dividing by the height of a single block (all in inches). Then measure the width of the space and divide by the width of each block to determine the number of blocks in a course. Multiply the two resulting figures for the total number of blocks needed.

Floor coverings. Sheet vinyl flooring comes on rolls in 6- and 12-foot widths. Buy enough to cover the area with about 3 inches of overhang on each side. If the floor is less than 6 feet wide (or more than 6 feet but less than 12 feet wide), buy a 6-foot (or 12-foot) piece the length of the floor plus 6 inches. If the area is more than 12 feet wide, buy two or more lengths of flooring and seam them, if possible, in an inconspicuous space such as under a sofa or bookcase. Be sure to get enough to cover the floors of any halls, closets, or odd-shaped areas that branch off the main space.

Vinyl, asphalt, and carpet tiles come in 9- and 12-inch squares. Ceramic tiles come in 1-, 2-, 4-, 6-, 8-, 12-, and 18-inch squares, and in rectangular, hexagonal, and octagonal shapes. They are all usually sold by the box, but sometimes they are sold by the piece as well.

To calculate the number of pieces you'll need to cover a large area with tiles of the same size and color, divide the area of the space to be tiled by the area of a single tile. If you are planning to lay tiles in patterns involving mixed sizes or colors, lay out the design on graph paper (p.338) and count the number of tiles needed in each size and color. Add 10 percent for waste for ceramic tiles, a bit more for brittle tiles or tiles laid in a diagonal pattern, and less for the others. Then divide the number of tiles needed by the number of tiles per box to determine the total number of boxes required.

When buying ceramic tiles, be sure to check them before leaving the supplier. Ceramic tile is susceptible to breakage during storage and shipment.

Hardware and miscellaneous. When estimating the materials you'll need for a job, include hardware, adhesives, and other installation materials. Buy enough nails or other fasteners for joining pieces or mounting them on walls, and don't forget anchors or toggles for use in plaster or wallboard. If you're joining pieces with nuts and bolts, remember to include any needed washers. Be sure to buy matching nails and trim for wood paneling. When replacing a windowpane, include the glazier's points and caulk or glazing compound that hold the glass. And don't forget hinges, brackets, braces, latches, and knobs or pulls, if needed.

By consulting your drawn plans, you can make a good estimate of all the hardware you will need. Because fasteners get lost easily and nails bend if not driven properly, it's a good idea to buy more fasteners than you will need for a job; you can always save the extras for future repairs and other jobs.

Nails are sold in bubble packs, loose, or in boxes (often by the pound) and may be measured in inches or by the penny. The penny measurement goes back to the days of ancient Rome, and is abbreviated *d* for *denarius,* the Roman equivalent of a penny. It originally indicated the price of a nail per hundred, but it now signifies only size; for example, a 2d nail is 1 inch long. The higher the penny number, the longer and (generally) heavier the nail. The table above gives the sizes of common and finishing nails and the approximate number of nails in a pound.

Other fasteners, including screws, are generally sold in small bubble packs or in larger boxes. The number of pieces is marked on the package.

There are a variety of sources for the tools, hardware, and materials found in this book. Home improvement centers carry just about everything under one roof. Hardware stores are a good source, and they often provide an experienced staff that can answer questions. Auctions, garage and liquidation sales, and classified ads in the newspaper are excellent places to find quality hand and power tools at bargain prices. Visit demolition sites—with the owner's permission—if you are interested in used bricks, doors, ornate woodwork, windows, and other supplies that are still in good condition.

If you can't find what you need at a local store—or just prefer at-home shopping convenience—look for desired tools, hardware, or materials in the following list of specialty catalog sources. All of the companies sell directly to the public, and many have toll-free (800) numbers that make it easy to obtain information, do price comparisons, and place orders. Although there might be a minimal fee for a catalog, the company may reimburse it when you make a purchase. Additionally, some catalog companies may waive their requirement for a minimum order.

GENERAL

Brookstone Co.
5 Vose Farm Rd.
Peterborough, NH 03458
(800) 926-7000
General merchandise, including hand tools. Small fee for catalog.

Busy Bee Machine Tools Ltd.
475 North Rivermede Rd.
Concord, Ont. L4K 3R2
(905) 738-1292
(800) 461-2879
Tools and equipment for the home handyman.

Northern
P.O. Box 1499
Burnsville, MN 55337
(800) 533-5545
General merchandise, including power tools.

Renovator's Supply
Renovator's Old Mill
Dept. 9126
Millers Falls, MA 01349
(413) 659-2211
Furniture, door, window, and bathroom hardware, wallcoverings, and light fittings.

Sears Canada Inc.
222 Jarvis St.
Toronto, Ont. M5B 2B8
(416) 362-1711
Hand and power tools. Catalog outlets are found in many communities. Small fee for catalog.

The Tool Crib of the North
P.O. Box 1716
Grand Forks, ND 58206
(800) 358-3096
Hand tools, power tools and accessories, masonry tools, and fasteners. Small fee for catalog.

Tools on Sale
Division of Seven Corners
    Ace Hardware, Inc.
216 W. 7th St.
St. Paul, MN 55102
(612) 224-4859
Hand tools, power tools and accessories.

Van Dyke's Restorers
P.O. Box 278
Woonsocket, SD 57385
(800) 843-3320
Ornamental wood trim, fasteners, milk paint. Small fee for catalog.

HARDWARE

*See also woodworking catalogs

American Home Supply
P.O. Box 697
191 Lost Lake Lane
Campbell, CA 95009
(408) 246-1962
Solid brass hardware

The Antique Hardware Store
9718 Easton Rd., Rte. 611
Kintnersville, PA 18930
(215) 847-2447
Bathroom, door, window, cabinet, and other hardware. Small fee for catalog.

Bainbridge Manufacturing, Inc.
7873 N.W. Day Rd.
Bainbridge Island, WA 98110
(206) 842-6696
Cabinet and furniture drawer and shelf supports. Minimum order required.

Ball and Ball
463 W. Lincoln Hwy.
Exton, PA 19341-2594
(215) 363-7330
Reproductions of antique house and cabinet hardware and accessories. Small fee for catalog.

Garrett Wade Company, Inc.
161 Ave. of the Americas
New York, NY 10013
(800) 221-2942
Brass furniture hardware. Small fee for catalog.

Handyman's Mail Order Store
Division of the Generis Corp.
1295 Kamato Rd.
Mississauga, Ont. L4W 2M2
(905) 625-5614
Fasteners. Small fee for catalog.

Horton Brasses
P.O. Box 95
Cromwell, CT 06416
(203) 635-4400
Brass and wrought-iron furniture hardware. Minimum order required.

Imported European Hardware
A Division of Woodworker's
    Emporium
4320 W. Bell Dr.
Las Vegas, NV 89118
(702) 871-0722
Furniture, cabinet, and door hardware. Small fee for catalog.

Lee Valley Tools Ltd.
1080 Morrison Dr.
Ottawa, Ont. K2H 8K7
(613) 596-0350
(800) 267-8767
Specialty fasteners and hardware. Small fee for catalog.

Paxton Hardware Ltd.
7818 Bradshaw Rd.
Upper Falls, MD 21156
(410) 592-8505
Antique reproduction furniture hardware; lamp fittings.

Tremont Nail Co.
P.O. Box 111
Wareham, MA 02571
(508) 295-0038
Fasteners and forged iron items.

The Wise Co.
6503 St. Claude Ave.
Arabi, LA 70032
(504) 277-7551
Brassware. Small fee for catalog.

**The Workshop Centre
Steve's Shop**
R.R. 3 Woodstock, Ont.
N4S 7V7
(519) 475-4947
(800) 387-5716
Specialty furniture hardware and fasteners.

WOODWORKING

Adams Wood Products, Inc.
974 Forest Dr.
Morristown, TN 37814
(615) 587-2942
Turning blocks, wood turnings, and unfinished kits.

Artistry In Veneers, Inc.
450 Oak Tree Ave.
South Plainfield, NJ 07080
(201) 668-1430
Veneers, tools, marquetry kits.

The Beall Tool Co.
541 Swans Rd. NE
Newark, OH 43055
(800) 331-4718
Power tool accessories for making threads in wood.

Bridge City Tool Works, Inc.
1104 N.E. 28th Ave.
Portland, OR 97232
(503) 282-6997
Specializes in squares, bevels, and gauges. Sells other hand tools and some power tools. Small fee for catalog.

Bristol Valley Hardwoods
4300 Bristol Valley Rd.
Canandaigua, NY 14424
(716) 229-5695
Domestic and exotic hardwood lumber, turning blocks, and flooring planks. Small fee for catalog.

Canadian Handcrafted Homebuilders Supply
P.O. Box 940
Minden, Ont. K0M 2K0
(705) 286-3305
Log home timber frames, and tools and equipment for log home builders.

Canadian Woodworker Ltd.
1391 St. James St., Unit 4
Winnipeg, Man. R3H OZ1
(204) 786-3196
(800) 665-2244
Router bits.

Cascade Tools, Inc.
P.O. Box 3110
Bellingham, WA 98227
(206) 647-1059
Router bits, shaper cutters, and miscellaneous accessories.

Certainly Wood
11753 Big Tree Rd.
East Aurora, NY 14052
(716) 655-0206
Veneers. Minimum order required.

Albert Constantine & Son, Inc.
2050 Eastchester Rd.
Bronx, NY 10461
(718) 792-1600
Veneers, inlays, tools, finishes, milk paint. Small fee for catalog.

Cooper and Horton Ltd.
1180 Lorimar Dr.
Mississauga, Ont. L5S 1N1
(905) 670-5110
Woodworking tools.

Dominion Saw Ltd.
600 Orwell St.
Mississauga, Ont. L5A 3R9
(905) 270-2200
Hand and power tools, abrasives, saw blades, router bits, cutters.

Eagle America Corp.
P.O. Box 1099
Chardon, OH 44024
(800) 872-2511
Router bits and drill bits. Small fee for catalog.

Farris Machinery
320 N. 11th St.
Blue Springs, MO 64015
(800) 872-5489
Hand and power tools.

Frog Tool Co. Ltd.
700 W. Jackson Blvd.
Chicago, IL 60606
(312) 648-1270
Hand and power tools, finishes and plans. Small fee for catalog.

Furnima Industrial Carbide Inc.
Biernacki Rd., Box 308
Barry's Bay, Ont. K0J 1B0
(613) 756-3657
(800) 267-8833
Carbide router bits and shaper cutters.

Garrett Wade Company, Inc.
161 Ave. of the Americas
New York, NY 10013
(800) 221-2942
Hand and power tools, inlays and finishes. Small fee for catalog.

Geneva Specialties
P.O. Box 542
Lake Geneva, WI 53147
(800) 556-2548
Hand tools, wood turnings.

Gesswein
Woodworking Products Div.
255 Hancock Ave.
Bridgeport, CT 06605
(800) 544-2043, ext. 22
Power carving tools and accessories. Minimum order required.

Grizzly Imports, Inc.
P.O. Box 2069
Bellingham, WA 98225
(206) 647-0801
Hand tools, power tools and accessories.

Highland Hardware
1045 N. Highland Ave. NE
Atlanta, GA 30306
(404) 872-4466
Hand tools, power tools and accessories, and veneers.

Homecraft Veneer
901 West Way
Latrobe, PA 15650
(412) 537-8435
Veneers. Minimum order required.

House of Tools
100 Mayfield Common
Edmonton, Alta. T5P 4K9
(403) 486-0123
(800) 661-3987
Hard-to-find woodworking tools and supplies. Small fee for catalog.

Klockit
P.O. Box 542
Lake Geneva, WI 53147
(800) 556-2548
Clockmaking accessories, ornamental wood trim, and furniture hardware.

Lee Valley Tools Ltd.
1080 Morrison Dr.
Ottawa, Ont. K2H 8K7
(613) 596-0350
(800) 267-8767
Woodworking hand tools. Small fee for catalog.

Leigh Industries Ltd.
P.O. Box 357
104–1585 Broadway St.
Port Coquitlam, B.C. V3C 4K6
(800) 663-8932
Dovetail jig and router accessories.

McFeely's Square Drive Screws
P.O. Box 3, 712 12th St.
Lynchburg, VA 24505-0003
(800) 443-7937
Screws, hand and power tools.

Penn State Industries
2850 Comly Rd.
Philadelphia, PA 19154
(800) 288-7297
Power tools and accessories.

The Sanding Catalogue
P.O. Box 3737
Hickory, NC 28603-3737
(800) 228-0000
Abrasive sheets and tools. Small fee for catalog.

Sharpco Canada Ltd.
960 Alness St., Unit 2
Downsview, Ont. M3J 2S1
(416) 736-0333
(800) 387-7071
Woodworking carbide tools. Small fee for catalogue.

Stamford Hardware
3639 Portage Rd.
Niagara Falls, Ont. L2J 2K8
(905) 356-2921
(800) 668-3332
Router bits, power tools and machinery

Tooltrend Limited
420 Millway Ave.
Concord, Ont. L4K 3V8
(416) 663-8665
(800) 387-7005
Cabinet hardware, woodworking tools and machinery. Small fee for catalog.

Trend-lines
375 Beacham St.
Chelsea, MA 02150
(800) 366-6966
Power and hand tools, fasteners, furniture hardware, and veneers.

Viel Tools Inc
33 Beland St.
Isle-Verte
Que. G0L 1K0
(418) 898-2601
(800) 463-1380
Woodworking and sharpening tools.

Vintage Wood Works
P.O. Box R
Hwy. 34 S.
Quinlan, TX 75474
(903) 356-2158

Turnings and architectural details. Small fee for catalog.

West Wind Hardwood Inc.
10230 Bowerbank Rd.
P.O. Box 2205
Sidney, B.C. V8L 3S8
(604) 656-0848
(800) 667-2275

*(Serving the Pacific Northwest.)
Specialty plywoods; fine hardwoods, softwoods, carving blocks, and veneers. Small fee for catalog.*

Wilke Machinery Co.
3230 Susquehanna Trail
York, PA 17402
(717) 764-5000

Power tools and accessories.

Willard Brothers Woodcutters
300 Basin Rd.
Trenton, NJ 08619
(609) 890-1990

Exotic hardwood lumber, moldings, and wainscoting.

Woodsmith Project Supplies
P.O. Box 10350
Des Moines, IA 50312
(800) 444-7002

Power tool accessories.

Woodturner's World
Site 21, Compartment 17
R.R. 2, Gabriola Island
B.C. V0R 1X0
(604) 722-2930
(800) 695-6496

Woodturning tools and accessories, and sharpening jigs.

The Woodworkers' Store
21801 Industrial Blvd.
Rogers, MN 55374
(612) 428-2199

Exotic hardwood lumber and turning blocks, veneers, inlays, moldings, turnings, hand tools, hardware, fasteners and finishes. Minimum order required. Small fee for catalog.

Woodworker's Supply Inc.
(800) 645-9292

Hand tools, power tools and accessories, fasteners, furniture hardware, and finishes. Small fee for catalog.

**The Workshop Centre
Steve's Shop**
R.R. 3 Woodstock, Ont.
N4S 7V7
(519) 475-4947
(800) 387-5716

More than 200 in-stock woodturnings, custom woodturnings up to 9 ft. long. Architectural components. Specialty furniture hardware and fasteners.

METALWORKING

Allcraft Tool and Supply Co.
666 Pacific St.
Brooklyn, NY 11217
(800) 645-7124

Metals, tools, and other supplies for jewelers and metalsmiths.

Alpha Supply
1225 Hollis St., Box 2133
Bremerton, WA 98310
(206) 373-3302

Metals, tools, and other supplies for jewelers and metalsmiths. Minimum order required. Small fee for catalog.

**Anchor Tool &
Supply Co., Inc.**
P.O. Box 265
Chatham, NJ 07928-0265
(201) 887-8888

Metals and tools for metalsmiths. Minimum order required.

ARE, Inc.
Box 8, Rte. 16
Greensboro Bend, VT 05842
(800) 736-4273

Metals, tools, and other supplies for jewelers and metalsmiths. Small fee for catalog.

Forge & Anvil Metal Studio Ltd.
30 King St.
St. Jacobs, Ont. N0B 2N0
(519) 664-3622

Cast-iron and brass grilles and grates, cut nails, house hardware (original and reproduction), blacksmithing supplies including hammers, anvils, forge welding compounds, forge pots and tools.

Gesswein
P.O. Box 3998
255 Hancock Ave.
Bridgeport, CT 06605
(203) 366-5400

Tools for jewelers and metalsmiths. Small fee for catalog.

Model Builders Supply (MBS)
40 Engelhard Dr., Unit 11
Aurora, Ont. L4G 3V2
(905) 841-8392
(800) 265-4445

Specialty tools, box hardware, molding and casting compounds. Small fee for catalog.

H. & W. Perrin Co. Ltd.
90 Thorncliffe Park Dr.
Toronto, Ont. M4H 1N5
(416) 422-4600
(800) 387-5117 (Ont./Que.)
(800) 267-3952 (all other provinces)

Tools for jewelers.

Steptoe & Wife Antiques Ltd.
322 Geary Ave.
Toronto, Ont. M6H 2C7
(416) 530-4200
(800) 461-0060

Cast-iron spiral and straight stairs, tin ceilings, ornamental plaster, cast-iron and brass railings. Small fee for catalog.

Travers Tool Co., Inc.
P.O. Box 1550
128–15 26th Ave.
Flushing, NY 11354
(800) 221-0270

Hand and power tools and fasteners. Small fee for catalog.

TSI Inc.
101 Nickerson St.
Seattle, WA 98109
(800) 426-9984

Metals, tools, and other supplies for jewelers and metalsmiths.

CERAMIC TILES

Designs in Tile
P.O. Box 358
Mt. Shasta, CA 96067
(916) 926-2629

Custom-colored and custom-designed tiles for kitchens, bathrooms, and other applications.

DeWittshire Studio
104 Paddock
DeWitt, NY 13214
(315) 446-6011

Custom-colored and custom-designed tiles for kitchens, bathrooms, and other applications.

Sun House/FerGene Studio
9986 Happy Acres W.
Bozeman, MT 59715
(406) 587-3651

Reproduction Victorian tiles for fireplaces. Will custom-color and custom-design tiles.

GLASS

S.A. Bendheim Co., Inc.
61 Willet St.
Passaic, NJ 07055
(201) 471-1733

Restoration glass. They do not do millwork.

Burlington Store
Rte. 1, Box 145
Omaha, AR 72662
(501) 426-5440

Stained glass, tools, plans, and other related supplies. Small fee for catalog.

Burtards Antiques
2034 N. 15th St.
Sheboygan, WI 53081
(414) 452-5466

Curved glass for china cabinets.

Delphi Stained Glass
2116 E. Michigan Ave.
Lansing, MI 48912
(517) 482-2617
*Stained glass, tools and kits.
Small fee for catalog.*

The Glass Place
50 Ste. Anne St.
Point Claire Village
Que. H9S 4P8
(800) 363-7855
*Stained glass, tools, and related
supplies.*

Whittemore-Durgin Glass Co.
P.O. Box 2065
Hanover, MA 02339
(617) 871-1743
*Stained glass, tools, and related
supplies.*

PLASTICS

AIN Plastics
249 Sandford Blvd., Box 151
Mt. Vernon, NY 10550
(800) 431-2451
Acrylic, fiberglass, and PVC.

Clark Craft Boat Shop
1640 Aqua Lane
Tonawanda, N.Y. 14150
(716) 873-2640
*Fiberglassing materials and
tools.*

Defender Industries Inc.
P.O. Box 820
255 Main St.
New Rochelle, NY 10802
(914) 632-3001
Fiberglassing materials and tools.

Model Builders Supply (MBS)
40 Engelhard Dr., Unit 11
Aurora, Ont. L4G 3V2
(905) 841-8392
(800) 265-4445
*Acrylic plastics--profiles, tubes
and fittings. Small fee for
catalog.*

Smithcraft Fiberglass Inc.
970 The Queensway
Toronto, Ont. M8Z 1P6
(416) 259-6946
*Fiberglass related products
and raw materials, composite
materials, epoxy.*

WALL COVERINGS, PAINTS AND FINISHES

*See also woodworking catalogs

Amity Finishing Products
P.O. Box 107, 1571 Ivory Dr.
Sun Prairie, WI 53590
(608) 837-8484
Wood finishes.

Auro/Sinan Co.
P.O. Box 857
Davis, CA 95617
(916) 753-3104
Organic paints, wood finishes.

**The Old Fashioned Milk
Paint Co.**
436 Main St.
Groton, MA 01450
(508) 448-6336
Milk paint and finishes.

Olde Mill Cabinet Shoppe
1660 Camp Betty
  Washington Rd.
York, PA 17402
(717) 755-8884
Wood finishes, dyes, milk paints.

Smithcraft Fiberglass Inc.
970 The Queensway
Toronto, Ont. M8Z 1P6
(416) 259-6946
Fiberglass paint.

Steptoe & Wife Antiques Ltd.
322 Geary Ave.
Toronto, Ont. M6H 2C7
(416) 530-4200
(800) 461-0060
*Embossed wall covering and trim,
decorative drapery hardware.*

Power tool companies

You can contact the following power tool companies for information about their products and to locate distributors near your home. If you already own one of their tools, you may want to call the company for maintenance and repair information. For difficult repairs that require professional experience, they will direct you to their nearest agent or service center.

Black & Decker Canada Inc.
100 Central Ave.
Brockville, Ont. K6V 5W6
(905) 635-6740
(800) 465-6070

Robert Bosch Inc.
6811 Century Ave.
Mississauga, Ont. L5N 1R1
(800) 387-8304

**Delta International
  Machinery**
644 Imperial Rd. N.
Guelph, Ont. N1H 6M7
(519) 836-2840

Dremel—distributed by **Giles
Tool Agencies Limited**
6520 Lawrence Ave. E.
Scarborough, Ont. M1C 4A7
(905) 287-3000

Freud-Westmore Tools Ltd.
7450 Pacific Circle
Mississauga, Ont. L5T 2A3
(905) 670-1025

Hitachi—distributed by **Jet
Equipment and Tools Ltd.**
1291 Parker St.
Vancouver, B.C. V6A 2H5
(604) 251-4711

Makita Canada Inc.
1950 Forbes St.
Whitby, Ont. L1N 7B7
(905) 571-2200 (Toronto)
(514) 323-1223 (Montreal)
(604) 278-3104 (Vancouver)

**Milwaukee Electric Tool
(Canada) Ltd.**
755 Progress Ave.
Scarborough, Ont. M1H 2W7
(416) 439-4181
(800) 268-4015

Porter-Cable Corp.
P.O. Box 2468
4825 Hwy. 45 N.
Jackson, TN 38302-2468
(901) 668-8600

Powermatic
Division of DeVlieg-
  Bullard, Inc.
Morrison Rd.
McMinnville, TN 37110
(615) 473-5551
*In Canada, Powermatic has
several agents, rather than
one distributor. Write or phone
for the name of your local
distributor.*

Ryobi Canada Inc.
P.O. Box 910
Cambridge, Ont. N1R 6K2
(416) 453-4195
(800) 265-6778

Shopsmith Canada Inc.
2500 Milltower Court
Mississauga, Ont. L5N 6A3
(905) 858-2400

Skil Canada Inc.
9999 Highway 48
Markham, Ont. L3P 3J3
(905) 294-9340

**Snap-on Tools
of Canada Ltd.**
2325 Skymark Ave.
Mississauga, Ont. L4W 5A9
(416) 624-0066
(800) 263-8665 (Alberta,
  British Columbia,
  Manitoba, Saskatchewan)
(800) 665-8665 (other
  provinces)

Stanley of Canada Ltd.
1110 Corporate Drive
Burlington, Ont. L7L 5R6
(905) 825-1981
(800) 263-6292

If you would like to find more information about a material, you can contact the manufacturer through the phone number or address listed below. Most of the companies are willing to send you brochures about their products. Many materials can be found in large home improvement centers; however, if you are having difficulty finding a product, the manufacturer will also give you the address of the distributor closest to your home.

WOODWORKING

Canadian Wood Council
1730 St. Laurent Blvd.
Suite 350
Ottawa, Ont. K1G 5L1
(800) 463-5091
All wood products.

Council of Forest Industries
1200--555 Burrard St.
Vancouver, B.C. V7X 1S7
(604) 684-0211
Manufactured wood products.

CONCRETE, BRICKS AND STONES

Brampton Brick Limited
225 Wanless Dr.
Brampton, Ont. L7A 1E9
(905) 840-1011
Clay bricks.

Brique Citadelle
111 Francheville
C.P. 5190
Beauport, Que. G1E 6B5
(418) 663-7821
(800) 463-1565
Clay bricks.

Canada Brick
P.O. Box 666
Streetsville, Ont. L5M 2C3
(905) 601-7314
(800) 268-5852
Clay bricks.

Hebron Brick Co.
Hebron, ND 58638
(701) 232-0781
Bricks.

Hidden Brick Co.
2610 Kauffman Ave.
Vancouver, WA 98660
(206) 696-4421
Bricks.

I-XL Industries Ltd.
P. O. Box 70
Medicine Hat, Alta. T1A 7E7
(403) 526-5901
Clay bricks, flue linings, firebrick.

LaChance Brick Co.
392 Mosher Rd.
Gorham, ME 04038
(207) 839-3301
Bricks.

Permacon Montreal
8140 Bombardier St.
Anjou, Que. H1J 1A4
(514) 351-2120
Concrete masonry products including blocks and bricks, and landscaping products such as pavers, curbs, retaining wall systems, and slabs.

Permacon Ottawa
S.S. 1
Stittsville, Ont. K2S 1B9
(613) 836-6194
Concrete masonry products including blocks and bricks, and landscaping products such as pavers, curbs, retaining wall systems, and slabs.

Permacon Toronto
R.R. 3
Bolton, Ont. L7E 5R9
(905) 857-6773
Concrete masonry products including blocks and bricks, and pavers, curbs, retaining wall systems, and slabs.

St-Lawrence Cement
Technical Services
435 Place Trans-Canada
Longueuil, Que. J4G 2P9
(914) 267-6700
Masonry and concrete.

L. E. Shaw Ltd.
P.O. Box 2130
Lantz, N.S. B0N 1R0
(902) 883-2201
Clay bricks, concrete bricks and blocks, clay and concrete pavers, curbs and patio slabs.

Webster & Sons Ltd.
2585 Côte-de-Liesse
Montreal, Que. H4N 2M8
(514) 332-0520
Clay brick, concrete masonry blocks, glass bricks.

CERAMIC TILE, GLASS, AND PLASTICS

Advanced Technology
311 Regional Rd. S.
Greensboro, NC 27409
(919) 668-0488
Information is also available from the Canadian distributor:

Octopus Products Ltd.
200 Geary Ave.
Toronto, Ont. M6H 2B9
(416) 531-5051
Sheet plastic laminates.

American Olean Tile Co.
1000 Cannon Ave.
Lansdale, PA 19446
(215) 393-2434
Ceramic tiles for walls, floors, countertops, and other applications.

Avonite
1945 Hwy. 304
Belen, NM 87002
(800) 428-6648
Solid-surface material.

BP Chemicals Inc.
7310 Turfway Rd., Suite 300
Florence, KY 41042
(800) 443-4566
Preformed fiberglass panels.

Corian Building Products of Dupont Canada
P.O. Box 2200, Streetsville
Mississauga, Ont. L5M 2H3
(905) 821-5348
(800) 426-7426
Solid-surface materials.

Country Floors
15 E. 16th St.
New York, NY 10003
(212) 627-8300 East Coast
(310) 657-0510 West Coast
Ceramic tiles for walls, floors, countertops, and other applications. Tiles are from around the world; many are handmade.

Deer Creek Pottery
305 Richardson St.
Grass Valley, CA 95945
(916) 272-3373
Hand-pressed ceramic tiles for walls, countertops, and other applications.

Euroglass Corp.
123 Main St., Suite 920
White Plains, NY 10601
(914) 683-1390
Glass blocks.

Fiberglas Canada Inc.
4100 Yonge St., Suite 600
Willowdale, Ont. M2B 2B6
(416) 733-1600
Fiberglassing materials.

Fibre Glass–Evercoat Company of Canada Incorporated
41 Brockley Dr., Unit 4
Hamilton, Ont. L8E 3C3
(800) 729-7600
Fiberglass materials.

Formica Canada Inc.
25 Mercier St.
St-Jean-sur-Richelieu
Que. J3B 6E9
(514) 347-7541
(800) 363-1405
Plastic laminates and solid-surface materials.

Fulper Tile
P.O. Box 373
Yardley, PA 19067
(215) 736-8512
Handmade tiles suitable for walls, fireplace surrounds, hearths, and backsplashes.

GE Plastics Canada Ltd.
2300 Meadowvale Blvd.
Mississauga, Ont. L5N 5P9
(905) 858-5700
Polycarbonate sheets.

Glasshaus, Inc.
415 W. Gold Rd., Suite 13
Arlington Heights, IL 60005
(708) 640-6910
Glass blocks.

Mannington Ceramic Tile
P.O. Box 1777
Victor St.
Lexington, NC 27292
(704) 249-3931
Ceramic tiles for walls, floors, and other applications.

Micarta Laminate
Westinghouse Electric Corp.
Hampton, SC 29924
(800) 845-4791
Sheet plastic laminates.

Olympia Tile International Inc.
Head Office
1000 Lawrence Ave. W.
Toronto, Ont. M6B 4A8
(800) 268-1613
Ceramic tiles, vinyl tiles, natural stone, and marble products.

Pittsburgh Corning Corp.
800 Presque Isle Dr.
Pittsburgh, PA 15239-2799
(800) 624-2120
Glass blocks.

Summitville Tiles Inc.
P.O. Box 73
Rte. 644
Summitville, OH 43962
(216) 223-1511
Ceramic tiles for floors, walls, and countertops.

Ralph Wilson Plastics Co.
600 S. General Bruce Dr.
Temple, TX 76504
(800) 433-3222
Sheet plastic laminates.

FLOORING

Aged Woods, Inc.
2331 E. Market St.
York, PA 17402
(800) 233-9307
Antique wood planks.

Armstrong World Industries Canada Ltd.
6911 boul. Décarie
Montreal, Que.
(514) 733-9981
Resilient sheet flooring and tiles.

Boen Hardwood Flooring Inc.
Rte. 5, Box 640
Bassett, VA 24055
(703) 629-3381
Planks, strips, and parquets.

Bruce Hardwood Floors
16803 Dallas Pkwy.
Dallas, TX 75248
(214) 931-3100, ext. 600
Planks, strips, and parquets.

Carlisle Restoration Lumber
HCR 32, Box 679
Stoddard, NH 03464-9712
(603) 446-3937
Wood planks, paneling, beams.

Congoleum Corporation
43--1313 Border Place
Winnipeg, Man. R3H 0X4
(800) 465-1652
Resilient sheet flooring.

Granville Manufacturing Co., Inc.
Granville, VT 05747
(802) 767-4747
Clapboard planks.

Harris-Tarkett, Inc.
P.O. Box 300
Johnson City, TN 37602-0300
(800) 842-7816
Wood planks, laminated floating planks, and parquets.

Kentile Floors Inc.
Kentile Rd.
South Plainfield, NJ 07080
(908) 757-3000
Resilient tiles.

Kentucky Wood Floors, Inc.
P.O. Box 33276
Louisville, KY 40432
(800) 235-5235
Wood planks, strips, and parquets.

Knights of Meaford Inc.
81 Edwin St. E.
Meaford, Ont. N0H 1Y0
(519) 538-2000
Oak and maple strips, hardwood flooring.

MacMillan Bloedel Building Materials Ltd.
925 West Georgia St.
Vancouver, B.C. V6C 3L2
(604) 661-8000
Hardwood flooring, floor underlayment.

MacMillan Bloedel Building Materials Ltd.
308, rue Saint-Patrick
Montreal, Que. H8N 1V1
(514) 366-2100
Hardwood flooring, floor underlayment.

MacMillan Bloedel Building Materials Ltd.
50 Oak St.
Weston, Ont. M9N 1S1
(416) 244-1741
Hardwood flooring, floor underlayment.

Mannington Wood Floors
1327 Lincoln Dr.
High Point, NC 27260
(919) 884-5600
Wood planks.

North American Hardwood Flooring
Hwy. 9 Spur
Melbourne, AK 72556
(501) 368-4850
Wood planks, laminated floating planks, and parquets.

Robbins Hardwood Flooring
4785 Eastern Ave.
Cincinnati, OH 45226
(513) 871-8510
Wood planks, parquets, and blocks.

Tarkett Inc.
215 Carlingview Dr.,
Suite 112
Rexdale, Ont. M9W 5X8
(416) 675-1133
Resilient sheet flooring and tiles.

Unicorn Universal Woods Ltd.
4190 Steeles Ave. W.
Woodbridge, Ont. L4L 3S8
(905) 851-2308
Exotic and domestic lumber; specialty marine plywood, veneers.

Windsor Plywood
Head Office & Distribution Office
10382-176th St.
Surrey, B.C. V3T 5M5
Plywood, molding, and flooring.

FINISHES

Benjamin Moore & Co. Ltd.
139 Mulock
Toronto, Ont. M6N 1G9
(416) 766-1173
Paints, stains, and clear finishes.

Benjamin Moore & Co. Ltd.
26680 Gloucester Way
Aldergrove, B.C. V0X 1H0
(604) 857-0600
Paints, stains, and clear finishes.

Glidden Paints
8200 Keele St.
Concord, Ont. L4K 2A5
(800) 387-3663
No-solvent latex paint in three finishes. Faux finish clinic.

INDEX

METRIC CONVERSION

In today's marketplace, the Canadian consumer can comfortably shop for imperial or metric sizes. Labels on many products will have both measurements. And suppliers still sell items by the foot or square foot, even if such goods (lumber and concrete for example) are produced by industries that have long since converted to metric measurements.

Once you know the metric system, it becomes much easier to calculate the amount of materials required for a job. Instead of 12 inches to a foot, 3 feet to a yard, and 1,760 yards to a mile, you'll find 1,000 millimetres in 100 centimetres or 1 metre, and 1,000 metres in a kilometre.

Tables and charts designed to help you readily convert from one system to the other appear on these pages. The linear conversion table, for example, provides already calculated equivalents for some common measurements. Other charts let you compare grams and ounces, litres and gallons, millimetres and inches.

Lumber Widths and Thicknesses

Lumber is ordered by thickness, width, and length. When you order in imperial measurements (2 inches x 4 inches x 8 feet, for example), the thickness and width figures (in this instance 2 x 4) refer to nominal size—the dimensions of the piece as it left the saw. But what you get is the smaller, actual size remaining when the piece has been planed smooth; in actual fact, a piece 1½ inches x 3½ inches x 8 feet. (Length is not reduced by the processing.)
Metric measurements on the other hand always describe the actual dimensions of the processed piece.

Imperial (in.) nominal size	(actual size)	Metric (mm) actual size
2 x 2	(1½ x 1½)	38 x 38
2 x 4	(1½ x 3½)	38 x 89
2 x 6	(1½ x 5½)	38 x 140
2 x 8	(1½ x 7¼)	38 x 184
2 x 10	(1½ x 9¼)	38 x 235
4 x 4	(3½ x 3½)	89 x 89
4 x 6	(3½ x 5½)	89 x 140

Linear conversion table

	1/64	1/32	1/25	1/16	1/8	1/4	3/8	2/5	1/2	5/8	3/4	7/8	1	2	3	4	5	6	7	8	9	10	11	12	36	39.4
Inches (in.)																										
Feet (ft)																								1	3	3¼†
Yards (yd)																									1	1½†
Millimetres* (mm)	0.40	0.79	1	1.59	3.18	6.35	9.53	10	12.7	15.9	19.1	22.2	25.4	50.8	76.2	101.6	127	152	178	203	229	254	279	305	914	1,000
Centimetres* (cm)							0.95	1	1.27	1.59	1.91	2.22	2.54	5.08	7.62	10.16	12.7	15.2	17.8	20.3	22.9	25.4	27.9	30.5	91.4	100
Metres* (m)																								.30	.91	1.00

† Approximate fractions.   * Metric values are rounded off.

Conversion factors

To change:	Into:	Multiply by:	To change:	Into:	Multiply by:
Imperial system to metric system			**Metric system to imperial system**		
Inches	Millimetres	25.4	Millimetres	Inches	0.039
Inches	Centimetres	2.54	Centimetres	Inches	0.394
Feet	Metres	0.305	Metres	Feet	3.28
Yards	Metres	0.914	Metres	Yards	1.09
Miles	Kilometres	1.609	Kilometres	Miles	0.621
Square inches	Square centimetres	6.45	Square centimetres	Square inches	0.155
Square feet	Square metres	0.093	Square metres	Square feet	10.8
Square yards	Square metres	0.836	Square metres	Square yards	1.2
Cubic inches	Cubic centimetres	16.4	Cubic centimetres	Cubic inches	0.061
Cubic feet	Cubic metres	0.0283	Cubic metres	Cubic feet	35.3
Cubic yards	Cubic metres	0.765	Cubic metres	Cubic yards	1.31
Pints (imperial)	Litres	0.568	Litres	Pints (imperial)	0.88
Quarts (imperial)	Litres	1.136	Litres	Quarts (imperial)	0.176
Gallons (imperial)	Litres	4.546	Litres	Gallons (imperial)	0.22
Gallons (U.S.)	Litres	3.79	Litres	Gallons (U.S.)	0.26
Ounces	Grams	28.4	Grams	Ounces	0.035
Pounds	Kilograms	0.454	Kilograms	Pounds	2.2
Tons	Tonnes	0.907	Tonnes	Tons	1.1